Edward B. Tylor

Primitive Culture Resaerches Into the Developement of Mythology

Edward B. Tylor

Primitive Culture Resaerches Into the Developement of Mythology

ISBN/EAN: 9783742817495

Manufactured in Europe, USA, Canada, Australia, Japa

Cover: Foto ©Thomas Meinert / pixelio.de

Manufactured and distributed by brebook publishing software
(www.brebook.com)

Edward B. Tylor

Primitive Culture Resaerches Into the Developement of

Mythology

PRIMITIVE CULTURE.

PRIMITIVE CULTURE:

RESEARCHES INTO THE DEVELOPMENT OF MYTHOLOGY, PHILOSOPHY,
RELIGION, LANGUAGE, ART, AND CUSTOM.

BY

EDWARD B. TYLOR, LL.D., F.R.S.,

AUTHOR OF " RESEARCHES INTO THE EARLY HISTORY OF MANKIND," &c.

IN TWO VOLUMES.

VOL. I.

SECOND EDITION.

LONDON:
JOHN MURRAY, ALBEMARLE STREET.
1873.

LONDON:

BRADBURY, AGNEW, & CO., PRINTERS, WHITEFRIARS.

PREFACE TO THE FIRST EDITION.

—◆—

THE present volumes, uniform with the previous volume of "Researches into the Early History of Mankind" (1st Ed. 1865; 2nd Ed. 1870), carry on the investigation of Culture into other branches of thought and belief, art and custom. During the past six years, I have taken occasion to bring tentatively before the public some of the principal points of new evidence and argument here advanced. The doctrine of survival in culture, the bearing of directly-expressive language and the invention of numerals on the problem of early civilization, the place of myth in the primitive history of the human mind, the development of the animistic philosophy of religion, and the origin of rites and ceremonies, have been discussed in various papers and lectures,* before being treated at large and with a fuller array of facts in this work.

The authorities for the facts stated in the text are

* Fortnightly Review : 'Origin of Language,' April 15, 1866 ; 'Religion of Savages,' August 15, 1866. Lectures at Royal Institution ; 'Traces of the Early Mental Condition of Man,' March 15, 1867 ; 'Survival of Savage Thought in Modern Civilization,' April 23, 1869. Lecture at University College, London : 'Spiritualistic Philosophy of the Lower Races of Mankind,' May 6, 1869. Paper read at British Association, Nottingham, 1866 : 'Phenomena of Civilization Traceable to a Rudimental Origin among Savage Tribes.' Paper read at Ethnological Society of London, April 26, 1870 : 'Philosophy of Religion among the Lower Races of Mankind,' &c. &c.

fully specified in the foot-notes, which must also serve as my general acknowledgment of obligations to writers on ethnography and kindred sciences, as well as to historians, travellers, and missionaries. I will only mention apart two treatises of which I have made especial use: the 'Mensch in der Geschichte,' by Professor Bastian of Berlin, and the 'Anthropologie der Naturvölker,' by the late Professor Waitz of Marburg.

In discussing problems so complex as those of the development of civilization, it is not enough to put forward theories accompanied by a few illustrative examples. The statement of the facts must form the staple of the argument, and the limit of needful detail is only reached when each group so displays its general law, that fresh cases come to range themselves in their proper niches as new instances of an already established rule. Should it seem to any readers that my attempt to reach this limit sometimes leads to the heaping up of too cumbrous detail, I would point out that the theoretical novelty as well as the practical importance of many of the issues raised, make it most unadvisable to stint them of their full evidence. In the course of ten years chiefly spent in these researches, it has been my constant task to select the most instructive ethnological facts from the vast mass on record, and by lopping away unnecessary matter to reduce the data on each problem to what is indispensable for reasonable proof.

E. B. T.

March, 1871.

PREFACE TO THE SECOND EDITION.

Since the publication of this work in 1871, translations have appeared in German and Russian. In the present edition, the form of page has been slightly altered, for convenience of re-issue at once in England and America. The matter, however, remains substantially the same. A few passages have been amplified or altered for greater clearness, and on some points additional or improved evidence has been put in. Among the anthropologists whose published reviews or private communications have enabled me to correct or strengthen various points, I will only mention by name Professor Felix Liebrecht, of Liége, Mr. Clements R. Markham, Professor Calderwood, Mr. Ralston, and Mr. Sebastian Evans.

It may have struck some readers as an omission, that in a work on civilization insisting so strenuously on a theory of development or evolution, mention should scarcely have been made of Mr. Darwin and Mr. Herbert Spencer, whose influence on the whole course of modern thought on such subjects should not be left without formal recognition. This absence of particular reference is accounted for by the present

work, arranged on its own lines, coming scarcely into
contact of detail with the previous works of these
eminent philosophers.

An objection made by several critics as to the accumulation of evidence in these volumes leads me to remark, with sincere gratification, that this objection has
in fact been balanced by solid advantage. The plan of
collecting wide and minute evidence, so that readers
may have actually before them the means of judging
the theory put forward, has been justified by the
reception of the book, even in circles to whose views
many of its arguments are strongly adverse, and that
in matters of the first importance. Writers of most
various philosophical and theological schools now
admit that the ethnological facts are real, and vital,
and have to be accounted for. It is not too much to
say that a perceptible movement of public opinion has
here justified the belief that the English mind, not
readily swayed by rhetoric, moves freely under the
pressure of facts.

                                        E. B. T.

September, 1873.

CONTENTS

OF

THE FIRST VOLUME.

— • —

CHAPTER I.

THE SCIENCE OF CULTURE.

CHAPTER II.

THE DEVELOPMENT OF CULTURE.

CHAPTER III.

SURVIVAL IN CULTURE.

CHAPTER IV.

SURVIVAL IN CULTURE (continued).

CHAPTER V.

EMOTIONAL AND IMITATIVE LANGUAGE.

CHAPTER VI.

EMOTIONAL AND IMITATIVE LANGUAGE (continued).

CHAPTER VII.

THE ART OF COUNTING.

CHAPTER VIII.

MYTHOLOGY.

CHAPTER IX.

MYTHOLOGY (continued).

PRIMITIVE CULTURE.

CHAPTER I.

THE SCIENCE OF CULTURE.

Culture or Civilisation—Its phenomena related according to definite Laws—
Method of classification and discussion of the evidence—Connexion of
successive stages of culture by Permanence, Modification, and Survival—
Principal topics examined in the present work.

CULTURE or Civilization, taken in its wide ethnographic
sense, is that complex whole which includes knowledge, belief, art, morals, law, custom, and any other capabilities and
habits acquired by man as a member of society. The condition of culture among the various societies of mankind, in
so far as it is capable of being investigated on general
principles, is a subject apt for the study of laws of human
thought and action. On the one hand, the uniformity
which so largely pervades civilization may be ascribed, in
great measure, to the uniform action of uniform causes;
while on the other hand its various grades may be regarded
as stages of development or evolution, each the outcome of
previous history, and about to do its proper part in shaping
the history of the future. To the investigation of these two
great principles in several departments of ethnography, with
especial consideration of the civilization of the lower tribes
as related to the civilization of the higher nations, the present volumes are devoted.

Our modern investigators in the sciences of inorganic nature are foremost to recognize, both within and without their special fields of work, the unity of nature, the fixity of its laws, the definite sequence of cause and effect through which every fact depends on what has gone before it, and acts upon what is to come after it. They grasp firmly the Pythagorean doctrine of pervading order in the universal Kosmos. They affirm, with Aristotle, that nature is not full of incoherent episodes, like a bad tragedy. They agree with Leibnitz in what he calls "my axiom, that nature never acts by leaps (la nature n'agit jamais par saut)," as well as in his "great principle, commonly little employed, that nothing happens without its sufficient reason." Nor, again, in studying the structure and habits of plants and animals, or in investigating the lower functions even of man, are these leading ideas unacknowledged. But when we come to talk of the higher processes of human feeling and action, of thought and language, knowledge and art, a change appears in the prevalent tone of opinion. The world at large is scarcely prepared to accept the general study of human life as a branch of natural science, and to carry out, in a large sense, the poet's injunction to "Account for moral as for natural things." To many educated minds there seems something presumptuous and repulsive in the view that the history of mankind is part and parcel of the history of nature, that our thoughts, wills, and actions accord with laws as definite as those which govern the motion of waves, the combination of acids and bases, and the growth of plants and animals.

The main reasons of this state of the popular judgment are not far to seek. There are many who would willingly accept a science of history if placed before them with substantial definiteness of principle and evidence, but who not unreasonably reject the systems offered to them, as falling too far short of a scientific standard. Through resistance such as this, real knowledge always sooner or later makes its way, while the habit of opposition to novelty does such excellent service against the invasions of speculative dogmatism, that we may sometimes even wish it were stronger than it is. But other obstacles to the investigation of laws of human nature arise from considerations of metaphysics and theology. The popular notion of free human will involves not only freedom to act in accordance with motive, but also a power of breaking loose from continuity and acting without cause,—a combination which may be roughly illustrated by the simile of a balance sometimes acting in the usual way, but also possessed of the faculty of turning by itself without or against its weights. This view of an anomalous action of the will, which it need hardly be said is incompatible with scientific argument, subsists as an opinion patent or latent in men's minds, and strongly affecting their theoretic views of history, though it is not, as a rule, brought prominently forward in systematic reasoning. Indeed the definition of human will, as strictly according with motive, is the only possible scientific basis in such enquiries. Happily, it is not needful to add here yet another to the list of dissertations on supernatural intervention and natural causation, on liberty, predestination, and accountability. We may hasten to escape from the regions of transcendental philosophy and theology, to start on a more hopeful journey over more practicable ground. None will deny that, as each man knows by the evidence of his own consciousness, definite and natural cause does, to a great extent, determine human action. Then, keeping aside from considerations of extra-natural interference and causeless spontaneity, let us take this admitted existence of natural cause and effect as our standing-ground, and travel on it so far as it will bear us. It is on this same basis that physical science pursues, with ever-increasing success, its quest of laws of nature. Nor need this restriction hamper the scientific study of human life, in which the real difficulties are the practical ones of enormous complexity of evidence, and imperfection of methods of observation.

■ 2

Now it appears that this view of human will and conduct,
as subject to definite law, is indeed recognized and acted
upon by the very people who oppose it when stated in
the abstract as a general principle, and who then complain
that it annihilates man's free will, destroys his sense of personal responsibility, and degrades him to a soulless machine.
He who will say these things will nevertheless pass much of
his own life in studying the motives which lead to human
action, seeking to attain his wishes through them, framing
in his mind theories of personal character, reckoning what
are likely to be the effects of new combinations, and giving
to his reasoning the crowning character of true scientific enquiry, by taking it for granted that in so far as his calculation turns out wrong, either his evidence must have been
false or incomplete, or his judgment upon it unsound.
Such a one will sum up the experience of years spent in
complex relations with society, by declaring his persuasion
that there is a reason for everything in life, and that where
events look unaccountable, the rule is to wait and watch in
hope that the key to the problem may some day be found.
This man's observation may have been as narrow as his inferences are crude and prejudiced, but nevertheless he has
been an inductive philosopher "more than forty years without knowing it." He has practically acknowledged definite
laws of human thought and action, and has simply thrown
out of account in his own studies of life the whole fabric of
motiveless will and uncaused spontaneity. It is assumed
here that they should be just so thrown out of account in
wider studies, and that the true philosophy of history lies
in extending and improving the methods of the plain people
who form their judgments upon facts, and check them
upon new facts. Whether the doctrine be wholly or but
partly true, it accepts the very condition under which we
search for new knowledge in the lessons of experience,
and in a word the whole course of our rational life is based
upon it.

"One event is always the son of another, and we must

never forget the parentage," was a remark made by a
Bechuana chief to Casalis the African missionary. Thus
at all times historians, so far as they have aimed at being
more than mere chroniclers, have done their best to show
not merely succession, but connexion, among the events upon
their record. Moreover, they have striven to elicit general
principles of human action, and by these to explain particular events, stating expressly or taking tacitly for granted
the existence of a philosophy of history. Should any one
deny the possibility of thus establishing historical laws,
the answer is ready with which Boswell in such a case
turned on Johnson: "Then, sir, you would reduce all
history to no better than an almanack." That nevertheless
the labours of so many eminent thinkers should have as yet
brought history only to the threshold of science, need cause
no wonder to those who consider the bewildering complexity
of the problems which come before the general historian.
The evidence from which he is to draw his conclusions is at
once so multifarious and so doubtful, that a full and distinct
view of its bearing on a particular question is hardly to be
attained, and thus the temptation becomes all but irre-
sistible to garble it in support of some rough and ready
theory of the course of events. The philosophy of history
at large, explaining the past and predicting the future phenomena of man's life in the world by reference to general
laws, is in fact a subject with which, in the present state of
knowledge, even genius aided by wide research seems but
hardly able to cope. Yet there are departments of it which,
though difficult enough, seem comparatively accessible. If
the field of inquiry be narrowed from History as a whole
to that branch of it which is here called Culture, the
history, not of tribes or nations, but of the condition of
knowledge, religion, art, custom, and the like among them,
the task of investigation proves to lie within far more
moderate compass. We suffer still from the same kind of
difficulties which beset the wider argument, but they are
much diminished. The evidence is no longer so wildly

heterogeneous, but may be more simply classified and compared, while the power of getting rid of extraneous matter, and treating each issue on its own proper set of facts, makes close reasoning on the whole more available than in general history. This may appear from a brief preliminary examination of the problem, how the phenomena of Culture may be classified and arranged, stage by stage, in a probable order of evolution.

Surveyed in a broad view, the character and habit of mankind at once display that similarity and consistency of phenomena which led the Italian proverb-maker to declare that "all the world is one country," "tutto il mondo è paese." To general likeness in human nature on the one hand, and to general likeness in the circumstances of life on the other, this similarity and consistency may no doubt be traced, and they may be studied with especial fitness in comparing races near the same grade of civilization. Little respect need be had in such comparisons for date in history or for place on the map; the ancient Swiss lake-dweller may be set beside the mediæval Aztec, and the Ojibwa of North America beside the Zulu of South Africa. As Dr. Johnson contemptuously said when he had read about Patagonians and South Sea Islanders in Hawkesworth's Voyages, "one set of savages is like another." How true a generalization this really is, any Ethnological Museum may show. Examine for instance the edged and pointed instruments in such a collection; the inventory includes hatchet, adze, chisel, knife, saw, scraper, awl, needle, spear and arrow-head, and of these most or all belong with only differences of detail to races the most various. So it is with savage occupations; the wood-chopping, fishing with net and line, shooting and spearing game, fire-making, cooking, twisting cord and plaiting baskets, repeat themselves with wonderful uniformity in the museum shelves which illustrate the life of the lower races from Kamchatka to Tierra del Fuego, and from Dahome to Hawaii. Even when it comes to comparing barbarous hordes with civilized nations, the consideration thrusts itself upon our minds, how far item after item of the life of the lower races passes into analogous proceedings of the higher, in forms not too far changed to be recognized, and sometimes hardly changed at all. Look at the modern European peasant using his hatchet and his hoe, see his food boiling or roasting over the log-fire, observe the exact place which beer holds in his calculation of happiness, hear his tale of the ghost in the nearest haunted house, and of the farmer's niece who was bewitched with knots in her inside till she fell into fits and died. If we choose out in this way things which have altered little in a long course of centuries, we may draw a picture where there shall be scarce a hand's breadth difference between an English ploughman and a negro of Central Africa. These pages will be so crowded with evidence of such correspondence among mankind, that there is no need to dwell upon its details here, but it may be used at once to override a problem which would complicate the argument, namely, the question of race. For the present purpose it appears both possible and desirable to eliminate considerations of hereditary varieties or races of man, and to treat mankind as homogeneous in nature, though placed in different grades of civilization. The details of the enquiry will, I think, prove that stages of culture may be compared without taking into account how far tribes who use the same implement, follow the same custom, or believe the same myth, may differ in their bodily configuration and the colour of their skin and hair.

A first step in the study of civilization is to dissect it into details, and to classify these in their proper groups. Thus, in examining weapons, they are to be classed under spear, club, sling, bow and arrow, and so forth; among textile arts are to be ranged matting, netting, and several grades of making and weaving threads; myths are divided under such headings as myths of sunrise and sunset, eclipse-myths, earthquake-myths, local myths which account for the names of places by some fanciful tale, eponymic myths which account

for the parentage of a tribe by turning its name into the
name of an imaginary ancestor ; under rites and ceremonies
occur such practices as the various kinds of sacrifice to the
ghosts of the dead and to other spiritual beings, the turning
to the east in worship, the purification of ceremonial or
moral uncleanness by means of water or fire. Such are a
few miscellaneous examples from a list of hundreds, and
the ethnographer's business is to classify such details with
a view to making out their distribution in geography and
history, and the relations which exist among them. What
this task is like, may be almost perfectly illustrated by comparing these details of culture with the species of plants and
animals as studied by the naturalist. To the ethnographer,
the bow and arrow is a species, the habit of flattening
children's skulls is a species, the practice of reckoning
numbers by tens is a species. The geographical distribution of these things, and their transmission from region to
region, have to be studied as the naturalist studies the
geography of his botanical and zoological species. Just as
certain plants and animals are peculiar to certain districts,
so it is with such instruments as the Australian boomerang,
the Polynesian stick-and-groove for fire-making, the tiny
bow and arrow used as a lancet or phleme by tribes about
the Isthmus of Panama, and in like manner with many an
art, myth, or custom, found isolated in a particular field.
Just as the catalogue of all the species of plants and animals
of a district represents its Flora and Fauna, so the list of
all the items of the general life of a people represents that
whole which we call its culture. And just as distant regions
so often produce vegetables and animals which are analogous,
though by no means identical, so it is with the details of the
civilization of their inhabitants. How good a working
analogy there really is between the diffusion of plants and
animals and the diffusion of civilization, comes well into
view when we notice how far the same causes have produced
both at once.¹ In district after district, the same causes
which have introduced the cultivated plants and domesti-

cated animals of civilization, have brought in with them a
corresponding art and knowledge.† The course of events
which carried horses and wheat to America carried with
them the use of the gun and the iron hatchet, while in
return the old world received not only maize, potatoes,
and turkeys, but the habit of smoking and the sailor's
hammock.

It is a matter worthy of consideration, that the accounts
of similar phenomena of culture, recurring in different parts
of the world, actually supply incidental proof of their own
authenticity. Some years since, a question which brings
out this point was put to me by a great historian—"How
can a statement as to customs, myths, beliefs, &c., of a
savage tribe be treated as evidence where it depends on the
testimony of some traveller or missionary, who may be a
superficial observer, more or less ignorant of the native
language, a careless retailer of unsifted talk, a man prejudiced or even wilfully deceitful?" This question is, indeed,
one which every ethnographer ought to keep clearly and
constantly before his mind. Of course he is bound to use
his best judgment as to the trustworthiness of all authors
he quotes, and if possible to obtain several accounts to
certify each point in each locality. But it is over and above
these measures of precaution, that the test of recurrence
comes in. If two independent visitors to different countries,
say a mediæval Mohammedan in Tartary and a modern
Englishman in Dahome, or a Jesuit missionary in Brazil
and a Wesleyan in the Fiji Islands, agree in describing some
analogous art or rite or myth among the people they have
visited, it becomes difficult or impossible to set down such
correspondence to accident or wilful fraud. A story by a
bushranger in Australia may, perhaps, be objected to as a
mistake or an invention, but did a Methodist minister in
Guinea conspire with him to cheat the public by telling the
same story there? The possibility of intentional or unin-
tentional mystification is often barred by such a state of
things as that a similar statement is made in two remote

lands, by two witnesses, of whom A lived a century before
D, and D appears never to have heard of A. How distant
are the countries, how wide apart the dates, how different
the creeds and characters of the observers, in the catalogue
of facts of civilization, needs no farther showing to any one
who will even glance at the foot-notes of the present work.
And the more odd the statement, the less likely that several
people in several places should have made it wrongly. This
being so, it seems reasonable to judge that the statements
are in the main truly given, and that their close and regular
coincidence is due to the cropping up of similar facts in
various districts of culture. Now the most important facts
of ethnography are vouched for in this way. Experience
leads the student after a while to expect and find that the
phenomena of culture, as resulting from widely-acting similar
causes, should recur again and again in the world. He even
mistrusts isolated statements to which he knows of no parallel
elsewhere, and waits for their genuineness to be shown by
corresponding accounts from the other side of the earth, or
the other end of history. So strong, indeed, is this means
of authentication, that the ethnographer in his library may
sometimes presume to decide, not only whether a particular
explorer is a shrewd and honest observer, but also whether
what he reports is conformable to the general rules of civilization. *Non quis, sed quid.*

To turn from the distribution of culture in different
countries, to its diffusion within these countries. The
quality of mankind which tends most to make the systematic study of civilization possible, is that remarkable tacit
consensus or agreement which so far induces whole populations to unite in the use of the same language, to follow the
same religion and customary law, to settle down to the same
general level of art and knowledge. It is this state of things
which makes it so far possible to ignore exceptional facts
and to describe nations by a sort of general average. It is
this state of things which makes it so far possible to represent
immense masses of details by a few typical facts, while, these

once settled, new cases recorded by new observers simply fall into their places to prove the soundness of the classification. There is found to be such regularity in the composition of societies of men, that we can drop individual differences out of sight, and thus can generalize on the arts and opinions of whole nations, just as, when looking down upon an army from a hill, we forget the individual soldier, whom, in fact, we can scarce distinguish in the mass, while we see each regiment as an organized body, spreading or concentrating, moving in advance or in retreat. In some branches of the study of social laws it is now possible to call in the aid of statistics, and to set apart special actions of large mixed communities of men by means of taxgatherers' schedules, or the tables of the insurance-office. Among modern arguments on the laws of human action, none have had a deeper effect than generalizations such as those of M. Quetelet, on the regularity, not only of such matters as average stature and the annual rates of birth and death, but of the recurrence, year after year, of such obscure and seemingly incalculable products of national life as the numbers of murders and suicides, and the proportion of the very weapons of crime. Other striking cases are the annual regularity of persons killed accidentally in the London streets, and of undirected letters dropped into post-office letter-boxes. But in examining the culture of the lower races, far from having at command the measured arithmetical facts of modern statistics, we may have to judge of the condition of tribes from the imperfect accounts supplied by travellers or missionaries, or even to reason upon relics of prehistoric races of whose very names and languages we are hopelessly ignorant. Now these may seem at the first glance sadly indefinite and unpromising materials for a scientific enquiry. But in fact they are neither indefinite nor unpromising, but give evidence that is good and definite, so far as it goes. They are data which, for the distinct way in which they severally denote the condition of the tribe they belong to, will actually bear comparison with the statistician's returns. The fact is that a stone arrow-head, a carved club, an idol, a grave-mound where slaves and property have been buried for the use of the dead, an account of a sorcerer's rites in making rain, a table of numerals, the conjugation of a verb, are things which each express the state of a people as to one particular point of culture, as truly as the tabulated numbers of deaths by poison, and of chests of tea imported, express in a different way other partial results of the general life of a whole community.

That a whole nation should have a special dress, special tools and weapons, special laws of marriage and property, special moral and religious doctrines, is a remarkable fact, which we notice so little because we have lived all our lives in the midst of it. It is with such general qualities of organized bodies of men that ethnography has especially to deal. Yet, while generalizing on the culture of a tribe or nation, and setting aside the peculiarities of the individuals composing it as unimportant to the main result, we must be careful not to forget what makes up this main result. There are people so intent on the separate life of individuals that they cannot grasp a notion of the action of a community as a whole—such an observer, incapable of a wide view of society, is aptly described in the saying that he "cannot see the forest for the trees." But, on the other hand, the philosopher may be so intent upon his general laws of society as to neglect the individual actors of whom that society is made up, and of him it may be said that he cannot see the trees for the forest. We know how arts, customs, and ideas are shaped among ourselves by the combined actions of many individuals, of which actions both motive and effect often come quite distinctly within our view. The history of an invention, an opinion, a ceremony, is a history of suggestion and modification, encouragement and opposition, personal gain and party prejudice, and the individuals concerned act each according to his own motives, as determined by his character and circumstances. Thus sometimes we watch individuals acting for their own ends with little thought of their effect on society at large, and sometimes we have to study movements of national life as a whole, where the individuals co-operating in them are utterly beyond our observation. But seeing that collective social action is the mere resultant of many individual actions, it is clear that these two methods of enquiry, if rightly followed, must be absolutely consistent.

In studying both the recurrence of special habits or ideas in several districts, and their prevalence within each district, there come before us ever-reiterated proofs of regular causation producing the phenomena of human life, and of laws of maintenance and diffusion according to which these phenomena settle into permanent standard conditions of society, at definite stages of culture. But, while giving full importance to the evidence bearing on these standard conditions of society, let us be careful to avoid a pitfall which may entrap the unwary student. Of course the opinions and habits belonging in common to masses of mankind are to a great extent the results of sound judgment and practical wisdom. But to a great extent it is not so. That many numerous societies of men should have believed in the influence of the evil eye and the existence of a firmament, should have sacrificed slaves and goods to the ghosts of the departed, should have handed down traditions of giants slaying monsters and men turning into beasts—all this is ground for holding that such ideas were indeed produced in men's minds by efficient causes, but it is not ground for holding that the rites in question are profitable, the beliefs sound, and the history authentic. This may seem at the first glance a truism, but, in fact, it is the denial of a fallacy which deeply affects the minds of all but a small critical minority of mankind. Popularly, what everybody says must be true, what everybody does must be right—"Quod ubique, quod semper, quod ab omnibus creditum est, hoc est vere proprieque Catholicum"—and so forth. There are various topics, especially in history, law, philosophy, and

theology, where even the educated people we live among
can hardly be brought to see that the cause why men do
hold an opinion, or practise a custom, is by no means
necessarily a reason why they ought to do so.   Now collections of ethnographic evidence, bringing so prominently into
view the agreement of immense multitudes of men as to
certain traditions, beliefs, and usages, are peculiarly liable
to be thus improperly used in direct defence of these institutions themselves, even old barbaric nations being polled
to maintain their opinions against what are called modern
ideas.   As it has more than once happened to myself to
find my collections of traditions and beliefs thus set up to
prove their own objective truth, without proper examination
of the grounds on which they were actually received, I take
this occasion of remarking that the same line of argument
will serve equally well to demonstrate, by the strong and
wide consent of nations, that the earth is flat, and nightmare the visit of a demon.

It being shown that the details of Culture are capable of
being classified in a great number of ethnographic groups of
arts, beliefs, customs, and the rest, the consideration comes
next how far the facts arranged in these groups are produced
by evolution from one another.   It need hardly be pointed
out that the groups in question, though held together each
by a common character, are by no means accurately defined.
To take up again the natural history illustration, it may be
said that they are species which tend to run widely into
varieties.   And when it comes to the question what relations
some of these groups bear to others, it is plain that the
student of the habits of mankind has a great advantage over
the student of the species of plants and animals.   Among
naturalists it is an open question whether a theory of
development from species to species is a record of transitions which actually took place, or a mere ideal scheme
serviceable in the classification of species whose origin was
really independent.   But among ethnographers there is no
such question as to the possibility of species of implements

or habits or beliefs being developed one out of another, for development in culture is recognized by our most familiar knowledge. Mechanical invention supplies apt examples of the kind of development which affects civilization at large. In the history of fire-arms, the clumsy wheel-lock, in which a notched steel wheel was turned by a handle against the flint till a spark caught the priming, led to the invention of the more serviceable flint-lock, of which a few still hang in the kitchens of our farm-houses, for the boys to shoot small birds with at Christmas; the flint-lock in time passed by an obvious modification into the percussion-lock, which is just now changing its old-fashioned arrangement to be adapted from muzzle-loading to breech-loading. The mediæval astrolabe passed into the quadrant, now discarded in its turn by the seaman, who uses the more delicate sextant, and so it is through the history of one art and instrument after another. Such examples of progression are known to us as direct history, but so thoroughly is this notion of development at home in our minds, that by means of it we reconstruct lost history without scruple, trusting to general knowledge of the principles of human thought and action as a guide in putting the facts in their proper order. Whether chronicle speaks or is silent on the point, no one comparing a long-bow and a cross-bow would doubt that the cross-bow was a development arising from the simpler instrument. So among the savage fire-drills for igniting by friction, it seems clear on the face of the matter that the drill worked by a cord or bow is a later improvement on the clumsier primitive instrument twirled between the hands. That instructive class of specimens which antiquaries sometimes discover, bronze celts modelled on the heavy type of the stone hatchet, are scarcely explicable except as first steps in the transition from the Stone Age to the Bronze Age, to be followed soon by the next stage of progress, in which it is discovered that the new material is suited to a handier and less wasteful pattern. And thus, in the other branches of our history, there will come again

and again into view series of facts which may be consistently arranged as having followed one another in a
particular order of development, but which will hardly bear
being turned round and made to follow in reversed order.
Such for instance are the facts I have here brought forward
in a chapter on the Art of Counting, which tend to prove
that as to this point of culture at least, savage tribes
reached their position by learning and not by unlearning, by
elevation from a lower rather than by degradation from a
higher state.

Among evidence aiding us to trace the course which the
civilization of the world has actually followed, is that great
class of facts to denote which I have found it convenient
to introduce the term "survivals." These are processes,
customs, opinions, and so forth, which have been carried on
by force of habit into a new state of society different from
that in which they had their original home, and they thus
remain as proofs and examples of an older condition of culture out of which a newer has been evolved. Thus, I know
an old Somersetshire woman whose hand-loom dates from
the time before the introduction of the "flying shuttle,"
which new-fangled appliance she has never even learnt to
use, and I have seen her throw her shuttle from hand to
hand in true classic fashion; this old woman is not a
century behind her times, but she is a case of survival.
Such examples often lead us back to the habits of hundreds
and even thousands of years ago. The ordeal of the Key
and Bible, still in use, is a survival; the Midsummer bonfire
is a survival; the Breton peasants' All Souls' supper for
the spirits of the dead is a survival. The simple keeping
up of ancient habits is only one part of the transition
from old into new and changing times. The serious
business of ancient society may be seen to sink into the
sport of later generations, and its serious belief to linger
on in nursery folk-lore, while superseded habits of old-world
life may be modified into new-world forms still powerful for
good and evil. Sometimes old thoughts and practices will

burst out afresh, to the amazement of a world that thought them long since dead or dying; here survival passes into revival, as has lately happened in so remarkable a way in the history of modern spiritualism, a subject full of instruction from the ethnographer's point of view. The study of the principles of survival has, indeed, no small practical importance, for most of what we call superstition is included within survival, and in this way lies open to the attack of its deadliest enemy, a reasonable explanation. Insignificant, moreover, as multitudes of the facts of survival are in themselves, their study is so effective for tracing the course of the historical development through which alone it is possible to understand their meaning, that it becomes a vital point of ethnographic research to gain the clearest possible insight into their nature. This importance must justify the detail here devoted to an examination of survival, on the evidence of such games, popular sayings, customs, superstitions, and the like, as may serve well to bring into view the manner of its operation.

Progress, degradation, survival, revival, modification, are all modes of the connexion that binds together the complex network of civilization. It needs but a glance into the trivial details of our own daily life to set us thinking how far we are really its originators, and how far but the transmitters and modifiers of the results of long past ages. Looking round the rooms we live in, we may try here how far he who only knows his own time can be capable of rightly comprehending even that. Here is the honeysuckle of Assyria, there the fleur-de-lis of Anjou, a cornice with a Greek border runs round the ceiling, the style of Louis XIV. and its parent the Renaissance share the looking-glass between them. Transformed, shifted, or mutilated, such elements of art still carry their history plainly stamped upon them; and if the history yet farther behind is less easy to read, we are not to say that because we cannot clearly discern it there is therefore no history there. It is thus even with the fashion of the clothes men wear. The

ridiculous little tails of the German postilion's coat show
of themselves how they came to dwindle to such absurd
rudiments; but the English clergyman's bands no longer
so convey their history to the eye, and look unaccountable
enough till one has seen the intermediate stages through
which they came down from the more serviceable wide
collars, such as Milton wears in his portrait, and which
gave their name to the "band-box" they used to be kept
in. In fact, the books of costume, showing how one
garment grew or shrunk by gradual stages and passed into
another, illustrate with much force and clearness the nature
of the change and growth, revival and decay, which go on
from year to year in more important matters of life. In
books, again, we see each writer not for and by himself, but
occupying his proper place in history; we look through
each philosopher, mathematician, chemist, poet, into the
background of his education,—through Leibnitz into Descartes, through Dalton into Priestley, through Milton into
Homer. The study of language has, perhaps, done more
than any other in removing from our view of human thought
and action the ideas of chance and arbitary invention, and
in substituting for them a theory of development by the co-
operation of individual men, through processes ever
reasonable and intelligible where the facts are fully known.
Rudimentary as the science of culture still is, the symptoms
are becoming very strong that even what seem its most
spontaneous and motiveless phenomena will, nevertheless,
be shown to come within the range of distinct cause and
effect as certainly as the facts of mechanics. What would
be popularly thought more indefinite and uncontrolled than
the products of the imagination in myths and fables? Yet
any systematic investigation of mythology, on the basis of a
wide collection of evidence, will show plainly enough in
such efforts of fancy at once a development from stage to
stage, and a production of uniformity of result from uniformity of cause. Here, as elsewhere, causeless spontaneity
is seen to recede farther and farther into shelter within the

dark precincts of ignorance; like chance, that still holds its place among the vulgar as a real cause of events otherwise unaccountable, while to educated men it has long consciously meant nothing but this ignorance itself. It is only when men fail to see the line of connexion in events, that they are prone to fall upon the notions of arbitrary impulses, causeless freaks, chance and nonsense and indefinite unaccountability. If childish games, purposeless customs, absurd superstitions are set down as spontaneous because no one can say exactly how they came to be, the assertion may remind us of the like effect that the eccentric habits of the wild rice-plant had on the philosophy of a Red Indian tribe, otherwise disposed to see in the harmony of nature the effects of one controlling personal will. The Great Spirit, said these Sioux theologians, made all things except the wild rice; but the wild rice came by chance.

"Man," said Wilhelm von Humboldt, "ever connects on from what lies at hand (der Mensch knüpft immer an Vorhandenes an)." The notion of the continuity of civilization contained in this maxim is no barren philosophic principle, but is at once made practical by the consideration that they who wish to understand their own lives ought to know the stages through which their opinions and habits have become what they are. Auguste Comte scarcely overstated the necessity of this study of development, when he declared at the beginning of his ' Positive Philosophy ' that "no conception can be understood except through its history," and his phrase will bear extension to culture at large. To expect to look modern life in the face and comprehend it by mere inspection, is a philosophy whose weakness can easily be tested. Imagine any one explaining the trivial saying, " a little bird told me," without knowing of the old belief in the language of birds and beasts, to which Dr. Dasent, in the introduction to the Norse Tales, so reasonably traces its origin. To ingenious attempts at explaining by the light of reason things which want the

c 2

light of history to show their meaning, much of the learned
nonsense of the world has indeed been due. Sir H. S. Maine,
in his 'Ancient Law,' gives a perfect instance. In all the
literature which enshrines the pretended philosophy of law,
he remarks, there is nothing more curious than the pages
of elaborate sophistry in which Blackstone attempts to
explain and justify that extraordinary rule of English law,
only recently repealed, which prohibited sons of the same
father by different mothers from succeeding to one another's
land. To Sir H. S. Maine, knowing the facts of the case, it
was easy to explain its real origin from the "Customs of
Normandy," where according to the system of agnation, or
kinship on the male side, brothers by the same mother but
by different fathers were of course no relations at all to one
another. But when this rule "was transplanted to England, the English judges, who had no clue to its principle,
interpreted it as a general prohibition against the succession of the half-blood, and extended it to consanguine-
ous brothers, that is to sons of the same father by different
wives." Then, ages after, Blackstone sought in this
blunder the perfection of reason, and found it in the
argument that kinship through both parents ought to
prevail over even a nearer degree of kinship through but
one parent.[1] Such are the risks that philosophers run in
detaching any phenomenon of civilization from its hold on
past events, and treating it as an isolated fact, to be simply
disposed of by a guess at some plausible explanation.

In carrying on the great task of rational ethnography,
the investigation of the causes which have produced the
phenomena of culture, and the laws to which they are
subordinate, it is desirable to work out as systematically as
possible a scheme of evolution of this culture along its

---

[1] Blackstone, 'Commentaries.' "As every man's own blood is compounded
of the bloods of his respective ancestors, he only is properly of the whole or
entire blood with another, who hath (so far as the distance of degrees will
permit), all the same ingredients in the composition of his blood that the
other hath," etc.

many lines. In the following chapter, on the Development of Culture, an attempt is made to sketch a theoretical course of civilization among mankind, such as appears on the whole most accordant with the evidence. By comparing the various stages of civilization among races known to history, with the aid of archæological inference from the remains of pre-historic tribes, it seems possible to judge in a rough way of an early general condition of man, which from our point of view is to be regarded as a primitive condition, whatever yet earlier state may in reality have lain behind it. This hypothetical primitive condition corresponds in a considerable degree to that of modern savage tribes, who, in spite of their difference and distance, have in common certain elements of civilization, which seem remains of an early state of the human race at large. If this hypothesis be true, then, notwithstanding the continual interference of degeneration, the main tendency of culture from primeval up to modern times has been from savagery towards civilization. On the problem of this relation of savage to civilized life, almost every one of the thousands of facts discussed in the succeeding chapters has its direct bearing. Survival in Culture, placing all along the course of advancing civilization way-marks full of meaning to those who can decipher their signs, even now sets up in our midst primeval monuments of barbaric thought and life. Its investigation tells strongly in favour of the view that the European may find among the Greenlanders or Maoris many a trait for reconstructing the picture of his own primitive ancestors. Next comes the problem of the Origin of Language. Obscure as many parts of this problem still remain, its clearer positions lie open to the investigation whether speech took its origin among mankind in the savage state, and the result of the enquiry is that, consistently with all known evidence, this may have been the case. From the examination of the Art of Counting a far more definite consequence is shown. It may be confidently asserted, that not only is this important art

found in a rudimentary state among savage tribes, but that
satisfactory evidence proves numeration to have been developed by rational invention from this low stage up to that
in which we ourselves possess it. The examination of
Mythology contained in the first volume, is for the most
part made from a special point of view, on evidence collected for a special purpose, that of tracing the relation
between the myths of savage tribes and their analogues
among more civilized nations. The issue of such enquiry
goes far to prove that the earliest myth-maker arose and
flourished among savage hordes, setting on foot an art
which his more cultured successors would carry on, till its
results came to be fossilized in superstition, mistaken for
history, shaped and draped in poetry, or cast aside as lying
folly.

Nowhere, perhaps, are broad views of historical development more needed than in the study of religion. Notwithstanding all that has been written to make the world
acquainted with the lower theologies, the popular ideas of
their place in history and their relation to the faiths of
higher nations are still of the mediæval type. It is wonderful to contrast some missionary journals with Max Müller's
Essays, and to set the unappreciating hatred and ridicule
that is lavished by narrow hostile zeal on Brahmanism,
Buddhism, Zoroastrism, beside the catholic sympathy with
which deep and wide knowledge can survey those ancient
and noble phases of man's religious consciousness; nor,
because the religions of savage tribes may be rude and
primitive compared with the great Asiatic systems, do they
lie too low for interest and even for respect. The question
really lies between understanding and misunderstanding
them. Few who will give their minds to master the
general principles of savage religion will ever again think it
ridiculous, or the knowledge of it superfluous to the rest of
mankind. Far from its beliefs and practices being a
rubbish-heap of miscellaneous folly, they are consistent
and logical in so high a degree as to begin, as soon as even

roughly classified, to display the principles of their formation and development; and these principles prove to be
essentially rational, though working in a mental condition
of intense and inveterate ignorance. It is with a sense of
attempting an investigation which bears very closely on the
current theology of our own day, that I have set myself to
examine systematically, among the lower races, the development of Animism; that is to say, the doctrine of souls
and other spiritual beings in general. More than half of
the present work is occupied with a mass of evidence from
all regions of the world, displaying the nature and meaning
of this great element of the Philosophy of Religion, and
tracing its transmission, expansion, restriction, modification, along the course of history into the midst of our own
modern thought. Nor are the questions of small practical
moment which have to be raised in a similar attempt to
trace the development of certain prominent Rites and Ceremonies—customs so full of instruction as to the inmost
powers of religion, whose outward expression and practical
result they are.

In these investigations, however, made rather from an
ethnographic than a theological point of view, there has
seemed little need of entering into direct controversial
argument, which indeed I have taken pains to avoid as far
as possible. The connexion which runs through religion,
from its rudest forms up to the status of an enlightened
Christianity, may be conveniently treated of with little
recourse to dogmatic theology. The rites of sacrifice and
purification may be studied in their stages of development
without entering into questions of their authority and value,
nor does an examination of the successive phases of the
world's belief in a future life demand a discussion of the
arguments adduced for or against the doctrine itself. The
ethnographic results may then be left as materials for professed theologians, and it will not perhaps be long before
evidence so fraught with meaning shall take its legitimate
place. To fall back once again on the analogy of natural

history, the time may soon come when it will be thought as
unreasonable for a scientific student of theology not to have
a competent acquaintance with the principles of the religions of the lower races, as for a physiologist to look with
the contempt of fifty years ago on evidence derived from
the lower forms of life, deeming the structure of mere
invertebrate creatures matter unworthy of his philosophic
study.

Not merely as a matter of curious research, but as an important practical guide to the understanding of the present
and the shaping of the future, the investigation into the
origin and early development of civilization must be pushed
on zealously. Every possible avenue of knowledge must be
explored, every door tried to see if it is open. No kind of
evidence need be left untouched on the score of remoteness
or complexity, of minuteness or triviality. The tendency
of modern enquiry is more and more toward the conclusion
that if law is anywhere, it is everywhere. To despair of
what a conscientious collection and study of facts may lead
to, and to declare any problem insoluble because difficult
and far off, is distinctly to be on the wrong side in science ;
and he who will choose a hopeless task may set himself to
discover the limits of discovery. One remembers Comte
starting in his account of astronomy with a remark on the
necessary limitation of our knowledge of the stars : we conceive, he tells us, the possibility of determining their form,
distance, size, and movement, whilst we should never by
any method be able to study their chemical composition,
their mineralogical structure, &c. Had the philosopher
lived to see the application of spectrum analysis to this
very problem, his proclamation of the dispiriting doctrine of
necessary ignorance would perhaps have been recanted in
favour of a more hopeful view. And it seems to be with
the philosophy of remote human life somewhat as with the
study of the nature of the celestial bodies. The processes
to be made out in the early stages of our mental evolution
lie distant from us in time as the stars lie distant from us

in space, but the laws of the universe are not limited with
the direct observation of our senses.   There is vast material to be used in our enquiry; many workers are now
busied in bringing this material into shape, though little
may have yet been done in proportion to what remains to
do; and already it seems not too much to say that the
vague outlines of a philosophy of primæval history are
beginning to come within our view.

CHAPTER II.

THE DEVELOPMENT OF CULTURE.

Stages of culture, industrial, intellectual, political, moral—Development of culture in great measure corresponds with transition from savage through barbaric to civilized life — Progression-theory — Degeneration-theory — Development-theory includes both, the one as primary, the other as secondary—Historical and traditional evidence not available as to low stages of culture—Historical evidence as to principles of Degeneration—Ethnological evidence as to rise and fall in culture, from comparison of different levels of culture in branches of the same race—Extent of historically recorded antiquity of civilization — Prehistoric Archæology extends the antiquity of man in low stages of civilization—Traces of Stone Age, corroborated by megalithic structures, lake dwellings, shell-heaps, burial-places, &c., prove original low culture throughout the world—Stages of Progressive Development in industrial arts.

In taking up the problem of the development of culture as a branch of ethnological research, a first proceeding is to obtain a means of measurement. Seeking something like a definite line along which to reckon progression and retrogression in civilization, we may apparently find it best in the classification of real tribes and nations, past and present. Civilization actually existing among mankind in different grades, we are enabled to estimate and compare it by positive examples. The educated world of Europe and America practically settles a standard by simply placing its own nations at one end of the social series and savage tribes at the other, arranging the rest of mankind between these limits according as they correspond more closely to savage or to cultured life. The principal criteria of classification are the absence or presence, high or low development, of the industrial arts, especially metal-working, manufacture of implements and vessels, agriculture, architecture, &c., the extent of scientific knowledge, the definiteness of moral principles, the condition of religious belief and ceremony, the degree of social and political organization, and so forth. Thus, on the definite basis of compared facts, ethnographers are able to set up at least a rough scale of civilization. Few would dispute that the following races are arranged rightly in order of culture :—Australian, Tahitian, Aztec, Chinese, Italian. By treating the development of civilization on this plain ethnographic basis, many difficulties may be avoided which have embarrassed its discussion. This may be seen by a glance at the relation which theoretical principles of civilization bear to the transitions to be observed as matter of fact between the extremes of savage and cultured life.

From an ideal point of view, civilization may be looked upon as the general improvement of mankind by higher organization of the individual and of society, to the end of promoting at once man's goodness, power, and happiness. This theoretical civilization does in no small measure correspond with actual civilization, as traced by comparing savagery with barbarism, and barbarism with modern educated life. So far as we take into account only material and intellectual culture, this is especially true. Acquaintance with the physical laws of the world, and the accompanying power of adapting nature to man's own ends, are, on the whole, lowest among savages, mean among barbarians, and highest among modern educated nations. Thus a transition from the savage state to our own would be, practically, that very progress of art and knowledge which is one main element in the development of culture.

But even those students who hold most strongly that the general course of civilization, as measured along the scale of races from savages to ourselves, is progress towards the benefit of mankind, must admit many and manifold exceptions. Industrial and intellectual culture by no means advances uniformly in all its branches, and in fact excellence in various of its details is often obtained under conditions which keep back culture as a whole. It is true that these exceptions seldom swamp the general rule; and the Englishman, admitting that he does not climb trees like the wild Australian, nor track game like the savage of the Brazilian forest, nor compete with the ancient Etruscan and the modern Chinese in delicacy of goldsmith's work and ivory carving, nor reach the classic Greek level of oratory and sculpture, may yet claim for himself a general condition above any of these races. But there actually have to be taken into account developments of science and art which tend directly against culture. To have learnt to give poison secretly and effectually, to have raised a corrupt literature to pestilent perfection, to have organized a successful scheme to arrest free enquiry and proscribe free expression, are works of knowledge and skill whose progress toward their goal has hardly conduced to the general good. Thus, even in comparing mental and artistic culture among several peoples, the balance of good and ill is not quite easy to strike.

If not only knowledge and art, but at the same time moral and political excellence, be taken into consideration, it becomes yet harder to reckon on an ideal scale the advance or decline from stage to stage of culture. In fact, a combined intellectual and moral measure of human condition is an instrument which no student has as yet learnt properly to handle. Even granting that intellectual, moral, and political life may, on a broad view, be seen to progress together, it is obvious that they are far from advancing with equal steps. It may be taken as man's rule of duty in the world, that he shall strive to know as well as he can find out, and to do as well as he knows how. But the parting asunder of these two great principles, that separation of intelligence from virtue which accounts for so much of the wrong-doing of mankind, is continually seen to happen in the great movements of civilization. As one conspicuous instance of what all history stands to prove, if we study the early ages of Christianity, we may see men with minds pervaded by the new religion of duty, holiness, and love, yet at the same time actually falling away in intellectual life, thus at once vigorously grasping one half of civilization, and contemptuously casting off the other. Whether in high ranges or in low of human life, it may be seen that advance of culture seldom results at once in unmixed good. Courage, honesty, generosity, are virtues which may suffer, at least for a time, by the development of a sense of value of life and property. The savage who adopts something of foreign civilization too often loses his ruder virtues without gaining an equivalent. The white invader or colonist, though representing on the whole a higher moral standard than the savage he improves or destroys, often represents his standard very ill, and at best can hardly claim to substitute a life stronger, nobler, and purer at every point than that which he supersedes. The onward movement from barbarism has dropped behind it more than one quality of barbaric character, which cultured modern men look back on with regret, and will even strive to regain by futile attempts to stop the course of history, and restore the past in the midst of the present. So it is with social institutions. The slavery recognized by savage and barbarous races is preferable in kind to that which existed for centuries in late European colonies. The relation of the sexes among many savage tribes is more healthy than among the richer classes of the Mahommedan world. As a supreme authority of government, the savage councils of chiefs and elders compare favourably with the unbridled despotism under which so many cultured races have groaned. The Creek Indians, asked concerning their religion, replied that where agreement was not to be had, it was best to "let every man paddle his canoe his own way:" and after long ages of theological strife and persecution, the modern world seems coming to think these savages not far wrong.

Among accounts of savage life, it is not, indeed, uncommon to find details of admirable moral and social excellence. To take one prominent instance, Lieut. Bruijn Kops and

Mr. Wallace have described, among the rude Papuans of the Eastern Archipelago, a habitual truthfulness, rightfulness, and kindliness which it would be hard to match in the general moral life of Persia or India, to say nothing of many a civilized European district.[1] Such tribes may count as the "blameless Ethiopians" of the modern world, and from them an important lesson may be learnt. Ethnographers who seek in modern savages types of the remotely ancient human race at large, are bound by such examples to consider the rude life of primæval man under favourable conditions to have been, in its measure, a good and happy life. On the other hand, the pictures drawn by some travellers of savagery as a kind of paradisaical state may be taken too exclusively from the bright side. It is remarked as to these very Papuans, that Europeans whose intercourse with them has been hostile become so impressed with the wild-beast-like cunning of their attacks, as hardly to believe in their having feelings in common with civilized men. Our Polar explorers may well speak in kindly terms of the industry, the honesty, the cheerful considerate politeness of the Esquimaux; but it must be remembered that these rude people are on their best behaviour with foreigners, and that their character is apt to be foul and brutal where they have nothing to expect or fear. The Caribs are described as a cheerful, modest, courteous race, and so honest among themselves that if they missed anything out of a house they said quite naturally, "There has been a Christian here." Yet the malignant ferocity with which these estimable people tortured their prisoners of war with knife and fire-brand and red pepper, and then cooked and ate them in solemn debauch, gave fair reason for the name of Carib (Cannibal) to become the generic name of man-eaters in European languages.[2] So when we read descriptions of the hospitality, the gentleness, the bravery, the deep religious feeling of the

[1] G. W. Earl, 'Papuans,' p. 79; A. R. Wallace, 'Eastern Archipelago.'
[2] Rochefort, 'Iles Antilles,' pp. 100—480.

North American Indians, we admit their claims to our
sincere admiration ; but we must not forget that they were
hospitable literally to a fault, that their gentleness would
pass with a flash of anger into frenzy, that their bravery
was stained with cruel and treacherous malignity, that their
religion expressed itself in absurd belief and useless ceremony. The ideal savage of the 18th century might be held
up as a living reproof to vicious and frivolous London ; but
in sober fact, a Londoner who should attempt to lead the
atrocious life which the real savage may lead with impunity
and even respect, would be a criminal only allowed to follow
his savage models during his short intervals out of gaol.
Savage moral standards are real enough, but they are far
looser and weaker than ours. We may, I think, apply the
often-repeated comparison of savages to children as fairly
to their moral as to their intellectual condition. The better
savage social life seems in but unstable equilibrium, liable
to be easily upset by a touch of distress, temptation, or
violence, and then it becomes the worse savage life, which
we know by so many dismal and hideous examples. Altogether, it may be admitted that some rude tribes lead a life
to be envied by some barbarous races, and even by the
outcasts of higher nations. But that any known savage
tribe would not be improved by judicious civilization, is a
proposition which no moralist would dare to make ; while
the general tenour of the evidence goes far to justify the
view that on the whole the civilized man is not only wiser
and more capable than the savage, but also better and
happier, and that the barbarian stands between.

It might, perhaps, seem practicable to compare the whole
average of the civilization of two peoples, or of the same
people in different ages, by reckoning each, item by item,
to a sort of sum-total, and striking a balance between them,
much as an appraiser compares the value of two stocks of
merchandise, differ as they may both in quantity and
quality. But the few remarks here made will have shown
how loose must be the working-out of these rough-and-ready

estimates of culture. In fact, much of the labour spent in investigating the progress and decline of civilization has been mis-spent, in premature attempts to treat that as a whole which is as yet only susceptible of divided study. The present comparatively narrow argument on the development of culture at any rate avoids this greatest perplexity. It takes cognizance principally of knowledge, art, and custom, and indeed only very partial cognizance within this field, the vast range of physical, political, social, and ethical considerations being left all but untouched. Its . standard of reckoning progress and decline is not that of ideal good and evil, but of movement along a measured line from grade to grade of actual savagery, barbarism, and civilization. The thesis which I venture to sustain, within limits, is simply this, that the savage state in some measure represents an early condition of mankind, out of which the higher culture has gradually been developed or evolved, by processes still in regular operation as of old, the result showing that, on the whole, progress has far prevailed over relapse.

On this proposition, the main tendency of human society during its long term of existence has been to pass from a savage to a civilized state. Now all must admit a great part of this assertion to be not only truth, but truism. Referred to direct history, a great section of it proves to belong not to the domain of speculation, but to that of positive knowledge. It is mere matter of chronicle that modern civilization is a development of mediæval civilization, which again is a development from civilization of the order represented in Greece, Assyria, or Egypt. Thus the higher culture being clearly traced back to what may be called the middle culture, the question which remains is, whether this middle culture may be traced back to the lower culture, that is, to savagery. To affirm this, is merely to assert that the same kind of development in culture which has gone on inside our range of knowledge has also gone on outside it, its course of proceeding being unaffected by our having or not having reporters present. If any one holds that human thought and action were worked out in primæval times according to laws essentially other than those of the modern world, it is for him to prove by valid evidence this anomalous state of things, otherwise the doctrine of permanent principle will hold good, as in astronomy or geology. That the tendency of culture has been similar throughout the existence of human society, and that we may fairly judge from its known historic course what its pre-historic course may have been, is a theory clearly entitled to precedence as a fundamental principle of ethnographic research.

Gibbon, in his 'Roman Empire,' expresses in a few vigorous sentences his theory of the course of culture, as from savagery upward. Judged by the knowledge of nearly a century later, his remarks cannot, indeed, pass unquestioned. Especially he seems to rely with misplaced confidence on traditions of archaic rudeness, to exaggerate the lowness of savage life, to underestimate the liability to decay of the ruder arts, and in his view of the effect of high on low civilization, to dwell too exclusively on the brighter side. But, on the whole, the great historian's judgment seems so substantially that of the unprejudiced modern student of the progressionist school, that I gladly quote the passage here at length, and take it as a text to represent the development-theory of culture :—" The discoveries of ancient and modern navigators, and the domestic history, or tradition, of the most enlightened nations, represent the *human savage* naked both in mind and body, and destitute of laws, of arts, of ideas, and almost of language. From this abject condition, perhaps the primitive and universal state of man, he has gradually arisen to command the animals, to fertilise the earth, to traverse the ocean, and to measure the heavens. His progress in the improvement and exercise of his mental and corporeal faculties has been irregular and various; infinitely slow in the beginning, and increasing by degrees with redoubled velocity: ages of laborious ascent have been followed by a moment of rapid downfall; and the several climates of the globe have felt the vicissitudes of light and darkness.   Yet the experience of four thousand years should enlarge our hopes, and diminish our apprehensions: we cannot determine to what height the human species may aspire in their advances towards perfection; but it may safely be presumed that no people, unless the face of nature is changed, will relapse into their original barbarism.   The improvements of society may be viewed under a threefold aspect.   1. The poet or philosopher illustrates his age and country by the efforts of a *single* mind; but these superior powers of reason or fancy are rare and spontaneous productions; and the genius of Homer, or Cicero, or Newton, would excite less admiration, if they could be created by the will of a prince, or the lessons of a preceptor.   2. The benefits of law and policy, of trade and manufactures, of arts and sciences, are more solid and permanent; and *many* individuals may be qualified, by education and discipline, to promote, in their respective stations, the interest of the community.   But this general order is the effect of skill and labour; and the complex machinery may be decayed by time, or injured by violence.   3. Fortunately for mankind, the more useful, or, at least, more necessary arts, can be performed without superior talents, or national subordination; without the powers of *one*, or the union of *many*. Each village, each family, each individual, must always possess both ability and inclination to perpetuate the use of fire and of metals; the propagation and service of domestic animals; the methods of hunting and fishing; the rudiments of navigation; the imperfect cultivation of corn, or other nutritive grain; and the simple practice of the mechanic trades.   Private genius and public industry may be extirpated; but these hardy plants survive the tempest, and strike an everlasting root into the most unfavourable soil. The splendid days of Augustus and Trajan were eclipsed by a cloud of ignorance; and the barbarians subverted the laws and palaces of Rome.   But the scythe, the invention or emblem of Saturn, still continued annually to mow the harvests of Italy; and the human feasts of the Læstrigons have never been renewed on the coast of Campania. Since the first discovery of the arts, war, commerce, and religious zeal, have diffused, among the savages of the Old and New World, these inestimable gifts; they have been successively propagated; they can never be lost. We may therefore acquiesce in the pleasing conclusion, that every age of the world has increased, and still increases, the real wealth, the happiness, the knowledge, and perhaps the virtue, of the human race."[1]

This progression-theory of civilization may be contrasted with its rival, the degeneration-theory, in the dashing invective of Count Joseph de Maistre, written toward the beginning of this century. "Nous partons toujours," he says, "de l'hypothèse banale que l'homme s'est élevé graduellement de la barbarie à la science et à la civilisation. C'est le rêve favori, c'est l'erreur-mère, et comme dit l'école, le proto-pseudes de notre siècle. Mais si les philosophes de ce malheureux siècle, avec l'horrible perversité que nous leur avons connue, et qui s'obstinent encore malgré les avertissements qu'ils ont reçus, avaient possédé de plus quelques-unes de ces connaissances qui ont du nécessairement appartenir aux premiers hommes, &c."[2] The degeneration-theory, which this eloquent antagonist of "modern ideas" indeed states in an extreme shape, has received the sanction of men of great learning and ability. It has practically resolved itself into two assumptions, first, that the history of culture began with the appearance on earth of a semi-civilized race of men, and second, that from this stage culture has proceeded in two ways, backward to produce savages, and forward to produce civilized men. The idea of the original condition of man being one of more or less high culture, must have a certain prominence

[1] Gibbon, 'Decline and Fall of the Roman Empire,' ch. xxxviii.
[2] De Maistre, 'Soirées de St. Pétersbourg,' vol. ii. p. 180.

given to it on account of its considerable hold on public
opinion. As to definite evidence, however, it does not
seem to have any ethnological basis whatever. Indeed, I
scarcely think that a stronger counter-persuasion could be
used on an intelligent student inclined to the ordinary
degeneration-theory than to induce him to examine criti-
cally and impartially the arguments of the advocates on his
own side. It must be borne in mind, however, that the
grounds on which this theory has been held have generally
been rather theological than ethnological. The strength
of the position it has thus occupied may be well instanced
from the theories adopted by two eminent French writers
of the last century, which in a remarkable way piece
together a belief in degeneration and an argument for progression. De Brosses, whose whole intellectual nature
turned to the progression-theory, argued that by studying
what actually now happens "we may trace men upward from
the savage state to which the flood and dispersion had
reduced them."[1]   And Goguet, holding that the pre-
existing arts perished at the deluge, was thus left free to
work out on the most thorough-going progressionist
principles his theories of the invention of fire, cooking,
agriculture, law, and so forth, among tribes thus reduced
to a condition of low savagery.[2] At the present time it is
not unusual for the origin of civilization to be treated as
matter of dogmatic theology. It has happened to me more
than once to be assured from the pulpit that the theories of
ethnologists who consider man to have risen from a low
original condition are delusive fancies, it being revealed
truth that man was originally in a high condition. Now as
a matter of Biblical criticism it must be remembered that a
large proportion of modern theologians are far from accepting such a dogma. But in investigating the problem of

---

[1] De Brosses, 'Dieux Fétiches,' p. 15; 'Formation des Langues,' vol. i.
p. 49; vol. ii. p. 52.
[2] Goguet, 'Origine des Lois, des Arts,' etc., vol. i. p. 88.

early civilization, the claim to ground scientific opinion upon a basis of revelation is in itself objectionable. It would be, I think, inexcusable if students who have seen in Astronomy and Geology the unhappy results of attempting to base science on religion, should countenance a similar attempt in Ethnology.

By long experience of the course of human society, the principle of development in culture has become so ingrained in our philosophy that ethnologists, of whatever school, hardly doubt but that, whether by progress or degradation, savagery and civilization are connected as lower and higher stages of one formation. As such, then, two principal theories claim to account for their relation. As to the first hypothesis, which takes savage life as in some sort representing an early human state whence higher states were, in time, developed, it has to be noticed that advocates of this progression-theory are apt to look back toward yet lower original conditions of mankind. It has been truly remarked that the modern naturalist's doctrine of progressive development has encouraged a train of thought singularly accordant with the Epicurean theory of man's early existence on earth, in a condition not far removed from that of the lower animals. On such a view, savage life itself would be a far advanced condition. If the advance of culture be regarded as taking place along one general line, then existing savagery stands directly intermediate between animal and civilized life ; if along different lines, then savagery and civilization may be considered as at least indirectly connected through their common origin. The method and evidence here employed are not, however, suitable for the discussion of this remoter part of the problem of civilization. Nor is it necessary to enquire how, under this or any other theory, the savage state first came to be on earth. It is enough that, by some means or other, it has actually come into existence ; and so far as it may serve as a guide in inferring an early condition of the human race at large, so far the argument takes the very

practicable shape of a discussion turning rather on actual
than imaginary states of society. The second hypothesis,
which regards higher culture as original, and the savage
condition as produced from it by a course of degeneration,
at once cuts the hard knot of the origin of culture. It
takes for granted a supernatural interference, as where
Archbishop Whately simply refers to miraculous revelation
that condition above the level of barbarism which he considers to have been man's original state.[1] It may be incidentally remarked, however, that the doctrine of original
civilization bestowed on man by divine intervention, by no
means necessarily involves the view that this original civilization was at a high level. Its advocates are free to choose
their starting-point of culture above, at, or below the savage
condition, as may on the evidence seem to them most
reasonable.

The two theories which thus account for the relation of
savage to cultured life may be contrasted according to their
main character, as the progression-theory and the degradation-theory. Yet of course the progression-theory recognizes degradation, and the degradation-theory recognizes
progression, as powerful influences in the course of culture.
Under proper limitations the principles of both theories are
conformable to historical knowledge, which shows us, on
the one hand, that the state of the higher nations was
reached by progression from a lower state, and, on the
other hand, that culture gained by progression may be lost
by degradation. If in this enquiry we should be obliged to
end in the dark, at any rate we need not begin there.
History, taken as our guide in explaining the different stages
of civilization, offers a theory based on actual experience.
This is a development-theory, in which both advance and
relapse have their acknowledged places. But so far as
history is to be our criterion, progression is primary and
degradation secondary; culture must be gained before it

[1] Whately, 'Essay on the Origin of Civilization,' in Miscellaneous Lectures,
etc. See also W. Cooke Taylor, 'Natural History of Society.'

can be lost. Moreover, in striking a balance between the effects of forward and backward movement in civilization, it must be borne in mind how powerfully the diffusion of culture acts in preserving the results of progress from the attacks of degeneration. A progressive movement in culture spreads, and becomes independent of the fate of its originators. What is produced in some limited district is diffused over a wider and wider area, where the process of effectual "stamping out" becomes more and more difficult. Thus it is even possible for the habits and inventions of races long extinct to remain as the common property of surviving nations; and the destructive actions which make such havoc with the civilizations of particular districts fail to destroy the civilization of the world.

The enquiry as to the relation of savagery to barbarism and semi-civilization lies almost entirely in præ-historic or extra-historic regions. This is of course an unfavourable condition, and must be frankly accepted. Direct history hardly tells anything of the changes of savage culture, except where in contact with and under the dominant influence of foreign civilization, a state of things which is little to our present purpose. Periodical examinations of low races otherwise left isolated to work out their own destinies, would be interesting evidence to the student of civilization if they could be made; but unfortunately they cannot. The lower races, wanting documentary memorials, loose in preserving tradition, and ever ready to clothe myth in its shape, can seldom be trusted in their stories of long-past ages. History is oral or written record which can be satisfactorily traced into contact with the events it describes ; and perhaps no account of the course of culture in its lower stages can satisfy this stringent criterion. Traditions may be urged in support either of the progression-theory or of the degradation-theory. These traditions may be partly true, and must be partly untrue ; but whatever truth or untruth they may contain, there is such difficulty in separating man's recollection of what was from his specu-

lation as to what might have been, that ethnology seems not
likely to gain much by attempts to judge of early stages of
civilization on a traditional basis. The problem is one
which has occupied the philosophic mind even in savage
and barbaric life, and has been solved by speculations
asserted as facts, and by traditions which are, in great
measure, mere realized theories. The Chinese can show,
with all due gravity, the records of their ancient dynasties,
and tell us how in old times their ancestors dwelt in caves,
clothed themselves in leaves, and ate raw flesh, till, under
such and such rulers, they were taught to build huts,
prepare skins for garments, and make fire.[1] Lucretius can
describe to us, in his famous lines, the large-boned, hardy,
lawless, primæval race of man, living the roving life of the
wild beasts which he overcame with stones and heavy clubs,
devouring berries and acorns, ignorant as yet of fire, and
agriculture, and the use of skins for clothing. From this
state the Epicurean poet traces up the development of
culture, beginning outside but ending inside the range of
human memory.[2] To the same class belong those legends
which, starting from an ancient savage state, describe its
elevation by divine civilizers: this, which may be called the
supernatural progression-theory, is exemplified in the
familiar culture-traditions of Peru and Italy.

But other minds, following a different ideal track from
the present to the past, have seen in a far different shape
the early stages of human life. Those men whose eyes are
always turned to look back on the wisdom of the ancients,
those who by a common confusion of thought ascribe to
men of old the wisdom of old men, those who hold fast to
some once-honoured scheme of life which new schemes are
superseding before their eyes, are apt to carry back their
thought of present degeneration into far-gone ages, till they
reach a period of primæval glory. The Parsi looks back to
the happy rule of King Yima, when men and cattle were
immortal, when water and trees never dried up and food

[1] Goguet, vol. iii. p. 270.   [2] Lucret. v. 923, etc.; see Hor. Sat. i. 3.

was inexhaustible, when there was no cold nor heat, no envy nor old age.[1] The Buddhist looks back to the age of glorious soaring beings who had no sin, no sex, no want of food, till the unhappy hour when, tasting a delicious scum that formed upon the surface of the earth, they fell into evil, and in time became degraded to eat rice, to bear children, to build houses, to divide property, and to establish caste. In after ages, record preserves details of the continuing course of degeneration. It was King Chetiya who told the first lie, and the citizens who heard of it, not knowing what a lie was, asked if it were white, black or blue. Men's lives grew shorter and shorter, and it was King Maha Sâgara who, after a brief reign of 252,000 years, made the dismal discovery of the first grey hair.[2]

Admitting the imperfection of the historical record as regards the lowest stages of culture, we must bear in mind that it tells both ways. Niebuhr, attacking the progressionists of the 18th century, remarks that they have overlooked the fact "that no single example can be brought forward of an actually savage people having independently become civilized."[3] Whately appropriated this remark, which indeed forms the kernel of his well-known Lecture on the Origin of Civilization : "Facts are stubborn things," he says, "and that no authenticated instance can be produced of savages that ever *did* emerge, unaided, from that state is no *theory*, but a statement, hitherto never disproved, of a matter of *fact*." He uses this as an argument in support of his general conclusion, that man could not have risen independently from a savage to a civilized state, and that savages are degenerate descendants of civilized men.[4] But he omits to ask the counter-question, whether we find one recorded instance of a civilized people falling independently into a savage

---

[1] 'Avesta,' trans. Spiegel & Bleeck, vol. II. p. 50.
[2] Hardy, 'Manual of Budhism,' pp. 64, 128.
[3] Niebuhr, 'Römische Geschichte,' part i. p. 88 : "Nur das haben sie übersehen, dass kein einziges Beyspiel von einem wirklich wilden Volk aufzuweisen ist, welches frey zur Cultur übergegangen wäre."
[4] Whately, 'Essay on Origin of Civilization.'

state? Any such record, direct and well vouched, would be of
high interest to ethnologists, though, of course, it would not
contradict the development-theory, for proving loss is not
disproving previous gain. But where is such a record to be
found ? The defect of historical evidence as to the transition between savagery and higher culture is a two-sided fact,
only half taken into Archbishop Whately's one-sided argument. Fortunately the defect is by no means fatal.
Though history may not account directly for the existence
and explain the position of savages, it at least gives evidence
which bears closely on the matter. Moreover, we are in
various ways enabled to study the lower course of culture on
evidence which cannot have been tampered with to support
a theory. Old traditional lore, however untrustworthy as
direct record of events, contains most faithful incidental
descriptions of manners and customs ; archæology displays
old structures and buried relics of the remote past; philology brings out the undesigned history in language, which
generation after generation have handed down without a
thought of its having such significance ; the ethnological
survey of the races of the world tells much ; the ethnographical comparison of their condition tells more.

Arrest and decline in civilization are to be recognized as
among the more frequent and powerful operations of national
life. That knowledge, arts, and institutions should decay in
certain districts, that peoples once progressive should lag
behind and be passed by advancing neighbours, that sometimes even societies of men should recede into rudeness and
misery—all these are phenomena with which modern history
is familiar. In judging of the relation of the lower to the
higher stages of civilization, it is essential to gain some idea
how far it may have been affected by such degeneration.
What kind of evidence can direct observation and history
give as to the degradation of men from a civilized condition
towards that of savagery ? In our great cities, the so-called
" dangerous classes " are sunk in hideous misery and de-
pravity. If we have to strike a balance between the

Papuans of New Caledonia and the communities of European beggars and thieves, we may sadly acknowledge that we have in our midst something worse than savagery. But it is not savagery; it is broken down civilization. Negatively, the inmates of a Whitechapel casual ward and of a Hottentot kraal agree in their want of the knowledge and virtue of the higher culture. But positively, their mental and moral characteristics are utterly different. Thus, the savage life is essentially devoted to gaining subsistence from nature, which is just what the proletarian life is not. Their relations to civilized life—the one of independence, the other of dependence—are absolutely opposite. To my mind the popular phrases about "city savages" and "street Arabs" seem like comparing a ruined house to a builder's yard. It is more to the purpose to notice how war and misrule, famine and pestilence, have again and again devastated countries, reduced their population to miserable remnants, and lowered their level of civilization, and how the isolated life of wild country districts seems sometimes tending towards savagery. So far as we know, however, none of these causes have ever really reproduced a savage community. For an ancient account of degeneration under adverse circumstances, Ovid's mention of the unhappy colony of Tomi on the Black Sea is a case in point, though perhaps not to be taken too literally. Among its mixed Greek and barbaric population, harassed and carried off into slavery by the Sarmatian horsemen, much as the Persians of to-day are by the Turkomans, the poet describes the neglect of the gardener's craft, the decay of textile arts, the barbaric clothing of hides.

> " Nec tamen hæc loca sunt ullo pretiosa metallo :
>   Hostis ab agricola vix sinit illa fodi.
> Purpura sæpe tuos fulgens protexit amictus,
>   Sed non Sarmatico tingitur illa mari.
> Vellera dura ferunt pecudes, et Palladis uti
>   Arte Tomitanæ non didicere nurus.
> Femina pro lana Corialia munera frangit,
>   Suppositoque gravem vertice portat aquam.

> Non hic pampineis amicitur vitibus ulmus,
> Nulla premunt ramos pondere poma sua.
> Tristia deformes pariunt absinthia campi,
> Terraque de fructu quam sit amara, docet."[1]

Cases of exceptionally low civilization in Europe may perhaps be sometimes accounted for by degeneration of this kind. But they seem more often the relics of ancient unchanged barbarism. The evidence from wild parts of Ireland two or three centuries ago is interesting from this point of view. Acts of Parliament were passed against the inveterate habits of fastening ploughs to the horses' tails, and of burning oats from the straw to save the trouble of threshing. In the 18th century Ireland could still be thus described in satire :—

> "The Western isle renowned for bogs,
> For tories and for great wolf-dogs,
> For drawing hobbies by the tails,
> And threshing corn with fiery flails."[2]

Fynes Moryson's description of the wild or "meere" Irish, about 1600, is amazing. The very lords of them, he says, dwelt in poor clay houses, or cabins of boughs covered with turf. In many parts men as well as women had in very winter time but a linen rag about the loins and a woollen mantle on their bodies, so that it would turn a man's stomach to see an old woman in the morning before breakfast. He notices their habit of burning oats from the straw, and making cakes thereof. They had no tables, but set their meat on a bundle of grass. They feasted on fallen horses, and seethed pieces of beef and pork with the unwashed entrails of beasts in a hollow tree, lapped in a raw cow's hide, and so set over the fire, and they drank milk warmed with a stone first cast into the fire.[3] Another

---

[1] Ovid. Ex Ponto, lil. 8 ; see Grote, 'History of Greece,' vol. xii. p. 641.

[2] W. C. Taylor, 'Nat. Hist. of Society,' vol. L p. 202.

[3] Fynes Moryson, 'Itinerary ;' London, 1617, part lil. p. 162, etc. ; J. Evans in 'Archæologia,' vol. xll. See description of hide-boiling, etc., among the wild Irish about 1550, in Andrew Boorde, 'Introduction of Knowledge,' ed. by F. J. Furnivall, Early English Text Soc. 1870.

district remarkable for a barbaric simplicity of life is the
Hebrides. In 1868 Mr. Walter Morrison there bought from
an old woman at Stornoway the service of earthenware she was
actually using, of which he gave me a crock. These earthen
vessels, unglazed and made by hand without the potter's
wheel, might pass in a museum as indifferent specimens of
savage manufacture. Such a modern state of the potter's
art in the Hebrides fits well with George Buchanan's statement in the 10th century that the islanders used to boil
meat in the beast's own paunch or hide.[1] Early in the
18th century Martin mentions as prevalent there the ancient
way of dressing corn by burning it dexterously from the ear,
which he notices to be a very quick process, thence called
" graddan " (Gaelic, grad=quick).[2] Thus we see that the
habit of burning out the grain, for which the " meere Irish "
were reproached, was really the keeping up of an old Keltic
art, not without its practical use. So the appearance in
modern Keltic districts of other widespread arts of the lower
culture—hide-boiling, like that of the Scythians in Herodotus, and stone-boiling, like that of the Assinaboins of North
America—seems to fit not so well with degradation from a
high as with survival from a low civilization. The Irish and
the Hebrideans had been for ages under the influence of comparatively high civilization, which nevertheless may have left
unaltered much of the older and ruder habit of the people.

Instances of civilized men taking to a wild life in outlying districts of the world, and ceasing to obtain or want
the appliances of civilization, give more distinct evidence of
degradation. In connexion with this state of things takes
place the nearest known approach to an independent degeneration from a civilized to a savage state. This happens
in mixed races, whose standard of civilization may be more
or less below that of the higher race. The mutineers of the
Bounty, with their Polynesian wives, founded a rude but

---

[1] Buchanan, ' Rerum Scoticarum Historia ;' Edinburgh, 1528, p. 7. See
' Early History of Mankind,' 2nd ed. p. 272.
    Martin, ' Description of Western Islands,' in Pinkerton, vol. iii. p. 639.

not savage community on Pitcairn's Island.[1] The mixed
Portuguese and native races of the East Indies and
Africa lead a life below the European standard, but not a
savage life.[2] The Gauchos of the South American Pampas,
a mixed European and Indian race of equestrian herdsmen,
are described as sitting about on ox-skulls, making broth in
horns with hot cinders heaped round, living on meat without vegetables, and altogether leading a foul, brutal,
comfortless, degenerate, but not savage life.[3] One step
beyond this brings us to the cases of individual civilized
men being absorbed in savage tribes and adopting the
savage life, on which they exercise little influence for improvement; the children of these men may come distinctly
under the category of savages. These cases of mixed
breeds, however, do not show a low culture actually
produced as the result of degeneration from a high one.
Their theory is that, given a higher and a lower civilization
existing among two races, a mixed race between the two
may take to the lower or an intermediate condition.

Degeneration probably operates even more actively in
the lower than in the higher culture. Barbarous nations
and savage hordes, with their less knowledge and scantier
appliances, would seem peculiarly exposed to degrading
influences. In Africa, for instance, there seems to have
been in modern centuries a falling off in culture, probably
due in a considerable degree to foreign influence. Mr. J.
L. Wilson, contrasting the 16th and 17th century accounts
of powerful negro kingdoms in West Africa with the present
small communities, with little or no tradition of their forefathers' more extended political orginazation, looks
especially to the slave-trade as the deteriorating cause.[4] In

    [1] 'Mutiny of the Bounty,' etc.
    [2] Wallace, 'Malay Archipelago,' vol. i. pp. 42, 471; vol. II. pp. 11, 43, 48;
Latham, 'Descr. Eth.,' vol. ii. pp. 492-5; D. and C. Livingstone, 'Exp. to
Zambesi,' p. 45.
    [3] Southey, 'History of Brazil,' vol. iii. p. 422.
    [4] J. L. Wilson, 'W. Afr.,' p. 189.

South-east Africa, also, a comparatively high barbaric culture, which we especially associate with the old descriptions of the kingdom of Monomotapa, seems to have fallen away, and the remarkable ruins of buildings of hewn stone fitted without mortar indicate a former civilization above that of the present native population.[1] In North America, Father Charlevoix remarks of the Iroquois of the last century, that in old times they used to build their cabins better than other nations, and better than they do themselves now; they carved rude figures in relief on them; but since in various expeditions almost all their villages have been burnt, they have not taken the trouble to restore them in their old condition.[2] The degradation of the Cheyenne Indians is matter of history. Persecuted by their enemies the Sioux, and dislodged at last even from their fortified village, the heart of the tribe was broken. Their numbers were thinned, they no longer dared to establish themselves in a permanent abode, they gave up the cultivation of the soil, and became a tribe of wandering hunters, with horses for their only valuable possession, which every year they bartered for a supply of corn, beans, pumpkins, and European merchandise, and then returned into the heart of the prairies.[3] When in the Rocky Mountains, Lord Milton and Dr. Cheadle came upon an outlying fragment of the Shushwap race, without horses or dogs, sheltering themselves under rude temporary slants of bark or matting, falling year by year into lower misery, and rapidly dying out; this is another example of the degeneration which no doubt has lowered or destroyed many a savage people.[4] There are tribes who are the very outcasts of savage life. There is reason to look upon the miserable Digger Indians

---

[1] Waitz, 'Anthropologie,' vol. II. p. 359, see 91; Du Chaillu, 'Ashango-land,' p. 110.

[2] Charlevoix, 'Nouvelle France,' vol. vi. p. 51.

[3] Irving, 'Astoria,' vol. ii. ch. v.

[4] Milton and Cheadle, 'North West Passage by Land,' p. 241; Waitz, vol. iii. pp. 74—6.

of North America and the Bushmen of South Africa as the
persecuted remnants of tribes who have seen happier days.[1]
The traditions of the lower races of their ancestors' better
life may sometimes be real recollections of a not far distant
past. The Algonquin Indians look back to old days as to
a golden age when life was better than now, when they had
better laws and leaders, and manners less rude.[2] And
indeed, knowing what we do of their history, we may admit
that they have cause to remember in misery happiness gone
by. Well, too, might the rude Kamchadal declare that the
world is growing worse and worse, that men are becoming fewer and viler, and food scarcer, for the hunter, and
the bear, and the reindeer are hurrying away from here to
the happier life in the regions below.[3] It would be a valuable
contribution to the study of civilization to have the action
of decline and fall investigated on a wider and more exact
basis of evidence than has yet been attempted. The cases
here stated are probably but part of a long series which
might be brought forward to prove degeneration in culture
to have been, by no means indeed the primary cause of the
existence of barbarism and savagery in the world, but a
secondary action largely and deeply affecting the general
development of civilization. It may perhaps give no unfair
idea to compare degeneration of culture, both in its kind of
operation and in its immense extent, to denudation in the
geological history of the earth.

In judging of the relations between savage and civilized
life, something may be learnt by glancing over the divisions
of the human race. For this end the classification by
families of languages may be conveniently used, if checked
by the evidence of bodily characteristics. No doubt speech
by itself is an insufficient guide in tracing national descent,
as witness the extreme cases of Jews in England, and three-
parts negro races in the West Indies, nevertheless speaking

[1] 'Early History of Mankind,' p. 187.
[2] Schoolcraft, 'Algic Res.,' vol. I. p. 80.
[3] Steller, 'Kamtschatka,' p. 272.

English as their mother-tongue. Still, under ordinary circumstances, connexion of speech does indicate more or less connexion of ancestral race. As a guide in tracing the history of civilization, language gives still better evidence, for common language to a great extent involves common culture. The race dominant enough to maintain or impose its language, usually more or less maintains or imposes its civilization also. Thus the common descent of the languages of Hindus, Greeks, and Teutons is no doubt due in great measure to common ancestry, but is still more closely bound up with a common social and intellectual history, with what Professor Max Müller well calls their " spiritual relationship." The wonderful permanence of language often enables us to detect among remotely ancient and distant tribes the traces of connected civilization. How, on such grounds, do savage and civilized tribes appear to stand related, within the various groups of mankind connected historically by the possession of kindred languages ?

The Semitic family, which represents one of the oldest known civilizations of the world, includes Arabs, Jews, Phœnicians, Syrians, etc., and may have an older as well as a newer connexion in North Africa. This family takes in some rude tribes, but none which would be classed as savages. The Aryan family has existed in Asia and Europe certainly for several thousand years, and there are well-known and well-marked traces of its early barbaric condition, which has perhaps survived with least change among secluded tribes in the valleys of the Hindu Kush and Himalaya. There seems, again, no known case of any full Aryan tribe having become savage. The Gypsies and other outcasts are, no doubt, partly Aryan in blood, but their degraded condition is not savagery. In India there are tribes Aryan by language, but whose physique is rather of indigenous type, and whose ancestry is mainly from indigenous stocks with more or less mixture of the dominant Hindu. Some tribes coming under this category, as among the Bhils and Kulis of the

Bombay Presidency, speak dialects which are Hindi in vocabulary at least, whether or not in grammatical structure, and yet the people themselves are lower in culture than some Hinduized nations who have retained their original Dravidian speech, the Tamils for instance. But these all appear to stand at higher stages of civilization than any wild forest tribes of the peninsula who can be reckoned as nearly savages ; all such are non-Aryan both in blood and speech.[1] In Ceylon, however, we seem to have the remarkable phenomenon of a distinctly savage race speaking an Aryan dialect.   This is the wild part of the race of Veddas or "hunters," of whom a remnant still inhabit the forest land.   These people are dark-skinned and flat-nosed, slight of frame, and very small of skull, and five feet is a full average man's height.   They are a shy, harmless, simple people, living principally by hunting ; they lime birds, take fish by poisoning the water, and are skilful in getting wild honey ; they have bows with iron-pointed arrows, which, with their hunting dogs, are their most valuable possessions. They dwell in caves or bark huts, and their very word for a house is Singhalese for a hollow tree (ruknla) ; a patch of bark was formerly their dress, but now a bit of linen hangs to their waist-cords ; their planting of patches of ground is said to be recent.   They count on their fingers, and produce fire with the simplest kind of fire-drill twirled by hand.   They are most truthful and honest.   Their monogamy and conjugal fidelity contrast strongly with the opposite habits of the more civilized Singhalese.   A remarkable Vedda marriage custom sanctioned a man's taking his younger (not elder) sister as his wife ; sister-marriage existing among the Singhalese, but being confined to the royal family.   Mistaken statements have been made as to the Veddas having no religion, no personal names, no language.   Their religion, in fact, corresponds with the animism of the ruder tribes of India ; some of their names are remarkable as being Hindu,

[1] See O. Campbell, 'Ethnology of India,' in Journ. As. Soc. Bengal, 1866, part ii.

but not in use among the modern Singhalese; their language is described as a kind of Singhalese patois, peculiar in dialect and utterance. There is no doubt attaching to the usual opinion that the Veddas are in the main descended from the "yakkos" or demons; i. e., from the indigenous tribes of the island. Legend and language concur to make probable an admixture of Aryan blood accompanying the adoption of Aryan speech, but the evidence of bodily characteristics shows the Vedda race to be principally of indigenous præ-Aryan type.[1]

The Tatar family of Northern Asia and Europe (Turanian, if the word be used in a restricted sense), displays evidence of quite a different kind. This wide-lying group of tribes and nations has members nearly or quite touching the savage level in ancient and even modern times, such as Ostyaks, Tunguz, Samoyeds, Lapps, while more or less high ranges of culture are represented by Mongols, Turks, and Hungarians. Here, however, it is unquestionable that the rude tribes represent the earlier condition of the Tatar race at large, from which its more mixed and civilized peoples, mostly by adopting the foreign culture of Buddhist, Moslem, and Christian nations, and partly by internal development, are well known to have risen. The ethnology of South-Eastern Asia is somewhat obscure; but if we may classify under one heading the native races of Siam, Birma, etc., the wilder tribes may be considered as representing earlier conditions, for the higher culture of this region is obviously foreign, especially of Buddhist origin. The Malay race is also remarkable for the range of civilization represented by tribes classed as belonging to it. If the wild tribes of the Malayan peninsula and Borneo be compared with the semi-civilized nations of Java and Sumatra, it appears that part of the race survives to represent an early savage state, while part is found in possession of a civiliza-

---

[1] J. Bailey, 'Veddahs,' in Tr. Eth. Soc., vol. ii. p. 278; see vol. III. p. 70. Compare Robert Knox, 'Historical Relation of Ceylon.' London, 1691, part iii. chap. i.; Sir J. E. Tennent, 'Ceylon,' etc.

tion which the first glance shows to have been mostly
borrowed from Hindu and Moslem sources. Some forest
tribes of the peninsula seem to be representatives of the
Malay race at a very low level of culture, how far original
and how far degraded it is not easy to say. Among them
the very rude Orang Sabimba, who have no agriculture and
no boats, give a remarkable account of themselves, that
they are descendants of shipwrecked Malays from the Bugis
country, but were so harassed by pirates that they gave up
civilization and cultivation, and vowed not to eat fowls,
which betrayed them by their crowing. So they plant
nothing, but eat wild fruit and vegetables, and all animals
but the fowl. This, if at all founded on fact, is an interesting
case of degeneration. But savages usually invent myths to
account for peculiar habits, as where, in the same district,
the Biduanda Kallang account for their not cultivating the
ground by the story that their ancestors vowed not to make
plantations. Another rude people of the Malay peninsula
are the Jakuns, a simple, kindly race, among whom some
trace their pedigree to a pair of white monkeys, while others
declare that they are descendants of white men; and indeed
there is some ground for supposing these latter to be really
of mixed race, for they use a few Portuguese words, and a report exists of some refugees having settled up the country.[1]
The Polynesians, Papuans, and Australians represent grades
of savagery spread each over its own vast area in a comparatively homogeneous way. Lastly, the relations of
savagery to higher conditions are remarkable, but obscure,
on the American continents. There are several great
linguistic families whose members were discovered in a
savage state throughout: such are the Esquimaux, Algonquin, and Guarani groups. On the other hand there were
three apparently unconnected districts of semi-civilization
reaching a high barbaric level, viz., in Mexico and Central
America, Bogota, and Peru. Between these higher and
lower conditions were races at the level of the Natchez of

[1] Journ. Ind. Archip., vol. i. pp. 295–9; vol. ii. p. 237.

Louisiana and the Apalaches of Florida. Linguistic connexion is not unknown between the more advanced peoples and the lower races around them.[1] But definite evidence showing the higher culture to have arisen from the lower, or the lower to have fallen from the higher, is scarcely forthcoming. Both operations may in degree have happened.

It is apparent, from such general inspection of this ethnological problem, that it would repay a far closer study than it has as yet received. As the evidence stands at present, it appears that when in any race some branches much excel the rest in culture, this more often happens by elevation than by subsidence. But this elevation is much more apt to be produced by foreign than by native action. Civilization is a plant much oftener propagated than developed. As regards the lower races, this accords with the results of European intercourse with savage tribes during the last three or four centuries; so far as these tribes have survived the process, they have assimilated more or less of European culture and risen towards the European level, as in Polynesia, South Africa, South America. Another important point becomes manifest from this ethnological survey. The fact that, during so many thousand years of known existence, neither the Aryan nor the Semitic stock appears to have thrown off any direct savage offshoot recognizable by the age-enduring test of language, tells, with some force, against the probability of degradation to the savage level ever happening from high-level civilization.

With regard to the opinions of older writers on early civilization, whether progressionists or degenerationists, it must be borne in mind that the evidence at their disposal

---

[1] For the connexion between the Aztec language and the Sonoran family extending N.W. toward the sources of the Missouri, see Buschmann, 'Spuren der Aztekischen Sprache im Nördlichen Mexico,' etc., in Abh. der Akad. der Wissensch. 1854; Berlin, 1859; also Tr. Eth. Soc., vol. II. p. 130. For the connexion between the Natchez and Maya languages, see Daniel G. Brinton, in 'American Historical Magazine,' 1867, vol. i. p. 16; and 'Myths of the New World,' p. 23.

fell far short of even the miserably imperfect data now
accessible. Criticizing an 18th century ethnologist is like
criticizing an 18th century geologist. The older writer may
have been far abler than his modern critic, but he had not
the same materials. Especially he wanted the guidance of
Prehistoric Archæology, a department of research only
established on a scientific footing within the last few years.
It is essential to gain a clear view of the bearing of this
newer knowledge on the old problem.

Chronology, though regarding as more or less fictitious
the immense dynastic schemes of the Egyptians, Hindus,
and Chinese, passing as they do into mere ciphering-book
sums with years for units, nevertheless admits that existing
monuments carry back the traces of comparatively high
civilization to a distance of above five thousand years. By
piecing together Eastern and Western documentary evidence,
it seems that the great religious divisions of the Aryan race,
to which modern Brahmanism, Zarathustrism, and Buddhism
are due, belong to a period of remotely ancient history.
Even if we are not quite sure, with Professor Max Müller,
in the preface to his translation of the "Rig Veda," that
this collection of Aryan hymns "will take and maintain for
ever its position as the most ancient of books in the library
of mankind," and if we do not fully admit the stringency of
his reckonings of its date in centuries B.C., yet we must
grant that he shows cause to refer its composition to a very
ancient period, where it then proves that a comparatively
high barbaric culture already existed. The linguistic argument for the remotely ancient common origin of the Indo-
European nations, in a degree as to their bodily descent,
and in a greater degree as to their civilization, tends toward
the same result. So it is again with Egypt. Baron Bunsen's
calculations of Egyptian dynasties in thousands of years are
indeed both disputable and disputed, but they are based on
facts which at any rate authorize the reception of a long
chronology. To go no further than the identification of two
or three Egyptian names mentioned in Biblical and Classical

history, we gain a strong impression of remote antiquity.
Such are the names of Shishank; of the Psammitichos line,
whose obelisks are to be seen in Rome; of Tirhakah, King
of Ethiopia, whose nurse's coffin is in the Florence Museum;
of the city of Rameses, plainly connected with that great
Ramesside line which Egyptologists call the 19th Dynasty.
Here, before classic culture had arisen, the culture of Egypt
culminated, and behind this time lies the somewhat less
advanced age of the Pyramid kings, and behind this again
the indefinite lapse of ages which such a civilization required
for its production. Again, though no part of the Old Testament can satisfactorily prove for itself an antiquity of
composition approaching that of the earliest Egyptian
hieroglyphic inscriptions, yet all critics must admit that the
older of the historical books give on the one hand contemporary documents showing considerable culture in the
Semitic world at a date which in comparison with classic
history is ancient, while on the other hand they afford
evidence by way of chronicle, carrying back ages farther the
record of a somewhat advanced barbaric civilization. Now
if the development-theory is to account for phenomena such
as these, its chronological demand must be no small one,
and the more so when it is admitted that in the lower ranges
of culture progress would be extremely slow in comparison
with that which experience shows among nations already far
advanced. On these conditions of the first appearance of
the middle civilization being thrown back to distant
antiquity, and of slow development being required to
perform its heavy task in ages still more remote, Prehistoric
Archæology cheerfully takes up the problem. And, indeed,
far from being dismayed by the vastness of the period
required on the narrowest computation, the prehistoric
archæologist shows even too much disposition to revel in
calculations of thousands of years, as a financier does in
reckonings of thousands of pounds, in a liberal and maybe
somewhat reckless way.

Prehistoric Archæology is fully alive to facts which may

bear on degeneration in culture. Such are the colossal
human figures of hewn stone in Easter Island, which may
possibly have been shaped by the ancestors of the existing
islanders, whose present resources, however, are quite un-
equal to the execution of such gigantic works.[1] A much
more important case is that of the former inhabitants of the
Mississippi Valley. In districts where the native tribes
known in modern times do not rank high even as savages,
there formerly dwelt a race whom ethnologists call the
Mound-Builders, from the amazing extent of their mounds
and enclosures, of which there is a single group occupying
an area of four square miles. To have constructed such
works the Mound-Builders must have been a numerous
population, mainly subsisting by agriculture, and indeed
vestiges of their ancient tillage are still to be found. The
civilization of these people has been, however, sometimes
overrated. Their earthworks did not require, as has been
thought, standards of measurement and means of determining angles, for a cord and a bundle of stakes would be a sufficient set of instruments to lay out any of them. Their
use of native copper, hammered into shape for cutting
instruments, is similar to that of some of the savage tribes
farther north. On the whole, judging by their earthworks,
fields, pottery, stone implements, and other remains, they
seem to have belonged to those high savage or barbaric
tribes of the Southern States, of whom the Creeks and
Cherokees, as described by Bartram, may be taken as
typical.[2] If any of the wild roving hunting tribes now found
living near the huge earthworks of the Mound-Builders are
the descendants of this somewhat advanced race, then a very
considerable degradation has taken place. The question is
an open one. The explanation of the traces of tillage may

---

[1] J. H. Lamprey, in Trans. of Prehistoric Congress, Norwich, 1868, p. 60 ;
J. Linton Palmer, in Journ. Eth. Soc., vol. i., 1869.

[2] Squier and Davis, 'Mon. of Mississippi Valley,' etc., in Smithsonian
Contr., vol. i. 1848. See Lubbock, 'Prehistoric Times,' chap. vii. ; Waitz,
'Anthropologie,' vol. iii. p. 72. Bartram, 'Creek and Cherokee Ind.,' in Tr.
Amer. Ethnol. Soc., vol. iii. part i.

perhaps in this case be like that of remains of old cultivation-terraces in Borneo, the work of Chinese colonists whose descendants have mostly been merged in the mass of the population and follow the native habits.[1] On the other hand, the evidence of locality may be misleading as to race. A traveller in Greenland, coming on the ruined stone buildings at Kakortok, would not argue justly that the Esquimaux are degenerate descendants of ancestors capable of such architecture, for in fact these are the remains of a church and baptistery built by the ancient Scandinavian settlers.[2] On the whole it is remarkable how little of colourable evidence of degeneration has been disclosed by archæology. Its negative evidence tells strongly the other way. As an instance may be quoted Sir John Lubbock's argument against the idea that tribes now ignorant of metallurgy and pottery formerly possessed but have since lost these arts. "We may also assert, on a general proposition, that no weapons or instruments of metal have ever been found in any country inhabited by savages wholly ignorant of metallurgy. A still stronger case is afforded by pottery. Pottery is not easily destroyed; when known at all it is always abundant, and it possesses two qualities, namely, those of being easy to break, and yet difficult to destroy, which render it very valuable in an archæological point of view. Moreover, it is in most cases associated with burials. It is, therefore, a very significant fact, that no fragment of pottery has ever been found in Australia, New Zealand, or the Polynesian Islands."[3] How different a state of things the popular degeneration-theory would lead us to expect is pointedly suggested by Sir Charles Lyell's sarcastic sentences in his ' Antiquity of Man.' Had the original stock of mankind, he argues, been really endowed with superior intellectual powers and inspired knowledge, while possessing the same improvable nature as their posterity, how extreme a point of advancement would

[1] St. John, 'Life in Forests of Far East,' vol. ii. p. 327.
[2] Rafn, 'American Arctiske Landes Gamle Geographie,' pl. vii., viii.
[3] Lubbock, in 'Report of British Association, Dundee, 1867,' p. 121.

they have reached. "Instead of the rudest pottery or flint tools, so irregular in form as to cause the unpractised eye to doubt whether they afford unmistakable evidence of design, we should now be finding sculptured forms surpassing in beauty the master-pieces of Phidias or Praxiteles; lines of buried railways or electric telegraphs, from which the best engineers of our day might gain invaluable hints; astronomical instruments and microscopes of more advanced construction than any known in Europe, and other indications of perfection in the arts and sciences, such as the nineteenth century has not yet witnessed. Still farther would the triumphs of inventive genius be found to have been carried, when the later deposits, now assigned to the ages of bronze and iron, were formed. Vainly should we be straining our imaginations to guess the possible uses and meaning of such relics—machines, perhaps, for navigating the air or exploring the depths of the ocean, or for calculating arithmetical problems beyond the wants or even the conception of living mathematicians."[1]

The master-key to the investigation of man's primæval condition is held by Prehistoric Archæology. This key is the evidence of the Stone Age, proving that men of remotely ancient ages were in the savage state. Ever since the long-delayed recognition of M. Boucher de Perthes' discoveries (1841 and onward) of the flint implements in the Drift gravels of the Somme Valley, evidence has been accumulating over a wide European area to show that the ruder Stone Age, represented by implements of the Palæolithic or Drift type, prevailed among savage tribes of the Quaternary period, the contemporaries of the mammoth and the woolly rhinoceros, in ages for which Geology asserts an antiquity far more remote than History can avail to substantiate for the human race. Mr. John Frere had already written in 1797 respecting such flint instruments discovered at Hoxne in Suffolk. "The situation in which these weapons were found may tempt us to refer them to a very remote period

[1] Lyell, 'Antiquity of Man,' chap. xix.

indeed, even beyond that of the present world."[1] The vast lapse of time through which the history of London has represented the history of human civilization, is to my mind one of the most suggestive facts disclosed by archæology. There the antiquary, excavating but a few yards deep, may descend from the débris representing our modern life, to relics of the art and science of the Middle Ages, to signs of Norman, Saxon, Romano-British times, to traces of the higher Stone Age. And on his way from Temple Bar to the Great Northern Station he passes near the spot (" opposite to black Mary's, near Grayes inn lane ") where a drift implement of black flint was found with the skeleton of an elephant by Mr. Conyers, about a century and a half ago, the relics side by side of the London mammoth and the London savage.[2] In the gravel-beds of Europe, the laterite of India, and other more superficial localities, where relics of the Palæolithic Age are found, what principally testifies to man's condition is the extreme rudeness of his stone implements, and the absence of even edge-grinding. The natural inference that this indicates a low savage state is confirmed in the caves of Central France. There a race of men, who have left indeed really artistic portraits of themselves and the reindeer and mammoths they lived among, seem, as may be judged from the remains of their weapons, implements, etc., to have led a life somewhat of Esquimaux type, but lower by the want of domesticated animals. The districts where implements of the rude primitive Drift type are found are limited in extent. It is to ages later in time and more advanced in development, that the Neolithic or Polished Stone Period belonged, when the manufacture of stone instruments was much improved, and grinding and polishing were generally introduced. During the long period of prevalence of this state of things, Man appears to have spread almost over the whole

[1] Frere, in 'Archæologia,' 1800.
[2] J. Evans, in 'Archæologia,' 1861 ; Lubbock, 'Prehistoric Times,' 2nd ed., p. 335.

habitable earth. The examination of district after district of the world has now all but established a universal rule that the Stone Age (bone or shell being the occasional substitutes for stone) underlies the Metal Age everywhere. Even the districts famed in history as seats of ancient civilization show, like other regions, their traces of a yet more archaic Stone Age. Asia Minor, Egypt, Palestine, India, China, furnish evidence from actual specimens, historical mentions, and survivals, which demonstrate the former prevalence of conditions of society which have their analogues among modern savage tribes.[1] The Duke of Argyll, in his 'Primeval Man,' while admitting the Drift implements as having been the ice hatchets and rude knives of low tribes of men inhabiting Europe toward the end of the Glacial Period, concludes thence " that it would be about as safe as to argue from these implements as to the condition of Man at that time in the countries of his Primeval Home, as it would be in our own day to argue from the habits and arts of the Eskimo as to the state of civilization in London or in Paris."[2] The progress of Archæology for years past, however, has been continually cutting away the ground on which such an argument as this can stand, till now it is all but utterly driven off the field. Where now is the district of the earth that can be pointed to as the " Primeval Home " of Man, and that does not show by rude stone implements buried in its soil the savage condition of its former inhabitants? There is scarcely a known province of the world of which we cannot say certainly, savages once dwelt here, and if in such a case an ethnologist asserts that these savages were the descendants or successors of a civilized nation, the burden of proof lies on him. Again, the Bronze Age and the Iron Age belong in great measure to history, but their relation to the Stone Age proves the soundness of the judgment of Lucretius, when, attaching experience of the present to memory and

[1] See 'Early History of Mankind,' 2nd ed. chap. viii.
[2] Argyll, 'Primeval Man,' p. 129.

inference from the past, he propounded what is now a tenet
of archæology, the succession of the Stone, Bronze, and Iron
Ages :

> "Arma antiqua manus ungues dentesque fuerunt,
> Et lapides, et item silvarum fragmina rami
>
> . . . .
>
> Posterius ferri vis est ærisque reperta,
> Et prior æris erat quam ferri cognitus usus." [1]

Throughout the various topics of Prehistoric Archæology,
the force and convergence of its testimony upon the development of culture are overpowering. The relics discovered in
gravel-beds, caves, shell-mounds, terramares, lake-dwellings,
earthworks, the results of an exploration of the superficial
soil in many countries, the comparison of geological evidence, of historical documents, of modern savage life, cor-
roborate and explain one another. The megalithic structures, menhirs, cromlechs, dolmens, and the like, only
known to England, France, Algeria, as the work of races of
the mysterious past, have been kept up as matters of modern
construction and recognized purpose among the ruder indigenous tribes of India. The series of ancient lake-settle-
ments which must represent so many centuries of successive
population fringing the shores of the Swiss lakes, have their
surviving representatives among rude tribes of the East
Indies, Africa, and South America. Outlying savages are
still heaping up shell-mounds like those of far-past Scandinavian antiquity. The burial-mounds still to be seen in
civilized countries have served at once as museums of early
culture and as proofs of its savage or barbaric type. It is
enough, without entering farther here into subjects fully
discussed in modern special works, to claim the general
support given to the development-theory of culture by Prehistoric Archæology. It was with a true appreciation of
the bearings of this science that one of its founders, the
venerable Professor Sven Nilsson, declared in 1843 in the

[1] Lucret. De Rerum Natura, v. 1281.

Introduction to his 'Primitive Inhabitants of Scandinavia,' that we are "unable properly to understand the significance of the antiquities of any individual country without at the same time clearly realizing the idea that they are the fragments of a progressive series of civilization, and that the human race has always been, and still is, steadily advancing in civilization." [1]

Enquiry into the origin and early development of the material arts, as judged of by comparing the various stages at which they are found existing, leads to a corresponding result. Not to take this argument up in its full range, a few typical details may serve to show its general character. Amongst the various stages of the arts, it is only a minority which show of themselves by mere inspection whether they are in the line of progress or of decline. Most such facts may be compared to an Indian's canoe, stem and stern alike, so that one cannot tell by looking at it which way it is set to go. But there are some which, like our own boats, distinctly point in the direction of their actual course. Such facts are pointers in the study of civilization, and in every branch of the enquiry should be sought out. A good example of these pointer-facts is recorded by Mr. Wallace. In Celebes, where the bamboo houses are apt to lean with the prevalent west wind, the natives have found out that if they fix some crooked timbers in the sides of the house, it will not fall. They choose such accordingly, the crookedest they can find, but they do not know the rationale of the contrivance, and have not hit on the idea that straight poles fixed slanting would have the same effect in making the structure rigid. [3] In fact, they have gone halfway toward inventing what builders call a "strut," but have stopped

[1] See Lyell, 'Antiquity of Man,' 3rd ed. 1863; Lubbock, 'Prehistoric Times,' 2nd ed. 1870; 'Trans. of Congress of Prehistoric Archæology,' (Norwich, 1868); Stevens, 'Flint Chips, etc.,' 1870; Nilsson, 'Primitive Inhabitants of Scandinavia' (ed. by Lubbock, 1868); Falconer, 'Palæontological Memoirs, etc.'; Lartet and Christy, 'Reliquiæ Aquitanicæ' (ed. by T. R. Jones); Keller, 'Lake Dwellings' (Tr. and Ed. by J. E. Lee), etc., etc.
[3] Wallace, 'Indian Archipelago,' vol. I. p. 357.

short. Now the mere sight of such a house would show
that the plan is not a remnant of higher architecture, but a
half-made invention. This is a fact in the line of progress,
but not of decline. I have mentioned elsewhere a number
of similar cases; thus the adaptation of a cord to the fire-
drill is obviously an improvement on the simpler instrument twirled by hand, and the use of the spindle for making thread is an improvement on the clumsier art of hand-
twisting; [1] but to reverse this position, and suppose the
hand-drill to have come into use by leaving off the use of
the cord of the cord-drill, or that people who knew the use
of the spindle left it off and painfully twisted their thread by
hand, is absurd. Again, the appearance of an art in a particular locality where it is hard to account for it as borrowed
from elsewhere, and especially if it concerns some special
native product, is evidence of its being a native invention.
Thus, what people can claim the invention of the hammock,
or the still more admirable discovery of the extraction of
the wholesome cassava from the poisonous manioc, but the
natives of the South American and West Indian districts to
which these things belong? As the isolated possession of
an art goes to prove its invention where it is found, so the
absence of an art goes to prove that it was never present.
The onus probandi is on the other side; if anyone thinks
that the East African's ancestors had the lamp and the
potter's wheel, and that the North American Indians once
possessed the art of making beer from their maize like the
Mexicans, but that these arts have been lost, at any rate let
him show cause for such an opinion. I need not, perhaps, go
so far as a facetious ethnological friend of mine, who argues
that the existence of savage tribes who do not kiss their
women is a proof of primæval barbarism, for, he says, if
they had ever known the practice they could not possibly
have forgotten it. Lastly and principally, as experience
shows us that arts of civilized life are developed through
successive stages of improvement, we may assume that the

[1] 'Early History of Mankind,' pp. 192, 248, etc., etc.

early development of even savage arts came to pass in a
similar way, and thus, finding various stages of an art
among the lower races, we may arrange these stages in a
series probably representing their actual sequence in
history. If any art can be traced back among savage tribes
to a rudimentary state in which its invention does not seem
beyond their intellectual condition, and especially if it may
be produced by imitating nature or following nature's direct
suggestion, there is fair reason to suppose the very origin of
the art to have been reached.

Professor Nilsson, looking at the remarkable similarity of
the hunting and fishing instruments of the lower races of
mankind, considers them to have been contrived instinc-
tively by a sort of natural necessity. As an example he takes
the bow and arrow.[1] The instance seems an unfortunate
one, in the face of the fact that the supposed bow-and-
arrow-making instinct fails among the natives of Australia,
to whom it would have been very useful, while even among
the Papuan natives of the New Hebrides there is reason to
think it not original, for the bow is called there *fana, pena,*
nfanga, &c., names apparently taken from the Malay *panah,*
and indicating a Malay origin for the instrument. It seems
to me that Dr. Klemm, in his dissertation on Implements
and Weapons, and Colonel Lane Fox, in his lectures on
Primitive Warfare, take a more instructive line in tracing
the early development of arts, not to a blind instinct, but to
a selection, imitation, and gradual adaptation and improvement of objects and operations which Nature, the instructor
of primæval man, sets before him. Thus Klemm traces
the stages by which progress appears to have been made
from the rough stick to the finished spear or club, from the
natural sharp-edged or rounded stone to the artistically
fashioned celt, spear-head, or hammer.[2] Fox traces connexion through the various types of weapons, pointing out
how a form once arrived at is repeated in various sizes, like

---

[1] Nilsson, 'Primitive Inhabitants of Scandinavia,' p. 104.
[2] Klemm, 'Allg. Culturwissenschaft,' part ii., Werkzeuge und Waffen.

the spear-head and arrow-point; how in rude conditions of
the arts the same instrument serves different purposes, as
where the Fuegians used their arrow-heads also for knives,
and Kafirs carve with their assagais, till separate forms are
adopted for special purposes; and how in the history of the
striking, cutting, and piercing instruments used by mankind, a continuity may be traced, which indicates a gradual
progressive development from the rudest beginnings to the
most advanced improvements of modern skill.　To show
how far the early development of warlike arts may have
been due to man's imitative faculty, he points out the
analogies in methods of warfare among animals and men,
classifying as defensive appliances hides, solid plates,
jointed plates, scales; as offensive weapons, the piercing,
striking, serrated, poisoned kinds, &c.; and under the head
of stratagems, flight, concealment, leaders, outposts, war-
cries, and so forth.[1]

The manufacture of stone implements is now almost
perfectly understood by archæologists.　The processes used
by modern savages have been observed and imitated.　Mr.
John Evans, for instance, by blows with a pebble, pressure
with a piece of stag's horn, sawing with a flint-flake, boring
with a stick and sand, and grinding on a stone surface,
succeeds in reproducing all but the finest kinds of stone
implements.[2]　On thorough knowledge we are now able to
refer in great measure the remarkable similarities of the
stone scrapers, flake-knives, hatchets, spear- and arrow-
heads, &c., as found in distant times and regions, to the
similarity of natural models, of materials, and of requirements which belong to savage life.　The history of the
Stone Age is clearly seen to be one of development.　Beginning with the natural sharp stone, the transition to the

[1] Lane Fox, 'Lectures on Primitive Warfare,' Journ. United Service Inst.
1867—9.
[2] Evans in 'Trans. of Congress of Prehistoric Archæology' (Norwich, 1868),
p. 191; Rau in 'Smithsonian Reports,' 1868; Sir E. Belcher in Tr. Eth. Soc.
vol. L p. 129.

rudest artificially shaped stone implement is imperceptibly gradual, and onward from this rude stage much independent progress in different directions is to be traced, and the manufacture at last arrives at admirable artistic perfection, by the time that the introduction of metal is superseding it. So with other implements and fabrics, of which the stages are known through their whole course of development from the merest nature to the fullest art. The club is traced from the rudest natural bludgeon up to the weapon of finished shape and carving. Pebbles held in the hand to hammer with, and cutting-instruments of stone shaped or left smooth at one end to be held in the hand, may be seen in museums, hinting that the important art of fixing instruments in handles was the result of invention, not of instinct. The stone hatchet, used as a weapon, passes into the battle-axe. The spear, a pointed stick or pole, has its point hardened in the fire, and a further improvement is to fix on a sharp point of horn, bone, or chipped stone. Stones are flung by hand, and then by the sling, a contrivance widely but not universally known among savage tribes. From first to last in the history of war the spear or lance is grasped as a thrusting weapon. Its use as a missile no doubt began as early, but it has hardly survived so far in civilization. Thus used, it is most often thrown by the unaided arm, but a sling for the purpose is known to various savage tribes. The short cord with an eye used in the New Hebrides, and called a "becket" by Captain Cook, and a whip-like instrument noticed in New Zealand, are used for spear-throwing. But the more usual instrument is a wooden handle, a foot or two long. This spear-thrower is known across the high northern districts of North America, among some tribes of South America, and among the Australians. These latter, it has been asserted, could not have invented it in their present state of barbarism. But the remarkable feature of the matter is that the spear-thrower belongs especially to savagery, and not to civilization. Among the higher nations the nearest approach to it seems to have been the

classic amentum, apparently a thong attached to the middle
of the javelin to throw it with. The highest people known
to have used the spear-thrower proper are the Aztecs. Its
existence among them is vouched for by representations in
the Mexican mythological pictures, by its name " atlatl,"
and by a beautifully artistic specimen of the thing itself in
the Christy Museum; but we do not hear of it as in
practical use at the Conquest, when it had apparently fallen
into survival. In fact the history of the instrument seems
in absolute opposition to the degradation-theory, representing as it does an invention belonging to savage culture, and
scarcely able to survive beyond. Nearly the same may be
said of the blow-tube, which as a serious weapon scarcely
ranges above rude tribes of the East Indies and South
America, though kept up in sport at higher levels. The
Australian boomerang has been claimed as derived from
some hypothetical high culture, whereas the transition-
stages through which it is connected with the club are to be
observed in its own country, while no civilized race possesses
the weapon.

The use of an elastic switch to fillip small missiles with,
and the remarkable elastic darts of the Pelew Islands, bent
and made to fly by their own spring, indicate inventions
which may have led to that of the bow, while the arrow is a
miniature form of the javelin. The practice of poisoning
arrows, after the manner of stings and serpents' fangs, is no
civilized device, but a characteristic of lower life, which is
generally discarded even at the barbaric stage. The art of
narcotizing fish, remembered but not approved by high
civilization, belongs to many savage tribes, who might
easily discover it in any forest pool where a suitable plant
had fallen in. The art of setting fences to catch fish at the
ebb of the tide, so common among the lower races, is a
simple device for assisting nature quite likely to occur to
the savage, in whom sharp hunger is no mean ally of dull
wit. Thus it is with other arts. Fire-making, cooking,
pottery, the textile arts, are to be traced along lines of

gradual improvement.[1] Music begins with the rattle and the drum, which in one way or another hold their places from end to end of civilization, while pipes and stringed instruments represent an advanced musical art which is still developing. So with architecture and agriculture. Complex, elaborate, and highly-reasoned as are the upper stages of these arts, it is to be remembered that their lower stages begin with mere direct imitation of nature, copying the shelters which nature provides, and the propagation of plants which nature performs. Without enumerating to the same purpose the remaining industries of savage life, it may be said generally that their facts resist rather than require a theory of degradation from higher culture. They agree with, and often necessitate, the same view of development which we know by experience to account for the origin and progress of the arts among ourselves.

In the various branches of the problem which will henceforward occupy our attention, that of determining the relation of the mental condition of savages to that of civilized men, it is an excellent guide and safeguard to keep before our minds the theory of development in the material arts. Throughout all the manifestations of the human intellect, facts will be found to fall into their places on the same general lines of evolution. The notion of the intellectual state of savages as resulting from decay of previous high knowledge, seems to have as little evidence in its favour as that stone celts are the degenerate successors of Sheffield axes, or earthen grave-mounds degraded copies of Egyptian pyramids. The study of savage and civilized life alike avail us to trace in the early history of the human intellect, not gifts of transcendental wisdom, but rude shrewd sense taking up the facts of common life and shaping from them schemes of primitive philosophy. It will be seen again and again, by examining such topics as language, mythology, custom, religion, that savage opinion is in a more or less rudimentary state, while the civilized

---

[1] See details in ‘Early History of Mankind,’ chap. vii.—ix.

mind still bears vestiges, neither few nor slight, of a past
condition from which savages represent the least, and
civilized men the greatest advance. Throughout the whole
vast range of the history of human thought and habit, while
civilization has to contend not only with survival from
lower levels, but also with degeneration within its own
borders, it yet proves capable of overcoming both and
taking its own course. History within its proper field, and
ethnography over a wider range, combine to show that the
institutions which can best hold their own in the world
gradually supersede the less fit ones, and that this incessant conflict determines the general resultant course of
culture. I will venture to set forth in mythic fashion how
progress, aberration, and retrogression in the general course
of culture contrast themselves in my own mind. We may
fancy ourselves looking on Civilization, as in personal
figure she traverses the world; we see her lingering or
resting by the way, and often deviating into paths that
bring her toiling back to where she had passed by long
ago; but, direct or devious, her path lies forward, and if
now and then she tries a few backward steps, her walk soon
falls into a helpless stumbling. It is not according to her
nature, her feet were not made to plant uncertain steps
behind her, for both in her forward view and in her onward
gait she is of truly human type.

CHAPTER III.

SURVIVAL IN CULTURE.

Survival and Superstition—Children's games—Games of chance—Traditional sayings—Nursery poems—Proverbs—Riddles—Significance and survival in Customs: meeting-formula, rite of foundation-sacrifice, prejudice against saving a drowning man.

WHEN a custom, an art, or an opinion is fairly started in the world, disturbing influences may long affect it so slightly that it may keep its course from generation to generation, as a stream once settled in its bed will flow on for ages. This is mere permanence of culture; and the special wonder about it is that the change and revolution of human affairs should have left so many of its feeblest rivulets to run so long. On the Tatar steppes, six hundred years ago, it was an offence to tread on the threshold or touch the ropes in entering a tent, and so it appears to be still.[1] Eighteen centuries ago Ovid mentions the vulgar Roman objection to marriages in May, which he not unreasonably explains by the occurrence in that month of the funeral rites of the Lemuralia :—

> "Nec viduæ tædis eadem, nec virginis apta
> Tempora. Quæ nupsit, non diuturna fuit.
> Hac quoque de causa, si te proverbia tangunt,
> Mense malas Maio nubere vulgus ait."[2]

The saying that marriages in May are unlucky survives

---

[1] Wil. de Bubruquis in Pinkerton, vol. vii. pp. 46, 87, 182; Michie, 'Siberian Overland Route,' p. 96.

[2] Ovid. Fast. v. 487. For modern Italy and France, see Edélestane du Méril, 'Études d' Archéol.' p. 121.

to this day in England, a striking example how an idea,
the meaning of which has perished for ages, may continue
to exist simply because it has existed.

Now there are thousands of cases of this kind which
have become, so to speak, landmarks in the course of
culture. When in the process of time there has come
general change in the condition of a people, it is usual,
notwithstanding, to find much that manifestly had not its
origin in the new state of things, but has simply lasted on
into it. On the strength of these survivals, it becomes
possible to declare that the civilization of the people they
are observed among must have been derived from an earlier
state, in which the proper home and meaning of these
things are to be found; and thus collections of such facts
are to be worked as mines of historic knowledge. In dealing with such materials, experience of what actually
happens is the main guide, and direct history has to teach
us, first and foremost, how old habits hold their ground in
the midst of a new culture which certainly would never
have brought them in, but on the contrary presses hard to
thrust them out. What this direct information is like, a
single example may show. The Dayaks of Borneo were
not accustomed to chop wood, as we do, by notching out
V-shaped cuts. Accordingly, when the white man intruded
among them with this among other novelties, they marked
their disgust at the innovation by levying a fine on any of
their own people who should be caught chopping in the
European fashion; yet so well aware were the native wood-
cutters that the white man's plan was an improvement on
their own, that they would use it surreptitiously when they
could trust one another not to tell.[1] The account is
twenty years old, and very likely the foreign chop may have
ceased to be an offence against Dayak conservatism, but its
prohibition was a striking instance of survival by ancestral
authority in the very teeth of common sense. Such a proceeding as this would be usually, and not improperly,

----

[1] 'Journ. Ind. Archip.' (ed. by J. R. Logan), vol. ii. p. liv.

described as a superstition; and, indeed, this name would be given to a large proportion of survivals generally. The very word "superstition," in what is perhaps its original sense of a "standing over" from old times, itself expresses the notion of survival. But the term superstition now implies a reproach, and though this reproach may be often cast deservedly on fragments of a dead lower culture embedded in a living higher one, yet in many cases it would be harsh, and even untrue. For the ethnographer's purpose, at any rate, it is desirable to introduce such a term as "survival," simply to denote the historical fact which the word "superstition" is now spoiled for expressing. Moreover, there have to be included as partial survivals the mass of cases where enough of the old habit is kept up for its origin to be recognizable, though in taking a new form it has been so adapted to new circumstances as still to hold its place on its own merits.

Thus it would be seldom reasonable to call the children's games of modern Europe superstitions, though many of them are survivals, and indeed remarkable ones. If the games of children and of grown-up people be examined with an eye to ethnological lessons to be gained from them, one of the first things that strikes us is how many of them are only sportive imitations of the serious business of life. As children in modern civilized times play at dining and driving horses and going to church, so a main amusement of savage children is to imitate the occupations which they will carry on in earnest a few years later, and thus their games are in fact their lessons. The Esquimaux children's sports are shooting with a tiny bow and arrow at a mark, and building little snow-huts, which they light up with scraps of lamp-wick begged from their mothers.[1] Miniature boomerangs and spears are among the toys of Australian children; and even as the fathers keep up the extremely primitive custom of getting themselves wives by carrying them off by violence from other tribes, so playing at such

[1] Klemm, 'Cultur-Geschichte,' vol ii. p. 309.

Sabine marriage has been noticed as one of the regular
games of the little native boys and girls.[1] Now it is quite
a usual thing in the world for a game to outlive the serious
practice of which it is an imitation. The bow and arrow is
a conspicuous instance. Ancient and wide-spread in savage
culture, we trace this instrument through barbaric and
classic life and onward to a high mediæval level. But now,
when we look on at an archery meeting, or go by country
lanes at the season when toy bows and arrows are "in"
among the children, we see, reduced to a mere sportive
survival, the ancient weapon which among a few savage
tribes still keeps its deadly place in the hunt and the battle.
The cross-bow, a comparatively late and local improvement
on the long-bow, has disappeared yet more utterly from
practical use; but as a toy it is in full European service,
and likely to remain so. For antiquity and wide diffusion
in the world, through savage up to classic and mediæval
times, the sling ranks with the bow and arrow. But in the
middle ages it fell out of use as a practical weapon, and it
was all in vain that the 15th century poet commended the
art of slinging among the exercises of a good soldier :—

> " Use eek the cast of stone, with slynge or honde :
> It falleth ofte, yf other shot there none is,
> Men harneysed in steel may not withstonde,
> The multitude and mighty cast of stonys ;
> And stonys in effecte, are every where,
> And slyngos are not noyous for to beare." [2]

Perhaps as serious a use of the sling as can now be pointed
out within the limits of civilization is among the herdsmen
of Spanish America, who sling so cleverly that the saying is
they can hit a beast on either horn and turn him which
way they will. But the use of the rude old weapon is
especially kept up by boys at play, who are here again the
representatives of remotely ancient culture.

[1] Oldfield in 'Tr. Eth. Soc.' vol. iii. p. 266 ; Dumont d'Urville, 'Voy. de
l'Astrolabe,' vol I. p. 411.
[2] Strutt, 'Sports and Pastimes,' book ii. chap. ii.

As games thus keep up the record of primitive warlike arts, so they reproduce, in what are at once sports and little children's lessons, early stages in the history of child-like tribes of mankind. English children delighting in the imitations of cries of animals and so forth, and New Zealanders playing their favourite game of imitating in chorus the saw hissing, the adze chipping, the musket roaring, and the other instruments making their proper noises, are alike showing at its source the imitative element so important in the formation of language.[1] When we look into the early development of the art of counting, and see the evidence of tribe after tribe having obtained numerals through the primitive stage of counting on their fingers, we find a certain ethnographic interest in the games which teach this earliest numeration. The New Zealand game of "ti" is described as played by counting on the fingers, a number being called by one player, and he having instantly to touch the proper finger; while in the Samoan game one player holds out so many fingers, and his opponent must do the same instantly or lose a point.[2] These may be native Polynesian games, or they may be our own children's games borrowed. In the English nursery the child learns to say how many fingers the nurse shows, and the appointed formula of the game is "Buck, Buck, how many horns do I hold up?" The game of one holding up fingers and the others holding up fingers to match is mentioned in Strutt. We may see small schoolboys in the lanes playing at the guessing-game, where one gets on another's back and holds up fingers, the other must guess how many. It is interesting to notice the wide distribution and long permanence of these trifles in history when we read the following passage from Petronius Arbiter, written in the time of Nero:— "Trimalchio, not to seem moved by the loss, kissed the

---

[1] Polack, 'New Zealanders,' vol. ii. p. 171.
[2] Polack, Ibid. ; Wilkes, 'U.S. Exp.' vol. i. p. 194. See the account of the game of lingi in Mariner, 'Tonga Is.' vol. ii. a. 339; and Yate, 'New Zealand,' p. 113.

boy and bade him get up on his back. Without delay the boy climbed on horseback on him, and slapped him on the shoulders with his hand, laughing and calling out "*bucca, bucca*, quot sunt hic ?"[1] The simple counting-games played with the fingers must not be confounded with the addition-game, where each player throws out a hand, and the sum of all the fingers shown has to be called, the successful caller scoring a point; practically each calls the total before he sees his adversary's hand, so that the skill lies especially in shrewd guessing. This game affords endless amusement to China, where it is called "tsoey-moey," and to Southern Europe, where it is known in Italian as "morra," and in French as "mourre." So peculiar a game would hardly have been invented twice over in Europe and Asia, but it is hard to guess whether the Chinese learnt it from the West, or whether it belongs to the remarkable list of clever inventions which Europe has borrowed from China. The ancient Egyptians, as their sculptures show, used to play at some kind of finger-game, and the Romans had their finger-flashing, "micare digitis," at which butchers used to gamble with their customers for bits of meat. It is not clear whether these were morra or some other games.[2]

When Scotch lads, playing at the game of "tappie-tousie," take one another by the forelock and say, "Will ye be my man ?"[3] they know nothing of the old symbolic manner of receiving a bondman which they are keeping up in survival. The wooden drill for making fire by friction, which so many rude or ancient races are known to have used as their common household instrument, and which lasts on among the modern Hindus as the time-honoured sacred means of lighting the pure sacrificial flame, has been

---

[1] Petron. Arbitri Satiræ rec. Büchler, p. 61 (other readings are *bucos* or *bucco*).

[2] Compare Davis, 'Chinese,' vol. I. p. 317 ; Wilkinson, Ancient Egyptians, vol. I. p. 188 ; Facciolati, Lexicon, s. v. 'micare' ; etc.

[3] Jamieson, 'Dict. of Scottish Lang.' s. v.

found surviving in Switzerland as a toy among the children, who made fire with it in sport, much as Esquimaux would have done in earnest.[1] In Gothland it is on record that the ancient sacrifice of the wild boar has actually been carried on into modern time in sportive imitation, by lads in masquerading clothes with their faces blackened and painted, while the victim was personated by a boy rolled up in furs and placed upon a seat, with a tuft of pointed straws in his mouth to imitate the bristles of the boar.[2] One innocent little child's sport of our own time is strangely mixed up with an ugly story of about a thousand years ago. The game in question is thus played in France :—The children stand in a ring, one lights a spill of paper and passes it on to the next, saying, "petit bonhomme vit encore," and so on round the ring, each saying the words and passing on the flame as quickly as may be, for the one in whose hands the spill goes out has to pay a forfeit, and it is then proclaimed that "petit bonhomme est mort." Grimm mentions a similar game in Germany, played with a burning stick, and Halliwell gives the nursery rhyme which is said with it when it is played in England :—

> "Jack's alive and in very good health,
> If he dies in your hand you must look to yourself."

Now, as all readers of Church history know, it used to be a favourite engine of controversy for the adherents of an established faith to accuse heretical sects of celebrating hideous orgies as the mysteries of their religion. The Pagans told these stories of the Jews, the Jews told them of the Christians, and Christians themselves reached a bad eminence in the art of slandering religious opponents whose moral life often seems in fact to have been exceptionally pure. The Manichæans were an especial mark for such aspersions, which were passed on to a sect considered as their successors—the Paulicians, whose name reappears in

---

[1] 'Early History of Mankind,' p. 244, etc. ; Grimm, 'Deutsche Myth.,' p. 572.   [2] Grimm, ibid., p. 1200.

the middle ages, in connexion with the Cathari. To these latter, apparently from an expression in one of their religious formulas, was given the name of Boni Homines, which became a recognized term for the Albigenses. It is clear that the early Paulicians excited the anger of the orthodox by objecting to sacred images, and calling those who venerated them idolaters; and about A.D. 700, John of Osun, Patriarch of Armenia, wrote a diatribe against the sect, urging accusations of the regular anti-Manichæan type, but with a peculiar feature which brings his statement into the present singular connexion. He declares that they blasphemously call the orthodox "image-worshippers;" that they themselves worship the sun; that, moreover, they mix wheaten flour with the blood of infants and therewith celebrate their communion, and "when they have slain by the worst of deaths a boy, the first-born of his mother, thrown from hand to hand among them by turns, they venerate him in whose hand the child expires, as having attained to the first dignity of the sect." To explain the correspondence of these atrocious details with the nursery sport, it is perhaps the most likely supposition, not that the game of "Petit Bonhomme" keeps up a recollection of a legend of the Boni Homines, but that the game was known to the children of the eighth century much as it is now, and that the Armenian Patriarch simply accused the Paulicians of playing at it with live babes.[1]

[1] Halliwell, 'Popular Rhymes,' p. 112; Grimm, 'D. M.' p. 512. Bastian, 'Mensch,' vol. iii. p. 106. Johannis Philosophi Ozniensis Opera (Aucher), Venice, 1834, p. 76—89. 'Infantium sanguini similam commiscentes illegitimam communionem deglutiant; quo pacto porcorum suos fœtus immaniter vescentium exsuperant edacitatem. Quique illorum cadavera super tecti culmen celantes, ac sursum oculis in cœlum defixis replelentes, jurant alieno verbo ac sensu: *Altissimus morit.* Solem vero deprecari volentes, ejunt: *Solicule, Lucicule;* atque aëreos, vagosque dæmones clam invocant, juxta Manichæorum Simonisque incantatoris errores. Similiter et primam parientis feminæ puerum de manu in manum inter eos invicem projectum, quum pessimâ morte occiderint, illum, in cujus manu exspiraverit puer, ad primam sectæ dignitatem provectum venerantur; atque per utriusque nomen audent insane jurare; *Juro,* dicunt, *per unigenitum Filium:* et iterum: *Fratem habeo tibi gloriam ejus, in cujus manum unigenitus filius spiritum*

It may be possible to trace another interesting group of sports as survivals from a branch of savage philosophy, once of high rank though now fallen into merited decay.   Games of chance correspond so closely with arts of divination belonging already to savage culture, that there is force in applying to several such games the rule that the serious practice comes first, and in time may dwindle to the sportive survival.   To a modern educated man, drawing lots or tossing up a coin is an appeal to chance, that is, to ignorance ; it is committing the decision of a question to a mechanical process, itself in no way unnatural or even extraordinary, but merely so difficult to follow that no one can say beforehand what will come of it.   But we also know that this scientific doctrine of chance is not that of early civilization, which has little in common with the mathematician's theory of probabilities, but much in common with such sacred divination as the choice of Matthias by lot as a twelfth apostle, or, in a later age, the Moravian Brethren's rite of choosing wives for their young men by casting lots with prayer.   It was to no blind chance that the Maoris looked when they divined by throwing up lots to find a thief among a suspected company ;[1] or the Guinea negroes when they went to the fetish-priest, who shuffled his bundle of little strips of leather and gave his sacred omen.[2]   The crowd with uplifted hands pray to the gods, when the heroes cast lots in the cap of Atreides Agamemnon, to know who shall go forth to do battle with Hektor and help the well-greaved Greeks.[3]   With prayer to the gods, and looking up to heaven, the German priest or father, as Tacitus relates, drew three lots from among the marked fruit-tree twigs scattered on a pure white garment, and interpreted the

suum tradidit . . . . Contra hos [the orthodox] audacter evomere præsumunt impietatis suæ bilem, atque insanientes, ea mali spiritus blasphemiâ, *Sculpticulas* vocant."

[1] Polack, vol. i. p. 270.
[2] Bosman, 'Ouinea Kust,' letter x. ; Eng. Trans. in Pinkerton, vol. xvi. p. 399.
[3] Homer. Iliad. vii. 171.

answer from their signs.[1] As in ancient Italy oracles gave responses by graven lots,[2] so the modern Hindus decide disputes by casting lots in front of a temple, appealing to the gods with cries of " Let justice be shown! Show the innocent! "[3]

The uncivilized man thinks that lots or dice are adjusted in their fall with reference to the meaning he may choose to attach to it, and especially he is apt to suppose spiritual beings standing over the diviner or the gambler, shuffling the lots or turning up the dice to make them give their answers. This view held its place firmly in the middle ages, and later in history we still find games of chance looked on as results of supernatural operation. The general change from mediæval to modern notions in this respect is well shown in a remarkable work published in 1619, which seems to have done much toward bringing the change about. Thomas Gataker, a Puritan minister, in his treatise ' Of the Nature and Use of Lots,' states, in order to combat them, the following among the current objections made against games of chance :—" Lots may not be used but with great reverence, because the disposition of them commeth immediately from God " . . . . " the nature of a Lot, which is affirmed to bee a worke of Gods speciall and immediate providence, a sacred oracle, a divine judgement or sentence : the light use of it therefore to be an abuse of Gods name ; and so a sinne against the third Commandement." Gataker, in opposition to this, argues that " to expect the issue and event of it, as by ordinarie meanes from God, is common to all actions : to expect it by an immediate and extraordinarie worke is no more lawfull here than elsewhere, yea is indeed mere superstition."[1] It took time, however, for this opinion to become prevalent in the educated world. After a lapse of forty years, Jeremy Taylor could still bring out a remnant of the

[1] Tacit. Germania. 10.
[2] Smith's ' Dic. of Gr. and Rom. Ant.,' arts. ' oraculum,' ' sortes.'
[3] Roberts, ' Oriental Illustrations, p. 163.
[4] Gataker, p. 141, 91 ; see Lecky, ' History of Rationalism,' vol. I. p. 307.

older notion, in the course of a generally reasonable argument in favour of games of chance when played for refreshment and not for money. "I have heard," he says, "from them that have skill in such things, there are such strange chances, such promoting of a hand by fancy and little arts of geomancy, such constant winning on one side, such unreasonable losses on the other, and these strange contingencies produce such horrible effects, that it is not improbable that God hath permitted the conduct of such games of chance to the devil, who will order them so where he can do most mischief; but, without the instrumentality of money, he could do nothing at all."[1] With what vitality the notion of supernatural interference in games of chance even now survives in Europe, is well shown by the still flourishing arts of gambler's magic. The folk-lore of our own day continues to teach that a Good Friday's egg is to be carried for luck in gaming, and that a turn of one's chair will turn one's fortune; the Tyrolese knows the charm for getting from the devil the gift of winning at cards and dice; there is still a great sale on the continent for books which show how to discover, from dreams, good numbers for the lottery; and the Lusatian peasant will even hide his lottery-tickets under the altar-cloth that they may receive the blessing with the sacrament, and so stand a better chance of winning.[2]

Arts of divination and games of chance are so similar in principle, that the very same instrument passes from one use to the other. This appears in the accounts, very suggestive from this point of view, of the Polynesian art of divination by spinning the "niu" or cocoa-nut. In the Tongan Islands, in Mariner's time, the principal purpose for which this was solemnly performed was to inquire if a sick person would recover; prayer was made aloud to the patron god of the family to direct the nut, which was then spun, and its direction at rest indicated the intention of the

[1] Jeremy Taylor, Ductor Dubitantium, in Works,' vol. xiv. p. 337.
[2] See Wuttke, 'Deutsche Volksaberglaube,' p. 95, 115, 178.

god. On other occasions, when the cocoa-nut was merely spun for amusement, no prayer was made, and no credit given to the result. Here the serious and the sportive use of this rudimentary teetotum are found together. In the Samoan Islands, however, at a later date, the Rev. G. Turner finds the practice passed into a different stage. A party sit in a circle, the cocoa-nut is spun in the middle, and the oracular answer is according to the person towards whom the monkey-face of the fruit is turned when it stops; but whereas formerly the Samoans used this as an art of divination to discover thieves, now they only keep it up as a way of casting lots, and as a game of forfeits.[1] It is in favour of the view of serious divination being the earlier use, to notice that the New Zealanders, though they have no cocoa-nuts, keep up a trace of the time when their ancestors in the tropical islands had them and divined with them; for it is the well-known Polynesian word "niu," i. e. cocoa-nut, which is still retained in use among the Maoris for other kinds of divination, especially that performed with sticks. Mr. Taylor, who points out this curiously neat piece of ethnological evidence, records another case to the present purpose. A method of divination was to clap the hands together while a proper charm was repeated; if the fingers went clear in, it was favourable, but a check was an ill omen; on the question of a party crossing the country in war-time, the locking of all the fingers, or the stoppage of some or all, were naturally interpreted to mean clear passage, meeting a travelling party, or being stopped altogether. This quaint little symbolic art of divination seems now only to survive as a game; it is called "puni-puni."[2] A similar connexion between divination and gambling is shown by more familiar instruments. The hucklebones or astragali were used in divination in ancient Rome, being converted into rude dice by numbering the four sides, and

[1] Mariner, 'Tonga Islands,' vol. ii. p. 239; Turner, 'Polynesia,' p. 214; Williams, 'Fiji,' vol. i. p. 228. Compare Cranz, 'Greenland,' p. 231.
[2] R. Taylor, 'New Zealand,' pp. 206, 348, 387.

even when the Roman gambler used the tali for gambling,
he would invoke a god or his mistress before he made his
throw.[1] Such implements are now mostly used for play,
but, nevertheless, their use for divination was by no means
confined to the ancient world, for hucklebones are mentioned in the 17th century among the fortune-telling instruments which young girls divined for husbands with,[2] and
Negro sorcerers still throw dice as a means of detecting
thieves.[3] Lots serve the two purposes equally well. The
Chinese gamble by lots for cash and sweetmeats, whilst
they also seriously take omens by solemn appeals to the
lots kept ready for the purpose in the temples, and professional diviners sit in the market-places, thus to open the
future to their customers.[4] Playing-cards are still in European use for divination. That early sort known as "tarots"
which the French dealer's license to sell "cartes et tarots"
still keeps in mind, is said to be preferred by fortune-tellers
to the common kind; for the tarot-pack, with its more
numerous and complex figures, lends itself to a greater
variety of omens. In these cases, direct history fails to tell
us whether the use of the instrument for omen or play came
first. In this respect, the history of the Greek "kottabos"
is instructive. This art of divination consisted in flinging
wine out of a cup into a metal basin some distance off without spilling any, the thrower saying or thinking his mistress's name, and judging from the clear or dull splash of
the wine on the metal what his fortune in love would be;
but in time the magic passed out of the process, and it
became a mere game of dexterity played for a prize.[5] If
this be a typical case, and the rule be relied on that the
serious use precedes the playful, then games of chance may
be considered survivals in principle or detail from corre-

[1] Smith's Dic. art. 'talus.'
[2] Brand, 'Popular Antiquities,' vol. ii. p. 412.
[3] D. & C. Livingstone, 'Exp. to Zambesi,' p. 51.
[4] Doolittle, 'Chinese,' vol. ii. p. 108, 285—7; see 384; Bastian, 'Oestl.
Asien,' vol. iii. pp. 76, 126.
[5] Smith's Dic. art. 'cottabos.'

sponding processes of magic—as divination in sport made gambling in earnest.

Seeking more examples of the lasting on of fixed habits among mankind, let us glance at a group of time-honoured traditional sayings, old saws which have a special interest as cases of survival. Even when the real signification of these phrases has faded out of men's minds, and they have sunk into sheer nonsense, or have been overlaid with some modern superficial meaning, still the old formulas are handed on, often gaining more in mystery than they lose in sense. We may hear people talk of "buying a pig in a poke," whose acquaintance with English does not extend to knowing what a poke is. And certainly those who wish to say that they have a great mind to something, and who express themselves by declaring that they have "a month's mind" to it, can have no conception of the hopeless nonsense they are making of the old term of the "month's mind" which was really the monthly service for a dead man's soul, whereby he was kept in mind or remembrance. The proper sense of the phrase "sowing his wild oats" seems generally lost in our modern use of it. No doubt it once implied that these ill weeds would spring up in later years, and how hard it would then be to root them out. Like the enemy in the parable, the Scandinavian Loki, the mischief-maker, is proverbially said in Jutland to sow his oats ("nu saaer Lokken sin havre"), and the name of "Loki's oats" (Lokeshavre) is given in Danish to the wild oats (avena fatua).[1] Sayings which have their source in some obsolete custom or tale, of course lie especially open to such ill-usage. It has become mere English to talk of an "unlicked cub" who "wants licking into shape," while few remember the explanation of these phrases from Pliny's story that bears are born as eyeless, hairless, shapeless lumps of white flesh, and have afterwards to be licked into form.[2]

Again, in relics of old magic and religion, we have some-

[1] Grimm, ' Deutsche Myth.' p. 222.
[2] Plin. viii. 54.

times to look for a deeper sense in conventional phrases than they now carry on their face, or for a real meaning in what now seems nonsense. How an ethnographical record may become embodied in a popular saying, a Tamil proverb now current in South India will show perfectly. On occasions when A hits B, and C cries out at the blow, the bystanders will say, "'Tis like a Koravan eating asafœtida when his wife lies in!" Now a Koravan belongs to a low race in Madras, and is defined as "gypsy, wanderer, ass-driver, thief, eater of rats, dweller in mat tents, fortune-teller, and suspected character;" and the explanation of the proverb is, that whereas native women generally eat asafœtida as strengthening medicine after childbirth, among the Koravans it is the husband who eats it to fortify himself on the occasion. This, in fact, is a variety of the world-wide custom of the "couvade," where at childbirth the husband undergoes medical treatment, in many cases being put to bed for days. It appears that the Koravans are among the races practising this quaint custom, and that their more civilized Tamil neighbours, struck by its oddity, but unconscious of its now-forgotten meaning, have taken it up into a proverb.[1] Let us now apply the same sort of ethnographical key to dark sayings in our own modern language. The maxim, "a hair of the dog that bit you" was originally neither a metaphor nor a joke, but a matter-of-fact recipe for curing the bite of a dog, one of the many instances of the ancient homœopathic doctrine, that what hurts will also cure: it is mentioned in the Scandinavian Edda, "Dog's hair heals dog's bite."[2] The phrase "raising the wind" now passes as humorous slang, but it once, in all seriousness, described one of the most dreaded of the sorcerer's arts, practised especially by the Finland wizards, of whose uncanny power over the weather our sailors have not to this day forgotten their old terror. The ancient

---

[1] From a letter of Mr. H. J. Stokes, Negapatam, to Mr. F. M. Jennings. General details of the Couvade in 'Early Hist. of Mankind,' p. 293.

[2] Hávamál, 138.

ceremony or ordeal of passing through a fire or leaping over burning brands has been kept up so vigorously in the British Isles, that Jamieson's derivation of the phrase " to haul over the coals " from this rite appears in no way far-fetched. It is not long since an Irishwoman in New York was tried for killing her child; she had made it stand on burning coals to find out whether it was really her own or a changeling.[1] The English nurse who says to a fretful child, " You got out of bed wrong foot foremost this morning," seldom or never knows the meaning of her saying; but this is still plain in the German folklore rule, that to get out of bed left foot first will bring a bad day,[2] one of the many examples of that simple association of ideas which connects right and left with good and bad respectively. To conclude, the phrase " cheating the devil" seems to belong to that familiar series of legends where a man makes a compact with the fiend, but at the last moment gets off scot-free by the interposition of a saint, or by some absurd evasion—such as whistling the gospel he has bound himself not to say, or refusing to complete his bargain at the fall of the leaf, on the plea that the sculptured leaves in the church are still on their boughs. One form of the mediæval compact was for the demon, when he had taught his black art to a class of scholars, to seize one of them for his professional fee, by letting them all run for their lives and catching the last—a story obviously connected with another popular saying: " devil take the hindmost." But even at this game the stupid fiend may be cheated, as is told in the folk-lore of Spain and Scotland, in the. legends of the Marqués de Villano and the Earl of Southesk, who attended the Devil's magic schools at Salamanca and Padua. The apt scholar only leaves the master his shadow to clutch as following hindmost in the race, and with this unsubstantial payment the demon must needs be satisfied, while the

[1] Jamieson, 'Scottish Dictionary,' s. v. 'coals;' R. Hunt, 'Popular Romances,' 1st ser. p. 85.

[2] Wuttke, 'Volksaberglaube,' p. 131.

new-made magician goes forth free, but ever after shadowless.[1]

It seems a fair inference to think folk-lore nearest to its
source where it has its highest place and meaning. Thus,
if some old rhyme or saying has in one place a solemn
import in philosophy or religion, while elsewhere it lies at
the level of the nursery, there is some ground for treating
the serious version as the more original, and the playful one
as its mere lingering survival. The argument is not safe,
but yet is not to be quite overlooked. For instance,
there are two poems kept in remembrance among the
modern Jews, and printed at the end of their book of Passover services in Hebrew and English. One is that known
as חד גדיא (Chad gadyâ): it begins, "A kid, a kid, my
father bought for two pieces of money;" and it goes on to
tell how a cat came and ate the kid, and a dog came and bit
the cat, and so on to the end.—"Then came the Holy One,
blessed be He! and slew the angel of death, who slew the
butcher, who killed the ox, that drank the water, that
quenched the fire, that burnt the stick, that beat the dog,
that bit the cat, that ate the kid, that my father bought for
two pieces of money, a kid, a kid." This composition is in
the 'Sepher Haggadah,' and is looked on by some Jews as
a parable concerning the past and future of the Holy Land.
According to one interpretation, Palestine, the kid, is devoured by Babylon the cat; Babylon is overthrown by
Persia, Persia by Greece, Greece by Rome, till at last the
Turks prevail in the land; but the Edomites (i.e. the
nations of Europe) shall drive out the Turks, the angel of
death shall destroy the enemies of Israel, and his children
shall be restored under the rule of Messiah. Irrespectively
of any such particular interpretation, the solemnity of the
ending may incline us to think that we really have the composition here in something like its first form, and that it

[1] Roehholz, ' Deutscher Glaube und Brauch,' vol. i, p. 120 ; R. Chambers,
' Popular Rhymes of Scotland,' Miscellaneous ; Grimm, pp. 969, 976 ; Wuttke,
p. 115.

was written to convey a mystic meaning. If so, then it
follows that our familiar nursery tale of the old woman who
couldn't get her kid (or pig) over the stile, and wouldn't get
home till midnight, must be considered a broken-down
adaptation of this old Jewish poem. The other composition
is a counting-poem, and begins thus:—

> "Who knoweth one? I (saith Israel) know One:
>   One is God, who is over heaven and earth.
> Who knoweth two? I (saith Israel) know two:
>   Two tables of the covenant; but One is our God who is over
>   the heavens and the earth."

(And so forth, accumulating up to the last verse, which
is—)

> "Who knoweth thirteen? I (saith Israel) know thirteen:
> Thirteen divine attributes, twelve tribes, eleven stars, ten com-
> mandments, nine months preceding childbirth, eight days pre-
> ceding circumcision, seven days of the week, six books of the
> Mishnah, five books of the Law, four matrons, three patriarchs,
> two tables of the covenant; but One is our God who is over the
> heavens and the earth."

This is one of a family of counting-poems, apparently
held in much favour in mediæval Christian times; for they
are not yet quite forgotten in country places. An old Latin
version runs: "Unus est Deus," etc., and one of the still-
surviving English forms begins, "One's One all alone, and
ever more shall be so," and reckons on as far as "Twelve,
the twelve apostles." Here both the Jewish and Christian
forms are or have been serious, so it is possible that the
Jew may have imitated the Christian, but the nobler form
of the Hebrew poem here again gives it a claim to be
thought the earlier.[1]

The old proverbs brought down by long inheritance into
our modern talk are far from being insignificant in themselves, for their wit is often as fresh, and their wisdom as

---

[1] Mendes, 'Service for the First Nights of Passover,' London, 1862 (in the
Jewish interpretation, the word shusra,—'cat,' is compared with Shinâr).
Halliwell, 'Nursery Rhymes,' p. 289; 'Popular Rhymes,' p. 6.

pertinent, as it ever was. Beyond these practical qualities, proverbs are instructive for the place in ethnography which they occupy. Their range in civilization is limited; they seem scarcely to belong to the lowest tribes, but appear first in a settled form among some of the higher savages. The Fijians, who were found a few years since living in what archæologists might call the upper Stone Age, have some well-marked proverbs. They laugh at want of forethought by the saying that "The Nakondo people cut the mast first" (i. e., before they had built the canoe); and when a poor man looks wistfully at what he cannot buy, they say, "Becalmed, and looking at the fish."[1] Among the list of the New Zealanders' "whakatauki," or proverbs, one describes a lazy glutton: "Deep throat, but shallow sinews;" another says that the lazy often profit by the work of the industrious: "The large chips made by Hardwood fall to the share of Sit-still;" a third moralizes that "A crooked part of a stem of toetoe can be seen; but a crooked part in the heart cannot be seen."[2] Among the Basutos of South Africa, "Water never gets tired of running," is a reproach to chatterers; "Lions growl while they are eating," means that there are people who never will enjoy anything; "The sowing-month is the headache-month," describes those lazy folks who make excuses when work is to be done; "The thief eats thunderbolts," means that he will bring down vengeance from heaven on himself.[3] West African nations are especially strong in proverbial philosophy; so much so that Captain Burton amused himself through the rainy season at Fernando Po in compiling a volume of native proverbs,[4] among which there are hundreds at about as high an intellectual level as those of Europe. "He fled from the sword and hid in the scabbard," is as good as our

1 Williams, 'Fiji,' vol. I. p. 110.
2 Shortland, 'Traditions of N. Z.' p. 196.
3 Casalis, 'Études sur la langue Séchuana.'
4 R. F. Burton, 'Wit and Wisdom from West Africa.' See also Waitz, vol. II. p. 245.

" Out of the frying-pan into the fire ; " and " He who has only his eyebrow for a cross-bow can never kill an animal," is more picturesque, if less terse, than our " Hard words break no bones." The old Buddhist aphorism, that " He who indulges in enmity is like one who throws ashes to windward, which come back to the same place and cover him all over," is put with less prose and as much point in the negro saying, " Ashes fly back in the face of him who throws them." When some one tries to settle an affair in the absence of the people concerned, the negroes will object that " You can't shave a man's head when he is not there," while, to explain that the master is not to be judged by the folly of his servant, they say, " The rider is not a fool because the horse is." Ingratitude is alluded to in " The sword knows not the head of the smith" (who made it), and yet more forcibly elsewhere, " When the calabash had saved them (in the famine), they said, let us cut it for a drinking-cup." The popular contempt for poor men's wisdom is put very neatly in the maxim, "When a poor man makes a proverb it does not spread," while the very mention of making a proverb as something likely to happen, shows a land where proverb-making is still a living art. Transplanted to the West Indies, the African keeps up this art, as witness these sayings : " Behind dog it is dog, but before dog it is Mr. Dog ; " and " Toute cabinette tini maringouin "—" Every cabin has its mosquito."

The proverb has not changed its character in the course of history ; but has retained from first to last a precisely definite type. The proverbial sayings recorded among the higher nations of the world are to be reckoned by tens of thousands, and have a large and well-known literature of their own. But though the range of existence of proverbs extends into the highest levels of civilization, this is scarcely true of their development. At the level of European culture in the middle ages, they have indeed a vast importance in popular education, but their period of actual growth seems already at an end. Cervantes raised the proverb-monger's

craft to a pitch it never surpassed; but it must not be forgotten that the incomparable Sancho's wares were mostly
heirlooms; for proverbs were even then sinking to remnants
of an earlier condition of society. As such, they survive
among ourselves, who go on using much the same relics of
ancestral wisdom as came out of the squire's inexhaustible
budget, old saws not to be lightly altered or made anew in
our changed modern times. We can collect and use the
old proverbs, but making new ones has become a feeble,
spiritless imitation, like our attempts to invent new myths
or new nursery rhymes.

Riddles start near proverbs in the history of civilization,
and they travel on long together, though at last towards
different ends. By riddles are here meant the old-fashioned
problems with a real answer intended to be discovered, such
as the typical enigma of the Sphinx, but not the modern
verbal conundrums set in the traditional form of question
and answer, as a way of bringing in a jest à propos of nothing. The original kind, which may be defined as "sense-
riddles," are found at home among the upper savages, and
range on into the lower and middle civilization; and while
their growth stops at this level, many ancient specimens have
lasted on in the modern nursery and by the cottage fireside.
There is a plain reason why riddles should belong only to
the higher grades of savagery; their making requires a fair
power of ideal comparison, and knowledge must have made
considerable advance before this process could become so
familiar as to fall from earnest into sport. At last, in
a far higher state of culture, riddles begin to be looked
on as trifling, their growth ceases, and they only survive
in remnants for children's play. Some examples chosen
among various races, from savagery upwards, will show
more exactly the place in mental history which the riddle
occupies.

The following are specimens from a collection of Zulu
riddles, recorded with quaintly simple native comments on
the philosophy of the matter:—Q. "Guess ye some men

who are many and form a row; they dance the wedding-
dance, adorned in white hip-dresses?" A. "The teeth;
we call them men who form a row, for the teeth stand like
men who are made ready for a wedding-dance, that they
may dance well. When we say, they are 'adorned with
white hip-dresses,' we put that in, that people may not at
once think of teeth, but be drawn away from them by thinking, 'It is men who put on white hip-dresses,' and continually have their thoughts fixed on men," etc. Q. "Guess
ye a man who does not lie down at night: he lies down in
the morning until the sun sets; he then awakes, and works
all night; he does not work by day; he is not seen when
he works?" A. "The closing-poles of the cattle-pen."
Q. "Guess ye a man whom men do not like to laugh, for it
is known that his laughter is a very great evil, and is followed
by lamentation, and an end of rejoicing. Men weep,
and trees, and grass; and everything is heard weeping in
the tribe where he laughs; and they say the man has
laughed who does not usually laugh?" A. "Fire. It is
called a man that what is said may not be at once evident,
it being concealed by the word 'man.' Men say many
things, searching out the meaning in rivalry, and missing
the mark. A riddle is good when it is not discernible at
once," etc.[1] Among the Basutos, riddles are a recognized part
of education, and are set like exercises to a whole company
of puzzled children. Q. "Do you know what throws itself
from the mountain-top without being broken?" A. "A
waterfall." Q. "There's a thing that travels fast without
legs or wings, and no cliff, nor river, nor wall can stop it?"
A. "The voice." Q. "Name the ten trees with ten flat
stones on the top of them." A. "The fingers." Q. "Who
is the little immovable dumb boy who is dressed up warm
in the day and left naked at night?" A. "The bed-
clothes' peg."[2] From East Africa, this Swahili riddle is an

[1] Callaway, 'Nursery Tales, etc. of Zulus,' vol. i. p. 364, etc.
[2] Casalis, 'Études sur la langue Séchuana,' p. 91; 'Basutos,' p. 337.

example : Q. "My hen has laid among thorns?" A. "A
pineapple." [1] From West Africa, this Yoruba one : "A
long slender trading woman who never gets to market?"
A. "A canoe (it stops at the landing-place)." [2] In Polynesia, the Samoan islanders are given to riddles. Q.
"There are four brothers, who are always bearing about
their father?" A. "The Samoan pillow," which is a
yard of three-inch bamboo resting on four legs. Q. "A
white-headed man stands above the fence, and reaches to
the heavens?" A. "The smoke of the oven." Q. "A
man who stands between two ravenous fish?" A. "The
tongue." [3] (There is a Zulu riddle like this, which compares the tongue to a man living in the midst of enemies
fighting.) The following are old Mexican enigmas : Q.
"What are the ten stones one has at his sides?" A. "The
finger-nails." Q. "What is it we get into by three parts
and out of by one?" A. "A shirt." Q. "What goes
through a valley and drags its entrails after it?" A. "A
needle." [4]

These riddles found among the lower races do not differ
at all in nature from those that have come down, sometimes
modernized in the setting, into the nursery lore of Europe.
Thus Spanish children still ask, "What is the dish of nuts
that is gathered by day, and scattered by night?" (the
stars.) Our English riddle of the pair of tongs : "Long
legs, crooked thighs, little head, and no eyes," is primitive
enough to have been made by a South Sea Islander. The
following is on the same theme as one of the Zulu riddles :
" A flock of white sheep, On a red hill ; Here they go, there
they go ; Now they stand still?" Another is the very
analogue of one of the Aztec specimens : " Old Mother
Twitchett had but one eye, And a long tail which she let fly ;

[1] Steere, ' Swahili Tales,' p. 418.
[2] Burton, ' Wit and Wisdom from West Africa,' p. 212.
[3] Turner, ' Polynesia,' p. 216. See Polack, 'New Zealanders,' vol. ii. p. 171.
[4] Sahagun, ' Historia de Nueva España,' in Kingsborough's 'Antiquities of
Mexico,' vol. vii. p. 178.

And every time she went over a gap, She left a bit of her
tail in a trap?"

So thoroughly does riddle-making belong to the mythologic stage of thought, that any poet's simile, if not too far-
fetched, needs only inversion to be made at once into an
enigma. The Hindu calls the Sun Saptásva, i. e., "seven-
horsed," while, with the same thought, the old German riddle
asks, "What is the chariot drawn by seven white and seven
black horses?" (the year, drawn by the seven days and
nights of the week.[1]) Such, too, is the Greek riddle of the
two sisters, Day and Night, who give birth each to the other,
to be born of her again:

> Εἰσὶ κασίγνηται δισσαί, ὧν ἡ μία τίκτει
> Τὴν ἑτέρην, αὐτὴ δὲ τεκοῦσ' ὑπὸ τῆσδε τεκνοῦται.

and the enigma of Kleoboulos, with its other like fragments
of rudimentary mythology:

> Εἷς ὁ πατήρ, παῖδες δὲ δυώδεκα· τῶν δὲ γ' ἑκάστῳ
> Παῖδες ἑξήκοντα τρίφανοι' διάνχα εἶδος ἔχουσαι·
> Ἁι μὲν λευκαὶ ἔασιν ἰδεῖν, ἡ δ' αὖτε μέλαιναι·
> Ἀθάνατοι δέ τ' ἐοῦσαι ἀποφθινύθουσιν ἅπασαι.

"One is the father, and twelve the children, and, born unto each one,
Maidens thirty, whose form in twain is parted asunder,
White to behold on the one side, black to behold on the other,
All immortal in being, yet doomed to dwindle and perish." [2]

Such questions as these may be fairly guessed now as in old
times, and must be distinguished from that scarcer class
which require the divination of some unlikely event to solve
them. Of such the typical example is Samson's riddle, and
there is an old Scandinavian one like it. The story is
that Gestr found a duck sitting on her nest in an ox's
horned skull, and thereupon propounded a riddle, describing
with characteristic Northman's metaphor the ox with its
horns fancied as already made into drinking-horns. The
following translation does not exaggerate the quaintness of

---

[1] Grimm, p. 699.   [2] Diog. Laert. L 91; Athenagoras, x. 451.

the original : — "Joying in children the bill-goose grew,
And her building-timbers together drew ; The biting grass-
shearer screened her bed, With the maddening drink-stream
overhead." [1]   Many of the old oracular responses are puzzles
of precisely this kind.   Such is the story of the Delphic
oracle, which ordered Temenos to find a man with three
eyes to guide the army, which injunction he fulfilled by
meeting a one-eyed man on horseback. [2]   It is curious to
find this idea again in Scandinavia, where Odin sets King
Heidrek a riddle, "Who are they two that fare to the
Thing with three eyes, ten feet, and one tail ? " the answer
being, the one-eyed Odin himself on his eight-footed horse
Sleipnir. [2]

The close bearing of the doctrine of survival on the study
of manners and customs is constantly coming into view
in ethnographic research.   It seems scarcely too much to
assert, once for all, that meaningless customs must be survivals, that they had a practical, or at least ceremonial,
intention when and where they first arose, but are now fallen
into absurdity from having been carried on into a new state
of society, where their original sense has been discarded.
Of course, new customs introduced in particular ages may
be ridiculous or wicked, but as a rule they have discernible
motives.   Explanations of this kind, by recourse to some
forgotten meaning, seem on the whole to account best for
obscure customs which some have set down to mere out-
breaks of spontaneous folly.   A certain Zimmermann, who
published a heavy 'Geographical History of Mankind' in
the last century, remarks as follows on the prevalence of
similar nonsensical and stupid customs in distant coun-

---

[1] Mannhardt's 'Zeitschr. für Deutsche Mythologie,' vol. iii. p. 2, etc. :

"Nóg er forthun nidegis raxin,
Barngiorn m er lar bútimbr saman ;
Hlifthu henni halms bitakálmir,
Thó lá drykkjar drynbróan yfir."

[2] See Grote, 'Hist. of Greece,' vol. ii. p. 5.
Mannhardt's 'Zeitschr.' l. c.

tries :—" For if two clever heads may, each for himself, hit
upon a clever invention or discovery, then it is far likelier,
considering the much larger total of fools and blockheads,
that like fooleries should be given to two far-distant lands.
If, then, the inventive fool be likewise a man of importance
and influence, as is, indeed, an extremely frequent case,
then both nations adopt a similar folly, and then, centuries
after, some historian goes through it to extract his evidence
for the derivation of these two nations one from the
other."[1]

Strong views as to the folly of mankind seem to have
been in the air about the time of the French Revolution.
Lord Chesterfield was no doubt an extremely different
person from our German philosopher, but they were quite
at one as to the absurdity of customs. Advising his son
as to the etiquette of courts, the Earl writes thus to him :—
" For example, it is respectful to bow to the King of
England, it is disrespectful to bow to the King of France ;
it is the rule to courtesy to the Emperor ; and the prostra-
tion of the whole body is required by Eastern Monarchs.
These are established ceremonies, and must be complied
with ; but why they were established, I defy sense and
reason to tell us. It is the same among all ranks, where
certain customs are received, and must necessarily be complied with, though by no means the result of sense and
reason. As for instance, the very absurd, though almost
universal custom of drinking people's healths. Can there
be anything in the world less relative to any other man's
health, than my drinking a glass of wine ? Common sense,
certainly, never pointed it out, but yet common sense tells
me I must conform to it."[2] Now, though it might be
difficult enough to make sense of the minor details of
court etiquette, Lord Chesterfield's example from it of

---

[1] E. A. W. Zimmermann, 'Geographische Geschichte des Menschen,' etc.,
1778—83, vol. iii. See Professor Rolleston's Inaugural Address, British
Association, 1870.

[2] Earl of Chesterfield, 'Letters to his Son,' vol. ii. No. lxviii.

the irrationality of mankind is a singularly unlucky one.
Indeed, if any one were told to set forth in few words the
relations of the people to their rulers in different states of
society, he might answer that men grovel on their faces
before the King of Siam, kneel on one knee or uncover
before a European monarch, and shake the hand of the
President of the United States as though it were a pump-
handle. These are ceremonies at once intelligible and
significant. Lord Chesterfield is more fortunate in his
second instance, for the custom of drinking healths is really
of obscure origin. Yet it is closely connected with an
ancient rite, practically absurd indeed, but done with a
conscious and serious intention which lands it quite outside
the region of nonsense. This is the custom of pouring out
libations and drinking at ceremonial banquets to gods and
the dead. Thus the old Northmen drank the "miuni" of
Thor, Odin, and Freya, and of kings likewise at their
funerals. The custom did not die out with the conversion
of the Scandinavian and Teutonic nations. Such formulas
as "God's minne!" "a bowl to God in heaven!" are on
record, while in like manner Christ, Mary, and the Saints
were drunk to in place of heathen gods and heroes, and
the habit of drinking to the dead and the living at the
same feast and in similar terms goes far to prove here a
common origin for both ceremonies. The "minne" was
at once love, memory, and the thought of the absent,
and it long survived in England in the "minnying" or
"mynde" days, on which the memory of the dead was celebrated by services or banquets. Such evidence as this
fairly justifies the writers, older and newer, who have
treated these ceremonial drinking usages as in their nature
sacrificial.[1] As for the practice of simply drinking the
health of living men, its ancient history reaches us from
several districts inhabited by Aryan nations. The Greeks

[1] See Hylten-Cavallius, 'Wärend och Wirdarne,' vol. i. p. 161—70; Grimm, pp. 52 5, 1201; Brand, vol. ii. pp. 314, 325, etc.

in symposium drank to one another, and the Romans adopted the habit (προπίνειν, propinare, Græco more bibere). The Goths cried " hails ! " as they pledged each other, as we have it in the curious first line of the verses " De conviviis barbaris " in the Latin Anthology, which sets down the shouts of a Gothic drinking-bout of the fifth century or so, in words which still partly keep their sense to an English ear :—

" Inter eils Goticum *scapiamatsiaia drincbn*
Non audet quisquam dignos educere versus."

As for ourselves, though the old drinking salutation of " wæs hæl ! " is no longer vulgar English, the formula remains with us, stiffened into a noun. On the whole, there is presumptive though not conclusive evidence that the custom of drinking healths to the living is historically related to the religious rite of drinking to the gods and the dead.

Let us now put the theory of survival to a somewhat severe test, by seeking from it some explanation of the existence, in practice or memory, within the limits of modern civilized society, of three remarkable groups of customs which civilized ideas totally fail to account for. Though we may not succeed in giving clear and absolute explanations of their motives, at any rate it is a step in advance to be able to refer their origins to savage or barbaric antiquity. Looking at these customs from the modern practical point of view, one is ridiculous, the others are atrocious, and all are senseless. The first is the practice of salutation on sneezing, the second the rite of laying the foundations of a building on a human victim, the third the prejudice against saving a drowning man.

In interpreting the customs connected with sneezing, it is needful to recognize a prevalent doctrine of the lower races, of which a full account will be given in another chapter. As a man's soul is considered to go in and out of his body, so it is with other spirits, particularly such as

enter into patients and possess them or afflict them with
disease. Among the less cultured races, the connexion of
this idea with sneezing is best shown among the Zulus, a
people firmly persuaded that kindly or angry spirits of the
dead hover about them, do them good or harm, stand
visibly before them in dreams, enter into them, and cause
diseases in them. The following particulars are abridged
from the native statements taken down by Dr. Callaway :—
When a Zulu sneezes, he will say, "I am now blessed.
The Idhlozi (ancestral spirit) is with me ; it has come to
me. Let me hasten and praise it, for it is it which causes
me to sneeze !" So he praises the manes of his family,
asking for cattle, and wives, and blessings. Sneezing is a
sign that a sick person will be restored to health ; he
returns thanks after sneezing, saying, "Ye people of ours,
I have gained that prosperity which I wanted. Continue
to look on me with favour !" Sneezing reminds a man
that he should name the Itongo (ancestral spirit) of his
people without delay, because it is the Itongo which causes
him to sneeze, that he may perceive by sneezing that the
Itongo is with him. If a man is ill and does not sneeze,
those who come to him ask whether he has sneezed or not ;
if he has not sneezed, they murmur, saying, "The disease
is great !" If a child sneezes, they say to it, "Grow !" it
is a sign of health. So then, it is said, sneezing among
black men gives a man strength to remember that the
Itongo has entered into him and abides with him. The
Zulu diviners or sorcerers are very apt to sneeze, which
they regard as an indication of the presence of the spirits,
whom they adore by saying "Makosi !" (i.e., lords or
masters). It is a suggestive example of the transition of
such customs as these from one religion to another, that
the Amakosa, who used to call on their divine ancestor
Utixo when they sneezed, since their conversion to Christianity say, "Preserver, look upon me !" or, "Creator of
heaven and earth !"[1] Elsewhere in Africa, similar ideas

[1] Callaway, 'Religion of Amazulu,' pp. 64, 222—3, 263.

are mentioned. Sir Thomas Browne, in his 'Vulgar
Errors,' made well known the story that when the King
of Monomotapa sneezed, acclamations of blessing passed
from mouth to mouth through the city; but he should
have mentioned that Godigno, from whom the original
account is taken, said that this took place when the king
drank, or coughed, or sneezed.[1] A later account from the
other side of the continent is more to the purpose. In
Guinea, in the last century, when a principal personage
sneezed, all present fell on their knees, kissed the earth,
clapped their hands, and wished him all happiness and
prosperity.[2] With a different idea, the negroes of Old
Calabar, when a child sneezes, will sometimes exclaim,
"Far from you!" with an appropriate gesture as if
throwing off some evil.[3] Polynesia is another region where
the sneezing salutation is well marked. In New Zealand,
a charm was said to prevent evil when a child sneezed;[4]
if a Samoan sneezed, the bystanders said, "Life to you!"[5]
while in the Tongan group a sneeze on the starting of an
expedition was a most evil presage.[6] A curious American
instance dates from Hernando de Soto's famous expedition
into Florida, when Guachoya, a native chief, came to pay
him a visit. "While this was going on, the cacique
Guachoya gave a great sneeze; the gentlemen who had
come with him and were lining the walls of the hall among
the Spaniards there all at once bowing their heads, opening
their arms and closing them again, and making other
gestures of great veneration and respect, saluted him with
different words, all directed to one end, saying, 'The Sun
guard thee, be with thee, enlighten thee, magnify thee,
protect thee, favour thee, defend thee, prosper thee, save
thee,' and other like phrases, as the words came, and for a

[1] Godignus, 'Vita Patris Gonzali Sylveriæ.' Col. Agripp. 1616; lib. il. c. x.
[2] Bosman, 'Guinea,' letter xviii. in Pinkerton, vol. xvi. p. 475.
[3] Burton, 'Wit and Wisdom from West Africa,' p. 373.
[4] Shortland, 'Trads. of New Zealand,' p. 131.
[5] Turner, 'Polynesia,' p. 348; see also Williams, 'Fiji,' vol. i. p. 250.
[6] Mariner, 'Tonga Is.' vol. i. p. 456.

good space there lingered the murmur of these words among
them, whereat the governor wondering said to the gentlemen and captains with him, ' Do you not see that all the
world is one ? ' This matter was well noted among the
Spaniards, that among so barbarous a people should be
used the same ceremonies, or greater, than among those
who hold themselves to be very civilized. Whence it may
be believed that this manner of salutation is natural among
all nations, and not caused by a pestilence, as is vulgarly
said," etc.[1]

In Asia and Europe, the sneezing superstition extends
through a wide range of race, age, and country.[2] Among
the passages relating to it in the classic ages of Greece and
Rome, the following are some of the most characteristic,—
the lucky sneeze of Telemachos in the Odyssey;[3] the
soldier's sneeze and the shout of adoration to the god which
rose along the ranks, and which Xenophon appealed to as a
favourable omen;[4] Aristotle's remark that people consider a sneeze as divine (τὸν μὲν πταρμὸν θεὸν ἡγούμεθα εἶναι),
but not a cough,[5] etc.; the Greek epigram on the man with
the long nose, who did not say Ζεῦ σῶσον when he sneezed,
for the noise was too far off for him to hear;[6] Petronius
Arbiter's mention of the custom of saying "Salve !" to one
who sneezed;[7] and Pliny's question, "Cur sternutamentis
salutamus ?" apropos of which he remarks that even Tiberius Cæsar, that saddest of men, exacted this observance.[8]

[1] Garcilaso de la Vega, 'Hist. de la Florida,' vol. iii. ch. xli.
[2] Among dissertations on the subject, see especially Sir Thos. Browne,
'Pseudodoxia Epidemica' (Vulgar Errors), book iv. chap. ix. ; Brand, 'Popular
Antiquities,' vol. iii. p. 119, etc. ; R. G. Haliburton, 'New Materials for the
History of Man.' Halifax, N. S. 1863 ; 'Encyclopædia Britannica,' art.
'sneezing ;' Wormsdorf, 'De Ritu Sternutantibus bene precandi.' Leipzig,
1741 ; see also Grimm, D. M. p. 1070, note.
[3] Homer. Odyss. xvii. 541.
[4] Xenophon. Anabasis, lib. 2, 9.
[5] Aristot. Problem. xxxiii. 7.
[6] Anthologia Græca, Branck, vol. iii. p. 95.
[7] Petron. Arb. Sat. 98.
[8] Plin. xxviii. 5.

Similar rites of sneezing have long been observed in Eastern Asia.[1] When a Hindu sneezes, bystanders say, "Live!" and the sneezer replies, "With you!" It is an ill omen, to which among others the Thugs paid great regard on starting on an expedition, and which even compelled them to let the travellers with them escape.[2]

The Jewish sneezing formula is, "Tobim chayim!" i.e., "Good life!"[3] The Moslem says, "Praise to Allah!" when he sneezes, and his friends compliment him with proper formulas, a custom which seems to be conveyed from race to race wherever Islam extends.[4] Lastly, the custom ranged through mediæval into modern Europe. To cite old German examples, "Die Heiden nicht endorften niesen, dâ man doch sprichet 'Nu helfiu Got!'" "Wir sprechen, swer niuset, Got helfe dir."[5] For a combined English and French example, the following lines (A.D. 1100) may serve, which show our old formula "wæs hæl!" ("may you be well!"—"wassail!") used also to avert being taken ill after a sneeze :—

> "E pur une feyze esternuer
> Tantot quident mal trouer,
> Si aznheil ne dies apres." [6]

In the 'Rules of Civility' (A.D. 1685, translated from the French) we read :—"If his lordship chances to sneeze, you are not to bawl out, 'God bless you, sir,' but, pulling off your hat, bow to him handsomely, and make that obsecration to yourself."[7] It is noticed that Anabaptists and

[1] Noel, 'Dic. des Origines;' Migne, 'Dic. des Superstitions,' etc.; Bastian, 'Oestl. Asien,' vol. II. p. 129.

[2] Ward, 'Hindoos,' vol. I. p. 142; Dubois, 'Peuples de l'Inde,' vol. I. p. 465; Sleeman, 'Ramaseeana,' p. 120.

[3] Buxtorf, 'Lexicon Chaldaicum;' Tendlau, 'Sprichwörter, etc. Deutsch-Jüdischer Vorzeit.' Frankf. a. M., 1860, p. 142.

[4] Lane, 'Modern Egyptians,' vol. I. p. 282. See Grant, in 'Tr. Eth. Soc.' vol. III. p. 90.

[5] Grimm, 'D. M.' pp. 1070, 1110.

[6] 'Manuel des Pecchés,' in Wedgwood, 'Dic. English Etymology,' s. v. 'wassail.'

[7] Brand, vol. III. p. 126.

Quakers rejected these with other salutations, but they
remained in the code of English good manners among high
and low till half a century or so ago, and are so little forgotten now, that most people still see the point of the story
of the fiddler and his wife, where his sneeze and her hearty
"God bless you!" brought about the removal of the fiddle
case. "Gott hilf!" may still be heard in Germany, and
"Felicità!" in Italy.

It is not strange that the existence of these absurd
customs should have been for ages a puzzle to curious
inquirers. Especially the legend-mongers took the matter
in hand, and their attempts to devise historical explanations
are on record in a group of philosophic myths,—Greek,
Jewish, Christian. Prometheus prays for the preservation
of his artificial man, when it gives the first sign of life by a
sneeze; Jacob prays that man's soul may not, as heretofore,
depart from his body when he sneezes; Pope Gregory prays
to avert the pestilence, in those days when the air was so
deadly that he who sneezed died of it; and from these
imaginary events legend declares that the use of the sneezing formulas was handed down. It is more to our purpose
to notice the existence of a corresponding set of ideas and
customs connected with gaping. Among the Zulus, repeated
yawning and sneezing are classed together as signs of
approaching spiritual possession.[1]   The Hindu, when he
gapes, must snap his thumb and finger, and repeat the name
of some God, as Rama: to neglect this is a sin as great as
the murder of a Brahman.[2] The Persians ascribe yawning,
sneezing, etc., to demoniacal possession. Among the modern
Moslems generally, when a man yawns, he puts the back of
his left hand to his mouth, saying, "I seek refuge with
Allah from Satan the accursed!" but the act of yawning is
to be avoided, for the Devil is in the habit of leaping into
a gaping mouth.[3] This may very likely be the meaning of

[1] Callaway, p. 263.   [2] Ward, l. c.
[3] 'Pend-Nameh,' tr. de Sacy, ch. lxiii.; Maury, 'Magie,' etc., p. 302;
Lane, l. c.

the Jewish proverb, "Open not thy mouth to Satan!" The other half of this idea shows itself clearly in Josephus' story of his having seen a certain Jew, named Eleazar, cure demoniacs in Vespasian's time, by drawing the demons out through their nostrils, by means of a ring containing a root of mystic virtue mentioned by Solomon.[1] The account of the sect of the Messalians, who used to spit and blow their noses to expel the demons they might have drawn in with their breath,[2] the records of the mediæval exorcists driving out devils through the patients' nostrils,[3] and the custom, still kept up in the Tyrol, of crossing oneself when one yawns, lest something evil should come into one's mouth,[4] involve similar ideas. In comparing the modern Kafir ideas with those of other districts of the world, we find a distinct notion of a sneeze being due to a spiritual presence. This, which seems indeed the key to the whole matter, has been well brought into view by Mr. Haliburton, as displayed in Keltic folklore, in a group of stories turning on the superstition that any one who sneezes is liable to be carried off by the fairies, unless their power be counteracted by an invocation, as "God bless you!"[5] The corresponding idea as to yawning is to be found in an Iceland folklore legend, where the troll, who has transformed herself into the shape of the beautiful queen, says, "When I yawn a little yawn, I am a neat and tiny maiden; when I yawn a half-yawn, then I am as a half-troll; when I yawn a whole yawn, then am I as a whole troll."[6] On the whole, though the sneezing superstition makes no approach to universality among mankind, its wide distribution is highly remarkable, and it would be an interesting problem to decide how far this wide distribution is due to independent growth in several regions,

[1] G. Drechter, 'Das Transcendentale im Talmud,' p. 169; Joseph. Ant. Jud. viii. 2, 5.
[2] Migne, 'Dic. des Hérésies,' s. v.
[3] Bastian, 'Mensch,' vol. ii. pp. 115, 322.
[4] Wuttke, 'Deutsche Volksaberglaube,' p. 137.
[5] Haliburton, op. cit.
[6] Powell and Magnusson, 'Legends of Iceland,' 2nd ser. p. 448.

how far to conveyance from race to race, and how far to
ancestral inheritance.   Here it has only to be maintained
that it was not originally an arbitrary and meaningless
custom, but the working out of a principle.[1]   The plain
statement by the modern Zulus fits with the hints to be
gained from the superstition and folklore of other races, to
connect the notions and practices as to sneezing with the
ancient and savage doctrine of pervading and invading
spirits, considered as good or evil, and treated accordingly.
The lingering survivals of the quaint old formulas in modern
Europe seem an unconscious record of the time when the
explanation of sneezing had not yet been given over to
physiology, but was still in the "theological stage."

There is current in Scotland the belief that the Picts,
to whom local legend attributes buildings of prehistoric
antiquity, bathed their foundation-stones with human
blood; and legend even tells that St. Columba found it
necessary to bury St. Oran alive beneath the foundation of
his monastery, in order to propitiate the spirits of the soil
who demolished by night what was built during the day.
So late as 1843, in Germany, when a new bridge was built
at Halle, a notion was abroad among the people that a child
was wanted to be built into the foundation.   These ideas of
church or wall or bridge wanting human blood or an im-
mured victim to make the foundation steadfast, are not only
widespread in European folklore, but local chronicle or tradition asserts them as matter of historical fact in district
after district.   Thus, when the broken dam of the Nogat
had to be repaired in 1463, the peasants, on the advice to
throw in a living man, are said to have made a beggar drunk
and buried him there.   Thuringian legend declares that to
make the castle of Liebenstein fast and impregnable, a child
was bought for hard money of its mother and walled in.   It

---

[1] The cases in which a sneeze is interpreted under special conditions, as with
reference to right and left, early morning, etc. (see Plutarch. De Genio
Socratis, etc.), are not considered here, as they belong to ordinary omen-
divination.

was eating a cake while the masons were at work, the story goes, and it cried out, "Mother, I see thee still;" then later, "Mother, I see thee a little still;" and, as they put in the last stone, "Mother, now I see thee no more." The wall of Copenhagen, legend says, sank as fast as it was built; so they took an innocent little girl, set her on a chair at a table with toys and eatables, and, as she played and ate, twelve master-masons closed a vault over her; then, with clanging music, the wall was raised, and stood firm ever after. Thus Italian legend tells of the bridge of Arta, that fell in and fell in till they walled in the master-builder's wife, and she spoke her dying curse that the bridge should tremble like a flower-stalk henceforth. The Slavonic chiefs founding Detinez, according to old heathen custom, sent out men to take the first boy they met and bury him in the foundation. Servian legend tells how three brothers combined to build the fortress of Skadra (Scutari); but, year after year, the demon (vila) razed by night what the three hundred masons built by day. The fiend must be appeased by a human sacrifice, the first of the three wives who should come bringing food to the workmen. All three brothers swore to keep the dreadful secret from their wives; but the two eldest gave traitorous warning to theirs, and it was the youngest brother's wife who came unsuspecting, and they built her in. But she entreated that an opening should be left for her to suckle her baby through, and for a twelve-month it was brought. To this day, Servian wives visit the tomb of the good mother, still marked by a stream of water which trickles, milky with lime, down the fortress wall. Lastly, there is our own legend of Vortigern, who could not finish his tower till the foundation-stone was wetted with the blood of a child born of a mother without a father. As is usual in the history of sacrifice, we hear of substitutes for such victims; empty coffins walled up in Germany, a lamb walled in under the altar in Denmark to make the church stand fast, and the churchyard in like manner hanselled by burying a live horse first. In modern Greece an evident

relic of the idea survives in the superstition that the first
passer-by after a foundation-stone is laid will die within the
year, wherefore the masons will compromise the debt by
killing a lamb or a black cock on the stone. With much
the same idea German legend tells of the bridge-building
fiend cheated of his promised fee, a soul, by the device of
making a cock run first across; and thus German folklore
says it is well, before entering a new house, to let a cat or
dog run in.[1] From all this it seems that, with due allowance for the idea having passed into an often-repeated and
varied mythic theme, yet written and unwritten tradition do
preserve the memory of a bloodthirsty barbaric rite, which
not only really existed in ancient times, but lingered long in
European history. If now we look to less cultured countries,
we shall find the rite carried on in our own day with a
distinctly religious purpose, either to propitiate the earth-
spirits with a victim, or to convert the soul of the victim
himself into a protecting demon.

In Africa, in Galam, a boy and girl used to be buried
alive before the great gate of the city to make it impregnable, a practice once executed on a large scale by a Dam-
barra tyrant; while in Great Bassam and Yarriba such
sacrifices were usual at the foundation of a house or village.[2]
In Polynesia, Ellis heard of the custom, instanced by the
fact that the central pillar of one of the temples at Maeva
was planted upon the body of a human victim.[3] In Borneo,

---

[1] W. Scott, 'Minstrelsy of Scottish Border;' Forbes Leslie, 'Early Races
of Scotland,' vol. L p. 149, 487 ; Grimm, 'Deutsche Mythologie,' p. 972,
1095 ; Bastian, 'Mensch,' vol. II. p. 92, 407, vol. III. p. 105, 112 ; Bowring,
'Servian Popular Poetry,' p. 64. A review of the First Edition of the present
work in 'Nature,' June 15, 1871, contains the following :—"It is not, for example, many years since the present Lord Leigh was accused of having built
an obnoxious person—one account, if we remember right, said eight obnoxious
persons—into the foundation of a bridge at Stoneleigh. Of course so preposterous a charge carried on its face its own sufficient refutation ; but the fact
that it was brought at all is a singular instance of the almost incredible
vitality of old traditions."
[2] Waitz, vol. II. p. 197.
[3] Ellis, 'Polyn. Res.' vol. L p. 346 ; Tyerman and Bennet, vol. II. p. 39.

among the Milanau Dayaks, at the erection of the largest
house a deep hole was dug to receive the first post, which
was then suspended over it; a slave girl was placed in the
excavation; at a signal the lashings were cut, and the
enormous timber descended, crushing the girl to death, a
sacrifice to the spirits. St. John saw a milder form of the
rite performed, when the chief of the Quop Dayaks set up a
flagstaff near his house, a chicken being thrown in to be
crushed by the descending pole.[1] More cultured nations of
Southern Asia have carried on into modern ages the rite of
the foundation-sacrifice. A 17th century account of Japan
mentions the belief there that a wall laid on the body of a
willing human victim would be secure from accident; accordingly, when a great wall was to be built, some wretched
slave would offer himself as foundation, lying down in the
trench to be crushed by the heavy stones lowered upon him.[2]
When the gate of the new city of Tavoy, in Tenasserim, was
built, perhaps twenty years ago, Mason was told by an eye-
witness that a criminal was put in each post-hole to become
a protecting demon. Thus it appears that such stories as
that of the human victims buried for spirit-watchers under
the gates of Mandalay, of the queen who was drowned
in a Birmese reservoir to make the dyke safe, of the
hero whose divided body was buried under the fortress of
Thatung to make it impregnable, are the records, whether
in historical or mythical form, of the actual customs of the

---

[1] St. John, 'Far East,' vol. L p. 46 ; see Bastian, vol. II. p. 407. I am
indebted to Mr. R. K. Douglas for a perfect example of one meaning of the
foundation-sacrifice, from the Chinese book, 'Yüh hea ke' ('Jewelled Casket
of Divination') : " Before beginning to build, the workmen should sacrifice
to the gods of the neighbourhood, of the earth and wood. Should the car-
penters be very apprehensive of the building falling, they, when fixing a post,
should take something living and put it beneath, and lower the post on it,
and to liberate [the evil influences] they should strike the post with an axe
and repeat—
                     ' It is well, it is well,
                     May those who live within
                     Be ever warm and well fed.' "

[2] Caron, 'Japan,' in Pinkerton, vol. vII. p. 623.

land.[1] Within our own dominion, when Rajah Sala Byne was building the fort of Sialkot in the Punjaub, the foundation of the south-east bastion gave way so repeatedly that he had recourse to a soothsayer, who assured him that it would never stand until the blood of an only son was shed there, wherefore the only son of a widow was sacrificed.[2] It is thus plain that hideous rites, of which Europe has scarcely kept up more than the dim memory, have held fast their ancient practice and meaning in Africa, Polynesia, and Asia, among races who represent in grade, if not in chronology, earlier stages of civilization.

When Sir Walter Scott, in the ' Pirate,' tells of Bryce the pedlar refusing to help Mordaunt to save the shipwrecked sailor from drowning, and even remonstrating with him on the rashness of such a deed, he states an old superstition of the Shetlanders. " Are you mad ?" says the pedlar ; " you that have lived sae lang in Zetland, to risk the saving of a drowning man ? Wot ye not, if you bring him to life again, he will be sure to do you some capital injury ?" Were this inhuman thought noticed in this one district alone, it might be fancied to have had its rise in some local idea now no longer to be explained. But when mentions of similar superstitions are collected among the St. Kilda islanders and the boatmen of the Danube, among French and English sailors, and even out of Europe and among less civilized races, we cease to think of local fancies, but look for some widely accepted belief of the lower culture to account for such a state of things. The Hindu does not save a man from drowning in the sacred Ganges, and the islanders of the Malay archipelago share the cruel notion.[3] Of all people the rude Kamchadals have the prohibition in the most remarkable form. They hold it a great fault, says Kracheninnikoff, to save a drown-

[1] Bastian, 'Oestl. Asien,' vol. i. pp. 193, 214 ; vol. ii. pp. 91, 270 ; vol. iii. p. 16. Roberts, 'Oriental Illustrations of Scriptures,' p. 283 (Ceylon).

[2] Bastian, 'Mensch,' vol. iii. p. 107. A modern Arnaut story is given by Prof. Liebrecht in 'Philologus,' vol. xxliii. (1865) p. 682.

[3] Bastian, 'Mensch,' vol. iii. p. 210   Ward, 'Hindoos,' vol. ii. p. 318.

ing man; he who delivers him will be drowned himself.[1]
Steller's account is more extraordinary, and probably applies
only to cases where the victim is actually drowning: he says
that if a man fell by chance into the water, it was a great
sin for him to get out, for as he had been destined to drown
he did wrong in not drowning, wherefore no one would let
him into his dwelling, nor speak to him, nor give him food
or a wife, but he was reckoned for dead; and even when a
man fell into the water while others were standing by, far
from helping him out, they would drown him by force. Now
these savages, it appears, avoided volcanoes because of the
spirits who live there and cook their food; for a like reason,
they held it a sin to bathe in hot springs; and they believed
with fear in a fish-like spirit of the sea, whom they called
Mitgk.[2] This spiritualistic belief among the Kamchadals is,
no doubt, the key to their superstition as to rescuing
drowning men. There is even to be found in modern
European superstition, not only the practice, but with it a
lingering survival of its ancient spiritualistic significance.
In Bohemia, a recent account (1864) says that the fishermen
do not venture to snatch a drowning man from the waters.
They fear that the "Waterman" (i. e., water-demon) would
take away their luck in fishing, and drown themselves at the
first opportunity.[3] This explanation of the prejudice
against saving the water-spirit's victim may be confirmed by
a mass of evidence from various districts of the world.
Thus, in discussing the doctrine of sacrifice, it will appear
that the usual manner of making an offering to a well, river,
lake, or sea, is simply to cast property, cattle, or men into
the water, which personally or by its in-dwelling spirit takes
possession of them.[4] That the accidental drowning of a
man is held to be such a seizure, savage and civilized folklore show by many examples. Among the Sioux Indians,

---

[1] Kracheninnikov, 'Descr. du Kamchatka, Voy. en Sibérie,' vol. iii. p. 71.
[2] Steller, 'Kamtschatka,' pp. 265, 274.
[3] J. V. Grohmann, 'Aberglauben und Gebräuche aus Böhmen,' p. 12.
[4] Chap. XVIII.

it is Unk-tahe the water-monster that drowns his victims in
flood or rapid ;[1] in New Zealand huge supernatural reptile-
monsters, called Taniwha, live in river-bends, and those who
are drowned are said to be pulled under by them ;[2] the
Siamese fears the Pnük or water-spirit that seizes bathers
and drags them under to his dwelling ;[3] in Slavonic lands
it is Topielec (the ducker) by whom men are always
drowned ;[4] when some one is drowned in Germany, people
recollect the religion of their ancestors, and say, "The
river-spirit claims his yearly sacrifice," or, more simply,
"The nix has taken him : "[5]—

> "Ich glaube, die Wellen verschlingen,
> Am Ende Fischer und Kahn ;
> Und das hat mit ihrem Singen
> Die Lorelei gethan."

From this point of view it is obvious that to save a sinking
man is to snatch a victim from the very clutches of the
water-spirit, a rash defiance of deity which would hardly pass
unavenged. In the civilized world the rude old theological
conception of drowning has long been superseded by physical explanation ; and the prejudice against rescue from
such a death may have now almost or altogether
disappeared. But archaic ideas, drifted on into modern
folklore and poetry, still bring to our view an apparent
connexion between the primitive doctrine and the surviving
custom.

As the social development of the world goes on, the
weightiest thoughts and actions may dwindle to mere
survival. Original meaning dies out gradually, each generation leaves fewer and fewer to bear it in mind, till it falls
out of popular memory, and in after-days ethnography has

[1] Eastman, 'Dacotah,' p. 118, 125.
[2] R. Taylor, 'New Zealand,' p. 48.
[3] Bastian, 'Oestl. Asien,' vol. iii. p. 34.
[4] Hanusch, 'Wissenschaft des Slawischen Mythus,' p. 299.
[5] Grimm, 'Deutsche Myth.' p. 462.

to attempt, more or less successfully, to restore it by piecing together lines of isolated or forgotten facts. Children's sports, popular sayings, absurd customs, may be practically unimportant, but are not philosophically insignificant, bearing as they do on some of the most instructive phases of early culture. Ugly and cruel superstitions may prove to be relics of primitive barbarism, for in keeping up such Man is like Shakspeare's fox,

> " Who, ne'er so tame, so cherish'd, and lock'd up,
> Will have a wild trick of his ancestors."

CHAPTER IV.

SURVIVAL IN CULTURE (continued).

Occult Sciences—Magical powers attributed by higher to lower races—Magical processes based on Association of Ideas—Omens—Augury, etc.—Oneiromancy—Haruspication, Scapulimancy, Chiromancy, etc.—Cartomancy, etc.—Rhabdomancy, Dactyliomancy, Coscinomancy, etc.—Astrology—Intellectual conditions accounting for the persistence of Magic—Survival passes into Revival—Witchcraft, originating in savage culture, continues in barbaric civilization ; its decline in early mediæval Europe followed by revival ; its practices and counter-practices belong to earlier culture—Spiritualism has its source in early stages of culture, in close connexion with witchcraft—Spirit-rapping and Spirit-writing—Rising in the air—Performances of tied mediums—Practical bearing of the study of Survival.

In examining the survival of opinions in the midst of conditions of society becoming gradually estranged from them, and tending at last to suppress them altogether, much may be learnt from the history of one of the most pernicious delusions that ever vexed mankind, the belief in Magic. Looking at Occult Science from this ethnographic point of view, I shall instance some of its branches as illustrating the course of intellectual culture. Its place in history is briefly this. It belongs in its main principle to the lowest known stages of civilization, and the lower races, who have not partaken largely of the education of the world, still maintain it in vigour. From this level it may be traced upward, much of the savage art holding its place substantially unchanged, and many new practices being in course of time developed, while both the older and newer developments have lasted on more or less among modern cultured nations. But during the ages in which progressive

races have been learning to submit their opinions to closer
and closer experimental tests, occult science has been breaking down into the condition of a survival, in which state we
mostly find it among ourselves.

The modern educated world, rejecting occult science as a
contemptible superstition, has practically committed itself
to the opinion that magic belongs to a lower level of
civilization. It is very instructive to find the soundness of
this judgment undesignedly confirmed by nations whose
education has not advanced far enough to destroy their
belief in magic itself. In any country an isolated or outlying race, the lingering survivor of an older nationality, is
liable to the reputation of sorcery. It is thus with the
Lavas of Birma, supposed to be the broken-down remains
of an ancient cultured race, and dreaded as man-tigers;[1]
and with the Budas of Abyssinia, who are at once the smiths
and potters, sorcerers and werewolves, of their district.[2] But
the usual and suggestive state of things is that nations who
believe with the sincerest terror in the reality of the magic
art, at the same time cannot shut their eyes to the fact that
it more essentially belongs to, and is more thoroughly at
home among, races less civilized than themselves. The
Malays of the Peninsula, who have adopted Mohammedan
religion and civilization, have this idea of the lower tribes
of the land, tribes more or less of their own race, but who have
remained in their early savage condition. The Malays have
enchanters of their own, but consider them inferior to the
sorcerers or poyangs belonging to the rude Mintira; to these
they will resort for the cure of diseases and the working of
misfortune and death to their enemies. It is, in fact, the
best protection the Mintira have against their stronger
Malay neighbours, that these are careful not to offend them
for fear of their powers of magical revenge. The Jakuns,
again, are a rude and wild race, whom the Malays despise
as infidels and little higher than animals, but whom at the

[1] Bastian, 'Oestl. Asien,' vol. i. p. 119.
[2] 'Life of Nath. Pearce,' ed. by J. J. Halls, vol. i. p. 286.

same time they fear extremely. To the Malay the Jakun
seems a supernatural being, skilled in divination, sorcery,
and fascination, able to do evil or good according to his
pleasure, whose blessing will be followed by the most
fortunate success, and his curse by the most dreadful consequences; he can turn towards the house of an enemy, at
whatever distance, and beat two sticks together till that
enemy will fall sick and die; he is skilled in herbal physic;
he has the power of charming the fiercest wild beasts.
Thus it is that the Malays, though they despise the Jakuns,
refrain, in many circumstances, from ill-treating them.[1]   In
India, in long-past ages, the dominant Aryans described the
rude indigenes of the land by the epithets of " possessed of
magical powers," " changing their shape at will."[2]   To this
day, Hindus settled in Chota-Nagpur and Singbhum firmly
believe that the Mundas have powers of witchcraft, whereby
they can transform themselves into tigers and other beasts
of prey to devour their enemies, and can witch away the
lives of man and beast; it is to the wildest and most
savage of the tribe that such powers are generally ascribed.[3]
In Southern India, again, we hear in past times of
Hinduized Dravidians, the Sudras of Canara, living in fear
of the dæmoniacal powers of the slave-caste below them.[4]
In our own day, among Dravidian tribes of the Nilagiri
district, the Todas and Badagas are in mortal dread of the
Kurumbas, despised and wretched forest outcasts, but
gifted, it is believed, with powers of destroying men and
animals and property by witchcraft.[5]   Northern Europe
brings the like contrast sharply into view. The Finns and
Lapps, whose low Tatar barbarism was characterized by
sorcery such as flourishes still among their Siberian kins-

[1] 'Journ. Ind. Archip.' vol. I. p. 328; vol. ii. p. 273; see vol. iv. p. 425.
[2] Muir, 'Sanskrit Texts,' part ii. p. 435.
[3] Dalton, 'Kols,' in 'Tr. Eth. Soc.' vol. vi. p. 6; see p. 16.
[4] Jas. Gardner, 'Faiths of the World,' s. v. 'Exorcism.'
[5] Shortt, 'Tribes of Neilgherries,' in 'Tr. Eth. Soc.' vol. vii. pp. 247, 277;
Sir W. Elliot in 'Trans. Congress of Prehistoric Archæology,' 1868, p. 253.

folk, were accordingly objects of superstitious fear to their
Scandinavian neighbours and oppressors. In the middle
ages the name of Finn was, as it still remains among sea-
faring men, equivalent to that of sorcerer, while Lapland
witches had a European celebrity as practitioners of the
black art. Ages after the Finns had risen in the social scale,
the Lapps retained much of their old half-savage habit of
life, and with it naturally their witchcraft, so that even the
magic-gifted Finns revered the occult powers of a people
more barbarous than themselves. Rühs writes thus early
in the present century: "There are still sorcerers in Finland, but the skilfullest of them believe that the Lapps far
excel them; of a well-experienced magician they say, 'That
is quite a Lapp,' and they journey to Lapland for such
knowledge."[1] All this is of a piece with the survival of
such ideas among the ignorant elsewhere in the civilized
world. Many a white man in the West Indies and Africa
dreads the incantations of the Obi-man, and Europe
ascribes powers of sorcery to despised outcast "races
maudites," Gypsies and Cagots. To turn from nations to
sects, the attitude of Protestants to Catholics in this matter
is instructive. It was remarked in Scotland: "There is
one opinion which many of them entertain, ... that a
popish priest can cast out devils and cure madness, and
that the Presbyterian clergy have no such power." So
Bourne says of the Church of England clergy, that the
vulgar think them no conjurors, and say none can lay
spirits but popish priests.[2] These accounts are not recent,
but in Germany the same state of things appears to exist
still. Protestants get the aid of Catholic priests and monks
to help them against witchcraft, to lay ghosts, consecrate
herbs, and discover thieves;[3] thus with unconscious irony
judging the relation of Rome toward modern civilization.

The principal key to the understanding of Occult Science

[1] F. Rühs, 'Finland,' p. 296; Bastian, 'Mensch.' vol. iii. p. 202.
[2] Brand, 'Pop. Ant.' vol. iii. pp. 81—3; see 813.
[3] Wuttke, 'Deutsche Volksaberglaube,' p. 126; see 239.

I 2

As to consider it as based on the Association of Ideas, a faculty which lies at the very foundation of human reason, but in no small degree of human unreason also. } Man, as yet in a low intellectual condition, having come to associate in thought those things which he found by experience to be connected in fact, proceeded erroneously to invert this action, and to conclude that association in thought must involve similar connexion in reality. He thus attempted to discover, to foretell, and to cause events by means of processes which we can now see to have only an ideal significance. By a vast mass of evidence from savage, barbaric, and civilized life, magic arts which have resulted from thus mistaking an ideal for a real connexion, may be clearly traced from the lower culture which they are of, to the higher culture which they are in.[1] Such are the practices whereby a distant person is to be affected by acting on something closely associated with him—his property, clothes he has worn, and above all cuttings of his hair and nails. Not only do savages high and low like the Australians and Polynesians, and barbarians like the nations of Guinea, live in deadly terror of this spiteful craft—not only have the Parsis their sacred ritual prescribed for burying their cut hair and nails, lest demons and sorcerers should do mischief with them, but the fear of leaving such clippings and parings about lest their former owner should be harmed through them, has by no means died out of European folklore, and the German peasant, during the days between his child's birth and baptism, objects to lend anything out of the house, lest witchcraft should be worked through it on the yet unconsecrated baby.[2] As the negro fetish-man, when his patient does not come in person, can

[1] For an examination of numerous magical arts, mostly coming under this category, see 'Early History of Mankind,' chaps. vi. and x.

[2] Stanbridge, 'Abor. of Victoria,' in 'Tr. Eth. Soc.' vol. i. p. 299; Ellis, 'Polyn. Res.' vol. i. p. 364; J. L. Wilson, 'W. Africa,' p. 215; Spiegel, 'Avesta,' vol. i. p. 124; Wuttke, 'Deutsche Volksberglaube,' p. 195; general references in 'Early History of Mankind,' p. 129.

divine by means of his dirty cloth or cap instead,[1] so the modern clairvoyant professes to feel sympathetically the sensations of a distant person, if communication be made through a lock of his hair or any object that has been in contact with him.[2] The simple idea of joining two objects with a cord, taking for granted that this communication will establish connexion or carry influence, has been worked out in various ways in the world. In Australia, the native doctor fastens one end of a string to the ailing part of the patient's body, and by sucking at the other end pretends to draw out blood for his relief.[3] In Orissa, the Joypore witch lets down a ball of thread through her enemy's roof to reach his body, that by putting the other end in her own mouth she may suck his blood.[4] When a reindeer is sacrificed at a sick Ostyak's tent-door, the patient holds in his hand a cord attached to the victim offered for his benefit.[5] Greek history shows a similar idea, when the citizens of Ephesus carried a rope seven furlongs from their walls to the temple of Artemis, thus to place themselves under her safeguard against the attack of Crœsus; and in the yet more striking story of the Kylonians, who tied a cord to the statue of the goddess when they quitted the asylum, and clung to it for protection as they crossed unhallowed ground; but by ill-fate the cord of safety broke and they were mercilessly put to death.[6] And in our own day, Buddhist priests in solemn ceremony put themselves in communication with a sacred relic, by each taking hold of a long thread fastened near it and around the temple.[7]

Magical arts in which the connexion is that of mere analogy or symbolism are endlessly numerous throughout

[1] Burton, 'W. and W. from West Africa,' p. 431.
[2] W. Gregory, 'Letters on Animal Magnetism,' p. 128.
[3] Eyre, 'Australia,' vol. ii. p. 341; Collins, 'New South Wales,' vol. i. pp. 561, 591.
[4] Shortt, in 'Tr. Eth. Soc.' vol. vi. p. 278.
[5] Bastian, 'Mensch.' vol. iii. p. 117.
[6] See Grote, vol. iii. pp. 113, 351.
[7] Hardy, 'Eastern Monachism,' p. 241.

the course of civilization. Their common theory may be
readily made out from a few typical cases, and thence applied
confidently to the general mass. The Australian will
observe the track of an insect near a grave, to ascertain the
direction where the sorcerer is to be found, by whose craft
the man died.[1] The Zulu may be seen chewing a bit of
wood, in order, by this symbolic act, to soften the heart of
the man he wants to buy oxen from, or of the woman he
wants for a wife.[2] The Obi-man of West Africa makes his
packet of grave-dust, blood, and bones, that this suggestive
representation of death may bring his enemy to the grave.[3]
The Khond sets up the iron arrow of the War-god in a
basket of rice, and judges from its standing upright that war
must be kept up also, or from its falling that the quarrel
may be let fall too; and when he tortures human victims
sacrificed to the Earth-goddess, he rejoices to see them shed
plentiful tears, which betoken copious showers to fall upon
his land.[4] These are fair examples of the symbolic magic
of the lower races, and they are fully rivalled in superstitions which still hold their ground in Europe. With quaint
simplicity, the German cottager declares that if a dog
howls looking downward, it portends a death; but if upward,
then a recovery from sickness.[5] Locks must be opened and
bolts drawn in a dying man's house, that his soul may not
be held fast.[6] The Hessian lad thinks that he may escape the
conscription by carrying a baby-girl's cap in his pocket—a
symbolic way of repudiating manhood.[7] Modern Servians,
dancing and singing, lead about a little girl dressed in
leaves and flowers, and pour bowls of water over her to
make the rain come.[8] Sailors becalmed will sometimes

[1] Oldfield, in 'Tr. Eth. Soc.' vol. iii. p. 246.
[2] Grout, 'Zulu-land,' p. 134.
[3] See specimen and description in the Christy Museum.
[4] Macpherson, 'India,' pp. 130, 363.
[5] Wuttke, 'Volksaberglaube,' p. 31.
[6] R. Hunt, 'Pop. Rom. of W. of England,' 2nd ser. p. 165 ; Brand, 'Pop.
Ant.' vol. ii. p. 231.
[7] Wuttke, p. 100.   [8] Grimm, 'D. M.' p. 560.

whistle for a wind; but in other weather they hate
whistling at sea, which raises a whistling gale.[1] Fish,
says the Cornishman, should be eaten from the tail
towards the head, to bring the other fishes' heads towards
the shore, for eating them the wrong way turns them from
the coast.[2] He who has cut himself should rub the
knife with fat, and as it dries, the wound will heal; this is
a lingering survival from days when recipes for sympathetic
ointment were to be found in the Pharmacopœia.[3] Fanciful
as these notions are, it should be borne in mind that they
come fairly under definite mental law, depending as they do
on a principle of ideal association, of which we can quite
understand the mental action, though we deny its practical
results. The clever Lord Chesterfield, too clever to understand folly, may again be cited to prove this. He relates in
one of his letters that the king had been ill, and that people
generally expected the illness to be fatal, because the oldest
lion in the Tower, about the king's age, had just died. "So
wild and capricious is the human mind," he exclaims, by
way of comment. But indeed the thought was neither wild
nor capricious, it was simply such an argument from analogy
as the educated world has at length painfully learnt to be
worthless; but which, it is not too much to declare, would
to this day carry considerable weight to the minds of four-
fifths of the human race.

A glance at those magical arts which have been systematized into pseudo-sciences, shows the same underlying
principle. The art of taking omens from seeing and meeting animals, which includes augury, is familiar to such
savages as the Tupis of Brazil[4] and the Dayaks of Borneo,[5]
and extends upward through classic civilization. The
Maoris may give a sample of the character of its rules : they

---

[1] Brand, vol. III. p. 240.
[2] Hunt, ibid. p. 148.
[3] Wuttke, p. 165; Brand, vol. III. p. 305.
[4] Magalhaues de Gandavo, p. 125 ; D'Orbigny, vol. II. p. 168.
[5] St. John, 'Far East,' vol. I. p. 202; 'Journ. Ind. Archip.' vol. II. p. 857.

hold it unlucky if an owl hoots during a consultation, but a
council of war is encouraged by prospect of victory when a
hawk flies overhead; a flight of birds to the right of the
war-sacrifice is propitious if the villages of the tribe are in
that quarter, but if the omen is in the enemy's direction
the war will be given up.[1] Compare these with the Tatar
rules, and it is obvious that similar thoughts lie at the
source of both. Here a certain little owl's cry is a sound of
terror, although there is a white owl which is lucky; but of
all birds the white falcon is most prophetic, and the Kalmuk
bows his thanks for the good omen when one flies by on the
right, but seeing one on the left turns away his face and
expects calamity.[2] So to the negro of Old Calabar, the cry
of the great kingfisher bodes good or evil, according as it is
heard on the right or left.[3] Here we have the obvious symbolism of the right and left hand, the foreboding of ill from
the owl's doleful note, and the suggestion of victory from
the fierce swooping hawk, a thought which in old Europe
made the bird of prey the warrior's omen of conquest.
Meaning of the same kind appears in the 'Angang,' the
omens taken from meeting animals and people, especially on
first going out in the morning, as when the ancient Slaves
held meeting a sick man or an old woman to bode ill-luck.
Any one who takes the trouble to go into this subject in
detail, and to study the classic, mediæval, and oriental codes
of rules, will find that the principle of direct symbolism still
accounts for a fair proportion of them, though the rest may
have lost their early significance, or may have been originally
due to some other reason, or may have been arbitrarily
invented (as a considerable proportion of such devices must
necessarily be) to fill up the gaps in the system. It is still
plain to us why the omen of the crow should be different on
the right or left hand, why a vulture should mean rapacity,
a stork concord, a pelican piety, an ass labour, why the

---

[1] Yate, 'New Zealand,' p. 90; Polack, vol. I. p. 248.
[2] Klemm, 'Cultur-Gesch.' vol. iii. p. 202.
[3] Burton, 'Wit and Wisdom from West Africa,' p. 351.

fierce conquering wolf should be a good omen, and the timid
hare a bad one, why bees, types of an obedient nation,
should be lucky to a king, while flies, returning however
often they are driven off, should be signs of importunity and
impudence.[1] And as to the general principle that animals
are ominous to those who meet them, the German peasant
who says a flock of sheep is lucky but a herd of swine unlucky to meet, and the Cornish miner who turns away in
horror when he meets an old woman or a rabbit on his way
to the pit's mouth, are to this day keeping up relics of early
savagery as genuine as any flint implement dug out of a
tumulus.

The doctrine of dreams, attributed as they are by the
lower and middle races to spiritual intercourse, belongs in
no far rather to religion than to magic. But oneiromancy,
the art of taking omens from dreams by non-natural interpretation, has its place here. Of the leading principle of such
mystical explanation, no better types could be chosen than
the details and interpretations of Joseph's dreams (Genesis
xxxvii., xl., xli.), of the sheaves and the sun and moon and
eleven stars, of the vine and the basket of meats, of the lean
and fat kine, and the thin and full corn-ears. Oneiromancy,
thus symbolically interpreting the things seen in dreams, is
not unknown to the lower races. A whole Australian tribe
has been known to decamp because one of them dreamt of a
certain kind of owl, which dream the wise men declared to
forebode an attack from a certain other tribe.[2] The Kamchadals, whose minds ran much on dreams, had special interpretations of some; thus to dream of lice or dogs betokened a visit of Russian travellers, &c.[3] The Zulus, experience having taught them the fallacy of expecting direct
fulfilment of dreams, have in some cases tried to mend

[1] See Cornelius Agrippa, 'De Occulta Philosophia,' L. 53; 'De Vanitate
Scient.' 37; Grimm, 'D. M.' p. 1073; Hanusch, 'Slaw. Myth.' p. 285;
Brand. vol. iii. pp. 184—227.
[2] Oldfield in 'Tr. Eth. Soc.' vol. iii. p. 241.
[3] Steller, 'Kamtschatka,' p. 279.

matters by rushing to the other extreme. If they dream of a sick man that he is dead, and they see the earth poured into the grave, and hear the funeral lamentation, and see all his things destroyed, then they say, "Because we have dreamt of his death he will not die." But if they dream of a wedding-dance, it is a sign of a funeral. So the Maoris hold that a kinsman dreamt of as dying will recover, but to see him well is a sign of death.[1] Both races thus work out, by the same crooked logic that guided our own ancestors, the axiom that "dreams go by contraries." It could not be expected, in looking over the long lists of precepts of classic, oriental, and modern popular dream-interpretation, to detect the original sense of all their readings. Many must turn on allusions intelligible at the time, but now obscure. The Moslem dream-interpretation of eggs as concerning women, because of a saying of Mohammed about women being like an egg hidden in a nest, is an example which will serve as well as a score to show how dream-rules may turn on far-fetched ideas, not to be recognized unless the key happens to have been preserved. Many rules must have been taken at random to fill up lists of omens, and of contingencies to match them. Why should a dream of roasting meat show the dreamer to be a backbiter, or laughter in sleep presage difficult circumstances, or a dream of playing on the clavicord the death of relatives? But the other side of the matter, the still apparent nonsensical rationality of so many dream-omens, is much more remarkable. It can only be considered that the same symbolism that lay at the root of the whole delusion, favoured the keeping up and new making of such rules as carried obvious meaning. Take the Moslem ideas that it is a good omen to dream of something white or green, or of water, but bad to dream of black or red, or of fire; that a palm-tree indicates an Arab, and a peacock a king; that he who dreams of devouring the stars will live free at some great man's table. Take the classic rules as in the 'Oneirocritica' of Artemidorus,

---

[1] Callaway, 'Rel. of Amazulu,' pp. 236, 241; R. Taylor, 'N. Z.' p. 334.

and pass on through the mediæval treatises down to such a
dream-dictionary as servant-maids still buy in penny chap-
books at the fair, and it will be seen that the ancient rules
still hold their places to a remarkable extent, while half the
mass of precepts still show their original mystic significance,
mostly direct, but occasionally according to the rule of contraries. An offensive odour signifies annoyance; to wash
the hands denotes release from anxieties; to embrace one's
best beloved is very fortunate; to have one's feet cut off
prevents a journey; to weep in sleep is a sign of joy; he
who dreams he hath lost a tooth shall lose a friend; and he
that dreams that a rib is taken out of his side shall ere long
see the death of his wife; to follow bees, betokens gain; to
be married signifies that some of your kinsfolk are dead; if
one sees many fowls together, that shall be jealousy and
chiding; if a snake pursue him, let him be on his guard
against evil women; to dream of death, denotes happiness
and long life; to dream of swimming and wading in the
water is good, so that the head be kept above water; to
dream of crossing a bridge, denotes you will leave a good
situation to seek a better; to dream you see a dragon is a
sign that you shall see some great lord your master, or a
magistrate.[1]

Haruspication belongs, among the lower races, especially
to the Malays and Polynesians,[2] and to various Asiatic
tribes.[3] It is mentioned as practised in Peru under the
Incas.[4] Captain Burton's account from Central Africa
perhaps fairly displays its symbolic principle. He
describes the mganga or sorcerer taking an ordeal by kill-

[1] Artemidorus, 'Oneirocritica;' Cockayne, 'Leechdoms,' etc., of Early England,' vol. iii.; Benfield, 'Literature, etc., of Dreams;' Brand, vol. iii.;
Halliwell, 'Pop. Rhymes,' etc., p. 217, etc., etc.

[2] St. John, 'Far East,' vol. i. pp. 74, 115; Ellis, 'Polyn. Res.' vol. iv.
p. 150; Polack, 'New Zealanders,' vol. i. p. 255.

[3] Georgi, 'Reise im Russ. Reich.' vol. i. p. 281; Hooker, 'Himalayan
Journals,' vol. i. p. 135; 'As. Res.' vol. iii. p. 27; Latham, 'Descr. Eth.'
vol. i. p. 61.

[4] Cieza de Leon, p. 289; Rivero and Tschudi, 'Peru,' p. 183.

ing and splitting a fowl and inspecting its inside : if black-
ness or blemish appears about the wings, it denotes the
treachery of children and kinsmen; the backbone convicts the
mother and grandmother ; the tail shows that the criminal
is the wife, &c.[1] In ancient Rome, where the art held so
great a place in public affairs, the same sort of interpretation
was usual, as witness the omen of Augustus, where the livers
of the victims were found folded, and the diviners prophesied
him accordingly a doubled empire.[2] Since then, haruspication has died out more completely than almost any magical
rite, yet even now a characteristic relic of it may be noticed
in Brandenburg; when a pig is killed and the spleen is
found turned over, there will be another overthrow, namely
a death in the family that year.[3] With haruspication may
be classed the art of divining by bones, as where North
American Indians would put in the fire a certain flat bone
of a porcupine, and judge from its colour if the porcupine
hunt would be successful.[4] The principal art of this kind is
divination by a shoulder-blade, technically called scapulimancy or omoplatoscopy. This is especially found in vogue
in Tartary, where it is ancient, and whence it may have
spread into all other countries where we hear of it. Its
simple symbolism is well shown in the elaborate account
with diagrams given by Pallas. The shoulder-blade is put
on the fire till it cracks in various directions, and then a
long split lengthwise is reckoned as the " way of life,"
while cross-cracks on the right and left stand for different
kinds and degrees of good and evil fortune ; or if the omen
is only taken as to some special event, then lengthwise splits
mean going on well, but crosswise ones stand for hindrance,
white marks portend much snow, black ones a mild winter,
&c.[5] To find this quaint art lasting on into modern times

[1] Burton, 'Central Afr.' vol. ii. p. 32 ; Waitz, vol. ii. pp. 417, 518.
[2] Plin. xi. 73. See Cic. de Divinatione, ii. 12.
[3] Wuttke, ' Volksaberglaube,' p. 32.
[4] Le Jeune, 'Nouvelle France,' vol. i. p. 90.
[5] Klemm, 'Cultur-Gesch.' vol. iii. pp. 109, 199 ; vol. iv. p. 221; Rubru-

in Europe, we can hardly go to a better place than our own
country; a proper English term for it is "reading the speal-
bone" (*speal* = *espaule*). In Ireland, Camden describes the
looking through the blade-bone of a sheep, to find a dark
spot which foretells a death, and Drayton thus commemorates the art in his Polyolbion :—

> "By th' shoulder of a ram from off the right side par'd,
> Which usually they boile, the spade-bone being bar'd,
> Which when the wizard takes, and gazing therupon
> Things long to come foreshowes, as things done long agone."[1]

Chiromancy, or palmistry, seems much like this, though it is
also mixed up with astrology. It flourished in ancient
Greece and Italy as it still does in India, where to say, "It
is written on the palms of my hands," is a usual way of expressing a sense of inevitable fate. Chiromancy traces in
the markings of the palm a line of fortune and a line of life,
finds proof of melancholy in the intersections on the satur-
nine mount, presages sorrow and death from black spots in
the finger-nails, and at last, having exhausted the powers of
this childish symbolism, it completes its system by details of
which the absurdity is no longer relieved by even an ideal
sense. The art has its modern votaries not merely among
Gypsy fortune-tellers, but in what is called "good
society."[2]

It may again and again thus be noticed in magic arts,
that the association of ideas is obvious up to a certain point.
Thus when the New Zealand sorcerer took omens by the
way his divining sticks (guided by spirits) fell, he quite
naturally said it was a good omen if the stick representing
his own tribe fell on top of that representing the enemy,
and vice versâ. Zulu diviners still work a similar process
with their magical pieces of stick, which rise to say yes and

quis, in Pinkerton, vol. vii. p. 65; Grimm, 'D. M.' p. 1067; R. F. Burton,
'Sindh,' p. 189; M. A. Walker, 'Macedonia,' p. 169.
[1] Brand, vol. III. p. 339; Forbes Leslie, vol. II. p. 491.
[2] Maury, 'Magie, etc.,' p. 74; Brand, vol. III. p. 348, etc. See figure in
Cornelius Agrippa, 'De Occult. Philosoph.' II. 27.

fall to say no, jump upon the head or stomach or other affected part of the patient's body to show where his complaint is, and lie pointing towards the house of the doctor who can cure him. So likewise, where a similar device was practised ages ago in the Old World, the responses were taken from staves which (by the operation of daemons) fell backward or forward, to the right or left.[1] But when processes of this kind are developed to complexity, the system has, of course, to be completed by more arbitrary arrangements. This is well shown in one of the divinatory arts mentioned in the last chapter for their connexion with games of chance. In cartomancy, the art of fortune-telling with packs of cards, there is a sort of nonsensical sense in such rules as that two queens mean friendship and four mean chattering, or that the knave of hearts prophesies a brave young man who will come into the family to be useful, unless his purpose be reversed by his card being upside down. But of course the pack can only furnish a limited number of such comparatively rational interpretations, and the rest must be left to such arbitrary fancy as that the seven of diamonds means a prize in the lottery, and the ten of the same suit an unexpected journey.[2]

A remarkable group of divining instruments illustrates another principle. In South-east Asia, the Sgau Karens, at funeral feasts, hang a bangle or metal ring by a thread over a brass basin, which the relatives of the dead approach in succession and strike on the edge with a bit of bamboo; when the one who was most beloved touches the basin, the dead man's spirit responds by twisting and stretching the string till it breaks and the ring falls into the cup, or at least till it rings against it.[3] Nearer Central Asia, in the

[1] R. Taylor, 'New Zealand,' p. 246; Shortland, p. 139; Callaway, 'Religion of Amazulu,' p. 330, etc.; Theophylact. in Brand, vol. III. p. 832. Compare mentions of similar devices; Herodot. iv. 67 (Scythia); Burton, 'Central Africa,' vol. ii. p. 350.
[2] Migne's 'Dic. des Sciences Occultes.'
[3] Mason, 'Karens,' in 'Journ. As. Soc. Bengal,' 1865, part ii. p. 209; Bastian, 'Oestl. Asien,' vol. I. p. 145.

north-east corner of India, among the Bodo and Dhimal, the professional exorcist has to find out what deity has entered into a patient's body to punish him for some impiety by an attack of illness ; this he discovers by setting thirteen leaves round him on the ground to represent the gods, and then holding a pendulum attached to his thumb by a string, till the god in question is persuaded by invocation to declare himself, making the pendulum swing towards his representative leaf.[1] These mystic arts (not to go into the question how these tribes came to use them) are rude forms of the classical dactyliomancy, of which so curious an account is given in the trial of the conspirators Patricius and Hilarius, who worked it to find out who was to supplant the emperor Valens. A round table was marked at the edge with the letters of the alphabet, and with prayers and mystic ceremonies a ring was held suspended over it by a thread, and by swinging or stopping towards certain letters gave the responsive words of the oracle.[2] Dactyliomancy has dwindled in Europe to the art of finding out what o'clock it is by holding a ring hanging inside a tumbler by a thread, till, without conscious aid by the operator, it begins to swing and strikes the hour. Father Schott, in his 'Physica Curiosa' (1662), refrains with commendable caution from ascribing this phenomenon universally to demoniac influence. It survives among ourselves in child's play, and though we are " no conjurors," we may learn something from the little instrument, which remarkably displays the effects of insensible movement. The operator really gives slight impulses till they accumulate to a considerable vibration, as in ringing a church-bell by very gentle pulls exactly timed. That he does, though unconsciously, cause and direct the swings, may be shown by an attempt to work the instrument with the operator's eyes shut, which will be found to fail, the directing power being lost. The action of the famous divining-rod with its curiously versatile sensibility to water, ore,

[1] Hodgson, 'Abor. of India,' p. 170. See Macpherson, p. 106 (Khonds).
[2] Ammian. Marcellin. xxix. 1.

treasure, and thieves, seems to belong partly to trickery by
professional Dousterswivels, and partly to more or less conscious direction by honester operators. It is still known
in England, and in Germany they are apt to hide it in
a baby's clothes, and so get it baptized for greater effi-
ciency.[1] To conclude this group of divinatory instruments,
chance or the operator's direction may determine the action
of one of the most familiar of classic and mediæval ordeals,
the so-called cosciuomancy, or, as it is described 'in
Hudibras, " th' oracle of sieve and shears, that turns as
certain as the spheres." The sieve was held hanging
by a thread, or by the points of a pair of shears stuck into
its rim, and it would turn, or swing, or fall, at the mention
of a thief's name, and give similar signs for other purposes.
Of this ancient rite, the Christian ordeal of the Bible and
key, still in frequent use, is a variation : the proper way
to detect a thief by this is to read the 50th Psalm to the
apparatus, and when it hears the verse, " When thou sawest
a thief, then thou consentedst with him," it will turn to the
culprit.[2]

Count de Maistre, with his usual faculty of taking an
argument up at the wrong end, tells us that judicial
astrology no doubt hangs to truths of the first order, which
have been taken from us as useless or dangerous, or which
we cannot recognize under their new forms.[3] A sober
examination of the subject may rather justify the contrary
opinion, that it is on an error of the first order that astrology depends, the error of mistaking ideal analogy for real
connexion. Astrology, in the immensity of its delusive
influence on mankind, and by the comparatively modern
period to which it remained an honoured branch of philosophy, may claim the highest rank among the occult

[1] Chevreul, ' De la Baguette Divinatoire, du Pendule dit Explorateur, et
des Tables Tournantes,' Paris, 1854 ; Brand, vol. iii. p. 332 ; Grimm, 'D. M.'
p. 926 ; H. B. Woodward, in 'Geological Mag.,' Nov. 1872 ; Wuttke, p. 94.
[2] Cornelius Agrippa, ' De Speciebus Magiæ,' xxl. ; Brand, vol. III. p. 351 ;
Grimm, 'D. M.' p. 1062.
[3] De Maistre, ' Soirées de St. Petersbourg,' vol. II. p. 212.

sciences. It scarcely belongs to very low levels of civilization, although one of its fundamental conceptions, namely,
that of the souls or animating intelligences of the celestial
bodies, is rooted in the depths of savage life. Yet the following Maori specimen of astrological reasoning is as real
an argument as could be found in Paracelsus or Agrippa, nor
is there reason to doubt its being home-made. When the
siege of a New Zealand "pa" is going on, if Venus is near the
moon, the natives naturally imagine the two as enemy and
fortress; if the planet is above, the foe will have the upper
hand; but if below, then the men of the soil will be able to
defend themselves.[1] Though the early history of astrology
is obscure, its great development and elaborate systema-
tization were undoubtedly the work of civilized nations of
the ancient and mediæval world. As might be well supposed,
a great part of its precepts have lost their intelligible sense,
or never had any, but the origin of many others is still
evident. To a considerable extent they rest on direct
symbolism. Such are the rules which connect the sun
with gold, with the heliotrope and pæony, with the cock
which heralds day, with magnanimous animals, such as the
lion and bull; and the moon with silver, and the changing
chamæleon, and the palm-tree, which was considered to
send out a monthly shoot. Direct symbolism is plain in
that main principle of the calculation of nativities, the
notion of the " ascendant " in the horoscope, which reckons
the part of the heavens rising in the east at the moment of
a child's birth as being connected with the child itself, and
prophetic of its future life.[2] It is an old story, that when
two brothers were once taken ill together, Hippokrates the
physician concluded from the coincidence that they were
twins, but Poseidonios the astrologer considered rather that
they were born under the same constellation : we may add,
that either argument would be thought reasonable by a

[1] Shortland, 'Trads, etc. of New Zealand,' p. 138.
[2] See Cicero, 'De Div.' i. ; Lucian. 'De Astrolog.' ; Cornelius Agrippa,
'De Occulta Philosophia; ' Sibly, 'Occult Sciences;' Brand, vol. iii.

savage. One of the most instructive astrological doctrines
which has kept its place in modern popular philosophy, is
that of the sympathy of growing and declining nature with
the waxing and waning moon. Among classical precepts
are these: to set eggs under the hen at new moon, but to
root up trees when the moon is on the wane, and after
midday. The Lithuanian precept to wean boys on a waxing, but girls on a waning moon, no doubt to make the
boys sturdy and the girls slim and delicate, is a fair match
for the Orkney islanders' objection to marrying except with
a growing moon, while some even wish for a flowing tide.
The following lines, from Tusser's 'Five Hundred Points
of Husbandry,' show neatly in a single case the two contrary lunar influences:—

> "Sow peason and beans in the wane of the moone
> Who soweth them sooner, he soweth too soone:
> That they, with the planet, may rest and rise,
> And flourish with bearing, most plentiful wise." [1]

The notion that the weather changes with the moon's
quarterings is still held with great vigour in England.
Yet the meteorologists, with all their eagerness to catch at
any rule which at all answers to facts, quite repudiate this
one, which indeed appears to be simply a maxim belonging
to popular astrology. Just as the growth and dwindling of
plants became associated with the moon's wax and wane, so
changes of weather became associated with changes of the
moon, while, by astrologers' logic, it did not matter
whether the moon's change were real, at new and full, or
imaginary, at the intermediate quarters. That educated
people to whom exact weather records are accessible should
still find satisfaction in the fanciful lunar rule, is an interesting case of intellectual survival.

In such cases as these, the astrologer has at any rate a
real analogy, deceptive though it be, to base his rule upon.

---

[1] Plin. xvi. 75; xviii. 75; Grimm, 'D. M.' p. 676; Brand, vol. ii. p. 169;
vol. iii. p. 144.

But most of his pseudo-science seems to rest on even weaker and more arbitrary analogies, not of things, but of names. Names of stars and constellations, of signs denoting regions of the sky and periods of days and years, no matter how arbitrarily given, are materials which the astrologer can work upon, and bring into ideal connexion with mundane events. That astronomers should have divided the sun's course into imaginary signs of the zodiac, was enough to originate astrological rules that these celestial signs have an actual effect on real earthly rams, bulls, crabs, lions, virgins. A child born under the sign of the Lion will be courageous; but one born under the Crab will not go forward well in life; one born under the Waterman is likely to be drowned, and so forth. Towards 1524, Europe was awaiting in an agony of prayerful terror a second deluge, prophesied for February in that year. As the fatal month drew nigh, dwellers by the waterside moved in crowds to the hills, some provided boats to save them, and the President Aurial, at Toulouse, built himself a Noah's Ark. It was the great astrologer Stoefler (the originator, it is said, of the weather-prophecies in our almanacks) who foretold this cataclysm, and his argument has the advantage of being still perfectly intelligible—at the date in question, three planets would be together in the aqueous sign of Pisces. Again, simply because astronomers chose to distribute among the planets the names of certain deities, the planets thereby acquired the characters of their divine namesakes. Thus it was that the planet Venus became connected with love, Mars with war, Jupiter (whose ♃ in altered shape still heads our physicians' prescriptions) with power and 'joviality.' Throughout the East, astrology even now remains a science in full esteem. The condition of medieval Europe may still be perfectly realized by the traveller in Persia, where the Shah waits for days outside the walls of his capital till the constellations allow him to enter, and where on the days appointed by the stars for letting blood, it literally flows in streams from the

barbers' shops into the street. Professor Wuttke declares,
that there are many districts in Germany where the child's
horoscope is still regularly kept with the baptismal certifi-
cate in the family chest. We scarcely reach this pitch of
conservatism in England, but I happen myself to live within
a mile of an astrologer, and I lately saw a grave paper on
nativities, offered in all good faith to the British
Association. The piles of 'Zadkiel's Almanack' in the
booksellers' windows in country towns about Christmas
are a symptom how much yet remains to be done in popular
education. As a specimen at once of the survival and of
the meaning of astrologic reasoning, I cannot do better
than quote a passage from a book published in London in
1861, and entitled, 'The Hand-Book of Astrology,' by
Zadkiel Tao-Sze.' At page 72 of his first volume, the
astrologer relates as follows: " The Map of the heavens
given at page 45 was drawn on the occasion of a young
lady having been arrested on a charge of the murder of her
infant brother. Having read in a newspaper, at twenty-
four minutes past noon on the 23rd July, 1860, that Miss
C. K. had been arrested on a charge of the murder of her
young brother, the author felt desirous to ascertain whether
she were guilty or not, and drew the map accordingly.
Finding the moon in the twelfth house, she clearly signifies
the prisoner. The moon is in a moveable sign, and moves
in the twenty-four hours, 14° 17'. She is, therefore, swift
in motion. These things indicated that the prisoner would
be very speedily released. Then we find a moveable sign
in the cusp of the twelfth, and its ruler, ♀, in a moveable
sign, a further indication of speedy release. Hence it was
judged and declared to many friends that the prisoner
would be immediately released, which was the fact. We
looked to see whether the prisoner were guilty of the deed
or not, and finding the Moon in Libra, a humane sign, and
having just past the ✳ aspect of the Sun and ♃, both
being on the M. C. we felt assured that she was a humane,
feeling, and honourable girl, and that it was quite im-

possible she could be guilty of any such atrocity. We declared her to be perfectly innocent, and as the Moon was so well aspected from the tenth house, we declared that her honour would be very soon perfectly established." Had the astrologer waited a few months longer, to have read the confession of the miserable Constance Kent, he would perhaps have put a different sense on his moveable signs, just balances, and sunny and jovial aspects. Nor would this be a difficult task, for these fancies lend themselves to endless variety of new interpretation. And on such fancies and such interpretations, the great science of the stars has from first to last been based.

Looking at the details here selected as fair samples of symbolic magic, we may well ask the question, is there in the whole monstrous farrago no truth or value whatever? It appears that there is practically none, and that the world has been enthralled for ages by a blind belief in processes wholly irrelevant to their supposed results, and which might as well have been taken just the opposite way. Pliny justly saw in magic a study worthy of his especial attention, "for the very reason that, being the most fraudulent of arts, it had prevailed throughout the world and through so many ages" (eo ipso quod fraudulentissima artium plurimum in toto terrarum orbe plurimisque seculis valuit). If it be asked how such a system could have held its ground, not merely in independence but in defiance of its own facts, a fair answer does not seem hard to give. In the first place, it must be borne in mind that occult science has not existed entirely in its own strength. Futile as its arts may be, they are associated in practice with other proceedings by no means futile. What are passed off as sacred omens, are often really the cunning man's shrewd guesses at the past and future. Divination serves to the sorcerer as a mask for real inquest, as when the ordeal gives him invaluable opportunity of examining the guilty, whose trembling hands and equivocating speech betray at once their secret and their utter belief in his power of

discerning it. Prophecy tends to fulfil itself, as where the
magician, by putting into a victim's mind the belief that
fatal arts have been practised against him, can slay him
with this idea as with a material weapon. Often priest as
well as magician, he has the whole power of religion at his
back ; often a man in power, always an unscrupulous
intriguer, he can work witchcraft and statecraft together,
and make his left hand help his right. Often a doctor, he
can aid his omens of life or death with remedy or poison,
while what we still call "conjurors' tricks" of sleight of
hand, have done much to keep up his supernatural prestige.
From the earliest known stages of civilization, professional
magicians have existed, who live by their craft, and keep it
alive. It has been said, that if somebody had endowed
lecturers to teach that two sides of a triangle are together
equal to the third, the doctrine would have a respectable
following among ourselves. At any rate, magic, with an
influential profession interested in keeping it in credit and
power, did not depend for its existence on mere evidence.

And in the second place, as to this evidence. Magic has
not its origin in fraud, and seems seldom practised as an
utter imposture. The sorcerer generally learns his time-
honoured profession in good faith, and retains his belief in
it more or less from first to last ; at once dupe and cheat,
he combines the energy of a believer with the cunning of a
hypocrite. Had occult science been simply framed for
purposes of deception, mere nonsense would have answered
the purpose, whereas, what we find is an elaborate and
systematic pseudo-science. It is, in fact, a sincere but
fallacious system of philosophy, evolved by the human
intellect by processes still in great measure intelligible to
our own minds, and it had thus an original standing-ground
in the world. And though the evidence of fact was dead
against it, it was but lately and gradually that this evidence
was brought fatally to bear. A general survey of the
practical working of the system may be made somewhat
thus. A large proportion of successful cases belong to

natural means disguised as magic. Also, a certain proportion of cases must succeed by mere chance. By far the
larger proportion, however, are what we should call failures;
but it is a part of the magician's profession to keep these
from counting, and this he does with extraordinary resource
of rhetorical shift and brazen impudence. He deals in
ambiguous phrases, which give him three or four chances
for one. He knows perfectly how to impose difficult
conditions, and to lay the blame of failure on their neglect.
If you wish to make gold, the alchemist in Central Asia
has a recipe at your service, only, to use it, you must
abstain three days from thinking of apes; just as our
English folklore says, that if one of your eyelashes comes
out, and you put it on your thumb, you will get anything
you wish for, if you can only avoid thinking of foxes' tails
at the fatal moment. Again, if the wrong thing happens,
the wizard has at least a reason why. Has a daughter
been born when he promised a son, then it is some hostile
practitioner who has turned the boy into a girl; does a
tempest come just when he is making fine weather, then
he calmly demands a larger fee for stronger ceremonies,
assuring his clients that they may thank him as it is, for
how much worse it would have been had he not done what
he did. And even setting aside all this accessory trickery,
if we look at honest but unscientific people practising
occult science in good faith, and face to face with facts,
we shall see that the failures which condemn it in our
eyes carry comparatively little weight in theirs. Part
escape under the elastic pretext of a " little more or less,"
as the loser in the lottery consoles himself that his lucky
number came within two of a prize, or the moon-observer
points out triumphantly that a change of weather has come
within two or three days before or after a quarter, so that
his convenient definition of near a moon's quarter applies
to four or six days out of every seven. Part escape through
incapacity to appreciate negative evidence, which allows
one success to outweigh half-a-dozen failures. How few

there are even among the educated classes now, who
have taken in the drift of that memorable passage in the
beginning of the 'Novum Organum:'—" The human understanding, when any proposition has been once laid down
(either from general admission and belief, or from the
pleasure it affords), forces everything else to add fresh
support and confirmation; and although most cogent and
abundant instances may exist to the contrary, yet either
does not observe or despises them, or gets rid of and
rejects them by some distinction, with violent and injurious
prejudice, rather than sacrifice the authority of its first
conclusions. It was well answered by him who was shown
in a temple the votive tablets suspended by such as had
escaped the peril of shipwreck, and was pressed as to
whether he would then recognize the power of the gods,
by an inquiry, ' But where are the portraits of those who
have perished in spite of their vows ?'"[1]

On the whole, the survival of symbolic magic through the
middle ages and into our own times is an unsatisfactory, but
not a mysterious fact. A once-established opinion, however
delusive, can hold its own from age to age, for belief can
propagate itself without reference to its reasonable origin,
as plants are propagated from slips without fresh raising
from the seed.

The history of survival in cases like those of the folklore
and occult arts which we have been considering, has for the
most part been a history of dwindling and decay. As men's
minds change in progressing culture, old customs and
opinions fade gradually in a new and uncongenial atmosphere, or pass into states more congruous with the new life
around them. But this is so far from being a law without
exception, that a narrow view of history may often make it
seem to be no law at all. For the stream of civilization winds
and turns upon itself, and what seems the bright onward
current of one age may in the next spin round in a whirling

[1] Bacon, 'Novum Organum.' The original story is that of Diagoras; see
Cicero, 'De Natura Deorum,' III. 37; Diog. Laert. lib. vi., Diogenes, 6.

eddy, or spread into a dull and pestilential swamp. Studying with a wide view the course of human opinion, we may
now and then trace on from the very turning-point the
change from passive survival into active revival. Some
well-known belief or custom has for centuries shown
symptoms of decay, when we begin to see that the state of
society, instead of stunting it, is favouring its new growth,
and it bursts forth again with a vigour often as marvellous
as it is unhealthy. And though the revival be not destined
to hold on indefinitely, and though when opinion turns
again its ruin may be more merciless than before, yet it
may last for ages, make its way into the inmost constitution
of society, and even become a very mark and characteristic
of its time.

Writers who desire to show that, with all our faults, we
are wiser and better than our ancestors, dwell willingly on
the history of witchcraft between the middle and modern
ages. They can quote Martin Luther, apropos of the
witches who spoil the farmers' butter and eggs, " I would
have no pity on these witches; I would burn them all."
They can show the good Sir Matthew Hale hanging witches
in Suffolk, on the authority of scripture and the consenting
wisdom of all nations; and King James presiding at the
torture of Dr. Fian for bringing a storm against the king's
ship on its course from Denmark, by the aid of a fleet of
witches in sieves, who carried out a christened cat to sea. In
those dreadful days, to be a blear-eyed wizened cripple was
to be worth twenty shillings to a witch-finder; for a woman
to have what this witch-finder was pleased to call the devil's
mark on her body was presumption for judicial sentence of
death; and not to bleed or shed tears or sink in a pond was
torture first and then the stake. Reform of religion was no
cure for the disease of men's minds, for in such things the
Puritan was no worse than the Inquisitor, and no better.
Papist and Protestant fought with one another, but both
turned against that enemy of the human race, the hag who
had sold herself to Satan to ride upon a broomstick, and to

suck children's blood, and to be for life and death of all
creatures the most wretched. But with new enlightenment
there came in the very teeth of law and authority a change
in European opinion. Toward the end of the seventeenth
century the hideous superstition was breaking down among
ourselves; Richard Baxter, of the 'Saint's Rest,' strove
with fanatic zeal to light again at home the witch-fires of
New England, but he strove in vain. Year by year the
persecution of witches became more hateful to the educated
classes, and though it died hard, it died at last down to a
vestige. In our days, when we read of a witch being
burnt at Camargo in 1860, we point to Mexico as a
country miserably in the rear of civilization. And if in
England it still happens that village boors have to be tried
at quarter-sessions for ill-using some poor old woman, who
they fancy has dried a cow or spoiled a turnip crop, we
comment on the tenacity with which the rustic mind clings
to exploded follies, and cry out for more schoolmasters.

True as all this is, the ethnographer must go wider and
deeper in his inquiry, to do his subject justice. The prevailing belief in witchcraft that sat like a nightmare on public
opinion from the 13th to the 17th centuries, far from being
itself a product of mediævalism, was a revival from the
remote days of primæval history. The disease that broke out
afresh in Europe had been chronic among the lower races
for how many ages we cannot tell. Witchcraft is part and
parcel of savage life. There are rude races of Australia
and South America whose intense belief in it has led them
to declare that if men were never bewitched, and never
killed by violence, they would not die at all. Like the
Australians, the Africans will inquire of their dead what
sorcerer slew them by his wicked arts, and when they have
satisfied themselves of this, blood must atone for blood.
In West Africa, it has been boldly asserted that the belief
in witchcraft costs more lives than the slave trade ever did.
In East Africa, Captain Burton, a traveller apt to draw his
social sketches in a few sharp lines, remarks that what with

slavery and what with black-magic, life is precarious among
the Wakhutu, and "no one, especially in old age, is safe from
being burnt at a day's notice;" and, travelling in the country
of the Wazaramo, he tells us of meeting every few miles with
heaps of ashes and charcoal, now and then such as seemed
to have been a father and mother, with a little heap hard by
that was a child.[1] Even in districts of British India a
state of mind ready to produce horrors like these is well
known to exist, and to be kept down less by persuasion
than by main force. From the level of savage life, we trace
witchcraft surviving throughout the barbarian and early
civilized world. It was existing in Europe in the centuries
preceding the 10th, but with no especial prominence, while
laws of Rothar and Charlemagne are actually directed
against such as should put men or women to death on the
charge of witchcraft. In the 11th century, ecclesiastical
influence was discouraging the superstitious belief in sorcery.
But now a period of reaction set in. The works of the
monastic legend and miracle-mongers more and more encouraged a baneful credulity as to the supernatural. In the
13th century, when the spirit of religious persecution had
begun to possess all Europe with a dark and cruel madness, the
doctrine of witchcraft revived with all its barbaric vigour.[2]
That the guilt of thus bringing down Europe intellectually
and morally to the level of negro Africa lies in the main
upon the Roman Church, the bulls of Gregory IX.
and Innocent VIII., and the records of the Holy
Inquisition, are conclusive evidence to prove. To us here
the main interest of mediæval witchcraft lies in the extent
and accuracy with which the theory of survival explains it.
In the very details of the bald conventional accusations that
were sworn against the witches, there may be traced

[1] Du Chaillu, 'Ashango-land,' pp. 428, 435 ; Burton, 'Central Afr.,' vol. l.
pp. 57, 113, 121.
[2] See Grimm, 'D. M.' ch. xxxiv. ; Lecky, 'Hist. of Rationalism,' vol. l.
chap. l ; Horst, 'Zauber-Bibliothek ;' 'The Pope and the Council,' by
'Janus,' xvii.

tradition often hardly modified from barbarous and savage
times.   They raised storms by magic rites, they had charms
against the hurt of weapons, they had their assemblies on
wild heath and mountain-top, they could ride through the
air on beasts and even turn into witch-cats and were-wolves
themselves, they had familiar spirits, they had intercourse
with incubi and succubi, they conveyed thorns, pins, feathers,
and such things into their victims' bodies, they caused disease
by demoniacal possession, they could bewitch by spells and
the evil eye, by practising on images and symbols, on food
and property. Now all this is sheer survival from præ-Christian ages, " in errore paganorum revolvitur," as Burchard
of Worms said of the superstition of his time.[1] Two of the
most familiar devices used against the mediæval witches may
serve to show the place in civilization of the whole craft.
The Oriental jinn are in such deadly terror of iron, that
its very name is a charm against them ; and so in European
folklore iron drives away fairies and elves, and destroys
their power. They are essentially, it seems, creatures
belonging to the ancient Stone Age, and the new metal is
hateful and hurtful to them. Now as to iron, witches are
brought under the same category as elves and nightmares.
Iron instruments keep them at bay, and especially iron
horseshoes have been chosen for this purpose, as half the
stable doors in England still show.[2] Again, one of the best
known of English witch ordeals is the trial by "fleeting"
or swimming. Bound hand and foot, the accused was flung
into deep water, to sink if innocent and swim if guilty, and
in the latter case, as Hudibras has it, to be hanged only for
not being drowned. King James, who seems to have had
a notion of the real primitive meaning of this rite, says in
his Dæmonology, "It appeares that God hath appointed

[1] See also Dasent, 'Introd. to Norse Tales ;' Maury, 'Magie, etc.,' ch. vii.
[2] Lane, 'Thousand and One Nights,' vol. i. p. 30 ; Grimm, 'D. M.' pp.
435, 465, 1056; Bastian, 'Mensch.' vol. ii. pp. 265, 287 : vol. iii. p. 204 ;
D. Wilson, 'Archæolog. of Scotland,' p. 439 ; Wuttke, 'Volksberglaube,'
pp. 16, 20, 122, 220.

for a supernatural signe of the monstrous impietie of witches, that the water shall refuse to receive them in her bosom that have shaken off them the sacred water of baptism," &c.   Now, in early German history this same trial by water was well known, and its meaning recognized to be that the conscious element rejects the guilty (si aqua illum velut innoxium receperit—innoxii submerguntur aqua, culpabiles supernatant). Already in the 9th century the laws were prohibiting this practice as a relic of superstition. Lastly, the same trial by water is recognized as one of the regular judicial ordeals in the Hindu code of Manu ; if the water does not cause the accused to float when plunged into it, his oath is true.   As this ancient Indian body of laws was itself no doubt compiled from materials of still earlier date, we may venture to take the correspondence of the water-ordeal among the European and Asiatic branches of the Aryan race as carrying back its origin to a period of remote antiquity.[1]

Let us hope that if the belief in present witchcraft, and the persecution necessarily ensuing upon such belief, once more come into prominence in the civilized world, they may appear in a milder shape than heretofore, and be kept down by stronger humanity and tolerance.   But any one who fancies from their present disappearance that they have necessarily disappeared for ever, must have read history to little purpose, and has yet to learn that " revival in culture " is something more than an empty pedantic phrase.   Our own time has revived a group of beliefs and practices which have their roots deep in the very stratum of early philosophy where witchcraft makes its first appearance.   This group of beliefs and practices constitutes what is now commonly known as Spiritualism.

Witchcraft and Spiritualism have existed for thousands of years in a closeness of union not unfairly typified in this

[1] Brand, 'Pop. Ant.' vol. iii. pp. 1—63 ; Wuttke, ' Volksaberglaube,' p. 50 ; Grimm, 'Deutsche Rechtsalterthümer,' p. 923 ; Pictet, 'Origines Indo-Europ.' part ii. p. 459 ; Manu, viii. 114—5 ; see Plin. vii. 2.

verse from John Bale's 16th-century Interlude concerning Nature, which brings under one head the art of bewitching vegetables and poultry, and causing supernatural movement of stools and crockery.

> " Theyr wells I can up drye,
> Cause trees and herbes to dye,
> And also all pulterye,
>   Whereas men doth me move:
> I can make stoles to daunce
> And earthen pottes to praunce,
> That none shall them enhaunce,
>   And do but cast my glove."

The same intellectual movement led to the decline of both witchcraft and spiritualism, till, early in the present century, men thought that both were dying or all but dead together. Now, however, not only are spiritualists to be counted by tens of thousands in America and England, but there are among them several men of distinguished mental power. I am well aware that the problem of the so-called "spirit-manifestations" is one to be discussed on its merits, in order to arrive at a distinct opinion how far it may be concerned with facts insufficiently appreciated and explained by science, and how far with superstition, delusion, and sheer knavery. Such investigation, pursued by careful observation in a scientific spirit, would seem apt to throw light on some most interesting psychological questions. But though it lies beyond my scope to examine the spiritualistic evidence for itself, the ethnographic view of the matter has, nevertheless, its value. This shows modern spiritualism to be in great measure a direct revival from the regions of savage philosophy and peasant folklore. It is not a simple question of the existence of certain phenomena of mind and matter. It is that, in connexion with these phenomena, a great philosophic-religious doctrine, flourishing in the lower culture but dwindling in the higher, has re-established itself in full vigour. The world is again swarming with intelligent and powerful disembodied spiritual beings, whose direct action on thought and matter is again confidently asserted, as in those times and countries where physical science had not as yet so far succeeded in extruding these spirits and their influences from the system of nature.

Apparitions have regained the place and meaning which they held from the level of the lower races to that of mediæval Europe. The regular ghost-stories, in which spirits of the dead walk visibly and have intercourse with corporeal men, are now restored and cited with new examples as "glimpses of the night-side of nature," nor have these stories changed either their strength to those who are disposed to believe them, or their weakness to those who are not. As of old, men live now in habitual intercourse with the spirits of the dead. Necromancy is a religion, and the Chinese manes-worshipper may see the outer barbarians come back, after a heretical interval of a few centuries, into sympathy with his time-honoured creed. As the sorcerers of barbarous tribes lie in bodily lethargy or sleep while their souls depart on distant journeys, so it is not uncommon in modern spiritualistic narratives for persons to be in an insensible state when their apparitions visit distant places, whence they bring back information, and where they communicate with the living. The spirits of the living as well as of the dead, the souls of Strauss and Carl Vogt as well as of Augustine and Jerome, are summoned by mediums to distant spirit-circles. As Dr. Bastian remarks, if any celebrated man in Europe feels himself at some moment in a melancholy mood, he may console himself with the idea that his soul has been sent for to America, to assist at the "rough fixings" of some backwoodsman. Fifty years ago, Dr. Macculloch, in his 'Description of the Western Islands of Scotland,' wrote thus of the famous Highland second-sight: "In fact it has undergone the fate of witchcraft; ceasing to be believed, it has ceased to exist." Yet a generation later he would have found it reinstated in a far larger range of society, and under far better circumstances of learning and material prosperity. Among the influences

which have combined to bring about the spiritualistic renaissance, a prominent place may, I think, be given to the effect
produced on the religious mind of Europe and America by
the intensely animistic teachings of Emanuel Swedenborg,
in the last century. The position of this remarkable
visionary as to some of the particular spiritualistic doctrines
may be judged of by the following statements from 'The
True Christian Religion.' A man's spirit is his mind, which
lives after death in complete human form, and this spirit
may be conveyed from place to place while the body remains at rest, as on some occasions happened to Swedenborg
himself. "I have conversed," he says, "with all my relations and friends, likewise with kings and princes, and men
of learning, after their departure out of this life, and this
now for twenty-seven years without interruption." And
foreseeing that many who read his 'Memorable Relations,'
will believe them to be fictions of imagination, he protests in
truth they are not fictions, but were really seen and heard ;
not seen and heard in any state of mind in sleep, but in a
state of complete wakefulness.[1]

I shall have to speak elsewhere of some of the doctrines
of modern spiritualism, where they seem to fall into their
places in the study of Animism. Here, as a means of illustrating the relation of the newer to the older spiritualistic
ideas, I propose to glance over the ethnography of two of the
most popular means of communicating with the spirit-world,
by rapping and writing, and two of the prominent spirit-
manifestations, the feat of rising in the air, and the trick of
the Davenport Brothers.

The elf who goes knocking and routing about the house
at night, and whose special German name is the "Polter-
geist," is an old and familiar personage in European folklore.[2]
From of old, such unexplained noises have been ascribed to
the agency of personal spirits, who more often than not are

---

[1] Swedenborg, 'The True Christian Religion,' London, 1855, Nos. 156, 157, 281, 851.

[2] Grimm, 'Deutsche Myth.' pp. 473, 181.

considered human souls. The modern Dayaks, Siamese, and
Singhalese agree with the Esths as to such routing and rapping being caused by spirits.[1] Knockings may be considered
mysterious but harmless, like those which in Swabia and
Franconia are expected during Advent on the Anklöpferleins-Nächte, or "Little Knockers' Nights."[2] Or they may be
useful, as when the Welsh miners think that the "knockers"
they hear underground are indicating the rich veins of lead
and silver.[3] Or they may be simply annoying, as when, in
the ninth century, a malignant spirit infested a parish by
knocking at the walls as if with a hammer, but being overcome with litanies and holy water, confessed itself to be
the familiar of a certain wicked priest, and to have been in
hiding under his cloak. Thus, in the seventeenth century,
the famous demon-drummer of Tedworth, commemorated
by Glanvil in the 'Saducismus Triumphatus,' thumped
about the doors and the outside of the house, and "for an
hour together it would beat *Roundheads and Cuckolds*, the
Tat-too, and several other *Points of War*, as well as any
Drummer."[4] But popular philosophy has mostly attached
to such mysterious noises a foreboding of death, the knock
being held as a signal or summons among spirits as among
men. The Romans considered that the genius of death
thus announced his coming. Modern folklore holds either
that a knocking or rumbling in the floor is an omen of a
death about to happen, or that dying persons themselves
announce their dissolution to their friends in such strange
sounds. The English rule takes in both cases: "Three loud
and distinct knocks at the bed's head of a sick person, or at
the bed's head or door of any of his relations, is an omen of
his death." We happen to have a good means of testing

[1] St. John, 'Far East,' vol. i. p. 82; Bastian, 'Psychologie,' p. 111; 'Oestl.
Aslen,' vol. iii. pp. 232, 259, 288; Boecler, 'Ehsten Aberglaube,' p. 147.
[2] Bastian, 'Mensch,' vol. ii. p. 74.
[3] Brand, vol. ii. p. 486.
[4] Glanvil, 'Saducismus Triumphatus,' part ii. The invisible drummer
appears to have been one William Drury; see 'Pepys' Diary,' vol. i. p. 227.

the amount of actual correspondence between omen and
event necessary to establish these rules: the illogical people
who were (and still are) able to discover a connexion between
the ticking of the "death-watch" beetle and an ensuing
death in the house, no doubt found it equally easy to give a
prophetic interpretation to any other mysterious knocks.[1]
There is a story, dated 1534, of a ghost that answered
questions by knocking in the Catholic Church of Orleans,
and demanded the removal of the provost's Lutheran wife,
who had been buried there; but the affair proved to be a
trick of a Franciscan friar.[2] The system of working an
alphabet by counted raps is a device familiar to prison-cells,
where it has long been at once the despair of gaolers and an
evidence of the diffusion of education even among the
criminal classes. Thus when, in 1847, the celebrated
rappings began to trouble the township of Arcadia in the
State of New York, the Fox family of Rochester, founders
of the modern spiritual movement, had on the one hand
only to revive the ancient prevalent belief in spirit-rappings,
which had almost fallen into the limbo of discredited superstitions, while, on the other hand, the system of communication with the spirits was ready made to their hand. The
system of a rapping-alphabet remains in full use, and
numberless specimens of messages thus received are in
print, possibly the longest being a novel, of which I can
only give the title, 'Juanita, Nouvelle par une Chaise. À
l'Imprimerie du Gouvernement, Basse Terre (Guadeloupe),
1853.' In the recorded communications, names, dates, etc.
are often alleged to have been stated under remarkable
circumstances, while the style of thought, language, and
spelling fits with the intellectual quality of the medium.
A large proportion of the communications being obviously
false and silly, even when the "spirit" has announced itself

[1] Brand, vol. iii. pp. 225, 233; Grimm, pp. 801, 1069, 1141; Wuttke, pp.
33—9, 208; Shortland, 'Trads. of New Zealand,' p. 137 (ominous ticking of
insect, doubtful whether idea native, or introduced by foreigners).
[2] Bastian, 'Mensch,' vol. ii. p. 393.

in the name of some great statesman, moralist, or philosopher of the past, the theory has been adopted by spiritualists that foolish or lying spirits are apt to personate those of higher degree, and give messages in their names.

Spirit-writing is of two kinds, according as it is done with or without a material instrument. The first kind is in full practice in China, where, like other rites of divination, it is probably ancient. It is called "descending of the pencil," and is especially used by the literary classes. When a Chinese wishes to consult a god, in this way, he sends for a professional medium. Before the image of the god are set candles and incense, and an offering of tea or mock money. In front of this, on another table, is placed an oblong tray of dry sand. The writing instrument is a V-shaped wooden handle, two or three feet long, with a wooden tooth fixed at its point. Two persons hold this instrument, each grasping one leg of it, and the point resting in the sand. Proper prayers and charms induce the god to manifest his presence by a movement of the point in the sand, and thus the response is written, and there only remains the somewhat difficult and doubtful task of deciphering it. To what state of opinion the rite belongs may be judged from this: when the sacred apricot-tree is to be robbed of a branch to make the spirit-pen, an apologetic inscription is scratched upon the trunk.[1] Notwithstanding theological differences between China and England, the art of spirit-writing is much the same in the two countries. A kind of "planchette" seems to have been known in Europe in the seventeenth century.[2] The instrument, which may now be bought at the toy-shops, is a heart-shaped board some seven inches long, resting on three supports, of which the two at the wide end are castors, and the third at the pointed end is a pencil thrust through

---

[1] Doolittle, 'Chinese,' vol. II. p. 112; Bastian, 'Oestl. Asien,' vol. III. p. 252; 'Psychologie,' p. 159.

[2] Toehla, 'Aurifontina Chymica,' cited by K. R. H. Mackenzie, in 'Spiritualist,' Mar. 15, 1870.

a hole in the board. The instrument is placed on a sheet of paper, and worked by two persons laying their fingers lightly on it, and waiting till, without conscious effort of the operators, it moves and writes answers to questions. It is not everybody who has the faculty of spirit-writing, but a powerful medium will write alone. Such mediums sometimes consider themselves acted on by some power separate from themselves, in fact, possessed.

Ecclesiastical history commemorates a miracle at the close of the Nicene Council. Two bishops, Chrysanthus and Mysonius, had died during its sitting, and the remaining crowd of Fathers brought the acts, signed by themselves, to the tomb, addressed the deceased bishops as if still alive, and left the document. Next day, returning, they found the two signatures added, to this effect :—" We, Chrysanthus and Mysonius, consenting with all the Fathers in the holy first and œcumenical Nicene Synod, although translated from the body, have also signed the volume with our own hands."[1] Such spirit-writing without material instrument has lately been renewed by the Baron de Guldenstubbé. This writer confirms by new evidence the truth of the tradition of all peoples as to souls of the dead keeping up their connexion with their mortal remains, and haunting the places where they dwelt "during their terrestrial incarnation." Thus Francis I. manifests himself principally at Fontainebleau, while Louis XV. and Marie-Antoinette roam about the Trianons. Moreover, if pieces of blank paper be set out in suitable places, the spirits, enveloped in their ethereal bodies, will concentrate by their force of will electric currents on the paper, and so form written characters. The Baron publishes, in his ' Pneumatologie Positive,' a mass of fac-similes of spirit-writings thus obtained. Julius and Augustus Cæsar give their names near their statues in the Louvre ; Juvenal produces a ludicrous attempt at a copy of verses ; Héloise at Père-la-

[1] Nicephor. Callist. Ecclesiast. Hist. viii. 22 ; Stanley, ' Eastern Church,' p. 172.

Chaise informs the world, in modern French, that Abelard and she are united and happy; St. Paul writes himself ἐλ(ιστος ἀποστολον (meaning, we may suppose, ἐλαχιστος ἀποστολων); and Hippokrates the physician (who spells himself Hippokratēs) attended M. de Guldenstubbé at his lodgings in Paris, and gave him a signature which of itself cured a sharp attack of rheumatism in a few minutes.[1]

The miracle of rising and floating in the air is one fully recognized in the literature of ancient India. The Buddhist saint of high ascetic rank attains the power called "perfection" (irdhi), whereby he is able to rise in the air, as also to overturn the earth and stop the sun. Having this power, the saint exercises it by the mere determination of his will, his body becoming imponderous, as when a man in the common human state determines to leap, and leaps. Buddhist annals relate the performance of the miraculous suspension by Gautama himself, as well as by other saints, as, for example, his ancestor Maha Sammata, who could thus seat himself in the air without visible support. Even without this exalted faculty, it is considered possible to rise and move in the air by an effort of ecstatic joy (udwega priti). A remarkable mention of this feat, as said to be performed by the Indian Brahmans, occurs in the third-century biography of Apollonius of Tyana; these Brahmans are described as going about in the air some two cubits from the ground, not for the sake of miracle (such ambition they despised), but for its being more suitable to solar rites.[2] Foreign conjurors were professing to exhibit this miracle among the Greeks in the second century, as witness Lucian's jocular account of the Hyperborean conjuror:—

---

[1] 'Pneumatologie Positive et Expérimentale; La Réalité des Esprits et le Phénomène Merveilleux de leur Écriture Directe démontrée,' par le Baron L. de Guldenstubbé. Paris, 1857.

[2] Hardy, 'Manual of Budhism,' pp. 38, 126, 150; 'Eastern Monachism,' pp. 272, 285, 332: Köppen, 'Religion des Buddha,' vol. I. p. 412; Bastian, 'Oestl. Asien,' vol. III. p. 390; Philostrati Vita Apollon. Tyan. iii. 15. See the mention among the Saadhs of India (17th century), in Trant, in 'Missionary Register,' July, 1820, pp. 291—6.

" Thou art joking, said Kleodemos, but I was once more incredulous than thou about such things, for I thought nothing
could have persuaded me to believe them; but when I first
saw that foreign barbarian flying—he was of the Hyperboreans, he said—I believed, and was overcome in spite of my
resistance.   For what was I to do, when I saw him carried
through the air in daylight, and walking on the water, and
passing leisurely and slowly through the fire?   What I
(said his interlocutor), you saw the Hyperborean man flying,
and walking on the water?   To be sure, said he, and he had
on undressed leather brogues as they generally wear them;
but what's the use of talking of such trifles, considering
what other manifestations he showed us,—sending loves,
calling up dæmons, raising the dead, and bringing in Hekate
herself visibly, and drawing down the moon? "   Kleodemos
then goes on to relate how the conjuror first had his four
minæ down for sacrificial expenses, and then made a clay
Cupid, and sent it flying through the air to fetch the girl
whom Glaukias had fallen in love with, and presently, lo
and behold, there she was "knocking at the door!"   The
interlocutor, however, comments in a sceptical vein on the
narrative.   It was scarce needful, he says, to have taken the
trouble to send for the girl with clay, and a magician from
the Hyperboreans, and even the moon, considering that for
twenty drachmas she would have let herself be taken to the
Hyperboreans themselves; and she seems, moreover, to have
been affected in quite an opposite way to spirits, for whereas
these beings take flight if they hear the noise of brass or
iron, Chrysis no sooner hears the chink of silver anywhere,
but she comes toward the sound.[1]   Another early instance
of the belief in miraculous suspension is in the life of
Iamblichus, the great Neo-Platonist mystic.   His disciples,
says Eunapius, told him they had heard a report from his
servants, that while in prayer to the gods he had been lifted
more than ten cubits from the ground, his body and clothes
changing to a beautiful golden colour, but after he ceased

[1] Lucian. Philopseudes, 13.

from prayer his body became as before, and then he came
down to the ground and returned to the society of his
followers. They entreated him therefore, "Why, O most
divine teacher, why dost thou do such things by thyself, and
not let us partake of the more perfect wisdom?" Then
Iamblichus, though not given to laughter, laughed at this
story, and said to them, "It was no fool who tricked you
thus, but the thing is not true."[1]

After a while, the prodigy which the Platonist disclaimed,
became a usual attribute of Christian saints. Thus St.
Richard, then chancellor to St. Edmund, Archbishop of
Canterbury, one day softly opening the chapel door, to see
why the archbishop did not come to dinner, saw him raised
high in the air, with his knees bent and his arms stretched
out; falling gently to the ground, and seeing the chancellor,
he complained that he had hindered him of great spiritual
delight and comfort. So St. Philip Neri used to be sometimes seen raised several yards from the ground during his
rapturous devotions, with a bright light shining from his
countenance. St. Ignatius Loyola is declared to have been
raised about two feet under the same circumstances, and
similar legends of devout ascetics being not only metaphorically but materially "raised above the earth" are told in the
lives of St. Dominic, St. Dunstan, St. Theresa, and other
less known saints. In the last century, Dom Calmet speaks
of knowing a good monk who rises sometimes from the
ground and remains involuntarily suspended, especially on
seeing some devotional image or hearing some devout
prayer, and also a nun who has often seen herself raised in
spite of herself to a certain distance from the earth. Unfortunately the great commentator does not specify any
witnesses as having seen the monk and nun rise in the air.
If they only thought themselves thus elevated, their stories
can only rank with that of the young man mentioned by De
Maistre, who so often seemed to himself to float in the air,
that he came to suspect that gravitation might not be natural

[1] Eunapius in Iambl.

to man.[1]   The hallucination of rising and floating in the air is extremely common, and ascetics of all religions are especially liable to it.

Among modern accounts of diabolic possession, also, the rising in the air is described as taking place not subjectively but objectively.   In 1657, Richard Jones, a sprightly lad of twelve years old, living at Shepton Mallet, was bewitched by one Jane Brooks; he was seen to rise in the air and pass over a garden wall some thirty yards, and at other times was found in a room with his hands flat against a beam at the top of the room, and his body two or three feet from the ground, nine people at a time seeing him in this latter position.   Jane Brooks was accordingly condemned and executed at Chard Assizes in March, 1658.   Richard, the Surrey demoniac of 1689, was hoisted up in the air and let down by Satan; at the beginning of his fits he was, as it were, blown or snatched or borne up suddenly from his chair, as if he would have flown away, but that those who held him hung to his arms and legs and clung about him.   One account (not the official medical one) of the demoniacal possessions at Morzine in Savoy, in 1864, relates that a patient was held suspended in the air by an invisible force during some seconds or minutes above the cemetery, in the presence of the archbishop.[2]   Modern spiritualists claim this power as possessed by certain distinguished living mediums, who, indeed, profess to rival in sober fact the aerostatic miracles of Buddhist and Catholic legend.   The force employed is of course considered to be that of the spirits.

The performances of tied mediums have been specially represented in England by the Davenport Brothers, who "are generally recognized by Spiritualists as genuine media, and

---

[1] Alban Butler, 'Lives of the Saints,' vol. i. p. 674; Calmet, 'Diss. sur les Apparitions, etc.,' chap. xxi.; De Maistre, 'Soirées de St. Pétersbourg,' vol. ii. pp. 158, 175. See also Bastian, 'Mensch,' vol. ii. p. 578; 'Psychologie,' p. 159.

[2] Glanvil, Sadducismus Triumphatus,' part II.; Bastian, 'Psychologie,' p. 161.

attribute the reverse opinion so deeply rooted in the public
mind, to the untruthfulness of the London and many other
newspapers." The performers were bound fast and shut by
themselves in a dark cabinet, with musical instruments,
whence not only musical sounds proceeded, but the coats of
the mediums were taken off and replaced; yet on inspection
their bodies were discovered still bound. The spirits would
also release the bound mediums from their cords, however
carefully tied about them.[1] Now the idea of supernatural
unbinding is very ancient, vouched for as it is by no less a
personage than the crafty Odysseus himself, in his adventure
on board the ship of the Thesprotians:

> "Me on the well-benched vessel, strongly bound,
> They leave, and snatch their meal upon the beach.
> But to my help the gods themselves unwound
> My cords with ease, though firmly twisted round."

In early English chronicle, we find it in a story told by the
Venerable Bede. A certain Imma was found all but dead
on the field of battle, and taken prisoner, but when he began
to recover and was put in bonds to prevent his escaping, no
sooner did his binders leave him but he was loose again.
The earl who owned him inquired whether he had about
him such "loosening letters" (literæ solutoriæ) as tales
were told of; the man replied that he knew nought of such
arts; yet when his owner sold him to another master, there
was still no binding him. The received explanation of this
strange power was emphatically a spiritual one. His brother
had sought for his dead body, and finding another like him,
buried it and proceeded to say masses for his brother's soul,
by the celebration whereof it came to pass that no one
could fasten him, for he was out of bonds again directly.
So they sent him home to Kent, whence he duly returned
his ransom, and his story, it is related, stimulated many to
devotion, who understood by it how salutary are masses to

---

[1] 'Spiritualist,' Feb. 15, 1870. Orrin Abbott, 'The Davenport Brothers,'
New York, 1864.

the redemption both of soul and body. Again, there prevailed in Scotland up to the last century this notion: when the lunatics who had been brought to St. Fillan's Pool to be bathed, were laid bound in the neighbouring church next night, if they were found loose in the morning their recovery was expected, but if at dawn they were still bound, their cure was doubtful.

The untying trick performed among savages is so similar to that of our mountebanks, that when we find the North American Indian jugglers doing both this and the familiar trick of breathing fire, we are at a loss to judge whether they inherited these two feats from their savage ancestors, or borrowed them from the white men. The point is not, however, the mere performance of the untying trick, but its being attributed to the help of spiritual beings. This notion is thoroughly at home in savage culture. It comes out well in the Esquimaux' accounts which date from early in the 18th century. Cranz thus describes the Greenland angekok setting out on his mystic journey to heaven and hell. When he has drummed awhile and made all sorts of wondrous contortions, he is himself bound with a thong by one of his pupils, his head between his legs, and his hands behind his back. All the lamps in the house are put out, and the windows darkened, for no one must see him hold intercourse with his spirit, no one must move or even scratch his head, that the spirit may not be interfered with—or rather, says the missionary, that no one may catch him at his trickery, for there is no going up to heaven in broad daylight. At last, after strange noises have been heard, and a visit has been received or paid to the torngak or spirit, the magician reappears unbound, but pale and excited, and gives an account of his adventures. Castrén's account of the similar proceedings of the Siberian shamans is as follows: "They are practised," he says, "in all sorts of conjuring-tricks, by which they know how to dazzle the simple crowd, and inspire greater trust in themselves. One of the most usual juggleries of the shamans in the Govern-

ment of Tomsk consists of the following hocus-pocus, a
wonder to the Russians as well as to the Samoieds. The
shaman sits down on the wrong side of a dry reindeer-hide
spread in the middle of the floor. There he lets himself be
bound hand and foot by the assistants. The shutters are
closed, and the shaman begins to invoke his ministering
spirits. All at once there arises a mysterious ghostliness in
the dark space. Voices are heard from different parts,
both within and without the yurt, while on the dry reindeer
skin there is a rattling and drumming in regular time.
Bears growl, snakes hiss, and squirrels leap about in the
room. At last this uncanny work ceases, and the audience
impatiently await the result of the game. A few moments
pass in this expectation, and behold, the shaman walks in
free and unbound from outside. No one doubts that it was
the spirits who were drumming, growling, and hissing, who
released the shaman from his bonds, and who carried him
by secret ways out of the yurt."[1]

On the whole, the ethnography of spiritualism bears on
practical opinion somewhat in this manner. Beside the
question of the absolute truth or falsity of the alleged
possessions, manes-oracles, doubles, brain-waves, furniture
movings, and floatings in the air, there remains the history
of spiritualistic belief as a matter of opinion. Hereby
it appears that the received spiritualistic theory of the
alleged phenomena belongs to the philosophy of savages.
As to such matters as apparitions or possessions this is
obvious, and it holds in more extreme cases. Suppose a
wild North American Indian looking on at a spirit-séance
in London. As to the presence of disembodied spirits,
manifesting themselves by raps, noises, voices, and other

[1] Homer. Odyss. xiv. 315 (Worsley's Trans.); Beda, 'Historia Ecclesiastica,' iv. 22; Grimm, 'D. M.,' p. 1180 (an old German loosing-charm is given from the Merseburg MS.); J. Y. Simpson, in 'Proc. Ant. Soc. Scotland,' vol. iv.; Keating, 'Long's Exp. to St. Peter's River,' vol. ii. p. 159; Fyede, 'Greenland,' p. 189; Cranz, 'Grönland,' p. 269; Castrén, 'Reiseberichte,' 1845—9, p. 173.

physical actions, the savage would be perfectly at home in
the proceedings, for such things are part and parcel of his
recognized system of nature. The part of the affair really
strange to him would be the introduction of such arts as
spelling and writing, which do belong to a different state of
civilization from his. The issue raised by the comparison
of savage, barbaric, and civilized spiritualism, is this: Do
the Red Indian medicine-man, the Tatar necromancer, the
Highland ghost-seer, and the Boston medium, share the
possession of belief and knowledge of the highest truth and
import, which, nevertheless, the great intellectual movement
of the last two centuries has simply thrown aside as worthless? Is what we are habitually boasting of and calling new
enlightenment, then, in fact a decay of knowledge? If so, this
is a truly remarkable case of degeneration, and the savages
whom some ethnographers look on as degenerate from a
higher civilization, may turn on their accusers and charge
them with having fallen from the high level of savage
knowledge.

Throughout the whole of this varied investigation, whether
of the dwindling survival of old culture, or of its bursting
forth afresh in active revival, it may perhaps be complained
that its illustrations should be chosen so much among things
worn out, worthless, frivolous, or even bad with downright
harmful folly. It is in fact so, and I have taken up this
course of argument with full knowledge and intent. For,
indeed, we have in such inquiries continual reason to be
thankful for fools. It is quite wonderful, even if we hardly
go below the surface of the subject, to see how large a share
stupidity and unpractical conservatism and dogged superstition have had in preserving for us traces of the history of
our race, which practical utilitarianism would have remorse-
lessly swept away. The savage is firmly, obstinately con-
servative. No man appeals with more unhesitating confidence
to the great precedent-makers of the past; the wisdom of
his ancestors can control against the most obvious evidence
his own opinions and actions. We listen with pity to the

rude Indian as he maintains against civilized science and
experience the authority of his rude forefathers.   We smile
at the Chinese appealing against modern innovation to the
golden precepts of Confucius, who in his time looked back
with the same prostrate reverence to sages still more
ancient, counselling his disciples to follow the seasons of
Hea, to ride in the carriage of Yin, to wear the ceremonial
cap of Chow.

The nobler tendency of advancing culture, and above all
of scientific culture, is to honour the dead without grovelling
before them, to profit by the past without sacrificing the
present to it.   Yet even the modern civilized world has but
half learnt this lesson, and an unprejudiced survey may lead
us to judge how many of our ideas and customs exist rather
by being old than by being good.   Now in dealing with
hurtful superstitions, the proof that they are things which
it is the tendency of savagery to produce, and of higher
culture to destroy, is accepted as a fair controversial
argument.   The mere historical position of a belief or
custom may raise a presumption as to its origin which
becomes a presumption as to its authenticity.   Dr. Middleton's celebrated Letter from Rome shows cases in point.
He mentions the image of Diana at Ephesus which fell
from the sky, thereby damaging the pretensions of the
Calabrian image of St. Dominic, which, according to pious
tradition, was likewise brought down from heaven.   He
notices that as the blood of St. Januarius now melts miracu-
lously without heat, so ages ago the priests of Gnatia tried
to persuade Horace, on his road to Brundusium, that the
frankincense in their temple had the habit of melting in like
manner:

> " . . . dehinc Gnatia lymphis
> Iratis exstructa dedit risusque jocosque;
> Dum flamma sine thura liquescere limine sacro,
> Persuadere cupit: credat Judæus Apella;
> Non ego." [1]

---

[1] Conyers Middleton, 'A Letter from Rome,' 1729 ; Hor. Sat. L. v. 98.

Thus ethnographers, not without a certain grim satisfaction, may at times find means to make stupid and evil superstitions bear witness against themselves.

Moreover, in working to gain an insight into the general laws of intellectual movement, there is practical gain in being able to study them rather among antiquarian relics of no intense modern interest, than among those seething problems of the day on which action has to be taken amid ferment and sharp strife. Should some moralist or politician speak contemptuously of the vanity of studying matters without practical moment, it will generally be found that his own mode of treatment will consist in partizan diatribes on the questions of the day, a proceeding practical enough, especially in confirming those who agree with him already, but the extreme opposite to the scientific way of eliciting truth. The ethnographer's course, again, should be like that of the anatomist who carries on his studies if possible rather on dead than on living subjects; vivisection is nervous work, and the humane investigator hates inflicting needless pain. Thus when the student of culture occupies himself in viewing the bearings of exploded controversies, or in unravelling the history of long-superseded inventions, he is gladly seeking his evidence rather in such dead old history, than in the discussions where he and those he lives among are alive with intense party feeling, and where his judgment is biassed by the pressure of personal sympathy, and even it may be of personal gain or loss. So, from things which perhaps never were of high importance, things which have fallen out of popular significance, or even out of popular memory, he tries to elicit general laws of culture, often to be thus more easily and fully gained than in the arena of modern philosophy and politics.

But the opinions drawn from old or worn-out culture are not to be left lying where they were shaped. It is no more reasonable to suppose the laws of mind differently constituted in Australia and in England, in the time of the cave-dwellers and in the time of the builders of sheet-iron houses, than to suppose that the laws of chemical combination were of one sort in the time of the coal-measures, and are of another now. The thing that has been will be; and we are to study savages and old nations to learn the laws that under new circumstances are working for good or ill in our own development. If it is needful to give an instance of the directness with which antiquity and savagery bear upon our modern life, let it be taken in the facts just brought forward on the relation of ancient sorcery to the belief in witchcraft which was not long since one of the gravest facts of European history, and of savage spiritualism to beliefs which so deeply affect our civilization now. No one who can see in these cases, and in many others to be brought before him in these volumes, how direct and close the connexion may be between modern culture and the condition of the rudest savage, will be prone to accuse students who spend their labour on even the lowest and most trifling facts of ethnography, of wasting their hours in the satisfaction of a frivolous curiosity.

CHAPTER V.

EMOTIONAL AND IMITATIVE LANGUAGE.

Element of directly expressive Sound in Language—Test by independent correspondence in distinct languages—Constituent processes of Language —Gesture—Expression of feature, etc.—Emotional Tone—Articulate sounds, vowels determined by musical quality and pitch, consonants— Emphasis and Accent—Phrase-melody, Recitative—Sound-Words—Inter- jections—Calls to Animals—Emotional Cries—Sense-Words formed from Interjections—Affirmative and Negative particles, etc.

In carrying on the inquiry into the development of culture, evidence of some weight is to be gained from an examination of Language. Comparing the grammars and dictionaries of races at various grades of civilization, it appears that, in the great art of speech, the educated man at this day substantially uses the method of the savage, only expanded and improved in the working out of details. It is true that the languages of the Tasmanian and the Chinese, of the Greenlander and the Greek, differ variously in structure; but this is a secondary difference, underlaid by a primary similarity in method, namely, the expression of ideas by articulate sounds habitually allotted to them. Now all languages are found on inspection to contain some articulate sounds of a directly natural and directly intelli- gible kind. These are sounds of interjectional or imitative character, which have their meaning not by inheritance from parents or adoption from foreigners, but by being taken up directly from the world of sound into the world of sense. Like pantomimic gestures, they are capable of conveying their meaning of themselves, without reference to the particular

language they are used in connexion with. From the
observation of these, there have arisen speculations as to
the origin of language, treating such expressive sounds as
the fundamental constituents of language in general, and
considering those of them which are still plainly recognizable
as having remained more or less in their original state, long
courses of adaptation and variation having produced from
such the great mass of words in all languages, in which no
connexion between idea and sound can any longer be
certainly made out. Thus grew up doctrines of a "natural"
origin of language, which, dating from classic times, were
developed in the eighteenth century into a system by that
powerful thinker, the President Charles de Brosses, and in
our own time are being expanded and solidified by a school
of philologers, among whom Mr. Hensleigh Wedgwood is
the most prominent.[1]   These theories have no doubt been
incautiously and fancifully worked.   No wonder that
students who found in nature real and direct sources of
articulate speech, in interjectional sounds like *ah! ugh!
h'm! eh!* and in imitative sounds like *purr, whis, tomtom,
cuckoo,* should have thought that the whole secret of language lay within their grasp, and that they had only to fit
the keys thus found into one hole after another to open
every lock.   When a philosopher has a truth in his hands,
he is apt to stretch it farther than it will bear.   The magic
umbrella must spread and spread till it becomes a tent wide
enough to shelter the king's army.   But it must be borne
in mind that what criticism touches in these opinions is
their exaggeration, not their reality.   That interjections
and imitative words are really taken up to some extent, be
it small or large, into the very body and structure of language, no one denies.   Such a denial, if any one offered it,
the advocates of the disputed theories might dispose of in
the single phrase, that they would neither be *pooh-poohed*

---

[1] C. de Brosses, 'Traité de la Formation Mécanique des Langues,' etc. (1st
ed. 1765); Wedgwood, 'Origin of Language' (1866); ' Dic. of English Etymology' (1859, 2nd ed. 1872); Farrar, 'Chapters on Language' (1865).

nor *hooted* down. It may be shown within the limits of the
most strict and sober argument, that the theory of the
origin of language in natural and directly expressive sounds
does account for a considerable fraction of the existing
copia verborum, while it raises a presumption that, could
we trace the history of words more fully, it would account
for far more.

In here examining interjectional and imitative sounds
with their derivative words, as well as certain other parts of
language of a more or less cognate character, I purpose to
bring forward as far as possible new evidence derived from
the languages of savage and barbarous races. By so doing
it becomes practicable to use a check which in great measure
stops the main source of uncertainty and error in such
enquiries, the habit of etymologizing words off-hand from
expressive sounds, by the unaided and often flighty fancy of
a philologer. By simply enlarging the survey of language,
the province of the imagination is brought within narrower
limits. If several languages, which cannot be classed as
distinctly of the same family, unite in expressing some
notion by a particular sound which may fairly claim to be
interjectional or imitative, their combined authority will go
far to prove the claim a just one. For if it be objected that
such words may have passed into the different languages
from a common source, of which the trace is for the most
part lost, this may be answered by the question, Why is there
not a proportionate agreement between the languages in
question throughout the far larger mass of words which
cannot pretend to be direct sound-words ? If several
languages have independently chosen like words to express
like meanings, then we may reasonably suppose that we are
not deluding ourselves in thinking such words highly appropriate to their purpose. They are words which answer the
conditions of original language, conforming as they do to
the saying of Thomas Aquinas, that the names of things
ought to agree with their natures, "nomina debent naturis
rerum congruere." Applied in such comparison, the lan-

guages of the lower races contribute evidence of excellent
quality to the problem. It will at the same time and by
the same proofs appear, that savages possess in a high
degree the faculty of uttering their minds directly in
emotional tones and interjections, of going straight to
nature to furnish themselves with imitative sounds, includ-
ing reproductions of their own direct emotional utterances,
as means of expression of ideas, and of introducing into
their formal language words so produced.   They have
clearly thus far the means and power of producing language.
In so far as the theories under consideration account for
the original formation of language, they countenance the
view that this formation took place among mankind in a
savage state, and even, for anything appearing to the contrary, in a still lower stage of culture than has survived to
our day.[1]

The first step in such investigation is to gain a clear idea
of the various elements of which spoken language is made
up.   These may be enumerated as gesture, expression of
feature, emotional tone, emphasis, force, speed, etc. of
utterance, musical rhythm and intonation, and the formation of the vowels and consonants which are the skeleton of
articulate speech.

In the common intercourse of men, speech is habitually
accompanied by gesture, the hands, head, and body aiding
and illustrating the spoken phrase.   So far as we can judge,
the visible gesture and the audible word have been thus
used in combination since times of most remote antiquity

[1] Among the principal savage and barbaric languages here used for evi-
dence, are as follows :—Africa : Galla (Tutschek, Gr. and Dic.), Yoruba
(Bowen, Gr. and Dic.), Zulu (Döhne, Dic.). Polynesia, etc.: Maori (Kendall,
Vocab., Williams, Dic.), Tonga (Mariner, Vocab.), Fiji (Hazlewood, Dic.),
Melanesia (Gabelentz, Melan. Spr.).   Australia (Grey, Moore, Schürmann,
Oldfield, Vocabs.)   N. America ; Pima, Yakama, Clallam, Lummi, Chinuk,
Mohawk, Micmac (Smithson. Contr. vol. III.), Chinook Jargon (Gibbs, Dic.),
Quiché (Brasseur, Gr. and Dic.), S. America : Tupi (Diaz, Dic.), Carib
(Rochefort, Vocab.), Quichua (Markham, Gr. and Dic.), Chilian (Febres,
Dic.), Brazilian tribes (Martius, ' Glossaria linguarum Brasiliensium ').   Many
details in Pott, ' Doppelung," etc.

in the history of our race. It seems, however, that in the daily intercourse of the lower races, gesture holds a much more important place than we are accustomed to see it fill, a position even encroaching on that which articulate speech holds among ourselves. Mr. Bonwick confirms by his experience Dr. Milligan's account of the Tasmanians as using "signs to eke out the meaning of monosyllabic expressions, and to give force, precision, and character to vocal sounds." Captain Wilson remarks on the use of gesticulation in modifying words in the Chinook Jargon. There is confirmation to Spix and Martius' description of low Brazilian tribes completing by signs the meaning of their scanty sentences, thus making the words "wood-go" serve to say "I will go into the wood," by pointing the mouth like a snout in the direction meant. The Rev. J. L. Wilson, describing the Grebo language of West Africa, remarks that they have personal pronouns, but seldom use them in conversation, leaving it to gesture to determine whether a verb is to be taken in the first or second person; thus the words "ni ne" will mean "I do it," or "you do it," according to the significant gestures of the speaker.[1] Beside such instances, it will hereafter be noticed that the lower races, in counting, habitually use gesture-language for a purpose to which higher races apply word-language. To this prominent condition of gesture as a means of expression among rude tribes, and to the development of pantomime in public show and private intercourse among such peoples as the Neapolitans of our own day, the most extreme contrast may be found in England, where, whether for good or ill, suggestive pantomime is now reduced to so small a compass in social talk, and even in public oratory.

Changes of the bodily attitude, corresponding in their fine gradations with changes of the feelings, comprise condi-

[1] Bonwick, 'Daily Life of Tasmanians,' p. 140; Capt. Wilson, in 'Tr. Eth. Soc.,' vol. iv. p. 322, etc.; J. L. Wilson, in 'Journ. Amer. Oriental Soc.,' vol. i. 1849, No. 4; also Cranz, 'Grönland,' p. 279 (cited below, p. 186). For other accounts, see 'Early Hist. of Mankind,' p. 77.

tions of the surface of the body, postures of the limbs, and also especially those expressive attitudes of the face to which our attention is particularly directed when we notice one another. The visible expression of the features is a symptom which displays the speaker's state of mind, his feelings of pleasure or disgust, of pride or humility, of faith or doubt, and so forth. Not that there is between the emotion and its bodily expression any originally intentional connexion. It is merely that a certain action of our physical machinery shows symptoms which we have learnt by experience to refer to a mental cause, as we judge by seeing a man sweat or limp that he is hot or footsore. Blushing is caused by certain emotions, and among Europeans it is a visible expression or symptom of them; not so among South American Indians, whose blushes, as Mr. David Forbes points out, may be detected by the hand or a thermometer, but being concealed by the dark skin cannot serve as a visible sign of feeling.[1] By turning these natural processes to account, men contrive to a certain extent to put on particular physical expressions, frowning or smiling for instance, in order to simulate the emotions which would naturally produce such expressions, or merely to convey the thought of such emotions to others. Now it is well known to every one that physical expression by feature, etc., forming a part of the universal gesture-language, thus serves as an important adjunct to spoken language. It is not so obvious, but on examination will prove to be true, that such expression by feature itself acts as a formative power in vocal language. Expression of countenance has an action beyond that of mere visible gesture. The bodily attitude brought on by a particular state of mind affects the position of the organs of speech, both the internal larynx, etc., and the external features whose change can be watched by the mere looker-on. Even though the expression of the speaker's face may not be seen by the hearer, the effect of the whole bodily attitude of

[1] Forbes, 'Aymara Indians,' in Journ. Eth. Soc. 1870, vol. II. p. 206.

which it forms part is not thereby done away with. For on
the position thus taken by the various organs concerned in
speech, depends what I have here called " emotional tone,"
whereby the voice carries direct expression of the speaker's
feeling.[1]

The ascertaining of the precise physical mode in which
certain attitudes of the internal and external face come to
correspond to certain moods of mind, is a physiological
problem as yet little understood; but the fact that particular
expressions of face are accompanied by corresponding and
dependent expressions of emotional tone, only requires an
observer or a looking-glass to prove it. The laugh made with
a solemn, contemptuous, or sarcastic face, is quite different
from that which comes from a joyous one; the *ah! oh! ho!
hey!* and so on, change their modulations to match the expression of countenance. The effect of the emotional tone does
not even require fitness in the meaning of the spoken words,
for nonsense or an unknown tongue may be made to convey,
when spoken with expressive intonation, the feelings which
are displayed upon the speaker's face. This expression
may even be recognized in the dark by noticing the tone it
gives forth, while the forced character given by the attempt
to bring out a sound not matching even the outward play
of the features can hardly be hidden by the most expert
ventriloquist, and in such forcing, the sound perceptibly
drags the face into the attitude that fits with it. The
nature of communication by emotional tone seems to me to
be somewhat on this wise. It does not appear that
particular tones at all belong directly and of themselves to
particular emotions, but that their action depends on the
vocal organs of the speaker and hearer. Other animals,
having vocal organs different from man's, have accordingly,
as we know, a different code of emotional tones. An
alteration in man's vocal organs would bring a corresponding alteration in the effect of tone in expressing feeling;

[1] Compare Herbert Spencer, 'Origin and Function of Music' in 'Essays'
(1858).

the tone which to us expresses surprise or anger might come to express pleasure, and so forth. As it is, children learn by early experience that such and such a tone indicates such and such an emotion, and this they make out partly by finding themselves uttering such tones when their feelings have brought their faces to the appropriate attitudes, and partly by observing the expression of voice in others. At three or four years old they are to be seen in the act of acquiring this knowledge, turning round to look at the speaker's face and gesture to make sure of the meaning of the tone. But in later years this knowledge becomes so familiar that it is supposed to have been intuitive. Then, when men talk together, the hearer receives from each emotional tone an indication, a signal, of the speaker's attitude of body, and through this of his state of mind, These he can recognize, and even reproduce in himself, as the operator at one end of a telegraphic wire can follow, by noticing his needles, the action of his colleague at the other. In watching the process which thus enables one man to take a copy of another's emotions through their physical effects on his vocal tone, we may admire the perfection with which a means so simple answers an end so complex, and apparently so remote.

By eliminating from speech all effects of gesture, of expression of face, and of emotional tone, we go far toward reducing it to that system of conventional articulate sounds which the grammarian and the comparative philologist habitually consider as language. These articulate sounds are capable of being roughly set down in signs standing for vowels and consonants, with the aid of accents and other significant marks; and they may then again be read aloud from these written signs, by any one who has learnt to give its proper sound to each letter.

What vowels are, is a matter which has been for some years well understood.[1] They are compound musical tones

[1] See Helmholtz, 'Tonempfindungen,' 2nd ed. p. 163; Tyndall, 'Sound,' lecture v.; Max Müller, 'Lectures,' 2nd series, p. 95, etc.

such as, in the vox humana stop of the organ, are sounded by reeds (vibrating tongues) fitted to organ-pipes of particular construction. The manner of formation of vowels by the voice is shortly this. There are situated in the larynx a pair of vibrating membranes called the vocal chords, which may be rudely imitated by stretching a piece of sheet india-rubber over the open end of a tube, so as to form two half-covers to it, "like the parchment of a drum split across the middle;" when the tube is blown through, the india-rubber flaps will vibrate as the vocal chords do in the larynx, and give out a sound. In the human voice, the musical effect of the vibrating chords is increased by the cavity of the mouth, which acts as a resonator or sounding-box, and which also, by its shape at any moment, modifies the musical "quality" of the sound produced. Quality, which is independent of pitch, depends on the harmonic overtones accompanying the fundamental tone which alone musical notation takes account of: this quality makes the difference between the same note on two instruments, flute and piano for instance, while some instruments, as the violin, can give to one note a wide variation of quality. To such quality the formation of vowels is due. This is perfectly shown by the common Jew's harp, which when struck can be made to utter the vowels a, e, i, o, u, &c., by simply putting the mouth in the proper position for speaking these vowels. In this experiment the player's voice emits no sound, but the vibrating tongue of the Jew's harp placed in front of the mouth acts as a substitute for the vocal chords, and the vowel-sounds are produced by the various positions of the cavity of the mouth modifying the quality of the note, by bringing out with different degrees of strength the series of harmonic tones of which it is composed. As to musical theory, emotional tone and vowel-tone are connected. In fact, an emotional tone may be defined as a vowel, whose particular musical quality is that produced by the human vocal organs, when adjusted to a particular state of feeling.

Europeans, while using modulation of musical pitch as
affecting the force of words in a sentence, know nothing of
making it alter the dictionary-meaning of a word.   But this
device is known elsewhere, especially in South-East Asia,
where rises and falls of tone, to some extent like those
which serve us in conveying emphasis, question and answer,
&c., actually give different signification.   Thus in Siamese,
há = to seek, *hā* = pestilence, *hà* = five.   The consequence of
this elaborate system of tone-accentuation is the necessity
of an accumulation of expletive particles, to supply the
place of the oratorical or emphatic intonation, which being
thus given over to the dictionary is lost for the grammar.
Another consequence is, that the system of setting poetry to
music becomes radically different from ours; to sing a
Siamese song to a European tune makes the meaning of the
syllables alter according to their rise and fall in pitch, and
turns their sense into the wildest nonsense.[1]   In West
Africa, again, the same device appears : Thus in Dahoman
so = stick, *só* = horse, *sò* = thunder; Yoruba, *bá* = with, *bí* =
bend.[2]   For practical purposes, this linguistic music is
hardly to be commended, but theoretically it is interesting,
as showing that man does not servilely follow an intuitive
or inherited scheme of language, but works out in various
ways the resources of sound as a means of expression.

The theory of consonants is much more obscure than that
of vowels.   They are not musical vibrations as vowels are,
but noises accompanying them.   To the musician such
noises as the rushing of the wind from the organ-pipe, the
scraping of the violin, the sputtering of the flute, are simply
troublesome as interfering with his musical tones, and he
takes pains to diminish them as much as may be.   But in
the art of language noises of this kind, far from being
avoided, are turned to immense account by being used as

[1] See Pallegoix, 'Gramm. Ling. Thai. ;' Bastian, in 'Monatsb. Berlin.
Akad.' June 6, 1867, and 'Roy. Asiatic Soc.' June, 1867.
[2] Burton, in 'Mem. Anthrop. Soc.,' vol. i. p. 313 ; Bowen, 'Yoruba Gr.
and Dic.' p. 5 ; see J. L. Wilson, 'W. Afr.,' p. 461.

consonants, in combination with the musical vowels. As to
the positions and movements of the vocal organs in producing consonants, an excellent account with anatomical
diagrams is given in Professor Max Müller's second series
of Lectures. For the present purpose of passing in review
the various devices by which the language-maker has contrived to make sound a means of expressing thought, perhaps
no better illustration of their nature can be mentioned than
Sir Charles Wheatstone's account of his speaking machine ;[1]
for one of the best ways of studying difficult phenomena is
to see them artificially imitated. The instrument in question pronounced Latin, French, and Italian words well: it
could say, " Je vous aime de tout mon cœur," " Leopoldus
Secundus Romanorum Imperator," and so forth, but it was
not so successful with German. As to the vowels, they
were of course simply sounded by suitable reeds and pipes.
To affect them with consonants, contrivances were arranged
to act like the human organs. Thus p was made by
suddenly removing the operator's hand from the mouth of
the figure, and b in the same way, except that the mouth
was not quite covered, while an outlet like the nostrils
was used in forming m ; f and v were rendered by modifying
the shape of the mouth by a hand ; air was made to rush
through small tubes to produce the sibilants s and sh ; and
the liquids r and l were sounded by the action of tremulous
reeds. As Wheatstone remarks, the most important use of
such ingenious mechanical imitations of speech may be to
fix and preserve an accurate register of the pronunciation of
different languages. A perfectly arranged speaking machine
would in fact represent for us that framework of language
which consists of mere vowels and consonants, though
without most of those expressive adjuncts which go to make
up the conversation of speaking men.

Of vowels and consonants capable of being employed in
language, man is able to pronounce and distinguish an

[1] C. W., in 'London and Westminster Review,' Oct. 1837.

enormous variety. But this great stock of possible sounds is nowhere brought into use altogether. Each language or dialect of the world is found in practice to select a limited series of definite vowels and consonants, keeping with tolerable exactness to each, and thus choosing what we may call its phonetic alphabet. Neglecting such minor differences as occur in the speech of individuals or small communities, each dialect of the world may be said to have its own phonetic system, and these phonetic systems vary widely. Our vowels, for instance, differ much from those of French and Dutch. French knows nothing of either of the sounds which we write as *th* in *thin* and *that*, while the Castilian lisped *c*, the so-called *ceceo*, is a third consonant which we must again make shift to write as *th*, though it is quite distinct in sound from both our own. It is quite a usual thing for us to find foreign languages wanting letters even near in sound to some of ours, while possessing others unfamiliar to ourselves. Among such cases are the Chinese difficulty in pronouncing *r*, and the want of *s* and *f* in Australian dialects. When foreigners tried to teach the Mohawks, who have no labials in their language, to pronounce words with *p* and *b* in them, they protested that it was too ridiculous to expect people to shut their mouths to speak; and the Portuguese discoverers of Brazil, remarking that the natives had neither *f*, *l*, nor *r* in their language, neatly described them as a people with neither *fé*, *ley*, nor *rey*, neither faith, law, nor king. It may happen, too, that sounds only used by some nations as interjectional noises, unwritten and unwriteable, shall be turned to account by others in their articulate language. Something of this kind occurs with the noises called "clicks." Such sounds are familiar to us as interjections; thus the lateral click made in the cheek (and usually in the left cheek) is continually used in driving horses, while varieties of the dental and palatal click made with the tongue against the teeth and the roof of the mouth, are common in the nursery as expressions of surprise, reproof, or satisfaction. Thus, too, the natives

of Tierra del Fuego express "no " by a peculiar cluck, as
do also the Turks, who accompany it with the gesture of
throwing back the head; and it appears from the accounts
of travellers that the clicks of surprise and admiration
among the natives of Australia are much like those we hear
at home. But though here these clicking noises are only
used interjectionally, it is well known that South African
races have taken such sounds up into their articulate speech
and have made, as we may say, letters of them. The very
name of Hottentots, applied to the Namaquas and other
kindred tribes, appears to be not a native name (as Peter
Kolb thought) but a rude imitative word coined by the
Dutch to express the clicking "*hot* en *tot*," and the term
Hottentotism has been thence adopted as a medical description of one of the varieties of stammering. North-West
America is another district of the world distinguished for the
production of strange clucking, gurgling, and grunting
letters, difficult or impossible to European voices. Moreover, there are many sounds capable of being used in
articulate speech, varieties of chirping, whistling, blowing,
and sucking noises, of which some are familiar to our own
use as calls to animals, or interjectional noises of contempt
or surprise, but which no tribe is known to have brought
into their alphabet. With all the vast phonetic variety of
known languages, the limits of possible utterance are far
from being reached.

Up to a certain point we can understand the reasons
which have guided the various tribes of mankind in the
selection of their various alphabets; ease of utterance to the
speaker, combined with distinctness of effect to the hearer,
have been undoubtedly among the principal of the selecting
causes. We may fairly connect with the close uniformity of
men's organs of speech all over the world, the general
similarity which prevails in the phonetic systems of the
most different languages, and which gives us the power of
roughly writing down so large a proportion of any one language
by means of an alphabet intended for any other. But while

we thus account by physical similarity for the existence of a
kind of natural alphabet common to mankind, we must look
to other causes to determine the selection of sounds used in
different languages, and to account for those remarkable
courses of change which go on in languages of a common
stock, producing in Europe such variations of one original
word as *pater*, *father*, *vater*, or in the islands of Polynesia
offering us the numeral 5 under the strangely-varied forms
of *lima*, *rima*, *dima*, *nima*, and *hima*.   Changes of this sort
have acted so widely and regularly, that since the enuncia-
tion of Grimm's law their study has become a main part of
philology.   Though their causes are as yet so obscure, we
may at least argue that such wide and definite operations
cannot be due to chance or arbitrary fancy, but must be the
result of laws as wide and definite as themselves.

Let us now suppose a book to be written with a tolerably
correct alphabet, for instance, an ordinary Italian book, or
an English one in some good system of phonetic letters.
To suppose English written in the makeshift alphabet which
we still keep in use, would be of course to complicate the
matter in hand with a new and needless difficulty.   If, then,
the book be written in a sufficient alphabet, and handed to
a reader, his office will by no means stop short at rendering
back into articulate sounds the vowels and consonants before
him, as though he were reading over proofs for the press.
For the emotional tone just spoken of has dropped out in
writing down the words in letters, and it will be the reader's
duty to guess from the meaning of the words what this tone
should be, and to put it in again accordingly.   He has moreover to introduce emphasis, whether by accent or stress, on
certain syllables or words, thereby altering their effect in
the sentence; if he says, for example, " I never sold you
that horse," an emphasis on any one of these six words will
alter the import of the whole phrase.   Now, in emphatic
pronunciation two distinct processes are to be remarked.
The effect produced by changes in loudness and duration of
words is directly imitative; it is a mere gesture made with

the voice, as we may notice by the way in which any one
will speak of "a *short sharp* answer," "a *long weary* year,"
"a *loud burst* of music," "a *gentle gliding* motion," as compared with the like manner in which the gesture-language
would adapt its force and speed to the kind of action to be
represented. Written language can hardly convey but by the
context the striking effects which our imitative faculty adds
to spoken language, in our continual endeavour to make the
sound of each word we speak a sort of echo to its sense.
We see this in the difference between writing and telling the
little story of the man who was worried by being talked to
about "good books." "Do you mean," he asked, speaking
shortly with a face of strong firm approval, "*good* books?"
"or," with a drawl and a fatuous-benevolent simper, "*goo-d*
books?" Musical accent (*accentus*,[1] musical tone) is turned to
account as a means of emphasis, as when we give prominence
to a particular syllable or word in a sentence by raising or
depressing it a semi-tone or more. The reader has to
divide his sentences with pauses, being guided in this to
some extent by stops; the rhythmic measure in which he
will utter prose as well as poetry is not without its effect;
and he has again to introduce music by speaking each
sentence to a kind of imperfect melody. Professor Helmholtz endeavours to write down in musical notes how a
German with a bass voice, speaking on B flat, might say,
"Ich bin spatzieren gegangen.—Bist du spatzieren gegang-
en?" falling a fourth (to F) at the end of the affirmative
sentence, and rising a fifth (to f) in asking the question,
thus ranging through an octave.[2] When an English speaker
tries to illustrate in his own language the rising and falling
tones of Siamese vowels, he compares them with the English
tones of question and answer, as in "Will you go? Yes."[3]
The rules of this imperfect musical intonation in ordinary
conversation have been as yet but little studied. But as a

[1] 'Accentus est etiam in dicendo cantus obscurior.'—Cic. de Orat.
[2] Helmholtz, p. 304.
[3] Caswell, in Bastian, 'Berlin. Akad.' l. c.

means of giving solemnity and pathos to language, it has been more fully developed and even systematized under exact rules of melody, and we thus have on the one hand ecclesiastical intoning and the less conventional half-singing so often to be heard in religious meetings, and on the other the ancient and modern theatrical recitative. By such intermediate stages we may cross the wide interval from spoken prose, with the musical pitch of its vowels so carelessly kept, and so obscured by consonants as to be difficult even to determine, to full song, in which the consonants are as much as possible suppressed, that they may not interfere with the precise and expressive music of the vowels.

Proceeding now to survey such parts of the vocabulary of mankind as appear to have an intelligible origin in the direct expression of sense by sound, let us first examine Interjections. When Horne Tooke spoke, in words often repeated since, of "the brutish inarticulate Interjection," he certainly meant to express his contempt for a mode of expression which lay outside his own too narrow view of language. But the epithets are in themselves justifiable enough. Interjections are undoubtedly to a certain extent "brutish" in their analogy to the cries of animals; and the fact gives them an especial interest to modern observers, who are thus enabled to trace phenomena belonging to the mental state of the lower animals up into the midst of the most highly cultivated human language. It is also true that they are "inarticulate," so far at least that the systems of consonants and vowels recognized by grammarians break down more hopelessly than elsewhere in the attempt to write down interjections. Alphabetic writing is far too incomplete and clumsy an instrument to render their peculiar and variously-modulated sounds, for which a few conventionally-written words do duty poorly enough. In reading aloud, and sometimes even in the talk of those who have learnt rather from books than from the living world, we may hear these awkward imitations, *ahem! hein! tush! tut! pshaw!* now carrying the unquestioned authority of words printed in a book, and reproduced letter for letter with a most amusing accuracy. But when Horne Tooke fastens upon an unfortunate Italian grammarian and describes him as "The industrious and exact Cinonio, who does not appear ever to have had a single glimpse of reason," it is not easy to see what the pioneer of English philology could find to object to in Cinonio's obviously true assertion, that a single interjection, ah! or ahi! is capable of expressing more than twenty different emotions or intentions, such as pain, entreaty, threatening, sighing, disdain, according to the tone in which it is uttered.[1] The fact that interjections do thus utter feelings is quite beyond dispute, and the philologist's concern with them is on the one hand to study their action in expressing emotion, and on the other to trace their passage into more fully-formed words, such as have their place in connected syntax and form part of logical propositions.

In the first place, however, it is necessary to separate from proper interjections the many sense-words which, often kept up in a mutilated or old-fashioned guise, come so close to them both in appearance and in use. Among classic examples are φέρε, δεῦτε, age! macte! Such a word is hail! which, as the Gothic Bible shows, was originally an adjective, "whole, hale, prosperous," used vocatively, just as the Italians cry bravo! brava! bravi! brave! When the African negro cries out in fear or wonder mámá! mámá![2] he might be thought to be uttering a real interjection, "a word used to express some passion or emotion of the mind," as Lindley Murray has it, but in fact he is simply calling, grown-up baby as he is, for his mother; and the very same

[1] Horne Tooke, 'Diversions of Purley,' 2nd ed. London, 1798, pt. i. pp. 60—8.

[2] R. F. Burton, 'Lake Regions of Central Africa,' vol. ii. p. 333; Livingstone, 'Missionary Tr. in S. Africa,' p. 298; 'Gr. of Mpongwe lang,' (A. B. C. F. Missions, Rev. J. L. Wilson), p. 27. See Callaway, 'Zulu Tales,' vol. i. p. 59.

thing has been noticed among Indians of Upper California, who as an expression of pain cry, *aná!* that is "mother."[1] Other exclamations consist of a pure interjection combined with a pronoun, as *οἴμοι! oime! ah me!* or with an adjective, as *alas! hélas!* (ah weary!) With what care interjections should be sifted, to avoid the risk of treating as original elementary sounds of language what are really nothing but sense-words, we may judge from the way in which the common English exclamation *well! well!* approaches the genuine interjectional sound in the Coptic expression "to make *ouelouele*," which signifies to wail, Latin *ululare*. Still better, we may find a learned traveller in the last century quite seriously remarking, apropos of the old Greek battle-shout, ἀλαλά! ἀλαλά! that the Turks to this day call out *Allah! Allah! Allah!* upon the like occasion.[2]

The calls to animals customary in different countries[3] are to a great extent interjectional in their use, but to attempt to explain them as a whole is to step upon as slippery ground as lies within the range of philology. Sometimes they may be in fact pure interjections, like the *schü schü!* mentioned as an old German cry to scare birds, as we should say *sh sh!* or the *ad!* with which the Indians of Brazil call their dogs. Or they may be set down as simple imitations of the animal's own cries, as the *clucking* to call fowls in our own farm-yards, or the Austrian calls of *pi pi!* or *tiet tiet!* to chickens, or the Swabian *kauter kaut!* to turkeys, or the shepherd's *baaing* to call sheep in India. In other cases, however, they may be sense-words more or less broken down, as when the creature is spoken to by a sound which seems merely taken from its own common name. If an English countryman meets a stray sheep-dog,

[1] Arroyo de la Cuesta, 'Gr. of Mutsun lang,' p. 39, in Smithsonian Contr., vol. iii.; Neapolitan *mamma mia!* exclamation of wonder, &c., Liebrecht in Götting. Gel. Anz. 1872, p. 1287.

[2] Shaw, 'Travels in Barbary,' in Pinkerton, vol. xv. p. 669.

[3] Some of the examples here cited, will be found in Grimm, 'Deutsche Gr.' vol. iii. p. 306; Pott, 'Doppelung.' p. 27; Wedgwood, 'Origin of Language.'

he will simply call to him *ship! ship!* So *schüp schüp!*
is an Austrian call to sheep, and *köss kuhel köss!* to cows.
In German districts *gus gus! gusch gusch! gös gös!* are set
down as calls to geese; and when we notice that the
Bohemian peasant calls *husy!* to them, we remember that
the name for goose in his language is *husa*, a word familiar
to English ears in the name of John Huss. The Bohemian,
again, will call to his dog *ps ps!* but then *pes* means
"dog."   Other sense-words addressed to animals break
down by long repetition into mutilated forms.   When we are
told that the *to to!* with which a Portuguese calls a dog is
short for *toma toma!* (*i.e.*, "take take!") which tells him
to come and take his food, we admit the explanation as
plausible; and the *coop coop!* which a cockney might so
easily mistake for a pure interjection, is only " Come up!
come up! "

> " Come uppe, Whitefoot, come uppe, Lightfoot,
> Come uppe, Jolly, rise and follow,
> Jetty, to the milking shed."

But I cannot offer a plausible guess at the origin of such
calls as *huf hüf!* to horses, *kühl kuhl!* to geese, *deckel deckel!*
to sheep.   It is fortunate for etymologists that such trivial
little words have not an importance proportioned to the
difficulty of clearing up their origin.   The word *puss!*
raises an interesting philological problem.   An English
child calling *puss puss!* is very likely keeping up the trace
of the old Keltic name for the cat, Irish *pus*, Erse *pusag*,
Gaelic *puis*.   Similar calls are known elsewhere in Europe
(as in Saxony, *pus pus!*), and there is some reason to think
that the cat, which came to us from the East, brought with
it one of its names, which is still current there, Tamil *pisei!*
Afghan *pusha*, Persian *pushak*, &c.   Mr. Wedgwood finds
an origin for the call in an imitation of the cat's spitting,
and remarks that the Servians cry *pis!* to drive a cat away,
while the Albanians use a similar sound to call it.   The
way in which the cry of *puss!* has furnished a name for the

cat itself, comes out curiously in countries where the animal
has been lately introduced by Englishmen.   Thus *boosi* is
the recognized word for cat in the Tonga Islands, no doubt
from Captain Cook's time.   Among Indian tribes of North-
west America, *pus͡h*, *pish-pish*, appear in native languages
with the meaning of cat; and not only is the European
cat called a *puss puss* in the Chinook jargon, but in the
same curious dialect the word is applied to a native
beast, the cougar, now called "hyas *puss-puss*," i.e., "great
cat".[1]

The derivation of names of animals in this manner from
calls to them, may perhaps not have been unfrequent.   It
appears that *huss!* is a cry used in Switzerland to set dogs
on to fight, as *s—s!* might be in England, and that the
Swiss call a dog *huss* or *hauss*, possibly from this.   We
know the cry of *dill! dilly!* as a recognized call to ducks in
England, and it is difficult to think it a corruption of any
English word or phrase, for the Bohemians also call *dlidli!*
to their ducks.   Now, though *dill* or *dilly* may not be found
in our dictionaries as the name for a duck, yet the way in
which Hood can use it as such in one of his best known
comic poems, shows perfectly the easy and natural step by
which such transitions can be made :—

> " For Death among the water-lilies,
>   Cried ' Due ad me ' to all her dillies."

In just the same way, because *gee!* is a usual call of the
English waggoner to his horses, the word *gee-gee* has become a familiar nursery noun meaning a horse.   And

---

[1] See Pictet, 'Origin. Indo-Europ.' part i. p. 382 ; Caldwell, 'Gr. of Dravidian Lang.,' p. 465 ; Wedgwood, Dic. s. v. 'puss,' etc. ; Mariner, 'Tonga
Is. Vocab.'; Gibbs, 'Dic. of Chinook Jargon,' Smithsonian Coll. No. 161 ;
Pandosy, 'Gr. and Dic. of Yakama,' Smithson. Contr. vol. iii. ; compare
J. L. Wilson, 'Mpongwe Gr.' p. 57.   The Hindu child's call to the cat *man
men!* may be from Hindust. *mano=*cat.   It. *micio*, Fr. *mite*, *minon*, Ger.
miezo, etc. = ' cat,' and Sp. *miz!* Ger. *minz!* etc. = ' puss !' are from imitations
of a *mew*.

neither in such nursery words, nor in words coined in jest,
is the evidence bearing on the origin of language to be set
aside as worthless; for it may be taken as a maxim of
ethnology, that what is done among civilized men in jest,
or among civilized children in the nursery, is apt to find its
analogue in the serious mental effort of savage, and therefore of primæval tribes.

Drivers' calls to their beasts, such as this *gee! gee-ho!*
to urge on horses, and *weh! woh!* to stop them, form part
of the vernacular of particular districts. The *geho!* perhaps
came to England in the Norman-French, for it is known in
France, and appears in the Italian dictionary as *gio!* The
traveller who has been hearing the drivers in the Grisons
stop their horses with a long *br-r-r!* may cross a pass and
hear on the other side a *hü-ü-ü!* instead. The ploughman's calls to turn the leaders of the team to right and left
have passed into proverb. In France they say of a stupid
clown " Il n'entend ni à *dia!* ni à *hurhaut!* " and the corresponding Platt-Deutsch phrase is "He weet nich *hutt!*
noch *koh!*" So there is a regular language to camels, as
Captain Burton remarks on his journey to Mekka : *ikh ikh!*
makes them kneel, *yahh yahh!* urges them on, *hai hai!*
induces caution, and so forth. In the formation of these
quaint expressions, two causes have been at work. The
sounds seem sometimes thoroughly interjectional, as the
Arab *hai!* of caution, or the French *hue!* North German
jö! Whatever their origin, they may be made to carry
their sense by imitative tones expressive to the ear of both
horse and man, as any one will say who hears the contrast
between the short and sharp high-pitched *hüp!* which tells
the Swiss horse to go faster, and the long-drawn *hü-ü-ü-ü!*
which brings him to a stand. Also, the way in which
common sense-words are taken up into calls like *gee-up!
woh-back!* shows that we may expect to find various old
broken fragments of formal language in the list, and such
on inspection we find accordingly. The following lines are
quoted by Halliwell from the Micro-Cynicon (1599) :—

> " A base borne issue of a baser syer,
> Bred in a cottage, wandering in the myer,
> With nailed shooes and whipstaffe in his hand,
> Who with a *hey* and *ree* the beasts command."

This *ree!* is equivalent to "right" (riddle-me-ree=riddle me right), and tells the leader of the team to bear to the right hand. The *hey!* may correspond with *heit!* or *camether!* which call him to bear "hither," i. e., to the left. In Germany *har! här! har-uh!* are likewise the same as "her," "hither, to the left." So *swude! schicude! zuwder!* "to the left," are of course simply "zuwider," "on the contrary way." Pairs of calls for "right" and "left" in German-speaking countries are *hot!—har!* and *hott!—wist!* This *wist!* is an interesting example of the keeping up of ancient words in such popular tradition. It is evidently a mutilated form of an old German word for the left hand, *winistrá*, Anglo-Saxon *winstre*, a name long since forgotten by modern High German, as by our own modern English.[1]

As quaint a mixture of words and interjectional cries as I have met with, is in an old French Cyclopædia,[2] which gives a minute description of the hunter's craft, and prescribes exactly what is to be cried to the hounds under all possible contingencies of the chase. If the creatures understood grammar and syntax, the language could not be more accurately arranged for their ears. Sometimes we have what seem pure interjectional cries. Thus, to encourage the hounds to work, the huntsman is to call to them *há halle halle halle!* while to bring them up before they are uncoupled it is prescribed that he shall call *hau hau!* or *hau tahaut!* and when they are uncoupled he is to

---

[1] For lists of drivers' words, see Grimm, l. c. ; Pott, 'Zählmethode,' p. 261 ; Halliwell, 'Dic. of Archaic and Provincial English,' s. v. 'ree;' Brand, vol. ii. p. 16 ; Pictet, part II. p. 439.

[2] 'Recueil de Planches sur les Sciences, les Arts, etc.' Paris, 1763, art. 'Chasse.' The traditional cries are still more or less in use. See 'A Week in a French Country-house.'

change his cry to *hau la y la la y la tayau!* a call which
suggests the Norman original of the English *tally-ho!*
With cries of this kind plain French words are intermixed,
*hà bellement li ila, li ila, hau valet!—hau l'ami, tau tau
après après, à route à route!* and so on. And sometimes
words have broken down into calls whose sense is not quite
gone, like the "*voilà ici*" and the "*voilà ce l'est,*" which
are still to be distinguished in the shout which is to tell the
hunters that the stag they have been chasing has made a
return, *raulcci rerari vauleceletz!* But the drollest thing
in the treatise is the grave set of English words (in very
Gallic shape) with which English dogs are to be spoken to,
because, as the author says, "there are many English
hounds in France, and it is difficult to get them to work
when you speak to them in an unknown tongue, that is, in
other terms than they have been trained to." Therefore,
to call them, the huntsman is to cry *here do-do ho ho!* to
get them back to the right track he is to say *houpe boy,
houpe boy!* when there are several on ahead of the rest of
the pack, he is to ride up to them and cry *saf me boy, saf
me boy!* and lastly, if they are obstinate and will not stop,
he is to make them go back with a shout of *cobat, cobat!*

How far the lower animals may attach any inherent
meaning to interjectional sounds is a question not easy to
answer. But it is plain that in most of the cases mentioned
here they only understand them as recognized signals
which have a meaning by regular association, as when they
remember that they are fed with one noise and driven away
with another, and they also pay attention to the gestures
which accompany the cries. Thus the well-known Spanish
way of calling the cat is *miz miz!* while *zape zape!* is used
to drive it away; and the writer of an old dictionary
mantains that there can be no real difference between these
words except by custom, for, he declares, he has heard that
in a certain monastery where they kept very handsome cats,
the brother in charge of the refectory hit upon the device of
calling *zape zape!* to them when he gave them their food,

and then he drove them away with a stick, crying angrily *miz miz;* and this of course prevented any stranger from calling and stealing them, for only he and the cats knew the secret![1] To philologists, the manner in which such calls to animals become customary in particular districts illustrates the consensus by which the use of words is settled. Each case of the kind indicates that a word has prevailed by selection among a certain society of men, and the main reasons of words holding their ground within particular limits, though it is so difficult to assign them exactly in each case, are probably inherent fitness in the first place, and traditional inheritance in the second.

When the ground has been cleared of obscure or mutilated sense-words, there remains behind a residue of real sound-words, or pure interjections. It has long and reasonably been considered that the place in history of these expressions is a very primitive one. Thus De Brosses describes them as necessary and natural words, common to all mankind, and produced by the combination of man's conformation with the interior affections of his mind. One of the best means of judging the relation between interjectional utterances and the feelings they express, is to compare the voices of the lower animals with our own. To a considerable extent there is a similarity. As their bodily and mental structure has an analogy with our own, so they express their minds by sounds which have to our ears a certain fitness for what they appear to mean. It is so with the bark, the howl, and the whine of the dog, the hissing of geese, the purring of cats, the crowing and clucking of cocks and hens. But in other cases, as with the hooting of owls and the shrieks of parrots and many other birds, we cannot suppose that these sounds are intended to utter anything like the melancholy or pain which such cries from a human being would be taken to convey. There are many animals that never utter any cry

[1] Aldrete, ' Lengua Castellana,' Madrid, 1673, a. vv. *ksvts, sts.*

but what, according to our notions of the meaning of
sounds, would express rage or discomfort ; how far are the
roars and howls of wild beasts to be thus interpreted? We
might as well imagine the tuning violin to be in pain, or
the moaning wind to express sorrow.   The connexion
between interjection and emotion depending on the physical
structure of the animal which utters or hears the sound, it
follows that the general similarity of interjectional utterance among all the varieties of the human race is an
important manifestation of their close physical and intellectual unity.

Interjectional sounds uttered by man for the expression
of his own feelings serve also as signs indicating these
feelings to another.   A long list of such interjections,
common to races speaking the most widely various languages, might be set down in a rough way as representing
the sighs, groans, moans, cries, shrieks, and growls by
which man gives utterance to various of his feelings.   Such,
for instance, are some of the many sounds for which *ah !*
oh ! ahi ! aie ! are the inexpressive written representatives ;
such is the sigh which is written down in the Wolof language of Africa as *hhihhe !* in English as *heigho !* in Greek
and Latin as *ii ! ii ! heu ! eheu !*   Thus the open-mouthed
wah wah ! of astonishment, so common in the East,
reappears in America in the *hwah ! hwah-wa !* of the
Chinook Jargon ; and the kind of groan which is represented in European languages by *weh ! ouais ! oval ! vae !* is
given in Coptic by *ouae !* in Galla by *wayo !* in the Ossetic
of the Caucasus by *voy !* among the Indians of British
Columbia by *woi !*   Where the interjections taken down in
the vocabularies of other languages differ from those
recognized in our own, we at any rate appreciate them and
see how they carry their meaning.   Thus with the Malagasy *u-u !* of pleasure, the North American Indian's often
described guttural *ugh !* the *kwish !* of contempt in the
Chinook Jargon, the Tunguz *yo yo !* of pain, the Irish *wb
wb !* of distress, the native Brazilian's *teh teh !* of wonder

and reverence, the *hi-yah!* so well known in the Pigeon-
English of the Chinese ports, and even, to take an extreme
case, the interjections of surprise among the Algonquin
Indians, where men say *tiau!* and women *nyau!* It is
much the same with expressions which are not uttered for
the speaker's satisfaction, but are calls addressed to
another. Thus the Siamese call of *hē!* the Hebrew *he!*
ha! for "lo! behold!" the *hói!* of the Clallam Indians for
"stop!" the Lummi *hái!* for "hold, enough!"—these
and others like them belong just as much to English.
Another class of interjections are such as any one conversant with the gesture-signs of savages and deaf-mutes would
recognize as being themselves gesture-signs, made with vocal
sound, in short, voice-gestures. The sound *m'm, n'n,* made
with the lips closed, is the obvious expression of the man
who tries to speak, but cannot. Even the deaf-and-dumb
child, though he cannot hear the sound of his own voice, makes
this noise to show that he is dumb, that he is *mu mu,* as
the Vei negroes of West Africa would say. To the speaking
man, the sound which we write as *mum!* says plainly
enough "hold your tongue!" "*mum's* the word!" and in
accordance with this meaning has served to form various
imitative words, of which a type is Tahitian *mamu,* to be
silent. Often made with a slight effort which aspirates
it, and with more or less continuance, this sound becomes
what may be indicated as *'m, 'n, h'm, h'n,* etc., interjections
which are conventionally written down as words, *hem!
ahem! hein!* Their primary sense seems in any case that
of hesitation to speak, of "humming and hawing," but this
serves with a varied intonation to express such hesitation
or refraining from articulate words as belongs either to
surprise, doubt or enquiry, approbation or contempt. In
the vocabulary of the Yorubas of West Africa, the nasal
interjection *huñ* is rendered, just as it might be in English,
as "fudge!" Rochefort describes the Caribs listening in
reverent silence to their chief's discourse, and testifying
their approval with a *hun-hun!* just as in his time (17th

cent.) an English congregation would have saluted a
popular preacher.[1] The gesture of blowing, again, is a
familiar expression of contempt and disgust, and when
vocalized gives the labial interjections which are written
pah! bah! pugh! pooh! in Welsh *pw!* in Low Latin
puppup! and set down by travellers among the savages in
Australia as *pooh!* These interjections correspond with
the mass of imitative words which express blowing, such as
Malay *puput*, to blow. The labial gestures of blowing pass
into those of spitting, of which one kind gives the dental
interjection *t' t' t'!* which is written in English or Dutch
tut tut! and that this is no mere fancy, a number of imitative verbs of various countries will serve to show, Tahitian
tutua, to spit, being a typical instance.

The place of interjectional utterance in savage intercourse is well shown in Cranz's description. The Greenlanders, he says, especially the women, accompany many
words with mien and glances, and he who does not well
apprehend this may easily miss the sense. Thus when
they affirm anything with pleasure they suck down air by
the throat with a certain sound, and when they deny anything with contempt or horror, they turn up the nose and
give a slight sound through it. And when they are out of
humour, one must understand more from their gestures
than their words.[2] Interjection and gesture combine to
form a tolerable practical means of intercourse, as where
the communication between French and English troops in
the Crimea is described as "consisting largely of such
interjectional utterances, reiterated with expressive emphasis

---

[1] "There prevailed in those days an indecent custom ; when the preacher
touched any favourite topick in a manner that delighted his audience, their
approbation was expressed by a loud hum, continued in proportion to their
zeal or pleasure. When Burnet preached, part of his congregation hummed
so loudly and so long, that he sat down to enjoy it, and rubbed his face with
his handkerchief. When Sprat preached, he likewise was honoured with the
like animating hum, but he stretched out his hand to the congregation, and
cried, 'Peace, peace ; I pray you, peace.' " Johnson, 'Life of Sprat.'
[2] Cranz, 'Grönland,' p. 279.

and considerable gesticulation."[1]   This description well brings before us in actual life a system of effective human intercourse, in which there has not yet arisen the use of those articulate sounds carrying their meaning by tradition, which are the inherited words of the dictionary.

When, however, we look closely into these inherited sense-words themselves, we find that interjectional sounds have actually had more or less share in their formation. Not stopping short at the function ascribed to them by grammarians, of standing here and there outside a logical sentence, the interjections have also served as radical sounds out of which verbs, substantives, and other parts of speech have been shaped.   In tracing the progress of interjections upward into fully developed language, we begin with sounds merely expressing the speaker's actual feelings. When, however, expressive sounds like *ah !* *ugh!* *pooh !* are uttered not to exhibit the speaker's actual feelings at the moment, but only in order to suggest to another the thought of admiration or disgust, then such interjections have little or nothing to distinguish them from fully formed words.   The next step is to trace the taking up of such sounds into the regular forms of ordinary grammar. Familiar instances of such formations may be found among ourselves in nursery language, where to *woh* is found in use with the meaning of to stop, or in that real though hardly acknowledged part of the English language to which belong such verbs as to *boo-hoo*.   Among the most obvious of such words are those which denote the actual utterance of an interjection, or pass thence into some closely allied meaning.   Thus the Fijian women's cry of lamentation *oile !* becomes the verb *oile* " to bewail," *oile-taka* " to lament for" (the men cry *ule !*) ; now this is in perfect analogy with such words as *ululare*, to *wail*.   With different grammatical terminations, another sound produces the Zulu verb *gigiteka* and its English equivalent to *giggle*.

[1] D. Wilson, 'Prehistoric Man,' p. 65.

The Galla *iya*, "to cry, scream, give the battle-cry" has
its analogues in Greek *lá*, *lŋ́*, "a cry," *iŋ́ios* "wailing,
mournful," etc. Good cases may be taken from a curious
modern dialect with a strong propensity to the use of
obvious sound-words, the Chinook Jargon of North-West
America. Here we find adopted from an Indian dialect
the verb to *kish-kish*, that is, "to drive cattle or horses";
humm stands for the word "stink," verb or noun; and the
laugh, *heehee*, becomes a recognized term meaning fun or
amusement, as in *mamook heehee*, "to amuse" (i. e., "to
make *heehee*") and *heehee house*, "a tavern." In Hawaii,
aa is "to insult;" in the Tonga Islands, *úi!* is at once
the exclamation "fie!" and the verb "to cry out against."
In New Zealand, *he!* is an interjection denoting surprise at
a mistake, *hé* as a noun or verb meaning "error, mistake,
to err, to go astray." In the Quiché language of Guatemala, the verbs *ay*, *oy*, *boy*, express the idea of "to call"
in different ways. In the Carajas language of Brazil, we
may guess an interjectional origin in the adjective *ei*,
"sorrowful" (compare Coptic *ciõiõ*, "to wear a sorrowful
countenance "); while we can scarcely fail to see a derivation from expressive sound in the verb *hai-hai* "to run
away" (compare the word *aie-aie*, used to mean "an
omnibus" in modern French slang). The Camacan
Indians, when they wish to express the notion of "much"
or "many," hold out their fingers and say *hi*. As this is
an ordinary savage gesture expressing multitude, it seems
likely that the *hi* is a mere interjection, requiring the
visible sign to convey the full meaning.[1] In the Quichua
language of Peru, *alalau!* is an interjection of complaint at
cold, whence the verb *alalauñini*, "to complain of the
cold." At the end of each strophe of the Peruvian hymns
to the Sun was sung the triumphant exclamation *haylli!*
and with this sound are connected the verbs *hayllini* "to
sing," *hayllicuni*, "to celebrate a victory." The Zulu

[1] Compare, in the same district, Camé *ii*, Coroxd *hiehíi*, *iuhíähíä*, multus,
·a, ·um.

halala ! of exultation, which becomes also a verb " to shout
for joy," has its analogues in the Tibetan *alala !* of joy,
and the Greek ἀλαλα, which is used as a noun meaning the
battle-cry and even the onset itself, ἀλαλάζω, " to raise the
war-cry," as well as Hebrew *hillel,* " to sing praise," whence
hallelujah ! a word which the believers in the theory that
the Red Indians were the Lost Tribes naturally recognized
in the native medicine-man's chant of *hi-le-li-lah !* The Zulu
makes his panting *ha !* do duty as an expression of heat,
when he says that the hot weather "says *ha ha* " ; his way of
pitching a song by a *ha ! ha !* is apparently represented in
the verb *haya,* " to lead a song," *hayo* " a starting song, a
fee given to the singing-leader for the *haya* " ; and his
interjectional expression *bà bà !* " as when one smacks his
lips from a bitter taste," becomes a verb-root meaning " to
be bitter or sharp to the taste, to prick, to smart."   The
Galla language gives some good examples of interjections
passing into words, as where the verbs *birr-djedn* (to say
brr !) and *birèfada* (to make *brr !*) have the meaning "to be
afraid."   Thus *o !* being the usual answer to a call, and
also a cry to drive cattle, there are formed from it by the
addition of verbal terminations, the verbs *oada,* " to
answer," and *ofa,* " to drive."

The capabilities of an interjection in modifying words,
when language chooses to avail itself thoroughly of them,
may be seen in the treatment of this same interjection *o !*
in the Japanese grammar.[1]   It is used before substantives
as a prefix of honour; *couni,* "country," thus becoming
ocouni.   When a man is talking to his superiors, he puts
o before the names of all objects belonging to them, while
these superiors drop the *o* in speaking of anything of their
own, or an inferior's; among the higher classes, persons of
equal rank put *o* before the names of each other's things,
but not before their own ; it is polite to say *o* before the
names of all women, and well-bred children are dis-

[1] J. H. Donker Curtius, ' Essai de Grammaire Japonaise,' p. 84, etc. 199.

tinguished from little peasants by the way in which they
are careful to put it even before the nursery names of father
and mother, *o toto*, *o caca*, which correspond to the *papa*
and *mama* of Europe. The *o* is also used to convey a
distinct notion of eminence, and even to distinguish the
male gender from the female; as *o m'ma*, a horse, from *me
m'ma*, a mare. A distinction is made in written language
between *o*, which is put to anything royal, and *oo* (pronounced *o-o* not *u*) which means great, as may be instanced
in the use of the word *mets'k*, or "spy" (literally "eye-
fixer"); *o mets'k* is a princely or imperial spy, while
oo mets'k is the spy in chief. This interjectional adjective
oo, great, is usually prefixed to the name of the capital city,
which it is customary to call *oo Yedo* in speaking to one of
its inhabitants, or when officials talk of it among themselves. And lastly, the *o* of honour is prefixed to verbs in all
their forms of conjugation, and it is polite to say *ominahai
matse*, "please to see," instead of the mere plebeian
minahai matse. Now the slightest consideration shows that
an English child of six years old would at once understand
these formations; and if we do not thus incorporate in our
grammar the *o !* of admiration and reverential embarrass-
ment, it is merely because we have not chosen to take
advantage of this rudimentary means of expression.
Another closely allied exclamation, the cry of *io !* has taken
its place in etymology. When added by the German to
his cry of "Fire!" "Murder!" *Feuerio ! Mordio !* it
remains indeed as mere an interjection as the *o !* in our
street cries of "Pease-*o !*" "Dust-*o !*" or the *ô !* in old
German *wafend ! "*to arms!" *hilfô ! "*help!" But the
Iroquois of North America makes a fuller use of his
materials, and carries his *io !* of admiration into the very
formation of compound words, adding it to a noun to say
that it is beautiful or good: thus, in Mohawk, *garonta*
means a tree, *garontio* a beautiful tree; in like manner,
Ohio means "river-beautiful:" and *Ontario*, "hill-rock-
beautiful," is derived in the same way. When, in the old

times of the French occupation of Canada, there was sent over a Governor-General of New France, Monsieur de Montmagny, the Iroquois rendered his name from their word *ononte*, "mountain," translating him into *Onontio*, or "Great Mountain," and thus it came to pass that the name of Onontio was handed down long after, like that of Cæsar, as the title of each succeeding governor, while for the King of France was reserved the yet higher style of "the great Onontio."[1]

The quest of interjectional derivations for sense-words is apt to lead the etymologist into very rash speculations. One of his best safeguards is to test forms supposed to be interjectional, by ascertaining whether anything similar has come into use in decidedly distinct languages. For instance, among the familiar sounds which fall on the traveller's ear in Spain is the muleteer's cry to his beasts, *arre! arre!* From this interjection, a family of Spanish words are reasonably supposed to be derived; the verb *arrear*, "to drive mules," *arriero*, the name for the "muleteer" himself, and so forth.[2] Now is this *arre!* itself a genuine interjectional sound? It seems likely to be so, for Captain Wilson found it in use in the Pelew Islands, where the paddlers in the canoes were kept up to their work by crying to them *arree! arree!* Similar interjections are noticed elsewhere with a sense of mere affirmation, as in an Australian dialect where *a-ree!* is set down as meaning "indeed," and in the Quichua language where *ari!* means "yes!" whence the verb *ariñi*, "to affirm." Two other cautions are desirable in such enquiries. These are, not to travel too far from the absolute meaning expressed by the interjection, unless there is strong corroborative evidence,

---

[1] Brayas, 'Mohawk Lang.' p. 16, in Smithson. Contr. vol. III. Schoolcraft, 'Indian Tribes,' Part III. p. 823, 502, 507. Charlevoix, 'Nouv. France,' vol. i., p. 350.

[2] The *arre!* may have been introduced into Europe by the Moors, as it is used in Arabic, and its use in Europe corresponds nearly with the limits of the Moorish conquest, in Spain *arre!* in Provence *arri!*

and not to override ordinary etymology by treating derivative words as though they were radical. Without these checks, even sound principle breaks down in application, as the following two examples may show. It is quite true that *h'm!* is a common interjectional call, and that the Dutch have made a verb of it, *hemmen,* " to hem after a person." We may notice a similar call in West Africa, in the *mma!* which is translated "hallo! stop!" in the language of Fernando Po. But to apply this as a derivation for German *hemmen,* " to stop, check, restrain," to *hem* in, and even to the *hem* of a garment, as Mr. Wedgwood does without even a perhaps,[1] is travelling too far beyond the record. Again, it is quite true that sounds of clicking and smacking of the lips are common expressions of satisfaction all over the world, and words may be derived from these sounds, as where a vocabulary of the Chinook language of North-West America expresses " good" as *t'k-tok-te,* or *e-tok-te,* sounds which we cannot doubt to be derived from such clicking noises, if the words are not in fact attempts to write down the very clicks themselves. But it does not follow that we may take such words as *deliciæ, delicatus,* out of a highly organized language like Latin, and refer them, as the same etymologist does, to an interjectional utterance of satisfaction, *click!*[2] To do this, is to ignore altogether the composition of words; we might as well explain Latin *dilectus* or English *delight* as direct formations from expressive sound. In concluding these remarks on interjections, two or three groups of words may be brought forward as examples of the application of collected evidence from a number of languages, mostly of the lower races.

The affirmative and negative particles, which bear in language such meanings as "yes!" "indeed!" and "no!" "not," may have their derivations from many different sources. It is thought that the Australian dialects all belong to a single stock, but so unlike are the sounds they

[1] Wedgwood, 'Origin of Language,' p. 62.
[2] Ibid., p. 72.

use for " no ! " and " yes ! " that tribes are actually named
from these words as a convenient means of distinction.
Thus the tribes known as *Gureang, Kamilaroi, Kogai,
Wolaroi, Wailwun, Wiratheroi*, have their names from the
words they use for "no," these being *gure, kamil, ko,
wol, wail, wiru*, respectively; and on the other hand the
Pikambul are said to be so called from their word *pika*,
" yes." The device of naming tribes, thus invented by the
savages of Australia, and which perhaps recurs in Brazil in
the name of the *Cocatapuya* tribe (*coca* "no," *tapuya* "man ")
is very curious in its similarity to the mediæval division of
Langue d'oc and *Langue d'oil*, according to the words for
" yes ! " which prevailed in Southern and Northern France :
oc ! is Latin *hoc*, as we might say " that's it ! " while the
longer form *hoc illud* was reduced to *oil !* and thence to
oui ! Many other of the words for " yes ! " and " no ! " may
be sense-words, as, again, the French and Italian *si !* is Latin
sic. But on the other hand there is reason to think that
many of these particles in use in various languages are not
sense-words, but sound-words of a purely interjectional
kind ; or, what comes nearly to the same thing, a feeling of
fitness of the sound to the meaning may have affected the
choice and shaping of sense-words—a remark of large application in such enquiries as the present. It is an old
suggestion that the primitive sound of such words as *non* is
a nasal interjection of doubt or dissent.[1] It corresponds in
sound with the visible gesture of closing the lips, while a
vowel-interjection, with or without aspiration, belongs
rather to open-mouthed utterance. Whether from this or
some other cause, there is a remarkable tendency among
most distant and various languages of the world, on the one
hand to use vowel-sounds, with soft or hard breathing, to
express " yes ! " and on the other hand to use nasal consonants to express " no ! " The affirmative form is much the
commoner. The guttural *i-i !* of the West Australian, the *ëë !*

[1] De Brosses, vol. i. p. 203. See Wedgwood.

of the Darien, the *a-ah !* of the Clallam, the *é !* of the Yakama Indians, the *e !* of the Basuto, and the *ai !* of the Kanuri, are some examples of a wide group of forms, of which the following are only part of those noted down in Polynesian and South American districts — ii *!* *é !* ia *!* ain *!* io *!* ya *!* ey *!* etc., *h' ! heh ! he-e ! hü ! hoehah ! uh-ha !* etc. The idea has most weight where pairs of words for " yes ! " and " no ! " are found both conforming. Thus in the very suggestive description by Dobrizhoffer among the Abipones of South America, for " yes ! " the men and youths say *héé !* the women say *héá !* and the old men give a grunt ; while for " no " they all say *yna !* and make the loudness of the sound indicate the strength of the negation. Dr. Martius's collection of vocabularies of Brazilian tribes, philologically very distinct, contains several such pairs of affirmatives and negatives, the equivalents of " yes ! " — " no ! " being in Tupi *ayé !—aau ! aani ! ;* in Guato *ii !—nau ! ;* in Jumana, *aeae !—maiu ! ;* in Miranha *ha ü !—nani !* The Quichua of Peru affirms by *y ! hu !* and expresses " no," " not," " not at all," by *ama ! manan !* etc., making from the latter the verb *manamñi,* " to deny." The Quiché of Guatemala has *e* or *ve* for the affirmative, *ma, man, mana,* for the negative. In Africa, again, the Galla language has *ee !* for " yes ! " and *kn, hin, hm,* for " not ! " ; the Fernandian *ee !* for " yes ! " and *'nt* for " not ; " while the Coptic dictionary gives the affirmative (Latin " sane ") as *eie, ie,* and the negative by a long list of nasal sounds such as *an, emmen, en, mmn,* etc. The Sanskrit particles *hi !* " indeed, certainly," *na,* " not," exemplify similar forms in Indo-European languages, down to our own *aye !* and *no ! ¹* There must be some meaning in all this, for otherwise I could hardly have noted down incidentally, without making any attempt at a general search, so many cases from such different languages, only finding a comparatively small number of contradictory cases.²

¹ Also Ormon *har—mako ;* Micmac *é—me.*

² A double contradiction in Carib *anhen ! = " yes ! " ona ! = " no ! "* Single contradictions in Catoquina *haag !* Tupi *eña !* Botorudo *koakem !* Yoruba

De Brosses maintained that the Latin *stare*, to *stand*,
might be traced to an origin in expressive sound. He
fancied he could hear in it an organic radical sign designating
fixity, and, could thus explain why *st!* should be used as a
call to make a man *stand still*. Its connexion with these
sounds is often spoken of in more modern books, and one
imaginative German philologer describes their origin among
primæval men as vividly as though he had been there
to see. A man stands beckoning in vain to a companion
who does not see him, till at last his effort relieves itself by
the help of the vocal nerves, and involuntarily there breaks
from him the sound *st !* Now the other hears the sound,
turns toward it, sees the beckoning gesture, knows that he
is called to stop ; and when this has happened again and
again, the action comes to be described in common talk by
uttering the now familiar *st!* and thus *sta* becomes a root,
the symbol of the abstract idea to stand ![1] This is a most
ingenious conjecture, but unfortunately nothing more. . It
would be at any rate strengthened, though not established,
if its supporters could prove that the *st !* used to call
people in Germany, *pst !* in Spain, is itself a pure interjectional sound. Even this, however, has never been made
out. The call has not yet been shown to be in use outside
our own Indo-European family of languages ; and so long as
it is only found in use within these limits, an opponent might
even plausibly claim it as an abbreviation of the very *sta !*
("stay! stop!") for which the theory proposes it as an
origin.[2]

st ! for "yes !" Culino *aiy !* Australian *yo !* for "no !" &c. How much
these sounds depend on peculiar intonation, we, who habitually use A'm *!*
either for "yes !" or "no !" can well understand.

[1] (Charles de Brosses) 'Traité de la Formation Mécanique des Langues,
etc.' Paris, An ix., vol. I. p. 238 ; vol. ii. p. 313. Lazarus and Steinthal,
'Zeitschrift für Völkerpsychologie,' etc., vol. i. p. 421. Heyse, 'System der
Sprachwissenschaft,' p. 73. Farrar, 'Chapters on Language,' p. 202.

[2] Similar sounds are used to command silence, to stop speaking as well as
to stop going. English *husht !* *whist !* *hist !* Welsh *ust !* French *chut !*
Italian *zitto !* Swedish *tyst !* Russian *st' !* and the Latin *st !* so well described

That it is not unfair to ask for fuller evidence of a sound being purely interjectional than its appearance in a single family of languages, may be shown by examining another group of interjections, which are found among the remotest tribes, and thus have really considerable claims to rank among the primary sounds of language. These are the simple sibilants, *s!* *sh!* *h'sh!* used especially to scare birds, and among men to express aversion or call for silence. Catlin describes a party of Sioux Indians, when they came to the portrait of a dead chief, each putting his hand over his mouth with a *hush-sh!* and when he himself wished to approach the sacred "medicine" in a Mandan lodge, he was called to refrain by the same *hush-sh!* Among ourselves the sibilant interjection passes into two exactly opposite senses, according as it is meant to put the speaker himself to silence, or to command silence for him to be heard; and thus we find the sibilant used elsewhere, sometimes in the one way and sometimes in the other. Among the wild Veddahs of Ceylon, *iss!* is an exclamation of disapproval, as in ancient or modern Europe; and the verb *shirak*, to hiss, is used in Hebrew with a like sense, "they shall hiss him out of his place." But in Japan reverence is expressed by a hiss, commanding silence. Captain Cook remarked that the natives of the New Hebrides expressed their admiration by hissing like geese. Casalis says of the Basutos, "Hisses are the most unequivocal marks of applause, and are as much courted in the African parliaments as they are dreaded by our candidates for popular favour."[1]   Among other sibilant interjec-

---

in the curious old line quoted by Mr. Farrar, which compares it with the gesture of the finger on the lips :—

"Isis, et Harpocrates digito qui significat *st!*"

This group of interjections, again, has not been proved to be in use outside Aryan limits.

[1] Catlin. 'North American Indians,' vol. i. pp. 231, 39, 151, 162.   Bailey in 'Tr. Eth. Soc.,' vol. ii. p. 318.   Job xxvii. 23.   (The verb *shárak* also signifies to call by a hiss, "and he will hiss unto them from the end of the

tions, are Turkish *süss!* Ossetic *ss! sos!* "silence!"
Fernandian *sia!* "listen!" "tush!" Yoruba *siá!* "pshaw!"
Thus it appears that these sounds, far from being special to
one linguistic family, are very wide-spread elements of
human speech. Nor is there any question as to their
passage into fully-formed words, as in our verb to *hush*,
which has passed into the sense of "to quiet, put to sleep"
(adjectively, "as *hush* as death"), metaphorically to *hush* up
a matter, or Greek σίζω "to hush, say hush! command
silence." Even Latin *silere* and Gothic *silan*, "to be silent,"
may with some plausibility be explained as derived from the
interjectional *s!* of silence.

Sanskrit dictionaries recognize several words which explicitly state their own interjectional derivation; such are
hūṅkāra (*hūṃ*-making), "the utterance of the mystic
religious exclamation *hūṃ!*" and *çiççabda* (*çiç*-sound), "a
hiss." Beside these obvious formations, the interjectional
element is present to some greater or less degree in the list of
Sanskrit radicals, which represent probably better than those
of any other language the verb-roots of the ancient Aryan
stock. In *ru*, "to roar, cry, wail," and in *kakh*, "to laugh,"
we have the simpler kind of interjectional derivation, that
which merely describes a sound. As to the more difficult
kind, which carry the sense into a new stage, Mr. Wedgwood
makes out a strong case for the connexion of interjections
of loathing and aversion, such as *pooh! fie!* etc., with that
large group of words which are represented in English by
foul and *fiend*, in Sanskrit by the verbs *pūy*, "to become
foul, to stink," and *piy, piy*, "to revile, to hate."[1] Further

earth, and behold, they shall come with speed," Is. v. 26; Jer. xix. 8.)
Alcock, 'The Capital of the Tycoon,' vol. i. p. 394. Cook, '2nd Voy.'
vol. ii. p. 30. Camilla, 'Basutos,' p. 234.

[1] Wedgwood, 'Origin of Language,' p. 53, 'Dictionary,' Introd. p. xliz.
and s. v. "foul." Prof. Max Müller, 'Lectures,' 2nd series, p. 92, protests
against the indiscriminate derivation of words directly from such cries and interjections, without the intervention of determinate roots. As to the present
topic, he points out that Latin *pus, putridus*, Gothic *fuls*, English *foul*, follow
Grimm's law as if words derived from a single root. Admitting this, how-

evidence may be here adduced in support of this theory.
The languages of the lower races use the sound *pu* to
express an evil smell; the Zulu remarks that "the meat
says *pu*" (inyama iti *pu*), meaning that it stinks; the
Timorese has *poip* "putrid;" the Quiché language has
puh, pch "corruption, pus," *puhir* "to turn bad, rot," *pnz*
"rottenness, what stinks;" the Tupi word for nasty, *puxi*,
may be compared with the Latin *putidus*, and the Columbia
River name for the "skunk," *o-pun-pun*, with similar names
of stinking animals, Sanskrit *putika* "civet-cat," and French
putois "pole-cat." From the French interjection *fi!* words
have long been formed belonging to the language, if not
authenticated by the Academy; in mediæval French 'maistre
fi-fi,' was a recognized term for a scavenger, and *fi-fi* books
are not yet extinct.

There has been as yet, unfortunately, too much separation between what may be called generative philology, which
examines into the ultimate origins of words, and historical
philology, which traces their transmission and change. It
will be a great gain to the science of language to bring these
two branches of enquiry into closer union, even as the
processes they relate to have been going on together since
the earliest days of speech. At present the historical philologists of the school of Grimm and Bopp, whose great
work has been the tracing of our Indo-European dialects to
an early Aryan form of language, have had much the
advantage in fulness of evidence and strictness of treatment.
At the same time it is evident that the views of the genera-

ever, the question has to be raised, how far pure interjections and their direct
derivatives, being self-expressive and so to speak living sounds, are affected
by phonetic changes such as that of Grimm's law, which act on articulate
sounds no longer fully expressive in themselves, but handed down by mere
tradition. Thus *p* and *f* occur in one and the same dialect in interjections of
disgust and aversion, *puh / fi /* being used in Venice or Paris, just as similar
sounds would be in London. In tracing this group of words from early Aryan
forms, it must also be noticed that Sanskrit is a very imperfect guide, for its
alphabet has no *f*, and it can hardly give the rôle in this matter to languages
possessing both *p* and *f*, and thus capable of nicer appreciation of this class
of interjections.

tive philologists, from De Brosses onward, embody a sound
principle, and that much of the evidence collected as to
emotional and other directly expressive words, is of the
highest value in the argument. But in working out the
details of such word-formation, it must be remembered that
no department of philology lies more open to Augustine's
caustic remark on the etymologists of his time, that like the
interpretation of dreams, the derivation of words is set
down by each man according to his own fancy. (Ut
somniorum interpretatio ita verborum origo pro cujusque
ingenio prædicatur.)

CHAPTER VI.

Imitative Words—Human actions named from sound—Animals' names from cries, etc.—Musical Instruments—Sounds reproduced—Words modified to adapt sound to sense—Reduplication—Gradation of vowels to express distance and difference—Children's Language—Sound-words as related to Sense-words—Language an original product of the lower Culture.

From the earliest times of language to our own day, it is unlikely that men ever quite ceased to be conscious that some of their words were derived from imitation of the common sounds heard about them. In our own modern English, for instance, results of such imitation are evident; flies *buzz*, bees *hum*, snakes *hiss*, a cracker or a bottle of ginger-beer *pops*, a cannon or a bittern *booms*. In the words for animals and for musical instruments in the various languages of the world, the imitation of their cries and tones is often to be plainly heard, as in the names of the *hoopoe*, the *ai-ai* sloth, the *kaka* parrot, the Eastern *tomtom*, which is a drum, the African *ulule*, which is a flute, the Siamese *khong-bong*, which is a wooden harmonicon, and so on through a host of other words. But these evident cases are far from representing the whole effects of imitation on the growth of language. They form, indeed, the easy entrance to a philological region, which becomes less penetrable the farther it is explored.

The operations of which we see the results before us in the actual languages of the world seem to have been somewhat as follows. Men have imitated their own emotional utterances or interjections, the cries of animals, the tones of musical instruments, the sounds of shouting, howling, stamping, breaking, tearing, scraping, and so forth, which are all day coming to their ears, and out of these imitations many current words indisputably have their source. But these words, as we find them in use, differ often widely, often beyond all recognition, from the original sounds they sprang from. In the first place, man's voice can only make a very rude copy of most sounds his ear receives; his possible vowels are very limited in their range compared with natural tones, and his possible consonants still more helpless as a means of imitating natural noises. Moreover, his voice is only allowed to use a part even of this imperfect imitative power, seeing that each language for its own convenience restricts it to a small number of set vowels and consonants, to which the imitative sounds have to conform, thus becoming conventionalized into articulate words with further loss of imitative accuracy. No class of words have a more perfect imitative origin than those which simply profess to be vocal imitations of sound. How ordinary alphabets to some extent succeed and to some extent fail in writing down these sounds may be judged from a few examples. Thus, the Australian imitation of a spear or bullet striking is given as *toop*; to the Zulu, when a calabash is beaten, it says *boo*; the Karens hear the flitting ghosts of the dead call in the wailing voice of the wind, *re re, ro ro*; the old traveller, Pietro della Valle, tells how the Shah of Persia sneered at Timur and his Tatars, with their arrows that went *ter ter*; certain Buddhist heretics maintained that water is alive, because when it boils it says *chichitá, chitichita*, a symptom of vitality which occasioned much theological controversy as to drinking cold and warm water. Lastly, sound-words taken up into the general inventory of a language have to follow its organic changes, and in the course of phonetic transition, combination, decay, and mutilation, to lose ever more and more their original shape. To take a single example, the French *huer* "to shout" (Welsh *hwa*) may be a perfect imitative verb; yet when it passes into modern

English *hue* and *cry*, our changed pronunciation of the vowel destroys all imitation of the call. Now to the language-makers all this was of little account. They merely wanted recognized words to express recognized thoughts, and no doubt arrived by repeated trials at systems which were found practically to answer this purpose. But to the modern philologist, who is attempting to work out the converse of the problem, and to follow backward the course of words to original imitative sound, the difficulty is most embarrassing. It is not only that thousands of words really derived from such imitation may now by successive change have lost all safe traces of their history; such mere deficiency of knowledge is only a minor evil. What is far worse is that the way is thrown open to an unlimited number of false solutions, which yet look on the face of them fully as like truth as others which we know historically to be true. One thing is clear, that it is of no use to resort to violent means, to rush in among the words of language, explaining them away right and left as derived each from some remote application of an imitative noise. The advocate of the Imitative Theory who attempts this, trusting in his own powers of discernment, has indeed taken in hand a perilous task, for, in fact, of all judges of the question at issue, he has nourished and trained himself up to become the very worst. His imagination is ever suggesting to him what his judgment would like to find true; like a witness answering the questions of the counsel on his own side, he answers in good faith, but with what bias we all know. It was thus with De Brosses, to whom this department of philology owes so much. It is nothing to say that he had a keen ear for the voice of Nature; she must have positively talked to him in alphabetic language, for he could hear the sound of hollowness in the *sk* of σκάπτω " to dig," of hardness in the *cal* of *callosity*, the noise of insertion of a body between two others in the *tr* of *trans*, *intra*. In enquiries so liable to misleading fancy, no pains should be spared in securing impartial testimony, and it fortunately

happens that there are available sources of such evidence,
which, when thoroughly worked, will give to the theory of
imitative words as near an approach to accuracy as has been
attained to in any other wide philological problem. By
comparing a number of languages, widely apart in their
general system and materials, and whose agreement
as to the words in question can only be accounted for by
similar formation of words from similar suggestion of sound,
we obtain groups of words whose imitative character is indisputable. The groups here considered consist in general
of imitative words of the simpler kind, those directly connected with the special sound they are taken from, but their
examination to some extent admits of words being brought
in, where the connexion of the idea expressed with the
sound imitated is more remote. This, lastly, opens the far
wider and more difficult problem, how far imitation of
sounds is the primary cause of the great mass of words in
the vocabularies of the world, between whose sound and sense
no direct connexion exists.

Words which express human actions accompanied with
sound form a very large and intelligible class. In remote
and most different languages, we find such forms as *pu, puf,
bu, buf, fu, fuf,* in use with the meaning of *puffing, fuffing,* or
blowing; Malay *puput;* Tongan *buhi;* Maori *pupui;* Australian *bobun, bwa-bun;* Galla *bufa, afufa;* Zulu *futa, punga,
pupuza (fu, pu,* used as expressive particles); Quiché *puba;*
Quichua *puhuni;* Tupi *ypeú;* Finnish *puhkia;* Hebrew
puach; Danish *puste;* Lithuanian *pūciu;* and in numbers
of other languages; [1] here, grammatical adjuncts apart, the
significant force lies in the imitative syllable. Savages have
named the European musket when they saw it, by the sound
pu, describing not the report but the *puff* of smoke issuing
from the muzzle. The Society Islanders supposed at first
that the white men blew through the barrel of the gun, and
they called it accordingly *pupuhi,* from the verb *puhi* to

---

[1] Mpongwe *puajina;* Basuto *fuka;* Carib *phoubâie;* Arawac *appadau*
(ignem sufflare). Other cases are given by Wedgwood, 'Or. of Lang.' p. 83.

blow, while the New Zealanders more simply called it a *pu*.
So the Amaxosa of South Africa call it *umpu*, from the
imitative sound *pu!* The Chinook Jargon of North West
America uses the phrase *mamook poo* (make *poo*) for a verb
"to shoot," and a six-chambered revolver is called *toham
poo*, i. e., a "six-poo." When a European uses the word
puff to denote the discharge of a gun, he is merely using the
same imitative word for blowing which describes a *puff* of
wind, or even a powder-*puff* or a *puff*-ball; and when a pistol
is called in colloquial German a *puffer*, the meaning of the
word matches that used for it in French Argot, a
"soufflant." It has often been supposed that the *puff*
imitates the actual sound, the *bang* of the gun, and this has
been brought forward to show by what extremely different
words one and the same sound may be imitated, but this is
a mistake.[1] These derivations of the name of the gun from
the notion of blowing correspond with those which give
names to the comparatively noiseless blow-tube of the bird-
hunter, called by the Indians of Yucatan a *pub*, in South
America by the Chiquitos a *pucuna*, by the Cocamas a *pu-
na*. Looking into vocabularies of languages which have
such verbs "to blow," it is usual to find with them other
words apparently related to them, and expressing more or
less distant ideas. Thus Australian *poo-yu, puyu* "smoke;"
Quichua *pukucuni* "to light a fire," *punquini* "to swell,"
puyu, puhuyu "a cloud;" Maori *puku* "to pant," *puka*
"to swell;" Tupi *pupú, pupúre* "to boil;" Galla *bubu*
"wind," *bubiza* "to cool by blowing;" Kanuri (root *fu*)
fungin "to blow, swell," *furúdu* "a stuffed pad or bolster,"
etc., *bubute* "bellows" (*bubute fungin* "I blow the
bellows"); Zulu (dropping the prefixes) *puku, pukupu*
"frothing, foam," whence *pukapuku* "an empty frothy
fellow," *pupuma* "to bubble, boil," *fu* "a cloud," *fumfu*
"blown about like high grass in the wind," whence *fumfuta*
"to be confused, thrown into disorder," *futo* "bellows," *fuba*
"the breast, chest," then figuratively "bosom, conscience."

[1] See Wedgwood, 'Dic.' Introd. p. viii.

The group of words belonging to the closed lips, of which *mum, mumming, mumble* are among the many forms belonging to European languages,[1] are worked out in like manner among the lower races—Vei *mu mn* "dumb"; Mpongwe *imamn* "dumb"; Zulu *momata* (from *moma*, "a motion with the mouth as in mumbling") "to move the mouth or lips," *mumata* "to close the lips as with a mouthful of water," *mamuta, numuza* "to eat mouthfuls of corn, etc., with the lips shut;" Tahitian *mamu* "to be silent," *omumu* "to murmur;" Fijian, *nomo, nomo-nomo* "to be silent;" Chilian, *ñomn* "to be silent;" Quiché, *mem* "mute," whence *memer* "to become mute;" Quichua, *amu* "dumb, silent," *amullini* "to have something in the mouth," *amullayacuni simicta* "to mutter, to grumble." The group represented by Sanskrit *t'hit'há* "the sound of spitting," Persian *thu kerdan* (make *thu*) "to spit," Greek πτύω, may be compared with Chinook *mamook toh, tooh,* (make *toh, tooh*); Chilian *tarcutun* (make *tuc*); Tahitian *tutua;* Galla *turu;* Yoruba *tu.* Among the Sanskrit verb-roots, none carries its imitative nature more plainly than *kahu* "to sneeze;" the following analogous forms are from South America:—Chilian, *echiun;* Quichua, *achhini;* and from various languages of Brazilian tribes, *techa-ai, haitschu, atchian, natschun, aritischune,* etc. Another imitative verb is well shown in the Negro-English dialect of Surinam, *njam* "to eat" (pron. *nyam*), *njam-njam* "food" (" en hem *njanjam* ben de sprinkhan nanga boesi-honi"—"and his meat was locusts and wild honey"). In Australia the imitative verb "to eat" re-appears as *g'nam-ang.* In Africa, the Susu language has *ninnim,* "to taste," and a similar formation is observed in the Zulu *nambita* "to smack the lips after eating or tasting, and thence to be tasteful, to be pleasant to the mind." This is an excellent instance of the transition of mere imitative sound to the expression of mental emotion, and it corresponds with the imitative way in which the Yakama language, in speaking of little children

[1] See Wedgwood, Dic., s. v. "mum," etc.

or pet animals, expresses the verb " to love " as *nem-no-sha*
(to make n'*m-n*'). In more civilized countries these forms
are mostly confined to baby-language. The Chinese child's
word for eating is *nam*, in English nurseries *nim* is noticed
as answering the same purpose, and the Swedish dictionary
even recognizes *namnam* " a tid-bit."

As for imitative names of animals derived from their cries
or noises, they are to be met with in every language, from
the Australian *tronk* " frog," the Yakama *rol-rol* " lark," to
the Coptic *criō* " ass," the Chinese *maou* " cat," and the
English *cuckoo* and *pewit*. Their general principle of
formation being acknowledged, their further philological
interest turns mostly on cases where corresponding words
have thus been formed independently in distant regions,
and those where the imitative name of the creature, or its
habitual sound, passes to express some new idea suggested
by its character. The Sanskrit name of the *kāka* crow re-
appears in the name of a similar bird in British Columbia,
the *kāh-kah*; a fly is called by the natives of Australia a
bamberoo, like Sanskrit *bambharāli* " a fly," Greek βομβύλιος,
and our *bumble-bee*. Analogous to the name of the *tse-tse*,
the terror of African travellers, is *ntaintsi*, the word for " a
fly" among the Basutos, which also, by a simple metaphor,
serves to express the idea of " a parasite." Mr. H. W.
Bates's description seems to settle the dispute among naturalists, whether the *toucan* had its name from its cry or
not. He speaks of its loud, shrill, yelping cries having " a
vague resemblance to the syllables *tocáno, tocáno*, and hence
the Indian name of this genus of birds." Granting this,
we can trace this sound-word into a very new meaning; for
it appears that the bird's monstrous bill has suggested a
name for a certain large-nosed tribe of Indians, who are
accordingly called the *Tucanos*.[1] The cock, gallo *quiqui-
riqui*, as the Spanish nursery-language calls him, has a long
list of names from various languages which in various ways

[1] Bates, ' Naturalist on the Amazons,' 2nd ed., p. 404 ; Markham in ' r.
Eth. Soc.,' vol. III. p. 143.

imitate his crowing; in Yoruba he is called *koklo*, in Ibo
okoko, akoka, in Zulu *kuku*, in Finnish *kukko*, in Sanskrit
kukkuta, and so on.   He is mentioned in the Zend-Avesta
in a very curious way, by a name which elaborately imitates
his cry, but which the ancient Persians seem to have held
disrespectful to their holy bird, who rouses men from sleep
to good thought, word, and work :—

> "The bird who bears the name of Parôdars, O holy Zarathustra ;
> Upon whom evil-speaking men impose the name *Kahrkataç*." [1]

The crowing of the cock (Malay *kôlaruk, kukuk*) serves to
mark a point of time, cockcrow. Other words originally
derived from such imitation of crowing have passed into
other curiously transformed meanings : Old French *cocart*
"vain ;" modern French *coquet* "strutting like a cock,
coquetting, a coxcomb ;" *cocarde* "a cockade" (from its
likeness to a cock's comb); one of the best instances is
coquelicot, a name given for the same reason to the wild
poppy, and even more distinctly in Languedoc, where
cacaracà means both the crowing and the flower. The hen
in some languages has a name corresponding to that of the
cock, as in Kussa *kukuduua* "cock," *kukukasi* "hen;" Ewe
koklo-tsu "cock," *koklo-no* "hen ;" and her *cackle* (whence
she has in Switzerland the name of *gugel, güggel*) has passed
into language as a term for idle gossip and chatter of
women, *caquet, caqueter, gackern*, much as the noise of a
very different creature seems to have given rise not only to
its name, Italian *cicala*, but to a group of words represented
by *cicalar* "to chirp, chatter, talk sillily." The *pigeon* is a
good example of this kind, both for sound and sense. It is
Latin *pipio*, Italian *pippione, piccione, pigione*, modern
Greek *πιπινον*, French *pipion* (old), *pigeon*; its derivation
is from the young bird's *peep*, Latin *pipire*, Italian *pipiare,
pigiolare*, modern Greek *πιπινιζω*, to chirp ; by an easy
metaphor, a *pigeon* comes to mean "a silly young fellow

<hr>

[1] 'Avesta,' Farg. xviii. 34-5.

easily caught," to *pigeon* "to cheat," Italian *pipione* "a silly gull, one that is soon caught and trepanned," *pippionare* "to pigeon, to gull one." In an entirely different family of languages, Mr. Wedgwood points out a curiously similar process of derivation; Magyar *pipegni, pipelni* "to peep or cheep;" *pipe, pipük* "a chicken, gosling;" *pipe-ember* (chicken-man), "a silly young fellow, booby."[1] The derivation of Greek βοῦς, Latin *bos*, Welsh *bu*, from the ox's lowing, or *booing* as it is called in the north country, has been much debated. With an excessive desire to make Sanskrit answer as a general Indo-European type, Bopp connected Sanskrit *go*, old German *chuo*, English *cow*, with these words, on the unusual and forced assumption of a change from guttural to labial.[2] The direct derivation from sound, however, is favoured by other languages, Cochin-Chinese *bo*, Hottentot *bou*. The beast may almost answer for himself in the words of that Spanish proverb which remarks that people talk according to their nature: "Habló el *buey, y dijó bu!*" "The ox spoke, and he said *boo!*"

Among musical instruments with imitative names are the following:—the *shee-shee-quoi*, the mystic rattle of the Red Indian medicine-man, an imitative word which re-appears in the Darien Indian *shak-shak*, the *shook-shook* of the Arawaks, the Chinook *shugh* (whence *shugh-opoots*, rattle-tail, *i. e.*, "rattlesnake;")—the drum, called *ganga* in Hausa, *gañgañ* in the Yoruba country, *ganguma* by the Gallas, and having its analogue in the Eastern *gong* :—the bell, called in Yakama (N. Amer.) *kwa-lal-kwa-lal*, in Yalof (W. Afr.) *walwal*, in Russian *kolokol*. The sound of the horn is imitated in English nurseries as *toot-toot*, and this is transferred to express the "omnibus" of which the bugle is the signal: with this nursery word is to be classed the

[1] Wedgwood, Dic., s. v. "pigeon;" Diez, 'Etym. Wörterb.,' s. v. "piccione."

[2] Bopp, 'Gloss. Sanscr.,' s. v. "go." See Pott, 'Wurzel-Wörterb. der Indo-Germ. Spr.,' s. v. "gu," Zählmeth., p. 227.

Peruvian name for the "shell-trumpet," *pututu*, and the Gothic *thuthaurn* (*thut-horn*), which is even used in the Gothic Bible for the last trumpet of the day of judgment,— "In spēdistin thuthaúrna. thuthaúrneith auk jah daúthans uslandand" (1 Cor. xv. 52). How such imitative words, when thoroughly taken up into language, suffer change of pronunciation in which the original sound-meaning is lost, may be seen in the English word *tabor*, which we might not recognize as a sound-word at all, did we not notice that it is French *tabour*, a word which in the form *tambour* obviously belongs to a group of words for drums, extending from the small rattling Arabic *tubl* to the Indian *dundhubi* and the *tombe*, the Moqui drum made of a hollowed log. The same group shows the transfer of such imitative words to objects which are like the instrument, but have nothing to do with its sound; few people who talk of *tambour*-work, and fewer still who speak of a footstool as a *tabouret*, associate these words with the sound of a drum, yet the connexion is clear enough. When these two processes go on together, and a sound-word changes its original sound on the one hand, and transfers its meaning to something else on the other, the result may soon leave philological analysis quite helpless, unless by accident historical evidence is forthcoming. Thus with the English word *pipe*. Putting aside the particular pronunciation which we give the word, and referring it back to its French or mediæval Latin sound in *pipe, pipa*, we have before us an evident imitative name of a musical instrument, derived from a familiar sound used also to represent the chirping of chickens, Latin *pipire*, English to *peep*, as in the translation of Isaiah viii. 19: "Seek . . . unto wizards that *peep*, and that mutter." The Algonquin Indians appear to have formed from this sound *pib* (with a grammatical suffix) their name for the *pib-e-guun* or native flute. Now just as *tuba, tubus*, "a trumpet" (itself very likely an imitative word) has given a name for any kind of *tube*, so the word *pipe* has been transferred from the musical instrument to which it first belonged, and is used to describe tubes of various sorts, gas-pipes, water-pipes, and pipes in general. There is nothing unusual in these transitions of meaning, which are in fact rather the rule than the exception. The *chibouk* was origi-nally a herdsman's pipe or flute in Central Asia. The *calumet*, popularly ranked with the tomahawk and the mocassin among characteristic Red Indian words, is only the name for a shepherd's pipe (Latin *calamus*) in the dialect of Normandy, corresponding with the *chalumeau* of literary French ; for when the early colonists in Canada saw the Indians performing the strange operation of smoking, "with a hollow piece of stone or wood like a pipe," as Jacques Cartier has it, they merely gave to the native tobacco-pipe the name of the French musical instrument it resembled. Now changes of sound and of sense like this of the English word *pipe* must have been in continual opera-tion in hundreds of languages where we have no evidence to follow them by, and where we probably may never obtain such evidence. But what little we do know must compel us to do justice to the imitation of sound as a really existing process, capable of furnishing an indefinitely large supply of words for things and actions which have no necessary connexion at all with that sound. Where the traces of the transfer are lost, the result is a stock of words which are the despair of philologists, but are perhaps none the less fitted for the practical use of men who simply want recog-nized symbols for recognized ideas.

The claim of the Eastern *tomtom* to have its name from a mere imitation of its sound seems an indisputable one ; but when we notice in what various languages the beating of a resounding object is expressed by something like *tum, tumb, tump, tup*, as in Javan *tumbuk*, Coptic *tmno*, " to pound in a mortar," it becomes evident that the admission involves more than at first sight appears. In Malay, *timpa, tampa*, is " to beat out, hammer, forge ; " in the Chinook Jargon *tum-tum* is " the heart," and by combining the same sound with the English word "water," a name is made for

" waterfall," *tum-arita*. The Gallas of East Africa declare that a box on the ear seems to them to make a noise like *tub*, for they call its sound *tubdjeda*, that is, " to say *tub*." In the same language, *tuma* is " to beat," whence *tumtu*, " a workman, especially one who beats, a smith." With the aid of another imitative word, *bufa* "to blow," the Gallas can construct this wholly imitative sentence, *tumtum bufa bufti*, " the workman blows the bellows," as an English child might say, " the *tumtum puffs* the *puffer*." This imitative sound seems to have obtained a footing among the Aryan verb-roots, as in Sanskrit *tup, tubh* " to smite," while in Greek, *tup, tump*, has the meaning of " to beat, to *thump*," producing for instance τύμπανον, *tympanum*, " a drum or *tomtom*." Again, the verb to *crack* has become in modern English as thorough a root-word as the language possesses. The mere imitation of the sound of breaking has passed into a verb to break; we speak of a *cracked* cup or a *cracked* reputation without a thought of imitation of sound; but we cannot yet use the German *krachen* or French *craquer* in this way, for they have not developed in meaning as our word has, but remain in their purely imitative stage. There are two corresponding Sanskrit words for the saw, *kra-kara, kra-kacha*, that is to say, the " *kra*-maker, *kra*-crier; " and it is to be observed that all such terms, which expressly state that they are imitations of sound, are particularly valuable evidence in these enquiries, for whatever doubt there may be as to other words being really derived from imitated sound, there can, of course, be none here. Moreover, there is evidence of the same sound having given rise to imitative words in other families of language, Dahoman *kra-kra*, " a watchman's rattle;" Grebo *grika* " a saw;" Aino *chacha* " to saw;" Malay *graji* " a saw," *karat* " to gnash the teeth," *karot* " to make a grating noise;" Coptic *khrij* " to gnash the teeth," *khrajrej* " to grate." Another form of the imitation is given in the descriptive Galla expression *cacakdjeda*, i. e., " to say *cacak*," " to crack, *krachen*." With this sound corresponds a whole family of Peruvian words, of which the root seems to be the guttural *cca*, coming from far back in the throat; *ccallani*, "to break," *ccatatani*, "to gnash the teeth," *ceacñiy*, "thunder," and the expressive word for "a thunder-storm," *ccaccaccahay*, which carries the imitative process so much farther than such European words as thunder-*clap*, donner-*klapf*. In Maori, *pata* is "to *patter* as water dropping, drops of rain." The Manchu language describes the noise of fruits falling from the trees as *pata pata* (so Hindustani *bhadbhad*); this is like our word *pat*, and we should say in the same manner that the fruit comes *pattering* down, while French. *patatra* is a recognized imitation of something falling. Coptic *potpt* is "to fall," and the Australian *badbadin* (or *patpatin*) is translated into almost literal English as *pitpatting*. On the strength of such non-Aryan languages, are we to assign an imitative origin to the Sanskrit verb-root *pat*, "to fall," and to Greek πίπτω ?

Wishing rather to gain a clear survey of the principles of language-making than to plunge into obscure problems, it is not necessary for me to discuss here questions of intricate detail. The point which continually arises is this,—granted that a particular kind of transition from sound to sense is possible in the abstract, may it be safely claimed in a particular case? In looking through the vocabularies of the world, it appears that most languages offer words which, by obvious likeliness or by their correspondence with similar forms elsewhere, may put forward a tolerable claim to be considered imitative. Some languages, as Aztec or Mohawk, offer singularly few examples, while in others they are much more numerous. Take Australian cases : *walle*, "to wail ; " *bung-bung-ween*, "thunder ; " *wirriti*, "to blow, as wind ; " *wirrirriti*, "to storm, rage, as in fight ; " *wirri*, *birirri*, "the native throwing stick," seemingly so called from its *whir* through the air ; *kurarriti*, "to hum, buzz ; " *kurrirrurriri*, "round about, unintelligible," etc. ; *pitata*, "to knock, pelt, as rain," *pitapitata*, "to knock ; "

wiiti, " to laugh, rejoice "—just as in our own " Turnament
of Tottenham ":—

> " ' *We te he !* ' quoth Tyb, and lngh,
> ' Ye er a dughty man !' "

The so-called Chinook jargon of British Columbia is a language crowded with imitative words, sometimes adopted
from the native Indian languages, sometimes made on the
spot by the combined efforts of the white man and the
Indian to make one another understand. Samples of its
quality are *hŏh-hoh,* " to cough," *kŏ-ko,* " to knock," *kwa-*
lal'-kwa-lal, " to gallop," *muck-a-muck,* " to eat," *chak-chak,*
" the bald eagle " (from its scream), *tsish,* " a grindstone,"
mamook tsish (make *tsish*), " to sharpen." It has been
remarked by Prof. Max Müller that the peculiar sound
made in blowing out a candle is not a favourite in civilized
languages, but it seems to be recognized here, for no doubt
it is what the compiler of the vocabulary is doing his best
to write down when he gives *mamook poh* (make *poh*) as the
Chinook expression for " to blow out or extinguish as a
candle." This jargon is in great measure of new growth
within the last seventy or eighty years, but its imitative
words do not differ in nature from those of the more
ordinary and old-established languages of the world. Thus
among Brazilian tribes there appear. Tupi *cororóng, cururuc,*
" to snore " (compare Coptic *kherkher,* Quichua *ccorcuni*
(ccor)), whence it appears that an imitation of a snore may
perhaps serve the Carajás Indians to express " to sleep "
arourou-cré, as well as the related idea of " night," *roou.*
Again Pimenteira *ebaung,* " to bruise, beat," compares with
Yoruba *gba,* " to slap," *gbá* (gbang) " to sound loudly, to
bang," and so forth. Among African languages, the Zulu
seems particularly rich in imitative words. Thus *bibiza,*
" to dribble like children, drivel in speaking " (compare
English *bib*); *babala,* " the larger bush-antelope " (from the
baa of the female) ; *boba,* " to babble, chatter, be noisy,"
bobi, " a babbler ;" *boboni,* " a throstle " (cries *bo! bo!* com-

pare American *bobolink*); *bomboloza*, "to rumble in the
bowels, to have a bowel-complaint;" *bubula*, "to *buzz* like
bees," *bubulela*, "a swarm of bees, a buzzing crowd of
people;" *bubuluza*, "to make a blustering noise, like frothing beer or boiling fat." These examples, from among
those given under one initial letter in one dictionary of one
barbaric language, may give an idea of the amount of the
evidence from the languages of the lower races bearing on
the present problem.

For the present purpose of giving a brief series of examples of the sort of words in which imitative sound seems
fairly traceable, the strongest and most manageable evidence
is of course found among such words as directly describe
sounds or what produces them, such as sounds of and
names for animals, the terms for action accompanied by
sound, and the materials and objects so acted upon. In
further investigation it becomes more and more requisite to
isolate the sound-type or root from the modifications and
additions to which it has been subjected for grammatical
and phonetical adaptation. It will serve to give an idea
of the extent and intricacy of this problem, to glance at a
group of words in one European language, and notice the
etymological network which spreads round the German
word *klapf*, in Grimm's dictionary, *klappen*, *klippen*,
klopfen, *kläffen*, *klimpern*, *klampern*, *klateren*, *kloteren*,
klitteren, *klatzen*, *klacken*, and so forth, to be matched
with allied forms in other languages. Setting aside the
consideration of grammatical inflexion, it belongs to the
present subject to notice that man's imitative faculty in
language is by no means limited to making direct copies of
sound and shaping them into words. It seizes upon ready-
made terms of whatever origin, alters and adapts them to
make their sound fitting to their sense, and pours into the
dictionaries a flood of adapted words of which the most
difficult to analyse are those which are neither altogether
etymological nor altogether imitative, but partly both.
How words, while preserving, so to speak, the same

skeleton, may be made to follow the variation of sound, of
force, of duration, of size, an imitative group more or less
connected with the last will show—*crick, creak, crack, crash,
crush, crunch, craunch, scrunch, scrannch.* It does not at
all follow that because a word suffers such imitative and
symbolic changes it must be, like this, directly imitative in
its origin. What, for instance, could sound more imitative
than the name of that old-fashioned cannon for throwing
grape-shot, the *patterero!* Yet the etymology of the word
appears in the Spanish form *pedrero*, French *perrier;* it
means simply an instrument for throwing stones (*piedra,
pierre*), and it was only when the Spanish word was adopted
in England that the imitative faculty caught and transformed it into an apparent sound-word, resembling the verb
to *patter.* The propensity of language to make sense of
strange words by altering them into something with an
appropriate meaning (like *beefeater* from *buffetier*) has been
often dwelt upon by philologists, but the propensity to alter
words into something with an appropriate sound has produced
results immensely more important. The effects of symbolic
change of sound acting upon verb-roots seem almost boundless. The verb to *waddle* has a strong imitative appearance,
and so in German we can hardly resist the suggestion
that imitative sound has to do with the difference between
wandern and *wandeln;* but all these verbs belong to a
family represented by Sanskrit *rad*, to go, Latin *rado*, and to
this root there seems no sufficient ground for assigning an
imitative origin, the traces of which it has at any rate lost
if it ever had them. Thus, again, to *stamp* with the foot,
which has been claimed as an imitation of sound, seems only
a "coloured" word. The root *sta*, "to stand," Sanskrit
sthâ, forms a causative *stap*, Sanskrit *sthâpay*, "to make to
stand," English to *stop*, and a foot-*step* is when the foot
comes to a stand, a foot-*stop*. But we have Anglo-Saxon
stapan, stæpan, steppan, English to *step*, varying to express
its meaning by sound in to *staup*, to *stamp*, to *stump*, and
to *stomp*, contrasting in their violence or clumsy weight

with the foot on the Dorset cottage-sill—in Barnes's
poem :—

> " Where love do seek the maiden's even'n vloor,
> Wi' stip-step light, an tip-tap slight
>   Agean the door."

By expanding, modifying, or, so to speak, colouring,
sound is able to produce effects closely like those of gesture-
language, expressing length or shortness of time, strength
or weakness of action, and then passing into a further stage
to describe greatness or smallness of size or of distance,
and thence making its way into the widest fields of metaphor.
And it does all this with a force which is surprising when
we consider how childishly simple are the means employed.
Thus the Bachapin of Africa call a man with the cry *hela !*
but according as he is far or farther off the sound of the
heela ! he-i-la ! is lengthened out.   Mr. Macgregor in his
' Rob Roy on the Jordan,' graphically describes this method
of expression, " ' But where is Zalmouda?' . . . Then
with rough eagerness the strongest of the Dowana faction
pushes his long forefinger forward, pointing straight enough
—but whither? and with a volley of words ends, *Ah-ah-a-
a-a —— a-a*.   This strange expression had long before
puzzled me when first heard from a shepherd in Bashan.
. . . But the simple meaning of this long string of 'ah's '
shortened, and quickened, and lowered in tone to the end,
is merely that the place pointed to is a ' very great way
off.' "   The Chinook jargon, as usual representing primitive
developments of language, uses a similar device in lengthen-
ing the sound of words to indicate distance.   The Siamese
can, by varying the tone-accent, make the syllable *non*,
" there," express a near, indefinite, or far distance, and in
like manner can modify the meaning of such a word as *ny*,
" little."   In the Gaboon, the strength with which such a
word as *mpolu*, " great," is uttered serves to show whether
it is great, very great, or very very great, and in this way,
as Mr. Wilson remarks in his ' Mpongwe Grammar,' " the

comparative degrees of greatness, smallness, hardness, rapidity, and strength, &c., may be conveyed with more accuracy and precision than could readily be conceived." In Madagascar *ratchi* means "bad," but *rátchi* is "very bad." The natives of Australia, according to Oldfield, show the use of this process in combination with that of symbolic reduplication: among the Watchandie tribe *jir-rie* signifies "already or past," *jir-rie jir-rie* indicates "a long time ago," while *jie-r-rie jirrie* (the first syllable being dwelt on for some time) signifies "an immense time ago." Again, *boo-rie* is "small," *boo-rie-boo-rie* "very small," and *b-o-rie boorie* "exceedingly small." Wilhelm von Humboldt notices the habit of the southern Guarani dialect of South America of dwelling more or less time on the suffix of the perfect tense, *yma*, *y—ma*, to indicate the length or shortness of the distance of time at which the action took place; and it is curious to observe that a similar contrivance is made use of among the aboriginal tribes of India, where the Ho language forms a future tense by adding *d* to the root, and prolonging its sound, *kajee* "to speak," Amg *kajēēā* "I will speak." As might be expected, the languages of very rude tribes show extremely well how the results of such primitive processes pass into the recognized stock of language. Nothing could be better for this than the words by which one of the rudest of living races, the Botocudos of Brazil, express the sea. They have a word for a stream, *ouatou*, and an adjective which means great, *ijipakijiou;* thence the two words "stream-great," a little strengthened in the vowels, will give the term for a river, *ouatou-ijiipakiiijou*, as it were, "stream-grea-at," and this, to express the immensity of the ocean, is amplified into *ouatou-ijiipakiijou-ou-ou-ou-ou-ou*. Another tribe of the same family works out the same result more simply; the word *ouatou*, "stream," becomes *ouatou-ou-ou-ou*, "the sea." The Chavantes very naturally stretch the expression *rom-o-wodi*, "I go a long way," into *rom-o-o-o-o-wodi*, "I go a very long way indeed," and when they are called upon to count beyond five they say it is *ka-o-o-oki*, by which they evidently mean it is a very great many. The Cauixanas in one vocabulary are described as saying *kauraungabi* for four, and drawling out the same word for five, as if to say a "long four," in somewhat the same way as the Aponegicrans, whose word for six is *itaircuna*, can expand this into a word for seven, *itaicuũna*, obviously thus meaning a "long six." In their earlier and simpler stages nothing can be more easy to comprehend than these, so to speak, pictorial modifications of words. It is true that writing, even with the aid of italics and capitals, ignores much of this symbolism in spoken language, but every child can see its use and meaning, in spite of the efforts of book-learning and school-teaching to set aside whatever cannot be expressed by their imperfect symbols, nor controlled by their narrow rules. But when we try to follow out to their full results these methods, at first so easy to trace and appreciate, we soon find them passing out of our grasp. The language of the Sahaptin Indians shows us a process of modifying words which is far from clear, and yet not utterly obscure. These Indians have a way of making a kind of disrespectful diminutive by changing the *n* in a word to *l*; thus *twinirt* means "tailless," but to indicate particular smallness, or to express contempt, they make this into *twilirt*, pronounced with an appropriate change of tone; and again, *wana* means "river," but this is made into a diminutive *wala* by "changing *n* into *l*, giving the voice a different tone, putting the lips out in speaking, and keeping them suspended around the jaw." Here we are told enough about the change of pronunciation to guess at least how it could convey the notions of smallness and contempt. But it is less easy to follow the process by which the Mpongwe language turns an affirmative into a negative verb by "an intonation upon, or prolongation of the radical vowel," *tŏnda*, to love, *tŏ̄nda*, not to love; *tŏndo* to be loved, *tŏ̄ndo*, not to be loved. So Yoruba, *biba*, "a great thing," *biba*, "a small thing," contrasted in a proverb, "*Baba* bo, *baba* molle "—"A great

matter puts a smaller out of sight." Language is, in fact,
full of phonetic modifications which justify a suspicion that
symbolic sound had to do with their production, though it
may be hard to say exactly how.

Again, there is the familiar process of reduplication, simple
or modified, which produces such forms as *murmur, pitpat,
helterskelter*. This action, though much restricted in literary
dialects, has such immense scope in the talk of children
and savages that Professor Pott's treatise on it[1] has become
incidentally one of the most valuable collections of facts ever
made with relation to early stages of language. Now up to a
certain point any child can see how and why such doubling is
done, and how it always adds something to the original idea.
It may make superlatives or otherwise intensify words, as in
Polynesia *loa* "long," *lololoa* "very long"; Mandingo *ding*
"a child," *dingding* "a very little child." It makes plurals,
as Malay *raja-raja* "princes," *orang-orang* "people." It
adds numerals, as Mosquito *walwal* "four" (two-two), or
distributes them, as Coptic·*ouai ouai* "singly" (one-one).
These are cases where the motive of doubling is comparatively
easy to make out. As an example of cases much more difficult to comprehend may be taken the familiar reduplication
of the perfect tense, Greek γέγραφα from γράφω, Latin
momordi from *mordeo*, Gothic *haihald* from *haldan*, "to
hold." Reduplication is habitually used in imitative words
to intensify them, and still more, to show that the sound is
repeated or continuous. From the immense mass of such
words we may take as instances the Botocudo *hou-hou-hou-
gitcha* "to suck" (compare Tongan *hūhū* "breast"), *kiaku-
käck-käck* "a butterfly"; Quichua *chiuiuiuiñichi* "wind
whistling in the trees"; Maori *haruru* "noise of wind";
hohoro "hurry"; Dayak *kakakkaka* "to go on laughing
loud"; Aino *shiriushlriukanni* "a rasp"; Tamil *murumuru*
"to murmur"; Akra *ewiewiewiewie* "he spoke repeatedly

[1] Pott, 'Doppelung (Reduplication, Gemination) als eines der wichtigsten
Bildungsmittel der Sprache,' 1862. Frequent use has been here made of this
work.

and continually "; and so on, throughout the whole range of the languages of the world.

The device of conveying different ideas of distance by the use of a graduated scale of vowels seems to me one of great philological interest, from the suggestive hint it gives of the proceedings of the language-makers in most distant regions of the world, working out in various ways a similar ingenious contrivance of expression by sound. A typical series is the Javan: *iki* "this" (close by); *ika* "that" (at some distance); *iku* "that" (farther off). It is not likely that the following list nearly exhausts the whole number of cases in the languages of the world, for about half the number have been incidentally noted down by myself without any especial search, but merely in the course of looking over vocabularies of the lower races.[1]

Javan	.	.	. *iki*, this; *ika*, that (intermediate); *iku*, that.
Malagasy	.		. *ao*, there (at a short distance); *eo*, there (at a shorter distance); *io*, there, (close at hand). *atsy*, there (not far off); *etsy*, there (nearer); *itsy*, this or these.
Japanese	.	.	. *ko*, here; *ka*, there. *korera*, these; *karera*, they (those).
Canarese	.	.	. *iranu*, this; *avanu*, that (intermediate); *avaru*, that.
Tamul	.	.	. *i*, this; *a*, that.
Rajmahali	.	.	. *ih*, this; *ah*, that.
Dhimal	.	.	. *isho*, *ita*, here; *usho*, *uta*, there. *iti*, *idong*, this; *uti*, *udong*, that [of things and persons respectively].
Abchasian	.	.	. *abri*, this; *ubri*, that.
Ossetic	.	.	. *am*, here; *um*, there.
Magyar	.	.	. *ez*, this; *oz*, that.
Zulu	.	.	. *apa*, here; *apo*, there. *lesi*, *leso*, *lesiya*; *abu*, *abo*, *abuya*; &c. = this, that, that (in the distance).

[1] For authorities see especially Pott, 'Doppelung,' p. 30, 47-49; W. v. Humboldt, 'Kawi-Spr.' vol. ii. p. 36; Max Müller in Bunsen, 'Philos. of Univ. Hist.,' vol. i. p. 329; Latham, 'Comp. Phil.' p. 200; and the grammars and dictionaries of the particular languages. The Guarani and Carib on authority of D'Orbigny, 'L'Homme Américain,' vol. ii. p. 268; Dhimal of Hodgson, 'Abor. of India,' p. 69, 79, 115; Colville Ind. of Wilson in 'Tr. Eth. Soc.,' vol. iv. p. 331; Botocudo of Martius, 'Gloss. Brasil.'

Yoruba . . . *na*, this; *ni*, that.
Fernandian . . *olo*, this; *ole*, that.
Tumale . . . *rr*, this; *ri*, that.
                 ngi, I; *ngo*, thou; *ngu*, he.
Greenlandish . . *uv*, here, there (where one points to); *iv*, there,
                 up there [found in comp.].
Snjelpa (Colville Ind.), *axa*, this; *ixi*, that.
Sahaptin . . . *kinn*, here; *kunn*, there.
Mutsun . . . *ne*, here; *nu*, there.
Tarahumara . . *ibe*, here; *abe*, there.
Guarani . . . *nde*, *ne*, thou; *ndi*, *ni*, he.
Botocudo . . *ati*, I; *oki*, thou, you, (prep.) to.
Carib . . . *ne*, thou; *ni*, he.
Chilian . . . *tva*, *vachi*, this; *tivy*, *veychi*, that.

It is obvious on inspection of this list of pronouns and
adverbs that they have in some way come to have their
vowels contrasted to match the contrast of here and there, this
and that. Accident may sometimes account for such cases.
For instance it is well known to philologists that our own
this and *that* are pronouns partly distinct in their formation,
thi-s being probably two pronouns run together, but yet the
Dutch neuters *dit* "this," and *dat* "that," have taken the
appearance of a single form with contrasted vowels.[1]   But
accident cannot account for the frequency of such words in
pairs, and even in sets of three, in so many different languages.   There must have been some common intention at
work, and there is evidence that some of these languages do
resort to a change of sound as a means of expressing change
of distance.   Thus the language of Fernando Po can not
only express "this" and "that" by *olo*, *ole*, but it can even
make a change of the pronunciation of the vowel distinguish
between *o boehe* "this month," and *oh boehe*, "that month."
In the same way the Grebo can make the difference between
"I" and "thou," "we," and "you," "solely by the intonation of the voice, which the final *h* of the second persons
mdh and *ñh* is intended to express."

> *mā* di, I eat; *mdh* di, thou eatest;
> *d* di, we eat; *ñh* di, ye eat.

[1] Also Old High German *diz* and *daz*.

The set of Zulu demonstratives which express the three distances of near, farther, furthest, are very complex, but a remark as to their use shows how thoroughly symbolic sound enters into their nature. The Zulus not only say *nansi,* "here is," *nanso,* "there is," *nansiya,* "there is in the distance," but they even express the greatness of this distance by the emphasis and prolongation of the *ya.* If we could discern a similar gradation of the vowels to express a corresponding gradation of distance throughout our list, the whole matter would be easier to explain; but it is not so, the *i*-words, for instance, are sometimes nearer and sometimes farther off than the *a*-words. We can only judge that, as any child can see that a scale of vowels makes a most expressive scale of distances, many pronouns and adverbs in use in the world have probably taken their shape under the influence of this simple device, and thus there have arisen sets of what we may call contrasted or "differential" words.

How the differencing of words by change of vowels may be used to distinguish between the sexes, is well put in a remark of Professor Max Müller's: "The distinction of gender . . . is sometimes expressed in such a manner that we can only explain it by ascribing an expressive power to the more or less obscure sound of vowels. *Ukko,* in Finnic, is an old man; *akka,* an old woman . . . In Mangu *chacha* is mas. . . . *checke,* femina. Again, *ama,* in Mangu, is father; *eme,* mother; *amcha,* father-in-law, *emche,* mother-in-law."[1] The Coretú language of Brazil has another curiously contrasted pair of words *tsiackö,* "father," *tsaacko* "mother," while the Carib has *baba* for father, and *bibi* for mother, and the Ibu of Africa has *nna* for father and *nne* for mother. This contrivance of distinguishing the male from the female by a difference of vowels is however but a small part of the process of formation which can be traced among such words as those for father and mother. Their conside-

[1] Max Müller, l. c.

rntion leads into a very interesting philological region, that
of " Children's Language."

If we set down a few of the pairs of words which stand
for " father " and " mother " in very different and distant
languages—*papa* and *mama*; Welsh, *tad* (*dad*) and *mam*;
Hungarian, *atya* and *anya*; Mandingo, *fa* and *ba*; Lummi
(N. America), *man* and *tan*; Catoquina (S. America), *payú*
and *nayá*; Watchandie (Australia), *amo* and *ago*—their
contrast seems to lie in their consonants, while many other
pairs differ totally, like Hebrew *ab* and *im*; Kuki, *p'ha* and
noo; Kayan, *amay* and *inei*; Tarnhumarn, *nono* and *jeje*.
Words of the class of *papa* and *mama*, occurring in remote
parts of the world, were once freely used as evidence of a
common origin of the languages in which they were found
alike.   But Professor Buschmann's paper on "Nature-
Sound," published in 1853,[1] effectually overthrew this
argument, and settled the view that such coincidences
might arise again and again by independent production.
It was clearly of no use to argue that Carib and English
were allied because the word *papa*, " father," belongs to
both, or Hottentot and English because both use *mama* for
" mother," seeing that these childish articulations may be
used in just the opposite way, for the Chilian word for
mother is *papa*, and the Tlatskanai for father is *mama*.
Yet the choice of easy little words for " father " and
" mother " does not seem to have been quite indiscriminate.
The immense list of such words collected by Buschmann
shows that the types *pa* and *ta*, with the similar forms *ap*
and *at*, preponderate in the world as names for " father,"
while *ma* and *na*, *am* and *an*, preponderate as names for
" mother."   His explanation of this state of things as
affected by direct symbolism choosing the hard sound for the
father, and the gentler for the mother, has very likely truth
in it, but it must not be pushed too far.   It cannot be, for

[1] J. C. E. Buschmann, 'Ueber den Naturlaut,' Berlin, 1853; and in 'Abh.
der K. Akad. d. Wissensch.' 1852.   An English trans. in 'Proc. Philological
Society,' vol. vi.   See De Brosses, 'Form. des L.,' vol. L p. 211.

instance, the same principle of symbolism which leads the
Welshman to say *tad* for "father" and *mam* for "mother,"
and the Indian of British Columbia to say *maan*, "father"
and *taan*, "mother," or the Georgian to say *mama*, "father"
and *deda*, "mother." Yet I have not succeeded in finding
anywhere our familiar *papa* and *mama* exactly reversed in
one and the same language; the nearest approach to it
that I can give is from the island of Meang, where *mama*
meant "father, man," and *babi*, "mother, woman."[1]

Between the nursery words *pepa* and *mama* and the more
formal *father* and *mother* there is an obvious resemblance in
sound. What, then, is the origin of these words *father* and
mother? Up to a certain point their history is clear. They
belong to the same group of organised words with *vater* and
mutter, *pater* and *mater*, *πατήρ* and *μήτηρ*, *pitar* and *mâtar*, and
other similar forms through the Indo-European family of
languages. There is no doubt that all these pairs of names
are derived from an ancient and common Aryan source, and
when they are traced back as far as possible towards that
source, they appear to have sprung from a pair of words
which may be roughly called *patar* and *matar*, and which
were formed by adding *tar*, the suffix of the actor, to the
verb-roots *pa* and *ma*. There being two appropriate Sanskrit
verbs *pâ* and *mâ*, it is possible to etymologize the two words
as *patar*, "protector," and *matar*, "producer." Now this
pair of Aryan words must have been very ancient, lying back
at the remote common source from which forms parallel to
our English *father* and *mother* passed into Greek and
Persian, Norse and Armenian, thus holding fixed type
through the eventful course of Indo-European history. Yet,
ancient as these words are, they were no doubt preceded
by simpler rudimentary words of the children's language,
for it is not likely that the primitive Aryans did without
baby-words for father and mother until they had an
organized system of adding suffixes to verb-roots to express

[1] One family of languages, the Athapascan, contains both *appa* and *mama*
as terms for "father," in the Tahkali and Tlatskanai.

such notions as "protector" or "producer." Nor can it
be supposed that it was by mere accident that the root-
words thus chosen happened to be the very sounds *pa* and
ma, whose types so often occur in the remotest parts of the
world as names for "father" and "mother." Prof. Adolphe
Pictet makes shift to account for the coincidence thus: he
postulates first the pair of forms *pá* and *má* as Aryan verb-
roots of unknown origin, meaning "to protect" and "to
create," next another pair of forms *pa* and *ma*, children's
words commonly used to denote father and mother, and
lastly he combines the two by supposing that the root-
verbs *pá* and *má* were chosen to form the Indo-European
words for parents, because of their resemblance to the
familiar baby-words already in use. This circuitous process at any rate saves those sacred monosyllables, the
Sanskrit verb-roots, from the disgrace of an assignable
origin. Yet those who remember that these verb-roots are
only a set of crude forms in use in one particular language
of the world at one particular period of its development,
may account for the facts more simply and more thoroughly.
It is a fair guess that the ubiquitous *pa* and *ma* of the
children's language were the original forms; that they were
used in an early period of Aryan speech as indiscriminately
substantive and verb, just as our modern English, which so
often reproduces the most rudimentary linguistic processes,
can form from the noun "father" a verb "to father;" and
that lastly they became verb-roots, whence the words
patar and *matar* were formed by the addition of the
suffix.[1]

The baby-names for parents must not be studied as though
they stood alone in language. They are only important
members of a great class of words, belonging to all times
and countries within our experience, and forming a children's language, whose common character is due to its con-

[1] See Pott, 'Indo-Ger. Wurzelwörterb.' s. v. "pá"; Böhtlingk and Roth,
'Sanskrit-Wörterb.' s. v. *mâtar*; Pictet, 'Origines Indo-Europ.,' part II.
p. 319. Max Müller, 'Lectures,' 2nd series, p. 212.

cerning itself with the limited set of ideas in which little children are interested, and expressing these ideas by the limited set of articulations suited to the child's first attempts to talk. This peculiar language is marked quite characteristically among the low savage tribes of Australia; *mamman* "father," *ngangan* "mother," and by metaphor "thumb," "great toe" (as is more fully explained in *jinnanamman* "great toe," i.e. foot's father), *tammin* "grandfather or grandmother," *bab-ba* "bad, foolish, childish," *bee-bee, beep* "breast," *pappi* "father," *pappa* "young one, pup, whelp," (whence is grammatically formed the verb *papparniti* "to become a young one, to be born." Or if we look for examples from India, it does not matter whether we take them from non-Hindu or Hindu languages, for in baby-language all races are on one footing. Thus Tamil *appá* "father," *ammó* "mother," Bodo *aphá* "father," *áyá* "mother;" the Koech group *nánó* and *náni* "paternal grandfather and grandmother," *mámá* "uncle," *dádá* "cousin," may be set beside Sanskrit *tata* "father," *nana* "mother," and the Hindustani words of the same class, of which some are familiar to the English ear by being naturalized in Anglo-Indian talk, *bábá* "father," *bábá* "child, prince, Mr.," *bíbí* "lady," *dadá* "nurse" (*áyá* "nurse" seems borrowed from Portuguese). Such words are continually coming fresh into existence everywhere, and the law of natural selection determines their fate. The great mass of the *nana's* and *dada's* of the nursery die out almost as soon as made. Some few take more root and spread over large districts as accepted nursery words, and now and then a curious philologist makes a collection of them. Of such, many are obvious mutilations of longer words, as French *faire dodo* "to sleep" (dormir), Brandenburg *wiwi*, a common cradle lullaby (wiegen). Others, whatever their origin, fall, in consequence of the small variety of articulations out of which they must be chosen, into a curiously indiscriminate and unmeaning mass, as Swiss *bobo* "a scratch;" *bambam* "all gone;" Italian *bobò* "something to drink," *gogo* "little boy," for *dede* "to play." These are words quoted by Pott, and for English examples *nana* "nurse," *tata!* "good-bye!" may serve. But all *baby*-words, as this very name proves, do not stop short even at this stage of publicity. A small proportion of them establish themselves in the ordinary talk of grown-up men and women, and when they have once made good their place as constituents of general language, they may pass on by inheritance from age to age. Such examples as have been here quoted of nursery words give a clue to the origin of a mass of names in the most diverse languages, for father, mother, grandmother, aunt, child, breast, toy, doll, &c. The negro of Fernando Po who uses the word *bubboh* for "a little boy," is on equal terms with the German who uses *bube;* the Congo-man who uses *tata* for "father" would understand how the same word could be used in classic Latin for "father" and in mediæval Latin for "pedagogue;" the Carib and the Caroline Islander agree with the Englishman that *papa* is a suitable word to express "father," and then it only remains to carry on the word, and make the baby-language name the priests of the Eastern Church and the great *Papa* of the Western. At the same time the evidence explains the indifference with which, out of the small stock of available materials, the same sound does duty for the most different ideas; why *mama* means here "mother," there "father," there "uncle," *maman* here "mother," there "father-in-law," *dada* here "father," there "nurse," there "breast," *tata* here "father," there "son." A single group of words may serve to show this character of this peculiar region of language: Blackfoot Indian *ninnah* "father;" Greek *νέννος* "uncle," *νέννα* "aunt;" Zulu *nina*, Sangir *nina*, Malagasy *nini* "mother;" Javan *nini* "grandfather or grandmother;" Vayu *nini* "paternal aunt;" Darien Indian *ninah* "daughter;" Spanish *niño, niña* "child;" Italian *ninna* "little girl;" Milanese *ninin* "bed;" Italian *ninnare* "to rock the cradle."

In this way a dozen easy child's articulations, *ba's* and *na's*, *ti's* and *de's*, *pa's* and *ma's*, serve almost as indiscrimi-

nately to express a dozen child's ideas as though they had
been shaken in a bag and pulled out at random to express
the notion that came first, doll or uncle, nurse or grandfather. It is obvious that among words cramped to such
scanty choice of articulate sounds, speculations as to derivation must be more than usually unsafe. Looked at from
this point of view, children's language may give a valuable
lesson to the philologist. He has before him a kind of
language, formed under peculiar conditions, and showing the
weak points of his method of philological research, only
exaggerated into extraordinary distinctness. In ordinary
language, the difficulty of connecting sound with sense lies
in great measure in the inability of a small and rigid set of
articulations to express an interminable variety of tones and
noises. In children's language, a still more scanty set of
articulations fails yet more to render these distinctly. The
difficulty of finding the derivation of words lies in great
measure in the use of more or less similar root-sounds for
most heterogeneous purposes. To assume that two words
of different meanings, just because they sound somewhat
alike, must therefore have a common origin, is even in
ordinary language the great source of bad etymology. But
in children's language the theory of root-sounds fairly
breaks down. Few would venture to assert, for instance,
that *papa* and *pap* have a common derivation or a common
root. All that we can safely say of connexion between
them is that they are words related by common acceptance
in the nursery language. As such, they are well marked in
ancient Rome as in modern England: *papas* "nutricius,
nutritor," *pappus* "senex;" "cum cibum et potum *buas ac
papas* dicunt, et matrem *mammam*, patrem *tatam* (or
papam.)"[1]

From children's language, moreover, we have striking
proof of the power of consensus of society, in establishing
words in settled use without their carrying traces of inherent

[1] Facciolati, 'Lex.' Varro ap. Nonn., ii. 97.

expressiveness. It is true that children are intimately acquainted with the use of emotional and imitative sound, and
their vocal intercourse largely consists of such expression.
The effects of this are in some degree discernible in the
class of words we are considering. But it is obvious that
the leading principle of their formation is not to adopt
words distinguished by the expressive character of their
sound, but to choose somehow a fixed word to answer a
given purpose. To do this, different languages have chosen
similar articulations to express the most diverse and opposite ideas. Now in the language of grown-up people, it is
clear that social consensus has worked in the same way.
Even if the extreme supposition be granted, that the ultimate
origin of every word of language lies in inherently expressive
sound, this only partly affects the case, for it would have to
be admitted that, in actual languages, most words have so far
departed in sound or sense from this originally expressive stage, that to all intents and purposes they might at first
have been arbitrarily chosen. The main principle of
language has been, not to preserve traces of original sound-
signification for the benefit of future etymologists, but to fix
elements of language to serve as counters for practical
reckoning of ideas. In this process much original expressiveness has no doubt disappeared beyond all hope of
recovery.

Such are some of the ways in which vocal sounds seem to
have commended themselves to the mind of the word-maker
as fit to express his meaning, and to have been used accordingly. I do not think that the evidence here adduced
justifies the setting-up of what is called the Interjectional
and Imitative Theory as a complete solution of the problem
of original language. Valid as this theory proves itself
within limits, it would be incautious to accept a hypothesis
which can perhaps satisfactorily account for a twentieth of
the crude forms in any language, as a certain and absolute
explanation of the nineteen-twentieths whose origin remains
doubtful. A key must unlock more doors than this, to be

taken as the master-key. Moreover, some special points
which have come under consideration in these chapters tend
to show the positive necessity of such caution in theorizing.
Too narrow a theory of the application of sound to sense
may fail to include the varied devices which the languages
of different regions turn to account. It is thus with the
distinction in meaning of a word by its musical accent, and
the distinction of distance by graduated vowels. These are
ingenious and intelligible contrivances, but they hardly
seem directly emotional or imitative in origin. A safer way
of putting the theory of a natural origin of language is
to postulate the original utterance of ideas in what may
be called self-expressive sounds, without defining closely
whether their expression lay in emotional tone, imitative
noise, contrast of accent or vowel or consonant, or other
phonetic quality. Even here, exception of unknown and
perhaps enormous extent must be made for sounds chosen
by individuals to express some notion, from motives which
even their own minds failed to discern, but which sounds
nevertheless made good their footing in the language of the
family, the tribe, and the nation. There may be many
modes even of recognizable phonetic expression, unknown
to us as yet. So far, however, as I have been able to trace
them here, such modes have in common a claim to belong
not exclusively to the scheme of this or that particular
dialect, but to wide-ranging principles of formation of language. Their examples are to be drawn with equal cogency
from Sanskrit or Hebrew, from the nursery-language of
Lombardy, or the half-Indian, half-European jargon of
Vancouver's Island; and wherever they are found, they
help to furnish groups of sound-words—words which have
not lost the traces of their first expressive origin, but still
carry their direct significance plainly stamped upon them.
In fact, the time has now come for a substantial basis to be
laid for Generative Philology. A classified collection of
words with any strong claim to be self-expressive should be
brought together out of the thousand or so of recognized

languages and dialects of the world. In such a Dictionary
of Sound-Words, half the cases cited might very likely be
worthless, but the collection would afford the practical
means of expurgating itself; for it would show on a large
scale what particular sounds have manifested their fitness to
convey particular ideas, by having been repeatedly chosen
among different races to convey them.

Attempts to explain as far as may be the primary formation of speech, by tracing out in detail such processes as
have been here described, are likely to increase our knowledge by sure and steady steps wherever imagination does
not get the better of sober comparison of facts. But there
is one side of this problem of the Origin of Language on
which such studies have by no means an encouraging effect.
Much of the popular interest in such matters is centred in
the question, whether the known languages of the world
have their source in one or many primæval tongues. On
this subject the opinions of the philologists who have compared the greatest number of languages are utterly at
variance, nor has any one brought forward a body of philological evidence strong and direct enough to make anything
beyond mere vague opinion justifiable. Now such processes as the growth of imitative or symbolic words form a
part, be it small or large, of the Origin of Language, but
they are by no means restricted to any particular place or
period, and are indeed more or less in activity now. Their
operation on any two dialects of one language will be to
introduce in each a number of new and independent words,
and words even suspected of having been formed in this
direct way become valueless as proof of genealogical connexion between the languages in which they are found.
The test of such genealogical connexion must, in fact, be
generally narrowed to such words or grammatical forms as
have become so far conventional in sound and sense, that
we cannot suppose two tribes to have arrived at them
independently, and therefore consider that both must have
inherited them from a common source. Thus the intro-

duction of new sound-words tends to make it practically of
less and less consequence to a language what its original
stock of words at starting may have been; and the philologist's extension of his knowledge of such direct formations
must compel him to strip off more and more of any language, as being possibly of later growth, before he can set
himself to argue upon such a residuum as may have come
by direct inheritance from times of primæval speech.

In concluding this survey, some general considerations
suggest themselves as to the nature and first beginnings of
language. In studying the means of expression among
men in stages of mental culture far below our own, one of
our first needs is to clear our minds of the kind of superstitious veneration with which articulate speech has so commonly been treated, as though it were not merely the
principal but the sole means of uttering thought. We must
cease to measure the historical importance of emotional
exclamations, of gesture-signs, and of picture-writing, by
their comparative insignificance in modern civilized life, but
must bring ourselves to associate the articulate words of the
dictionary in one group with cries and gestures and pictures,
as being all of them means of manifesting outwardly the
inward workings of the mind. Such an admission, it must
be observed, is far from being a mere detail of scientific
classification. It has really a most important bearing on
the problem of the Origin of Language. For as the
reasons are mostly dark to us, why particular words are
currently used to express particular ideas, language has
come to be looked upon as a mystery, and either occult
philosophical causes have been called in to explain its
phenomena, or else the endowment of man with the faculties of thought and utterance has been deemed insufficient,
and a special revelation has been demanded to put into his
mouth the vocabulary of a particular language. In the
debate which has been carried on for ages over this much-
vexed problem, the saying in the 'Kratylos' comes back to
our minds again and again, where Sokrates describes the

etymologists who release themselves from their difficulties
as to the origin of words by saying that the first words were
divinely made, and therefore right, just as the tragedians,
when they are in perplexity, fly to their machinery and
bring in the gods.[1] Now I think that those who soberly
contemplate the operation of cries, groans, laughs, and
other emotional utterances, as to which some considerations
have been here brought forward, will admit that, at least,
our present crude understanding of this kind of expression
would lead us to class it among the natural actions of man's
body and mind. Certainly, no one who understands anything of the gesture-language or of picture-writing would
be justified in regarding either as due to occult causes, or
to any supernatural interference with the course of man's
intellectual development. Their cause evidently lies in
natural operations of the human mind, not such as were
effective in some long past condition of humanity and have
since disappeared, but in processes existing amongst us,
which we can understand and even practise for ourselves.
When we study the pictures and gestures with which
savages and the deaf-and-dumb express their minds, we can
mostly see at a glance the direct relation between the outward sign and the inward thought which it makes manifest.
We may see the idea of "sleep" shown in gesture by the
head with shut eyes, leant heavily against the open hand ;
or the idea of "running" by the attitude of the runner,
with chest forward, mouth half open, elbows and shoulders
well back ; or "candle" by the straight forefinger held up,
and as it were blown out; or "salt" by the imitated act
of sprinkling it with thumb and finger. The figures of the
child's picture-book, the sleeper and the runner, the candle
and the salt-cellar, show their purport by the same sort of
evident relation between thought and sign. We so far
understand the nature of these modes of utterance, that we
are ready ourselves to express thought after thought by such

[1] Plato Cratylus. 90.

means, so that those who see our signs shall perceive our meaning.

When, however, encouraged by our ready success in making out the nature and action of these ruder methods, we turn to the higher art of speech, and ask how such and such words have come to express such and such thoughts, we find ourselves face to face with an immense problem, as yet but in small part solved. The success of investigation has indeed been enough to encourage us to push vigorously forward in the research, but the present explorations have not extended beyond corners and patches of an elsewhere unknown field. Still the results go far to warrant us in associating expression by gestures and pictures with articulate language as to principles of original formation, much as men associate them in actual life by using gesture and word at once. Of course, articulate speech, in its far more complex and elaborate development, has taken up devices to which the more simple and rude means of communication offer nothing comparable. Still, language, so far as its constitution is understood, seems to have been developed like writing or music, like hunting or fire-making, by the exercise of purely human faculties in purely human ways. This state of things by no means belongs exclusively to rudimentary philological operations, such as the choosing expressive sounds to name corresponding ideas by. In the higher departments of speech, where words already existing are turned to account to express new meanings and shade off new distinctions, we find these ends attained by contrivances ranging from extreme dexterity down to utter clumsiness. For a single instance, one great means of giving new meaning to old sound is metaphor, which transfers ideas from hearing to seeing, from touching to thinking, from the concrete of one kind to the abstract of another, and can thus make almost anything in the world help to describe or suggest anything else. What the German philosopher described as the relation of a cow to a comet, that both have tails, is enough and more than

enough for the language-maker. It struck the Australians,
when they saw a European book, that it opened and shut
like a mussel-shell, and they began accordingly to call
books "mussels" (*mäyäm*). The sight of a steam engine
may suggest a whole group of such transitions in our own
language; the steam passes along "fifes" or "trumpets,"
that is, *pipes* or *tubes*, and enters by "folding-doors" or
valves, to push a "pestle" or *piston* up and down in a
"roller" or *cylinder*, while the light pours from the furnace
in "staves" or "poles," that is, in *rays* or *beams*. The
dictionaries are full of cases compared with which such as
these are plain and straightforward. Indeed, the processes
by which words have really come into existence may often
enough remind us of the game of "What is my thought
like?" When one knows the answer, it is easy enough to
see what *junketting* and cathedral *canons* have to do with
reeds; Latin *juncus* "a reed," Low Latin *juncata*, "cheese
made in a reed-basket," Italian *giuncata*, "cream cheese in
a rush frail," French *joncade* and English *junket*, which are
preparations of cream, and lastly *junketting* parties where
such delicacies are eaten; Greek κάνη, "reed, cane,"
κανών, "measure, rule," thence *canonicus*, "a clerk under
the ecclesiastical rule or canon." But who could guess the
history of these words, who did not happen to know these
intermediate links ?

Yet there is about this process of derivation a thoroughly
human artificial character. When we know the whole facts
of any case, we can generally understand it at once, and see
that we might have done the same ourselves had it come in
our way. And the same thing is true of the processes of
making sound-words detailed in these chapters. Such a
view is, however, in no way inconsistent with the attempt
to generalise upon these processes, and to state them as
phases of the development of language among mankind. If
certain men under certain circumstances produce certain
results, then we may at least expect that other men much
resembling these and placed under roughly similar circum-

stances will produce more or less like results; and this has
been shown over and over again in these pages to be what
really happens. Now Wilhelm von Humboldt's view that
language is an "organism" has been considered a great
step in philological speculation; and so far as it has led
students to turn their minds to the search after general
laws, no doubt it has been so. But it has also caused an
increase of vague thinking and talking, and thereby no
small darkening of counsel. Had it been meant to say that
human thought, language, and action generally, are organic
in their nature, and work under fixed laws, this would be a
very different matter; but this is distinctly not what is
meant, and the very object of calling language an organism
is to keep it apart from mere human arts and contrivances.
It was a hateful thing to Humboldt's mind to "bring down
speech to a mere operation of the understanding." "Man,"
he says, "does not so much form language, as discern with
a kind of joyous wonder its developments, coming forth as
of themselves." Yet, if the practical shifts by which words
are shaped or applied to fit new meanings are not devised by
an operation of the understanding, we ought consistently to
carry the stratagems of the soldier in the field, or the contrivances of the workman at his bench, back into the dark
regions of instinct and involuntary action. That the actions
of individual men combine to produce results which may be
set down in those general statements of fact which we call
laws, may be stated once again as one of the main propositions of the Science of Culture. But the nature of a fact is
not altered by its being classed in common with others of
the same kind, and a man is not less the intelligent inventor
of a new word or a new metaphor, because twenty other
intelligent inventors elsewhere may have fallen on a similar
expedient.

The theory that the original forms of language are to be
referred to a low or savage condition of culture among the
remotely ancient human race, stands in general consistency
with the known facts of philology. The causes which have

produced language, so far as they are understood, are notable for that childlike simplicity of operation which befits the infancy of human civilization. The ways in which sounds are in the first instance chosen and arranged to express ideas, are practical expedients at the level of nursery philosophy. A child of five years old could catch the meaning of imitative sounds, interjectional words, symbolism of sex or distance by contrast of vowels. Just as no one is likely to enter into the real nature of mythology who has not the keenest appreciation of nursery tales, so the spirit in which we guess riddles and play at children's games is needed to appreciate the lower phases of language. Such a state of things agrees with the opinion that such rudimentary speech had its origin among men while in a childlike intellectual condition, and thus the self-expressive branch of savage language affords valuable materials for the problem of primitive speech. If we look back in imagination to an early period of human intercourse, where gesture and self-expressive utterance may have had a far greater comparative importance than among ourselves, such a conception introduces no new element into the problem, for a state of things more or less answering to this is described among certain low savage tribes. If we turn from such self-expressive utterance, to that part of articulate language which carries its sense only by traditional and seemingly arbitrary custom, we shall find no contradiction to the hypothesis. Sound carrying direct meaning may be taken up as an element of language, keeping its first significance recognizable to nations yet unborn. But it may far more probably become by wear of sound and shift of sense an expressionless symbol, such as might have been chosen in pure arbitrariness—a philological process to which the vocabularies of savage dialects bear full witness. In the course of the development of language, such traditional words with merely an inherited meaning have in no small measure driven into the background the self-expressive words, just as the Eastern

figures 2, 3, 4, which are not self-expressive, have driven
into the background the Roman numerals II., III., IIII.,
which are—this, again, is an operation which has its place
in savage as in cultivated speech.   Moreover, to look
closely at language as a practical means of expressing
thought, is to face evidence of no slight bearing on the
history of civilization.   We come back to the fact, so full of
suggestion, that the languages of the world represent
substantially the same intellectual art, the higher nations
indeed gaining more expressive power than the lowest
tribes, yet doing this not by introducing new and more
effective central principles, but by mere addition and
improvement in detail.   The two great methods of naming
thoughts and stating their relation to one another, viz.,
metaphor and syntax, belong to the infancy of human expression, and are as thoroughly at home in the language of
savages as of philosophers.   If it be argued that this
similarity in principles of language is due to savage tribes
having descended from higher culture, carrying down with
them in their speech the relics of their former excellence,
the answer is that linguistic expedients are actually worked
out with as much originality, and more extensively if not
more profitably, among savages than among cultured men.
Take for example the Algonquin system of compounding
words, and the vast Esquimaux scheme of grammatical
inflexion.   Language belongs in essential principle both to
low grades and high of civilization, to which should its
origin be attributed ?   An answer may be had by comparing
the methods of language with the work it has to do.   Take
language all in all over the world, it is obvious that the
processes by which words are made and adapted have far
less to do with systematic arrangement and scientific classification, than with mere rough and ready ingenuity and the
great rule of thumb.   Let any one whose vocation it is to
realize philosophical or scientific conceptions and to express
them in words, ask himself whether ordinary language is an
instrument planned for such purposes.   Of course it is not.

It is hard to say which is the more striking, the want of scientific system in the expression of thought by words, or the infinite cleverness of detail by which this imperfection is got over, so that he who has an idea does somehow make shift to get it clearly in words before his own and other minds. The language by which a nation with highly developed art and knowledge and sentiment must express its thoughts on these subjects, is no apt machine devised for such special work, but an old barbaric engine added to and altered, patched and tinkered into some sort of capability. Ethnography reasonably accounts at once for the immense power and the manifest weakness of language as a means of expressing modern educated thought, by treating it as an original product of low culture, gradually adapted by ages of evolution and selection, to answer more or less sufficiently the requirements of modern civilization.

CHAPTER VII.

Mr. J. S. Mill, in his ' System of Logic,' takes occasion
to examine the foundations of the art of arithmetic. Against
Dr. Whewell, who had maintained that such propositions
as that two and three make five are "necessary truths,"
containing in them an element of certainty beyond that
which mere experience can give, Mr. Mill asserts that " two
and one are equal to three" expresses merely "a truth
known to us by early and constant experience : an inductive
truth ; and such truths are the foundation of the science of
Number. The fundamental truths of that science all rest on
the evidence of sense ; they are proved by showing to our
eyes and our fingers that any given number of objects, ten
balls for example, may by separation and re-arrangement
exhibit to our senses all the different sets of numbers the sum
of which is equal to ten. All the improved methods of teach-
ing arithmetic to children proceed on a knowledge of this
fact. All who wish to carry the child's *mind* along with
them in learning arithmetic ; all who wish to teach
numbers, and not mere ciphers—now teach it through the
evidence of the senses, in the manner we have described."

Mr. Mill's argument is taken from the mental conditions of people among whom there exists a highly advanced arithmetic. The subject is also one to be advantageously studied from the ethnographer's point of view. The examination of the methods of numeration in use among the lower races not only fully bears out Mr. Mill's view, that our knowledge of the relations of numbers is based on actual experiment, but it enables us to trace the art of counting to its source, and to ascertain by what steps it arose in the world among particular races, and probably among all mankind.

In our advanced system of numeration, no limit is known either to largeness or to smallness. The philosopher cannot conceive the formation of any quantity so large or of any atom so small, but the arithmetician can keep pace with him, and can define it in a simple combination of written signs. But as we go downwards in the scale of culture, we find that even where the current language has terms for hundreds and thousands, there is less and less power of forming a distinct notion of large numbers, the reckoner is sooner driven to his fingers, and there increases among the most intelligent that numerical indefiniteness that we notice among children—if there were not a thousand people in the street there were certainly a hundred, at any rate there were twenty. Strength in arithmetic does not, it is true, vary regularly with the level of general culture. Some savage or barbaric peoples are exceptionally skilled in numeration. The Tonga Islanders really have native numerals up to 100,000. Not content even with this, the French explorer Labillardière pressed them farther and obtained numerals up to 1000 billions, which were duly printed, but proved on later examination to be partly nonsense-words and partly indelicate expressions,[1] so that the supposed series of high numerals forms at once a little vocabulary of Tongan indecency, and a warning as to the

[1] Mariner, 'Tonga Islands,' vol. II. p. 390.

probable results of taking down unchecked answers from
question-worried savages.   In West Africa, a lively and
continual habit of bargaining has developed a great power
of arithmetic, and little children already do feats of computation with their heaps of cowries.   Among the Yorubas of
Abeokuta, to say "you don't know nine times nine " is
actually an insulting way of saying "you are a dunce."[1]
This is an extraordinary proverb, when we compare it with
the standard which our corresponding European sayings set
for the limits of stupidity: the German says, "he can
scarce count five "; the Spaniard, "I will tell you how
many make five" (cuantos son cinco); and we have the
same saw in England :—

> "... as sure as I'm alive,
> And knows how many beans make five."

A Siamese law-court will not take the evidence of a witness
who cannot count or reckon figures up to ten; a rule which
reminds us of the ancient custom of Shrewsbury, where a
person was deemed of age when he knew how to count up to
twelve pence.[2]

Among the lowest living men, the savages of the South
American forests and the deserts of Australia, 5 is actually
found to be a number which the languages of some tribes do
not know by a special word.   Not only have travellers
failed to get from them names for numbers above 2, 3, or
4, but the opinion that these are the real limits of their
numeral series is strengthened by the use of their highest
known number as an indefinite term for a great many.
Spix and Martius say of the low tribes of Brazil, "They
count commonly by their finger joints, so up to three only.
Any larger number they express by the word 'many.'"[3]   In

---

[1] Crowther, 'Yoruba Vocab.'; Burton, 'W. & W. from W. Africa,' p. 253,
"O daju dann, o ke mo eman meman.—You (may seem) very clever, (but)
you can't tell 9 × 9."
[2] Low in 'Journ. Ind. Archip.,' vol. I. p. 408; Year-Books Edw. I. (xx.—I.
ed. Horwood, p. 220.
[3] Spix and Martius, 'Reise in Brasilien,' p. 387.

a Puri vocabulary the numerals are given as 1. *omi*; 2. *curiri*; 8. *prica*, "many": in a Botocudo vocabulary, 1. *mokenam*; 2. *uruhū*, "many." The numeration of the Tasmanians is, according to Jorgenson, 1. *parmery*; 2. *calabawa*; more than 2, *cardia*; as Backhouse puts it, they count "one, two, plenty"; but an observer who had specially good opportunities, Dr. Milligan, gives a word found among them for 5, which we shall recur to.[1] Mr. Oldfield (writing especially of Western tribes) says, "The New Hollanders have no names for numbers beyond *two*. The Watchandie scale of notation is *co-ote-on* (one), *u-tan-ra* (two), *bool-tha* (many), and *bool-tha-bat* (very many). If absolutely required to express the numbers three or four, they say *u-tar-ra coo-te-oo* to indicate the former number, and *u-tar-ra u-tar-ra* to denote the latter." That is to say, their names for one, two, three, and four, are equivalent to "one," "two," "two-one," "two-two." Dr. Lang's numerals from Queensland are just the same in principle, though the words are different: 1. *ganar*; 2. *burla*; 8. *burla-ganar*, "two-one"; 4. *burla-burla*, "two-two"; *korumba*, "more than four, much, great." The Kamilaroi dialect, though with the same 2 as the last, improves upon it by having an independent 8, and with the aid of this it reckons as far as 6: 1. *mal*; 2. *bularr*; 8. *guliba*; 4. *bularr-bularr*, "two-two"; 5. *bulaguliba*, "two-three"; 6. *guliba-guliba* "three-three." These Australian examples are at least evidence of a very scanty as well as clumsy numeral system among certain tribes.[2] Yet here again higher forms will have to be noticed, which in one district at least carry the native numerals up to 15 or 20.

It is not to be supposed, because a savage tribe has no current words for numbers above 8 or 5 or so, that therefore they cannot count beyond this. It appears that

[1] Bonwick, 'Tasmanians,' p. 143; Backhouse, 'Narr.' p. 104; Milligan in Papers, etc. Roy. Soc. Tasmania, vol. iii. part ii. 1859.
[2] Oldfield in Tr. Eth. Soc. vol. iii. p. 291; Lang, 'Queensland,' p. 433; Latham, 'Comp. Phil.' p. 352. Other terms in Bonwick, l. c.

they can and do count considerably farther, but it is by
falling back on a lower and ruder method of expression
than speech—the gesture-language.   The place in intellectual development held by the art of counting on
one's fingers, is well marked in the description which
Massieu, the Abbé Sicard's deaf-and-dumb pupil, gives of
his notion of numbers in his comparatively untaught
childhood : "I knew the numbers before my instruction,
my fingers had taught me them.   I did not know the
ciphers ; I counted on my fingers, and when the number
passed 10 I made notches on a bit of wood."[1]   It is thus
that all savage tribes have been taught arithmetic by their
fingers.   Mr. Oldfield, after giving the account just quoted
of the capability of the Watchandie language to reach 4
by numerals, goes on to describe the means by which the
tribe contrive to deal with a harder problem in numeration.
"I once wished to ascertain the exact number of natives
who had been slain on a certain occasion.   The individual
of whom I made the enquiry, began to think over the
names . . . . assigning one of his fingers to each, and it
was not until after many failures, and consequent fresh
starts, that he was able to express so high a number, which
he at length did by holding up his hand three times, thus
giving me to understand that fifteen was the answer to this
most difficult arithmetical question."   Of the aborigines of
Victoria, Mr. Stanbridge says : "They have no name for
numerals above two, but by repetition they count to five ;
they also record the days of the moon by means of the
fingers, the bones and joints of the arms and the head."[2]
The Bororos of Brazil reckon : 1. *couai;* 2. *macouai;* 3.
ouai; and then go on counting on their fingers, repeating
this *ouai.*[3]   Of course it no more follows among savages
than among ourselves that, because a man counts on his

[1] Sicard, 'Théorie des Signes pour l'Instruction des Sourds-Muets,' vol. II.
p. 634.
[2] Stanbridge in 'Tr. Eth. Soc.' vol. I. p. 304.
[3] Martius, 'Gloss. Brasil,' p. 16.

fingers, his language must be wanting in words to express
the number he wishes to reckon.   For example it was noticed
that when natives of Kamchatka were set to count, they
would reckon all their fingers, and then all their toes, so
getting up to 20, and then would ask, " What are we to do
next ? "   Yet it was found on examination that numbers up
to 100 existed in their language.[1]   Travellers notice the use
of finger-counting among tribes who can, if they choose,
speak the number, and who either silently count it upon their
fingers, or very usually accompany the word with the action ;
nor indeed are either of these modes at all unfamiliar in
modern Europe.   Let Father Gumilla, one of the early
Jesuit missionaries in South America, describe for us the
relation of gesture to speech in counting, and at the same
time bring to our minds very remarkable examples (to be
paralleled elsewhere) of the action of consensus, whereby
conventional rules become fixed among societies of men,
even in so simple an art as that of counting on one's fingers.
" Nobody among ourselves," he remarks, " except incidentally, would say for instance ' one,' ' two,' etc., and
give the number on his fingers as well, by touching them
with the other hand.   Exactly the contrary happens among
Indians.   They say, for instance, ' give me one pair of
scissors,' and forthwith they raise one finger ; ' give me two,'
and at once they raise two, and so on.   They would never
say ' five ' without showing a hand, never ' ten ' without
holding out both, never ' twenty ' without adding up the
fingers, placed opposite to the toes.   Moreover, the mode
of showing the numbers with the fingers differs in each
nation.   To avoid prolixity, I give as an example the
number ' three.'   The Otomacs to say ' three ' unite the
thumb, forefinger, and middle finger, keeping the others
down.   The Tamanacs show the little finger, the ring
finger, and the middle finger, and close the other two.
The Maipures, lastly, raise the fore, middle, and ring

[1] Kracheninnikow, 'Kamtchatka.' p. 17.

fingers, keeping the other two hidden."[1]   Throughout the
world, the general relation between finger-counting and
word-counting may be stated as follows. For readiness
and for ease of apprehension of numbers, a palpable
arithmetic, such as is worked on finger-joints or fingers,[2] or
heaps of pebbles or beans, or the more artificial contrivances of the rosary or the abacus, has so great an
advantage over reckoning in words as almost necessarily
to precede it. Thus not only do we find finger-counting
among savages and uneducated men, carrying on a part of
their mental operations where language is only partly able
to follow it, but it also retains a place and an undoubted
use among the most cultured nations, as a preparation for
and means of acquiring higher arithmetical methods.

Now there exists valid evidence to prove that a child
learning to count upon its fingers does in a way reproduce
a process of the mental history of the human race ; that in
fact men counted upon their fingers before they found
words for the numbers they thus expressed; that in this
department of culture, Word-language not only followed
Gesture-language, but actually grew out of it. The evidence in question is principally that of language itself,
which shows that, among many and distant tribes, men
wanting to express 5 in words called it simply by their
name for the *hand* which they held up to denote it, that in
like manner they said *two hands* or *half a man* to denote
10, that the word *foot* carried on the reckoning up to 15,

---

[1] Gumilla, 'Historia del Orenoco,' vol. iii. ch. xlv. ; Pott, 'Zählmethode,'
p. 16.

[2] The Eastern brokers have used for ages, and still use, the method of
secretly indicating numbers to one another in bargaining, "by snipping
fingers under a cloth." "Every joynt and every finger hath his signification," as an old traveller says, and the system seems a more or less artificial
development of ordinary finger-counting, the thumb and little finger stretched
out, and the other fingers closed, standing for 6 or 60, the addition of the
fourth finger making 7 or 70, and so on. It is said that between two brokers
settling a price by thus snipping with the fingers, cleverness in bargaining,
offering a little more, hesitating, expressing an obstinate refusal to go farther,
etc., comes out just as in chaffering in words.

and to 20, which they described in words as in gesture by
the *hands and feet* together, or as *one man*, and that
lastly, by various expressions referring directly to the
gestures of counting on the fingers and toes, they gave
names to these and intermediate numerals. As a definite
term is wanted to describe significant numerals of this class,
it may be convenient to call them "hand-numerals" or
"digit-numerals." A selection of typical instances will
serve to make it probable that this ingenious device was not,
at any rate generally, copied from one tribe by another or
inherited from a common source, but that its working out
with original character and curiously varying detail displays
the recurrence of a similar but independent process of
mental development among various races of man.

Father Gilij, describing the arithmetic of the Tamanacs
on the Orinoco, gives their numerals up to 4: when they
come to 5, they express it by the word *amgnaitòne*, which
being translated means "a whole hand"; 6 is expressed by
a term which translates the proper gesture into words,
itaconò amynaponà tevinitpe "one of the other hand," and
so on up to 9. Coming to 10, they give it in words as
amgna acrponáre "both hands." To denote 11 they stretch
out both the hands, and adding the foot they say *puitta-
ponà tevinitpe* "one to the foot," and so on up to 15, which
is *iptaitòne* "a whole foot." Next follows 16, "one to the
other foot," and so on to 20, *tevin itòto*, "one Indian;" 21,
itaconò itòto jamgnàr bonà tevinitpe "one to the hands of the
other Indian;" 40, *acciaché itòto*, "two Indians," and so on
for 60, 80, 100, "three, four, five Indians," and beyond if
needful. South America is remarkably rich in such evidence of an early condition of finger-counting recorded in
spoken language. Among its many other languages which
have recognizable digit-numerals, the Cayriri, Tupi, Abi-
pone, and Carib rival the Tamanac in their systematic way
of working out "hand," "hands," "foot," "feet," etc.
Others show slighter traces of the same process, where, for
instance, the numerals 5 or 10 are found to be connected

with words for "hand," etc., as when the Omagua uses *pua*,
"hand," for 5, and reduplicates this into *upapua* for 10.   In
some South American languages a man is reckoned by
fingers and toes up to 20, while in contrast to this, there are
two languages which display a miserably low mental state,
the man counting only one hand, thus stopping short at 5;
the Juri *ghomen apa* " one man," stands for 5; the Cayriri
ibichó is used to mean both "person" and 5.   Digit-
numerals are not confined to tribes standing, like these, low
or high within the limits of savagery.   The Muyscas of Bogota
were among the more civilized native races of America,
ranking with the Peruvians in their culture, yet the same
method of formation which appears in the language of the
rude Tamanacs is to be traced in that of the Muyscas, who,
when they come to 11, 12, 13, counted *quihicha ata, bosa,
mica*, i.e., "foot one, two, three."[1]   To turn to North
America, Cranz, the Moravian missionary, thus describes
about a century ago the numeration of the Greenlanders.
" Their numerals," he says, "go not far, and with them the
proverb holds that they can scarce count five, for they
reckon by the five fingers and then get the help of the toes
on their feet, and so with labour bring out twenty."   The
modern Greenland grammar gives the numerals much as
Cranz does, but more fully.   The word for 5 is *tatdlimat*,
which there is some ground for supposing to have once
meant "hand;" 6 is *arfinek-attausek*, " on the other hand
one," or more shortly *arfinigdlit*, " those which have on the
other hand;" 7 is *arfinek-mardluk*, "on the other hand
two;" 13 is *arkanek-pingasut*, "on the first foot three;"
18 is *arfersanek-pingasut*, " on the other foot three;" when
they reach 20, they can say *inuk nǎvdlugo*, "a man ended,"
or *inúp aratai nǎvdlugit*, " the man's outer members ended;"
and thus by counting several men they reach higher

. [1] Gilij; 'Saggio di Storia Americana,' vol. ii. p. 332 (Tamanac, Maypure).
Martius, 'Gloss. Brasil.' (Cayriri, Tupi, Carib, Omagua, Juri, Guachi, Coreto,
Charentes, Maxuruna, Curipuna, Canixana, Carajás, Coruado, etc); Dobri-
hoffer, 'Abipones,' vol. ii. p. 169; Humboldt, 'Monumens,' pl. xliv. (Muysca).

numbers, thus expressing, for example, 58 as *inup pinga-jugsdne arkanek-pingasut*, " on the third man on the first foot three." [1] If we pass from the rude Greenlanders to the comparatively civilized Aztecs, we shall find on the Northern as on the Southern continent traces of early finger-numeration surviving among higher races. The Mexican names for the first four numerals are as obscure in etymology as our own. But when we come to 5 we find this expressed by *macuilli*, and as *ma* (ma-itl) means " hand," and *cuiloa* " to paint or depict," it is likely that the word for 5 may have meant something like " hand-depicting." In 10, *matlactli*, the word *ma*, " hand," appears again, while *tlactli* means half, and is represented in the Mexican picture-writings by the figure of half a man from the waist upward; thus it appears that the Aztec 10 means the " hand-half " of a man, just as among the Towka Indians of South America 10 is expressed as " half a man," a whole man being 20. When the Aztecs reach 20 they call it *cempoalli*, " one counting," with evidently the same meaning as elsewhere, one whole man, fingers and toes.

Among races of the lower culture elsewhere, similar facts are to be observed. The Tasmanian language again shows the man stopping short at the reckoning of himself when he has held up one hand and counted its fingers; for here, as in the two South American tribes before mentioned, *puggana* " man," stands for 5. Some of the West Australian tribes have done much better than this, using their word for " hand," *marh-ra ; marh-jin-bang-ga*, " half the hands," is 5 ; *marh-jin-bang-ga-gudjir-gyn*, " half the hands and one," is 6, and so on; *marh-jin-belli-belli-gudjir-jina-bang-ga*, " the hand on either side and half the feet," is 15. [2] As an example from the Melanesian languages the Maré will serve ; it reckons 10 as *ome re rue tubenine*, apparently " the two

[1] Crane, 'Grünland,' p. 286 ; Kleinschmidt. ' Gr. der Grönl. Spr. ;' Rae in ' Tr. Eth. Soc.' vol. iv. p. 145.
[2] Milligan, l. c. ; G. F. Moore, ' Vocab. W. Australia.' Compare a series of quinary numerals to 9, from Sydney, in Pott, ' Zählmethode,' p. 46.

sides " (i. e. both hands), 20 as *sa re ngome*, "one man," etc.;
thus in John v. 5 "which had an infirmity thirty and eight
years," the numeral 38 is expressed by the phrase, "one
man and both sides five and three."[1]   In the Malayo-
Polynesian languages, the typical word for 5 is *lima* or *rima*
"hand," and the connexion is not lost by the phonetic
variations among different branches of this family of languages, as in Malagasy *dimy*, Marquesan *fima*, Tongan
nima, but while *lima* and its varieties mean 5 in almost all
Malayo-Polynesian dialects, its meaning of "hand" is confined to a much narrower district, showing that the word
became more permanent by passing into the condition of a
traditional numeral. In languages of the Malayo-Polynesian
family, it is usually found that 6 etc., are carried on with
words whose etymology is no longer obvious, but the forms
lima-sa, *lima-zua* "hand-one," "hand-two," have been found
doing duty for 6 and 7.[2]   In West Africa, Kölle's account of
the Vei language gives a case in point. These negroes are
so dependent on their fingers that some can hardly count
without, and their toes are convenient as the calculator squats
on the ground. The Vei people and many other African
tribes, when counting, first count the fingers of their left
hand, beginning, be it remembered, from the little one, then
in the same manner those of the right hand, and afterwards
the toes. The Vei numeral for 20, *mõ bánde*, means obviously "a person (mo) is finished (bande)," and so on with
40, 60, 80, etc. "two men, three men, four men, etc., are
finished." It is an interesting point that the negroes who
used these phrases had lost their original descriptive sense
—the words have become mere numerals to them.[3]   Lastly,
for bringing before our minds a picture of the man counting
upon his fingers, and being struck by the idea that if he
describes his gestures in words, these words may become an

[1] Gabelentz, 'Melanesische Sprachen,' p. 183.
[2] W. v. Humboldt, 'Kawi Spr,' vol. ii. p. 308; corroborated by 'As.
Res.' vol. vi. p. 90; 'Journ. Ind. Archip.' vol. iii. p. 182, etc.
[3] Koelle, 'Gr. of Vei Lang.' p. 27.

actual name for the number, perhaps no language in the
world surpasses the Zulu. The Zulu counting on his
fingers begins in general with the little finger of his left
hand. When he comes to 5, this he may call *edesanta*
"finish hand;" then he goes on to the thumb of the right
hand, and so the word *tatisitupa* "taking the thumb"
becomes a numeral for 6. Then the verb *komba* "to point,"
indicating the forefinger, or "pointer," makes the next
numeral, 7. Thus, answering the question "How much
did your master give you?" a Zulu would say "U *kombile*"
"He pointed with his forefinger," *i.e.*, "He gave me
seven," and this curious way of using the numeral verb is
shown in such an example as "amahasi *akombile*" "the
horses have pointed," *i.e.*, "there were seven of them." In
like manner, *Kijangalobili* "keep back two fingers," *i.e.* 8,
and *Kijangalolunje* "keep back one finger," *i.e.* 9, lead on to
kumi, 10; at the completion of each ten the two hands with
open fingers are clapped together.[1]

The theory that man's primitive mode of counting was
palpable reckoning on his hands, and the proof that many
numerals in present use are actually derived from such a
state of things, is a great step towards discovering the origin
of numerals in general. Can we go farther, and state
broadly the mental process by which savage men, having no
numerals as yet in their language, came to invent them?
What was the origin of numerals not named with reference
to hands and feet, and especially of the numerals below five,
to which such a derivation is hardly appropriate? The
subject is a peculiarly difficult one. Yet as to principle it
is not altogether obscure, for some evidence is forthcoming as to the actual formation of new numeral words,
these being made by simply pressing into the service
names of objects or actions in some way appropriate to the
purpose.

People possessing full sets of inherited numerals in their

[1] Schrœder, 'Gr. for Zulu Sproget,' p. 30; Döhne, 'Zulu Dic.;' Grout,
'Zulu Gr.' See Hahn, 'Gr. des Herero.'

own languages have nevertheless sometimes found it convenient to invent new ones.   Thus the scholars of India,
ages ago, selected a set of words for a memoria technica in
order to record dates and numbers.   These words they chose
for reasons which are still in great measure evident; thus
"moon" or "earth" expressed 1, there being but one of
each; 2 might be called "eye," "wing," "arm," "jaw,"
as going in pairs; for 3 they said "Rama," "fire," or
"quality," there being considered to be three Ramas, three
kinds of fire, three qualities (guna); for 4 were used "veda"
"age," or "ocean," there being four of each recognized;
"season" for 6, because they reckoned six seasons; "sage"
or "vowel" for 7, from the seven sages and the seven
vowels; and so on with higher numbers, "sun" for 12,
because of his twelve annual denominations, or "zodiac"
from its twelve signs, and "nail" for 20, a word incidentally
bringing in a finger-notation.   As Sanskrit is very rich in
synonyms, and as even the numerals themselves might be
used, it became very easy to draw up phrases or nonsense-
verses to record series of numbers by this system of artificial memory.   The following is a Hindu astronomical
formula, a list of numbers referring to the stars of the lunar
constellations.   Each word stands as the mnemonic equivalent of the number placed over it in the English translation.
The general principle on which the words are chosen to
denote the numbers is evident without further explanation :—

> "Vahni tri rtvishu gunendu kritAgnibhúta
> BánAsvinetra çara bhúku yugabdhi rámáh
> RudrAbdhirámagunavodaçatá dviyugma
> Dantá budhairabhihitáh kramaço bhatáráh."

i. e., "Fire, three, season, arrow, quality, moon, four-side of die,
fire, element,

Arrow, Asvin, eye, arrow, earth, earth, age, ocean, Ramas,

11   4   3   3   4   100   2   2

Budra, ocean, Rama, quality, Veda, hundred, two, couple,

32

Teeth: by the wise have been set forth in order the mighty lords."[1]

It occurred to Wilhelm von Humboldt, in studying this curious system of numeration, that he had before his eyes the evidence of a process very like that which actually produced the regular numeral words *one, two, three,* and so forth, in the various languages of the world. The following passage in which, more than thirty years ago, he set forth this view, seems to me to contain a nearly perfect key to the theory of numeral words. "If we take into consideration the origin of actual numerals, the process of their formation appears evidently to have been the same as that here described. The latter is nothing else than a wider extension of the former. For when 5 is expressed, as in several languages of the Malay family, by ' hand' (*lima*), this is precisely the same thing as when in the description of numbers by words, 2 is denoted by 'wing.' Indisputably there lie at the root of all numerals such metaphors as these, though they cannot always be now traced. But people seem early to have felt that the multiplicity of such signs for the same number was superfluous, too clumsy, and leading to misunderstandings." Therefore, he goes on to argue, synonyms of numerals are very rare. And to nations with a deep sense of language, the feeling must soon have been present, though perhaps without rising to distinct consciousness, that recollections of the original etymology and descriptive meaning of numerals had best be allowed to disappear, so as to leave the numerals themselves to become mere conventional terms.

[1] Sir W. Jones in 'As. Res.' vol. ii. 1790, p. 296 ; E. Jacquet in 'Nouv. Journ. Asiat.' 1835 ; W. v. Humboldt, 'Kawi-Spr.' vol. i. p. 19. This system of recording dates, etc., extended as far as Tibet and the Indian Archipelago. Many important points of Oriental chronology depend on such formulæ. Unfortunately their evidence is more or less vitiated by inconsistencies in the use of words for numbers.

The most instructive evidence I have found bearing on the formation of numerals, other than digit-numerals, among the lower races, appears in the use on both sides of the globe of what may be called numeral-names for children. In Australia a well-marked case occurs. With all the poverty of the aboriginal languages in numerals, 3 being commonly used as meaning "several or many," the natives in the Adelaide district have for a particular purpose gone far beyond this narrow limit, and possess what is to all intents a special numeral system, extending perhaps to 9. They give fixed names to their children in order of age, which are set down as follows by Mr. Eyre: 1. Kertameru; 2. Warritya; 8. Kudnutya; 4. Monaitya; 5. Milaitya; 6. Marrutya; 7. Wangutya; 8. Ngarlaitya; 9. Pouarna. These are the male names, from which the female differ in termination. They are given at birth, more distinctive appellations being soon afterwards chosen.[1] A similar habit makes its appearance among the Malays, who in some districts are reported to use a series of seven names in order of age, beginning with 1. *Sulung* ("eldest"); 2. *Awang* ("friend, companion"), and ending with *Kechil* ("little one"), or *Bongsu* ("youngest"). These are for sons; daughters have *Meh* prefixed, and nicknames have to be used for practical distinction.[2] In Madagascar, the Malay connexion manifests itself in the appearance of a similar set of appellations given to children in lieu of proper names, which are, however, often substituted in after years. Males; *Lahimatoa* ("first male"), *Lah-iro* ("intermediate male"); *Ra-fara-lahy* ("last born male"). Females; *Ramatoa* ("eldest female"), *Ra-iro* ("intermediate"), *Ra-fara-vavy* ("last born female").[3] Lastly, the system has

---

[1] Eyre, 'Australia,' vol. II. p. 324 : Shürmann, 'Vocab. of Parnkalla Lang.' gives forms partially corresponding.

[2] 'Journ. Ind. Archip.' New Ser. vol. II. 1858, p. 118 [Sulong, Awang, Itam ('black'), Putah ('white'), Allang, Pandeh, Kechil or Bongsu] ; Bastian, 'Oestl. Asien,' vol. II. p. 494. The details are imperfectly given, and seem not all correct.

[3] Ellis, 'Madagascar,' vol. I. p. 154. Also Andriampaivo, or Lahi-Zan-

come into existence among a North American group of
tribes, the Dacotas or Sioux. There have been found in
use among them the following two series of names for
sons and daughters in order of birth. Eldest son, *Chaské*;
second, *Haparm*; third, *Ha-pe-dah*; fourth, *Chatun*; fifth,
Harka. Eldest daughter, *Wenonah*; second, *Harpen*;
third, *Harpstenah*; fourth, *Waska*; fifth, *We-harka*.
These mere numeral appellations they retain through childhood, till their relations or friends find occasion to replace them by bestowing some more distinctive personal
name.[1]

As to numerals in the ordinary sense, Polynesia shows
remarkable cases of new formation. Besides the well-
known system of numeral words prevalent in Polynesia,
exceptional terms have from time to time grown up. Thus
the habit of altering words which sounded too nearly like a
king's name, has led the Tahitians on the accession of new
chiefs to make several new words for numbers. Thus,
wanting a new term for 2 instead of the ordinary *rua*, they
for obvious reasons took up the word *piti*, "together," and
made it a numeral, while to get a new word for 5 instead of
rima, "hand," which had to be discontinued, they substituted *pae*, "part, division," meaning probably division of
the two hands. Such words as these, introduced in
Polynesia for ceremonial reasons, are expected to be
dropped again and the old ones replaced, when the reason
for their temporary exclusion ceases, yet the new 2 and 5,
piti and *pae*, became so positively the proper numerals of
the language, that they stand instead of *rua* and *rima* in the
Tahitian translation of the Gospel of St. John made at the
time. Again, various special habits of counting in the
South Sea Islands have had their effect on language. The
Marquesans, counting fish or fruit by one in each hand,

---

drina, for last male; Andrianivo for intermediate male. Malagasy *lahy*
'male' = Malay *laki*; Malagasy *vavy*, 'female' = Tongan *fafine*, Maori *wahine*,
'woman;' comp. Malay *bétina*, 'female.'

[1] M. Eastman, 'Dahcotah; or, Life and Legends of the Sioux,' p. xxv.

have come to use a system of counting by pairs instead of
by units. They start with *tauna*, "a pair," which thus
becomes a numeral equivalent to 2; then they count
onward by pairs, so that when they talk of *takau* or 10, they
really mean 10 pair or 20. For bread-fruit, as they are
accustomed to tie them up in knots of four, they begin with
the word *pona*, "knot," which thus becomes a real numeral
for 4, and here again they go on counting by knots, so that
when they say *takau* or 10, they mean 10 knots or 40.
The philological mystification thus caused in Polynesian
vocabularies is extraordinary; in Tahitian, etc., *rau* and
mano, properly meaning 100 and 1,000, have come to
signify 200 and 2,000, while in Hawaii a second doubling
in their sense makes them equivalent to 400 and 4,000.
Moreover, it seems possible to trace the transfer of suitable
names of objects still farther in Polynesia in the Tongan
and Maori word *tekau*, 10, which seems to have been a word
for "parcel" or "bunch," used in counting yams and
fish, as also in *tefuhi*, 100, derived from *fuhi*, "sheaf or
bundle."[1]

In Africa, also, special numeral formations are to be
noticed. In the Yoruba language, 40 is called *ogodzi*, "a
string," because cowries are strung by forties, and 200 is
igba, "a heap," meaning again a heap of cowries. Among
the Dahomans in like manner, 40 cowries make a *kade* or
"string," 50 strings make one *afo* or "head;" these words
becoming numerals for 40 and 2,000. When the king of
Dahome attacked Abeokuta, it is on record that he was
repulsed with the heavy loss of "two heads, twenty strings,
and twenty cowries" of men, that is to say, 4,820.[2]

Among cultured nations, whose languages are most
tightly bound to the conventional and unintelligible

---

[1] H. Hale, 'Ethnography and Philology,' vol. vi. of Wilkes, U. S. Exploring Exp., Philadelphia, 1846, pp. 172, 289. (N.B. The ordinary editions do not contain this important volume.)

[2] Bowen, 'Gr. and Dic. of Yoruba.' Burton in 'Mem. Anthrop. Soc.' vol. i. p. 314.

numerals of their ancestors, it is likewise usual to find
other terms existing which are practically numerals already,
and might drop at once into the recognized place of such, if
by any chance a gap were made for them in the traditional
series. Had we room, for instance, for a new word instead
of *two*, then either *pair* (Latin *par*, "equal") or *couple*
(Latin *copula*, "bond or tie,") is ready to fill its place.
Instead of *twenty*, the good English word *score*, "notch,"
will serve our turn, while, for the same purpose, German
can use *stiege*, possibly with the original sense of "a stall
full of cattle, a sty;" Old Norse *drótt*, "a company,"
Danish, *snees*. A list of such words used, but not grammatically classed as numerals in European languages, shows
great variety: examples are, Old Norse, *flockr* (flock), 5;
sveit, 6; *drótt* (party), 20; *thiodh* (people), 30; *folk*
(people), 40; *öld* (people), 80; *her* (army), 100; Sleswig,
schilk, 12 (as though we were to make a numeral out of
"shilling"); Mid High-German, *rotte*, 4; New High-
German, *mandel*, 15; *schock* (sheaf), 60. The Letts give a
curious parallel to Polynesian cases just cited. They
throw crabs and little fish three at a time in counting them,
and therefore the word *mettens*, "a throw," has come to
mean 3; while flounders being fastened in lots of thirty,
the word *kahlis*, "a cord," becomes a term to express this
number.[1]

In two other ways, the production of numerals from
merely descriptive words may be observed both among
lower and higher races. The Gallas have no numerical
fractional terms, but they make an equivalent set of terms
from the division of the cakes of salt which they use as
money. Thus *tchabnana*, "a broken piece" (from *tchaba*,
"to break," as we say "a fraction"), receives the meaning
of one-half; a term which we may compare with Latin
dimidium, French *demi*. Ordinal numbers are generally
derived from cardinal numbers, as *third, fourth, fifth*, from

---

[1] See Pott, 'Zählmethode,' pp. 78, 99, 124, 161; Grimm, 'Deutsche
Rechtsalterthümer,' ch. v.

three, four, five. But among the very low ones there is to be seen evidence of independent formation quite unconnected with a conventional system of numerals already existing. Thus the Greenlander did not use his " one" to make " first," but calls it *sujugdlek,* " foremost," nor "two" to make " second," which he calls *aipá,* " his companion ; " it is only at "third" that he takes to his cardinals, and forms *pingajuat* in connexion with *pingasut,* 3. So, in Indo-European languages, the ordinal *prathamas,* πρῶτος, *primus, first,* has nothing to do with a numerical "one," but with the preposition *pra,* "before," as meaning simply " foremost ; " and although Greeks and Germans call the next ordinal δεύτερος, *zweite,* from δύο, *zwei,* we call it *second,* Latin *secundus,* "the following" (*sequi*), which is again a descriptive sense-word.

If we allow ourselves to mix for a moment what is with what might be, we can see how unlimited is the field of possible growth of numerals by mere adoption of the names of familiar things. Following the example of the Sleswigers we might make *shilling* a numeral for 12, and go on to express 4 by *groat; week* would provide us with a name for 7, and *clover* for 8. But this simple method of description is not the only available one for the purpose of making numerals. The moment any series of names is arranged in regular order in our minds, it becomes a counting-machine. I have read of a little girl who was set to count cards, and she counted them accordingly, January, February, March, April. She might, of course, have reckoned them as Monday, Tuesday, Wednesday. It is interesting to find a case coming under the same class in the language of grown people. We know that the numerical value of the Hebrew letters is given with reference to their place in the alphabet, which was arranged for reasons that can hardly have had anything to do with arithmetic. The Greek alphabet is modified from a Semitic one, but instead of letting the numeral value of their letters follow throughout their newly-arranged alphabet, they reckon α, β, γ, δ, ε, properly as 1, 2, 3, 4, 5,

then put in ϝ for 6, and so manage to let ι stand for 10,
as ' does in Hebrew, where it is really the 10th letter. Now,
having this conventional arrangement of letters made, it is
evident that a Greek who had to give up the regular 1, 2, 3,
—εἷς, δύο, τρεῖς, could supply their places at once by
adopting the names of the letters which had been settled to
stand for them, thus calling 1 alpha, 2 bêta, 3 gamma, and
so forth. The thing has actually happened; a remarkable
slang dialect of Albania, which is Greek in structure,
though full of borrowed and mystified words and metaphors
and epithets understood only by the initiated, has, as its
equivalent for "four" and "ten," the words δίλτα and
λῶρα.[1]

While insisting on the value of such evidence as this in
making out the general principles of the formation of
numerals, I have not found it profitable to undertake the
task of etymologizing the actual numerals of the languages
of the world, outside the safe limits of the systems of digit-
numerals among the lower races, already discussed. There
may be in the languages of the lower races other relics of
the etymology of numerals, giving the clue to the ideas
according to which they were selected for an arithmetical
purpose, but such relics seem scanty and indistinct.[2] There
may even exist vestiges of a growth of numerals from descriptive words in our Indo-European languages, in Hebrew
and Arabic, in Chinese. Such etymologies have been

[1] Francisque-Michel, 'Argot,' p. 483.
[2] Of evidence of this class, the following deserves attention:—Dobrizhoffer,
'Abipones,' vol. ii. p. 169, gives geyenknate, 'ostrich-toes,' as the numeral
for 4, their ostrich having three toes before and one behind, and netakalek,
'a five-coloured spotted hide,' as the numeral 5. D'Orbigny, 'L'Homme
Américain,' vol. ii. p. 163, remarks:—" Les Chiquitos ne savent compter que
jusqu'à un (toma), n'ayant plus ensuite que des termes de comparaison."
Kölle, 'Gr. of Vei Lang.,' notices that féra means both 'with' and 2, and
thinks the former meaning original, (compare the Tah. piti, 'together,' thence
2). Quichua chunca, 'heap,' chunca, 10, may be connected. Aztec, ce, 1,
ce-tli, 'grain,' may be connected. On possible derivation of 2 from
hand, &c., especially Hottentot t'koam, 'hand, 2,' see Pott, 'Zählmethode,'
p. 29.

s 2

brought forward,[1] and they are consistent with what is
known of the principles on which numerals or quasi-
numerals are really formed.   But so far as I have been able
to examine the evidence, the cases all seem so philologically
doubtful, that I cannot bring them forward in aid of the
theory before us, and, indeed, think that if they succeed in
establishing themselves, it will be by the theory supporting
them, rather than by their supporting the theory.   This
state of things, indeed, fits perfectly with the view here
adopted, that when a word has once been taken up to
serve as a numeral, and is thenceforth wanted as a mere
symbol, it becomes the interest of language to allow it to
break down into an apparent nonsense-word, from which all
traces of original etymology have disappeared.

Etymological research into the derivation of numeral
words thus hardly goes with safety beyond showing in the
languages of the lower culture frequent instances of digit
numerals, words taken from direct description of the gestures of counting on fingers and toes.   Beyond this,
another strong argument is available, which indeed covers
almost the whole range of the problem.   The numerical
systems of the world, by the actual schemes of their arrangement, extend and confirm the opinion that counting on
fingers and toes was man's original method of reckoning,
taken up and represented in language.   To count the
fingers on one hand up to 5, and then go on with a second

[1] See Farrar, 'Chapters on Language,' p. 223. Benloew, 'Recherches sur
l'Origine des Noms de Nombre ;' Pictet, 'Origines Indo-Europ.' part II. ch.
II. ; Pott, 'Zählmethode,' p. 128, etc.; A. v. Humboldt's plausible comparison between Skr. *pancha*, 5, and Pers. *penjeh*, 'the palm of the hand with the
fingers spread out; the outspread foot of a bird,' as though 5 were called
pancha from being like a hand, is erroneous. The Persian *penjeh* is itself
derived from the numeral 5, as in Skr. the hand is called *panchaçâkha*, 'the
five-branched.' The same formation is found in English ; slang describes a
man's hand as his 'fives,' or 'bunch of fives,' thence the name of the game
of fives, played by striking the ball with the open hand, a term which has made
its way out of slang into accepted language.   Burton describes the polite
Arab at a meal, calling his companion's attention to a grain of rice fallen into
his beard. "The gazelle is in the garden," he says, with a smile. "We
will hunt her with the *five*," is the reply.

five, is a notation by fives, or as it is called, a quinary notation. To count by the use of both hands to 10, and thence
to reckon by tens, is a decimal notation. To go on by
hands and feet to 20, and thence to reckon by twenties, is a
vigesimal notation. Now though in the larger proportion of
known languages, no distinct mention of fingers and toes,
hands and feet, is observable in the numerals themselves,
yet the very schemes of quinary, decimal, and vigesimal notation remain to vouch for such hand-and-foot-counting
having been the original method on which they were
founded. There seems no doubt that the number of the
fingers led to the adoption of the not especially suitable
number 10 as a period in reckoning, so that decimal
arithmetic is based on human anatomy. This is so obvious,
that it is curious to see Ovid in his well-known lines putting
the two facts close together, without seeing that the second
was the consequence of the first.

> "Annus erat, decimum cum luna receperat orbem.
> Hic numerus magno tunc in honore fuit.
> Seu quia tot digiti, per quos numerare solemus:
> Seu quia bis quino femina mense parit:
> Seu quod adusque decem numero crescente venitur,
> Principium spatiis sumitur inde novis."[1]

In surveying the languages of the world at large, it is
found that among tribes or nations far enough advanced in
arithmetic to count up to five in words, there prevails, with
scarcely an exception, a method founded on hand-counting,
quinary, decimal, vigesimal, or combined of these. For
perfect examples of the quinary method, we may take a
Polynesian series which runs 1, 2, 3, 4, 5, 5·1, 5·2, &c.; or
a Melanesian series which may be rendered as 1, 2, 3, 4, 5,
2nd 1, 2nd 2, &c. Quinary leading into decimal is well
shown in the Fellata series 1 . . . 5, 5·1 . . . 10, 10·1 . . .
10·5, 10·5·1 . . . 20, . . . 30, . . . 40, &c. Pure decimal
may be instanced from Hebrew 1, 2 . . . 10, 10·1 . . . 20,
20·1 . . . &c. Pure vigesimal is not usual, for the obvious

[1] Ovid. Fast. lib. 121.

reason that a set of independent numerals to 20 would be inconvenient, but it takes on from quinary, as in Aztec, which may be analyzed as 1, 2 . . . 5, 5·1 . . . 10, 10·1 . . . 10·5, 10·5·1 . . . 20, 20·1 . . . 20·10, 20·10·1 . . . 40, &c.; or from decimal, as in Basque, 1 . . . 10, 10·1 . . . 20, 20·1 . . . 20·10, · 20·10·1 . . . 40, etc.[1] It seems unnecessary to bring forward here the mass of linguistic details required for any general demonstration of these principles of numeration among the races of the world. Prof. Pott, of Halle, has treated the subject on elaborate philological evidence, in a special monograph,[2] which is incidentally the most extensive collection of details relating to numerals, indispensable to students occupied with such inquiries. For the present purpose the following rough generalization may suffice, that the quinary system is frequent among the lower races, among whom also the vigesimal system is considerably developed, but the tendency of the higher nations has been to avoid the one as too scanty, and the other as too cumbrous, and to use the intermediate decimal system. These differences in the usage of various tribes and nations do not interfere with, but rather confirm, the general principle which is their common cause, that man originally learnt to reckon from his fingers and toes, and in various ways stereotyped in language the result of this primitive method.

Some curious points as to the relation of these systems may be noticed in Europe. It was observed of a certain deaf-and-dumb boy, Oliver Caswell, that he learnt to count as high as 50 on his fingers, but always "fived," reckoning, for instance, 18 objects as "both hands, one hand, three fingers."[3] The suggestion has been made that the Greek use

[1] The actual word-numerals of the two quinary series are given as examples. Triton's Bay, 1, *somani*; 2, *rokti*; 3, *touwroe*; 4, *faat*; 5, *rimi*; 6, *rim-samon*; 7, *rim-rokti*; 8, *rim-touwroe*; 9, *rim-fani*; 10, *wortyïa*. Lifu, 1. *pacha*; 2, *lo*; 3, *kun*; 4, *thack*; 5, *thabumb*; 6, *lo-acha*; 7, *lo-a-lo*; 8, *lo-kunu*; 9, *lo-thack*; 10, *le-bennete*.

[2] A. F. Pott, 'Die Quinäre und Vigesimale Zählmethode bei Völkern aller Welttheile,' Halle, 1847; supplemented in 'Festgabe zur xxv. Versammlung Deutscher Philologen, etc., in Halle' (1867).

[3] 'Account of Laura Bridgman,' London, 1845, p. 159.

of πεμπάζειν, " to five," as an expression for counting, is a trace of rude old quinary numeration (compare Finnish lokket "to count," from lokke "ten"). Certainly, the Roman numerals I, II, . . . V, VI . . . X, XI . . . XV, XVI, etc., form a remarkably well-defined written quinary system. Remains of vigesimal counting are still more instructive. Counting by twenties is a strongly marked Keltic characteristic. The cumbrous vigesimal notation could hardly be brought more strongly into view in any savage race than in such examples as Gaelic aon deng is da fhichead " one, ten, and two twenties," i.e., 51; or Welsh unarbymtheg ar ugain " one and fifteen over twenty," i.e., 36; or Breton unnek ka tri-ugent " eleven and three twenties," i.e., 71. Now French, being a Romance language, has a regular system of Latin tens up to 100; cinquante, soixante, septante, huitante, nonante, which are to be found still in use in districts with-in the limits of the French language, as in Belgium. Nevertheless, the clumsy system of reckoning by twenties has broken out through the decimal system in France. The septante is to a great extent suppressed, soixante-quatorze, for instance, standing for 74; quatre-ringts has fairly established itself for 80, and its use continues into the nineties, quatre-vingt-treize for 93; in numbers above 100 we find six-vingts, sept-ringts, huit-vingts, for 120, 140, 160, and a certain hospital has its name of Les Quinze-vingts from its 300 inmates. It is, perhaps, the most reasonable explanation of this curious phenomenon, to suppose the earlier Keltic system of France to have held its ground, modelling the later French into its own ruder shape. In England, the Anglo-Saxon numeration is decimal, hund-seofontig, 70; hund-eahtntig, 80; hund-ni-gontig, 90; hund-teontig, 100; hund-enlufontig, 110; hund-twelftig, 120. It may be here also by Keltic survival that the vigesimal reckoning by the " score," threescore and ten, fourscore and thirteen, etc., gained a position in English which it has not yet totally lost.[1]

---

[1] Compare the Rajmahali tribes adopting Hindi numerals, yet reckoning by

From some minor details in numeration, ethnological hints may be gained. Among rude tribes with scanty series of numerals, combination to make out new numbers is very soon resorted to. Among Australian tribes addition makes "two-one," "two-two," express 8 and 4; in Guachi "two-two" is 4; in San Antonio "four and two-one" is 7. The plan of making numerals by subtraction is known in North America, and is well shown in the Aino language of Yesso, where the words for 8 and 9 obviously mean "two from ten," "one from ten." Multiplication appears, as in San Antonio, "two-and-one-two," and in a Tupi dialect "two-three," to express 6. Division seems not known for such purposes among the lower races, and quite exceptional among the higher. Facts of this class show variety in the inventive devices of mankind, and independence in their formation of language. They are consistent at the same time with the general principles of hand-counting. The traces of what might be called binary, ternary, quaternary, senary reckoning, which turn on 2, 8, 4, 6, are mere varieties, leading up to, or lapsing into, quinary and decimal methods.

The contrast is a striking one between the educated European, with his easy use of his boundless numeral series, and the Tasmanian, who reckons 8, or anything beyond 2, as "many," and makes shift by his whole hand to reach the limit of "man," that is to say, 5. This contrast is due to arrest of development in the savage, whose mind remains in the childish state which one of our nursery number-rhymes illustrates in a curiously perfect way. It runs—

> "One's none,
> Two's some,
> Three's a many,
> Four's a penny,
> Five's a little hundred."

twentics. Shaw, l. c. The use of a 'score' as an indefinite number in England, and similarly of 20 in France, of 40 in the Hebrew of the Old Testament and the Arabic of the Thousand and One Nights, may be among other traces of vigesimal reckoning.

To notice this state of things among savages and children
raises interesting points as to the early history of grammar.
W. von Humboldt suggested the analogy between the
savage notion of 3 as "many" and the grammatical use of 3
to form a kind of superlative, in forms of which "tris-
megistus," "ter felix," "thrice blest," are familiar instances.
The relation of single, dual, and plural is well shown pic-
torially in the Egyptian hieroglyphics, where the picture of
an object, a horse for instance, is marked by a single line |
if but one is meant, by two lines ⫿ | if two are meant, by
three lines | | | if three or an indefinite plural number are
meant. The scheme of grammatical number in some of the
most ancient and important languages of the world is laid
down on the same savage principle. Egyptian, Arabic,
Hebrew, Sanskrit, Greek, Gothic, are examples of languages
using singular, dual, and plural number; but the tendency
of higher intellectual culture has been to discard the plan as
inconvenient and unprofitable, and only to distinguish singular and plural. No doubt the dual held its place by inheritance from an early period of culture, and Dr. D. Wilson
seems justified in his opinion that it "preserves to us the
memorial of that stage of thought when all beyond two was
an idea of indefinite number." [1]

When two races at different levels of culture come into
contact, the ruder people adopt new art and knowledge, but
at the same time their own special culture usually comes to
a standstill, and even falls off. It is thus with the art of
counting. We may be able to prove that the lower race
had actually been making great and independent progress
in it, but when the higher race comes with a convenient
and unlimited means of not only naming all imaginable
numbers, but of writing them down and reckoning with
them by means of a few simple figures, what likelihood is
there that the barbarian's clumsy methods should be farther
worked out? As to the ways in which the numerals of the

[1] D. Wilson, 'Prehistoric Man,' p. 616.

superior race are grafted on the language of the inferior,
Captain Grant describes the native slaves of Equatorial
Africa occupying their lounging hours in learning the
numerals of their Arab masters.[1] Father Dobrizhoffer's
account of the arithmetical relations between the native
Brazilians and the Jesuits is a good description of the
intellectual contact between savages and missionaries.
The Guaranis, it appears, counted up to 4 with their native
numerals, and when they got beyond, they would say
"innumerable." "But as counting is both of manifold use
in common life, and in the confessional absolutely indispensable in making a complete confession, the Indians were
daily taught at the public catechising in the church to
count in Spanish. On Sundays the whole people used to
count with a loud voice in Spanish, from 1 to 1,000." The
missionary, it is true, did not find the natives use the
numbers thus learnt very accurately—"We were washing
at a blackamoor," he says.[2] If, however, we examine the
modern vocabularies of savage or low barbarian tribes, they
will be found to afford interesting evidence how really
effective the influence of higher on lower civilization has
been in this matter. So far as the ruder system is complete and moderately convenient, it may stand, but where
it ceases or grows cumbrous, and sometimes at a lower
limit than this, we can see the cleverer foreigner taking it
into his own hands, supplementing or supplanting the
scanty numerals of the lower race by his own. The higher
race, though advanced enough to act thus on the lower,
need not be itself at an extremely high level. Markham
observes that the Jivaras of the Marañon, with native
numerals up to 5, adopt for higher numbers those of the
Quichua, the language of the Peruvian Incas.[3] The cases
of the indigenes of India are instructive. The Khonds
reckon 1 and 2 in native words, and then take to borrowed

[1] Grant in 'Tr. Eth. Soc.' vol. iii. p. 90.

[2] Dobrizhoffer, 'Gesch. der Abiponer,' p. 205 ; Eng. Trans. vol. II. p. 171.

[3] Markham in 'Tr. Eth. Soc.' vol. iii. p. 166.

Hindi numerals. The Oraon tribes, while belonging to a race of the Dravidian stock, and having had a series of native numerals accordingly, appear to have given up their use beyond 4, or sometimes even 2, and adopted Hindi numerals in their place.[1] The South American Conibos were observed to count 1 and 2 with their own words, and then to borrow Spanish numerals, much as a Brazilian dialect of the Tupi family is noticed in the last century as having lost the native 5, and settled down into using the old native numerals up to 8, and then continuing in Portuguese.[2] In Melanesia, the Annatom language can only count in its own numerals to 5, and then borrows English *siks*, *seven*, *eet*, *nain*, etc. In some Polynesian islands, though the native numerals are extensive enough, the confusion arising from reckoning by pairs and fours as well as units, has induced the natives to escape from perplexity by adopting *huneri* and *tausani*.[3] And though the Esquimaux counting by hands, feet, and whole men, is capable of expressing high numbers, it becomes practically clumsy even when it gets among the scores, and the Greenlander has done well to adopt *untrite* and *tusinte* from his Danish teachers. Similarity of numerals in two languages is a point to which philologists attach great and deserved importance in the question whether they are to be considered as sprung from a common stock. But it is clear that so far as one race may have borrowed numerals from another, this evidence breaks down. The fact that this borrowing extends as low as 3, and may even go still lower for all we know, is a reason for using the argument from connected numerals cautiously, as tending rather to prove intercourse than kinship.

At the other end of the scale of civilization, the adoption

<hr />

[1] Latham. 'Comp. Phil.' p. 186; Shaw in 'As. Res.' vol. iv. p. 96; Journ. As. Soc. Bengal,' 1866, part ii. pp. 27, 201, 251.

[2] St. Cricq in 'Bulletin de la Soc. de Geog.' 1853, p. 286; Pott. Zählmethode,' p. 7.

[3] Gabelentz, . 89 Hale, l. c.

of numerals from nation to nation still presents interesting philological points. Our own language gives curious instances, as *second* and *million*. The manner in which English, in common with German, Dutch, Danish, and even Russian, has adopted Mediæval Latin *dozena* (from *duodecim*) shows how convenient an arrangement it was found to buy and sell by the *dozen*, and how necessary it was to have a special word for it. But the borrowing process has gone farther than this. If it were asked how many sets of numerals are now in use among English-speaking people in England, the probable reply would be one set, the regular *one, two, three*, etc. There exist, however, two borrowed sets as well. One is the well-known dicing-set, *ace, deuce, tray, cater, cinque, size*; thus *size-ace* is " 6 and one," *cinques* or *sinks*, " double five." These came to us from France, and correspond with the common French numerals, except *ace*, which is Latin *as*, a word of great philological interest, meaning " one." The other borrowed set is to be found in the Slang Dictionary. It appears that the English street-folk have adopted as a means of secret communication a set of Italian numerals from the organ-grinders and image-sellers, or by other ways through which Italian or Lingua Franca is brought into the low neighbourhoods of London. In so doing, they have performed a philological operation not only curious, but instructive. By copying such expressions as Italian *due soldi, tre soldi*, as equivalent to "twopence," " threepence," the word *saltee* became a recognized slang term for " penny;" and pence are reckoned as follows:—

Oney saltee	. . . .	1d. uno soldo.
Doee saltee	. . . .	2d. due soldi.
Tray saltee	. . . .	3d. tre soldi.
Quarterer saltee	. . . . . .	4d. quattro soldi.
Chinker saltee	. . . .	5d. cinque soldi.
Say saltee	. . . . . .	6d. sei soldi.
Say oney saltee or *setter saltee*	. . .	7d. sette soldi.
Say doee saltee or *otter saltee*	. .	8d. otto soldi.
Say tray saltee or *nobba saltee*	. . .	9d. nove soldi.

Say quarterer saltee or dacha saltee	. .	10d. dieci soldi.
Say chinker saltee or dacha oney saltee	. .	11d. undici soldi.
Oney beong	. .	1s.
A beong say saltee . . .	. .	1s. 6d.
Doue beong say saltee or madsa caroon	. .	2s. 6d. (half crown, matza corona.[1])

One of these series simply adopts Italian numerals
decimally. But the other, when it has reached 6, having
had enough of novelty, makes 7 by "six-one," and so
forth. It is for no abstract reason that 0 is thus made the
turning-point, but simply because the costermonger is
adding pence up to the silver sixpence, and then adding
pence again up to the shilling. Thus our duodecimal coinage
has led to the practice of counting by sixes, and produced a
philological curiosity, a real senary notation.

On evidence such as has been brought forward in this
essay, the apparent relations of savage to civilized culture,
as regards the Art of Counting, may now be briefly stated
in conclusion. The principal methods to which the
development of the higher arithmetic are due, lie outside
the problem. They are mostly ingenious plans of expressing numerical relations by written symbols. Among them
are the Semitic scheme, and the Greek derived from it, of
using the alphabet as a series of numerical symbols, a plan
not quite discarded by ourselves, at least for ordinals, as in
schedules A, B, &c.; the use of initials of numeral words
as figures for the numbers themselves, as in Greek Π and
Δ for 5 and 10, Roman C and M for 100 and 1,000, and
the Indian numerals themselves, if their originals are
the initials of "eka," "dvi," "tri," &c.; the device of
expressing fractions, shown in a rudimentary stage in Greek
γ', δ', for $\frac{1}{3}$, $\frac{1}{4}$, γ'' for $\frac{2}{3}$; the introduction of the cipher or
zero, and the arrangement of the Indian numerals in order,
so that position distinguishes units, tens, hundreds, &c.;
and lastly, the modern notation of decimal fractions by
carrying down below the unit the proportional order which

[1] J. C. Hotten, 'Slang Dictionary,' p. 218.

for ages had been in use above it. The ancient Egyptian
and the still-used Roman and Chinese numeration are
indeed founded on savage picture-writing,[1] while the abacus
and the swan-pan, the one still a valuable school-instru-
ment, and the other in full practical use, have their germ
in the savage counting by groups of objects, as when South
Sea Islanders count with cocoa-nut stalks, putting a little
one aside every time they come to 10, and a large one when
they come to 100, or when African negroes reckon with
pebbles or nuts, and every time they come to 5 put them
aside in a little heap.[2]

We are here expecially concerned with gesture-counting
on the fingers, as an absolutely savage art still in use among
children and peasants, and with the system of numeral
words, as known to all mankind, appearing scantily among
the lowest tribes, and reaching within savage limits to developments which the highest civilization has only improved in
detail. These two methods of computation by gesture and
word tell the story of primitive arithmetic in a way that can
be hardly perverted or misunderstood. We see the savage
who can only count to 2 or 3 or 4 in words, but can go
farther in dumb show. He has words for hands and fingers,
feet and toes, and the idea strikes him that the words which
describe the gesture will serve also to express its meaning,
and they become his numerals accordingly. This did not
happen only once, it happened among different races in
distant regions, for such terms as "hand" for 5, "hand-
one" for 6, "hands" for 10, "two on the foot" for 12,
"hands and feet" or "man" for 20, "two men" for 40, etc.,
show such uniformity as is due to common principle, but
also such variety as is due to independent working-out.
These are "pointer-facts" which have their place and
explanation in a development-theory of culture, while a
degeneration-theory totally fails to take them in. They are
distinct records of development, and of independent deve-

[1] 'Early History of Mankind,' p. 106.
[2] Ellis, 'Polyn. Res.' vol. i. p. 91 ; Klemm, C. G. vol. iii. p. 383.

lopment, among savage tribes to whom some writers on
civilization have rashly denied the very faculty of self-
improvement. The original meaning of a great part of the
stock of numerals of the lower races, especially of those from
1 to 4, not suited to be named as hand-numerals, is obscure.
They may have been named from comparison with objects,
in a way which is shown actually to happen in such forms
as "together" for 2, "throw" for 3, "knot" for 4; but
any concrete meaning we may guess them to have once had
seems now by modification and mutilation to have passed
out of knowledge.

Remembering how ordinary words change and lose their
traces of original meaning in the course of ages, and that in
numerals such breaking down of meaning is actually
desirable, to make them fit for pure arithmetical symbols,
we cannot wonder that so large a proportion of existing
numerals should have no discernible etymology. This is
especially true of the 1, 2, 3, 4, among low and high races
alike, the earliest to be made, and therefore the earliest to
lose their primary significance. Beyond these low numbers
the languages of the higher and lower races show a remarkable difference. The hand-and-foot numerals, so prevalent
and unmistakeable in savage tongues like Esquimaux and
Zulu, are scarcely if at all traceable in the great languages
of civilization, such as Sanskrit and Greek, Hebrew and
Arabic. This state of things is quite conformable to the
development-theory of language. We may argue that
it was in comparatively recent times that savages arrived
at the invention of hand-numerals, and that therefore the etymology of such numerals remains obvious. But
it by no means follows from the non-appearance of such
primitive forms in cultured Asia and Europe, that they did
not exist there in remote ages; they may since have been
rolled and battered like pebbles by the stream of time, till
their original shapes can no longer be made out. Lastly,
among savage and civilized races alike, the general framework of numeration stands throughout the world as an

abiding monument of primæval culture. This framework, the all but universal scheme of reckoning by fives, tens, and twenties, shows that the childish and savage practice of counting on fingers and toes lies at the foundation of our arithmetical science. Ten seems the most convenient arithmetical basis offered by systems founded on hand-counting, but twelve would have been better, and duodecimal arithmetic is in fact a protest against the less convenient decimal arithmetic in ordinary use. The case is the not uncommon one of high civilization bearing evident traces of the rudeness of its origin in ancient barbaric life.

CHAPTER VIII.

MYTHOLOGY.

AMONG those opinions which are produced by a little
knowledge, to be dispelled by a little more, is the belief in
an almost boundless creative power of the human imagination. The superficial student, mazed in a crowd of seemingly wild and lawless fancies, which he thinks to have no
reason in nature nor pattern in this material world, at first
concludes them to be new births from the imagination of the
poet, the tale-teller, and the seer. But little by little, in
what seemed the most spontaneous fiction, a more comprehensive study of the sources of poetry and romance begins
to disclose a cause for each fancy, an education that has led
up to each train of thought, a store of inherited materials
from out of which each province of the poet's land has been
shaped, and built over, and peopled. Backward from our
own times, the course of mental history may be traced

through the changes wrought by modern schools of thought
and fancy, upon an intellectual inheritance handed down to
them from earlier generations. And through remoter
periods, as we recede more nearly towards primitive conditions of our race, the threads which connect new thought
with old do not always vanish from our sight. It is in
large measure possible to follow them as clues leading back
to that actual experience of nature and life, which is the
ultimate source of human fancy. What Matthew Arnold
has written of Man's thoughts as he floats along the River
of Time, is most true of his mythic imagination :—

> " As is the world on the banks
> So is the mind of the man.
>
> Only the tract where he sails
> He wots of : only the thoughts,
> Raised by the objects he passes, are his."

Impressions thus received the mind will modify and work
upon, transmitting the products to other minds in shapes
that often seem new, strange, and arbitrary, but which yet
result from processes familiar to our experience, and to be
found at work in our own individual consciousness. The
office of our thought is to develope, to combine, and to
derive, rather than to create ; and the consistent laws it
works by are to be discerned even in the unsubstantial
structures of the imagination. Here, as elsewhere in the
universe, there is to be recognized a sequence from cause to
effect, a sequence intelligible, definite, and where knowledge
reaches the needful exactness, even calculable.

There is perhaps no better subject-matter through which
to study the processes of the imagination, than the well-
marked incidents of mythical story, ranging as they do
through every known period of civilization, and through all
the physically varied tribes of mankind. Here Maui, the
New Zealand Sun-god, fishing up the island with his en-
chanted hook from the bottom of the sea, will take his place
in company with the Indian Vishnu, diving to the depth of the

ocean in his avatar of the Boar, to bring up the submerged earth on his monstrous tusks; and here Daiame the creator, whose voice the rude Australians hear in the rolling thunder, will sit throned by the side of Olympian Zeus himself. Starting with the bold rough nature-myths into which the savage moulds the lessons he has learnt from his childlike contemplation of the universe, the ethnographer can follow these rude fictions up into times when they were shaped and incorporated into complex mythologic systems, gracefully artistic in Greece, stiff and monstrous in Mexico, swelled into bombastic exaggeration in Buddhist Asia. He can watch how the mythology of classic Europe, once so true to nature and so quick with her ceaseless life, fell among the commentators to be plastered with allegory or euhemerized into dull sham history. At last, in the midst of modern civilization, he finds the classic volumes studied rather for their manner than for their matter, or mainly valued for their antiquarian evidence of the thoughts of former times; while relics of structures reared with skill and strength by the myth-makers of the past must now be sought in scraps of nursery folk-lore, in vulgar superstitions and old dying legends, in thoughts and allusions carried on from ancient days by the perennial stream of poetry and romance, in fragments of old opinion which still hold an inherited rank gained in past ages of intellectual history. But this turning of mythology to account as a means of tracing the history of laws of mind, is a branch of science scarcely discovered till the present century. Before entering here on some researches belonging to it, there will be advantage in glancing at the views of older mythologists, to show through what changes their study has at length reached a condition in which it has a scientific value.

It is a momentous phase of the education of mankind, when the regularity of nature has so imprinted itself upon men's minds, that they begin to wonder how it is that the ancient legends that they were brought up to hear with such reverent delight, should describe a world so strangely

different from their own.   Why, they ask, are the gods and
giants and monsters no longer seen to lead their prodigious
lives on earth—is it perchance that the course of things is
changed since the old days?   Thus it seemed to Pausanias
the historian, that the wide-grown wickedness of the world
had brought it to pass that times were no longer as of old,
when Lykaon was turned into a wolf, and Niobe into a
stone, when men still sat as guests at table with the gods,
or were raised like Herakles to become gods themselves.
Up to modern times, the hypothesis of a changed world has
more or less availed to remove the difficulty of belief in
ancient wonder-tales.   Yet though always holding firmly a
partial ground, its application was soon limited for these
obvious reasons, that it justified falsehood and truth alike
with even-handed favour, and utterly broke down that
barrier of probability which in some measure has always
separated fact from fancy.   The Greek mind found other
outlets to the problem.   In the words of Mr. Grote, the
ancient legends were cast back into an undefined past, to
take rank among the hallowed traditions of divine or heroic
antiquity, gratifying to extol by rhetoric, but repulsive to
scrutinize in argument.   Or they were transformed into
shapes more familiar to experience, as when Plutarch,
telling the tale of Theseus, begs for indulgent hearers to
accept mildly the archaic story, and assures them that he
has set himself to purify it by reason, that it may receive
the aspect of history.[1]   This process of giving fable the
aspect of history, this profitless art of transforming untrue
impossibilities into untrue possibilities, has been carried on
by the ancients, and by the moderns after them, especially
according to the two following methods.

Men have for ages been more or less conscious of that
great mental district lying between disbelief and belief, where
room is found for all mythic interpretation, good or bad.
It being admitted that some legend is not the real narrative

---

[1] Grote, 'History of Greece,' vol. i. chaps. ix. xi. ; Pausanias viii. 2; Plutarch. Theseus 1.

which it purports to be, they do not thereupon wipe it out
from book and memory as simply signifying nothing, but
they ask what original sense may be in it, out of what older
story it may be a second growth, or what actual event or
current notion may have suggested its development into the
state in which they find it? Such questions, however,
prove almost as easy to answer plausibly as to set; and
then, in the endeavour to obtain security that these off-hand
answers are the true ones, it becomes evident that the problem
admits of an indefinite number of apparent solutions, not
only different but incompatible. This radical uncertainty
in the speculative interpretation of myths is forcibly stated
by Lord Bacon, in the preface to his 'Wisdom of the
Ancients.' "Neither am I ignorant," he says, "how fickle
and inconstant a thing fiction is, as being subject to be
drawn and wrested any way, and how great the commodity
of wit and discourse is, that is able to apply things well, yet
so as never meant by the first authors." The need of such
a caution may be judged of from the very treatise to which
Bacon prefaced it, for there he is to be seen plunging head-
long into the very pitfall of which he had so discreetly
warned his disciples. He undertakes, after the manner of
not a few philosophers before and after him, to interpret
the classic myths of Greece as moral allegories. Thus the
story of Memnon depicts the destinies of rash young men
of promise; while Perseus symbolizes war, and when of the
three Gorgons he attacks only the mortal one, this means
that only practicable wars are to be attempted. It would
not be easy to bring out into a stronger light the difference
between a fanciful application of a myth, and its analysis
into its real elements. For here, where the interpreter believed himself to be reversing the process of myth-making,
he was in fact only carrying it a stage farther in the old
direction, and out of the suggestion of one train of thought
evolving another connected with it by some more or less
remote analogy. Any of us may practise this simple art,
each according to his own fancy. If, for instance, political

economy happens for the moment to lie uppermost in our mind, we may with due gravity expound the story of Perseus as an allegory of trade: Perseus himself is Labour, and he finds Andromeda, who is Profit, chained and ready to be devoured by the monster Capital; he rescues her, and carries her off in triumph. To know anything of poetry or of mysticism is to know this reproductive growth of fancy as an admitted and admired intellectual process. But when it comes to sober investigation of the processes of mythology, the attempt to penetrate to the foundation of an old fancy will scarcely be helped by burying it yet deeper underneath a new one.

Nevertheless, allegory has had a share in the development of myths which no interpreter must overlook. The fault of the rationalizer lay in taking allegory beyond its proper action, and applying it as a universal solvent to reduce dark stories to transparent sense. The same is true of the other great rationalizing process, founded also, to some extent, on fact. Nothing is more certain than that real personages often have mythic incidents tacked on to their history, and that they even figure in tales of which the very substance is mythic. No one disbelieves in the existence of Solomon because of his legendary adventure in the Valley of Apes, nor of Attila because he figures in the Nibelungen Lied. Sir Francis Drake is made not less but more real to us by the cottage tales which tell how he still leads the Wild Hunt over Dartmoor, and still rises to his revels when they beat at Buckland Abbey the drum that he carried round the world. The mixture of fact and fable in traditions of great men shows that legends containing monstrous fancy may yet have a basis in historic fact. But, on the strength of this, the mythologists arranged systematic methods of reducing legend to history, and thereby contrived at once to stultify the mythology they professed to explain, and to ruin the history they professed to develope. So far as the plan consisted in mere suppression of the marvellous, a notion of its trustworthiness may be obtained, as Mr. G. W. Cox well

puts it, in rationalizing Jack the Giant-Killer by leaving
out the giants. So far as it treated legendary wonders as
being matter-of-fact disguised in metaphor, the mere naked
statement of the results of the method is to our minds its
most cruel criticism. Thus already in classic times men
were declaring that Atlas was a great astronomer who taught
the use of the sphere, and was therefore represented with
the world resting on his shoulders. To such a pass had
come the decay of myth into commonplace, that the great
Heaven-god of the Aryan race, the living personal Heaven
himself, Zeus the Almighty, was held to have been a king
of Krete, and the Kretans could show to wondering strangers
his sepulchre, with the very name of the great departed
inscribed upon it. The modern "euhemerists" (so called
from Eubemeros of Messenia, a great professor of the art
in the time of Alexander) in part adopted the old interpretations, and sometimes fairly left their Greek and Roman
teachers behind in the race after prosaic possibility. They
inform us that Jove smiting the giants with his thunderbolts
was a king repressing a sedition; Danae's golden shower
was the money with which her guards were bribed; Prometheus made clay images, whence it was hyperbolically
said that he created man and woman out of clay; and when
Daidalos was related to have made figures which walked,
this meant that he improved the shapeless old statues, and
separated their legs. Old men still remember as the guides
of educated opinion in their youth the learned books in
which these fancies are solemnly put forth; some of our
school manuals still go on quoting them with respect, and a
few straggling writers carry on a remnant of the once
famous system of which the Abbé Dauier was so distinguished an exponent.[1] But it has of late fallen on evil days,
and mythologists in authority have treated it in so high-
handed a fashion as to bring it into general contempt. So
far has the feeling against the abuse of such argument gone,

---

[1] See Banier, 'La Mythologie et les Fables expliquées par l'Histoire,' Paris,
1738; Lempriere, 'Classical Dictionary,' etc.

that it is now really desirable to warn students that it has a reasonable as well as an unreasonable side, and to remind them that some wild legends undoubtedly do, and therefore that many others may, contain a kernel of historic truth.

Learned and ingenious as the old systems of rationalizing myth have been, there is no doubt that they are in great measure destined to be thrown aside. It is not that their interpretations are proved impossible, but that mere possibility in mythological speculation is now seen to be such a worthless commodity, that every investigator devoutly wishes there were not such plenty of it. In assigning origins to myths, as in every other scientific enquiry, the fact is that increased information, and the use of more stringent canons of evidence, have raised far above the old level the standard of probability required to produce conviction. There are many who describe our own time as an unbelieving time, but it is by no means sure that posterity will accept the verdict. No doubt it is a sceptical and a critical time, but then scepticism and criticism are the very conditions for the attainment of reasonable belief. Thus, where the positive credence of ancient history has been affected, it is not that the power of receiving evidence has diminished, but that the consciousness of ignorance has grown. We are being trained to the facts of physical science, which we can test and test again, and we feel it a fall from this high level of proof when we turn our minds to the old records which elude such testing, and are even admitted on all hands to contain statements not to be relied on. Historical criticism becomes hard and exacting, even where the chronicle records events not improbable in themselves; and the moment that the story falls out of our scheme of the world's habitual course, the ever repeated question comes out to meet it—Which is the more likely, that so unusual an event should have really happened, or that the record should be misunderstood or false? Thus we gladly seek for sources of history in antiquarian relics, in undesigned and collateral proofs, in documents not written

to be chronicles. But can any reader of geology say we are
too incredulous to believe wonders, if the evidence carry
any fair warrant of their truth? Was there ever a time
when lost history was being reconstructed, and existing
history rectified, more zealously than they are now by a
whole army of travellers, excavators, searchers of old
charters, and explorers of forgotten dialects? The very
myths that were discarded as lying fables, prove to be
sources of history in ways that their makers and transmitters
little dreamed of. Their meaning has been misunderstood,
but they have a meaning. Every tale that was ever told
has a meaning for the times it belongs to; even a lie, as
the Spanish proverb says, is a lady of birth ("la mentira es
hija de algo"). Thus, as evidence of the development of
thought, as records of long past belief and usage, even in
some measure as materials for the history of the nations
owning them, the old myths have fairly taken their place
among historic facts; and with such the modern historian,
so able and willing to pull down, is also able and willing to
rebuild.

Of all things, what mythologic work needs is breadth of
knowledge and of handling. Interpretations made to suit a
narrow view reveal their weakness when exposed to a wide
one. See Herodotus rationalizing the story of the infant
Cyrus, exposed and suckled by a bitch; he simply relates
that the child was brought up by a herdsman's wife named
Spakô (in Greek Kynô), whence arose the fable that a real
bitch rescued and fed him. So far so good—for a single
case. But does the story of Romulus and Remus likewise
record a real event, mystified in the self-same manner by
a pun on a nurse's name, which happened to be a she-
beast's? Did the Roman twins also really happen to be
exposed, and brought up by a foster-mother who happened
to be called Lupa? Positively, the 'Lempriere's Dictionary' of our youth (I quote the 16th edition of 1831) gravely
gives this as the origin of the famous legend. Yet, if we
look properly into the matter, we find that these two stories

are but specimens of a widespread mythic group, itself only
a section of that far larger body of traditions in which
exposed infants are saved to become national heroes.   For
other examples, Slavonic folk-lore tells of the she-wolf and
she-bear that suckled those superhuman twins, Waligora
the mountain-roller and Wyrwidab the oak-uprooter;
Germany has its legend of Dieterich, called Wolfdieterich
from his foster-mother the she-wolf; in India, the episode
recurs in the tales of Satavahana and the lioness, and Sing-
Baba and the tigress; legend tells of Burta-Chino, the boy
who was cast into a lake, and preserved by a she-wolf to
become founder of the Turkish kingdom; and even the
savage Yuracarés of Brazil tell of their divine hero Tiri,
who was suckled by a jaguar.[1]

Scientific myth-interpretation, on the contrary, is actually
strengthened by such comparison of similar cases.   Where
the effect of new knowledge has been to construct rather
than to destroy, it is found that there are groups of myth-
interpretations for which wider and deeper evidence makes
a wider and deeper foundation.   The principles which
underlie a solid system of interpretation are really few and
simple.   The treatment of similar myths from different
regions, by arranging them in large compared groups, makes
it possible to trace in mythology the operation of imaginative
processes recurring with the evident regularity of mental
law; and thus stories of which a single instance would have
been a mere isolated curiosity, take their place among
well-marked and consistent structures of the human mind.
Evidence like this will again and again drive us to admit
that even as "truth is stranger than fiction," so myth may
be more uniform than history.

There lies within our reach, moreover, the evidence of

[1] Hanusch, 'Slav. Myth.' p. 323; Grimm, D. M. p. 363; Latham,
'Descr. Eth.' vol. ii. p. 448; I. J. Schmidt, 'Forschungen,' p. 13; J. G.
Muller, 'Amer. Urrelig.' p. 268.   See also Plutarch. Parallela xxxvi.;
Campbell, 'Highland Tales,' vol. i. p. 278; Max Müller, 'Chips,' vol. ii. p.
169; Tylor, 'Wild Men and Beast-children,' in Anthropological Review, May
1863.

races both ancient and modern, who so faithfully represent
the state of thought to which myth-development belongs,
as still to keep up both the consciousness of meaning in
their old myths, and the unstrained unaffected habit of
creating new ones. Savages have been for untold ages, and
still are, living in the myth-making stage of the human
mind. It was through sheer ignorance and neglect of this
direct knowledge how and by what manner of men myths
are really made, that their simple philosophy has come to
be buried under masses of commentators' rubbish. Though
never wholly lost, the secret of mythic interpretation was
all but forgotten. Its recovery has been mainly due to
modern students who have with vast labour and skill
searched the ancient language, poetry, and folk-lore of our
own race, from the cottage tales collected by the brothers
Grimm to the Rig-Veda edited by Max Müller. Aryan
language and literature now open out with wonderful
range and clearness a view of the early stages of mythology,
displaying those primitive germs of the poetry of nature,
which later ages swelled and distorted till childlike fancy
sank into superstitious mystery. It is not proposed here
to enquire specially into this Aryan mythology, of which so
many eminent students have treated, but to compare some of
the most important developments of mythology among the
various races of mankind, especially in order to determine
the general relation of the myths of savage tribes to the
myths of civilized nations. The argument does not aim at a
general discussion of the mythology of the world, numbers
of important topics being left untouched which would have
to be considered in a general treatise. The topics chosen
are mostly such as are fitted, by the strictness of evidence
and argument applying to them, to make a sound basis for
the treatment of myth as bearing on the general ethnological problem of the development of civilization. The
general thesis maintained is that Myth arose in the savage
condition prevalent in remote ages among the whole human
race, that it remains comparatively unchanged among the

modern rude tribes who have departed least from these primitive conditions, while higher and later grades of civilization, partly by retaining its actual principles, and partly by carrying on its inherited results in the form of ancestral tradition, continued it not merely in toleration but in honour.

To the human intellect in its early childlike state may be assigned the origin and first development of myth. It is true that learned critics, taking up the study of mythology at the wrong end, have almost habitually failed to appreciate its childlike ideas, conventionalized in poetry or disguised as chronicle. Yet the more we compare the mythic fancies of different nations, in order to discern the common thoughts which underlie their resemblances, the more ready we shall be to admit that in our childhood we dwelt at the very gates of the realm of myth. In mythology, the child is, in a deeper sense than we are apt to use the phrase in, father of the man. Thus, when in surveying the quaint fancies and wild legends of the lower tribes, we find the mythology of the world at once in its most distinct and most rudimentary form, we may here again claim the savage as a representative of the childhood of the human race. Here Ethnology and Comparative Mythology go hand in hand, and the development of Myth forms a consistent part of the development of Culture. If savage races, as the nearest modern representatives of primæval culture, show in the most distinct and unchanged state the rudimentary mythic conceptions thence to be traced onward in the course of civilization, then it is reasonable for students to begin, so far as may be, at the beginning. Savage mythology may be taken as a basis, and then the myths of more civilized races may be displayed as compositions sprung from like origin, though more advanced in art. This mode of treatment proves satisfactory through almost all the branches of the enquiry, and eminently so in investigating those most beautiful of poetic fictions, to which may be given the title of Nature-Myths.

First and foremost among the causes which transfigure into myths the facts of daily experience, is the belief in the animation of all nature, rising at its highest pitch to personification. This, no occasional or hypothetical action of the mind, is inextricably bound in with that primitive mental state where man recognizes in every detail of his world the operation of personal life and will. This doctrine of Animism will be considered elsewhere as affecting philosophy and religion, but here we have only to do with its bearing on mythology. To the lower tribes of man, sun and stars, trees and rivers, winds and clouds, become personal animate creatures, leading lives conformed to human or animal analogies, and performing their special functions in the universe with the aid of limbs like beasts, or of artificial instruments like men; or what men's eyes behold is but the instrument to be used or the material to be shaped, while behind it there stands some prodigious but yet half-human creature, who grasps it with his hands or blows it with his breath. The basis on which such ideas as these are built is not to be narrowed down to poetic fancy and transformed metaphor. They rest upon a broad philosophy of nature, early and crude indeed, but thoughtful, consistent, and quite really and seriously meant.

Let us put this doctrine of universal vitality to a test of direct evidence, lest readers new to the subject should suppose it a modern philosophical fiction, or think that if the lower races really express such a notion, they may do so only as a poetical way of talking. Even in civilized countries, it makes its appearance as the child's early theory of the outer world, nor can we fail to see how this comes to pass. The first beings that children learn to understand something of are human beings, and especially their own selves; and the first explanation of all events will be the human explanation, as though chairs and sticks and wooden horses were actuated by the same sort of personal will as nurses and children and kittens. Thus infants take their first step in mythology by contriving, like Cosette

with her doll, " se figurer que quelque chose est quelqu'un ; "
and the way in which this childlike theory has to be
unlearnt in the course of education shows how primitive it
is. Even among full-grown civilized Europeans, as Mr.
Grote appositely remarks, "The force of momentary
passion will often suffice to supersede the acquired habit,
and even an intelligent man may be impelled in a moment
of agonizing pain to kick or beat the lifeless object from
which he has suffered." In such matters the savage mind
well represents the childish stage. The wild native of
Brazil would bite the stone he stumbled over, or the arrow
that had wounded him. Such a mental condition may be
traced along the course of history, not merely in impulsive
habit, but in formally enacted law. The rude Kukis of
Southern Asia were very scrupulous in carrying out their
simple law of vengeance, life for life; if a tiger killed a
Kuki, his family were in disgrace till they had retaliated by
killing and eating this tiger, or another; but further, if a
man was killed by a fall from a tree, his relatives would
take their revenge by cutting the tree down, and scattering
it in chips.[1]   A modern king of Cochin-China, when one of
his ships sailed badly, used to put it in the pillory as he
would any other criminal.[2]   In classical times, the stories
of Xerxes flogging the Hellespont and Cyrus draining the
Gyndes occur as cases in point, but one of the regular
Athenian legal proceedings is a yet more striking relic.
A court of justice was held at the Prytaneum, to try any
inanimate object, such as an axe or a piece of wood or
stone, which had caused the death of anyone without
proved human agency, and this wood or stone, if condemned, was in solemn form cast beyond the border.[3]
The spirit of this remarkable procedure reappears in the
old English law (repealed in the present reign), whereby not

[1] Macrae in 'As. Res.' vol vii. p. 189.
[2] Bastian, 'Oestl. Asien,' vol. i. p. 51.
[3] Grote, vol. iii. p. 104 ; vol. v. p. 22 ; Herodot. i. 159 ; vii. 34 ; Porphyr.
de Abstinentia, ii. 30 ; Pausan. i. 28 ; Pollux, 'Onomasticon.'

only a beast that kills a man, but a cart-wheel that runs over him, or a tree that falls on him and kills him, is deodand, or given to God, i. e., forfeited and sold for the poor: as Bracton says, " Omnia quæ movent ad mortem sunt Deodanda." Dr. Reid comments on this law, declaring that its intention was not to punish the ox or the cart as criminal, but " to inspire the people with a sacred regard to the life of man." [1] But his argument rather serves to show the worthlessness of off-hand speculations on the origin of law, like his own in this matter, unaided by the indispensable evidence of history and ethnography. An example from modern folklore shows still at its utmost stretch this primitive fancy that inert things are alive and conscious. The pathetic custom of " telling the bees" when the master or mistress of a house dies, is not unknown in our own country. But in Germany the idea is more fully worked out; and not only is the sad message given to every bee-hive in the garden and every beast in the stall, but every sack of corn must be touched and everything in the house shaken, that they may know the master is gone. [2]

Animism takes in several doctrines which so forcibly conduce to personification, that savages and barbarians, apparently without an effort, can give consistent individual life to phenomena that our utmost stretch of fancy only avails to personify in conscious metaphor. An idea of pervading life and will in nature far outside modern limits, a belief in personal souls animating even what we call inanimate bodies, a theory of transmigration of souls as well in life as after death, a sense of crowds of spiritual beings sometimes flitting through the air, but sometimes also inhabiting trees and rocks and waterfalls, and so lending their own personality to such material objects—all these thoughts work in mythology with such manifold coincidence, as to make it hard indeed to unravel their separate action.

[1] Reid, 'Essays,' vol. iii. p. 113.
[2] Waitke, 'Volksberglaube,' p. 210.

Such animistic origin of nature-myths shows out very
clearly in the great cosmic group of Sun, Moon, and Stars.
In early philosophy throughout the world, the Sun and
Moon are alive and as it were human in their nature.
Usually contrasted as male and female, they nevertheless
differ in the sex assigned to each, as well as in their
relations to one another. Among the Mbocobis of South
America, the Moon is a man and the Sun his wife, and the
story is told how she once fell down and an Indian put her
up again, but she fell a second time and set the forest
blazing in a deluge of fire.[1] To display the opposite of this
idea, and at the same time to illustrate the vivid fancy
with which savages can personify the heavenly bodies, we
may read the following discussion concerning eclipses,
between certain Algonquin Indians and one of the early
Jesuit missionaries to Canada in the 17th century, Father
Le Jeune :—"Je leur ay demandé d'où venoit l'Eclipse de
Lune et de Soleil ; ils m'ont respondu que la Lune s'éclip-
soit ou paroissoit noire, à cause qu'elle tenoit son fils entre
ses bras, qui empeschoit que l'on ne vist sa clarté. Si la
Lune a un fils, elle est mariée, ou l'a été, leur dis-je. Oüy
dea, me dirent-ils, le Soleil est son mary, qui marche tout
le jour, et elle toute la nuict ; et s'il s'éclipse, ou s'il
s'obscurcit, c'est qu'il prend aussi par fois le fils qu'il a eu
de la Lune entre ses bras. Oüy, mais ny la Lune ny le
Soleil n'ont point de bras, leur disois-je. Tu n'as point
d'esprit ; ils tiennent tousiours leurs arcs bandés deuant
eux, voilà pourquoy leurs bras ne paroissent point. Et sur
qui veulent-ils tirer ? Hô qu'en sçauons nous ?"[2] A
mythologically important legend of the same race, the
Ottawa story of Iosco, describes Sun and Moon as brother
and sister. Two Indians, it is said, sprang through a
chasm in the sky, and found themselves in a pleasant

[1] D'Orbigny, 'L'Homme Américain,' vol. ii. p. 102. See also De la
Borde, 'Caraïbes,' p. 525.
[2] Le Jeune in 'Relations des Jesuites dans la Nouvelle France,' 1634,
p. 26. See Charlevoix, 'Nouvelle France,' vol. ii. p. 170.

moonlit land; there they saw the Moon approaching as
from behind a hill, they knew her at the first sight, she was
an aged woman with white face and pleasing air; speaking
kindly to them, she led them to her brother the Sun, and
he carried them with him in his course and sent them home
with promises of happy life.[1] As the Egyptian Osiris and
Isis, identified with Sun and Moon, were at once brother and
sister, and husband and wife, so it was with the Peruvian Sun
and Moon, and thus the sister-marriage of the Incas had in
their religion at once a meaning and a justification.[2] The
myths of other countries, where such relations of sex may
not appear, carry on the same lifelike personification in
telling the ever-reiterated, never tedious tale of day and
night. Thus to the Mexicans it was an ancient hero who,
when the old sun was burnt out, and had left the world in
darkness, sprang into a huge fire, descended into the shades
below, and arose deified and glorious in the east as Tonatiuh
the Sun. After him there leapt in another hero, but now
the fire had grown dim, and he arose only in milder radiance
as Metztli the Moon.[3]

If it be objected that all this may be mere expressive
form of speech, like a modern poet's fanciful metaphor,
there is evidence which no such objection can stand against.
When the Aleutians thought that if any one gave offence
to the moon, he would fling down stones on the offender
and kill him,[4] or when the moon came down to an Indian
squaw, appearing in the form of a beautiful woman with a
child in her arms, and demanding an offering of tobacco
and fur robes,[5] what conceptions of personal life could be

---

[1] Schoolcraft, 'Algic Researches,' vol. ii. p. 54; compare 'Tanner's
Narrative,' p. 517; see also 'Prose Edda,' i. 11; 'Early Hist. of Mankind.'
p. 327.

[2] Prescott, 'Peru,' vol. i. p. 86; Garcilaso de la Vega, 'Comm. Real.' i.
c. 4.

[3] Torquemada, 'Monarquia Indiana,' vi. 42; Clavigero, vol. ii. p. 9;
Sahagun in Kingsborough, 'Antiquities of Mexico.'

[4] Bastian, 'Mensch,' vol. ii. p. 59.

[5] Le Jeune, in 'Relations des Jésuites dans la Nouvelle France,' 1639,
p. 38.

more distinct than these? When the Apache Indian pointed to the sky and asked the white man, "Do you not believe that God, this Sun (que Dios, este Sol) sees what we do and punishes us when it is evil?" it is impossible to say that this savage was talking in rhetorical simile.[1] There was something in the Homeric contemplation of the living personal Helios, that was more and deeper than metaphor. Even in far later ages, we may read of the outcry that arose in Greece against the astronomers, those blasphemous materialists who denied, not the divinity only, but the very personality of the sun, and declared him a huge hot ball. Later again, how vividly Tacitus brings to view the old personification dying into simile among the Romans, in contrast with its still enduring religious vigour among the German nations, in the record of Boiocalcus pleading before the Roman legate that his tribe should not be driven from their lands. Looking toward the sun, and calling on the other heavenly bodies as though, says the historian, they had been there present, the German chief demanded of them if it were their will to look down upon a vacant soil? (Solem deinde respiciens, et cætera sidera vocans, quasi coram interrogabat, vellentne contueri inane solum?)[2]

So it is with the stars. Savage mythology contains many a story of them, agreeing through all other difference in attributing to them animate life. They are not merely talked of in fancied personality, but personal action is attributed to them, or they are even declared once to have lived on earth. The natives of Australia not only say the stars in Orion's belt and scabbard are young men dancing a corroboree; they declare that Jupiter, whom they call "Foot of Day" (Ginabong-Bearp), was a chief among the Old Spirits, that ancient race who were translated to heaven before man came on earth.[3] The Esquimaux did not stop short at calling the stars of Orion's belt the Lost Ones, and

[1] Froebel, 'Central America,' p. 490.   [2] Tac. Ann. xiii. 55.
[3] Stanbridge, in 'Tr. Eth. Soc.' vol. I. p. 301.

telling a tale of their being seal-hunters who missed their
way home; but they distinctly held that the stars were in
old times men and animals, before they went up into the
sky.[1] So the North American Indians had more than
superficial meaning in calling the Pleiades the Dancers, and
the morning-star the Day-bringer; for among them stories
are told like that of the Iowas, of the star that an Indian
had long gazed upon in childhood, and who came down and
talked with him when he was once out hunting, weary and
luckless, and led him to a place where there was much
game.[2] The Kasia of Bengal declare that the stars were once
men: they climbed to the top of a tree (of course the great
heaven-tree of the mythology of so many lands), but others
below cut the trunk and left them up there in the branches.[3]
With such savage conceptions as guides, the original meaning in the familiar classic personification of stars can
scarcely be doubted. The explicit doctrine of the animation of stars is to be traced through past centuries, and
down to our own. Origen declares that the stars are
animate and rational, moved with such order and reason as
it would be absurd to say irrational creatures could fulfil.
Pamphilius, in his apology for this Father, lays it down
that whereas some have held the luminaries of heaven to be
animate and rational creatures, while others have held them
mere spiritless and senseless bodies, no one may call
another a heretic for holding either view, for there is no
open tradition on the subject, and even ecclesiastics have
thought diversely of it.[4] It is enough to mention here the
well-known mediæval doctrine of star-souls and star-angels,
so intimately mixed up with the delusions of astrology. In
our own time the theory of the animating souls of stars
finds still here and there an advocate, and De Maistre,

---

[1] Cranz, 'Grönland,' p. 293; Hayes, 'Arctic Boat Journey,' p. 254.
[2] Schoolcraft, 'Indian Tribes,' part iii. p. 276; see also De la Borde,
'Caraibes,' p. 525.
[3] Latham, 'Descr. Eth.' vol. i. p. 119.
[4] Origen. de Principiis, i. 7, 8; Pamphil. Apolog. pro Origine, ix. 84.

prince and leader of reactionary philosophers, maintains
against modern astronomers the ancient doctrine of personal will in astronomic motion, and even the theory of
animated planets.[1]

Poetry has so far kept alive in our minds the old anima-
tive theory of nature, that it is no great effort to us to fancy
the waterspout a huge giant or sea-monster, and to depict
in what we call appropriate metaphor its march across the
fields of ocean. But where such forms of speech are current
among less educated races, they are underlaid by a distinct
prosaic meaning of fact. Thus the waterspouts which the
Japanese see so often off their coasts are to them long-tailed
dragons, "flying up into the air with a swift and violent
motion," wherefore they call them "tatsmaki," "spouting
dragons."[2] Waterspouts are believed by some Chinese to
be occasioned by the ascent and descent of the dragon;
although the monster is never seen head and tail at once for
clouds, fishermen and sea-side folk catch occasional glimpses
of him ascending from the water and descending to it.[3]
In the mediæval Chronicle of John of Bromton there is
mentioned a wonder which happens about once a month in
the Gulf of Satalia, on the Pamphylian coast. A great
black dragon seems to come in the clouds, letting down his
head into the waves, while his tail seems fixed to the sky,
and this dragon draws up the waves to him with such avidity
that even a laden ship would be taken up on high, so that to
avoid this danger the crews ought to shout and beat boards
to drive the dragon off. However, concludes the chronicler,
some indeed say that this is not a dragon, but the sun drawing up the water, which seems more true.[4] The Moslems still
account for waterspouts as caused by gigantic demons, such
as that one described in the "Arabian Nights:"—"The

[1] De Maistre, 'Soirées de Saint-Pétersbourg,' vol. ii. p. 210, see 184.

[2] Kaempfer, 'Japan,' in Pinkerton, vol. vii. p. 684.

[3] Doolittle, 'Chinese,' vol. ii. p. 265; see Ward, 'Hindoos,' vol. i. p. 140
(Indra's elephants drinking).

[4] Chron. Joh. Bromton, in 'Hist. Angl. Scriptores,' x. Ric. I. p. 1216.

sea became troubled before them, and there arose from it a black pillar, ascending towards the sky, and approaching the meadow . . . and behold it was a Jinnee, of gigantic stature."[1] The difficulty in interpreting language like this is to know how how far it is seriously and how far fancifully meant. But this doubt in no way goes against its original animistic meaning, of which there can be no question in the following story of a "great sea-serpent" current among a barbarous East African tribe. A chief of the Wanika told Dr. Krapf of a great serpent which is sometimes seen out at sea, reaching from the sea to the sky, and appearing especially during heavy rain. "I told them," says the missionary, "that this was no serpent, but a waterspout."[2] Out of the similar phenomenon on land there has arisen a similar group of myths. The Moslem fancies the whirling sand-pillar of the desert to be caused by the flight of an evil jinn, and the East African simply calls it a demon (p'hepo). To traveller after traveller who gazes on these monstrous shapes gliding majestically across the desert, the thought occurs that the well-remembered "Arabian Nights'" descriptions rest upon personifications of the sand-pillars themselves, as the gigantic demons into which fancy can even now so naturally shape them.[3]

Rude and distant tribes agree in the conception of the Rainbow as a living monster. New Zealand myth, describing the battle of the Tempest against the Forest, tells how the Rainbow arose and placed his mouth close to Tane-mahuta, the Father of Trees, and continued to assault him till his trunk was snapt in two, and his broken branches strewed the ground.[4] It is not only in mere nature-myth like this, but in actual awe-struck belief and terror, that the idea of the

[1] Lane, 'Thousand and One N.' vol. i, p. 30, 7.

[2] Krapf, 'Travels,' p. 198.

[3] Lane, ibid. pp. 30, 42; Burton, 'El Medinah and Meccah,' vol. ii. p. 69; 'Lake Regions,' vol. i. p. 297; J. D. Hooker, 'Himalayan Journals,' vol. i. p. 79; Tylor, 'Mexico,' p. 30; Tyerman and Bennet, vol. ii. p. 362. [Illudu jigicha = demon, whirlwind.]

[4] Taylor, 'New Zealand,' p. 121.

live Rainbow is worked out. The Karens of Birma say it is
a spirit or demon. "The Rainbow can devour men. . . .
When it devours a person, he dies a sudden or violent
death. All persons that die badly, by falls, by drowning,
or by wild beasts, die because the Rainbow has devoured
their ka-la, or spirit. On devouring persons it becomes
thirsty and comes down to drink, when it is seen in the sky
drinking water. Therefore when people see the Rainbow,
they say, 'The Rainbow has come to drink water. Look
out, some one or other will die violently by an evil death.'
If children are playing, their parents will say to them, 'The
Rainbow has come down to drink. Play no more, lest some
accident should happen to you.' And after the Rainbow
has been seen, if any fatal accident happens to anyone, it is
said the Rainbow has devoured him."[1] The Zulu ideas
correspond in a curious way with these. The Rainbow lives
with a snake, that is, where it is there is also a snake; or
it is like a sheep, and dwells in a pool. When it touches
the earth, it is drinking at a pool. Men are afraid to
wash in a large pool; they say there is a Rainbow in it, and
if a man goes in, it catches and eats him. The Rainbow,
coming out of a river or pool and resting on the ground,
poisons men whom it meets, affecting them with eruptions.
Men say, "The Rainbow is disease. If it rests on a man,
something will happen to him."[2] Lastly in Dahome, Danh
the Heavenly Snake, which makes the Popo beads and
confers wealth on man, is the Rainbow.[3]

To the theory of Animism belong those endless tales
which all nations tell of the presiding genii of nature, the
spirits of cliffs, wells, waterfalls, volcanos, the elves and wood-
nymphs seen at times by human eyes when wandering by
moonlight or assembled at their fairy festivals. Such beings
may personify the natural objects they belong to, as when,
in a North American tale, the guardian spirit of waterfalls

[1] Mason, 'Karens,' in 'Journ. As. Soc. Bengal,' 1865, part ii. p. 217.
[2] Callaway, 'Zulu Tales,' vol. I. p. 294.
[3] Burton, 'Dahome,' vol. II. p. 143; see 242.

rushes through the lodge as a raging current, bearing rocks
and trees along in its tremendous course, and then the
guardian spirit of the islands of Lake Superior enters in
the guise of rolling waves covered with silver-sparkling
foam.[1] Or they may be guiding and power-giving spirits of
nature, like the spirit Fugamu, whose work is the cataract
of the Nguyai, and who still wanders night and day around
it, though the negroes who tell of him can no longer see his
bodily form.[2] The belief prevailing through the lower
culture that the diseases which vex mankind are brought
by individual personal spirits, is one which has produced
striking examples of mythic development. Thus the savage
Karen lives in terror of the mad "la," the epileptic "la,"
and the rest of the seven evil demons who go about seeking
his life; and it is with a fancy not many degrees removed
from this early stage of thought that the Persian sees in
bodily shape the apparition of Al, the scarlet fever :—

"Would you know Al? she seems a blushing maid,
With locks of flame and cheeks all rosy red."[3]

It is with this deep old spiritualistic belief clearly in view
that the ghastly tales are to be read where pestilence and
death come on their errand in weird human shape. To the
mind of the Israelite, death and pestilence took the personal
form of the destroying angel who smote the doomed.[4] When
the great plague raged in Justinian's time, men saw on the
sea brazen barks whose crews were black and headless men,
and where they landed, the pestilence broke out.[5] When the
plague fell on Rome in Gregory's time, the saint rising from
prayer saw Michael standing with his bloody sword on
Hadrian's castle—the archangel stands there yet in bronze,
giving the old fort its newer name of the Castle of St. Angelo.

[1] Schoolcraft, 'Algic Res.' vol. II. p. 146.
[2] Du Chaillu, 'Ashango-land,' p. 106.
[3] Jas. Atkinson, 'Customs of the Women of Persia,' p. 49.
[4] 2 Sam. xxiv. 16 ; 2 Kings xix, 35.
[5] G. S. Assemanni 'Bibliotheca Orientalis,' II. 86.

Among a whole group of stories of the pestilence seen in personal shape travelling to and fro in the land, perhaps there is none more vivid than this Slavonic one. There sat a Russian under a larch-tree, and the sunshine glared like fire. He saw something coming from afar; he looked again —it was the Pest-maiden, huge of stature, all shrouded in linen, striding towards him. He would have fled in terror, but the form grasped him with her long outstretched hand. "Knowest thou the Pest?" she said; "I am she. Take me on thy shoulders and carry me through all Russia; miss no village, no town, for I must visit all. But fear not for thyself, thou shalt be safe amid the dying." Clinging with her long hands, she clambered on the peasant's back; he stepped onward, saw the form above him as he went, but felt no burden. First he bore her to the towns; they found there joyous dance and song; but the form waved her linen shroud, and joy and mirth were gone. As the wretched man looked round, he saw mourning, he heard the tolling of the bells, there came funeral processions, the graves could not hold the dead. He passed on, and coming near each village heard the shriek of the dying, saw all faces white in the desolate houses. But high on the hill stands his own hamlet: his wife, his little children are there, and the aged parents, and his heart bleeds as he draws near. With strong gripe he holds the maiden fast, and plunges with her beneath the waves. He sank: she rose again, but she quailed before a heart so fearless, and fled far away to the forest and the mountain."[1]

Yet, if mythology be surveyed in a more comprehensive view, it is seen that its animistic development falls within a broader generalization still. The explanation of the course and change of nature, as caused by life such as the life of the thinking man who gazes on it, is but a part of a far wider mental process. It belongs to that great doctrine of

[1] Hanusch, 'Slav. Mythus,' p. 322. Compare Torquemada, 'Monarqia Indiana,' i. c. 11 (Mexico); Bastian, 'Psychologie,' p. 197.

analogy, from which we have gained so much of our apprehension of the world around us. Distrusted as it now is by severer science for its misleading results, analogy is still to us a chief means of discovery and illustration, while in earlier grades of education its influence was all but paramount. Analogies which are but fancy to us were to men of past ages reality. They could see the flame licking its yet undevoured prey with tongues of fire, or the serpent gliding along the waving sword from hilt to point; they could feel a live creature gnawing within their bodies in the pangs of hunger; they heard the voices of the hill-dwarfs answering in the echo, and the chariot of the Heaven-god rattling in thunder over the solid firmament. Men to whom these were living thoughts had no need of the schoolmaster and his rules of composition, his injunctions to use metaphor cautiously, and to take continual care to make all similes consistent. The similes of the old bards and orators were consistent, because they seemed to see and hear and feel them: what we call poetry was to them real life, not as to the modern versemaker a masquerade of gods and heroes, shepherds and shepherdesses, stage heroines and philosophic savages in paint and feathers. It was with a far deeper consciousness that the circumstance of nature was worked out in endless imaginative detail in ancient days and among uncultured races.

Upon the sky above the hill-country of Orissa, Pidzu Pennu, the Rain-god of the Khonds, rests as he pours down the showers through his sieve.[1] Over Peru there stands a princess with a vase of rain, and when her brother strikes the pitcher, men hear the shock in thunder and see the flash in lightning.[2] To the old Greeks the rainbow seemed stretched down by Jove from heaven, a purple sign of war and tempest, or it was the personal Iris, messenger between gods and men.[3] To the South Sea islander it was the

---

[1] Macpherson, 'India,' p. 357.
[2] Markham, 'Quichua Gr. and Dic.' p. 9.
[3] Welcker, 'Griech. Götterl.' vol. i. p. 690.

heaven-ladder where heroes of old climbed up and down;[1]
and so to the Scandinavian it was Bifröst, the trembling
bridge, timbered of three hues and stretched from sky to
earth; while in German folk-lore it is the bridge where the
souls of the just are led by their guardian angels across to
paradise.[2] As the Israelite called it the bow of Jehovah in
the clouds, it is to the Hindu the bow of Rama,[3] and to the
Finn the bow of Tiermes the Thunderer, who slays with it
the sorcerers that hunt after men's lives;[4] it is imagined,
moreover, as a gold-embroidered scarf, a head-dress of
feathers, St. Bernard's crown, or the sickle of an Esthonian
deity.[5] And yet through all such endless varieties of mythic
conception, there runs one main principle, the evident suggestion and analogy of nature. It has been said of the
savages of North America, that "there is always something
actual and physical to ground an Indian fancy on."[6] The
saying goes too far, but within limits it is emphatically true,
not of North American Indians alone, but of mankind.

Such resemblances as have just been displayed thrust
themselves directly on the mind, without any necessary intervention of words. Deep as language lies in our mental
life, the direct comparison of object with object, and action
with action, lies yet deeper. The myth-maker's mind shows
forth even among the deaf-and-dumb, who work out just
such analogies of nature in their wordless thought. Again
and again they have been found to suppose themselves
taught by their guardians to worship and pray to sun, moon,
and stars, as personal creatures. Others have described
their early thoughts of the heavenly bodies as analogous to
things within their reach, one fancying the moon made like
a dumpling and rolled over the tree-tops like a marble across

[1] Ellis, 'Polyn. Res.' vol i. p. 231; Polack, 'New. Z.' vol. i. p. 273.
[2] Grimm, 'D. M.' pp. 694—6.
[3] Ward, 'Hindoos,' vol. i. p. 140.
[4] Castren, 'Finnische Mythologie,' pp. 48, 49.
[5] Delbrück in Lazarus and Steinthal's Zeitschrift, vol. iii. p. 269.
[6] Schoolcraft, part iii, p. 520.

a table, and the stars cut out with great scissors and stuck against the sky, while another supposed the moon a furnace and the stars fire-grates, which the people above the firmament light up as we kindle fires.[1] Now the mythology of mankind at large is full of conceptions of nature like these, and to assume for them no deeper original source than metaphorical phrases, would be to ignore one of the great transitions of our intellectual history.

Language, there is no doubt, has had a great share in the formation of myth. The mere fact of its individualizing in words such notions as winter and summer, cold and heat, war and peace, vice and virtue, gives the myth-maker the means of imagining these thoughts as personal beings. Language not only acts in thorough unison with the imagination whose product it expresses, but it goes on producing of itself, and thus, by the side of the mythic conceptions in which language has followed imagination, we have others in which language has led, and imagination has followed in the track. These two actions coincide too closely for their effects to be thoroughly separated, but they should be distinguished as far as possible. For myself, I am disposed to think (differing here in some measure from Professor Max Müller's view of the subject) that the mythology of the lower races rests especially on a basis of real and sensible analogy, and that the great expansion of verbal metaphor into myth belongs to more advanced periods of civilization. In a word, I take material myth to be the primary, and verbal myth to be the secondary formation. But whether this opinion be historically sound or not, the difference in nature between myth founded on fact and myth founded on word is sufficiently manifest. The want of reality in verbal metaphor cannot be effectually hidden by the utmost stretch of imagination. In spite of this essential weakness, however, the habit of realizing everything that words can describe is

[1] Sicard, 'Théorie des Signes, etc.' Paris, 1808, vol. ii. p. 631; 'Personal Recollections' by Charlotte Elizabeth, London, 1841, p. 132; Dr. Orpen, 'The Contrast,' p. 25. Compare Meiners, vol. I. p. 42.

one which has grown and flourished in the world. Descriptive names become personal, the notion of personality stretches to take in even the most abstract notions to which a name may be applied, and realized name, epithet, and metaphor pass into interminable mythic growths by the process which Max Müller has so aptly characterized as "a disease of language." It would be difficult indeed to define the exact thought lying at the root of every mythic conception, but in easy cases the course of formation can be quite well followed. North American tribes have personified Nipinûkhe and Pipûnûkhe, the beings who bring the spring (nipin) and the winter (pipûn); Nipinûkhe brings the heat and birds and verdure, Pipûnûkhe ravages with his cold winds, his ice and snow; one comes as the other goes, and between them they divide the world.[1] Just such personification as this furnishes the staple of endless nature-metaphor in our own European poetry. In the springtime it comes to be said that May has conquered Winter, his gate is open, he has sent letters before him to tell the fruit that he is coming, his tent is pitched, he brings the woods their summer clothing. Thus, when Night is personified, we see how it comes to pass that Day is her son, and how each in a heavenly chariot drives round the world. To minds in this mythologic stage, the Curse becomes a personal being, hovering in space till it can light upon its victim; Time and Nature arise as real entities; Fate and Fortune become personal arbiters of our lives. But at last, as the change of meaning goes on, thoughts that once had a more real sense fade into mere poetic forms of speech. We have but to compare the effect of ancient and modern personification on our own minds, to understand something of what has happened in the interval. Milton may be consistent, classical, majestic, when he tells how Sin and Death sat within the gates of hell, and how they built their bridge of length prodigious across the deep abyss to earth. Yet such

[1] Le Jeune, in 'Rel. des Jés. dans la Nouvelle France,' 1634, p. 13.

descriptions leave but scant sense of meaning on modern
minds, and we are apt to say, as we might of some counter-
feit bronze from Naples, "For a sham antique how cleverly
it is done." Entering into the mind of the old Norseman,
we guess how much more of meaning than the cleverest
modern imitation can carry, lay in his pictures of Hel, the
death-goddess, stern and grim and livid, dwelling in her
high and strong-barred house, and keeping in her nine
worlds the souls of the departed; Hunger is her dish,
Famine is her knife, Care is her bed, and Misery her
curtain. When such old material descriptions are transferred to modern times, in spite of all the accuracy of re-
production their spirit is quite changed. The story of the
monk who displayed among his relics the garments of St.
Faith is to us only a jest; and we call it quaint humour
when Charles Lamb, falling old and infirm, once wrote to a
friend, "My bed-fellows are Cough and Cramp; we sleep
three in a bed." Perhaps we need not appreciate the
drollery any the less for seeing in it at once a consequence
and a record of a past intellectual life.

The distinction of grammatical gender is a process
intimately connected with the formation of myths. Grammatical gender is of two kinds. What may be called sexual
gender is familiar to all classically-educated Englishmen,
though their mother tongue has mostly lost its traces.
Thus in Latin not only are such words as *homo* and *femina*
classed naturally as masculine and feminine, but such words
as *pes* and *gladius* are made masculine, and *biga* and *navis*
feminine, and the same distinction is actually drawn
between such abstractions as *honos* and *fides*. That sexless
objects and ideas should thus be classed as male and female,
in spite of a new gender—the neuter or "neither" gender
—having been defined, seems in part explained by considering this latter to have been of later formation, and the
original Indo-European genders to have been only masculine
and feminine, as is actually the case in Hebrew. Though
the practice of attributing sex to objects that have none is

not easy to explain in detail, yet there seems nothing mysterious in its principles, to judge from one at least of its main ideas, which is still quite intelligible. Language makes an admirably appropriate distinction between strong and weak, stern and gentle, rough and delicate, when it contrasts them as male and female. It is possible to understand even such fancies as those which Pietro della Valle describes among the mediæval Persians, distinguishing between male and female, that is to say, practically between robust and tender, even in such things as food and cloth, air and water, and prescribing their proper use accordingly.[1] And no phrase could be more plain and forcible than that of the Dayaks of Borneo, who say of a heavy downpour of rain, "ujatn arai, 'sa!'"—"a *he* rain this!"[2] Difficult as it may be to decide how far objects and thoughts were classed in language as male and female because they were personified, and how far they were personified because they were classed as male and female, it is evident at any rate that these two processes fit together and promote each other.[3]

Moreover, in studying languages which lie beyond the range of common European scholarship, it is found that the theory of grammatical gender must be extended into a wider field. The Dravidian languages of South India make the interesting distinction between a "high-caste or major gender," which includes rational beings, *i. e.*, deities and men, and a "caste-less or minor gender," which includes irrational objects, whether living animals or lifeless things.[4] The distinction between an animate and an inanimate gender appears with especial import in a family of North American Indian languages, the Algonquin. Here not only

[1] Pietro della Valle, 'Viaggi,' letter xvi.
[2] 'Journ. Ind. Archip.' vol. ii. p. xxvii.
[3] See remarks on the tendency of sex-denoting language to produce myth in Africa, in W. H. Bleek, 'Reynard the Fox in S. Afr.' p. xx. ; 'Origin of Lang.' p. xxiii.
[4] Caldwell, 'Comp. Gr. of Dravidian Langs.' p. 172.

do all animals belong to the animate gender, but also the sun, moon, and stars, thunder and lightning, as being personified creatures. The animate gender, moreover, includes not only trees and fruits, but certain exceptional lifeless objects which appear to owe this distinction to their special sanctity or power; such are the stone which serves as the altar of sacrifice to the manitus, the bow, the eagle's feather, the kettle, tobacco-pipe, drum, and wampum. Where the whole animal is animate, parts of its body considered separately may be inanimate—hand or foot, beak or wing. Yet even here, for special reasons, special objects are treated as of animate gender; such are the eagle's talons, the bear's claws, the beaver's castor, the man's nails, and other objects for which there is claimed a peculiar or mystic power.[1] If to any one it seems surprising that savage thought should be steeped through and through in mythology, let him consider the meaning that is involved in a grammar of nature like this. Such a language is the very reflexion of a mythic world.

There is yet another way in which language and mythology can act and re-act on one another. Even we, with our blunted mythologic sense, cannot give an individual name to a lifeless object, such as a boat or a weapon, without in the very act imagining for it something of a personal nature. Among nations whose mythic conceptions have remained in full vigour, this action may be yet more vivid. Perhaps very low savages may not be apt to name their implements or their canoes as though they were live people, but races a few stages above them show the habit in perfection. Among the Zulus we hear of names for clubs, Igumgehle or Glutton, U-nothlola-mazibuko or He-who-watches-the-fords; among names for assagais are Imbubuzi or Groan-causer, U-silo-si-lambile or Hungry Leopard, and the weapon being also used as an implement, a certain

[1] Schoolcraft, 'Indian Tribes,' part II. p. 366. For other cases see especially Pott in Erach and Gruber's 'Allg. Encyclop.' art. 'Geschlecht;' also D. Forbes, 'Persian Gr.' p. 26; Latham, 'Descr. Eth.' vol. II. p. 60.

assagai bears the peaceful name of U-simbela-banta-bami,
He-digs-up-for-my-children.[1]   A similar custom prevailed
among the New Zealanders.   The traditions of their
ancestral migrations tell how Ngahue made from his jasper
stone those two sharp axes whose names were Tutauru and
Hauhau-te-rangi; how with these axes were shaped the
canoes Arawa and Tainui; how the two stone anchors of
Te Arawa were called Toka-parore or Wrystone, and
Tu-te-rangi-harum or Like-to-the-roaring-sky.   These
legends do not break off in a remote past, but carry on a
chronicle which reaches into modern times.   It is only
lately, the Maoris say, that the famous axe Tutauru was
lost, and as for the ear-ornament named Kaukau-matua,
which was made from a chip of the same stone, they declare
that it was not lost till 1846, when its owner, Te Heuheu,
perished in a landslip.[2]   Up from this savage level the same
childlike habit of giving personal names to lifeless objects
may be traced, as we read of Thor's hammer, Miölnir,
whom the giants know as he comes flying through the air,
or of Arthur's brand, Excalibur, caught by the arm clothed
in white samite when Sir Bedivere flung him back into the
lake, or of the Cid's mighty sword Tizona, the Firebrand,
whom he vowed to bury in his own breast were she overcome through cowardice of his.

The teachings of a childlike primæval philosophy ascribing personal life to nature at large, and the early tyranny
of speech over the human mind, have thus been two great
and, perhaps, greatest agents in mythologic development.
Other causes, too, have been at work, which will be noticed
in connexion with special legendary groups, and a full list,
could it be drawn up, might include as contributories many
other intellectual actions.   It must be thoroughly understood, however, that such investigation of the processes of
myth-formation demands a lively sense of the state of men's

[1] Callaway, 'Relig. of Amazulu,' p. 166.
[2] Grey, 'Polyn. Myth.' pp. 132, etc., 211 ; Shortland, 'Traditions of N. Z.'
p. 15.

minds in the mythologic period. When the Russians in
Siberia listened to the talk of the rude Kirgis, they stood
amazed at the barbarians' ceaseless flow of poetic improvisa-
tion, and exclaimed, " Whatever these people see gives
birth to fancies!" Just so the civilized European may
contrast his own stiff orderly prosaic thought with the wild
shifting poetry and legend of the old myth-maker, and may
say of him that everything he saw gave birth to fancy.
Wanting the power of transporting himself into this imaginative atmosphere, the student occupied with the analysis
of the mythic world may fail so pitiably in conceiving its
depth and intensity of meaning, as to convert it into stupid
fiction. Those can see more justly who have the poet's gift
of throwing their minds back into the world's older life, like
the actor who for a moment can forget himself and become
what he pretends to be. Wordsworth, that " modern
ancient," as Max Müller has so well called him, could write
of Storm and Winter, or of the naked Sun climbing the
sky, as though he were some Vedic poet at the head-spring
of the Aryan race, " seeing " with his mind's eye a mythic
hymn to Agni or Varuna. Fully to understand an old-world
myth needs not evidence and argument alone, but deep
poetic feeling.

Yet such of us as share but very little in this rare gift,
may make shift to let evidence in some measure stand in its
stead. In the poetic stage of thought we may see that
ideal conceptions once shaped in the mind must have
assumed some such reality to grown-up men and women as
they still do to children. I have never forgotten the vivid-
ness with which, as a child, I fancied I might look through
a great telescope, and see the constellations stand round the
sky, red, green, and yellow, as I had just been shown them
on the celestial globe. The intensity of mythic fancy may
be brought even more nearly home to our minds by comparing it with the morbid subjectivity of illness. Among
the lower races, and high above their level, morbid ecstasy
brought on by meditation, fasting, narcotics, excitement, or

disease, is a state common and held in honour among the
very classes specially concerned with mythic idealism, and
under its influence the barriers between sensation and
imagination break utterly away. A North American Indian
prophetess once related the story of her first vision : At her
solitary fast at womanhood she fell into an ecstasy, and at
the call of the spirits she went up to heaven by the path
that leads to the opening of the sky ; there she heard a
voice, and, standing still, saw the figure of a man standing
near the path, whose head was surrounded by a brilliant
halo, and his breast was covered with squares ; he said,
" Look at me, my name is Oshauwauegeeghick, the Bright
Blue Sky ! " Recording her experience afterwards in the
rude picture-writing of her race, she painted this glorious
spirit with the hieroglyphic horns of power and the brilliant
halo round his head.[1] We know enough of the Indian
pictographs, to guess how a fancy with these familiar details
of the picture-language came into the poor excited creature's mind ; but how far is our cold analysis from her
utter belief that in vision she had really seen this bright
being, this Red Indian Zeus. Far from being an isolated
case, this is scarcely more than a fair example of the rule
that any idea shaped and made current by mythic fancy,
may at once acquire all the definiteness of fact. Even if to
the first shaper it be no more than lively imagination, yet,
when it comes to be embodied in words and to pass from
house to house, those who hear it become capable of the
most intense belief that it may be seen in material shape,
that it has been seen, that they themselves have seen it.
The South African who believes in a god with a crooked leg
sees him with a crooked leg in dreams and visions.[2] In the
time of Tacitus it was said, with a more poetic imagination,
that in the far north of Scandinavia men might see the very
forms of the gods and the rays streaming from their heads.[3]

[1] Schoolcraft, ' Indian Tribes,' part I. p. 391 and pl. 55.
[2] Livingstone, ' S. Afr.' p. 121.
[3] Tac. Germania, 15.

In the 6th century the famed Nile-god might still be seen,
in gigantic human form, rising waist-high from the waters
of his river.[1] Want of originality indeed seems one of the
most remarkable features in the visions of mystics. The
stiff Madonnas with their crowns and petticoats still
transfer themselves from the pictures on cottage walls to
appear in spiritual personality to peasant visionaries, as the
saints who stood in vision before ecstatic monks of old were
to be known by their conventional pictorial attributes.
When the devil with horns, hoofs, and tail had once become
a fixed image in the popular mind, of course men saw him
in this conventional shape. So real had St. Anthony's
satyr-demon become to men's opinion, that there is a grave
13th century account of the mummy of such a devil being
exhibited at Alexandria; and it is not fifteen years back
from the present time that there was a story current at
Teignmouth of a devil walking up the walls of the houses,
and leaving his fiendish backward footprints in the snow.
Nor is it vision alone that is concerned with the delusive
realization of the ideal; there is, as it were, a conspiracy of
all the senses to give it proof. To take a striking instance :
there is an irritating herpetic disease which gradually
encircles the body as with a girdle, whence its English name
of the *shingles* (Latin, *cingulum*). By an imagination not
difficult to understand, this disease is attributed to a sort of
coiling snake; and I remember a case in Cornwall where a
girl's family waited in great fear to see if the creature
would stretch all round her, the belief being that if the
snake's head and tail met, the patient would die. But a yet
fuller meaning of this fantastic notion is brought out in an
account by Dr. Bastian of a physician who suffered in a
painful disease, as though a snake were twined round him,
and in whose mind this idea reached such reality that in
moments of excessive pain he could see the snake and touch
its rough scales with his hand.

The relation of morbid imagination to myth is peculiarly

[1] Maury, 'Magie, etc.' p. 175.

well instanced in the history of a widespread belief, extending through savage, barbaric, classic, oriental, and mediæval
life, and surviving to this day in European superstition.
This belief, which may be conveniently called the Doctrine of
Werewolves, is that certain men, by natural gift or magic
art, can turn for a time into ravening wild beasts. The
origin of this idea is by no means sufficiently explained.
What we are especially concerned with is the fact of its prevalence in the world. It may be noticed that such a notion
is quite consistent with the animistic theory that a man's
soul may go out of his body and enter that of a beast or
bird, and also with the opinion that men may be transformed
into animals; both these ideas having an important place in
the belief of mankind, from savagery onward. The doctrine
of werewolves is substantially that of a temporary metempsychosis or metamorphosis. Now it really occurs that, in
various forms of mental disease, patients prowl shyly, long to
bite and destroy mankind, and even fancy themselves transformed into wild beasts. Belief in the possibility of such
transformation may have been the very suggesting cause
which led the patient to imagine it taking place in his own
person. But at any rate such insane delusions do occur,
and physicians apply to them the mythologic term of lycanthropy. The belief in men being werewolves, man-tigers,
and the like, may thus have the strong support of the very
witnesses who believe themselves to be such creatures.
Moreover, professional sorcerers have taken up the idea, as
they do any morbid delusion, and pretend to turn themselves
and others into beasts by magic art. Through the mass of
ethnographic details relating to this subject, there is manifest
a remarkable uniformity of principle.

Among the non-Aryan indigenes of India, the tribes of the
Garo Hills describe as "transformation into a tiger" a kind
of temporary madness, apparently of the nature of delirium
tremens, in which the patient walks like a tiger, shunning
society.[1] The Khonds of Orissa say that some among them

[1] Eliot in 'As. Res.' vol. III. p. 82.

have the art of "mleepa," and by the aid of a god become "mleepa" tigers for the purpose of killing enemies, one of the man's four souls going out to animate the bestial form. Natural tigers, say the Khonds, kill game to benefit men, who find it half devoured and share it, whereas man-killing tigers are either incarnations of the wrathful Earth-goddess, or they are transformed men.[1] Thus the notion of man-tigers serves, as similar notions do elsewhere, to account for the fact that certain individual wild beasts show a peculiar hostility to man. Among the Ho of Singbhoom it is related, as an example of similar belief, that a man named Mora saw his wife killed by a tiger, and followed the beast till it led him to the house of a man named Poosa. Telling Poosa's relatives of what had occurred, they replied that they were aware that he had the power of becoming a tiger, and accordingly they brought him out bound, and Mora deliberately killed him. Inquisition being made by the authorities, the family deposed, in explanation of their belief, that Poosa had one night devoured an entire goat, roaring like a tiger whilst eating it, and that on another occasion he told his friends he had a longing to eat a particular bullock, and that very night that very bullock was killed and devoured by a tiger.[2] South-eastern Asia is not less familiar with the idea of sorcerers turning into man-tigers and wandering after prey ; thus the Jakuns of the Malay Peninsula believe that when a man becomes a tiger to revenge himself on his enemies, the transformation happens just before he springs, and has been seen to take place.[3] How vividly the imagination of an excited tribe, once inoculated with a belief like this, can realize it into an event, is graphically told by Dobrizhoffer among the Abipones of South America. When a sorcerer, to get the better of an enemy, threatens to change himself into a tiger and tear his

[1] Macpherson, 'India,' pp. 92, 99, 108.
[2] Dalton, 'Kols of Chota-Nagpore' in 'Tr. Eth. Soc.' vol. vi. p. 32.
[3] J. Cameron, 'Malayan India,' p. 393; Bastian, 'Oestl. Asien,' vol. i. p. 119; vol. iii. pp. 201, 273; 'As. Res.' vol. vi. p. 173.

tribesmen to pieces, no sooner does he begin to roar, than
all the neighbours fly to a distance; but still they hear the
feigned sounds. "Alas!" they cry, "his whole body is
beginning to be covered with tiger-spots!" "Look, his
nails are growing!" the fear-struck women exclaim, although
they cannot see the rogue, who is concealed within his tent,
but distracted fear presents things to their eyes which have
no real existence. "You daily kill tigers in the plain without dread," said the missionary; "why then should you
weakly fear a false imaginary tiger in the town?" "You
fathers don't understand these matters," they reply with a
smile. "We never fear, but kill tigers in the plain, because
we can see them. Artificial tigers we do fear, because they
can neither be seen nor killed by us."[1] The sorcerers who
induced assemblies of credulous savages to believe in this
monstrous imposture, were also the professional spiritualistic
mediums of the tribes, whose business it was to hold intercourse with the spirits of the dead, causing them to appear
visibly, or carrying on audible dialogues with them behind a
curtain. Africa is especially rich in myths of man-lions,
man-leopards, man-hyænas. In the Kanuri language of
Bornu, there is grammatically formed from the word
"bultu," a hyæna, the verb "bultungin," meaning "I transform myself into a hyæna;" and the natives maintain that
there is a town called Kabutiloa, where every man possesses
this faculty.[2] The tribe of Budas in Abyssinia, iron-workers
and potters, are believed to combine with these civilized
avocations the gift of the evil eye and the power of turning
into hyænas, wherefore they are excluded from society and
the Christian sacrament. In the 'Life of Nathaniel Pearce,'
the testimony of one Mr. Coffin is printed. A young Buda,
his servant, came for leave of absence, which was granted;
but scarcely was Mr. Coffin's head turned to his other

---

[1] Dobrizhoffer, 'Abipones,' vol. II. p. 77. See J. G. Müller, 'Amer.
Urrelig.' p. 68; Martius, 'Ethn. Amer.' vol. I. p. 652; Oviedo, 'Nicaragua,'
p. 239; Piedrahita, 'Nuevo Reyno de Granada,' part I. lib. I. c. 3.
[2] Koelle, 'Afr. Lit. and Kanuri Vocab.' p. 275.

servants, when some of them called out, pointing in the direction the Buda had taken, "Look, look, he is turning himself into a hyæna." Mr. Coffin instantly looked round, the young man had vanished, and a large hyæna was running off at about a hundred paces' distance, in full light on the open plain, without tree or bush to intercept the view. The Buda came back next morning, and as usual rather affected to countenance than deny the prodigy. Coffin says, moreover, that the Budas wear a peculiar gold ear-ring, and this he has frequently seen in the ears of hyænas shot in traps, or speared by himself and others; the Budas are dreaded for their magical arts, and the editor of the book suggests that they put ear-rings in hyæna's ears to encourage a profitable superstition.[1] Mr. Mansfield Parkyns' more recent account shows how thoroughly this belief is part and parcel of Abyssinian spiritualism. Hysterics, lethargy, morbid insensibility to pain, and the "demoniacal posses-sion," in which the patient speaks in the name and language of an intruding spirit, are all ascribed to the spiritual agency of the Budas. Among the cases described by Mr. Parkyns was that of a servant-woman of his, whose illness was set down to the influence of one of these blacksmith-hyænas, who wanted to get her out into the forest and devour her. One night, a hyæna having been heard howling and laughing near the village, the woman was bound hand and foot and closely guarded in the hut, when suddenly, the hyæna calling close by, her master, to his astonishment, saw her rise "without her bonds" like a Davenport Brother, and try to escape.[2] In Ashango-land, M. Du Chaillu tells the follow-ing suggestive story. He was informed that a leopard had killed two men, and many palavers were held to settle the affair; but this was no ordinary leopard, but a transformed man. Two of Akondogo's men had disappeared, and only

[1] 'Life and Adventures of Nathaniel Pearce' (1810–9), ed. by J. J. Halls, London, 1831, vol. i. p. 286; also 'Tr. Eth. Soc.' vol. vi. p. 233; Waitz, vol. ii. p. 504.
[2] Parkyns, 'Life in Abyssinia' (1853), vol. ii. p. 140.

their blood was found, so a great doctor was sent for, who
said it was Akondogo's own nephew and heir Akosho. The
lad was sent for, and when asked by the chief, answered
that it was truly he who had committed the murders, that he
could not help it, for he had turned into a leopard, and his
heart longed for blood, and after each deed he had turned
into a man again. Akondogo loved the boy so much that he
would not believe his confession, till Akosho took him to a
place in the forest, where lay the mangled bodies of the two
men, whom he had really murdered under the influence of
this morbid imagination. He was slowly burnt to death, all
the people standing by.[1]

Brief mention is enough for the comparatively well-
known European representatives of these beliefs. What
with the mere continuance of old tradition, what with the
tricks of magicians, and what with cases of patients under
delusion believing themselves to have suffered transformation, of which a number are on record, the European series
of details from ancient to modern ages is very complete.
Virgil in the Bucolics shows the popular opinion of his
time that the arts of the werewolf, the necromancer or
"medium," and the witch, were different branches of one
craft, where he tells of Mœris as turning into a wolf by the
use of poisonous herbs, as calling up souls from the tombs,
and as bewitching away crops :—

> " Has herbas, atque hæc Ponto mihi lecta venena
> Ipse dedit Mœris ; nascuntur plurima Ponto.
> His ego sæpe lupum fieri, et se condere sylvis
> Mœrin, sæpe animas imis excire sepulcris,
> Atque satas alio vidi traducere messes." [2]

Of the classic accounts, one of the most remarkable is
Petronius Arbiter's story of the transformation of a "versi-
pellis" or "turnskin;" this contains the episode of the

---

[1] Du Chaillu, 'Ashango-land,' p. 52. For other African details, see Waitz,
vol. II. p. 343; J. L. Wilson, 'W. Afr.' pp. 222, 365, 398; Burton, 'E. Afr.'
p. 57; Livingstone, 'S. Afr.' pp. 615, 642; Magyar, 'S. Afr.' p. 156.
[2] Virg. Bucol. ec'. viii. 95.

wolf being wounded and the man who wore its shape found
with a similar wound, an idea not sufficiently proved to
belong originally to the lower races, but which becomes a
familiar feature in European stories of werewolves and
witches. In Augustine's time magicians were persuading
their dupes that by means of herbs they could turn them to
wolves, and the use of salve for this purpose is mentioned
at a comparatively modern date. Old Scandinavian sagas
have their werewolf warriors, and "shape-changers" (ham-
rammr) raging in fits of furious madness. The Danes still
know a man who is a werewolf by his eyebrows meeting,
and thus resembling a butterfly, the familiar type of the
soul, ready to fly off and enter some other body. In the
last year of the Swedish war with Russia, the people of
Kalmar said the wolves which overran the land were transformed Swedish prisoners. From Herodotus' legend of the
Neuri who turned every year for a few days to wolves, we
follow the idea on Slavonic ground to where Livonian
sorcerers bathe yearly in a river and turn for twelve days to
wolves; and widespread Slavonic superstition still declares
that the wolves that sometimes in bitter winters dare to
attack men, are themselves "wilkolak," men bewitched into
wolf's shape. The modern Greeks, instead of the classic
λυκάνθρωπος, adopt the Slavonic term βρύκολακας (Bulga-
rian "vrkolak"); it is a man who falls into a cataleptic
state, while his soul enters a wolf and goes ravening for
blood. Modern Germany, especially in the north, still
keeps up the stories of wolf-girdles, and in December you
must not "talk of the wolf" by name, lest the werewolves
tear you. Our English word "werewolf," that is "man-
wolf" (the "verevulf" of Cnut's Laws), still reminds us of
the old belief in our own country, and if it has had for
centuries but little place in English folklore, this has been
not so much for lack of superstition, as of wolves. To
instance the survival of the idea, transferred to another
animal, in the more modern witch-persecution, the following
Scotch story may serve. Certain witches at Thurso for a

long time tormented an honest fellow under the usual form of cats, till one night he put them to flight with his broad-sword, and cut off the leg of one less nimble than the rest; taking it up, to his amazement he found it to be a woman's leg, and next morning he discovered the old hag its owner with but one leg left. In France the creature has what is historically the same name as our "werewolf;" viz. in early forms "gerulphus," "garoul," and now pleonastically "loup-garou." The parliament of Franche-Comté made a law in 1578 to expel the werewolves; in 1598 the werewolf of Angers gave evidence of his hands and feet turning to wolf's claws; in 1603, in the case of Jean Grenier, the judge declared lycanthropy to be an insane delusion, not a crime. In 1658, a French satirical description of a magician could still give the following perfect account of the witch-werewolf: "I teach the witches to take the form of wolves and eat children, and when anyone has cut off one of their legs (which proves to be a man's arm) I forsake them when they are discovered, and leave them in the power of justice." Even in our own day the idea has by no means died out of the French peasant's mind. Not ten years ago in France, Mr. Baring-Gould found it impossible to get a guide after dark across a wild place haunted by a loup-garou, an incident which led him afterwards to write his "Book of Werewolves," a monograph of this remarkable combination of myth and madness.[1]

If we judged the myths of early ages by the unaided power of our modern fancy, we might be left unable to account for their immense effect on the life and belief of mankind. But by the study of such evidence as this, it

[1] For collections of European evidence, see W. Hertz, 'Der Werwolf;' Baring-Gould, 'Book of Werewolves;' Grimm, 'D. M.' p. 1047; Dasent, 'Norse Tales,' Introd. p. cxix.; Bastian, 'Mensch.' vol. II. pp. 32, 566; Brand, 'Pop. Ant.' vol. I. p. 312, vol. III. p. 33; Lecky, 'Hist. of Rationalism,' vol. I. p. 82. Particular details in Petron. Arbiter, Satir. lxii.; Virgil. Eclog. viii. 97; Plin. viii. 31; Herodot. iv. 105; Mela ii. 1; Augustin. De Civ. Dei, xviii. 17; Hanusch, 'Slaw. Myth.' pp. 286, 320; Wuttke, 'Deutsche Volksaberglaube,' p. 118.

becomes possible to realize a usual state of the imagination
among ancient and savage peoples, intermediate between
the conditions of a healthy prosaic modern citizen and of a
raving fanatic or a patient in a fever-ward.   A poet of our
own day has still much in common with the minds of
uncultured tribes in the mythologic stage of thought.   The
rude man's imaginations may be narrow, crude, and
repulsive, while the poet's more conscious fictions may be
highly wrought into shapes of fresh artistic beauty, but
both share in that sense of the reality of ideas, which fortunately or unfortunately modern education has proved so
powerful to destroy.   The change of meaning of a single
word will tell the history of this transition, ranging from
primæval to modern thought.   From first to last, the
processes of *phantasy* have been at work; but where the
savage could see *phantasms*, the civilized man has come to
amuse himself with *fancies*.

CHAPTER IX.

MYTHOLOGY—*continued*.

Nature-myths, their origin, canon of interpretation, preservation of original sense and significant names—Nature-myths of upper savage races compared with related forms among barbaric and civilized nations—Heaven and Earth as Universal Parents—Sun and Moon : Eclipse and Sunset, as Hero or Maiden swallowed by Monster; Rising of Sun from Sea and Descent to Under-World; Jaws of Night and Death, Symplegades; Eye of Heaven, eye of Odin and the Grail—Sun and Moon as mythic civilizers—Moon, her inconstancy, periodical death and revival—Stars, their generation—Constellations, their place in Mythology and Astronomy—Wind and Tempest—Thunder—Earthquake.

From laying down general principles of myth-development, we may now proceed to survey the class of Nature-myths, such especially as seem to have their earliest source and truest meaning among the lower races of mankind.

Science, investigating nature, discusses its facts and announces its laws in technical language which is clear and accurate to trained students, but which falls only as a mystic jargon on the ears of barbarians, or peasants, or children. It is to the comprehension of just these simple unschooled minds that the language of poetic myth is spoken, so far at least as it is true poetry, and not its quaint affected imitation. The poet contemplates the same natural world as the man of science, but in his so different craft strives to render difficult thought easy by making it visible and tangible, above all by referring the being and movement of the world to such personal life as his hearers feel within themselves, and thus working out in far-stretched fancy the maxim that "Man is the measure of all things." Let but the key be recovered to this mythic dialect, and its complex and shifting terms will translate themselves into reality, and show how far legend, in its sympathetic fictions of war, love, crime, adventure, fate, is only telling the perennial story of the world's daily life. The myths shaped out of those endless analogies between man and nature which are the soul of all poetry, into those half-human stories still so full to us of unfading life and beauty, are the masterpieces of an art belonging rather to the past than to the present. The growth of myth has been checked by science, it is dying of weights and measures, of proportions and specimens—it is not only dying, but half dead, and students are anatomising it. In this world one must do what one can, and if the moderns cannot feel myth as their forefathers did, at least they can analyse it. There is a kind of intellectual frontier within which he must be who will sympathise with myth, while he must be without who will investigate it, and it is our fortune that we live near this frontier-line, and can go in and out. European scholars can still in a measure understand the belief of Greeks or Aztecs or Maoris in their native myths, and at the same time can compare and interpret them without the scruples of men to whom such tales are history, and even sacred history. Moreover, were the whole human race at a uniform level of culture with ourselves, it would be hard to bring our minds to conceive of tribes in the mental state to which the early growth of nature-myth belongs, even as it is now hard to picture to ourselves a condition of mankind lower than any that has been actually found. But the various grades of existing civilization preserve the landmarks of a long course of history, and there survive by millions savages and barbarians whose minds still produce, in rude archaic forms, man's early mythic representations of nature.

Those who read for the first time the dissertations of the modern school of mythologists, and sometimes even those who have been familiar with them for years, are prone to ask, with half-incredulous appreciation of the beauty and

simplicity of their interpretations, can they be really true?
Can so great a part of the legendary lore of classic, barbarian, and mediæval Europe be taken up with the everlasting depiction of Sun and Sky, Dawn and Gloaming,
Day and Night, Summer and Winter, Cloud and Tempest;
can so many of the personages of tradition, for all their
heroic human aspect, have their real origin in anthropomorphic myths of nature? Without any attempt to
discuss these opinions at large, it will be seen that inspection of nature-mythology from the present point of
view tells in their favour, at least as to principle. The
general theory that such direct conceptions of nature as
are so naïvely and even baldly uttered in the Veda, are
among the primary sources of myth, is enforced by
evidence gained elsewhere in the world. Especially the
traditions of savage races display mythic conceptions of the
outer world, primitive like those of the ancient Aryans,
agreeing with them in their general character, and often
remarkably corresponding in their very episodes. At the
same time it must be clearly understood that the truth of
such a general principle is no warrant for all the particular
interpretations which mythologists claim to base upon it,
for of these in fact many are wildly speculative, and many
hopelessly unsound. Nature-myth demands indeed a
recognition of its vast importance in the legendary lore of
mankind, but only so far as its claim is backed by strong
and legitimate evidence.

The close and deep analogies between the life of nature
and the life of man have been for ages dwelt upon by poets
and philosophers, who in simile or in argument have told of
light and darkness, of calm and tempest, of birth, growth,
change, decay, dissolution, renewal. But no one-sided interpretation can be permitted to absorb into a single theory
such endless many-sided correspondences as these. Rash
inferences which on the strength of mere resemblance derive
episodes of myth from episodes of nature must be regarded
with utter mistrust, for the student who has no more strin-

gent criterion than this for his myths of sun and sky and
dawn, will find them wherever it pleases him to seek them.
It may be judged by simple trial what such a method may
lead to; no legend, no allegory, no nursery rhyme, is safe
from the hermeneutics of a thorough-going mythologic
theorist.   Should he, for instance, demand as his property
the nursery " Song of Sixpence," his claim would be easily
established : obviously the four-and-twenty blackbirds are
the four-and-twenty hours, and the pie that holds them is
the underlying earth covered with the overarching sky; how
true a touch of nature it is that when the pie is opened,
that is, when day breaks, the birds begin to sing; the
King is the Sun, and his counting out his money is pouring
out the sunshine, the golden shower of Danae ; the Queen
is the Moon, and her transparent honey the moonlight; the
Maid is the "rosy-fingered" Dawn who rises before the Sun
her master, and hangs out the clouds, his clothes, across
the sky; the particular blackbird who so tragically ends the
tale by snipping off her nose, is the hour of sunrise.   The
time-honoured rhyme really wants but one thing to prove it
a Sun-myth, that one thing being a proof by some argument
more valid than analogy.   Or if historical characters be
selected with any discretion, it is easy to point out the solar
episodes embodied in their lives.   See Cortès landing in
Mexico, and seeming to the Aztecs their very Sun-priest
Quetzalcoatl, come back from the East to renew his reign
of light and glory; mark him deserting the wife of his
youth, even as the Sun leaves the Dawn, and again in later
life abandoning Marina for a new bride; watch his sun-like
career of brilliant conquest, checkered with intervals of
storm, and declining to a death clouded with sorrow and
disgrace.   The life of Julius Cæsar would fit as plausibly
into a scheme of solar myth ; his splendid course as in each
new land he came, and saw, and conquered ; his desertion
of Cleopatra; his ordinance of the solar year for men; his
death at the hand of Brutus, like Sifrit's death at the hand
of Hagen in the Nibelungen Lied ; his falling pierced with

many bleeding wounds, and shrouding himself in his cloak
to die in darkness. Of Cæsar, better than of Cassius his
slayer, it might have been said in the language of sun-
myth :

> ". . . O setting sun,
> As in thy red rays thou dost sink to-night,
> So in his red blood Cassius' day is set ;
> The sun of Rome is set ! "

Thus, in interpreting heroic legend as based on nature-
myth, circumstantial analogy must be very cautiously appealed to, and at any rate there is need of evidence more
cogent than vague likenesses between human and cosmic
life. Now such evidence is forthcoming at its strongest in
a crowd of myths, whose open meaning it would be wanton
incredulity to doubt, so little do they disguise, in name or
sense, the familiar aspects of nature which they figure as
scenes of personal life. Even where the tellers of legend
may have altered or forgotten its earlier mythic meaning,
there are often sufficient grounds for an attempt to restore
it. In spite of change and corruption, myths are slow to
lose all consciousness of their first origin ; as for instance,
classical literature retained enough of meaning in the great
Greek sun-myth, to compel even Lempriere of the Classical
Dictionary to admit that Apollo or Phœbus "is often confounded with the sun." For another instance, the Greeks
had still present to their thoughts the meaning of Argos
Panoptes, Io's hundred-eyed, all-seeing guard who was slain
by Hermes and changed into the Peacock, for Macrobius
writes as recognizing in him the star-eyed heaven itself ; [1]
even as the Aryan Indra, the Sky, is the "thousand-
eyed" (*sahasrâksha, sahasranayana*). In modern times the
thought is found surviving or reviving in a strange region of
language : whoever it was that brought *argo* as a word for
"heaven" into the Lingua Furbesca or Robbers' Jargon of
Italy,[2] must have been thinking of the starry sky watching

---

[1] Macrob. 'Satum.' I. 19, 19. See Eurip. 'Phœn.' 1116, etc. and Schol.
Welcker, vol. I. p. 336 ; Max Müller, 'Lectures,' vol. II. p. 380.
[2] Francisque-Michel, 'Argot,' p. 425.

him like Argus with his hundred eyes. The etymology of names, moreover, is at once the guide and safeguard of the mythologist. The obvious meaning of words did much to preserve vestiges of plain sense in classic legend, in spite of all the efforts of the commentators. There was no disputing the obvious facts that Hēlios was the Sun, and Selēnē the Moon; and as for Jove, all the nonsense of pseudo-history could not quite do away the idea that he was really Heaven, for language continued to declare this in such expressions as "sub Jove frigido." The explanation of the rape of Persephone, as a nature-myth of summer and winter, does not depend alone on analogy of incident, but has the very names to prove its reality, Zeus, Hēlios, Dēmētēr—Heaven, and Sun, and Mother Earth. Lastly, in stories of mythic beings who are the presiding genii of star or mountain, tree or river, or heroes and heroines actually metamorphosed into such objects, personification of nature is still plainly evident; the poet may still as of old see Atlas bear the heavens on his mighty shoulders, and Alpheus in impetuous course pursue the maiden Arethusa.

In a study of the nature-myths of the world, it is hardly practicable to start from the conceptions of the very lowest human tribes, and to work upwards from thence to fictions of higher growth; partly because our information is but meagre as to the beliefs of these shy and seldom quite intelligible folk, and partly because the legends they possess have not reached that artistic and systematic shape which they attain to among races next higher in the scale. It therefore answers better to take as a foundation the mythology of the North American Indians, the South Sea Islanders, and other high savage tribes who best represent in modern times the early mythologic period of human history. The survey may be fitly commenced by a singularly perfect and purposeful cosmic myth from New Zealand.

It seems long ago and often to have come into men's

minds, that the overarching Heaven and the all-producing
Earth are, as it were, a Father and a Mother of the world,
whose offspring are the living creatures, men, and beasts,
and plants. Nowhere, in the telling of this oft-told tale, is
present nature veiled in more transparent personification,
nowhere is the world's familiar daily life repeated with more
childlike simplicity as a story of long past ages, than in the
legend of ' The Children of Heaven and Earth ' written down
by Sir George Grey among the Maoris not twenty years
ago. From Rangi, the Heaven, and Papa, the Earth, it is
said, sprang all men and things, but sky and earth clave
together, and darkness rested upon them and the beings
they had begotten, till at last their children took counsel
whether they should rend apart their parents, or slay them.
Then Tane-mahuta, father of forests, said to his five great
brethren, "It is better to rend them apart, and to let the
heaven stand far above us, and the earth lie under our feet.
Let the sky become as a stranger to us, but the earth remain
close to us as our nursing mother." So Rongo-ma-tane,
god and father of the cultivated food of man, arose and
strove to separate the heaven and the earth; he struggled,
but in vain, and vain too were the efforts of Tangaroa,
father of fish and reptiles, and of Haumia-tikitiki, father of
wild-growing food, and of Tu-matauenga, god and father of
fierce men. Then slow uprises Tane-mahuta, god and
father of forests, and wrestles with his parents, striving to
part them with his hands and arms. "Lo, he pauses; his
head is now firmly planted on his mother the earth, his feet
he raises up and rests against his father the skies, he strains
his back and limbs with mighty effort. Now are rent apart
Rangi and Papa, and with cries and groans of woe they
shriek aloud . . . . But Tane-mahuta pauses not; far, far
beneath him he presses down the earth; far, far above him
he thrusts up the sky." But Tawhiri-ma-tea, father of
winds and storms, had never consented that his mother
should be torn from her lord, and now there arose in his
breast a fierce desire to war against his brethren. So the

Storm-god rose and followed his father to the realms above, hurrying to the sheltered hollows of the boundless skies, to hide and cling and nestle there. Then came forth his progeny, the mighty winds, the fierce squalls, the clouds, dense, dark, fiery, wildly drifting, wildly bursting; and in their midst their father rushed upon his foe. Tane-mahuta and his giant forests stood unconscious and unsuspecting when the raging hurricane burst on them, snapping the mighty trees across, leaving trunks and branches rent and torn upon the ground for the insect and the grub to prey on. Then the father of storms swooped down to lash the waters into billows whose summits rose like cliffs, till Tangaroa, god of ocean and father of all that dwell therein, fled affrighted through his seas. His children, Ika-tere, the father of fish, and Tu-te-wehiwehi, the father of reptiles, sought where they might escape for safety; the father of fish cried, " Ho, ho, let us all escape to the sea," but the father of reptiles shouted in answer, "Nay, nay, let us rather fly inland," and so these creatures separated, for while the fish fled into the sea, the reptiles sought safety in the forests and scrubs. But the sea-god Tangaroa, furious that his children the reptiles should have deserted him, has ever since waged war on his brother Tane who gave them shelter in his woods. Tane attacks him in return, supplying the offspring of his brother Tu-matauenga, father of fierce men, with canoes and spears and fish-hooks made from his trees, and with nets woven from his fibrous plants, that they may destroy withal the fish, the Sea-god's children; and the Sea-god turns in wrath upon the Forest-god, overwhelms his canoes with the surges of the sea, sweeps with floods his trees and houses into the boundless ocean. Next the god of storms pushed on to attack his brothers the gods and progenitors of the tilled food and the wild, but Papa, the Earth, caught them up and hid them, and so safely were these her children concealed by their mother, that the Storm-god sought for them in vain. So he fell upon the last of his brothers, the father of fierce men, but him he could not even shake, though he put forth all his strength. What cared Tu-matauenga for his brother's wrath? He it was who had planned the destruction of their parents, and had shown himself brave and fierce in war; his brethren had yielded before the tremendous onset of the Storm-god and his progeny; the Forest-god and his offspring had been broken and torn in pieces; the Sea-god and his children had fled to the depths of the ocean or the recesses of the shore; the gods of food had been safe in hiding; but Man still stood erect and unshaken upon the bosom of his mother Earth, and at last the hearts of the Heaven and the Storm became tranquil, and their passion was assuaged.

But now Tu-matauenga, father of fierce men, took thought how he might be avenged upon his brethren who had left him unaided to stand against the god of storms. He twisted nooses of the leaves of the whanake tree, and the birds and beasts, children of Tane the Forest-god, fell before him; he netted nets from the flax-plant, and dragged ashore the fish, the children of Tangaroa the Sea-god; he found in their hiding-place underground the children of Rongo-ma-tane, the sweet potato and all cultivated food, and the children of Haumia-tikitiki, the fern-root and all wild-growing food, he dug them up and let them wither in the sun. Yet, though he overcame his four brothers, and they became his food, over the fifth he could not prevail, and Tawhiri-ma-tea, the Storm-god, still ever attacks him in tempest and hurricane, striving to destroy him both by sea and land. It was the bursting forth of the Storm-god's wrath against his brethren that caused the dry land to disappear beneath the waters: the beings of ancient days who thus submerged the land were Terrible-rain, Long-continued-rain, Fierce-hailstorms; and their progeny were Mist, and Heavy-dew, and Light-dew, and thus but little of the dry land was left standing above the sea. Then clear light increased in the world, and the beings who had been hidden between Rangi and Papa before they were parted, now multiplied upon the earth. "Up to this time the vast Heaven has still ever remained

separated from his spouse the Earth. Yet their mutual
love still continues; the soft warm sighs of her loving
bosom still ever rise up to him, ascending from the woody
mountains and valleys, and men call these mists; and the
vast Heaven, as he mourns through the long nights his
separation from his beloved, drops frequent tears upon her
bosom, and men seeing these term them dew-drops." [1]

The rending asunder of heaven and earth is a far-spread
Polynesian legend, well known in the island groups that
lie away to the north-east.[2] Its elaboration, however, into
the myth here sketched out was probably native New
Zealand work. Nor need it be supposed that the particular form in which the English governor took it down
among the Maori priests and tale-tellers, is of ancient date.
The story carries in itself evidence of an antiquity of
character which does not necessarily belong to mere lapse
of centuries. Just as the adzes of polished jade and the
cloaks of tied flax-fibre, which these New Zealanders were
using but yesterday, are older in their place in history than
the bronze battle-axes and linen mummy cloths of ancient
Egypt, so the Maori poet's shaping of nature into nature-
myth belongs to a stage of intellectual history which was
passing away in Greece five-and-twenty centuries ago.
The myth-maker's fancy of Heaven and Earth as father
and mother of all things naturally suggested the legend
that they in old days abode together, but have since been
torn asunder. In China the same idea of the universal
parentage is accompanied by a similar legend of the separation. Whether or not there is historical connexion here
between the mythology of Polynesia and China I will not
guess, but certainly the ancient Chinese legend of the

---

[1] Sir G. Grey, 'Polynesian Mythology,' p. 1 etc., translated from the
original Maori text published by him under the title 'Ko nga Mahinga a nga
Tapuna Maori, etc.' London, 1854. Compare with Shortland, 'Trads. of ' N.
Z.' p. 55, etc.; R. Taylor, 'New Zealand,' p. 114, etc.

[2] Schirren, 'Wandersagen der Neuseeländer, etc.' p. 42; Ellis, 'Polyn.
Res.' vol. i. p. 116; Tyerman and Bennet, p. 526; Turner, 'Polynesia,'
p. 245.

separation of heaven and earth in the primæval days of Puang-Ku seems to have taken the very shape of the Polynesian myth: "Some say a person called Puang-Ku opened or separated the heavens and the earth, they previously being pressed down close together."[1] As to the mythic details in the whole story of 'The Children of Heaven and Earth,' there is scarcely a thought that is not still transparent, scarcely even a word that has lost its meaning to us. The broken and stiffened traditions which our fathers fancied relics of ancient history are, as has been truly said, records of a past which was never present; but the simple nature-myth, as we find it in its actual growth, or reconstruct it from its legendary remnants, may be rather called the record of a present which is never past. The battle of the storm against the forest and the ocean is still waged before our eyes; we still look upon the victory of man over the creatures of the land and sea; the food-plants still hide in their mother earth, and the fish and reptiles find shelter in the ocean and the thicket; but the mighty forest-trees stand with their roots firm planted in the ground, while with their branches they push up and up against the sky. And if we have learnt the secret of man's thought in the childhood of his race, we may still realize with the savage the personal being of the ancestral Heaven and Earth.

The idea of the Earth as a mother is more simple and obvious, and no doubt for that reason more common in the world, than the idea of the Heaven as a father. Among the native races of America the Earth-mother is one of the great personages of mythology. The Peruvians worshipped her as Mama-Ppacha or "Mother-Earth;" the Caribs, when there was an earthquake, said it was their mother Earth dancing, and signifying to them to dance and make merry likewise, which accordingly they did. Among the North-American Indians the Comanches call on the Earth

[1] Premare in Pauthier, 'Livres Sacrés de l'Orient,' p. 19; Doolittle, 'Chinese,' vol. II. p. 396.

as their mother, and the Great Spirit as their father. A story told by Gregg shows a somewhat different thought of mythic parentage. General Harrison once called the Shawnee chief Tecumseh for a talk:—"Come here, Tecumseh, and sit by your father!" he said. "You my father!" replied the chief, with a stern air. "No! yonder sun (pointing towards it) is my father, and the earth is my mother, so I will rest on her bosom," and he sat down on the ground. Like this was the Aztec fancy, as it seems from this passage in a Mexican prayer to Tezcatlipoca, offered in time of war: "Be pleased, O our Lord, that the nobles who shall die in the war be peacefully and joyously received by the Sun and the Earth, who are the loving father and mother of all."[1] In the mythology of Finns, Lapps, and Esths, Earth-Mother is a divinely honoured personage.[2] Through the mythology of our own country the same thought may be traced, from the days when the Anglo-Saxon called upon the Earth, "Hál wes thu folde, fira modor," "Hail thou Earth, men's mother," to the time when mediæval Englishmen made a riddle of her, asking "Who is Adam's mother?" and poetry continued what mythology was letting fall, when Milton's archangel promised Adam a life to last

> " . . . . till like ripe fruit, thou drop
> Into thy mother's lap." [3]

Among the Aryan race, indeed, there stands, wide and firm, the double myth of the "two great parents," as the Rig-Veda calls them. They are *Dyaushpitar*, Ζεὺς πατήρ, *Jupiter*, the "Heaven-father," and *Prthivi mátar*, the

---

[1] J. G. Müller, 'Amer. Urrelig.' pp. 108, 110, 117, 221, 369, 494, 620; Rivero and Tschudi, 'Ant of Peru,' p. 161; Gregg, 'Journal of a Santa Fé Trader,' vol. ii. p. 257; Sahagun, 'Retorica, etc., Mexicana,' cap. 3, in Kingsborough, 'Ant. of Mexico,' vol. v.

[2] Castrén, 'Finn. Myth.' p. 86.

[3] Grimm, 'D. M.' p. xix. 229-33, 608; Halliwell, 'Pop. Rhymes,' p. 153; Milton, 'Paradise Lost,' ix. 273, l. 535; see Lucretius, i. 250.

"Earth-mother;" and their relation is still kept in mind
in the ordinance of Brahman marriage according to the
Yajur-Veda, where the bridegroom says to the bride, "I
am the sky, thou art the earth, come let us marry." When
Greek poets called Ouranos and Gaia, or Zeus and Dêmêtěr,
husband and wife, what they meant was the union of Heaven
and Earth; and when Plato said that the earth brought
forth men, but God was their shaper, the same old mythic
thought must have been present to his mind.[1] It re-appears
in ancient Scythia;[2] and again in China, where Heaven and
Earth are called in the Shu-King "Father and Mother of
all things." Chinese philosophy naturally worked this idea
into the scheme of the two great principles of nature, the
Yu and Yang, male and female, heavenly and earthly, and
from this disposition of nature they drew a practical moral
lesson: Heaven, said the philosophers of the Sung dynasty,
made man, and Earth made woman, and therefore woman
is to be subject to man as Earth to Heaven.[3]

Entering next upon the world-wide myths of Sun, Moon,
and Stars, the regularity and consistency of human imagination may be first displayed in the beliefs connected with
eclipses. It is well known that these phenomena, to us
now crucial instances of the exactness of natural laws, are,
throughout the lower stages of civilization, the very embodi-
ment of miraculous disaster. Among the native races of
America it is possible to select a typical series of myths
describing and explaining, according to the rules of savage
philosophy, these portents of dismay. The Chiquitos of
the southern continent thought the Moon was hunted
across the sky by huge dogs, who caught and tore her till
her light was reddened and quenched by the blood flowing
from her wounds, and then the Indians, raising a frightful

[1] Max Müller, 'Lectures,' 2nd series, p. 459 ; Pictet, 'Origines Indo-Europ.'
part IL pp. 603-7 ; Colebrooke, 'Essays,' vol. i. p. 220.
[2] Herod. iv. 59.
[3] Plath, 'Religion der alten Chinesen,' part. L p. 37 ; Davis, 'Chinese,'
vol. ii. p. 64 ; Legge, 'Confucius,' p. 106 ; Bastian, 'Mensch,' vol. ii. p. 437 ;
vol. iii. p. 302.

howl and lamentation, would shoot across into the sky to
drive the monsters off. The Caribs, thinking that the
demon Maboya, hater of all light, was seeking to devour
the Sun and Moon, would dance and howl in concert all
night long to scare him away. The Peruvians, imagining
such an evil spirit in the shape of a monstrous beast, raised
the like frightful din when the Moon was eclipsed, shouting, sounding musical instruments, and beating the dogs
to join their howls to the hideous chorus. Nor are such
ideas extinct in our own days. In the Tupi language, the
proper description of a solar eclipse is "onrasu jaguareté
vû," that is, "Jaguar has eaten Sun;" and the full meaning of this phrase is displayed by tribes who still shout and
let fly burning arrows to drive the devouring beast from his
prey. On the northern continent, again, some savages
believed in a great sun-swallowing dog, while others would
shoot up arrows to defend their luminaries against the
enemies they fancied attacking them. By the side of these
prevalent notions there occur, however, various others;
thus the Caribs could imagine the eclipsed Moon hungry,
sick; or dying; the Peruvians could fancy the Sun angry
and hiding his face, and the sick Moon likely to fall in
total darkness, and bring on the end of the world; the
Hurons thought the Moon sick, and explained their
customary charivari of shouting men and howling dogs as
performed to recover her from her complaint. Passing
on from these most primitive conceptions, it appears that
natives of both South and North America fell upon philosophic myths somewhat nearer the real facts of the case,
insomuch as they admit that the Sun and Moon cause
eclipses of one another. In Cumana, men thought that
the wedded Sun and Moon quarrelled, and that one of them
was wounded; and the Ojibwas endeavoured by tumultuous
noise to distract the two from such a conflict. The course
of progressive science went far beyond this among the
Aztecs, who, as part of their remarkable astronomical
knowledge, seem to have had an idea of the real cause of

eclipses, but who kept up a relic of the old belief by continuing to speak in mythologic phrase of the Sun and Moon
being eaten.[1] Elsewhere in the lower culture, there prevailed
similar mythic conceptions. In the South Sea Islands,
some supposed the Sun and Moon to be swallowed by an
offended deity, whom they therefore induced, by liberal
offerings, to eject the luminaries from his stomach.[2] In
Sumatra we have the comparatively scientific notion that
an eclipse has to do with the action of Sun and Moon on
one another, and, accordingly, they make a loud noise with
sounding instruments to prevent the one from devouring
the other.[3] So, in Africa, there may be found both the
rudest theory of the Eclipse-monster, and the more
advanced conception that a solar eclipse is "the Moon
catching the Sun."[4]

It is no cause for wonder that an aspect of the heavens so
awful as an eclipse should in times of astronomic ignorance
have filled men's minds with terror of a coming destruction
of the world. It may help us still to realize this thought if
we consider how, as Calmet pointed out many years ago, the
prophet Joel adopted the plainest words of description of
the solar and lunar eclipse, "The sun shall be turned into
darkness, and the moon into blood;" nor could the thought
of any catastrophe of nature have brought his hearers face
to face with a more lurid and awful picture. But to our
minds, now that the eclipse has long passed from the realm
of mythology into the realm of science, such words can
carry but a feeble glimmer of their early meaning. The

[1] J. G. Muller, 'Amer. Urrelig.' pp. 59, 219, 231, 255, 395, 420; Martius,
'Ethnog. Amer.' vol. i. pp. 329, 467, 583; vol. ii. p. 109; Southey, 'Brazil,'
vol. i. p. 352, vol. ii. p. 371; De la Borde, 'Caraïbes,' p. 525; Dobrizhoffer,
'Abipones,' vol. ii. p. 84; Smith and Lowe, 'Journey from Lima to Para,'
p. 230; Schoolcraft, 'Indian Tribes of N. A.' part i. p. 271; Charlevoix,
'Nouv. France,' vol. vi p. 149; Cranz, 'Grönland,' p. 295; Bastian, 'Mensch,'
vol. iii. p. 191; 'Early Hist. of Mankind,' p. 163.
[2] Ellis, 'Polyn. Res.' vol. i. p. 331.
[3] Marsden, 'Sumatra,' p. 194.
[4] Grant in 'Tr. Eth. Soc.' vol. iii. p. 90; Koelle, 'Kanuri Proverbs, etc.'
p. 207.

ancient doctrine of the eclipse has not indeed lost its whole interest. To trace it upward from its early savage stages to the period when astronomy claimed it, and to follow the course of the ensuing conflict over it between theology and science—ended among ourselves but still being slugggishly fought out among less cultured nations—this is to lay open a chapter of the history of opinion, from which the student who looks forward as well as back may learn grave lessons.

There is reason to consider most or all civilized nations to have started from the myth of the Eclipse-monster in forms as savage as those of the New World. It prevails still among the great Asiatic nations. The Hindus say that the demon Ráhu insinuated himself among the gods, and obtained a portion of the amrita, the drink of immortality; Vishnu smote off the now immortal head, which still pursues the Sun and Moon whose watchful gaze detected his presence in the divine assembly. Another version of the myth is that there are two demons, Ráhu and Ketu, who devour Sun and Moon respectively, and who are described in conformity with the phenomena of eclipses, Ráhu being black, and Ketu red; the usual charivari is raised by the populace to drive them off, though indeed, as their bodies have been cut off at the neck, their prey must of natural course slip out as soon as swallowed. Or Ráhu and Ketu are the head and body of the dissevered demon, by which conception the Eclipse-monster is most ingeniously adapted to advanced astronomy, the head and tail being identified with the ascending and descending nodes. The following remarks on the eclipse-controversy, made by Mr. Samuel Davis eighty years ago in the Asiatick Researches, are still full of interest. "It is evident, from what has been explained, that the Pûndits, learned in the Jyotish shastrû, have truer notions of the form of earth and the economy of the universe than are ascribed to the Hindoos in general: and that they must reject the ridiculous belief of the common Brahmûns, that eclipses are occasioned by the intervention of the monster Rahoo, with many other particulars equally unscientific and absurd. But as this belief is founded on explicit and positive declarations contained in the védás and poorantis, the divine authority of which writings no devout Hindoo can dispute, the astronomers have some of them cautiously explained such passages in those writings as disagree with the principles of their own science: and where recon-ciliation was impossible, have apologized, as well as they could, for propositions necessarily established in the practice of it, by observing, that certain things, as stated in other shastrûs, might have been so formerly, and may be so still; but for astronomical purposes, astronomical rules must be followed."[1]   It is not easy to give a more salient example than this of the consequence of investing philosophy with the mantle of religion, and allowing priests and scribes to convert the childlike science of an early age into the sacred dogma of a late one. Asiatic peoples under Buddhist influence show the eclipse-myth in its different stages. The rude Mongols make a clamour of rough music to drive the attacking Aracho (Ráhu) from Sun or Moon. A Buddhist version mentioned by Dr. Bastian describes Indra the Heaven-god pursuing Ráhu with his thunderbolt, and ripping open his belly, so that although he can swallow the heavenly bodies, he lets them slip out again.[2] The more civilized nations of South-East Asia, accepting the eclipse-demons Ráhu and Ketu, were not quite staggered in their belief by the foreigners' power of foretelling eclipses, nor even by learning roughly to do the same themselves. The Chinese have official announcement of an eclipse duly made beforehand, and then proceed to encounter the ominous monster, when he comes, with

[1] H. H. Wilson, 'Vishnupurana,' pp. 78, 140; Skr. Dic. s. v. ráhu; Sir W. Jones in 'As. Res.' vol. ii. p. 290; S. Davis, ibid., p. 258; Pictet, 'Ori-gines Indo-Europ.,' part. ii. p. 581; Roberts, 'Oriental Illustrations,' p. 7; Hardy, 'Manual of Buddhism.'
[2] Castrén, 'Finn. Myth.' p. 63; Bastian, 'Oestl. Asien,' vol. ii. p. 311.

gongs and bells and the regularly appointed prayers. Travellers of a century or two ago relate curious details of such combined belief in the dragon and the almanac, culminating in an ingenious argument to account for the accuracy of the Europeans' predictions. These clever people, the Siamese said, know the monster's mealtimes, and can tell how hungry he will be, that is, how large an eclipse will be required to satisfy him.[1]

In Europe popular mythology kept up ideas, either of a fight of sun or moon with celestial enemies, or of the moon's fainting or sickness; and especially remnants of such archaic belief are manifested in the tumultuous clamour raised in defence or encouragement of the afflicted luminary. The Romans flung firebrands into the air, and blew trumpets, and clanged brazen pots and pans, "laboranti succurrere lunæ." Tacitus, relating the story of the soldiers' mutiny against Tiberius, tells how their plan was frustrated by the moon suddenly languishing in a clear sky (luna claro repente cœlo visa languescere): in vain by clang of brass and blast of trumpet they strove to drive away the darkness, for clouds came up and covered all, and the plotters saw, lamenting, that the gods turned away from their crime.[2] In the period of the conversion of Europe, Christian teachers began to attack the pagan superstition, and to urge that men should no longer clamour and cry "vince luna!" to aid the moon in her sore danger; and at last there came a time when the picture of the sun or moon in the dragon's mouth became a mere old-fashioned symbol to represent eclipses in the calendar, and the saying, "Dieu garde la lune des loups" passed into a mocking proverb against fear of remote danger. Yet the ceremonial charivari is mentioned in our own country in the seventeenth century:

[1] Klemm, 'C. G.' vol. vi. p. 449; Doolittle, 'Chinese,' vol. l. p. 309; Turpin, Richard, and Dorri in Pinkerton, vol. iv. pp. 579, 725, 815; Hanlon, 'Ocnli Asien,' vol. ii. p. 109; vol. iii. p. 242. See Eisenmenger, 'Entdecktes Judenthum,' vol. l. p. 398 (Talmudic myth).

[2] Plutarch. de Facie in Orbe Lunæ; Juvenal, Sat. vi. 441; Plin. ii. 9; Tacit. Annal. l. 28.

"The Irish or Welsh during eclipses run about beating
kettles and pans, thinking their clamour and vexations
available to the assistance of the higher orbes." In 1654,
Nuremberg went wild with terror of an impending solar
eclipse; the markets ceased, the churches were crowded
with penitents, and a record of the event remains in the
printed thanksgiving which was issued (Danckgebeth nach
vergangener höchstbedrohlich und hochschädlicher Sonnen-
finsternuss), which gives thanks to the Almighty for granting to poor terrified sinners the grace of covering the sky
with clouds, and sparing them the sight of the awful sign in
heaven. In our own times, a writer on French folklore was
surprised during a lunar eclipse to hear sighs and exclamations, "Mon Dieu, qu'elle est souffrante!" and found on
inquiry that the poor moon was believed to be the prey of
some invisible monster seeking to devour her.[1] No doubt
such late survivals have belonged in great measure to the
ignorant crowd, for the educated classes of the West have
never suffered in its extreme the fatal Chinese union of
scepticism and superstition. Yet if it is our mood to bewail
the slowness with which knowledge penetrates the mass of
mankind, there stand dismal proofs before us here. The
eclipse remained an omen of fear almost up to our own
century, and could rout a horror-stricken army, and fill
Europe with dismay, a thousand years after Pliny had
written in memorable words his eulogy of the astronomers;
those great men, he said, and above ordinary mortals, who,
by discovering the laws of the heavenly bodies, had freed the
miserable mind of men from terror at the portents of eclipses.

Day is daily swallowed up by Night, to be set free again
at dawn, and from time to time suffers a like but shorter
durance in the maw of the Eclipse and the Storm-cloud;

---

[1] Grimm, 'D. M.' 668-78, 224; Hanusch, 'Slav. Myth.' p. 268; Brand,
'Pop. Ant.' vol. iii. p. 152; Horst, 'Zauber Bibliothek,' vol. iv. p. 350; D.
Monnier, 'Traditions populaires comparées,' p. 135; see Migne, 'Dict. des
Superstitions,' art. 'Eclipse;' Cornelius Agrippa, 'De Occulta Philosophia,'
ii. c. 45, gives a picture of the lunar eclipse-dragon.

Summer is overcome and prisoned by dark Winter, to be again set free. It is a plausible opinion that such scenes from the great nature-drama of the conflict of light and darkness are, generally speaking, the simple facts, which in many lands and ages have been told in mythic shape, as legends of a Hero or Maiden devoured by a Monster, and hacked out again or disgorged. The myths just displayed show with absolute distinctness, that myth can describe eclipse as the devouring and setting free of the personal sun and moon by a monster. The following Maori legend will supply proof as positive that the episode of the Sun's or the Day's death in sunset may be dramatized into a tale of a personal solar hero plunging into the body of the personal Night.

Maui, the New Zealand cosmic hero, at the end of his glorious career came back to his father's country, and was told that here, perhaps, he might be overcome, for here dwelt his mighty ancestress, Hine-nui-te-po, Great-Woman-Night, whom " you may see flashing, and as it were opening and shutting there, where the horizon meets the sky; what you see yonder shining so brightly-red, are her eyes, and her teeth are as sharp and hard as pieces of volcanic glass; her body is like that of a man; and as for the pupils of her eyes, they are jasper; and her hair is like the tangles of long sea-weed, and her mouth is like that of a barra-couta." Maui boasted of his former exploits, and said, " Let us fearlessly seek whether men are to die or live for ever;" but his father called to mind an evil omen, that when he was baptizing Maui he had left out part of the fitting prayers, and therefore he knew that his son must perish. Yet he said, " O, my last-born, and the strength of my old age, . . . be bold, go and visit your great ancestress, who flashes so fiercely there where the edge of the horizon meets the sky." Then the birds came to Maui to be his companions in the enterprise, and it was evening when they went with him, and they came to the dwelling of Hine-nui-te-po, and found her fast asleep. Maui charged

the birds not to laugh when they saw him creep into the old
chieftainess, but when he had got altogether inside her, and
was coming out of her mouth, then they might laugh long
and loud. So Maui stripped off his clothes, and the skin
on his hips, tattooed by the chisel of Uetonga, looked
mottled and beautiful, like a mackerel's, as he crept in.
The birds kept silence, but when he was in up to his waist,
the little tiwakawaka could hold its laughter in no longer,
and burst out loud with its merry note; then Maui's ancestress awoke, closed on him and caught him tight, and he
was killed. Thus died Maui, and thus death came into the
world, for Hine-nui-te-po is the goddess both of night and
death, and had Maui entered into her body and passed
safely through her, men would have died no more. The
New Zealanders hold that the Sun descends at night into
his cavern, bathes in the Wai Ora Tane, the Water of Life,
and returns at dawn from the under-world; hence we may
interpret their thought that if Man could likewise descend
into Hades and return, his race would be immortal.[1] It is
seldom that solar characteristics are more distinctly marked
in the several details of a myth than they are here. Hine-nui-
te-po, Great-Woman-Night, who dwells on the horizon, is
the New Zealand Hades, or goddess of Hades. The birds
are to keep silence as the Sun enters the Night, but may sing
when he comes forth from her mouth, the mouth of Hades.
Lastly, I have been able to use an unexceptionable means of
testing whether the legend is or is not a real sun-myth. If
it is so, then the tiwakawaka (also called the piwakawaka)
ought to be a bird that sings at sunset. I have had inquiry

[1] Grey, 'Polyn. Myth.' p. 54—58; in his editions of the Maori text, Ko
nga Mahinga, pp. 28-30, Ko nga Mateatea, pp. xlviii-lx. I have to thank
Sir G. Grey for a more explicit and mythologically more consistent translation of the story of Maui's entrance into the womb of Hine-nui-te-po and her
crushing him to death between her thighs, than is given in his English version. Compare H. Taylor, 'New Zealand,' p. 132; Schirren, 'Wanderungen
der Neuseel.' p. 33; Shortland, 'Trads. of N. Z.' p. 63 (a curious version of
the myth of Maui's death); see also pp. 171, 180, and Baker in 'Tr. Eth.
Soc.' vol. i. p. 63.

made in New Zealand to ascertain whether this is the case, and have thus obtained a perfect confirmation of my interpretation of the legend of the death of Maui, as being a nature-myth of the setting sun; the reply is that the name " describes the cry of the bird, which is only heard at sunset."

In the list of myths of engulphing monsters, there are others which seem to display, with a clearness almost approaching this, an origin suggested by the familiar spectacle of Day and Night, or Light and Darkness. The simple story of the Day may well be told in the Karen tale of Ta Ywa, who was born a tiny child, and went to the Sun to make him grow; the Sun tried in vain to destroy him by rain and heat, and then blew him up large till his head touched the sky; then he went forth and travelled from his home far over the earth; and among the adventures which befel him was this—a snake swallowed him, but they ripped the creature up, and Ta Ywa came back to life,[1] like the Sun from the ripped up serpent-demon in the Buddhist eclipse-myth. In North American Indian mythology, a principal personage is Manabozho, an Algonquin hero or deity whose solar character is well brought into view in an Ottawa myth which tells us that Manabozho (whom it calls Na-na-bou-jou) is the elder brother of Ning-gah-be-ar-nong Manito, the Spirit of the West, god of the country of the dead in the region of the setting sun. Manabozho's solar nature is again revealed in the story of his driving the West, his father, across mountain and lake to the brink of the world, though he cannot kill him. This sun-hero Manabozho, when he angled for the King of Fishes, was swallowed, canoe and all; then he smote the monster's heart with his war-club till he would fain have cast him up into the lake again, but the hero set his canoe fast across the fish's throat inside, and finished slaying him; when the dead monster drifted ashore, the gulls pecked an opening for Manabozho to come out. This is a story familiar to

[1] Mason, Karens in 'Journ. As. Soc. Bengal,' 1865, part II. p. 173, etc.

English readers from its introduction into the poem of Hiawatha. In another version, the tale is told of the Little Monedo of the Ojibwas, who also corresponds with the New Zealand Maui in being the Sun-Catcher; among his various prodigies, he is swallowed by the great fish, and cut out again by his sister.[1] South Africa is a region where there prevail myths which seem to tell the story of the world imprisoned in the monster Night, and delivered by the dawning Sun. The Basutos have their myth of the hero Litaolane; he came to man's stature and wisdom at his birth; all mankind save his mother and he had been devoured by a monster; he attacked the creature and was swallowed whole, but cutting his way out he set free all the inhabitants of the world. The Zulus tell stories as pointedly suggestive. A mother follows her children into the maw of the great elephant, and finds forests and rivers and highlands, and dogs and cattle, and people who had built their villages there; a description which is simply that of the Zulu Hades. When the Princess Untombinde was carried off by the Isikqukqumadevu, the "bloated, squatting, bearded monster," the King gathered his army and attacked it, but it swallowed up men, and dogs, and cattle, all but one warrior; he slew the monster, and there came out cattle, and horses, and men, and last of all the princess herself. The stories of these monsters being cut open imitate, in graphic savage fashion, the cries of the imprisoned creatures as they came back from darkness into daylight. "There came out first a fowl, it said, 'Kukuluku! I see the world!' For, for a long time it had been without seeing it. After the fowl there came out a man, he said 'Hau! I at length see the world!'" and so on with the rest.[2]

---

[1] Schoolcraft, 'Indian Tribes,' part iii. p. 318; 'Algic Res.' vol. i. p. 135, etc., 144; John Tanner, 'Narrative,' p. 357; see Brinton, 'Myths of New World,' p. 166. For legends of Sun-Catcher, see 'Early History of Mankind,' ch. xii.

[2] Casalis, 'Basutos,' p. 347; Callaway, 'Zulu Tales,' vol. i. pp. 56, 69, 84, 334 (see also the story, p. 241, of the frog who swallowed the princess and carried her safe home). See Cranz, p. 271 (Greenland angekok swallowed by

The well-known modern interpretation of the myth of
Perseus and Andromeda, or of Herakles and Hesione, as a
description of the Sun slaying the Darkness, has its connexion with this group of legends. It is related in a
remarkable version of this story, that when the Trojan
King Laomedon had bound his daughter Hesione to the
rock, a sacrifice to Poseidon's destroying sea-monster,
Herakles delivered the maiden, springing full-armed into
the fish's gaping throat, and coming forth hairless after
three days hacking within. This singular story, probably
in part of Semitic origin, combines the ordinary myth of
Hesione or Andromeda with the story of Jonah's fish, for
which indeed the Greek sculpture of Andromeda's monster
served as the model in early Christian art, while Joppa was
the place where vestiges of Andromeda's chains on a rock in
front of the town were exhibited in Pliny's time, and whence
the bones of a whale were carried to Rome as relics of
Andromeda's monster. To recognize the place which the
nature-myth of the Man swallowed by the Monster occupies
in mythology, among remote and savage races and onward
among the higher nations, affects the argument on a point
of Biblical criticism. It strengthens the position of the
critics who, seeing that the Book of Jonah consists of two
wonder-episodes adapted to enforce two great religious
lessons, no longer suppose intention of literal narrative in
what they may fairly consider as the most elaborate parable
of the Old Testament. Had the Book of Jonah happened
to be lost in old times, and only recently recovered, it is
indeed hardly likely that any other opinion of it than this
would find acceptance among scholars.[1]

bear and walrus and thrown up again), and Bastian, 'Mensch,' vol. ii pp.
505-7 ; J. M. Harris in 'Mem. Anthrop. Soc,' vol. ii. p. 81 (similar notions
in Africa and New Guinea).

[1] Tretzus ap. Lycophron, Cassandra, 35. As to connexion with Joppa and
Phœnicia, see Plin. v. 14 ; ix. 4 ; Mela, i. 11; Strabo, xvi. 2, 28 ; Movers,
Phönizier, vol. i. pp. 422-3. The expression in Jonah, ii. 2, "out of the
belly of Hades" (mibten sheol, ἐκ κοιλίας ᾅδου) seems a relic of the original
meaning of the myth.

The conception of Hades as a monster swallowing men in death, was actually familiar to Christian thought. Thus, to take instances from different periods, the account of the Descent into Hades in the Apocryphal Gospel of Nicodemus makes Hades speak in his proper personality, complaining that his belly is in pain, when the Saviour is to descend and set free the saints imprisoned in it from the beginning of the world ; and in mediæval representations of this deliverance, the so-called " Harrowing of Hell," Christ is depicted standing before a huge fish-like monster's open jaws, whence Adam and Eve are coming forth first of mankind.[1] With even more distinctness of mythical meaning, the man-devouring monster is introduced in the Scandinavian Eireks-Saga. Eirek, journeying toward Paradise, comes to a stone bridge guarded by a dragon, and entering into its maw, finds that he has arrived in the world of bliss.[2] But in another wonder-tale, belonging to that legendary growth which formed round early Christian history, no such distinguishable remnant of nature-myth survives. St. Margaret, daughter of a priest of Antioch, had been cast into a dungeon, and there Satan came upon her in the form of a dragon, and swallowed her alive :

" Maiden Mergrete the Loked her beside,
And sees a loathly dragon, Out of an hirn glide :
His eyen were full grisely, His mouth opened wide,
And Margrete might no where flee There she must abide,
Maiden Margrete Stood still as any stone,
And that loathly worm, To her-ward gan gone
Took her in his foul mouth, And swallowed her flesh and bone,
Anon he brast—Damage hath she none !
Maiden Mergrete Upon the dragon stood ;
Blyth was her harte, And joyful was her mood."[3]

Stories belonging to the same group are not unknown to

[1] 'Apoc. Gosp.' Nicodemus, ch. xx. ; Mrs. Jameson, 'History of our Lord in Art,' vol. il. p. 258.
[2] Eireks Saga, 3, 4, in 'Flateyjarbok,' vol. i., Christiania, 1859 ; Baring-Gould, 'Myths of the Middle Ages,' p. 233.
[3] Mrs. Jameson, 'Sacred and Legendary Art,' vol. il. p. 138.

European folklore. One is the story of Little Red Riding Hood, mutilated in the English nursery version, but known more perfectly by old wives in Germany, who can tell that the lovely little maid in her shining red satin cloak was swallowed with her grandmother by the Wolf, but they both came out safe and sound when the hunter cut open the sleeping beast. Any one who can fancy with Prince Hal, "the blessed sun himself a fair hot wench in flame-coloured taffeta," and can then imagine her swallowed up by Sköll, the Sun-devouring Wolf of Scandinavian mythology, may be inclined to class the tale of Little Red Ridinghood as a myth of sunset and sunrise. There is indeed another story in Grimm's Märchen, partly the same as this one, which we can hardly doubt to have a quaint touch of sun-myth in it. It is called the Wolf and Seven Kids, and tells of the wolf swallowing the kids all but the youngest of the seven, who was hidden in the clock-case. As in Little Red Ridinghood they cut open the wolf and fill him with stones. This tale, which took its present shape since the invention of clocks, looks as though the tale-teller was thinking, not of real kids and wolf, but of days of the week swallowed by night, or how should he have hit upon such a fancy as that the wolf could not get at the youngest of the seven kids, because it was hidden (like to-day) in the clock-case ?[1]

It may be worth while to raise the question apropos of this nursery tale, does the peasant folklore of modern Europe really still display episodes of nature-myth, not as

[1] J. and W. Grimm, 'Kinder und Hausmärchen, vol. i. pp. 26, 110 ; vol. iii. p. 15. [See ref. to these two stories, 'Early Hist. of M.' 1st ed. (1865) p. 332. I find that Mr. G. W. Cox, 'Mythology' (1870), vol. i. p. 358, had noticed the Wolf and Seven Kids as a myth of the days of the week (Note to 2nd ed.)]. For mentions of the wolf of darkness, see Max Müller, 'Lectures,' 2nd series, p. 506, see 370, 'Chips, etc.,' vol. ii. p. 103 ; Hanusch, p. 192 ; Edda, Gylfaginning, 12 ; Grimm, 'D. M.' pp. 224, 668. With the episode of the stones substituted, compare the myth of Zeus and Kronos. For various other stories belonging to the group of the Man swallowed by the Monster, see Hardy, 'Manual of Buddhism,' p. 501 ; Lane, 'Thousand and One Nights,' vol. iii. p. 104 ; Halliwell, 'Pop. Rhymes,' p. 98 ; 'Nursery Rhymes,' p. 43 ; 'Early Hist. of Mankind,' p. 337.

mere broken-down and senseless fragments, but in full shape and significance ? In answer it will be enough to quote the story of Vasilissa the Beautiful, brought forward by Mr. W. Ralston in a recent lecture on Russian Folklore. Vasilissa's stepmother and two sisters, plotting against her life, send her to get a light at the house of Bába Yagá, the witch, and her journey contains the following history of the Day, told in truest mythic fashion. Vasilissa goes and wanders, wanders in the forest. She goes, and she shudders. Suddenly before her bounds a rider, he himself white, and clad in white, the horse under him white, and the trappings white. And day began to dawn. She goes farther, when a second rider bounds forth, himself red, clad in red, and on a red horse. The sun began to rise. She goes on all day, and towards evening arrives at the witch's house. Suddenly there comes again a rider, himself black, clad in all black, and on a black horse ; he bounded to the gates of the Bába Yagá and disappeared as if he had sunk through the earth. Night fell. After this, when Vasilissa asks the witch, who was the white rider, she answered, " That is my clear Day ; " who was the red rider, " That is my red Sun ; " who was the black rider, " That is my black Night ; they are all my trusty friends." Now, considering that the story of Little Red Ridinghood belongs to the same class of folklore tales as this story of Vasilissa the Beautiful, we need not be afraid to seek in the one for traces of the same archaic type of nature-myth which the other not only keeps up, but keeps up with the fullest consciousness of meaning.

The development of nature-myth into heroic legend seems to have taken place among the savage tribes of the South Sea Islands and North America much as it took place among the ancestors of the classic nations of the Old World. We are not to expect accurate consistency or proper sequence of episodes in the heroic cycles, but to judge from the characteristics of the episodes themselves as to the ideas which suggested them. As regards the less cultured races, a glance at two legendary cycles, one from Polynesia and the

other from North America, will serve to give an idea of the
varieties of treatment of phases of sun-myth. The New
Zealand myth of Maui, mixed as it may be with other
fancies, is in its most striking features the story of Day and
Night. The story of the Sun's birth from the ocean is thus
told. There were five brothers, all called Maui, and it was
the youngest Maui who had been thrown into the sea by
Taranga his mother, and ...ied by his ancestor Tama-
nui-ki-te-Rangi, Great-Man-in-Heaven, who took him to his
house, and hung him in the roof. Then is given in fanciful
personality the tale of the vanishing of Night at dawn. One
night, when Taranga came home, she found little Maui with
his brothers, and when she knew her last born, the child of
her old age, she took him to sleep with her, as she had been
used to take the other Mauis his brothers, before they were
grown up. But the little Maui grew vexed and suspicious,
when he found that every morning his mother rose at dawn
and disappeared from the house in a moment, not to return
till nightfall. So one night he crept out and stopped every
crevice in the wooden window and the doorway, that the day
might not shine into the house; then broke the faint light
of early dawn, and then the sun rose and mounted into the
heavens, but Taranga slept on, for she knew not it was broad
day outside. At last she sprang up, pulled out the stopping
of the chinks, and fled in dismay. Then Maui saw her
plunge into a hole in the ground and disappear, and thus he
found the deep cavern by which his mother went down below
the earth as each night departed. After this, follows the
episode of Maui's visit to his ancestress Muri-ranga-whenua,
at that western Land's End where Maori souls descend into
the subterranean region of the dead. She sniffs as he comes
towards her, and distends herself to devour him, but when
she has sniffed round from south by east to north, she smells
his coming by the western breeze, and so knows that he is
a descendant of hers. He asks for her wondrous jawbone,
she gives it to him, and it is his weapon in his next exploit
when he catches the sun, Tama-nui-te-Ra, Great-Man-Sun,

in the noose, and wounds him and makes him go slowly. With a fishhook pointed with the miraculous jawbone, and smeared with his own blood for bait, Maui next performs his most famous feat of fishing up New Zealand, still called Te-Ika-a-Maui, the fish of Maui. To understand this, we must compare the various versions of the story in these and other Pacific Islands, which show that it is a general myth of the raising of dry land from beneath the ocean. It is said elsewhere that it was Maui's grandfather, Rangi-Wenua, Heaven-Earth, who gave the jawbone. More distinctly, it is also said that Maui had two sons, whom he slew when young to take their jawbones; now these two sons must be the Morning and Evening, for Maui made the morning and evening stars from an eye of each; and it was with the jaw-bone of the eldest that he drew up the land from the deep. Thus the bringing up of the land from the ocean by the blood-stained jawbone of the morning seems to be a myth of the dawn. The metaphor of the jawbone of morning, somewhat far-fetched as it may seem, re-appears in the Rig-Veda, if Professor Max Müller's interpretation of Sârameya as the Dawn will hold good in this passage : "When thou, bright Sârameya, openest thy teeth, O red one, spears seem to glitter on thy jaws as thou swallowest. Sleep, sleep."[1] Another Maori legend tells how Maui takes fire in his hands, it burns him, and he springs with it into the sea: "When he sank in the waters, the sun for the first time set, and darkness covered the earth. When he found that all was night, he immediately pursued the sun, and brought him back in the morning." When Maui carried or flung the fire into the sea, he set a volcano burning. It is told, again, that when Maui had put out all fires on earth, his mother sent him to get new fire from her ancestress Mahuika. The Tongans, in their version of the myth, relate how the youngest Maui discovers the cavern that leads to Bulotu, the west-land of the dead, and how his father, another Maui, sends him to the yet older Maui who sits by his great

[1] Rig-Veda, vii. 54 ; Max Müller, 'Lectures,' 2nd ser. p. 473.

fire; the two wrestle, and Maui brings away fire for men,
leaving the old earthquake-god lying crippled below. The
legendary group thus dramatizes the birth of the sun from
the ocean and the departure of the night, the extinction of
the light at sunset and its return at dawn, and the descent
of the sun to the western Hades, the under-world of night
and death, which is incidentally identified with the region of
subterranean fire and earthquake. Here, indeed, the
characteristics of true nature-myth are not indistinctly
marked, and Maui's death by his ancestress the Night fitly
ends his solar career.[1]

It is a sunset-story, very differently conceived, that
begins the beautiful North American .Indian myth of the
Red Swan. The story belongs to the Algonquin race.
The hunter Ojibwa had just killed a bear and begun to
skin him, when suddenly something red tinged all the air
around. Reaching the shore of a lake, the Indian saw it
was a beautiful red swan, whose plumage glittered in the
sun. In vain the hunter shot his shafts, for the bird
floated unharmed and unheeding, but at last he remembered
three magic arrows at home, which had been his father's.
The first and second arrow flew near and nearer, the third
struck the swan, and flapping its wings, it flew off slowly
towards the sinking of the sun. With full sense of the
poetic solar meaning of this episode, Longfellow has adapted
it as a sunset picture, in one of his Indian poems:

> " Can it be the sun descending
> O'er the level plain of water?
> Or the Red Swan floating, flying,
> Wounded by the magic arrow,

[1] Grey, 'Polyn. Myth.' p. 16, etc., see 144. Other details in Schirren,
'Wanderungen der Neuseeländer,' pp. 32–7, 143–51; R. Taylor, 'New Zea-
land,' p. 124, etc.; compare 116, 141, etc., and volcano-myth, p. 248; Yate,
'New Zealand,' p. 142; Polack, 'M. and C. of New. Z.' vol. I. p. 15; S. S.
Farmer, 'Tonga Is.' p. 134. See also Turner, 'Polynesia,' pp. 252, 527
(Samoan version). In comparing the group of Maui-legends it is to be ob-
served that New Zealand Mahuika and Maui-Tikitiki correspond to Tongan
Mafuike and Kijikiji, Samoan Mafule and Tiitli.

Staining all the waves with crimson,
With the crimson of its life-blood,
Filling all the air with splendour,
With the splendour of its plumage!"

The story goes on to tell how the hunter speeds westward
in pursuit of the Red Swan. At lodges where he rests,
they tell him she has often passed there, but those who
followed her have never returned. She is the daughter of
an old magician who has lost his scalp, which Ojibwa
succeeds in recovering for him and puts back on his head,
and the old man rises from the earth, no longer aged and
decrepit, but splendid in youthful glory. Ojibwa departs,
and the magician calls forth the beautiful maiden, now not
his daughter but his sister, and gives her to his victorious
friend. It was in after days, when Ojibwa had gone home
with his bride, that he travelled forth, and coming to an
opening in the earth, descended and came to the abode of
departed spirits; there he could behold the bright western
region of the good, and the dark cloud of wickedness. But
the spirits told him that his brethren at home were quarrel-
ling for the possession of his wife, and at last, after long
wandering, this Red Indian Odysseus returned to his
mourning constant Penelope, laid the magic arrows to his
bow, and stretched the wicked suitors dead at his feet.[1]
Thus savage legends from Polynesia and America may well
support the theory[2] that Odysseus visiting the Elysian fields,
or Orpheus descending to the land of Hades to bring back
the "wide-shining" Eurydikê, are but the Sun himself
descending to, and ascending from, the world below.

Where Night and Hades take personal shape in myth,

[1] 'Schoolcraft, 'Algic Res.' vol. ii. pp. 1-33. The three arrows recur in
Manabozho's slaying the Shining Manitu, vol. i. p. 153. See the remarkably
corresponding three magic arrows in Orvar Odd's Saga; Nilsson, 'Stone Age,'
p. 197. The Red-Swan myth of sunset is introduced in George Eliot's
'Spanish Gypsy,' p. 69; Longfellow, 'Hiawatha,' xii.
[2] See Kuhn's 'Zeitschrift,' 1866, vol. ix. p. 212; Max Müller, 'Chips,'
vol. ii. p. 127; Cox, 'Mythology,' vol. i. p. 256, vol. ii. p. 239.

we may expect to find conceptions like that simply shown
in a Sanskrit word for evening, "rajanimukha," i. e.,
"mouth of night." Thus the Scandinavians told of Hel
the death-goddess, with mouth gaping like the mouth of
Fenrir her brother, the moon-devouring wolf; and an old
German poem describes Hell's abyss yawning from heaven
to earth:

> " der was der Hallen gelich
> diu dax abgrundo
> begenit mit ir munde
> unde den himel zuo der erden." [1]

The sculptures on cathedrals still display for the terror of
the wicked the awful jaws of Death, the mouth of Hell
wide yawning to swallow its victims. Again, where barbaric
cosmology accepts the doctrine of a firmament arching
above the earth, and of an under world whither the sun
descends when he sets and man when he dies, here the
conception of gates or portals, whether really or metaphorically meant, has its place. Such is the great gate which
the Gold Coast negro describes the Heaven as opening in
the morning for the Sun; such were the ancient Greek's
gates of Hades, and the ancient Jew's gates of Sheol.
There are three mythic descriptions connected with these
ideas found among the Karens, the Algonquins, and the
Aztecs, which are deserving of special notice. The Karens
of Birma, a race among whose special ideas are curiously
mixed thoughts borrowed from the more cultured races
they have been in contact with, have precedence here for
the distinctness of their statement. They say that in the
west there are two massive strata of rocks which are continually opening and shutting, and between these strata the
sun descends at sunset, but how the upper stratum is supported, no one can describe. The idea comes well into
view in the description of a Bghai festival, where sacrificed
fowls are thus addressed,—"The seven heavens, thou

[1] Grimm, 'D. M.' pp. 291, 767.

ascendest to the top; the seven earths, thou descendest to
the bottom. Thou arrivest at Khu-the; thou goest unto
Tha-ma (i. e., Yama, the Judge of the Dead in Hades).
Thou goest through the crevices of rocks, thou goest
through the crevices of precipices. At the opening and
shutting of the western gates of rock, thou goest in between;
thou goest below the earth where the Sun travels. I employ
thee, I exhort thee. I make thee a messenger, I make thee
an angel, etc."[1] Passing from Birma to the region of the
North American lakes, we find a corresponding description
in the Ottawa tale of Iosco, already quoted here for its
clearly marked personification of Sun and Moon. This
legend, though modern in some of its description of the
Europeans, their ships, and their far-off land across the
sea, is evidently founded on a myth of Day and Night.
Iosco seems to be Ioskeha, the White One, whose contest
with his brother Tawiscara, the Dark One, is an early and
most genuine Huron nature-myth of Day and Night. Iosco
and his friends travel for years eastward and eastward to
reach the sun, and come at last to the dwelling of Manabozho near the edge of the world, and then, a little beyond,
to the chasm to be passed on the way to the land of the
Sun and Moon. They began to hear the sound of the
beating sky, and it seemed near at hand, but they had far
to travel before they reached the place. When the sky
came down, its pressure would force gusts of wind from the
opening, so strong that the travellers could hardly keep
their feet, and the sun passed but a short distance
above their heads. The sky would come down with
violence, but it would rise slowly and gradually. Iosco and
one of his friends stood near the edge, and with a great
effort leapt through and gained a foothold on the other
side; but the other two were fearful and undecided, and

---

[1] Mason, 'Karens' in 'Journ. As. Soc. Bengal,' 1865, part II. pp. 233-4.
Prof. Liebrecht, in his notice of the 1st ed. of the present work, in Gött. Gel.
Anz. 1872, p. 1290, refers to a Birmese legend in Italian, O. A. vol. ii.
p. 515, and a Mongol legend, Geaser Chan, book iv.

when their companions called to them through the darkness,
"Leap! leap! the sky is on its way down," they looked up
and saw it descending, but paralyzed by fear they sprang so
feebly that they only reached the other side with their
hands, and the sky at the same moment striking violently
on the earth with a terrible sound, forced them into the
dreadful black abyss.[1] Lastly, in the funeral ritual of the
Aztecs there is found a like description of the first peril
that the shade had to encounter on the road leading to that
subterranean Land of the Dead, which the sun lights when
it is night on earth. Giving the corpse the first of the
passports that were to carry him safe to his journey's end,
the survivors said to him, "With these you will pass
between the two mountains that smite one against the
other."[2] On the suggestion of this group of solar conceptions and that of Mani's death, we may perhaps explain as
derived from a broken-down fancy of solar-myth, that
famous episode of Greek legend, where the good ship Argo
passed between the Symplégades, those two huge cliffs that
opened and closed again with swift and violent collision.[3]
Can any effort of baseless fancy have brought into the poet's
mind a thought so quaint in itself, yet so fitting with the
Karen and Aztec myths of the gates of Night and Death?
With the Maori legend, the Argonautic tale has a yet deeper
coincidence. In both the event is to determine the future;
but this thought is worked out in two converse ways. If

---

[1] Schoolcraft, 'Algic Researches,' vol. ii. p. 40, etc.; Loskiel, 'Gesch. der
Mission,' Barby, 1789, p. 47 (the English edition, part i. p. 35, is incorrect).
See also Brinton, 'Myths of New World,' p. 63. In an Esquimaux tale,
Giviok comes to the two mountains which shut and open; paddling swiftly
between, he gets through, but the mountains clashing together crush the
stern of his kayak, Rink, ' Eskimoische Eventyr og Sagn, p. 98, referred to
by Liebrecht, l. c.

[2] Torquemada, 'Monarquia Indiana,' xiii. 47; "Con estos has de pasar por
medio de dos Sierras, que se estan batiendo, y encontrando la una con la otra.'
Clavigero, vol. ii. p. 91.

[3] Apollodor. i. 9, 22; Apollon. Rhod. Argonautica, ii. 310–616; Pindar,
Pythia Carm. iv. 370. See Kuhn, ' Herabkunft des Feuers,' p. 152 (mention
of Hnitbjörg'.

Maui passed through the entrance of Night and returned to Day, death should not hold mankind ; if the Argo passed the Clashers, the way should lie open between them for ever. The Argo sped through in safety, and the Symplégades can clash no longer on the passing ship ; Maui was crushed, and man comes not forth again from Hades.

There is another solar metaphor which describes the sun, not as a personal creature, but as a member of a yet greater being. He is called in Java and Sumatra "Mata-ari," in Madagascar " Maso-andro," the "Eye of Day." If we look for translation of this thought from metaphor into myth, we may find it in the New Zealand stories of Maui setting his own eye up in heaven as the Sun, and the eyes of his two children as the Morning and the Evening Stars.[1] The nature-myth thus implicitly and explicitly stated is one widely developed on Aryan ground. It forms part of that macrocosmic description of the universe well known in Asiatic myth, and in Europe expressed in that passage of the Orphic poem which tells of Jove, at once the world's ruler and the world itself: his glorious head irradiates the sky where hangs his starry hair, the waters of the sounding ocean are the belt that girds his sacred body the earth omniparent, his eyes are sun and moon, his mind, moving and ruling by counsel all things, is the royal æther that no voice nor sound escapes :

" Sunt oculi Phœbus, Phœboque adversa recurrens
Cynthia. Mens verax nullique obnoxius æther
Regius interitu', qui cuncta movetque regitque
Consilia. Vox nulla potest, sonitusve, nec ullus
Hancce Jovis sobolem strepitus, nec fama latere.
Sic animi sensum, et caput immortale beatus
Obtinet : illustro, immensum, immutabile pandens,
Atque incertorum valido stans robore cœtus." [2]

Where the Aryan myth-maker takes no thought of the

[1] Polack, 'Manners of N. Z.' vol. L p. 16 ; 'New Zealand,' vol. L p. 358 ; Yate, p. 142 ; Schirren, pp. 68, 165.
[2] Euseb. Præp. Evang. lit. 9.

lesser light, he can in various terms describe the sun as the eye of heaven. In the Rig-Veda it is the "eye of Mitra, Varuna, and Agni"—"chakshuh Mitrasya Varunasyah Agneh."[1] In the Zend-Avesta it is "the shining sun with the swift horses, the eye of Ahura-Mazda and Mithra, the lord of the region."[2] To Hesiod it is the "all-seeing eye of Zeus"—"πάντα ἰδὼν Διὸς ὀφθαλμός:" Macrobius speaks of antiquity calling the sun the eye of Jove—"τί ἥλιος; οὐράνιος ὀφθαλμός."[3] The old Germans, in calling the sun "Wuotan's eye,"[4] recognized Wuotan, Woden, Odhin, as being himself the divine Heaven. These mythic expressions are of the most unequivocal type. By the hint they give, conjectural interpretations may be here not indeed asserted, but suggested, for two of the quaintest episodes of ancient European myth. Odin, the All-father, say the old scalds of Scandinavia, sits among his Æsir in the city Asgard, on his high throne Hlidskialf (Lid-shelf), whence he can look down over the whole world discerning all the deeds of men. He is an old man wrapped in his wide cloak, and clouding his face with his wide hat, "os pileo ne cultu proderetur obnubens," as Saxo Grammaticus has it. Odin is one-eyed; he desired to drink from Mimir's well, but he had to leave there one of his eyes in pledge, as it is said in the Völuspa:

> " All know I, Odin! Where thou hiddest thine eye
> In Mimir's famous well.
> Mead drinks Mimir every morning
> From Wale-father's pledge—Wit ye what this is?"

As Odin's single eye seems certainly to be the sun in heaven, one may guess what is the lost eye in the well— perhaps the sun's own reflection in any pool, or more likely

---

[1] Rig-Veda, I. 115; Böhtlingk and Roth, s. v. 'mitra.'
[2] Avesta, tr. Spiegel and Bleeck, Yaçna, I. 85; compare Burnouf, Yaçna.
[3] Macrob. Saturnal. I. 21, 13. See Max Müller, 'Chips,' vol. II. p. 85.
[4] Grimm, 'Deutsche Myth.' p. 665. See also Hanusch, 'Slaw. Myth.' p. 213.

the moon, which in popular myth from the time of the Veda has been found in the well.[1] Possibly, too, some such solar fancy may explain part of the myth of Perseus. There are three Scandinavian Norns, whose names are Urdhr, Verdhandi, and Skuld—Was, and Is, and Shall-be—and these three maidens are the "Weird sisters" who fix the lifetime of all men. So the Fates, the Parkai, daughters of the inevitable Anangke, divide among them the periods of time: Lachesis sings the past, Klôthô the present, Atropos the future. Now is it allowable to consider these fatal sisters as of common nature with two other mythic sister-triads—the Graiai and their kinsfolk the Gorgons?[2] If it be so, it is easy to understand why of the three Gorgons one alone was mortal, whose life her two immortal sisters could not save, for the deathless past and future cannot save the ever-dying present. Nor would the riddle be hard to read, what is the one eye that the Graiai had between them, and passed from one to another?—the eye of day—

---

[1] Edda, 'Völuspa,' 22; 'Gylfaginning,' 15. See Grimm, 'D. M.' p. 133; De Gubernatis, 'Zoological Mythology,' vol. i. p. 18, 81.

[2] As to the identification of the Norns and the Fates, see Grimm, 'D. M.' pp. 376–86; Max Müller, 'Chips,' vol. ii. p. 154. It is to be observed in connexion with the Perseus-myth, that another of its obscure episodes, the Gorgon's head turning those who look on it into stone, corresponds with myths of the sun itself. In Hispaniola, men came out of two caves (thus being born of their mother Earth); the giant who guarded these caves strayed one night, and the rising sun turned him into a great rock called Xauta, just as the Gorgon's head turned Atlas the Earth-bearer into the mountain that bears his name; after this, others of the early cave-men were surprised by the sunlight, and turned into stones, trees, plants or beasts (Friar Roman Pane in 'Life of Columbus' in Pinkerton, vol. xii. p. 80; J. G. Müller, 'Amer. Urrelig.' p. 179). In Central America a Quiché legend relates how the ancient animals were petrified by the Sun (Brasseur, 'Popol Vuh,' p. 245. Thus the Americans have the analogue of the Scandinavian myths of giants and dwarfs surprised by daylight outside their hiding-places, and turned to stones. Such fancies appear connected with the fancied human shapes of rocks or "standing-stones" which peasants still account for as transformed creatures. Thus in Fiji, two rocks are a male and female deity turned to stone at daylight, Seemann, 'Viti,' p. 66; see Liebrecht in Heidelberg. Jahrb. 1864, p. 214. This idea is brought also into the Perseus-myth, for the rocks abounding in Seriphos are the islanders thus petrified by the Gorgon's head.

the sun, that the past gives up to the present, and the present to the future.

Compared with the splendid Lord of Day, the pale Lady of Night takes, in myth as in nature, a lower and lesser place. Among the wide legendary group which associates together Sun and Moon, two striking examples are to be seen in the traditions by which half-civilized races of South America traced their rise from the condition of the savage tribes around them. These legends have been appealed to even by modern writers as gratefully-remembered records of real human benefactors, who carried long ago to America the culture of the Old World. But happily for historic truth, mythic tradition tells its tales without expurgating the episodes which betray its real character to more critical observation. The Muyscas of the high plains of Bogota were once, they said, savages without agriculture, religion or law; but there came to them from the East an old and bearded man, Bochica, the child of the Sun, and he taught them to till the fields, to clothe themselves, to worship the gods, to become a nation. But Bochica had a wicked, beautiful wife, Huythaca, who loved to spite and spoil her husband's work; and she it was who made the river swell till the land was covered by a flood, and but a few of mankind escaped upon the mountain-tops. Then Bochica was wroth, and he drove the wicked Huythaca from the earth, and made her the Moon, for there had been no moon before; and he cleft the rocks and made the mighty cataract of Tequendama, to let the deluge flow away. Then, when the land was dry, he gave to the remnant of mankind the year and its periodic sacrifices, and the worship of the Sun. Now the people who told this myth had not forgotten, what indeed we might guess without their help, that Bochica was himself Zuhé, the Sun, and Huythaca, the Sun's wife, the Moon.[1]

[1] Piedrahita, 'Hist. Gen. de las Conquistas del Nuevo Reyno de Granada,' Antwerp, 1688, part i. lib. i. c. 3; Humboldt, 'Monumens,' pl. vi.; J. G. Müller, 'Amer. Urrelig.' pp. 423—30.

Like to this in meaning, though different in fancy, is the civilization-myth of the Incas. Men, said this Qqichua legend, were savages dwelling in caves like wild beasts, devouring wild roots and fruit and human flesh, covering themselves with leaves and bark or skins of animals. But our father the Sun took pity on them, and sent two of his children, Manco Ccapac and his sister-wife, Mama Ocello: these rose from the lake of Titicaca, and gave to the uncultured hordes law and government, marriage and moral order, tillage and art and science. Thus was founded the great Peruvian empire, where in after ages each Inca and his sister-wife, continuing the mighty race of Manco Ccapac and Mama Ocello, represented in rule and religion not only the first earthly royal ancestors, but the heavenly father and mother of whom we can see these to be personifications, namely, the Sun himself, and his sister-wife the Moon.[1] Thus the nations of Bogota and Peru, remembering their days of former savagery, and the association of their culture with their national religion, embodied their traditions in myths of an often-recurring type, ascribing to the gods themselves, in human shape, the establishment of their own worship.

The "inconstant moon" figures in a group of characteristic stories. Australian legend says that Mityan, the Moon, was a native cat, who fell in love with some one else's wife, and was driven away to wander ever since.[2] The Khasias of the Himalaya say that the Moon falls monthly in love with his mother-in-law, who throws ashes in his face, whence his spots.[3] Slavonic legend, following the

---

[1] Garcilaso de la Vega, 'Commentarios Reales,' i. c. 15; Prescott, 'Peru,' vol. i. p. 7; J. G. Müller, pp. 308–9, 328–39. Other Peruvian versions show the fundamental solar idea in different mythic shapes (Tr. of Cieza de Leon, tr. and ed. by C. R. Markham, Hakluyt Soc. 1864, p. xlix. 298, 316, 372). W. B. Stevenson ('Residence in S. America,' vol. i. p. 394) and Bastian ('Mensch,' vol. iii. p. 347) met with a curious perversion of the myth, in which *Ixcu Manco Ccapac*, corrupted into *Ingasman Ccapac*, gave rise to a story of an *Englishman* figuring in the midst of Peruvian mythology.

[2] Stanbridge, 'Abor. of Australia,' in 'Tr. Eth. Soc.' vol. i. p. 301.

[3] J. D. Hooker, 'Himalayan Journals,' vol. ii. p. 276.

same track, says that the Moon, King of Night and husband
of the Sun, faithlessly loved the Morning Star, wherefore
he was cloven through in punishment, as we see him in the
sky.[1] By a different train of thought, the Moon's periodic
death and revival has suggested a painful contrast to the
destiny of man, in one of the most often-repeated and
characteristic myths of South Africa, which is thus told
among the Namaqua. The Moon once sent the Hare to
Men to give this message, "Like as I die and rise to life
again, so you also shall die and rise to life again," but the
Hare went to the Men and said, "Like as I die and do not
rise again, so you shall also die and not rise to life again."
Then the Hare returned and told the Moon what he had
done, and the Moon struck at him with a hatchet and slit
his lip, as it has remained ever since, and some say the
Hare fled and is still fleeing, but others say he clawed at
the Moon's face and left the scars that are still to be seen
on it, and they also say that the reason why the Namaqua
object to eating the hare (a prejudice which in fact they
share with very different races) is because he brought to
men this evil message.[2] It is remarkable that a story so
closely resembling this, that it is difficult not to suppose
both to be versions from a common original, is told in the
distant Fiji Islands. There was a dispute between two
gods as to how man should die: "Ra Vula (the Moon)
contended that man should be like himself—disappear
awhile and then live again. Ra Kalavo (the Rat) would
not listen to this kind proposal, but said, 'Let man die as
a rat dies.' And he prevailed." The dates of the versions
seem to show that the presence of these myths among the
Hottentots and Fijians, at the two opposite sides of the
globe, is at any rate not due to transmission in modern times.[3]

[1] Hanusch, 'Slaw. Myth.' p. 249.

[2] Bleek, 'Reynard in S. Africa,' pp. 69-71; C. J. Andersson, 'Lake Ngami,'
p. 328; see Grout, 'Zulu-land,' p. 148; Arbousset and Daumas, p. 471. As
to connexion of the moon with the hare, cf. Skr. "çaçanka;" and in Mexico,
Sahagun, book vii. c. 2, in Kingsborough, vol. vii.

[3] Williams, 'Fiji,' vol. i. p. 205. Compare the Caroline Island myth that

There is a very elaborate savage nature-myth of the generation of the Stars, which may unquestionably serve as a clue connecting the history of two distant tribes. The rude Mintira of the Malayan Peninsula express in plain terms the belief in a solid firmament, usual in the lower grades of civilization; they say the sky is a great pot held over the earth by a cord, and if this cord broke, everything on earth would be crushed. The Moon is a woman, and the Sun also: the Stars are the Moon's children, and the Sun had in old times as many. Fearing, however, that mankind could not bear so much brightness and heat, they agreed each to devour her children; but the Moon, instead of eating up her Stars, hid them from the Sun's sight, who, believing them all devoured, ate up her own; no sooner had she done it, than the Moon brought her family out of their hiding-place. When the Sun saw them, filled with rage she chased the Moon to kill her; the chase has lasted ever since, and sometimes the Sun even comes near enough to bite the Moon, and that is an eclipse; the Sun, as men may still see, devours his Stars at dawn, and the Moon hides hers all day while the Sun is near, and only brings them out at night when her pursuer is far away. Now among a tribe of North East India, the Ho of Chota-Nagpore, the myth reappears, obviously from the same source, but with a varied ending; the Sun cleft the Moon in twain for her deceit, and thus cloven and growing old again she remains, and her daughters with her which are the Stars.[1]

From savagery up to civilization, there may be traced in the mythology of the Stars a course of thought, changed

In the beginning men only quitted life on the last day of the waning moon, and resuscitated as from a peaceful sleep when she reappeared; but the evil spirit Erigirers inflicted a death from which there is no revival: De Brosses, 'Hist. des. Navig. aux Terres Australes,' vol. II. p. 479. Also in a song of the Indians of California it is said, that even as the moon dies and returns to life, so they shall be re-born after death; Duflot de Mofras in Bastian, 'Rechtsverhältnisse,' p. 385, see 'Psychologie,' p. 51.

[1] Journ. Ind. Archip. vol. I. p. 291; vol. iv. p. 333; Tickell in 'Journ. As. Soc.' vol. ix. part ii. p. 797; Latham, 'Descr. Eth.' vol. II. p. 423.

indeed in application, yet never broken in its evident connexion from first to last. The savage sees individual stars
as animate beings, or combines star-groups into living
celestial creatures, or limbs of them, or objects connected
with them; while at the other extremity of the scale of
civilization, the modern astronomer keeps up just such
ancient fancies, turning them to account in useful survival,
as a means of mapping out the celestial globe. The savage
names and stories of stars and constellations may seem at
first but childish and purposeless fancies; but it always
happens in the study of the lower races, that the more
means we have of understanding their thoughts, the more
sense and reason do we find in them. The aborigines of
Australia say that Yurree and Wanjel, who are the stars we
call Castor and Pollux, pursue Purra the Kangaroo (our
Capella), and kill him at the beginning of the great heat,
and the mirage is the smoke of the fire they roast him by.
They say also that Marpean-Kurrk and Neilloan (Arcturus
and Lyra) were the discoverers of the ant-pupas and the eggs
of the loan-bird, and taught the aborigines to find them for
food. Translated into the language of fact, these simple
myths record the summer place of the stars in question,
and the seasons of ant-pupas and loan-eggs, which seasons
are marked by the stars who are called their discoverers.[1]
Not less transparent is the meaning in the beautiful Algonquin myth of the Summer-Maker. In old days eternal
winter reigned upon the earth, till a sprightly little animal
called the Fisher, helped by other beasts his friends, broke
an opening through the sky into the lovely heaven-land
beyond, let the warm winds pour forth and the summer
descend to earth, and opened the cages of the prisoned
birds: but when the dwellers in heaven saw their birds let
loose and their warm gales descending, they started in pursuit, and shooting their arrows at the Fisher, hit him at
last in his one vulnerable spot at the tip of his tail; thus
he died for the good of the inhabitants of earth, and became

[1] Stanbridge in 'Tr. Eth. Soc.' vol. i. pp. 301-3.

the constellation that bears his name, so that still at the
proper season men see him lying as he fell toward the north
on the plains of heaven, with the fatal arrow still sticking
in his tail.[1]   Compare these savage stories with Orion pursuing the Pleiad sisters who take refuge from him in the
sea, and the maidens who wept themselves to death and
became the starry cluster of the Hyades, whose rising and
setting betokened rain: such mythic creatures might for
simple significance have been invented by savages, even as
the savage constellation-myths might have been made by
ancient Greeks.   When we consider that the Australians
who can invent such myths, and invent them with such
fulness of meaning, are savages who put two and one together to make their numeral for three, we may judge how
deep in the history of culture those conceptions lie, of
which the relics are still represented in our star-maps by
Castor and Pollux, Arcturus and Sirius, Boötes and Orion,
the Argo and the Charles's Wain, the Toucan and the
Southern Cross.   Whether civilized or savage, whether
ancient or new made after the ancient manner, such names
are so like in character that any tribe of men might adopt
them from any other, as American tribes are known to
receive European names into their own skies, and as our
constellation of the Royal Oak is said to have found its
way in new copies of the old Hindu treatises, into the
company of the Seven Sages and the other ancient constellations of Brahmanic India.

Such fancies are so fanciful, that two peoples seldom fall
on the same name for a constellation, while, even within
the limits of the same race, terms may differ altogether.
Thus the stars which we call Orion's Belt are in New
Zealand either the Elbow of Maui, or they form the stern

_____

[1] Schoolcraft, 'Algic Res.' vol. I. pp. 57-66.   The story of the hero or
deity invulnerable like Achilles save in one weak spot, recurs in the tales
of the slaying of the Shining Manitu, whose scalp alone was vulnerable, and
of the mighty Kwasind, who could be killed only by the cone of the white
pine wounding the vulnerable place on the crown of his head (vol. I. p. 153;
vol. II. p. 163).

of the Canoe of Tamarerete, whose anchor dropped from
the prow is the Southern Cross.[1] The Great Bear is equally
like a Wain, Orion's Belt serves as well for Frigga's or
Mary's Spindle, or Jacob's Staff. Yet sometimes natural
correspondences occur. The seven sister Pleiades seem to
the Australians a group of girls playing to a corroboree;
while the North American Indians call them the Dancers,
and the Lapps the Company of Virgins.[2] Still more
striking is the correspondence between savages and cultured
nations in fancies of the bright starry band that lies like a
road across the sky. The Basutos call it the "Way of the
Gods;" the Ojis say it is the "Way of Spirits," which
souls go up to heaven by.[3] North American tribes know it
as "the Path of the Master of Life," the "Path of Spirits,"
"the Road of Souls," where they travel to the land beyond
the grave, and where their camp-fires may be seen blazing
as brighter stars.[4] Such savage imaginations of the Milky
Way fit with the Lithuanian myth of the "Road of the
Birds," at whose end the souls of the good, fancied as
flitting away at death like birds, dwell free and happy.[5]
That souls dwell in the Galaxy was a thought familiar to
the Pythagoreans, who gave it on their master's word that
the souls that crowd there descend, and appear to men as
dreams,[6] and to the Manichæans whose fancy transferred
pure souls to this "column of light," whence they could

[1] Taylor, 'New Zealand,' p. 343.

[2] Stanbridge, l. c.; Charlevoix, vol. vi. p. 148; Leems, Lapland, in Pinkerton, vol. l. p. 411. The name of the Bear occurring in North America in
connexion with the stars of the Great and Little Bear (Charlevoix, l. c.;
Cotton Mather in Schoolcraft, 'Tribes,' vol. i. p. 284) has long been remarked
on (Goguet, vol. l. p. 262; vol. ii. p. 366, but with reference to Greenland, see
Cranz, p. 294). See observations on the history of the Aryan name in Max
Müller, 'Lectures,' 2nd series, p. 361.

[3] Casalis, p. 196; Waitz, vol. ii. p. 191.

[4] Long's Exp. vol. l. p. 288; Schoolcraft, part l. p. 272; Le Jeune in 'Rel.
des Jés. de la Nouvelle France,' 1634, p. 18; Loskiel, part l. p. 35; J. G.
Müller, p. 63.

[5] Hanusch, pp. 272, 407, 415.

[6] Porphyr. de Antro Nympharum, 28; Macrob. de Somn. Scip. l. 12.

come down to earth and again return.[1] It is a fall from
such ideas of the Galaxy to the Siamese "Road of the
White Elephant," the Spaniards' "Road of Santiago," or
the Turkish "Pilgrims' Road," and a still lower fall to the
"Straw Road" of the Syrian, the Persian, and the Turk,
who thus compare it with their lanes littered with the
morsels of straw that fall from the nets they carry it in.[2]
But of all the fancies which have attached themselves to
the celestial road, we at home have the quaintest. Passing
along the short and crooked way from St. Paul's to Cannon
Street, one thinks to how small a remnant has shrunk the
name of the great street of the Wœtlingas, which in old
days ran from Dover through London into Wales. But
there is a Watling Street in heaven as well as on earth,
once familiar to Englishmen, though now almost forgotten
even in local dialect. Chaucer thus speaks of it in his
'House of Fame:'—

> " Lo there (quod he) cast up thine eye
> Se yondir, lo, the Galaxie,
> The whiche men clepe The Milky Way,
> For It is white, and some parfay,
> Ycallin it han Watlynge strete." [3]

Turning from the mythology of the heavenly bodies, a
glance over other districts of nature-myth will afford fresh
evidence that such legend has its early home within the
precincts of savage culture. It is thus with the myths of
the Winds. The New Zealanders tell how Maui can ride
upon the other Winds or imprison them in their caves, but
he cannot catch the West Wind nor find its cave to roll a

---

[1] Beausobre, 'Hist. de Manichée, vol. II. p. 513.

[2] Bastian, 'Oestl. Asien,' vol. iii. p. 341 ; 'Chronique de Tabari,' tr. Dubeux,
p. 24 ; Grimm, 'D. M.' p. 330, etc.

[3] Chaucer, 'House of Fame,' ii. 427. With reference to questions of Aryan
mythology illustrated by the savage galaxy-myths, see Pictet, 'Origines,'
part ii. p. 582, etc. Mr. J. Jeremiah informs me that 'Watling Street,' is
still (1871) a name for the Milky Way in Scotland ; see also his paper on
'Welsh names of the Milky Way,' Philological Soc., Nov. 17, 1871. The
corresponding name 'London Road' is used in Suffolk.

stone against the mouth, and therefore it prevails, yet
from time to time he all but overtakes it, and hiding in its
cave for shelter it dies away.[1] Such is the fancy in classic
poetry of Æolus holding the prisoned winds in his dungeon
cave :—

> " Hic vasto rex Æolus antro
> Luctantes ventos, tempestatesque sonoras
> Imperio premit, ac vinclis et carcere frœnat."[2]

The myth of the Four Winds is developed among the
native races of America with a range and vigour and beauty
scarcely rivalled elsewhere in the mythology of the world.
Episodes belonging to this branch of Red Indian folklore
are collected in Schoolcraft's ' Algic Researches,' and thence
rendered with admirable taste and sympathy, though unfortunately not with proper truth to the originals, in Longfellow's master-piece, the ' Song of Hiawatha.' The West
Wind Mudjekeewis is Kabeyun, Father of the Winds,
Wabun is the East Wind, Shawondasee the South Wind,
Kabibonokka the North Wind. But there is another
mighty wind not belonging to the mystic quaternion,
Manabozho the North-West Wind, therefore described with
mythic appropriateness as the unlawful child of Kabeyun.
The fierce North Wind, Kabibonokka, in vain strives to
force Shingebis, the lingering diver-bird, from his warm
and happy winter-lodge ; and the lazy South Wind, Shawondasee, sighs for the maiden of the prairie with her sunny
hair, till it turns to silvery white, and as he breathes upon
her, the prairie dandelion has vanished.[3] Man naturally
divides his horizon into four quarters, before and behind,
right and left, and thus comes to fancy the world a square,
and to refer the winds to its four corners. Dr. Brinton, in
his ' Myths of the New World,' has well traced from these
ideas the growth of legend after legend among the native

[1] Yate, ' New Zealand,' p. 144, see Ellis, ' Polyn. Res.' vol. ii. p. 417.
[2] Virg. Æneid. L 56 ; Homer. Odys. x. l.
[3] Schoolcraft, ' Algic Res.' vol. L p. 200 ; vol. ii. pp. 122, 214 ; ' Indian
Tribes,' part III. p. 324.

races of America, where four brother heroes, or mythic ancestors or divine patrons of mankind, prove, on closer view,
to be in personal shape the Four Winds.[1]

The Vedic hymns to the Maruts, the Storm Winds, who
tear asunder the forest kings and make the rocks shiver,
and assume again, after their wont, the form of new-born
babes, the mythic feats of the child Hermes in the Homeric
hymn, the legendary birth of Boreas from Astraios and Eös,
Starry Heaven and Dawn, work out, on Aryan ground,
mythic conceptions that Red Indian tale-tellers could
understand and rival.[2] The peasant who keeps up in fireside talk the memory of the Wild Huntsman, Wodejäger,
the Grand Veneur of Fontainebleau, Herne the Hunter of
Windsor Forest, has almost lost the significance of this
grand old storm-myth. By mere force of tradition, the
name of the "Wish" or "Wush" hounds of the Wild
Huntsman has been preserved through the west of England;
the words must for ages past have lost their meaning among
the country folk, though we may plainly recognize in them
Woden's ancient well-known name, old German "Wunsch."
As of old, the Heaven-god drives the clouds before him in
raging tempest across the sky, while, safe within the cottage
walls, the tale-teller unwittingly describes in personal
legendary shape this same Wild Hunt of the Storm.[3]

It has many a time occurred to the savage poet or philo-
sopher to realize the thunder, or its cause, in myths of a
Thunder-bird. Of this wondrous creature North American
legend has much to tell. He is the bird of the great
Manitu, as the eagle is of Zeus, or he is even the great
Manitu himself incarnate. The Assiniboins not only know

[1] Brinton, 'Myths of the New World,' ch. iii.

[2] 'Rig-Veda,' tr. by Max Müller, vol. I. (Hymns to Maruts); Welcker,
'Griech. Götterl.' vol. iii. p. 67 ; Cox, 'Mythology of Aryan Nations,' vol. II.
ch. v.

[3] Grimm, 'D. M.' pp. 126, 599, 894 ; Hunt, 'Pop. Rom.' 1st ser. p. xix. ;
Baring-Gould, 'Book of Werewolves,' p. 101 ; see 'Myths of the Middle
Ages,' p. 25 ; Wuttke, 'Deutsche Volksaberglaube,' pp. 13, 236 ; Monnier,
'Traditions,' pp. 75, etc., 711, 717.

of his existence, but have even seen him, and in the far
north the story is told how he created the world. The
Ahts of Vancouver's Island talk of Tootooch, the mighty
bird dwelling aloft and far away, the flap of whose wings
makes the thunder (Tootah), and his tongue is the forked
lightning. There were once four of these birds in the land,
and they fed on whales; but the great deity Quawteaht,
entering into a whale, enticed one thunder-bird after another
to swoop down and seize him with its talons, when plunging
to the bottom of the sea he drowned it. Thus three of them
perished, but the last one spread his wings and flew to the
distant height where he has since remained. The meaning
of the story may perhaps be that thunderstorms come
especially from one of the four quarters of heaven. Of such
myths, perhaps that told among the Dacotas is the
quaintest: Thunder is a large bird, they say; hence its
velocity. The old bird begins the thunder; its rumbling
noise is caused by an immense quantity of young birds, or
thunders, who continue it, hence the long duration of the
peals. The Indian says it is the young birds, or thunders,
that do the mischief; they are like the young mischievous
men who will not listen to good counsel. The old thunder
or bird is wise and good, and does not kill anybody, nor do
any kind of mischief. Descending southward to Central
America, there is found mention of the bird Voc, the
messenger of Hurakan, the Tempest-god (whose name has
been adopted in European languages as huracano, ouragan,
hurricane) of the Lightning and of the Thunder. So among
Caribs, Brazilians, Harvey Islanders and Karens, Bechuanas
and Basutos, we find legends of a flapping or flashing
Thunder-bird, which seem simply to translate into myth
the thought of thunder and lightning descending from the
upper regions of the air, the home of the eagle and the
vulture.[1]

[1] Pr. Max v. Wied, 'Reise in N. A.' vol. L pp. 416, 455; vol. ii. pp. 152,
223; Sir Alex. Mackenzie, 'Voyages,' p. cxvii.; Sproat, 'Scenes of Savage
Life' (Vancouver's I.), p. 177, 213; Irving, 'Astoria,' vol. ii. ch. xxii.; Lo

The Heaven-god dwells in the regions of the sky, and thus what form could be fitter for him and for his messengers than the likeness of a bird?   But to cause the ground to quake beneath our feet, a being of quite different nature is needed, and accordingly the office of supporting the solid earth is given in various countries to various monstrous creatures, human or animal in character, who make their office manifest from time to time by a shake given in negligence or sport or anger to their burden.   Wherever earthquakes are felt, we are likely to find a version of the great myth of the Earth-bearer.   Thus in Polynesia the Tongans say that Maui upholds the earth on his prostrate body, and when he tries to turn over into an easier posture there is an earthquake, and the people shout and beat the ground with sticks to make him lie still.   Another version forms part of the interesting myth lately mentioned, which connects the under-world whither the sun descends at night, with the region of subterranean volcanic fire and of earth- quake.   The old Maui lay by his fire in the dead-land of Bulotu, when his grandson Maui came down by the cavern entrance; the young Maui carried off the fire, they wrestled, the old Maui was overcome, and has lain there bruised and drowsy ever since, underneath the earth, which quakes when he turns over in his sleep.[1]   In Celebes we hear of the world-supporting Hog, who rubs himself against a tree, and then there is an earthquake.[2]   Among the Indians of North America, it is said that earthquakes come of the movement of the great world-bearing Tortoise.   Now this Tortoise seems but a mythic picture of the Earth itself,

Jenne, op. cit. 1634, p. 26; Schoolcraft, 'Indian Tribes,' part III. p. 233 'Algic Res.' vol. II. pp. 114-6, 199; Catlin, vol. ii. p. 164; Brasseur, 'Popol Vuh,' p. 71 and Index, 'Hurakan;' J. G. Muller, 'Amer. Urrel.' pp. 222 271; Ellis, 'Polyn. Res.' vol. ii. p. 417; Jno. Williams, 'Missionary Enter- prise,' p. 93; Mason, l. c. p. 217; Moffat, 'South Africa,' p. 339; Casalis, 'Basutos,' p. 266; Callaway, 'Religion of Amazulu,' p. 119.

[1] Mariner, 'Tonga Is.' vol. II. p. 120; S. S. Farmer, 'Tonga,' p. 135; Schirren, pp. 35-7.

[2] 'Journ. Ind. Archip.' vol. ii. p. 537.

and thus the story only expresses in mythic phrase the very
fact that the earth quakes; the meaning is but one degree
less distinct than among the Caribs, who say when there is
an earthquake that their Mother Earth is dancing.[1] Among
the higher races of the continent, such ideas remain little
changed in nature; the Tlascalans said that the tired world-
supporting deities shifting their burden to a new relay
caused the earthquake;[2] the Chibchas said it was their
god Chibchacum moving the earth from shoulder to
shoulder.[3] The myth ranges in Asia through as wide a
stretch of culture. The Kamchadals tell of Tuil the Earthquake-god, who sledges below ground, and when his dog
shakes off fleas or snow there is an earthquake;[4] Ta Ywa,
the solar hero of the Karens, set Shie-oo beneath the earth
to carry it, and there is an earthquake when he moves.[5]
The world-bearing elephants of the Hindus, the world-
supporting frog of the Mongol Lamas, the world-bull of the
Moslems, the gigantic Omophore of the Manichæan cosmology, are all creatures who carry the earth on their backs or
heads, and shake it when they stretch or shift.[6] Thus in
European mythology the Scandinavian Loki, strapped down
with thongs of iron in his subterranean cavern, writhes
when the overhanging serpent drops venom on him; or
Prometheus struggles beneath the earth to break his bonds;
or the Lettish Drebkuls or Poseidon the Earth-shaker
makes the ground rock beneath men's feet.[7] From
thorough myths of imagination such as most of these, it
may be sometimes possible to distinguish philosophic myths
like them in form, but which appear to be attempts at

[1] J. G. Müller, 'Amer. Urrelig.' pp. 61, 122.

[2] Brasseur, 'Mexique,' vol. III. p. 492.

[3] Pouchot, 'Plurality of Races,' p. 2.

[4] Steller, 'Kamtschatka,' p. 267.

[5] Mason, 'Karens,' l. c. p. 182.

[6] Bell, 'Tr. in Asia' in Pinkerton, vol. VII. p. 369; Bastian, 'Oestl. Asien,'
vol. II. p. 168; Lane, 'Thousand and one Nights,' vol. I. p. 21; see Latham,
'Descr. Eth.' vol. II. p. 171; Beausobre, 'Manichée,' vol. I. p. 243.

[7] Edda, 'Gylfaginning,' 50 Grimm, 'D. M.' p. 777, etc.

serious explanation without even a metaphor. The Japanese
think that earthquakes are caused by huge whales creeping
underground, having been probably led to this idea by
finding the fossil bones which seem the remains of such
subterranean monsters, just as we know that the Siberians
who find in the ground the mammoth-bones and tusks,
account for them as belonging to huge burrowing beasts,
and by force of this belief, have brought themselves to think
they can sometimes see the earth heave and sink as the
monsters crawl below. Thus, in investigating the earthquake-myths of the world, it appears that two processes,
the translation into mythic language of the phenomenon
itself, and the crude scientific theory to account for it by a
real moving animal underground, may result in legends of
very striking similarity.[1]

In thus surveying the mythic wonders of heaven and
earth, sun, moon, and stars, wind, thunder, and earthquake,
it is possible to set out in investigation under conditions of
actual certainty. So long as such beings as Heaven or Sun
are consciously talked of in mythic language, the meaning
of their legends is open to no question, and the actions
ascribed to them will as a rule be natural and apposite. But
when the phenomena of nature take a more anthropomorphic
form, and become identified with personal gods and heroes,
and when in after times these beings, losing their first consciousness of origin, become centres round which floating
fancies cluster, then their sense becomes obscure and corrupt, and the consistency of their earlier character must no
longer be demanded. In fact, the unreasonable expectation
of such consistency in nature-myths, after they have passed
into what may be called their heroic stage, is one of the
mythologist's most damaging errors. The present examination of nature-myths has mostly taken them in their
primitive and unmistakable condition, and has only been
in some degree extended to include closely-corresponding

---

[1] Kaempfer, 'Japan,' in Pinkerton, vol. vii. p. 684; see mammoth-myths in
'Early Hist. of Mankind,' p. 316.

legends in a less easily interpretable state. It has lain beyond my scope to enter into any systematic discussion of the views of Grimm, Grote, Max Müller, Kuhn, Schirren, Cox, Bréal, Dasent, Kelly, and other mythologists. Even the outlines here sketched out have been purposely left without filling in surrounding detail which might confuse their shape, although this strictness has caused the neglect of many a tempting hint to work out episode after episode, by tracing their relation to the myths of far-off times and lands. It has rather been my object to bring prominently into view the nature-mythology of the lower races, that their clear and fresh mythic conceptions may serve as a basis in studying the nature-myths of the world at large. The evidence and interpretation here brought forward, imperfect as they are, seem to countenance a strong opinion as to the historical development of legends which describe in personal shape the life of nature. The state of mind to which such imaginative fictions belong is found in full vigour in the savage condition of mankind, its growth and inheritance continue into the higher culture of barbarous or half-civilized nations, and at last in the civilized world its effects pass more and more from realized belief into fanciful, affected, and even artificial poetry.

CHAPTER X.

MYTHOLOGY (continued.)

ALTHOUGH the attempt to reduce to rule and system the
whole domain of mythology would as yet be rash and premature, yet the piecemeal invasion of one mythic province
after another proves feasible and profitable. Having discussed the theory of nature-myths, it is worth while to gain
in other directions glimpses of the crude and child-like
thought of mankind, not arranged in abstract doctrines,
but embodied by mythic fancy. We shall find the result in
masses of legends, full of interest as bearing on the early
history of opinion, and which may be roughly classified
under the following headings: myths philosophical or explanatory; myths based on real descriptions misunderstood,
exaggerated, or perverted; myths attributing inferred events
to legendary or historical personages; myths based on realization of fanciful metaphor; and myths made or adapted to
convey moral or social or political instruction.

Man's craving to know the causes at work in each event
he witnesses, the reasons why each state of things he sur-

veys is such as it is and no other, is no product of high
civilization, but a characteristic of his race down to its
lowest stages. Among rude savages it is already an intellectual appetite whose satisfaction claims many of the moments not engrossed by war or sport, food or sleep. Even
to the Botocudo or Australian, scientific speculation has its
germ in actual experience: he has learnt to do definite acts
that definite results may follow, to see other acts done and
their results following in course, to make inference from the
result back to the previous action, and to find his inference
verified in fact. When one day he has seen a deer or a
kangaroo leave footprints in the soft ground, and the next
day he has found new footprints and inferred that such an
animal made them, and has followed up the track and
killed the game, then he knows that he has reconstructed a
history of past events by inference from their results. But
in the early stages of knowledge the confusion is extreme
between actual tradition of events, and ideal reconstruction
of them. To this day there go about the world endless
stories told as matter of known reality, but which a critical
examination shows to be mere inferences, often utterly illu-
sory ones, from facts which have stimulated the invention of
some curious enquirer. Thus a writer in the Asiatick Researches of some eighty years ago relates the following
account of the Andaman islanders, as a historical fact of
which he had been informed: "Shortly after the Portuguese had discovered the passage to India round the Cape
of Good Hope, one of their ships, on board of which were
a number of Mozambique negroes, was lost on the Andaman
islands, which were till then uninhabited. The blacks remained in the island and settled it: the Europeans made a
small shallop in which they sailed to Pegu." Many readers
must have had their interest excited by this curious story,
but at the first touch of fact it dissolves into a philosophic
myth, made by the easy transition from what might have
been to what was. So far from the islands having been
uninhabited at the time of Vasco de Gama's voyage, their

population of naked blacks with frizzled hair had been described six hundred years earlier, and the story, which
sounded reasonable to people puzzled by the appearance of
a black population in the Andaman islands, is of course
repudiated by ethnologists aware of the wide distribution
of the negroid Papuans; really so distinct from any race of
African negroes.[1] Not long since, I met with a very perfect
myth of this kind. In a brick field near London, there had
been found a number of fossil elephant bones, and soon
afterwards a story was in circulation in the neighbourhood
somewhat in this shape : " A few years ago, one of Wombwell's caravans was here, an elephant died, and they buried
him in the field, and now the scientific gentlemen have
found his bones, and think they have got a pre-Adamite
elephant." It seemed almost cruel to spoil this ingenious
myth by pointing out that such a prize as a living mammoth was beyond the resources even of Wombwell's menagerie. But so exactly does such a story explain the facts
to minds not troubled with nice distinctions between existing and extinct species of elephants, that it was on
another occasion invented elsewhere under similar circumstances. This was at Oxford, where Mr. Buckland found
the story of the Wombwell's caravan and dead elephant
current to explain a similar find of fossil bones.[2] Such
explanations of the finding of fossils are easily devised and
used to be freely made, as when fossil bones found in the
Alps were set down to Hannibal's elephants, or when a
petrified oyster-shell near the Mount Cenis sets Voltaire
reflecting on the crowd of pilgrims on their way to Rome,
or when theologians supposed such shells on mountains to
have been left on their slopes and summits by a rising deluge.
Such theoretical explanations are unimpeachable in their
philosophic spirit, until further observation may prove them

[1] Hamilton in ' As. Res.' vol. II. p. 344 ; Colebrooke, ibid. vol. iv. p. 385 ;
Earl in ' Journ. Ind. Archip.' vol. iii. p. 682 ; vol. iv. p. 9. See Renaudot,
Travels of Two Mahommedans,' in Pinkerton, vol. vii. p. 183.
[2] F. Buckland, ' Curiosities of Nat. Hist.' 3rd series, vol. ii. p. 39.

to be unsound. Their disastrous effect on the historic conscience of mankind only begins when the inference is turned upside down, to be told as a recorded fact.

In this connexion brief notice may be taken of the doctrine of miracles in its special bearing on mythology. The mythic wonder-episodes related by a savage tale-teller, the amazing superhuman feats of his gods and heroes, are often to his mind miracles in the original popular sense of the word, that is, they are strange and marvellous events; but they are not to his mind miracles in a frequent modern sense of the word, that is, they are not violations or supersessions of recognized laws of nature. Exceptio probat regulam; to acknowledge anything as an exception is to imply the rule it departs from; but the savage recognizes neither rule nor exception. Yet a European hearer, brought up to use a different canon of evidence, will calmly reject this savage's most revered ancestral traditions, simply on the ground that they relate events which are impossible. The ordinary standards of possibility, as applied to the credibility of tradition, have indeed changed vastly in the course of culture through its savage, barbaric, and civilized stages. What concerns us here is that there is an important department of legend which this change in public opinion, generally so resistless, left to a great extent unaltered. In the middle ages the long-accepted practice rose to its height, of allowing the mere assertion of supernatural influence by angels or devils, saints or sorcerers, to override the rules of evidence and the results of experience. The consequence was that the doctrine of miracles became as it were a bridge along which mythology travelled from the lower into the higher culture. Principles of myth-formation belonging properly to the mental state of the savage, were by its aid continued in strong action in the civilized world. Mythic episodes which Europeans would have rejected contemptuously if told of savage deities or heroes, only required to be adapted to appropriate local details, and to be set forth as miracles in the life of some superhuman per-

B B 2

sonage, to obtain as of old a place of credit and honour in history.

From the enormous mass of available instances in proof of this let us take two cases belonging to the class of geological myths. The first is the well-known legend of St. Patrick and the serpents. It is thus given by Dr. Andrew Boorde in his description of Ireland and the Irish in Henry VIII.'s time. "Yet in Ierland is stupendyous thynges; for there is neyther Pyes nor venymus wormes. There is no Adder, nor Snake, nor Toode, nor Lyzerd, nor no Euyt, nor uone such lyke. I haue sene stones the whiche haue had the forme and shap of a snake and other venimus wormes. And the people of the countre sayth that suche stones were wormes, and they were turned into stones by the power of God and the prayers of saynt Patryk. And Englysh marchauntes of England do fetch of the erth of Irlonde to caste in their gardens, to kepe out and to kyll venimus wormes." [1]   In treating this passage, the first step is to separate pieces of imported foreign myth, belonging properly not to Ireland, but to islands of the Mediterranean; the story of the earth of the island of Krete being fatal to venomous serpents is to be found in Ælian,[2] and St. Honoratus clearing the snakes from his island (one of the Lerins opposite Cannes)[3] seems to take precedence of the Irish saint. What is left after these deductions is a philosophic myth accounting for the existence of fossil ammonites as being petrified snakes, to which myth a historical position is given by claiming it as a miracle, and ascribing it to St. Patrick. The second myth is valuable for the historical and geological evidence which it incidentally preserves. At the celebrated ruins of the temple of Jupiter Serapis at Pozzuoli, the ancient Puteoli, the marble columns, encircled half-way up by borings of Lithodomi, stand to prove that the ground of the temple must have been formerly submerged

[1] Andrew Boorde, 'Introduction of Knowledge,' ed. by F. J. Furnivall, Early Eng. Text Soc. 1870, p. 133.
[2] Ælian, De Nat. Animal. v. 2, see 8.
[3] Acta Sanctorum Bolland. Jan. xvi.

many feet below the sea, and afterwards upheaved to become again dry land. History is remarkably silent as to the events demonstrated by this remarkable geological evidence; between the recorded adornment of the temple by Roman emperors from the second to the third century, and the mention of its existence in ruins in the 16th century, no documentary information was till lately recognized. It has now been pointed out by Mr. Tuckett that a passage in the Apocryphal Acts of Peter and Paul, dating apparently more or less before the end of the 9th century, mentions the subsidence of the temple, ascribing it to a miracle of St. Paul. The legend is as follows: "And when he (Paul) came out of Messina he sailed to Didymus, and remained there one night. And having sailed thence, he came to Pontiole (Puteoli) on the second day. And Dioscorus the shipmaster, who brought him to Syracuse, sympathizing with Paul because he had delivered his son from death, having left his own ship in Syracuse, accompanied him to Pontiole. And some of Peter's disciples having been found there, and having received Paul, exhorted him to stay with them. And he stayed a week in hiding, because of the command of Cæsar (that he should be put to death). And all the toparchs were waiting to seize and kill him. But Dioscorus the shipmaster, being himself also bald, wearing his shipmaster's dress, and speaking boldly, on the first day went out into the city of Pontiole. Thinking therefore that he was Paul, they seized him and beheaded him, and sent his head to Cæsar. . . . . And Paul, being in Pontiole, and having heard that Dioscorus had been beheaded, being grieved with great grief, gazing into the height of the heaven, said: 'O Lord Almighty in Heaven, who hast appeared to me in every place whither I have gone on account of Thine only-begotten Word, our Lord Jesus Christ, punish this city, and bring out all who have believed in God and followed His word.' He said to them, therefore, 'Follow me.' And going forth from Pontiole with those who had believed in the word of God, they came to a place called Baias (Baiæ), and looking up with their eyes, they all see that city called Pontiole sunk into the sea-shore about one fathom; and there it is until this day, for a remembrance, under the sea. . . . And those who had been saved out of the city of Pontiole, that had been swallowed up, reported to Cæsar in Rome that Pontiole had been swallowed up with all its multitude." [1]

Episodes of popular myth, which are often items of the serious belief of the times they belong to, may serve as important records of intellectual history. As an example belonging to the class of philosophical or explanatory myths, let us glance at an Arabian Nights' story, which at first sight may seem an effort of the wildest imagination, but which is nevertheless traceable to a scientific origin; this is the story of the Magnetic Mountain. The Third Kalenter relates in his tale how a contrary wind drove his ships into a strange sea, and there, by the attraction of their nails and other ironwork, they were violently drawn towards a mountain of black loadstone, till at last the iron flew out to the mountain, and the ships went to pieces in the surf. The episode is older than the date when the 'Thousand and One Nights' were edited. When, in Henry of Veldeck's 12th century poem, Duke Ernest and his companions sail into the Klebermeer, they see the rock that is called Magnes, and are themselves dragged in below it among "many a work of keels," whose masts stand like a forest.[2] Turning from tale-tellers to grave geographers and travellers who talk of the loadstone mountain, we find El Kazwini, like Serapion before him, believing such boats as may be still seen in Ceylon, pegged and sewn without metal nails, to be so built lest the magnetic rock should attract them from their course at sea. This quaint notion is to be found in Sir John

[1] 'Acts of Peter and Paul,' trans. by A. Walker, in Ante-Nicene Library, vol. xvi. p. 257; F. F. Tuckett in 'Nature,' Oct. 20, 1870. See Lyell, 'Principles of Geology,' ch. xxx.; Phillips, 'Vesuvius,' p. 211.

[2] Lane, 'Thousand and One N.' vol. i. pp. 161, 217; vol. iii. p. 78; Hole, 'Remarks on the Ar. N.' p. 104; Helurich von Veldeck, 'Herzog Ernst's von Bayern Erhöhung, etc.' ed. Rixner, Amberg, 1830, p. 65; see Ludlow, 'Popular Epics of Middle Ages,' p. 221.

Mandeville: "In an isle clept Cruca, ben schippes withouten nayles of iren, or bonds, for the rockes of the adamandes; for they ben alle fulle there aboute in that see, that it is marveyle to spaken of. And gif a schipp passed by the marches, and hadde either iren bandes or iren nayles, anon he sholde ben perisbet. For the adamande of this kinde draws the iren to him; and so wolde it drnw to him the schipp, because of the iren; that he sholde never departen fro it, ne never go thens."[1] Now it seems that accounts of the magnetic mountain have been given not only as belonging to the southern seas, but also to the north, and that men have connected with such notions the pointing of the magnetic needle, as Sir Thomas Browne says, "ascribing thereto the cause of the needle's direction, and conceeving the effluxions from these mountains and rocks invite the lilly toward the north."[2] On this evidence we have, I think, fair ground for supposing that hypotheses of polar magnetic mountains were first devised to explain the action of the compass, and that these gave rise to stories of such mountains exerting what would be considered their proper effect on the iron of passing ships. The argument is clenched by the consideration that Europeans, who colloquially say the needle points to the north, naturally required their loadstone mountain in high northern latitudes, while on the other hand it was as natural that Orientals should place this wondrous rock in the south, for they say it is to the south that the needle points. The conception of magnetism among peoples who had not reached the idea of double polarity may be gathered from the following quaint remarks in the 17th century cyclopædia of the Chinese emperor Kang-hi. "I now hear the Europeans say it is towards the North pole that the compass turns; the ancients said it was toward the South; which have judged most rightly? Since neither give any reason why, we come to no more with the one side than with the other. But the

---

[1] Sir John Maundevile, 'Voiage and Travaile.'
[2] Sir Thomas Browne, 'Vulgar Errours,' ii. 3.

ancients are the earlier in date, and the farther I go the more
I perceive that they understood the mechanism of nature.
All movement languishes and dies in proportion as it
approaches the north; it is hard to believe it to be from
thence that the movement of the magnetic needle comes." [1]

To suppose that theories of a relation between man and
the lower mammalia are only a product of advanced science,
would be an extreme mistake. Even at low levels of culture,
men addicted to speculative philosophy have been led to
account for the resemblance between apes and themselves by
solutions satisfactory to their own minds, but which we must
class as philosophic myths. Among these, stories which
embody the thought of an upward change from ape to man,
more or less approaching the last-century theory of development, are to be found side by side with others which in the
converse way account for apes as degenerate from a previous
human state.

Central American mythology works out the idea that
monkeys were once a human race.[2] In South-East Africa,
Father Dos Santos remarked long since that "they hold
that the apes were anciently men and women, and thus they
call them in their tongue the first people." The Zulus still
tell the tale of an Amafene tribe who became baboons.
They were an idle race who did not like to dig, but wished
to eat at other people's houses, saying, "We shall live,
although we do not dig, if we eat the food of those who
cultivate the soil." So the chief of that place, of the house
of Tusi, assembled the tribe, and they prepared food and
went out into the wilderness. They fastened on behind them

[1] 'Mémoires conc. l'Hist., etc., des Chinois,' vol. iv. p. 457. Compare the
story of the magnetic (?) horseman in 'Thousand and One N.' vol. iii. p. 119,
with the old Chinese mention of magnetic cars with a movable-armed pointing figure, A. v. Humboldt, 'Asie Centrale,' vol. i. p. xi.; Goguet, vol. iii.
p. 284. (The loadstone mountain has its power from a horseman on the top
with brazen bow.)

[2] Brasseur, 'Popol Vuh,' pp. 23-31. Compare this Central American myth
of the ancient senseless mannikins who became monkeys, with a Pottowatom
legend in Schoolcraft, 'Indian Tribes,' part i. p. 320.

the handles of their now useless digging picks, these grew
and became tails, hair made its appearance on their bodies,
their foreheads became overhanging, and so they became
baboons, who are still called " Tusi's men." [1] Mr. Kingsley's
story of the great and famous nation of the Doasyoulikes,
who degenerated by natural selection into gorillas, is the
civilized counterpart of this savage myth. Or monkeys may
be transformed aborigines, as the Mbocobis relate in South
America : in the great conflagration of their forests a man
and woman climbed a tree for refuge from the fiery deluge,
but the flames singed their faces and they became apes.[2]
Among more civilized nations these fancies have graphic
representatives in Moslem legends, of which one is as
follows :—There was a Jewish city which stood by a river
full of fish, but the cunning creatures, noticing the habits of
the citizens, ventured freely in sight on the Sabbath, though
they carefully kept away on working-days. At last the
temptation was too strong for the Jewish fishermen, but
they paid dearly for a few days' fine sport by being miracu-
lously turned into apes as a punishment for Sabbath-breaking.
In after times, when Solomon passed through the Valley of
Apes, between Jerusalem and Mareb, he received from their
descendants, monkeys living in houses and dressed like men,
an account of their strange history.[3] So, in classic times,
Jove had chastised the treacherous race of the Cercopes ;
he took from them the use of tongues, born but to perjure,
leaving them to bewail in hoarse cries their fate, transformed
into the hairy apes of the Pithecusæ, like and yet unlike the
men they had been :—

" In deforme viros animal mutavit, ut idem
Dissimiles homini possent similesque videri." [4]

[1] Dos Santos, ' Ethiopia Oriental '; Evora, 1609, part L chap. lx. ; Callaway,
' Zulu Tales,' vol. L p. 177. See also Burton, 'Footsteps in E. Afr.' p. 271 ;
Waitz, 'Anthropologie,' vol. II. p. 173 (W. Afr.).
[2] D'Orbigny, ' L'Homme Américain,' vol. II. p. 102.
[3] Weil, ' Bibl. Leg. der Muselmänner,' p. 267 ; Lane, ' Thousand and One
N.' vol. iii. p. 350 ; Burton, ' El Medinah, etc.' vol. II. p. 313.
[4] Ovid, ' Metamm.' xiv. 89-100 ; Welcker, ' Griechische Götterlehre, vol. iiL
.109.

Turning from degeneration to development, it is found
that legends of the descent of human tribes from apes are
especially applied to races despised as low and beast-like by
some higher neighbouring people, and the low race may
even acknowledge the humiliating explanation. Thus the
aboriginal features of the robber-caste of the Marawars of
South India are the justification for their alleged descent
from Rama's monkeys, as for the like genealogy of the
Kathkuri, or catechu-gatherers, which these small, dark,
low-browed, curly-haired tribes actually themselves believe
in. The Jaitwas of Rajputana, a tribe reckoned politically
as Rajputs, nevertheless trace their descent from the
monkey-god Hanuman, and confirm it by alleging that their
princes still bear its evidence in a tail-like prolongation of
the spine; a tradition which has probably a real ethnological meaning, pointing out the Jaitwas as of non-Aryan
race.[1] Wild tribes of the Malay peninsula, looked down on
as lower animals by the more warlike and civilized Malays,
have among them traditions of their own descent from a
pair of the "unka puteh," or "white monkeys," who reared
their young ones and sent them into the plains, and there
they perfected so well that they and their descendants
became men, but those who returned to the mountains still
remained apes.[2] Thus Buddhist legend relates the origin
of the flat-nosed, uncouth tribes of Tibet, offspring of two
miraculous apes, transformed to people the snow-kingdom.
Taught to till the ground, when they had grown corn and
eaten it, their tails and hair gradually disappeared, they
began to speak, became men, and clothed themselves with
leaves. The population grew closer, the land was more and
more cultivated, and at last a prince of the race of Sakya,
driven from his home in India, united their isolated tribes
into a single kingdom.[3] In these traditions the develop-

[1] Campbell in 'Journ. As. Soc. Bengal,' 1866, part ii. p. 132; Latham,
'Descr. Eth.' vol. II. p. 456; Tod, 'Annals of Rajasthan,' vol. I. p. 114.
[2] Bourien in 'Tr. Eth. Soc.' vol. iii. p. 73; see 'Journ. Ind. Archip.' vol. II.
p. 271.
[3] Bastian, 'Oestl. Asien,' vol. iii. p. 435; 'Menab, vol. III. pp. 347, 348,

ment from ape to man is considered to have come in successive generations, but the negroes are said to attain the result in the individual, by way of metempsychosis. Froebel speaks of negro slaves in the United States believing that in the next world they shall be white men and free, nor is there anything strange in their cherishing a hope so prevalent among their kindred in West Africa. But from this the traveller goes on to quote another story, which, if not too good to be true, is a theory of upward and downward development, almost thorough enough for a Buddhist philosopher. He says, " A German whom I met here told me that the blacks believe the damned among the negroes to become monkeys ; but if in this state they behave well, they are advanced to the state of a negro again, and bliss is eventually possible to them, consisting in their turning white, becoming winged, and so on." [1]

To understand these stories (and they are worth some attention for the ethnological hints they contain), it is necessary that we should discard the results of modern scientific zoology, and bring our minds back to a ruder condition of knowledge. The myths of human degeneration and development have much more in common with the speculations of Lord Monboddo than with the anatomical arguments of Professor Huxley. On the one hand, uncivilized men deliberately assign to apes an amount of human quality which to modern naturalists is simply ridiculous. Everyone has heard the story of the negroes declaring that apes really can speak, but judiciously hold their tongues lest they should be made to work ; but it is not so generally known that this is found as serious matter of belief in several distant regions—West Africa, Madagascar, South America, &c.— where monkeys or apes are found.[2] With this goes another

[2] Froebel, 'Central America,' p. 230 ; see Bosman, 'Guinea,' in Pinkerton, vol. xvi. p. 401. For other traditions of human descent from apes, see Farrar, 'Chapters on Language,' p. 45.

[3] Bosman, 'Guinea,' p. 440 ; Waitz, vol. ii. p. 178 ; Canche, 'Relation de

widely-spread anthropoid story, which relates how great
apes like the gorilla and the orang-utan carry off women
to their homes in the woods, much as the Apaches and
Comanches of our own time carry off to their prairies
the women of North Mexico.[1] And on the other hand,
popular opinion has under-estimated the man as much as it
has over-estimated the monkey. We know how sailors and
emigrants can look on savages as senseless, ape-like brutes,
and how some writers on anthropology have contrived to
make out of the moderate intellectual difference between an
Englishman and a negro something equivalent to the immense interval between a negro and a gorilla. Thus we
can have no difficulty in understanding how savages may
seem mere apes to the eyes of men who hunt them like wild
beasts in the forests, who can only hear in their language a
sort of irrational gurgling and barking, and who fail totally
to appreciate the real culture which better acquaintance
always shows among the rudest tribes of man. It is well
known that when Sanskrit legend tells of the apes who
fought in the army of King Hanuman, it really refers to
those aborigines of the land who were driven by the Aryan
invaders to the hills and jungles, and whose descendants are
known to us as Bhils, Kols, Sonthals, and the like, rude
tribes such as the Hindu still speaks of as "monkey-
people."[2] One of the most perfect identifications of the
savage and the monkey in Hindustan is the following description of the *bunmanus*, or "man of the woods" (Sanskr.
vana = wood, *manusha* = man). "The *bunmanus* is an animal
of the monkey kind. His face has a near resemblance to

Madagascar,' p. 127 ; Dobrizhoffer, 'Abipones,' vol. i. p. 298 ; Bastian,
'Mensch,' vol. II. p. 16 ; Pouchet, 'Plurality of Human Race,' p. 22.

[1] Monboddo, 'Origin and Progress of Lang.' 2nd ed. vol. I. p. 277 ; Du
Chaillu, 'Equatorial Africa,' p. 61 ; St. John, 'Forests of Far East,' vol. I.
p. 17 ; vol. II. p. 230.

[2] Max Müller in Bunsen, 'Phil. Univ. Hist.' vol. i. p. 340 ; 'Journ. As.
Soc. Bengal,' vol. xxiv. p. 207. See Marsden in 'As. Res.' vol. iv. p. 226 ;
Fitch in Pinkerton, vol. ix. p. 115 ; Bastian, 'Oestl. Asien,' vol. I. p. 465 ;
vol. II. p. 201.

the human; he has no tail, and walks erect. The skin of his body is black, and slightly covered with hair." That this description really applies not to apes, but to the dark-skinned, non-Aryan aborigines of the land, appears further in the enumeration of the local dialects of Hindustan, to which, it is said, "may be added the jargon of the bunmanus, or wild men of the woods."[1] In the islands of the Indian Archipelago, whose tropical forests swarm both with high apes and low savages, the confusion between the two in the minds of the half-civilized inhabitants becomes almost inextricable. There is a well-known Hindu fable in the Hitopadesa, which relates as a warning to stupid imitators the fate of the ape who imitated the carpenter, and was caught in the cleft when he pulled out the wedge; this fable has come to be told in Sumatra as a real story of one of the indigenous savages of the island.[2] It is to rude forest-men that the Malays habitually give the name of orang-utan, i.e., "man of the woods." But in Borneo this term is applied to the miyas ape, whence we have learnt to call this creature the orang-utan, and the Malays themselves are known to give the name in one and the same district to both the savage and the ape.[3] This term "man of the woods" extends far beyond Hindu and Malay limits. The Siamese talk of the Khon pa, "men of the wood," meaning apes;[4] the Brazilians of Caniari, or "wood-men," meaning a certain savage tribe.[5] The name of the Bosjesman, so amusingly mispronounced by Englishmen, as though it were some outlandish native word, is merely the Dutch equivalent for Bush-man, "man of the woods or bush."[6] In our own language the

---

[1] Ayeen Akbaree, trans. by Gladwin; 'Report of Ethnological Committee Jabbulpore Exhibition, 1866-7,' part i. p. 3. See the mention of the bunmanush in Kumaon and Nepal, Campbell; 'Ethnology of India,' in 'Journ. As. Soc. Bengal,' 1866, part ii. p. 46.

[2] Marsden, 'Sumatra,' p. 41.

[3] Logan in 'Journ. Ind. Archip.' vol. i. p. 246; vol. iii. p. 490; Thomson, ibid. vol. i. p. 350; Crawfurd, ibid. vol. iv. p. 186.

[4] Bastian, 'Oestl. Asien,' vol. i. p. 123; vol. iii. p. 435.

[5] Martius, 'Ethnog. Amer.' vol. i. pp. 425, 471.

[6] Its analogue is bosjesbok, "bush-goat," the African antelope. The deri-

"homo silraticus" or "forest-man" has become the
"salvage man" or savage. European opinion of the native
tribes of the New World may be judged of by the fact that,
in 1537, Pope Paul III. had to make express statement that
these Indians were really men (attendentes Indos ipsos
utpote veros homines).[1] Thus there is little cause to
wonder at the circulation of stories of ape-men in South
America, and at there being some indefiniteness in the local
accounts of the selvage or "savage," that hairy wild man
of the woods who, it is said, lives in the trees, and sometimes carries off the native women.[2] The most perfect of
these mystifications is to be found in a Portuguese manu-
script quoted in the account of Castelnau's expedition, and
giving, in all seriousness, the following account of the
people called Cuatas: "This populous nation dwells east
of the Juruena, in the neighbourhood of the rivers San João
and San Thome, advancing even to the confluence of the
Juruena and the Arinos. It is a very remarkable fact that
the Indians composing it walk naturally like the quadru-
peds, with their hands on the ground ; they have the belly,
breast, arms, and legs covered with hair, and are of small
stature ; they are fierce, and use their teeth as weapons ;
they sleep on the ground, or among the branches of trees ;
they have no industry, nor agriculture, and live only on
fruits, wild roots, and fish."[3] The writer of this record
shows no symptom of being aware that cuata or coata is the
name of the large black Simia Paniscus, and that he has
been really describing, not a tribe of Indians, but a species
of apes.

Various reasons may have led to the growth of another
quaint group of legends, describing human tribes with tails

---

vation of the Bosjesman's name from his nest-like shelter in a bush, given by
Kolben and others since, is newer and far-fetched.

　[1] Martius, vol. i. 50.

　[2] Humboldt and Bonpland, vol. v. p. 81 ; Southey, 'Brazil,' vol. i. p. xxx. ;
Bates, 'Amazons,' vol. i. p. 73 ; vol. ii. p. 204.

　[3] Castelnau, 'Exp. dans l'Amér. du Sud,' vol. iii. p. 118. See Martius,
vol. i. pp. 246, 414, 563, 633.

like beasts. To people who at once believe monkeys a kind
of savages, and savages a kind of monkeys, men with tails
are creatures coming under both definitions. Thus the
Homo caudatus, or satyr, often appears in popular belief as
a half-human creature, while even in old-fashioned works
on natural history he may be found depicted on the evident
model of an anthropoid ape. In East Africa, the imagined
tribe of long-tailed men are also monkey-faced,[1] while in
South America the coata tapuya, or "monkey-men," are as
naturally described as men with tails.[2] European travellers
have tried to rationalize the stories of tailed men which
they meet with in Africa and the East. Thus Dr. Krapf
points to a leather appendage worn behind from the girdle
by the Wakamba, and remarks, "It is no wonder that
people say there are men with tails in the interior of
Africa," and other writers have called attention to hanging
mats or waist-cloths, fly-flappers or artificial tails worn for
ornament, as having made their wearers liable to be mistaken at a distance for tailed men.[3] But these apparently
silly myths have often a real ethnological significance,
deeper at any rate than such a trivial blunder. When an
ethnologist meets in any district with the story of tailed
men, he ought to look for a despised tribe of aborigines, outcasts, or heretics, living near or among a dominant population, who look upon them as beasts, and furnish them with
tails accordingly. Although the aboriginal Miau-tsze, or
"children of the soil," come down from time to time into
Canton to trade, the Chinese still firmly believe them to
have short tails like monkeys;[4] the half-civilized Malays
describe the ruder forest tribes as tailed men;[5] the
Moslem nations of Africa tell the same story of the Niam-

[1] Petherick, 'Egypt, etc.' p. 367.
[2] Southey, 'Brazil,' vol. i. p. 685 ; Martius, vol. i. pp. 425, 633.
[3] Krapf, p. 142 ; Baker, 'Albert Nyanza,' vol. i. p. 83 ; St. John, vol. I.
pp. 81, 405 ; and others.
[4] Lockhart, 'Abor. of China,' in 'Tr. Eth. Soc.' vol. i. p. 181.
[5] Journ. Ind. Archip.' vol. ii. p. 358 ; vol. iv. p. 374 ; Cameron, 'Malayan
India,' p. 120 ; Marsden, p. 7 ; Antonio Galvano, pp. 120, 218.

Nam of the interior.[1] The outcast race of Cagots, about
the Pyrenees, were said to be born with tails; and in Spain
the mediæval superstition still survives that the Jews have
tails, like the devil, as they say.[2] In England the notion
was turned to theological profit by being claimed as a judgment on wretches who insulted St. Augustine and St.
Thomas of Canterbury. Horne Tooke quotes thus from
that zealous and somewhat foul-mouthed reformer, Bishop
Bale: "Johan Capgrave and Alexander of Esseby sayth,
that for castynge of fyshe tayles at thys Augustyne, Dorsett
Shyre menne hadde tayles ever after. But Polydorus
applieth it unto Kentish men at Stroud by Rochester, for
cuttinge of Thomas Becket's horse's tail. Thus hath England in all other land a perpetuall infamy of tayles by theyr
wrytten legendes of lyes, yet can they not well tell, where to
bestowe them truely . . . . . . an Englyshman
now cannot travayle in an other land, by way of marchan-
dyse or any other honest occupyinge, but it is most con-
tumeliously thrown in his tethe, that al Englishmen have
tailes."[3] The story at last sank into a commonplace of
local slander between shire and shire, and the Devonshire
belief that Cornishmen had tails lingered at least till a few
years ago.[4] Not less curious is the tradition among savage
tribes, that the tailed state was an early or original condition of man. In the Fiji Islands there is a legend of a tribe
of men with tails like dogs, who perished in the great
deluge, while the Tasmanians declared that men originally
had tails and no knee-joints. Among the natives of Brazil,
it is related by a Portuguese writer of about 1600, after a
couple have been married, the father or father-in-law cuts a
wooden stick with a sharp flint, imagining that by this ceremony he cuts off the tails of any future grandchildren, so

[1] Davis, 'Carthage,' p. 230; Bostock and Riley's Pliny (Bohn's ed.), vol. ii.
p. 134, note.
[2] Francisque-Michel, 'Races Maudites,' vol. i. p. 17; 'Argot,' p. 319;
Fernan Caballero, 'La Gaviota,' vol. i. p. 59.
[3] Horne Tooke, 'Diversions of Purley,' vol. i. p. 397.
[4] Baring-Gould, 'Myths,' p. 137.

that they will be born tailless.[1] There seems no evidence
to connect the occasional occurrence of tail-like projections
by malformation with the stories of tailed human tribes.[2]

Anthropology, until modern times, classified among its
facts the particulars of monstrous human tribes, gigantic or
dwarfish, mouthless or headless, one-eyed or one-legged,
and so forth. The works of ancient geographers and
naturalists abound in descriptions of these strange creatures;
writers such as Isidore of Seville and Roger Bacon collected
them, and sent them into fresh and wider circulation in the
middle ages, and the popular belief of uncivilized nations
retains them still. It was not till the real world had been
so thoroughly explored as to leave little room in it for the
monsters, that about the beginning of the present century
science banished them to the ideal world of mythology.
Having had to glance here at two of the principal species
in this amazing semi-human menagerie, it may be worth
while to look among the rest for more hints as to the
sources of mythic fancy.[3]

That some of the myths of giants and dwarfs are connected with traditions of real indigenous or hostile tribes is
settled beyond question by the evidence brought forward by
Grimm, Nilsson, and Hanusch. With all the difficulty of
analyzing the mixed nature of the dwarfs of European folklore, and judging how far they are elves, or gnomes, or such
like nature-spirits, and how far human beings in mythic
aspect, it is impossible not to recognize this latter element

[1] Williams, 'Fiji,' vol. i. p. 252; Backhouse, 'Austr.' p. 557; Purchas,
vol. iv. p. 1250; De Laet, 'Novus Orbis,' p. 541.

[2] For various other stories of tailed men, see 'As. Res.' vol. iii. p. 119;
'Mem. Anthrop. Soc.' vol. i. p. 151; 'Journ. Ind. Archip.' vol. iii. p. 261, etc.
(Nicobar Islands); Klemm, 'C. G.' vol. ii. pp. 246, 316 (Sarytschew Is.);
'Letters of Columbus,' Hakluyt Soc. p. 11 (Cuba), etc., etc.

[3] Details of monstrous tribes have been in past centuries specially collected
in the following works: ' Anthropometamorphosis : Man Transformed, or the
Artificiall Changeling, etc.,' scripsit J. B. cognomento Chirosophus, M.D.,
London, 1653; Calorius, 'De Thaumatauthropologia, vera pariter atque ficta
tractatus historico-physicus,' Rostock, 1685; J. A. Fabricius, ' Dissertatio de
hominibus orbis nostri insolis, etc.,' Hamburg, 1721. Only a few principal
references are here given.

in the kindly or mischievous aborigines of the land, with
their special language, and religion, and costume. The
giants appear in European folklore as Stone-Age heathen,
shy of the conquering tribes of men, loathing their agriculture and the sound of their church-bells. The rude native's
fear of the more civilized intruder in his land is well depicted in the tale of the giant's daughter, who found the
boor ploughing his field and carried him home in her apron
for a plaything—plough, and oxen, and all ; but her mother
bade her carry them back to where she found them, for,
said she, they are of a people that can do the Huns much
ill. The fact of the giant tribes bearing such historic names
as Hun or Chud is significant, and Slavonic men have,
perhaps, not yet forgotten that the dwarfs talked of in their
legends were descended from the aborigines whom the Old-
Prussians found in the land. Beyond a doubt the old
Scandinavians are describing the ancient and ill-used Lapp
population, once so widely spread over Northern Europe,
when their sagas tell of the dwarfs, stunted and ugly, dressed
in reindeer kirtle and coloured cap, cunning and cowardly,
shy of intercourse even with friendly Norsemen, dwelling in
caves or in the mound-like Lapland " gamm," armed only
with arrows tipped with stone and bone, yet feared and
hated by their conquerors for their fancied powers of witchcraft.[1] Moslem legend relates that the race of Gog and
Magog (Yajuj and Majuj) are of tiny stature, but with ears
like elephants ; they are a numerous people, and ravaged
the world ; they dwell in the East, separated from Persia
by a high mountain, with but one pass ; and the nations
their neighbours, when they heard of Alexander the Great
(Dhu l' Karnein) traversing the world, paid tribute to him,
and he made them a wall of bronze and iron, to keep in the
nation of Gog and Magog.[2] Who can fail to recognize in

[1] Grimm, 'D. M.' ch. xvii. xviii. ; Nilsson, ' Primitive Inhabitants of Scandinavia,' ch. vi. ; Hanusch, 'Slav. Myth.' pp. 230, 325–7 ; Wuttke, ' Volksa-
bergl.' p. 231.
[2] 'Chronique de Tabari,' tr. Dubeux, part i. ch. viii. See Koran, xviii. 92.

this a mystified description of the Tatars of High Asia? Professor Nilsson tries to account in a general way for the huge or tiny stature of legendary tribes, as being mere exaggeration of their actual largeness or smallness. We must admit that this sometimes really happens. The accounts which European eye-witnesses brought home of the colossal stature of the Patagonians, to whose waists they declared their own heads reached, are enough to settle once for all the fact that myths of giants may arise from the sight of really tall men;[1] and it is so, too, with the dwarf-legends of the same region, as where Knivet, the old traveller, remarks of the little people of Rio de la Plata, that they are "not so very little as described."[2]

Nevertheless, this same group of giant and dwarf myths may serve as a warning not to stretch too widely a partial explanation, however sound within its proper limits. There is plenty of evidence that giant-legends are sometimes philosophic myths, made to account for the finding of great fossil bones. To give but a single instance of such connexion, certain huge jaws and teeth, found in excavating on the Hoe at Plymouth, were recognized as belonging to the giant Gogmagog, who in old times fought his last fight there against Corineus, the eponymic hero of Cornwall.[3] As to the dwarfs, again, stories of them are curiously associated with those long-enduring monuments of departed races—their burial-cysts and dolmens. Thus, in the United States, ranges of rude stone cysts, often only two or three feet long, are connected with the idea of a pygmy race buried in them, while in India it is a usual legend of the prehistoric dolmens, that they were dwarfs' houses—the dwellings of the ancient

[1] Pigafetta in Pinkerton, vol. xi. p. 314. See Blumenbach, 'De Generis Humanæ Varietate;' Fitzroy, 'Voy. of Adventure and Beagle,' vol. ii.; Waitz, 'Anthropologie,' vol. iii. p. 488.

[2] Knivet in Purchas, vol. iv. p. 1231; compare Humboldt and Bonpland, vol. v. p. 564, with Martius, 'Ethnog. Amer.' p. 424; see also Krapf, 'East Africa,' p. 51; Du Chaillu, 'Ashango-land,' p. 319.

[3] 'Early Hist. of Mankind,' ch. xi.; Hunt, 'Pop. Rom.' 1st series, pp. 18, 304.

pygmies, who here again appear as representatives of prehistoric tribes.[1] But a very different meaning is obvious in
a mediæval traveller's account of the hairy, man-like
creatures of Cathay, one cubit high, and that do not bend
their knees as they walk, or in an Arab geographer's description of an island people in the Indian seas, four spans
high, naked, with red downy hair on their faces, and who
climb up trees and shun mankind. If any one could possibly doubt the real nature of these dwarfs, his doubt may
be resolved by Marco Polo's statement that in his time
monkeys were regularly embalmed in the East Indies, and
sold in boxes to be exhibited over the world as pigmies.[2]
Thus various different facts have given rise to stories of
giants and dwarfs, more than one mythic element perhaps
combining to form a single legend—a result perplexing in
the extreme to the mythological interpreter.

Descriptions of strange tribes made in entire good faith
may come to be understood in now extravagant senses, when
carried among people not aware of the original facts. The
following are some interpretations of this kind, among
which some far-fetched cases are given, to show that the
method must not be trusted too much. The term "nose-
less" is apt to be misunderstood, yet it was fairly enough
applied to flat-nosed tribes, such as Turks of the steppes,
whom Rabbi Benjamin of Tudela thus depicts in the twelfth
century :—"They have no noses, but draw breath through
two small holes."[3] Again, among the common ornamental
mutilations of savages is that of stretching the ears to an
enormous size by weights or coils, and it is thus verbally
quite true that there are men whose ears hang down upon
their shoulders. Yet without explanation such a phrase

---

[1] Squier, 'Abor. Monuments of N. Y.' p. 68 ; Long's 'Exp.' vol. i. pp. 62,
275 ; Meadows Taylor in 'Journ. Eth. Soc.' vol. i. p. 157.

[2] Gul. de Rubruquis in Pinkerton, vol. vii. p. 69 ; Lane, 'Thousand and
One N.' vol. iii. pp. 61, 91, see 21, 52, 97 ; Hole, p. 63 ; Marco Polo, book iii.
ch. xi.

[3] Benjamin of Tudela, 'Itinerary,' ed. and tr. by Asher, 83 ; Plin. vii. 2.
See Max Müller in Bunsen, vol. i. pp. 346, 358.

would be understood to describe, not the appearance of a
real savage with his ear-lobes stretched into pendant fleshy
loops, but rather that of Piny's *Panotii*, or of the Indian
Karnaprdvarana, " whose ears serve them for cloaks," or of
the African dwarfs, said to use their ears one for mattress
and the other for coverlet when they lie down. One of the
most extravagant of these stories is told by Fray Pedro
Simou in California, where in fact the territory of *Oregon*
has its name from the Spanish term of *Orejones*, or " Dig-
Ears," given to the inhabitants from their practice of
stretching their ears with ornaments.[1] Even purely metaphorical descriptions, if taken in a literal sense, are capable
of turning into catches, like the story of the horse with its
head where its tail should be. I have been told by a
French Protestant from the Nismes district that the epithet
of *gorgeo negro*, or " black-throat," by which Catholics
describe a Huguenot, is taken so literally that heretic
children are sometimes forced to open their mouths to
satisfy the orthodox of their being of the usual colour
within. On examining the descriptions of savage tribes by
higher races, it appears that several of the epithets usually
applied only need literalizing to turn into the wildest of the
legendary monster-stories. Thus the Birmese speak of the
rude Karens as " dog-men;"[2] Marco Polo describes the
Angaman (Andaman) islanders as brutish and savage cannibals, with heads like dogs.[3] Ælian's account of the dog-
headed people of India is on the face of it an account of a
savage race. The Kynokephali, he says, are so called from
their bodily appearance, but otherwise they are human, and

---

[1] Plin. iv. 27 ; Mela, iii. 6 ; Bastian, 'Oestl. Asien,' vol. i. p. 120 ; vol. ii.
p. 93 ; St. John, vol. ii. p. 117 ; Marsden, p. 53 ; Lane, 'Thousand and One
N.' vol. iii. pp. 92, 305 ; Petherick, ' Egypt, etc.' p. 367 ; Burton, 'Central
Afr.' vol. i. p. 235 ; Pedro Simon, ' Indias Occidentales,' p. 7. A name
similar to *Orejones* is *Patagones*, or ' Dig-feet,' which remains in *Patagonia* :
compare with this the stories of men with feet so large as to serve for parasols,
the *Skiapdes* or 'Shadowfeet,' Plin. vii. 2 ; see Rawlinson's Herodotus,
vol. i. p. 50.

[2] Bastian, 'Oestl. Asien,' vol. i. p. 133.

[3] Marco Polo, book iii. ch. xviii.

they go dressed in the skins of beasts; they are just, and
harm not men; they cannot speak, but roar, yet they
understand the language of the Indians; they live by
hunting, being swift of foot, and they cook their game not
by fire, but by tearing it into fragments and drying it in the
sun; they keep goats and sheep, and drink the milk. The
naturalist concludes by saying that he mentions these fitly
among the irrational animals, because they have not articulate, distinct, and human language.[1] This last suggestive
remark well states the old prevalent notion that barbarians
have no real language, but are "speechless," "tongueless,"
or even mouthless.[2] Another monstrous people of wide
celebrity are Pliny's Blemmyæ, said to be headless, and
accordingly to have their mouths and eyes in their breasts;
creatures over whom Prester John reigned in Asia, who
dwelt far and wide in South American forests, and who to
our mediæval ancestors were as real as the cannibals with
whom Othello couples them.

> " The Anthropophagi, and men whose heads
> Do grow beneath their shoulders."

If, however, we look in dictionaries for the *Acephali*, we
may find not actual headless monsters, but heretics so called
because their original head or founder was not known; and
when the kingless Turkoman hordes say of themselves "We
are a people without a head," the metaphor is even more
plain and natural.[3] Again, Moslem legend tells of the

[1] Ælian, iv. 46; Plin. vi. 35; vii. 2. See for other versions, Purchas,
vol. iv. p. 1191; vol. v. p. 901; Cranz, p. 267; Lane, 'Thousand and One
Nights,' vol. iii. pp. 36, 94, 97, 305; Davis, 'Carthage,' p. 230; Latham,
'Descr. Eth.' vol. ii. p. 83.

[2] Plin. v. 8; vi. 24, 35; vii. 2; Mela, iii. 9; Herberstein in Hakluyt,
vol. i. p. 593; Latham, 'Descr. Eth.' vol. i. p. 433; Davis, l. c.; see 'Early
Hist. of Mankind,' p. 77.

[3] Plin. v. 8; Lane, vol. i. p. 33; vol. ii. p. 577; vol. iii. p. 31; Eisenmenger, vol. ii. p. 559; Mandeville, p. 243; Raleigh in Hakluyt, vol. iii.
pp. 652, 665; Humboldt and Bonpland, vol. v. p. 176; Purchas, vol. iv.
p. 1295; vol. v. p. 901; Isidor. Hispal. s. v. 'Acephali;' Vambéry, p. 310,
see p. 436.

Shikk and the Nesnas, creatures like one half of a split man, with one arm, leg, and eye. Possibly it was thence that the Zulus got their idea of a tribe of half-men, who in one of their stories found a Zulu maiden in a cave and thought she was two people, but on closer inspection of her admitted, "The thing is pretty! But oh the two legs!" This odd fancy coincides with the simple metaphor which describes a savage as only "half a man," *semihomo*, as Virgil calls the ferocious Cacus.[1] Again, when the Chinese compared themselves to the outer barbarians, they said " We see with two eyes, the Latins with one, and all other nations are blind." Such metaphors, proverbial among ourselves, verbally correspond with legends of one-eyed tribes, such as the savage cave-dwelling Kyklopes.[2] Verbal coincidence of this kind, untrustworthy enough in these latter instances, passes at last into the vaguest fancy. The negroes called Europeans " long-headed," using the phrase in our familiar metaphorical sense; but translate it into Greek, and at once Hesiod's *Makrokephaloi* come into being.[3] And, to conclude the list, one of the commonest of the monster-tribes of the Old and New World is that distinguished by having feet turned backward. Now there is really a people whose name, memorable in scientific controversy, describes them as " having feet the opposite

[1] Lane, vol. I. p. 33; Callaway, 'Zulu Tales,' vol. I. pp. 199, 202. Virg. Æn. viii. 194; a similar metaphor is the name of the *Nimchas*, from Persian *nim*—half, 'Journ. Eth. Soc.' vol. i. p. 192, cf. French *demi-monde*. Compare the 'one-legged' tribes, Plin. vii. 2; Schoolcraft, 'Indian Tribes,' part iii. p. 521; Charlevoix, vol. I. p. 25. The Australians use the metaphor 'of one leg' (matta gyn) to describe tribes as of one stock, G. F. Moore, 'Vocab.' pp. 5, 71.

[2] Hayton in Purchas, vol. III. p. 108; see Klemm, 'C. G.' vol. vi. p. 129; Vambéry, p. 49; Homer. Odyss. ix. ; Strabo, i. 2, 12; see Schortzer, 'Voy. of Novara,' vol. II. p. 10; C. J. Andersson, 'Lake Ngami, etc.,' p. 453; Du Chaillu, 'Equatorial Africa,' p. 440; Sir J. Richardson, 'Polar Regions,' p. 300. For tribes with more than two eyes, see Pliny's metaphorically explained Nisacorthos and Nisyti, Plin. vi. 35; also Bastian, 'Mensch,' vol. ii. p. 414; 'Oestl. Asien,' vol. I. pp. 25, 76; Petherick, l. c.; Bowen, 'Yoruba Gr.' p. xx.; Schirren, p. 196.

[3] Koelle, 'Vei Gr.' p. 229; Strabo, i. 2, 35.

way," and they still retain that ancient name of *Anti-
podes*.[1]

Returning from this digression to the region of philosophic myth, we may examine new groups of explanatory
stories, produced from that craving to know causes and
reasons which ever besets mankind. When the attention
of a man in the myth-making stage of intellect is drawn to
any phenomenon or custom which has to him no obvious
reason, he invents and tells a story to account for it, and
even if he does not persuade himself that this is a real
legend of his forefathers, the story-teller who hears it from
him and repeats it is troubled with no such difficulty. Our
task in dealing with such stories is made easy when the
criterion of possibility can be brought to bear upon them.
It has become a mere certainty to moderns that asbestos is
not really salamander's wool; that morbid hunger is not
really caused by a lizard or a bird in a man's stomach; that
a Chinese philosopher cannot really have invented the fire-
drill by seeing a bird peck at the branches of a tree till
sparks came. The African Wakuafi account for their cattle-
lifting proclivities by the calm assertion that Engai, that is,
Heaven, gave all cattle to them, and so wherever there is
any it is their call to go and seize it.[2] So in South America
the fierce Mbayas declare they received from the Caracara
a divine command to make war on all other tribes, killing
the men and adopting the women and children.[3] But
though it may be consistent with the notions of these
savages to relate such explanatory legends, it is not consistent with our notions to believe them. Fortunately, too,
the ex post facto legends are apt to come into collision with
more authentic sources of information, or to encroach on
the domain of valid history. It is of no use for the
Chinese to tell their stupid story of written characters
having been invented from the markings on a tortoise's

[1] Plin. vii. 2; Humboldt and Bonpland, vol. v. p. 81.
[2] Krapf, p. 359.
[3] Southey, 'Brazil,' vol. ii. p. 390.

shell, for the early forms of such characters, plain and simple pictures of objects, have been preserved in China to this day. Nor can we praise anything but ingenuity in the West Highland legend that the Pope once laid an interdict on the land, but forgot to curse the hills, so the people tilled them, this story being told to account for those ancient traces of tillage still to be seen on the wild hill-sides, the so-called "elf-furrows."[1] The most embarrassing cases of explanatory tradition are those which are neither impossible enough to condemn, nor probable enough to receive. Ethnographers who know how world-wide is the practice of defacing the teeth among the lower races, and how it only dies gradually out in higher civilization, naturally ascribe the habit to some general reason in human nature, at a particular stage of development. But the mutilating tribes themselves have local legends to account for local customs; thus the Penongs of Birmah and the Batoka of East Africa both break their front teeth, but the one tribe says its reason is not to look like apes, the other that it is to be like oxen and not like zebras.[2] Of the legends of tattooing, one of the oddest is that told to account for the fact that while the Fijians tattoo only the women, their neighbours, the Tongans, tattoo only the men. It is related that a Tongan, on his way from Fiji to report to his countrymen the proper custom for them to observe, went on his way repeating the rule he had carefully learnt by heart, "Tattoo the women, but not the men," but unluckily he tripped over a stump, got his lesson wrong, and reached Tonga repeating "Tattoo the men, but not the women," an ordinance which they observed ever after. How reasonable such an explanation seemed to the Polynesian mind, may be judged from the Samoans having a version with different details, and applied to their own instead of the Tongan islands.[3]

[1] D. Wilson, 'Archæology, etc. of Scotland,' p. 123.
[2] Bastian, 'Oestl. Asien,' vol. I. p. 128; Livingstone, p. 532.
[3] Williams, 'Fiji,' p. 160; Seemann, 'Viti,' p. 118; Turner, 'Polynesia,'

All men feel how wanting in sense of reality is a story
with no personal name to hang it to. This want is thus
graphically expressed by Sprenger the historian in his life
of Mohammed : " It makes, on me at least, quite a different
impression when it is related that ' the Prophet said to
Alkama,' even if I knew nothing whatever else of this
Alkama, than if it were merely stated that ' he said to
somebody.' " The feeling which this acute and learned
critic thus candidly confesses, has from the earliest times,
and in the minds of men troubled with no such nice historic conscience, germinated to the production of much
mythic fruit. Thus it has come to pass that one of the
leading personages to be met with in the tradition of the
world is really no more than—Somebody. There is nothing this wondrous creature cannot achieve, no shape he
cannot put on ; one only restriction binds him at all, that
the name he assumes shall have some sort of congruity
with the office he undertakes, and even from this he often-
times breaks loose. So rife in our own day is this manufacture of personal history, often filled up with details of
place and date into the very semblance of real chronicle,
that it may be guessed how vast its working must have been
in days of old. Thus the ruins of ancient buildings, of
whose real history and use no trustworthy tradition survives
in local memory, have been easily furnished by myth with a
builder and a purpose. In Mexico the great Somebody
assumes the name of Montezuma, and builds the aqueduct
of Tezcuco ; to the Persian any huge and antique ruin is
the work of the heroic Antar ; in Russia, says Dr. Bastian,
buildings of the most various ages are set down to Peter
the Great, as in Spain to Boabdil or Charles V.; and
European folklore may attribute to the Devil any old building of unusual massiveness, and especially those stone
structures which antiquaries now class as pre-historic monuments. With a more graceful thought, the Indians of

p. 182) a similar legend told by the Samoans). Another tattooing legend in
Latham, ' Descr. Eth.' vol. L p. 152 ; Bastian, ' Oestl. Asien,' vol. i. p. 112.

North America declare that the imitative tumuli of Ohio, great mounds laid out in rude imitation of animals, were shaped in old days by the great Manitu himself, in promise of a plentiful supply of game in the world of spirits. The New Zealanders tell how the hero Kupe separated the North and South Islands, and formed Cook's Straits. Greek myth placed at the gate of the Mediterranean the twin pillars of Herakles; in more recent times the opening of the Straits of Gibraltar became one of the many feats of Alexander of Macedon.[1] Such a group of stories as this is no unfair test of the value of mere traditions of personal names which simply answer the questions that mankind have been asking for ages about the origin of their rites, laws, customs, arts. Some such traditions are of course genuine, and we may be able, especially in the more modern cases, to separate the real from the imaginary. But it must be distinctly laid down that, in the absence of corroborative evidence, every tradition stands suspect of mythology, if it can be made by the simple device of fitting some personal name to the purely theoretical assertion that somebody must have introduced into the world fire-making, or weapons, or ornaments, or games, or agriculture, or marriage, or any other of the elements of civilization.

Among the various matters which have excited curiosity, and led to its satisfaction by explanatory myths, are local names. These, when the popular ear has lost their primitive significance, become in barbaric times an apt subject for the myth-maker to explain in his peculiar fashion. Thus the Tibetans declare that their lake *Chomoriri* was named from a woman (*chomo*) who was carried into it by the yak she was riding, and cried in terror *ri-ri!* The Arabs say the founders of the city of *Sennaar* saw on the river bank a beautiful woman with teeth glittering like fire,

[1] Bastian, 'Mensch,' vol. iii. pp. 167-8; Wilkinson in Rawlinson's 'Herodotus,' vol. ii. p. 79; Grimm, 'D. M.' pp. 972-6; W. G. Palgrave, 'Arabia,' vol. i. p. 251; Squier and Davis, 'Monuments of Mississippi Valley,' p. 131; Taylor, 'New Zealand,' p. 258.

whence they called the place *Sinadr*, i. e., "tooth of fire."
The Arkadians derived the name of their town *Trapezus*
from the table (*trapeza*), which Zeus overturned when the
wolfish Lykaon served a child on it for a banquet to him.[1]
Such crude fancies no way differ in nature from English
local legends current up to recent times, such as that which
relates how the Romans, coming in sight of where *Exeter*
now stands, exclaimed in delight, "*Ecce terra!*" and thus
the city had its name. Not long ago, a curious enquirer
wished to know from the inhabitants of *Fordingbridge*, or
as the country people call it, *Fardenbridge*, what the origin
of this name might be, and heard in reply that the bridge
was thought to have been built when wages were so cheap
that masons worked for a "farden" a day. The Falmouth
folks' story of Squire Pendarvis and his ale is well known,
how his servant excused herself for selling it to the sailors,
because, as she said, "The *penny come so quick*," whence
the place came to be called *Pennycomequick*; this nonsense
being invented to account for an ancient Cornish name,
probably *Penycumgwic*, "head of the creek valley." Mythic
fancy had fallen to a low estate when it dwindled to such
remnants as this.

That personal names may pass into nouns, we, who talk
of *broughams* and *bluchers*, cannot deny. But any such
etymology ought to have contemporary document or some
equally forcible proof in its favour, for this is a form of explanation taken by the most flagrant myths. David the
painter, it is related, had a promising pupil named *Chieque*,
the son of a fruiterer; the lad died at eighteen, but his
master continued to hold him up to later students as a
model of artistic cleverness, and hence arose the now

---

[1] Latham, 'Descr. Eth.' vol. I. p. 43 ; Lejean in 'Rev. des Deux Mondes,'
15 Feb. 1862, p. 856 ; Apollodor. iii. 8.   Compare the derivation of *Arequipa*
by the Peruvians from the words *ari I quepay* = 'yes I remain,' said to have
been addressed to the colonists by the Inca : Markham, 'Quichua Gr. and
Dic.;' also the supposed etymology of *Dahome*, *Dauh-ho-men* = 'on the belly
of Dauh,' from the story of King Dako building his palace on the body of the
conquered King Dauh : Burton, in 'Tr. Eth. Soc.' vol. iii. p. 401.

familiar term of *chic*. Etymologists, a race not wanting
in effrontery, have hardly ever surpassed this circumstantial
canard; the word *chic* dates at any rate from the seventeenth
century.[1] Another word with which similar liberty has
been taken, is *cant*. Steele, in the 'Spectator,' says that
some people derive it from the name of one Andrew *Cant*,
a Scotch minister, who had the gift of preaching in such a
dialect that he was understood by none but his own congregation, and not by all of them. This is, perhaps, not a
very accurate delineation of the real Andrew Cant, who is
mentioned in 'Whitelock's Memorials,' and seems to have
known how to speak out in very plain terms indeed. But
at any rate he flourished about 1650, whereas the verb to
cant was then already an old word. To *cante*, meaning to
speak, is mentioned in Harman's 'List of Rogues' Words,'
in 1566, and in 1587 Harrison says of the beggars and
gypsies that they have devised a language among themselves, which they name *canting*, but others "Pedlars'
Frenche."[2] Of all etymologies ascribed to personal
names, one of the most curious is that of the Danse *Macabre*, or Dance of Death, so well known from Holbein's
pictures. Its supposed author is thus mentioned in the
'Biographie Universelle:' "Macaber, poëte allemand, se-
rait tout-à-fait inconnu sans l'ouvrage qu'on a sous son
nom." This, it may be added, is true enough, for there
never was such a person at all, the Danse *Macabre* being
really Chorea *Machabæorum*, the Dance of the *Maccabees*,

[1] Charnock, 'Verba Nominalia,' s. v. 'chic;' see Francisque-Michel,
'Argot,' s. v.

[2] 'Spectator,' No. 147; Brand, 'Pop. Ant.' vol. iii. p. 93; Hotten, 'Slang
Dictionary,' p. 8; Charnock, s. v. 'cant.' As to the real etymology, that
from the beggar's whining *chaunt* is defective, for the beggar drops this tone
exactly when he *cants*, i. e., talks jargon with his fellows. If *cant* is directly
from Latin *cantare*, it will correspond with Italian *cantare* and French *chanter*,
both used as slang words for to speak (Francisque-Michel, 'Argot'). A Keltic
origin is more probable, Gaelic and Irish *caint*, *caint* = talk, language, dialect (see Wedgwood 'Etymological Dictionary'). The Gaelic equivalents for
pedlars' French or tramps' slang, are 'Lahlionn nan ceard,' 'ceinnt cheard,'
i. e., tinkers' Latin or jargon, or exactly 'cairds' *cant*.' A deeper connexion
between *caint* and *cantare* does not affect this.

a kind of pious pantomime of death performed in churches in the fifteenth century. Why the performance received this name, is that the rite of Mass for the dead is distinguished by the reading of that passage from the twelfth chapter of Book II. of the *Maccabees*, which relates how the people betook themselves to prayer, and besought the Lord that the sin of those who had been slain among them might be wholly blotted out; for if Judas had not expected that the slain should rise again, it had been superfluous and vain to pray for the dead.[1] Traced to its origin, it is thus seen that the Danse *Macabre* is neither more nor less than the Dance of the Dead.

It is not an unusual thing for tribes and nations to be known by the name of their chief, as in books of African travel we read of " Eyo's people," or " Kamrazi's people." Such terms may become permanent, like the name of the *Osmanli* Turks taken from the great *Othman*, or *Osman*. The notions of kinship and chieftainship may easily be combined, as where some individual Brian or Alpine may have given his name to a clan of *O'Briens* or *Mac Alpines*. How far the tribal names of the lower races may have been derived from individual names of chiefs or forefathers, is a question on which distinct evidence is difficult to obtain. In Patagonia bands or subdivisions of tribes are designated by the names of temporary chiefs, every roving party having such a leader, who is sometimes even styled " yank," i. e. " father,"[2] The Zulus and Maoris were races who paid great attention to the traditional genealogies of their clan-ancestors, who were, indeed, not only their kinsfolk but their gods; and they distinctly recognize the possibility of tribes being named from a deceased ancestor or chief. The Kafir tribe of *Ama-Xosa* derives its name from a chief, *U-Xosa*;[3] and the Maori tribes of *Ngate-Wakaue* and *Nga-Puhi* claim

[1] See also Francisque-Michel, ' Argot,' s. v. 'maccabe, maccabée ' = noyé.
[2] Musters, ' Patagonians,' p. 69, 184.
[3] Döhne, ' Zulu Dic.' p. 417; Arbousset and Daumas, p. 269; Waitz, vol. ii. pp. 349, 352.

descent from chiefs called *Wakaue* and *Puhi*.[1] Around this
nucleus of actuality, however, there gathers an enormous
mass of fiction simulating its effects. The myth-maker,
curious to know how any people or country gained its name,
had only to conclude that it came from a great ancestor or
ruler, and then the simple process of turning a national or
local title into a personal name at once added a new genealogy
to historical tradition. In some cases, the name of the
imagined ancestor is invented in such form that the local or
gentile name may stand as grammatically derived from it, as
usually happens in real cases, like the derivation of *Cæsarea*
from *Cæsar*, or of the *Benedictines* from *Benedict*. But in
the fictitious genealogy or history of the myth-maker, the
mere unaltered name of the nation, tribe, country, or city
often becomes without more ado the name of the eponymic
hero. It has to be remembered, moreover, that countries
and nations can be personified by an imaginative process
which has not quite lost its sense in modern speech. *France*
is talked of by politicians as an individual being, with particular opinions and habits, and may even be embodied as a
statue or picture with suitable attributes. And if one were
to say that *Britannia* has two daughters, *Canada* and
Australia, or that she has gone to keep house for a decrepit
old aunt called *India*, this would be admitted as plain fact
expressed in fantastic language. The invention of ancestries
from eponymic heroes or name-ancestors has, however, often
had a serious effect in corrupting historic truth, by helping
to fill ancient annals with swarms of fictitious genealogies.
Yet, when surveyed in a large view, the nature of the eponymic fictions is patent and indisputable, and so regular are
their forms, that we could scarcely choose more telling
examples of the consistent processes of imagination, as shown
in the development of myths.

The great number of the eponymic ancestors of ancient
Greek tribes and nations makes it easy to test them by comparison, and the test is a destructive one. Treat the heroic

---

[1] Shortland, 'Trads. of N. Z.' p. 224.

genealogies they belong to as traditions founded on real history, and they prove hopelessly independent and incompatible; but consider them as mostly local and tribal myths, and such independence and incompatibility become their proper features. Mr. Grote, whose tendency is to treat all myths as fictions not only unexplained but unexplainable, here makes an exception, tracing the eponymic ancestors from whom Greek cities and tribes derived their legendary parentage, to mere embodied local and gentile names. Thus, of the fifty sons of Lykaôn, a whole large group consists of personified cities of Arkadia, such as *Mantinêus*, *Phigalos*, *Tegeatês*, who, according to the simply inverting legend, are called founders of *Mantinêa*, *Phigalia*, *Tegea*. The father of King Æakos was Zeus, his mother his own personified land, *Ægina*; the city of *Mykênai* had not only an ancestress *Mykênê*, but an eponymic ancestor as well, *Mykêneus*. Long afterwards, mediæval Europe, stimulated by the splendid genealogies through which Rome had attached herself to Greece and the Greek gods and heroes, discovered the secret of rivalling them in the chronicles of Geoffry of Monmouth and others, by claiming, as founders of *Paris* and *Tours*, the Trojans *Paris* and *Turnus*, and connecting *France* and *Britain* with the Trojan war through *Francus*, son of Hector, and *Brutus*, great grandson of Æneas. A remarkably perfect eponymic historical myth accounting for the Gypsies or Egyptians, may be found cited seriously in 'Blackstone's Commentaries:' when Sultan Selim conquered Egypt in 1517, several of the natives refused to submit to the Turkish yoke, and revolted under one *Zinganeus*, whence the Turks called them *Zinganees*, but, being at length surrounded and banished, they agreed to disperse in small parties over the world, etc., etc. It is curious to watch Milton's mind emerging, but not wholly emerging, from the state of the mediæval chronicler. He mentions in the beginning of his 'History of Britain,' the "outlandish figment" of the four kings, *Magus*, *Saron*, *Druis*, and *Bardus*; he has no approval for the giant *Albion*, son of Neptune, who subdued the island and called it after his own name; he scoffs at the four sons of Japhet, called *Francus, Romanus, Alemannus,* and *Britto.* But when he comes to *Brutus* and the Trojan legends of old English history, his sceptical courage fails him: "those old and inborn names of successive kings, never any to have bin real persons, or don in their lives at least som part of what so long hath bin remember'd, cannot be thought without too strict an incredulity." [1]

Among ruder races of the world, asserted genealogies of this class may be instanced in South American tribes called the *Amoipira* and *Potyuara*,[2] Khond clans called *Baska* and *Jukso*,[3] Turkoman hordes called *Yomut, Tekke,* and *Chaudor*,[4] all of them professing to derive their designations from ancestors or chiefs who bore as individuals these very names. Where criticism can be brought to bear on these genealogies, its effect is often such as drove Brutus and his Trojans out of English history. When there appear in the genealogy of Haussa, in West Africa, plain names of towns like *Kano* and *Katsena*,[5] it is natural to consider these towns to have been personified into mythic ancestors. Mexican tradition assigns a whole set of eponymic ancestors or chiefs to the various races of the land, as *Mexi* the founder of *Mexico, Chichimecatl* the first king of the *Chichimecs,* and so forth, down to *Otomitl* the ancestor of the *Otomis,* whose very name by its termination betrays its Aztec invention.[6] The Brazilians account for the division of the *Tupis* and *Guaranis,* by the legend of two ancestral brothers, *Tupi* and *Guarani,* who

---

[1] On the adoption of imaginary ancestors as connected with the fiction of a common descent, and the important political and religious effects of these proceedings, see especially Grote, 'History of Greece,' vol. i.; McLennan, 'Primitive Marriage;' Maine, 'Ancient Law.' Interesting details on eponymic ancestors in Pott, 'Anti-Kaulen, oder Mythische Vorstellungen vom Ursprunge der Völker und Sprachen.'

[2] Martius, 'Ethnog. Amer.' vol. i. p. 51; see 293.

[3] Macpherson, 'India,' p. 78.

[4] Vambéry, 'Central Asia,' p. 325; see also Latham, 'Descr. Eth.' vol. i. p. 456 (Ostyaks); Georgi, 'Reise im Russ. Reich,' vol. i. 242 (Tungus).

[5] Barth, 'N. & Centr. Afr.' vol. ii. p. 71.

[6] J. G. Müller, 'Amer. Urrelig.' p. 574.

quarrelled and separated, each with his followers : but an
eponymic origin of the story is made likely by the word
Guarani not being an old national name at all, but merely
the designation of " warriors " given by the missionaries to
certain tribes.[1] And when such facts are considered as that
North American clans named after animals, *Bearer, Cray-
fish,* and the like, account for these names by simply claiming the very creatures themselves as ancestors,[2] the tendency
of general criticism will probably be not so much in favour
of real forefathers and chiefs who left their names to their
tribes, as of eponymic ancestors created by backwards imitation of such inheritance.

The examination of eponymic legend, however, must by
no means stop short at the destructive stage. In fact, when
it has undergone the sharpest criticism, it only displays the
more clearly a real historic value, not less perhaps than if
all the names it records were real names of ancient chiefs.
With all their fancies, blunders, and shortcomings, the heroic
genealogies preserve early theories of nationality, traditions
of migration, invasion, connexion by kindred or intercourse.
The ethnologists of old days, borrowing the phraseology of
myth, stated what they looked on as the actual relations of
races, in a personifying language of which the meaning may
still be readily interpreted. The Greek legend of the twin
brothers *Danaos* and *Ægyptos,* founders of the nations of
the *Danaoi* or Homeric Greeks and of the *Ægyptians,*
represents a distinct though weak ethnological theory.
Their eponymic myth of *Hellên,* the personified race of the
Hellênes, is another and more reasonable ethnological document stating kinship among four great branches of the
Greek race : the three sons of *Hellên,* it relates, were
Aiolos, Dôros, and *Xouthos;* the first two gave their names
to the *Æolians* and *Dorians,* the third had sons called
Achaios and *Iôn,* whose names passed as a heritage to the

[1] Martius, vol. I. pp. 180—4 ; Waitz, vol. iii. p. 416.
[2] Schoolcraft, ' Indian Tribes,' part I. p. 319, part iii. p. 263, see part ii.
p. 49 ; Catlin, vol. ii. p. 128 ; J. G. Müller, pp. 134, 327.

Achaioi and *Ionians.* The belief of the *Lydians, Mysians,* and *Karians* as to their national kinship is well expressed in the genealogy in Herodotus, which traces their descent from the three brothers *Lydos, Mysos,* and *Kar.*[1] The Persian legend of Feridun (Thraetaona) and his three sons, *Irej, Tur,* and *Selm,* distinguishes the two nationalities of *Iranian* and *Turanian, i. e.* Persian and Tatar.[2] The national genealogy of the Afghans is worthy of remark. It runs thus: Melik Talut (King Saul) had two sons, Berkia and Irmia (Berekiah and Jeremiah), who served David; the son of Berkia was *Afghan,* and the son of Irmia was *Usbek.* Thanks to the aquiline noses of the Afghans, and to their use of Biblical personal names derived from Biblical sources, the idea of their being descendants of the lost tribes of Israel found great credence among European scholars up to the present century.[3] Yet the pedigree is ethnologically absurd, for the whole source of the imagined cousinship of the Aryan *Afghan* and the Turanian *Usbek,* so distinct both in feature and in language, appears to be in their union by common Mohammedanism, while the reckless jumble of sham history, which derives both from a Semitic source, is only too characteristic of Moslem chronicle. Among the Tatars is found a much more reasonable national pedigree; in the 13th century, William of Ruysbroek relates, as sober circumstantial history, that they were originally called *Turks* from *Turk* the eldest son of Japhet, but one of their princes left his dominions to his twin sons, *Tatar* and *Mongol,* which gave rise to the distinction that has ever since prevailed between these two nations.[4] Historically absurd, this legend states what appears the unimpeachable ethnological

---

[1] Grote, 'Hist. of Greece;' Pausan. iii. 20; Diod. Sic. v. ; Apollodor. Bibl. i. 7, 3, vi. 1, 4 ; Herodot. i. 171.

[2] Max Müller in Bunsen, vol. i. p. 338 ; Tabari, part i. ch. xlv. lxix.

[3] Sir W. Jones in 'As. Res.' vol. ii. p. 24 ; Vansittart, *ibid.* p. 67 ; see Campbell, in 'Journ. As. Soc., Bengal,' 1866, part ii. p. 7.

[4] Gul de Rubruquis in Pinkerton, vol. vii. p. 23 ; Gabelentz in 'Zeitschrift für die Kunde des Morgenlandes,' vol. ii. p. 73 ; Schmidt, 'Volker Mittel. Asien,' p. 6.

fact, that the *Turks*, *Mongols*, and *Tatars* are closely-connected branches of one national stock, and we can only dispute in it what seems an exorbitant claim on the part of the *Turks* to represent the head of the family, the ancestor of the *Mongol* and the *Tatar*. Thus these eponymic national genealogies, mythological in form but ethnological in substance, embody opinions of which we may admit or deny the truth or value, but which we must recognize as distinctly ethnological documents.[1]

It thus appears that early ethnology is habitually expressed in a metaphorical language, in which lands and nations are personified, and their relations indicated by terms of personal kinship. This description applies to that important document of ancient ethnology, the table of nations in the 10th chapter of Genesis. In some cases it is a problem of minute and difficult criticism to distinguish among its ancestral names those which are simply local or national designations in personal form. But to critics conversant with the ethnic genealogies of other peoples, such as have here been quoted, simple inspection of this national list may suffice to show that part of its names are not names of real men, but of personified cities, lands, and races. The city *Zidon* (צידן) is brother to *Heth* (חת) the father of the *Hittites*, and next follow in person the Jebusite and the Amorite. Among plain names of countries, *Cush* or Æthiopia (כוש) begets Nimrod, *Asshur* or *Assyria* (אשור) builds Nineveh, and even the dual *Mizraim* (מצרים), the "two Egypts" (apparently meaning Upper and Lower Egypt, the "two lands," as the Egyptians themselves wrote it in their inscriptions), appears as a personal son and brother of other countries, and ancestor of populations. The Aryan stock is clearly recognized in personifications of at least two of its members, *Madai* (מדי) the *Mede*, and *Javan* (יון) the *Ionian*. And as regards the family to which the Israelites themselves belong, if *Canaan* (כנען), the father

[1] See also Pott, 'Anti-Kaulen,' pp. 19, 23 ; 'Rawn,' pp. 70, 153 ; and remarks on colonization-myths in Max Müller, 'Chips,' vol. ii. p. 68.

of *Zidon* (צידן), be transferred to it to represent the Phœnicians, by the side of *Asshur* (אשור), *Aram* (ארם), *Eber* (עבר), and the other descendants of Shem, the result will be mainly to arrange the Semitic stock according to the ordinary classification of modern comparative philology.

Turning now from cases where mythologic phrase serves as a medium for expressing philosophic opinion, let us quickly cross the district where fancy assumes the semblance of explanatory legend. The mediæval schoolmen have been justly laughed at for their habit of translating plain facts into the terms of metaphysics, and then solemnly offering them in this scientific guise as explanations of themselves—accounting for opium making people sleep, by its possession of a dormitive virtue. The mythmaker's proceedings may in one respect be illustrated by comparing them with this. Half mythology is occupied, as many a legend cited in these chapters has shown, in shaping the familiar facts of daily life into imaginary histories of their own cause and origin, childlike answers to those world-old questions of whence and why, which the savage asks as readily as the sage. So familiar is the nature of such description in the dress of history, that its easier examples translate off hand. When the Samoans say that ever since the great battle among the plaintains and bananas, the vanquished have hung down their heads, while the victor stands proudly erect,[1] who can mistake the simple metaphor which compares the upright and the drooping plants to a conqueror standing among his beaten foes. In simile just as obvious lies the origin of another Polynesian legend, which relates the creation of the coco-nut from a man's head, the chestnuts from his kidneys, and the yams from his legs.[2] To draw one more example from the mythology of plants, how transparent is the Ojibwa fancy of that heavenly youth with green robe and waving feathers, whom for the good of men the Indian overcame and buried, and

[1] Seemann, 'Viti,' p. 311 ; Turner, 'Polynesia,' p. 252.
[2] Ellis, 'Polyn. Res.' vol. I. p. 69.

who sprang again from his grave as the Indian corn, Mon-
damin, the " Spirit's grain." [1]   The New Forest peasant
deems that the marl he digs is still red with the blood of
his ancient foes the Danes; the Maori sees on the red cliffs
of Cook's Straits the blood stains that Kupe made when,
mourning for the death of his daughter, he cut his forehead
with pieces of obsidian; in the spot where Buddha offered
his own body to feed the starved tigress's cubs, his blood
for ever reddened the soil and the trees and flowers.   The
modern Albanian still sees the stain of slaughter in streams
running red with earth, as to the ancient Greek the river
that flowed by Byblos bore down in its summer floods the
red blood of Adonis.   The Cornishman knows from the red
filmy growth on the brook pebbles that murder has been
done there; John the Baptist's blood still grows in
Germany on his day, and peasants still go out to search for
it; the red meal fungus is blood dropped by the flying
Huns when they hurt their feet against the high tower-
roofs.   The traveller in India might see on the ruined walls
of Ganga Raja the traces of the blood of the citizens spilt
in the siege, and yet more marvellous to relate, at St.
Denis's church in Cornwall, the blood-stains on the stones
fell there when the saint's head was cut off somewhere else. [2]
Of such translations of descriptive metaphor under thin
pretence of history, every collection of myth is crowded
with examples, but it strengthens our judgment of the combined consistency and variety of what may be called the
mythic language, to extract from its dictionary such a group
as this, which in such variously imaginative fashion describes the appearance of a blood-red stain.

[1] Schoolcraft, 'Algic Res.' vol. I. p. 122; 'Indian Tribes,' part i. p. 320,
part II. p. 230.
[2] J. R. Wise, 'The New Forest,' p. 160; Taylor, 'New Zealand,' p. 268;
Max Müller, 'Chips,' vol. I. p. 249; M. A. Walker, 'Macedonia,' p. 192;
Movers, 'Phönizier,' vol. I. p. 665; Lucian. de Dea Syria, 8; Hunt, 'Pop.
Rom.' 2nd Series, p. 15; Wuttke, 'Volksaberglaube,' pp. 16, 91; Bastian,
'Mensch,' vol. II. p. 59, vol. III. p. 185; Buchanan, 'Mysore, etc.' in Pinker-
ton, vol. viii. p. 711.

The merest shadowy fancy or broken-down metaphor, when once it gains a sense of reality, may begin to be spoken of as an actual event. The Moslems have heard the very stones praise Allah, not in simile only but in fact, and among them the saying that a man's fate is written on his forehead has been materialized into a belief that it can be deciphered from the letter-like markings of the sutures of his skull. One of the miraculous passages in the life of Mohammed himself is traced plausibly by Sprenger to such a pragmatized metaphor. The angel Gabriel, legend declares, opened the prophet's breast, and took a black clot from his heart, which he washed with Zemzem water and replaced; details are given of the angel's dress and golden basin, and Anas ibn Malik declared he had seen the very mark where the wound was sewn up. We may venture with the historian to ascribe this marvellous incident to the familiar metaphor that Mohammed's heart was divinely opened and cleansed, and indeed he does say in the Koran that God opened his heart.' A single instance is enough to represent the same habit in Christian legend. Marco Polo relates how in 1225 the Khalif of Bagdad commanded the Christians of his dominions, under penalty of death or Islam, to justify their Scriptural text by removing a certain mountain. Now there was among them a shoemaker, who, having been tempted to excess of admiration for a woman, had plucked out his offending eye. This man commanded the mountain to remove, which it did to the terror of the Khalif and all his people, and since then the anniversary of the miracle has been kept holy. The Venetian traveller, after the manner of mediæval writers, records the story without a symptom of suspicion;² yet to our minds its whole origin so obviously lies in three verses of St. Matthew's gospel, that it is needless to quote them. To modern taste such wooden fictions as these are far from attractive. In fact the pragmatizer is a stupid creature;

¹ Sprenger, 'Leben des Mohammad,' vol. I. pp. 78, 119, 162, 310.
² Marco Polo, book I. ch. viii.

nothing is too beautiful or too sacred to be made dull and
vulgar by his touch, for it is through the very incapacity of
his mind to hold an abstract idea that he is forced to
embody it in a material incident. Yet wearisome as he
may be, it is none the less needful to understand him, to
acknowledge the vast influence he has had on the belief of
mankind, and to appreciate him as representing in its
extreme abuse that tendency to clothe every thought in a
concrete shape, which has in all ages been a mainspring of
mythology.

Though allegory cannot maintain the large place often
claimed for it in mythology, it has yet had too much influence to be passed over in this survey. It is true that the
search for allegorical explanation is a pursuit that has led
many a zealous explorer into the quagmires of mysticism.
Yet there are cases in which allegory is certainly used with
historical intent, as for instance in the apocryphal Book of
Enoch, with its cows and sheep which stand for Israelites,
and asses and wolves for Midianites and Egyptians, these
creatures figuring in a pseudo-prophetic sketch of Old
Testament chronicles. As for moral allegory, it is immensely plentiful in the world, although its limits are
narrower than mythologists of past centuries have supposed. It is now reasonably thought preposterous to interpret the Greek legends as moral apologues, after the manner
of Herakleides the philosopher, who could discern a parable
of repentant prudence in Athene seizing Achilles when just
about to draw his sword on Agamemnon.' Still, such a
mode of interpretation has thus much to justify it, that
numbers of the fanciful myths of the world are really allegories. There is allegory in the Hesiodic myth of Pandora,
whom Zeus sent down to men, decked with golden band
and garland of spring flowers, fit cause of longing and the
pangs of love, but using with a dog-like mind her gifts of
lies and treachery and pleasant speech. Heedless of his
wiser brother's words, the foolish Epimetheus took her;

Grote, vol. I. p. 347.

she raised the lid of the great cask and shook out the evils
that wander among mankind, and the diseases that by day
and night come silently bringing ill; she set on the lid
again and shut Hope in, that evil might be ever hopeless to
mankind. Shifted to fit a different moral, the allegory
remained in the later version of the tale, that the cask held
not curses but blessings; these were let go and lost to men
when the vessel was too curiously opened, while Hope alone
was left behind for comfort to the luckless human race.[1]
Yet the primitive nature of such legends underlies the
moral shape upon them. Zeus is no allegoric fiction, and
Prometheus, unless modern mythologists judge him very
wrongly, has a meaning far deeper than parable. Xenophon
tells (after Prodikos) the story of Herakles choosing between
the short and easy path of pleasure and the long and toilsome path of virtue,[2] but though the mythic hero may thus
be made to figure in a moral apologue, an imagination so
little in keeping with his unethic nature jars upon the
reader's mind.

The general relation of allegory to pure myth can hardly
be brought more clearly into view than in a class of stories
familiar to every child, the Beast-fables. From the ordinary civilized point of view the allegory in such fictions seems
fundamental, the notion of a moral lesson seems bound up
with their very nature, yet a broader examination tends to
prove the allegorical growth as it were parasitic on an older
trunk of myth without moral. It is only by an effort of intellectual reaction that a modern writer can imitate in parable
the beast of the old Beast-fable. No wonder, for the
creature has become to his mind a monster, only con-
ceivable as a caricature of man made to carry a moral lesson
or a satire. But among savages it is not so. To their
minds the semi-human beast is no fictitious creature, invented to preach or sneer, he is all but a reality. Beast-
fables are not nonsense to men who ascribe to the lower
animals a power of speech, and look on them as partaking

<hr/>

[1] Welcker, vol. i. p. 756.   [2] Xenoph. Memorabilia, ii. 1.

of moral human nature; to men in whose eyes any wolf or
hyæna may probably be a man-hyæna or a werewolf; to
men who so utterly believe "that the soul of our grandam
might haply inhabit a bird" that they will really regulate
their own diet so as to avoid eating an ancestor; to men an
integral part of whose religion may actually be the worship
of beasts. Such beliefs belong even now to half mankind,
and among such the beast-stories had their first home.
Even the Australians tell their quaint beast-tales, of the
Rat, the Owl, and the fat Blackfellow, or of Pussy-brother
who singed his friends' noses while they were asleep.[1]
The Kamchadals have an elaborate myth of the adventures
of their stupid deity Kutka with the Mice who played tricks
upon him, such as painting his face like a woman's, so that
when he looked in the water he fell in love with himself.[2]
Beast-tales abound among such races as the Polynesians
and the North American Indians, who value in them ingenuity of incident and neat adaptation of the habits and
characters of the creatures. Thus in a legend of the Flat-
head Indians, the Little Wolf found in cloudland his grand-
sires the Spiders with their grizzled hair and long crooked
nails, and they spun balls of thread to let him down to
earth; when he came down and found his wife the Speckled
Duck, whom the Old Wolf had taken from him, she fled in
confusion, and that is why she lives and dives alone to this
very day.[3] In Guinea, where beast-fable is one of the great
staples of native conversation, the following story is told as
a type of the tales which in this way account for peculiarities of animals. The great Engena-monkey offered his
daughter to be bride of the champion who should perform
the feat of drinking a whole barrel of rum. The dignified
Elephant, the graceful Leopard, the surly Boar, tried the
first mouthful of the fire-water, and retreated. Then the
tiny Telinga-monkey came, who had cunningly hidden in

---

[1] Oldfield in 'Tr. Eth. Soc.' vol. iii. p. 259.
[2] Steller, 'Kamtschatka,' p. 255.
[3] Wilson in 'Tr. Eth. Soc.' vol. iv. p. 306.

the long grass thousands of his fellows; he took his first glass and went away, but instead of his coming back, another just like him came for the second, and so on till the barrel was emptied and Telinga walked off with the Monkey-king's daughter. But in the narrow path the Elephant and Leopard attacked him and drove him off, and he took refuge in the highest boughs of the trees, vowing never more to live on the ground and suffer such violence and injustice. This is why to this day the little telingas are only found in the highest tree-tops.[1] Such stories have been collected by scores from savage tradition in their original state, while as yet no moral lesson has entered into them. Yet the easy and natural transition from the story into the parable is made among savages, perhaps without help from higher races. In the Hottentot Tales, side by side with the myths of the cunning Jackal tricking the Lion out of the best of the carcase, and getting the black stripe burnt on his own back by carrying off the Sun, there occurs the moral apologue of the Lion who thought himself wiser than his Mother, and perished by the Hunter's spear, for want of heed to her warning against the deadly creature whose head is in a line with his breast and shoulders.[2] So the Zulus have a thorough moral apologue in the story of the hyrax, who did not go to fetch his tail on the day when tails were given out, because he did not like to be out in the rain; he only asked the other animals to bring it for him, and so he never got it.[3] Among the North American legends of Manabozho, there is a fable quite Æsopian in its humour. Manabozho, transformed into a Wolf, killed a fat moose, and being very hungry sat down to eat. But he fell into great doubts as to where to begin, for, said he, if I begin at the head, people will laugh and say, he ate him backwards,

---

[1] J. L. Wilson, 'W. Afr.' p. 882.

[2] Bleek, 'Reynard in S. Afr.' pp. 5, 47, 67 (these are not among the stories which seem recently borrowed from Europeans). See 'Early History of Mankind,' p. 10.

[3] Callaway, 'Zulu Tales,' vol. L p. 355.

but if I begin at the side they will say, he ate him sideways.
At last he made up his mind, and was just putting a delicate
piece into his mouth, when a tree close by creaked. Stop,
stop! said he to the tree, I cannot eat with such a noise,
and in spite of his hunger he left the meat and climbed up
to quiet the creaking, but was caught between two branches
and held fast, and presently he saw a pack of wolves coming.
Go that way! Go that way! he cried out, whereupon the
wolves said, he must have something there, or he would not
tell us to go another way. So they came on, and found the
moose, and ate it to the bones while Manabozho looked
wistfully on. The next heavy blast of wind opened the
branches and let him out, and he went home thinking to
himself "See the effect of meddling with frivolous things
when I had certain good in my possession." [1]

In the Old World, the moral Beast-fable was of no mean
antiquity, but it did not at once supplant the animal-myths
pure and simple. For ages the European mind was capable
at once of receiving lessons of wisdom from the Æsopian
crows and foxes, and of enjoying artistic but by no means
edifying beast-stories of more primitive type. In fact the
Babrius and Phædrus collections were over a thousand years
old, when the genuine Beast-Epic reached its fullest growth
in the incomparable ' Reynard the Fox;' traceable in Jacob
Grimm's view to an original Frankish composition of the
12th century, itself containing materials of far earlier date.[2]
Reynard is not a didactic poem, at least if a moral hangs on
to it here and there it is oftenest a Macchiavellian one;
nor is it essentially a satire, sharply as it lashes men in
general and the clergy in particular. Its creatures are incarnate qualities, the Fox of cunning, the Bear of strength,
the Ass of dull content, the Sheep of guilelessness. The
charm of the narrative, which every class in mediæval
Europe delighted in, but which we have allowed to drop
out of all but scholars' knowledge, lies in great measure in

[1] Schoolcraft, 'Algic Res.' vol. i. p. 160; see 13, 51.
[2] Jacob Grimm, 'Reinhart Fuchs,' Introd.

the cleverly sustained combination of the beast's nature and the man's. How great the influence of the Reynard Epic was in the middle ages, may be judged from *Reynard, Bruin, Chanticleer*, being still names familiar to people who have no idea of their having been originally names of the characters in the great beast-fable. Even more remarkable are its traces in modern French. The donkey has its name of *baudet* from *Bauloin*, Baldwin the Ass. Common French dictionaries do not even contain the word *goupil* (*vulpes*), so effectually has the Latin name of the fox been driven out of use by his Frankish title in the Beast-Epic, *Raginhard* the Counsellor, *Reinhart, Reynard, Renart, renard.* The moralized apologues like Æsop's which Grimm contemptuously calls "fables thinned down to mere moral and allegory," "a fourth watering of the old grapes into an insipid moral infusion," are low in æsthetic quality as compared with the genuine beast-myths. Mythological critics will be apt to judge them after the manner of the child who said how convenient it was to have "Moral" printed in Æsop's Fables, that everybody might know what to skip.

The want of power of abstraction which has ever had such disastrous effect on the beliefs of mankind, confounding myth and chronicle, and crushing the spirit of history under the rubbish of literalized tradition, comes very clearly into view in the study of parable. The state of mind of the deaf, dumb, and blind Laura Bridgman, so instructive in illustrating the mental habits of uneducated though full-sensed men, displays in an extreme form the difficulty such men have in comprehending the unreality of any story. She could not be made to see that arithmetical problems were anything but statements of concrete fact, and when her teacher asked her, "If you can buy a barrel of cider for four dollars, how much can you buy for one dollar?" she replied quite simply, "I cannot give much for cider, because it is very sour."[1] It is a surprising instance of this tendency to concretism, that among people so civilized

[1] Account of Laura Bridgman, p. 120.

as the Buddhists, the most obviously moral beast-fables
have become literal incidents of sacred history. Gautama,
during his 550 jatakas or births, took the form of a frog, a
fish, a crow, an ape, and various other animals, and so far
were the legends of these transformations from mere myth
to his followers, that there have been preserved as relics in
Buddhist temples the hair, feathers, and bones of the
creatures whose bodies the great teacher inhabited. Now
among the incidents which happened to Buddha during
his series of animal births, he appeared as an actor in the
familiar fable of the Fox and the Stork, and it was he who,
when he was a Squirrel, set an example of parental virtue
by trying to dry up the ocean with his tail, to save his
young ones whose nest had drifted out to sea, till his per-
severing courage was rewarded by a miracle.[1] To our
modern minds, a moral which seems the very purpose of a
story is evidence unfavourable to its truth as fact. But if
even apologues of talking birds and beasts have not been
safe from literal belief, it is clear that the most evident
moral can have been but slight protection to parables told
of possible and life-like men. It was not a needless precaution to state explicitly of the New Testament parables
that they were parables, and even this guard has not availed
entirely. Mrs. Jameson relates some curious experience in
the following passage :—" I know that I was not very
young when I entertained no more doubt of the substantial
existence of Lazarus and Dives than of John the Baptist
and Herod; when the Good Samaritan was as real a personage as any of the Apostles ; when I was full of sincerest
pity for those poor foolish Virgins who had forgotten to
trim their lamps, and thought them—in my secret soul—
rather hardly treated. This impression of the literal actual
truth of the parables I have since met with in many children,
and in the uneducated but devout hearers and readers of

[1] Bowring, 'Siam,' vol. i. p. 313 ; Hardy, 'Manual of Budhism,' p. 98. See
the fable of the 'Crow and Pitcher,' in Plin. x. 60, and Bastian, 'Mensch,'
vol. i. p. 76.

the Bible; and I remember that when I once tried to explain to a good old woman the proper meaning of the word parable, and that the story of the Prodigal Son was not a fact, she was scandalized—she was quite sure that Jesus would never have told anything to his disciples that was not true. Thus she settled the matter in her own mind, and I thought it best to leave it there undisturbed."[1] Nor, it may be added, has such misconception been confined to the minds of the poor and ignorant. St. Lazarus, patron saint of lepers and their hospitals, and from whom the *lazzarone* and the *lazzaretto* take their name, obviously derives these qualities from the Lazarus of the parable.

The proof of the force and obstinacy of the mythic faculty, thus given by the relapse of parable into pseudo-history, may conclude this dissertation on mythology. In its course there have been examined the processes of animating and personifying nature, the formation of legend by exaggeration and perversion of fact, the stiffening of metaphor by mistaken realization of words, the conversion of speculative theories and still less substantial fictions into pretended traditional events, the passage of myth into miracle-legend, the definition by name and place given to any floating imagination, the adaptation of mythic incident as moral example, and the incessant crystallization of story into history. The investigation of these intricate and devious operations has brought ever more and more broadly into view two principles of mythologic science. The first is that legend, when classified on a sufficient scale, displays a regularity of development which the notion of motiveless fancy quite fails to account for, and which must be attributed to laws of formation whereby every story, old and new, has arisen from its definite origin and sufficient cause. So uniform indeed is such development, that it becomes possible to treat myth as an organic product of mankind at large, in which individual, national, and even racial distinctions stand subordinate to universal qualities of the

[1] Jameson, 'History of Our Lord in Art,' vol. i. p. 375.

human mind. The second principle concerns the relation
of myth to history. It is true that the search for mutilated
and mystified traditions of real events, which formed so
main a part of old mythological researches, seems to grow
more hopeless the farther the study of legend extends.
Even the fragments of real chronicle found embedded in
the mythic structure are mostly in so corrupt a state, that,
far from their elucidating history, they need history to
elucidate them. Yet unconsciously, and as it were in spite
of themselves, the shapers and transmitters of poetic legend
have preserved for us masses of sound historical evidence.
They moulded into mythic lives of gods and heroes their
own ancestral heirlooms of thought and word, they displayed
in the structure of their legends the operations of their own
minds, they placed on record the arts and manners, the
philosophy and religion of their own times, times of which
formal history has often lost the very memory. Myth is
the history of its authors, not of its subjects; it records the
lives, not of superhuman heroes, but of poetic nations.

CHAPTER XI.

ANIMISM.

Religious ideas generally appear among low races of Mankind—Negative statements on this subject frequently misleading and mistaken': many cases uncertain—Minimum definition of Religion—Doctrine of Spiritual Beings, here termed Animism—Animism treated as belonging to Natural Religion—Animism divided into two sections, the philosophy of Souls, and of other Spirits—Doctrine of Souls, its prevalence and definition among the lower races—Definition of Apparitional Soul or Ghost-Soul—It is a theoretical conception of primitive Philosophy, designed to account for phenomena now classed under Biology, especially Life and Death, Health and Disease, Sleep and Dreams, Trance and Visions—Relation of Soul in name and nature to Shadow, Blood, Breath—Division or Plurality of Souls—Soul cause of Life; its restoration to body when supposed absent—Exit of Soul in Trances—Dreams and Visions: theory of exit of dreamer's or seer's own soul; theory of visits received by them from other souls—Ghost-Soul seen in Apparitions—Wraiths and Doubles—Soul has form of body; suffers mutilation with it—Voice of Ghost—Soul treated and defined as of Material Substance; this appears to be the original doctrine—Transmission of Souls to service in future life by Funeral Sacrifice of wives, attendants, &c.—Souls of Animals—Their transmission by Funeral Sacrifice—Souls of Plants—Souls of Objects—Their transmission by Funeral Sacrifice—Relation of savage doctrine of Object-Souls to Epicurean theory of Ideas—Historical development of Doctrine of Souls, from the Ethereal Soul of primitive Biology to the Immaterial Soul of modern Theology.

ARE there, or have there been, tribes of men so low in culture as to have no religious conceptions whatever? This is practically the question of the universality of religion, which for so many centuries has been affirmed and denied, with a confidence in striking contrast to the imperfect evidence on which both affirmation and denial have been based. Ethnographers, if looking to a theory of development to explain civilization, and regarding its successive

stages as arising one from another, would receive with peculiar interest accounts of tribes devoid of all religion.
Here, they would naturally say, are men who have no religion because their forefathers had none, men who represent
a pre-religious condition of the human race, out of which
in the course of time religious conditions have arisen. It
does not, however, seem advisable to start from this ground
in an investigation of religious development. Though the
theoretical niche is ready and convenient, the actual statue
to fill it is not forthcoming. The case is in some degree
similar to that of the tribes asserted to exist without language
or without the use of fire ; nothing in the nature of things
seems to forbid the possibility of such existence, but as a
matter of fact the tribes are not found. Thus the assertion
that rude non-religious tribes have been known in actual
existence, though in theory possible, and perhaps in fact
true, does not at present rest on that sufficient proof
which, for an exceptional state of things, we are entitled to
demand.

It is not unusual for the very writer who declares in
general terms the absence of religious phenomena among
some savage people, himself to give evidence that shows
his expressions to be misleading. Thus Dr. Lang not only
declares that the aborigines of Australia have no idea of a
supreme divinity, creator, and judge, no object of worship,
no idol, temple, or sacrifice, but that " in short, they have
nothing whatever of the character of religion, or of religious observance, to distinguish them from the beasts that
perish." More than one writer has since made use of this
telling statement, but without referring to certain details
which occur in the very same book. From these it appears
that a disease like small-pox, which sometimes attacks the
natives, is ascribed by them " to the influence of Budyah,
an evil spirit who delights in mischief;" that when the
natives rob a wild bees' hive, they generally leave a little of
the honey for Buddai; that at certain biennial gatherings
of the Queensland tribes, young girls are slain in sacrifice

to propitiate some evil divinity; and that, lastly, according to the evidence of the Rev. W. Ridley, "whenever he has conversed with the aborigines, he found them to have definite traditions concerning supernatural beings—Baiame, whose voice they hear in thunder, and who made all things, Turramullun the chief of demons, who is the author of disease, mischief, and wisdom, and appears in the form of a serpent at their great assemblies, etc."[1] By the concurring testimony of a crowd of observers, it is known that the natives of Australia were at their discovery, and have since remained, a race with minds saturated with the most vivid belief in souls, demons, and deities. In Africa, Mr. Moffat's declaration as to the Bechuanas is scarcely less surprising —that "man's immortality was never heard of among that people," he having remarked in the sentence next before, that the word for the shades or manes of the dead is "liriti."[2] In South America, again, Don Felix de Azara comments on the positive falsity of the ecclesiastics' assertion that the native tribes have a religion. He simply declares that they have none; nevertheless in the course of his work he mentions such facts as that the Payaguas bury arms and clothing with their dead and have some notions of a future life, and that the Guanas believe in a Being who rewards good and punishes evil. In fact, this author's reckless denial of religion and law to the lower races of this region justifies D'Orbigny's sharp criticism, that "this is indeed what he says of all the nations he describes, while actually proving the contrary of his thesis by the very facts he alleges in its support."[3]

Such cases show how deceptive are judgments to which breadth and generality are given by the use of wide words in narrow senses. Lang, Moffat, and Azara are authors to whom ethnography owes much valuable knowledge of the tribes

[1] J. D. Lang, 'Queensland,' pp. 340, 371, 380, 386, 444 (Buddai appears, p. 379, as causing a deluge; he is probably identical with Budyah).

[2] Moffat, 'South Africa,' p. 261.

[3] Azara, 'Voy. dans l'Amérique Méridionale,' vol. II. pp. 3, 11, 25, 51, 60, 91, 119, etc.; D'Orbigny, 'L'Homme Américain,' vol. ii. p. 318.

they visited, but they seem hardly to have recognized anything short of the organized and established theology of the
higher races as being religion at all. They attribute irre-
ligion to tribes whose doctrines are unlike theirs, in much
the same manner as theologians have so often attributed
atheism to those whose deities differed from their own, from
the time when the ancient invading Aryans described the
aboriginal tribes of India as *adeva*, i. e., "godless," and
the Greeks fixed the corresponding term ἄθεοι on the early
Christians as unbelievers in the classic gods, to the comparatively modern ages when disbelievers in witchcraft and
apostolical succession were denounced as atheists ; and down
to our own day, when controversialists are apt to infer, as in
past centuries, that naturalists who support a theory of
development of species therefore necessarily hold atheistic
opinions.[1] These are in fact but examples of a general
perversion of judgment in theological matters, among the
results of which is a popular misconception of the religions
of the lower races, simply amazing to students who have
reached a higher point of view. Some missionaries, no
doubt, thoroughly understand the minds of the savages
they have to deal with, and indeed it is from men like
Cranz, Dobrizhoffer, Charlevoix, Ellis, Hardy, Callaway,
J. R. Wilson, T. Williams, that we have obtained our best
knowledge of the lower phases of religious belief. But for
the most part the "religious world" is so occupied in
hating and despising the beliefs of the heathen whose vast
regions of the globe are painted black on the missionary
maps, that they have little time or capacity left to understand them. It cannot be so with those who fairly seek to
comprehend the nature and meaning of the lower phases of
religion. These, while fully alive to the absurdities believed and the horrors perpetrated in its name, will yet

[1] Muir, 'Sanskrit Texts,' part ii. p. 435; Euseb. 'Hist. Eccl.' iv. 15;
Bingham, book l. ch. ii. ; Vanini, ' De Admirandis Naturæ Arcanis,' dial. 37 ;
Lecky, 'Hist. of Rationalism,' vol. l. p. 126 ; Encyclop. Brit. s. v. 'Super-
stition.'

regard with kindly interest all record of men's earnest
seeking after truth with such light as they could find. Such
students will look for meaning, however crude and childish,
at the root of doctrines often most dark to the believers
who accept them most zealously; they will search for the
reasonable thought which once gave life to observances now
become in seeming or reality the most abject and superstitious folly. The reward of these enquirers will be a
more rational comprehension of the faiths in whose midst
they dwell, for no more can he who understands but one
religion understand even that religion, than the man who
knows but one language can understand that language. No
religion of mankind lies in utter isolation from the rest,
and the thoughts and principles of modern Christianity
are attached to intellectual clues which run back through
far pre-Christian ages to the very origin of human civilization, perhaps even of human existence.

While observers who have had fair opportunities of studying the religions of savages have thus sometimes done scant
justice to the facts before their eyes, the hasty denials of
others who have judged without even facts can carry no
great weight. A 16th-century traveller gave an account of
the natives of Florida which is typical of such : " Touching
the religion of this people, which wee have found, for want
of their language wee could not understand neither by signs
nor gesture that they had any religion or lawe at all. . . . .
We suppose that they have no religion at all, and that they
live at their own libertie." [1]   Better knowledge of these
Floridans nevertheless showed that they had a religion, and
better knowledge has reversed many another hasty assertion to the same effect; as when writers used to declare
that the natives of Madagascar had no idea of a future state,
and no word for soul or spirit ; [2] or when Dampier inquired
after the religion of the natives of Timor, and was told

[1] J. de Verrazano in Hakluyt, vol. iii. p. 300.
[2] See Ellis, 'Madagascar,' vol. I. p. 429 ; Flacourt, 'Hist. de Madagascar,'
p. 50.

that they had none;[1] or when Sir Thomas Roe landed in
Saldanha Bay on his way to the court of the Great Mogul,
and remarked of the Hottentots that "they have left off
their custom of stealing, but know no God or religion."[2]
Among the numerous accounts collected by Sir John Lubbock as evidence bearing on the absence or low development of religion among low races,[3] some may be selected
as lying open to criticism from this point of view. Thus
the statement that the Samoan Islanders had no religion
cannot stand, in face of the elaborate description by the
Rev. G. Turner of the Samoan religion itself; and the
assertion that the Tupinambas of Brazil had no religion is
one not to be received without some more positive proof,
for the religious doctrines and practices of the Tupi race
have been recorded by Lery, De Laet, and other writers.
Even with much time and care and knowledge of language,
it is not always easy to elicit from savages the details of
their theology. · They try to hide from the prying and contemptuous foreigner their worship of gods who seem to
shrink, like their worshippers, before the white man and his
mightier Deity. Mr. Sproat's experience in Vancouver's Island is an apt example of this state of things. He says:
"I was two years among the Ahts, with my mind constantly
directed towards the subject of their religious beliefs, before
I could discover that they possessed any ideas as to an
overruling power or a future state of existence. The traders
on the coast, and other persons well acquainted with the
people, told me that they had no such ideas, and this
opinion was confirmed by conversation with many of the
less intelligent savages; but at last I succeeded in getting
a satisfactory clue."[4] It then appeared that the Ahts had
all the time been hiding a whole characteristic system of
religious doctrines as to souls and their migrations, the

[1] Dampier, 'Voyages,' vol. ii. part ii. p. 76.
[2] Roe in Pinkerton, vol. viii. p. 2.
[3] Lubbock, 'Prehistoric Times,' p. 564: see also 'Origin of Civilization,'
p. 138.
[4] Sproat, 'Scenes and Studies of Savage Life,' p. 205.

spirits who do good and ill to men, and the great gods above
all. Thus, even where no positive proof of religious ideas
among any particular tribe has reached us, we should dis-
trust its denial by observers whose acquaintance with the
tribe in question has not been intimate as well as kindly.
Assertions of this sort are made very carelessly. Thus it
is said of the Andaman Islanders that they have not the
rudest elements of a religious faith; Dr. Mouat states this
explicitly,[1] yet it appears that the natives did not even
display to the foreigners the rude music which they actually
possessed, so that they could scarcely have been expected to
be communicative as to their theology, if they had any. In
our time the most striking negation of the religion of savage
tribes is that published by Sir Samuel Baker, in a paper
read in 1866 before the Ethnological Society of London, as
follows: "The most northern tribes of the White Nile are
the Dinkas, Shillooks, Nuehr, Kytch, Dohr, Aliab, and
Shir. A general description will suffice for the whole,
excepting the Kytch. Without any exception, they are
without a belief in a Supreme Being, neither have they any
form of worship or idolatry; nor is the darkness of their
minds enlightened by even a ray of superstition." Had this
distinguished explorer spoken only of the Latukas, or of
other tribes hardly known to ethnographers except through
his own intercourse with them, his denial of any religious
consciousness to them would have been at least entitled to
stand as the best procurable account, until more intimate
communication should prove or disprove it. But in speaking thus of comparatively well known tribes such as the
Dinkas, Shilluks, and Nuehr, Sir S. Baker ignores the
existence of published evidence, such as describes the
sacrifices of the Dinkas, their belief in good and evil spirits
(adjok and djyok), their good deity and heaven-dwelling
creator, Dendid, as likewise Néar the deity of the Nuehr,
and the Shilluks' creator, who is described as visiting, like
other spirits, a sacred wood or tree. Kaufmann, Brun-

[1] Mouat, 'Andaman Islanders,' pp. 2, 279, 803.

Rollet, Lejean, and other observers, had thus placed on
record details of the religion of these White Nile tribes,
years before Sir S. Baker's rash denial that they had any
religion at all.[1]

The first requisite in a systematic study of the religions
of the lower races, is to lay down a rudimentary definition
of religion. By requiring in this definition the belief in a
supreme deity or of judgment after death, the adoration of
idols or the practice of sacrifice, or other partially-diffused
doctrines or rites, no doubt many tribes may be excluded
from the category of religious. But such narrow definition
has the fault of identifying religion rather with particular
developments than with the deeper motive which underlies
them. It seems best to fall back at once on this essential
source, and simply to claim, as a minimum definition of
Religion, the belief in Spiritual Beings. If this standard
be applied to the descriptions of low races as to religion,
the following results will appear. It cannot be positively
asserted that every existing tribe recognizes the belief in
spiritual beings, for the native condition of a considerable
number is obscure in this respect, and from the rapid change
or extinction they are undergoing, may ever remain so. It
would be yet more unwarranted to set down every tribe
mentioned in history, or known to us by the discovery of
antiquarian relics, as necessarily having possessed the
defined minimum of religion. Greater still would be the
unwisdom of declaring such a rudimentary belief natural or
instinctive in all human tribes of all times; for no evidence

[1] Baker, 'Races of the Nile Basin,' in Tr. Eth. Soc. vol. v. p. 231; 'The
Albert Nyanza,' vol. l. p. 246. See Kaufmann, 'Schilderungen aus Central-
afrika,' p. 123; Brun-Rollet, 'Le Nil Blanc et le Soudan,' pp. 100, 222, also
pp. 164, 200, 234; G. Lejean in 'Rev. des Deux M.' April 1, 1862, p. 760;
Waitz, 'Anthropologie,' vol. ll. pp. 72—5; Bastian, 'Mensch,' vol. lll. p. 208.
Other recorded cases of denial of religion of savage tribes on narrow definition
or inadequate evidence may be found in Meiners, 'Gesch. der Rel.' vol. l.
pp. 11—15 (Australians and Californians); Waitz, 'Anthropologie,' vol. l.
p. 323 (Arru Islanders, etc.); Farrar in 'Anthrop. Rev.' Aug. 1864, p. ccxvii.
(Kafirs, etc.); Martius, 'Ethnog. Amer.' vol. l. p. 583 (Manaos); J. G.
Palfrey, 'Hist. of New England,' vol. l. p. 46 (New Eng. tribes).

justifies the opinion that man, known to be capable of so vast an intellectual development, cannot have emerged from a non-religious condition, previous to that religious condition in which he happens at present to come with sufficient clearness within our range of knowledge. It is desirable, however, to take our basis of enquiry in observation rather than from speculation. Here, so far as I can judge from the immense mass of accessible evidence, we have to admit that the belief in spiritual beings appears among all low races with whom we have attained to thoroughly intimate acquaintance ; whereas the assertion of absence of such belief must apply either to ancient tribes, or to more or less imperfectly described modern ones. The exact bearing of this state of things on the problem of the origin of religion may be thus briefly stated. Were it distinctly proved that non-religious savages exist or have existed, these might be at least plausibly claimed as representatives of the condition of Man before he arrived at the religious stage of culture. It is not desirable, however, that this argument should be put forward, for the asserted existence of the non-religious tribes in question rests, as we have seen, on evidence often mistaken and never conclusive. The argument for the natural evolution of religious ideas among mankind is not invalidated by the rejection of an ally too weak at present to give effectual help. Non-religious tribes may not exist in our day, but the fact bears no more decisively on the development of religion, than the impossibility of finding a modern English village without scissors or books or lucifer-matches bears on the fact that there was a time when no such things existed in the land.

I purpose here, under the name of Animism, to investigate the deep-lying doctrine of Spiritual Beings, which embodies the very essence of Spiritualistic as opposed to Materialistic philosophy. Animism is not a new technical term, though now seldom used.[1] From its special relation to the doctrine

[1] The term has been especially used to denote the doctrine of Stahl, the promulgator also of the phlogiston-theory. The Animism of Stahl is a revival

of the soul, it will be seen to have a peculiar appropriateness to the view here taken of the mode in which theological ideas have been developed among mankind. The word Spiritualism, though it may be, and sometimes is, used in a general sense, has this obvious defect to us, that it has become the designation of a particular modern sect, who indeed hold extreme spiritualistic views, but cannot be taken as typical representatives of these views in the world at large. The sense of Spiritualism in its wider acceptation, the general belief in spiritual beings, is here given to Animism.

Animism characterizes tribes very low in the scale of humanity, and thence ascends, deeply modified in its transmission, but from first to last preserving an unbroken continuity, into the midst of high modern culture. Doctrines adverse to it, so largely held by individuals or schools, are usually due not to early lowness of civilization, but to later changes in the intellectual course, to divergence from, or rejection of, ancestral faiths; and such newer developments do not affect the present enquiry as to the fundamental religious condition of mankind. Animism is, in fact, the groundwork of the Philosophy of Religion, from that of savages up to that of civilized men. And although it may at first sight seem to afford but a bare and meagre definition of a minimum of religion, it will be found practically sufficient; for where the root is, the branches will generally be produced. It is habitually found that the theory of Animism divides into two great dogmas, forming parts of one consistent doctrine; first, concerning souls of individual creatures, capable of continued existence after the death or destruction of the body; second, concerning other spirits, upward to the rank of powerful deities. Spiritual beings are held to affect or control the events of the material world, and man's life here and hereafter; and it being considered

and development in modern scientific shape of the classic theory identifying vital principle and soul. See his 'Theoria Medica Vera,' Halle, 1737; and the critical dissertation on his views, Lemoine, 'Le Vitalisme et l'Animisme e Stahl,' Paris, 1864.

that they hold intercourse with men, and receive pleasure or displeasure from human actions, the belief in their existence leads naturally, and it might almost be said inevitably, sooner or later to active reverence and propitiation. Thus Animism, in its full development, includes the belief in souls and in a future state, in controlling deities and subordinate spirits, these doctrines practically resulting in some kind of active worship. One great element of religion, that moral element which among the higher nations forms its most vital part, is indeed little represented in the religion of the lower races. It is not that these races have no moral sense or no moral standard, for both are strongly marked among them, if not in formal precept, at least in that traditional consensus of society which we call public opinion, according to which certain actions are held to be good or bad, right or wrong. It is that the conjunction of ethics and Animistic philosophy, so intimate and powerful in the higher culture, seems scarcely yet to have begun in the lower. I propose here hardly to touch upon the purely moral aspects of religion, but rather to study the animism of the world so far as it constitutes, as unquestionably it does constitute, an ancient and world-wide philosophy, of which belief is the theory and worship is the practice. Endeavouring to shape the materials for an enquiry hitherto strangely undervalued and neglected, it will now be my task to bring as clearly as may be into view the fundamental animism of the lower races, and in some slight and broken outline to trace its course into higher regions of civilization. Here let me state once for all two principal conditions under which the present research is carried on. First, as to the religious doctrines and practices examined, these are treated as belonging to theological systems devised by human reason, without supernatural aid or revelation; in other words, as being developments of Natural Religion. Second, as to the connexion between similar ideas and rites in the religions of the savage and the civilized world. While dwelling at some length on doctrines and ceremonies of the lower

races, and sometimes particularizing for special reasons the
related doctrines and ceremonies of the higher nations, it
has not seemed my proper task to work out in detail the
problems thus suggested among the philosophies and creeds
of Christendom. Such applications, extending farthest
from the direct scope of a work on primitive culture, are
briefly stated in general terms, or touched in slight allusion,
or taken for granted without remark. Educated readers
possess the information required to work out their general
bearing on theology, while more technical discussion is left
to philosophers and theologians specially occupied with
such arguments.

The first branch of the subject to be considered is the
doctrine of human and other Souls, an examination of
which will occupy the rest of the present chapter. What
the doctrine of the soul is among the lower races, may be
explained in stating the present theory of its development.
It seems as though thinking men, as yet at a low level of
culture, were deeply impressed by two groups of biological
problems. In the first place, what is it that makes the
difference between a living body and a dead one ; what
causes waking, sleep, trance, disease, death ?   In the
second place, what are those human shapes which appear in
dreams and visions ?   Looking at these two groups of phenomena, the ancient savage philosophers probably made
their first step by the obvious inference that every man has
two things belonging to him, namely, a life and a phantom.
These two are evidently in close connexion with the body,
the life as enabling it to feel and think and act, the phantom
as being its image or second self ; both, also, are perceived
to be things separable from the body, the life as able to go
away and leave it insensible or dead, the phantom as appearing to people at a distance from it.   The second step would
seem also easy for savages to make, seeing how extremely
difficult civilized men have found it to unmake. It is merely to
combine the life and the phantom.   As both belong to the
body, why should they not also belong to one another, and

be manifestations of one and the same soul? Let them
then be considered as united, and the result is that well-
known conception which may be described as an appari-
tional-soul, a ghost-soul. This, at any rate, corresponds
with the actual conception of the personal soul or spirit
among the lower races, which may be defined as follows: It
is a thin unsubstantial human image, in its nature a sort of
vapour, film, or shadow; the cause of life and thought in
the individual it animates; independently possessing the
personal consciousness and volition of its corporeal owner,
past or present; capable of leaving the body far behind, to
flash swiftly from place to place; mostly impalpable and invisible, yet also manifesting physical power, and especially
appearing to men waking or asleep as a phantasm separate
from the body of which it bears the likeness; continuing to
exist and appear to men after the death of that body; able
to enter into, possess, and act in the bodies of other men,
of animals, and even of things. Though this definition is by
no means of universal application, it has sufficient generality to be taken as a standard, modified by more or less
divergence among any particular people. Far from these
world-wide opinions being arbitrary or conventional products, it is seldom even justifiable to consider their uniformity among distant races as proving communication of
any sort. They are doctrines answering in the most forcible
way to the plain evidence of men's senses, as interpreted by
a fairly consistent and rational primitive philosophy. So
well, indeed, does primitive animism account for the facts
of nature, that it has held its place into the higher levels of
education. Though classic and mediæval philosophy modified it much, and modern philosophy has handled it yet
more unsparingly, it has so far retained the traces of its
original character, that heirlooms of primitive ages may be
claimed in the existing psychology of the civilized world.
Out of the vast mass of evidence, collected among the
most various and distant races of mankind, typical details
may now be selected to display the earlier theory of the

soul, the relation of the parts of this theory, and the manner in which these parts have been abandoned, modified, or kept up, along the course of culture.

To understand the popular conceptions of the human soul or spirit, it is instructive to notice the words which have been found suitable to express it. The ghost or phantasm seen by the dreamer or the visionary is an unsubstantial form, like a shadow, and thus the familiar term of the *shade* comes in to express the soul. Thus the Tasmanian word for the shadow is also that for the spirit;[1] the Algonquin Indians describe a man's soul as *otahchuk*, "his shadow;"[2] the Quiché language uses *natub* for "shadow, soul;"[3] the Arawac *ueja* means "shadow, soul, image;"[4] the Abipones made the one word *loákal* serve for "shadow, soul, echo, image."[5] The Zulus not only use the word *tunzi* for "shadow, spirit, ghost," but they consider that at death the shadow of a man will in some way depart from the corpse, to become an ancestral spirit.[6] The Basutos not only call the spirit remaining after death the *seriti* or "shadow," but they think that if a man walks on the river bank, a crocodile may seize his shadow in the water and draw him in;"[7] while in Old Calabar there is found the same identification of the spirit with the *ukpon* or "shadow," for a man to lose which is fatal.[8] There are thus found among the lower races not only the types of those familiar classic terms, the *skia* and *umbra*, but also what seems the fundamental thought of the stories of shadowless men still current in the folklore of Europe, and familiar to modern readers in Chamisso's tale of Peter

[1] Bonwick, 'Tasmanians,' p. 182.

[2] Tanner's 'Narr.' ed. by James, p. 291. Also Sproat, p. 300 (Ahts).

[3] Brasseur, 'Langue Quichée,' s. v.

[4] Martius, 'Ethnog. Amer.' vol. i. p. 795; vol. ii. p. 310.

[5] Dobrizhoffer, 'Abipones,' vol. ii. p. 194.

[6] Döhne, 'Zulu Dic.' s. v. 'tunzi;' Callaway, 'Rel. of Amazulu,' pp. 91, 126; 'Zulu Tales,' vol. i. p. 342.

[7] Casalis, 'Basutos,' p. 245; Arbousset and Daumas, 'Voyage,' p. 12.

[8] Burton, 'W. and W. fr. W. Afr.' p. 389; see Koelle, 'Afr. Native Lit.' p. 324 (Kanuri). Also 'Journ. Ind. Archip.' vol. v. p. 713 (Australian).

Schlemihl. Thus the dead in Purgatory knew that Dante was alive when they saw that, unlike theirs, his figure cast a shadow on the ground.[1] Other attributes are taken into the notion of soul or spirit, with especial regard to its being the cause of life. Thus the Caribs, connecting the pulses with spiritual beings, and especially considering that in the heart dwells man's chief soul, destined to a future heavenly life, could reasonably use the one word *iouanni* for "soul, life, heart."[2] The Tongans supposed the soul to exist throughout the whole extension of the body, but particularly in the heart. On one occasion, the natives were declaring to a European that a man buried months ago was nevertheless still alive. "And one, endeavouring to make me understand what he meant, took hold of my hand, and squeezing it, said, ' This will die, but the life that is within you will never die ;' with his other hand pointing to my heart."[3] So the Basutos say of a dead man that his heart is gone out, and of one recovering from sickness that his heart is coming back.[4] This corresponds to the familiar Old World view of the heart as the prime mover in life, thought, and passion. The connexion of soul and blood, familiar to the Karens and Papuas, appears prominently in Jewish and Arabic philosophy.[5] To educated moderns the idea of the Macusi Indians of Guiana may seem quaint, that although the body will decay, "the man in our eyes" will not die, but wander about.[6] Yet the association of personal animation with the pupil of the eye is familiar to European folklore, which not unreasonably discerned a sign of bewitchment or approaching death in the disappearance of the image, pupil, or baby, from the dim eyeballs of the sick man.[7]

[1] Dante, 'Div. Comm. Purgatorio,' canto iii. Compare Grohmann, 'Aberglauben aus Böhmen,' p. 221. See *ante*, p. 85.

[2] Rochefort, pp. 429, 516; J. G. Müller, p. 207.

[3] Mariner, 'Tonga Is.' vol. ii. p. 135 ; S. S. Farmer, 'Tonga,' etc. p. 131.

[4] Casalis, l. c. See also Mariner, 'Tonga Is.' etc. p. 135.

[5] Bastian, 'Psychologie,' pp. 15—23.

[6] J. H. Bernau, 'Brit. Guiana,' p. 134.

[7] Grimm, 'D. M.' pp. 1028, 1133. Anglo-Saxon *man-lícn*.

The act of breathing, so characteristic of the higher animals during life, and coinciding so closely with life in its departure, has been repeatedly and naturally identified with the life or soul itself. Laura Bridgman showed in her instructive way the analogy between the effects of restricted sense and restricted civilization, when one day she made the gesture of taking something away from her mouth : " I dreamed," she explained in words, "that God took away my breath to heaven."[1] It is thus that West Australians used one word *wang* for " breath, spirit, soul;"[2] that in the Netela language of California, *piuts* means "life, breath, soul;"[3] that certain Greenlanders reckoned two souls to man, namely his shadow and his breath;[4] that the Malays say the soul of the dying man escapes through his nostrils, and in Java use the same word *ñawa* for "breath, life, soul."[5] How the notions of life, heart, breath, and phantom unite in the one conception of a soul or spirit, and at the same time how loose and vague such ideas are among barbaric races, is well brought into view in the answers to a religious inquest held in 1528 among the natives of Nicaragua. " When they die, there comes out of their mouth something that resembles a person, and is called *julio* [Aztec *yuli*=to live]. This being goes to the place where the man and woman are. It is like a person, but does not die, and the body remains here." *Question.* " Do those who go up on high keep the same body, the same face, and the same limbs, as here below ?" *Answer.* "No; there is only the heart." *Question.* "But since they tear out their hearts (i.e., when a captive was sacrificed), what happens then ?" *Answer.* " It is not precisely the heart, but that in them which makes them live, and that quits the body when they die." Or, as stated in another interro-

[1] Lieber, 'Laura Bridgman,' in Smithsonian Contrib. vol. ii. p. 8.
[2] G. F. Moore, 'Vocab. of W. Australia,' p. 103.
[3] Brinton, p. 50, see 235 ; Bastian, ' Psychologie,' p. 15.
[4] Crans, 'Grönland,' p. 257.
[5] Crawfurd, ' Malay Gr. and Dic.' s. v.; Marsden, 'Sumatra,' p. 336.

gatory, " It is not their heart that goes up above, but what
makes them live, that is to say, the breath that issues from
their mouth and is called *julio*."[1] The conception of the
soul as breath may be followed up through Semitic and
Aryan etymology, and thus into the main streams of the
philosophy of the world. Hebrew shows *nephesh*, " breath,"
passing into all the meanings of " life, soul, mind, animal,"
while *ruach* and *neshamah* make the like transition from
" breath " to " spirit;" and to these the Arabic *nefs* and
ruh correspond. The same is the history of Sanskrit *âtman*
and *prâna*, of Greek *psychê* and *pneuma*, of Latin *animus,
anima, spiritus*. So Slavonic *duch* has developed the meaning of " breath " into that of soul or spirit ; and the dialects
of the Gypsies have this word *dûk* with the meanings of
" breath, spirit, ghost," whether these pariahs brought the
word from India as part of their inheritance of Aryan
speech, or whether they adopted it in their migration across
Slavonic lands.[2] German *geist* and English *ghost*, too, may
possibly have the same original sense of breath. And if
any should think such expressions due to mere metaphor,
they may judge the strength of the implied connexion between
breath and spirit by cases of most unequivocal significance.
Among the Seminoles of Florida, when a woman died in
childbirth, the infant was held over her face to receive her
parting spirit, and thus acquire strength and knowledge for
its future use. These Indians could have well understood
why at the death-bed of an ancient Roman, the nearest
kinsman leant over to inhale the last breath of the departing (et excipies hanc animam ore pio). Their state of mind
is kept up to this day among Tyrolese peasants, who can
still fancy a good man's soul to issue from his mouth at
death like a little white cloud.[3]

[1] Oviedo, 'Hist. du Nicaragua,' pp. 21-51.
[2] Pott, 'Zigeuner,' vol. ii. p. 306 ; 'Indo-Germ. Wurzel-Wörterbuch,' vol. i.
p. 1073 ; Borrow, 'Lavengro,' vol. ii. ch. xxvi. "write the lil of him whose
duok gallops down that hill every night," see vol. iii. ch. iv.
[3] Brinton, 'Myths of New World,' p. 253 ; Comm. in Virg. Æn. iv. 684 ;

It will be shown that men, in their composite and confused notions of the soul, have brought into connexion a
list of manifestations of life and thought even more multifarious than this. But also, seeking to avoid such perplexity of combination, they have sometimes endeavoured
to define and classify more closely, especially by the theory
that man has a combination of several kinds of spirit, soul,
or image, to which different functions belong. Already
among savage races such classification appears in full
vigour. Thus the Fijians distinguish between a man's
" dark spirit " or shadow, which goes to Hades, and his
" light spirit " or reflexion in water or a mirror, which stays
near where he dies.[1] The Malagasy say that the *saina* or
mind vanishes at death, the *aina* or life becomes mere air,
but the *matoatoa* or ghost hovers round the tomb.[2] In
North America, the duality of the soul is a strongly marked
Algonquin belief; one soul goes out and sees dreams while
the other remains behind; at death one of the two abides
with the body, and for this the survivors leave offerings of
food, while the other departs to the land of the dead. A
division into three souls is also known, and the Dakotas
say that man has four souls, one remaining with the corpse,
one staying in the village, one going in the air, and one to
the land of spirits.[3] The Karens distinguish between the
' là ' or ' kelah,' which may be defined as the personal life-
phantom, and the ' thah ' which is the responsible moral
soul.[4] The fourfold division among the Khonds of Orissa
is as follows: the first soul is that capable of beatification
or restoration to Boora the Good Deity; the second is
attached to a Khond tribe on earth and is re-born genera-

Cic. Verr. v. 45; Wuttke, 'Volksaberglaube,' p. 210; Rochholz, 'Deutscher
Glaube,' etc. vol. i. p. 111.
[1] Williams, 'Fiji,' vol. i. p. 241.
[2] Ellis, 'Madagascar,' vol. i. p. 393.
[3] Charlevoix, vol. vi. pp. 75-8; Schoolcraft, 'Indian Tribes,' part i. pp. 33,
83, part iii. p. 229, part iv. p. 70; Waitz, vol. iii. p. 194; J. G. Muller,
pp. 66, 207, 8.
[4] Cross in 'Journ. Amer. Oriental Soc.' vol. iv. p. 316.

tion after generation, so that at the birth of each child the
priest asks which member of the tribe has returned; the
third goes out to hold spiritual intercourse, leaving the
body in a languid state, and it is this soul which can migrate
for a time into a tiger; the fourth dies on the dissolution
of the body.[1] Such classifications resemble those of higher
races, as for instance the three-fold division of shade, manes,
and spirit :

> " Bis duo sunt homini, manes, caro, spiritus, umbra :
> Quatuor hæc loci bis duo suscipiunt.
> Terra tegit carnem, tumulum circumvolat umbra,
> Manes Orcus habet, spiritus astra petit."

Not attempting to follow up the details of such psychical
division into the elaborate systems of literary nations, I
shall not discuss the distinction which the ancient Egyptians
seem to have made in the Ritual of the Dead between the
man's *ba, akh, ka, khaba,* translated by Mr. Birch as his
" soul," " mind," " existence," " shade," or the Rabbinical
division into what may be roughly described as the bodily,
spiritual, and celestial souls, or the distinction between the
emanative and genetic souls in Hindu philosophy, or the
distribution of life, apparition, ancestral spirit, among the
three souls of the Chinese, or the demarcations of the *nous,
psyche,* and *pneuma,* or of the *anima* and *animus,* or the
famous classic and mediæval theories of the vegetal, sensi-
tive, and rational souls. Suffice it to point out here that
such speculation dates back to the savage condition of our
race, in a state fairly comparing as to scientific value with
much that has gained esteem within the precincts of higher
culture. It would be a difficult task to treat such classification on a consistent logical basis. Terms corresponding
with those of life, mind, soul, spirit, ghost, and so forth,
are not thought of as describing really separate entities, so
much as the several forms and functions of one individual

---

[1] Macpherson, pp. 91, 2. See also Klemm, 'C. G.,' vol. iii. p. 71 (Lapp);
St. John, ' Far East,' vol. i. p. 189 (Dayaks).

being. Thus the confusion which here prevails in our own thought and language, in a manner typical of the thought and language of mankind in general, is in fact due not merely to vagueness of terms, but to an ancient theory of substantial unity which underlies them. Such ambiguity of language, however, will be found to interfere little with the present enquiry, for the details given of the nature and action of spirits, souls, phantoms, will themselves define the exact sense such words are to be taken in.

The early animistic theory of vitality, regarding the functions of life as caused by the soul, offers to the savage mind an explanation of several bodily and mental conditions, as being effects of a departure of the soul or some of its constituent spirits. This theory holds a wide and strong position in savage biology. The South Australians express it when they say of one insensible or unconscious, that he is "wilyamarraba," i. e., "without soul."[1] Among the Algonquin Indians of North America, we hear of sickness being accounted for by the patient's "shadow" being unsettled or detached from his body, and of the convalescent being reproached for exposing himself before his shadow was safely settled down in him; where we should say that a man was ill and recovered, they would consider that he died, but came again. Another account from among the same race explains the condition of men lying in lethargy or trance; their souls have travelled to the banks of the River of Death, but have been driven back and return to re-animate their bodies.[2] Among the Fijians, "when any one faints or dies, their spirit, it is said, may sometimes be brought back by calling after it; and occasionally the ludicrous scene is witnessed of a stout man lying at full length, and bawling out lustily for the return of his own soul."[3] To the negroes of North Guinea, derange-

[1] Schürmann, 'Vocab, of Parnkalla Lang.' s. v.
[2] Tanner's 'Narr.' p. 291; Keating 'Narr. of Long's Exp.' vol. ii. p. 154.
[3] Williams, 'Fiji,' vol. i. p. 242; see the converse process of catching away a man's soul, causing him to pine and die, p. 250.

ment or dotage is caused by the patient being prematurely
deserted by his soul, sleep being a more temporary with-
drawal.[1] Thus, in various countries, the bringing back of
lost souls becomes a regular part of the sorcerer's or priest's
profession.   The Salish Indians of Oregon regard the spirit
as distinct from the vital principle, and capable of quitting
the body for a short time without the patient being conscious of its absence; but to avoid fatal consequences it
must be restored as soon as possible, and accordingly the
medicine-man in solemn form replaces it down through the
patient's head.[2]   The Turanian or Tatar races of Northern
Asia strongly hold the theory of the soul's departure in
disease, and among the Buddhist tribes the Lamas carry
out the ceremony of soul-restoration in most elaborate
form.   When a man has been robbed by a demon of his
rational soul, and has only his animal soul left, his senses
and memory grow weak and he falls into a dismal state.
Then the Lama undertakes to cure him, and with quaint
rites exorcises the evil demon. But if this fails, then it is the
patient's soul itself that cannot or will not find its way back.
So the sick man is laid out in his best attire and surrounded
with his most attractive possessions, the friends and relatives go thrice round the dwelling, affectionately calling back
the soul by name, while as a further inducement the Lama
reads from his book descriptions of the pains of hell, and
the dangers incurred by a soul which wilfully abandons its
body, and then at last the whole assembly declare with one
voice that the wandering spirit has returned and the patient
will recover.[3]   The Karens of Birma will run about pre-
tending to catch a sick man's wandering soul, or as they
say with the ancient Greeks, his "butterfly" (*leip-pya*),
and at last drop it down upon his head. The Karen doctrine of the "là" is indeed a perfect and well-marked

[1] J. L. Wilson, 'W. Afr.' p. 220.
[2] Bastian, 'Mensch,' vol. ii. p. 319; also Sproat, p. 213 (Vancouver's I.).
[3] Bastian, 'Psychologie,' p. 34. Gmelin, 'Reise durch Sibirien,' vol. ii
p. 359 (Yakuts); Ravenstein, 'Amur,' p. 351 (Tunguz).

vitalistic system. This là, soul, ghost, or genius, may be separated from the body it belongs to, and it is a matter of the deepest interest to the Karen to keep his là with him, by calling it, making offerings of food to it, and so forth. It is especially when the body is asleep, that the soul goes out and wanders; if it is detained beyond a certain time, disease ensues, and if permanently, then its owner dies. When the " wee " or spirit-doctor is employed to call back the departed shade or life of a Karen, if he cannot recover it from the region of the dead, he will sometimes take the shade of a living man and transfer it to the dead, while its proper owner, whose soul has ventured out in a dream, sickens and dies. Or when a Karen becomes sick, languid and pining from his là having left him, his friends will perform a ceremony with a garment of the invalid's and a fowl which is cooked and offered with rice, invoking the spirit with formal prayers to come back to the patient.[1] This ceremony is perhaps ethnologically connected, though it is not easy to say by what manner of diffusion or when, with a rite still practised in China. When a Chinese is at the point of death, and his soul is supposed to be already out of his body, a relative may be seen holding up the patient's coat on a long bamboo, to which a white cock is often fastened, while a Tauist priest by incantations brings the departed spirit into the coat, in order to put it back into the sick man. If the bamboo after a time turns round slowly in the holder's hands, this shows that the spirit is inside the garment.[2]

Such temporary exit of the soul has a world-wide application to the proceedings of the sorcerer, priest, or seer himself. He professes to send forth his spirit on distant journeys, and probably often believes his soul released for a

[1] Bastian, 'Oestl. Asien,' vol. i. p. 143; vol. ii. pp. 388, 418; vol. iii. p. 236. Mason, 'Karens,' l. c. p. 196, etc.; Cross, 'Karens,' in 'Journ. Amer. Oriental Soc.' vol. iv. 1854, p. 307. See also St. John, 'Far East,' l. c. (Dayaks).

[2] Doolittle, 'Chinese,' vol. i. p. 150.

time from its bodily prison, as in the case of that remarkable dreamer and visionary Jerome Cardan, who describes himself as having the faculty of passing out of his senses as into ecstasy whenever he will, feeling when he goes into this state a sort of separation near the heart as if his soul were departing, this state beginning from his brain and passing down his spine, and he then feeling only that he is out of himself.[1] Thus the Australian native doctor is alleged to obtain his initiation by visiting the world of spirits in a trance of two or three days' duration;[2] the Khond priest authenticates his claim to office by remaining from one to fourteen days in a languid and dreamy state, caused by one of his souls being away in the divine presence;[3] the Greenland angekok's soul goes forth from his body to fetch his familiar demon;[4] the Turanian shaman lies in lethargy while his soul departs to bring hidden wisdom from the land of spirits.[5] The literature of more progressive races supplies similar accounts. A characteristic story from old Scandinavia is that of the Norse chief Ingimund, who shut up three Finns in a hut for three nights, that they might visit Iceland and inform him of the lie of the country where he was to settle; their bodies became rigid, they sent their souls on the errand, and awakening after the three days they gave a description of the Vatnsdœl.[6] The typical classic case is the story of Hermotimos, whose prophetic soul went out from time to time to visit distant regions, till at last his wife burnt the lifeless body on the funeral pile, and when the poor soul came back, there was no longer a dwelling for it to animate.[7] A group of the legendary visits to the spirit-world, which will be described in the next chapter,

[1] Cardan, 'De Varietate Rerum,' Basel, 1556, cap. xliii.
[2] Stanbridge, 'Abor. of Victoria,' in 'Tr. Eth. Soc.' vol. l. p. 300.
[3] Macpherson, 'India,' p. 108.
[4] Cranz, 'Grönland,' p. 269. See also Sproat, l. c.
[5] Hube, 'Fluland,' p. 303; Castrén, 'Finn. Myth,' p. 134; Bastian, 'Mensch,' vol. il. p. 319.
[6] Vatnsdœla Saga; Baring-Gould, 'Werewolves,' p. 29.
[7] Plin. vii. 53; Lucian. Hermotimus, Musc. Encom. 7.

belong to this class. A typical spiritualistic instance may
be quoted from Jung-Stilling, who says that examples have
come to his knowledge of sick persons who, longing to see
absent friends, have fallen into a swoon during which they
have appeared to the distant objects of their affection.[1] As
an illustration from our own folklore, the well-known superstition may serve, that fasting watchers on St. John's Eve
may see the apparitions of those doomed to die during the
year come with the clergyman to the church door and knock;
these apparitions are spirits who come forth from their
bodies, for the minister has been noticed to be much troubled
in his sleep while his phantom was thus engaged, and when
one of a party of watchers fell into a sound sleep and could
not be roused, the others saw his apparition knock at the
church door.[2] Modern Europe has indeed kept closely
enough to the lines of early philosophy, for such ideas to
have little strangeness to our own time. Language preserves record of them in such expressions as "out of oneself," "beside oneself," "in an ecstasy," and he who says
that his spirit goes forth to meet a friend, can still realize
in the phrase a meaning deeper than metaphor.

This same doctrine forms one side of the theory of dreams
prevalent among the lower races. Certain of the Greenlanders, Cranz remarks, consider that the soul quits the
body in the night and goes out hunting, dancing, and visiting; their dreams, which are frequent and lively, having
brought them to this opinion.[3] Among the Indians of
North America, we hear of the dreamer's soul leaving his
body and wandering in quest of things attractive to it.
These things the waking man must endeavour to obtain,
lest his soul be troubled, and quit the body altogether.[4]

[1] R. D. Owen, 'Footfalls on the Boundary of another World,' p. 259. See
A. R. Wallace, 'Scientific Aspect of the Supernatural,' p. 43.
[2] Brand, 'Pop. Ant.' vol. i. p. 331, vol. iii. p. 236. See Calmet, 'Diss.
sur les Esprits;' Maury, 'Magie,' part II. ch. iv.
[3] Cranz, 'Grönland,' p. 257.
[4] Waitz, vol. iii. p. 195.

The New Zealanders considered the dreaming soul to leave the body and return, even travelling to the region of the dead to hold converse with its friends.[1] The Tagals of Luzon object to waking a sleeper, on account of the absence of his soul.[2] The Karens, whose theory of the wandering soul has just been noticed, explain dreams to be what this là sees and experiences in its journeys when it has left the body asleep. They even account with much acuteness for the fact that we are apt to dream of people and places which we knew before; the leip-pya, they say, can only visit the regions where the body it belongs to has been already.[3] Onward from the savage state, the idea of the spirit's departure in sleep may be traced into the speculative philosophy of higher nations, as in the Vedanta system, and the Kabbala.[4] St. Augustine tells one of the double narratives which so well illustrate theories of this kind. The man who tells Augustine the story relates that, at home one night before going to sleep, he saw coming to him a certain philosopher, most well known to him, who then expounded to him certain Platonic passages, which when asked previously he had refused to explain. And when he (afterwards) enquired of this philosopher why he did at his house what he had refused to do when asked at his own: "I did not do it," said the philosopher, "but I dreamt I did." And thus, says Augustine, that was exhibited to one by phantastic image while waking, which the other saw in dream.[5] European folklore, too, has preserved interesting details of this primitive dream-theory, such as the fear of turning a sleeper over lest the absent soul should

[1] Taylor, 'New Zealand,' pp. 104, 184, 333; Baker in 'Tr. Eth. Soc.' vol. i. p 57.
[2] Bastian, 'Mensch,' vol. II. p. 319; Jagor in Journ. Eth. Soc. vol. II. p. 175.
[3] Mason, 'Karens,' l. c. p. 199; Cross, l. a.; Bastian, 'Oestl. Asien,' vol. l. p. 141, vol. II. p. 389, vol. III. p. 256.
[4] Bastian, 'Psychologie,' pp. 16-20; Eisenmenger, vol. i. p. 458, vol. II. pp. 13, 20, 453; Franck, 'Kabbale,' p. 235.
[5] Augustin. De Civ. Dei, xviii. 18.

miss the way back. King Gunthram's legend is one of a group interesting from the same point of view. The king lay in the wood asleep with his head in his faithful hench-man's lap; the servant saw as it were a snake issue from his lord's mouth and run to the brook, but it could not pass, so the servant laid his sword across the water, and the creature ran along it and up into a mountain; after a while it came back and returned into the mouth of the sleeping king, who waking told him how he had dreamt that he went over an iron bridge into a mountain full of gold.[1] This is one of those instructive legends which preserve for us, as in a museum, relics of an early intellectual condition of our Aryan race, in thoughts which to our modern minds have fallen to the level of quaint fancy, but which still remain sound and reasonable philosophy to the savage. A Karen at this day would appreciate every point of the story; the familiar notion of spirits not crossing water, which he ex-emplifies in his Burmese forests by stretching threads across the brook for the ghosts to pass along; the idea of the soul going forth embodied in an animal; and the theory of the dream being a real journey of the sleeper's soul. Finally, this old belief still finds, as such beliefs so often do, a refuge in modern poetry:

> " Yon child is dreaming far away,
> And is not where he seems."

This opinion, however, only constitutes one of several parts of the theory of dreams in savage psychology. An-other part has also a place here, the view that human souls come from without to visit the sleeper, who sees them as dreams. These two views are by no means incompatible. The North American Indians allowed themselves the alterna-tive of supposing a dream to be either a visit from the soul of the person or object dreamt of, or a sight seen by the rational soul, gone out for an excursion while the sensi-

[1] Grimm, ' D. M.' p. 1036.

tive soul remains in the body.[1] So the Zulu may be visited
in a dream by the shade of an ancestor, the itongo, who
comes to warn him of danger, or he may himself be taken
by the itongo in a dream to visit his distant people, and see
that they are in trouble; as for the man who is passing into
the morbid condition of the professional seer, phantoms are
continually coming to talk to him in his sleep, till he becomes,
as the expressive native phrase is, "a house of dreams."[2]
In the lower range of culture, it is perhaps most frequently
taken for granted that a man's apparition in a dream is a
visit from his disembodied spirit, which the dreamer, to use
an expressive Ojibwa idiom, "sees when asleep." Such a
thought comes out clearly in the Fijian opinion that a living
man's spirit may leave the body, to trouble other people in
their sleep;[3] or in a recent account of an old Indian woman
of British Columbia sending for the medicine-man to drive
away the dead people who came to her every night.[4] A
modern observer's description of the state of mind of the
negroes of South Guinea in this respect is extremely characteristic and instructive. "All their dreams are construed
into visits from the spirits of their deceased friends. The
cautions, hints, and warnings which come to them through
this source, are received with the most serious and deferential
attention, and are always acted upon in their waking hours.
The habit of relating their dreams, which is universal,
greatly promotes the habit of dreaming itself, and hence
their sleeping hours are characterized by almost as much
intercourse with the dead as their waking are with the
living. This is, no doubt, one of the reasons of their excessive superstitiousness. Their imaginations become so lively
that they can scarcely distinguish between their dreams and
their waking thoughts, between the real and the ideal, and

[1] Charlevoix, 'Nouvelle France,' vol. vi. p. 78; Loskiel, part L p. 76;
Sproat, 'Savage Life,' p. 172.
[2] Callaway, 'Relig. of Amazulu,' pp. 228, 260, 316; 'Journ. Anthrop.
Inst.' vol. i. p. 170. See also St. John, 'Far East,' vol. i. p. 199 (Dayaks).
[3] Williams, 'Fiji,' vol. i. p. 242.
[4] Mayne, 'Brit. Columbia,' p. 261; see Sproat l. c.

they consequently utter falsehood without intending, and profess to see things which never existed."[1]

To the Greek of old, the dream-soul was what to the modern savage it still is. Sleep, loosing cares of mind, fell on Achilles as he lay by the sounding sea, and there stood over him the soul of Patroklos, like to him altogether in stature, and the beauteous eyes, and the voice, and the garments that wrapped his skin; he spake, and Achilles stretched out to grasp him with loving hands, but caught him not, and like a smoke the soul sped twittering below the earth. Along the ages that separate us from Homeric times, the apparition in dreams of men living or dead has been a subject of philosophic speculation and of superstitious fear.[2] Both the phantom of the living and the ghost of the dead figure in Cicero's typical tale. Two Arcadians came to Megara together, one lodged at a friend's house, the other at an inn. In the night this latter appeared to his fellow-traveller, imploring his help, for the innkeeper was plotting his death; the sleeper sprang up in alarm, but thinking the vision of no consequence went to sleep again. Then a second time his companion appeared to him, to entreat that though he had failed to help, he would at least avenge, for the innkeeper had killed him and hidden his body in a dung-cart, wherefore he charged his fellow-traveller to be early next morning at the city-gate before the cart passed out. Struck with this second dream, the traveller went as bidden, and there found the cart; the body of the murdered man was in it, and the innkeeper was brought to justice. "Quid hoc somnio dici potest divinius?"[3] Augustine discusses with reference to the nature of the soul various dream-stories of his time, where the apparitions of men dead or living are seen in dreams.

[1] J. L. Wilson, 'W. Africa,' p. 395, see 210. See also Ellis, 'Polyn. Res.' vol. i. p. 396; J. G. Müller, 'Amer. Urrel.' p. 287; Buchanan, 'Mysore,' in Pinkerton, vol. viii. p. 577; 'Early Hist. of Mankind,' p. 8.

[2] Homer. Il. xxiii. 59. See also Odyss. xi. 207, 222; Porphyr. De Antro Nympharum; Virgil. Æn. ii. 794; Ovid. Fast v. 475.

[3] Cicero De Divinatione, i. 27.

In one of the latter he himself figured, for when a disciple
of his, Eulogius the rhetor of Carthage, once could not get
to sleep for thinking of an obscure passage in Cicero's
Rhetoric, that night Augustine came to him in a dream and
explained it. But Augustine's tendency was toward the
modern theory of dreams, and in this case he says it was
certainly his image that appeared, not himself, who was far
across the sea, neither knowing nor caring about the matter.[1]
As we survey the immense series of dream-stories of similar
types in patristic, mediæval, and modern literature, we may
find it difficult enough to decide which are truth and which
are fiction. But along the course of these myriad narratives of human phantoms appearing in dreams to cheer or
torment, to warn or inform, or to demand fulfilment of their
own desires, the problem of dream-apparitions may be traced
in progress of gradual determination, from the earlier conviction that a disembodied soul really comes into the presence
of the sleeper, toward the later opinion that such a phantasm
is produced in the dreamer's mind without the perception of
any external objective figure.

The evidence of visions corresponds with the evidence of
dreams in their bearing on primitive theories of the soul,[2]
and the two classes of phenomena substantiate and supple-
ment one another. Even in healthy waking life, the savage
or barbarian has never learnt to make that rigid distinction
between subjective and objective, between imagination and
reality, to enforce which is one of the main results of
scientific education. Still less, when disordered in body and
mind he sees around him phantom human forms, can he dis-
trust the evidence of his very senses. Thus it comes to
pass that throughout the lower civilization men believe, with
the most vivid and intense belief, in the objective reality of
the human spectres which they see in sickness, exhaustion, or
excitement. As will be hereafter noticed, one main reason
of the practices of fasting, penance, narcotising by drugs, and

[1] Augustin. De Curâ pro Mortuis, x.-xii. Epist. clviii.
[2] Compare Voltaire's remarks, 'Dict. Phil.' art. "ame," etc.

other means of bringing on morbid exaltation, is that the
patients may obtain the sight of spectral beings, from whom
they look to gain spiritual knowledge and even worldly power.
Human ghosts are among the principal of these phantasmal
figures. There is no doubt that honest visionaries describe
ghosts as they really appear to their perception, while even the
impostors who pretend to see them conform to the descriptions thus established; thus, in West Africa, a man's *kla* or
soul, becoming at his death a *sisa* or ghost, can remain in the
house with the corpse, but is only visible to the wong-man,
the spirit-doctor.[1] Sometimes the phantom has the characteristic quality of not being visible to all of an assembled
company. Thus the natives of the Antilles believed that
the dead appeared on the roads when one went alone, but
not when many went together;[2] thus among the Finns the
ghosts of the dead were to be seen by the shamans, but not
by men generally unless in dreams.[3] Such is perhaps the
meaning of the description of Samuel's ghost, visible to
the witch of Endor, but not to Saul, for he has to ask her
what it is she sees.[4] Yet this test of the nature of an
apparition is one which easily breaks down. We know well
how in civilized countries a current rumour of some one
having seen a phantom is enough to bring a sight of it to
others whose minds are in a properly receptive state. The
condition of the modern ghost-seer, whose imagination
passes on such slight excitement into positive hallucination,
is rather the rule than the exception among uncultured and
intensely imaginative tribes, whose minds may be thrown off
their balance by a touch, a word, a gesture, an unaccustomed
noise. Among savage tribes, however, as among civilized
races who have inherited remains of early philosophy formed
under similar conditions, the doctrine of visibility or in-

[1] Steinhauser, 'Religion des Negers,' in 'Magazin der Evang. Missionen,'
Basel, 1856, No. 2, p. 135.
[2] 'Historie del S. D. Fernando Colombo,' tr. Alfonso Ulloa, Venice, 1571,
p. 127; Eng. Tr. in Pinkerton, vol. xii. p. 80.
[3] Castrén, 'Finn. Myth.' p. 120.
[4] I. Sam. xxviii. 12.

visibility of phantoms has been obviously shaped with
reference to actual experience. To declare that souls or
ghosts are necessarily either visible or invisible, would
directly contradict the evidence of men's senses. But to
assert or imply, as the lower races do, that they are visible
sometimes and to some persons, but not always or to every
one, is to lay down an explanation of facts which is not
indeed our usual modern explanation, but which is a perfectly rational and intelligible product of early science.

Without discussing on their merits the accounts of what
is called "second sight," it may be pointed out that they are
related among savage tribes, as when Captain Jonathan
Carver obtained from a Cree medicine-man a true prophecy
of the arrival of a canoe with news next day at noon; or
when Mr. J. Mason Brown, travelling with two voyageurs
on the Coppermine River, was met by Indians of the very
band he was seeking, these having been sent by their
medicine-man, who, on enquiry, stated that "He saw them
coming, and heard them talk on their journey."[1] These are
analogous to accounts of the Highland second-sight, as when
Pennant heard of a gentleman of the Hebrides, said to have
the convenient gift of foreseeing visitors in time to get ready
for them, or when Dr. Johnson was told by another laird
that a labouring man of his had predicted his return to the
island, and described the peculiar livery his servant had been
newly dressed in.[2]

As a general rule, people are apt to consider it impossible
for a man to be in two places at once, and indeed a saying
to that effect has become a popular saw. But the rule is so
far from being universally accepted, that the word "bilocation" has been invented to express the miraculous faculty
possessed by certain Saints of the Roman Church, of being
in two places at once; like St. Alfonso di Liguori, who had
the useful power of preaching his sermon in church while

[1] Brinton, 'Myths of New World,' p. 269.
[2] Pennant, '2nd Tour in Scotland,' in Pinkerton, vol. iii. p. 315; Johnson,
'Journey to the Hebrides.'

he was confessing penitents at home.[1] The reception and explanation of these various classes of stories fits perfectly with the primitive animistic theory of apparitions, and the same is true of the following most numerous class of the second-sight narratives.

Death is the event which, in all stages of culture, brings thought to bear most intensely, though not always most healthily, on the problems of psychology. The apparition of the disembodied soul has in all ages been thought to bear especial relation to its departure from its body at death. This is well shown by the reception not only of a theory of ghosts, but of a special doctrine of " wraiths" or " fetches." Thus the Karens say that a man's spirit, appearing after death, may thus announce it.[2] In New Zealand it is ominous to see the figure of an absent person, for if it be shadowy and the face not visible, his death may ere long be expected, but if the face be seen he is dead already. A party of Maoris (one of whom told the story) were seated round a fire in the open air, when there appeared, seen only by two of them, the figure of a relative left ill at home; they exclaimed, the figure vanished, and on the return of the party it appeared that the sick man had died about the time of the vision.[3] Examining the position of the doctrine of wraiths among the higher races, we find it especially prominent in three intellectual districts, Christian hagiology, popular folk-lore, and modern spiritualism. St. Anthony saw the soul of St. Ammonius carried to heaven in the midst of choirs of angels, the same day that the holy hermit died five days' journey off in the desert of Nitria; when St. Ambrose died on Easter Eve, several newly-baptized children saw the holy bishop, and pointed him out to their parents, but these with their less pure eyes could not behold him; and so forth.[4]

[1] J. Gardner, 'Faiths of the World,' s. v. 'Bilocation.'
[2] Mason, 'Karens' l. c. p. 198.
[3] Shortland, 'Trads. of New Zealand,' p. 140; Polack, 'M. and C. of New Zealanders,' vol. I. p. 268. See also Ellis, 'Madagascar,' vol. I. p. 393; J. G. Müller, p. 261.
[4] Calmet, 'Diss. sur les Esprits,' vol. i. ch. xl.

Folk-lore examples abound in Silesia and the Tyrol, where
the gift of wraith-seeing still flourishes, with the customary
details of funerals, churches, four-cross-roads, and headless
phantoms, and an especial association with New Year's Eve.
The accounts of " second-sight " from North Britain mostly
belong to a somewhat older date. Thus the St. Kilda people
used to be haunted by their own spectral doubles, fore-
runners of impending death, and in 1799 a traveller writes
of the peasants of Kircudbrightshire, " It is common among
them to fancy that they see the wraiths of persons dying,
which will be visible to one and not to others present with
him.   Within these last twenty years, it was hardly possible
to meet with any person who had not seen many wraiths and
ghosts in the course of his experience." Those who discuss
the authenticity of the second-sight stories as actual
evidence, must bear in mind that they prove a little too
much ; they vouch not only for human apparitions, but for
such phantoms as demon-dogs, and for still more fanciful
symbolic omens.   Thus a phantom shroud seen in spiritual
vision on a living man predicts his death, immediate if it is
up to his head, less nearly approaching if it is only up to
his waist ; and to see in spiritual vision a spark of fire fall
upon a person's arm or breast, is a forerunner of a dead
child to be seen in his arms.[1]   As visionaries often see
phantoms of living persons without any remarkable event
coinciding with their hallucinations, it is naturally admitted
that a man's phantom or " double " may be seen without
portending anything in particular. The spiritualistic theory
specially insists on cases of apparition where the person's
death corresponds more or less nearly with the time when
some friend perceives his phantom.[2] Narratives of this class,
which I can here only specify without arguing on them, are

[1] Wuttke, 'Volksberglaube,' pp. 44, 56, 208 ; Brand, 'Popular Antiquities,'
vol. iii. pp. 155, 235 ; Johnson, 'Journey to the Hebrides ;' Martin, 'Western
Islands of Scotland,' in Pinkerton, vol. iii. p. 670.

[2] See R. D. Owen, 'Footfalls on the Boundary of another World '; Mrs.
Crowe, 'Night-Side of Nature ;' Howitt's Tr. of Ennemoser's 'Magic,' etc.

abundantly in circulation. Thus, I have an account by a lady, who " saw, as it were, the form of some one laid out," near the time when a brother died at Melbourne, and who mentions another lady known to her, who thought she saw her own father look in at the church window at the moment he was dying in his own house. Another account is sent me by a Shetland lady, who relates that about twenty years ago she and a girl leading her pony recognized the familiar figure of one Peter Sutherland, whom they knew to be at the time in ill-health in Edinburgh ; he turned a corner and they saw no more of him, but next week came the news of his sudden death.

That the apparitional human soul bears the likeness of its fleshly body, is the principle implicitly accepted by all who believe it really and objectively present in dreams and visions. My own view is that nothing but dreams and visions could have ever put into men's minds such an idea as that of souls being ethereal images of bodies. It is thus habitually taken for granted in animistic philosophy, savage or civilized, that souls set free from the earthly body are recognized by a likeness to it which they still retain, whether as ghostly wanderers on earth or inhabitants of the world beyond the grave. Man's spirit, says Swedenborg, is his mind, which lives after death in complete human form, and this is the poet's dictum in ' In Memoriam : '

> " Eternal form shall still divide
> The eternal soul from all beside ;
> And I shall know him when we meet."

This world-wide thought, coming into view here in a multitude of cases from all grades of culture, needs no collection of ordinary instances to illustrate it.[1] But a quaint and special group of beliefs will serve to display the thorough-

---

[1] The conception of the soul as a small human image is found in various districts ; see Eyre, 'Australia,' vol. ii. p. 356 ; St. John, 'Far East,' vol. i. p. 189 (Dayaks) ; Waitz, vol. iii. p. 104 (N. A. Ind.). The idea of a soul as a sort of "thumbling" is familiar to the Hindus and to German folk-lore ; compare the representations of tiny souls in mediæval pictures.

ness with which the soul is thus conceived as an image of
the body. As a consistent corollary to such an opinion, it
is argued that the mutilation of the body will have a corresponding effect upon the soul, and very low savage races
have philosophy enough to work out this idea. Thus it was
recorded of the Indians of Brazil by one of the early
European visitors, that they " believe that the dead arrive
in the other world wounded or hacked to pieces, in fact just
as they left this.[1] Thus, too, the Australian who has slain
his enemy will cut off the right thumb of the corpse, so that
although the spirit will become a hostile ghost, it cannot
throw with its mutilated hand the shadowy spear, and may
be safely left to wander, malignant but harmless.[2] The
negro fears long sickness before death, such as will send
him lean and feeble into the next world. His theory of the
mutilation of soul with body could not be brought more
vividly into view than in that ugly story of the West India
planter, whose slaves began to seek in suicide at once relief
from present misery and restoration to their native land ;
but the white man was too cunning for them, he cut off the
heads and hands of the corpses, and the survivors saw that
not even death could save them from a master who could
maim their very souls in the next world.[3] The same rude
and primitive belief continues among nations risen far
higher in intellectual rank. The Chinese hold in especial
horror the punishment of decapitation, considering that he
who quits this world lacking a member will so arrive in the
next, and a case is recorded lately of a criminal at Amoy
who for this reason begged to die instead by the cruel death
of crucifixion, and was crucified accordingly.[4] The series
ends as usual in the folk-lore of the civilized world. The
phantom skeleton in chains that haunted the house at

---

[1] Magalhanes de Gandavo, p. 110; Maffei, ' Indie Orientali,' p. 107.
[2] Oldfield in 'Tr. Eth. Soc.' vol. iii. p. 287.
[3] Waitz, vol. ii. p. 194 ; Römer, ' Guinea,' p. 42.
[4] Meiners, vol. ii. p. 756, 763 ; Purchas, vol. iii. p. 495 ; J. Jones in 'Tr.
Eth. Soc.' vol. iii. p. 138.

Bologna, showed the way to the garden where was buried the real chained fleshless skeleton it belonged to, and came no more when the remains had been duly buried. When the Earl of Cornwall met the fetch of his friend William Rufus carried black and naked on a black goat across the Bodmin moors, he saw that it was wounded through the midst of the breast; and afterwards he heard that at that very hour the king had been slain in the New Forest by the arrow of Walter Tirell.[1]

In studying the nature of the soul as conceived among the lower races, and in tracing such conceptions onward among the higher, circumstantial details are available. It is as widely recognized among mankind that souls or ghosts have voices, as that they have visible forms, and indeed the evidence for both is of the same nature. Men who perceive evidently that souls do talk when they present themselves in dream or vision, naturally take for granted at once the objective reality of the ghostly voice, and of the ghostly form from which it proceeds. This is involved in the series of narratives of spiritual communications with living men, from savagery onward to civilization, while the more modern doctrine of the subjectivity of such phenomena recognizes the phenomena themselves, but offers a different explanation of them. One special conception, however, requires particular notice. This defines the spirit-voice as being a low murmur, chirp, or whistle, as it were the ghost of a voice. The Algonquin Indians of North America could hear the shadow-souls of the dead chirp like crickets.[2] The divine spirits of the New Zealand dead, coming to converse with the living, utter their words in whistling tones, and such utterances by a squeaking noise are mentioned elsewhere in Polynesia.[3] The Zulu diviner's familiar spirits

[1] Calmet, vol. L ch. xxxvi. ; Flin. Ep. 7 27 ; Hunt, 'Pop. Romances,' vol II. p. 156.

[2] Le Jeune in 'Rel. des Jésuites,' 1639, p. 43 ; also 1634, p. 13.

[3] Shortland, 'Trads. of N. Z.' p. 92 ; Yate, p. 140 ; R. Taylor, p. 104 153 ; Ellis, 'Polyn. Res.' vol. I. p. 106.

are ancestral manes, who talk in a low whistling tone short
of a full whistle, whence they have their name of "imilozi"
or whistlers.[1] These ideas correspond with classic descriptions of the ghostly voice, as a "twitter" or "thin
murmur :"

" Ψυχὴ δὲ κατὰ χθονὸς ἠΰτε καπνὸς,
Ὤχετο τετριγυῖα." [2]

" Umbra cruenta Remi visa est assistere lecto,
Atque haec exiguo murmure verba loqui." [3]

As the attributes of the soul or ghost extend to other
spiritual beings, and the utterances of such are to a great
extent given by the voice of mediums, we connect these
accounts with the notion that the language of demons is
also a low whistle or mutter, whence the well-known practice
of whispering or murmuring charms, the "susurrus necro-
manticus" of sorcerers, to whom the already cited description of "wizards that peep (i. e. chirp) and mutter" is
widely applicable.[4]

The conception of dreams and visions as caused by present objective figures, and the identification of such phantom
souls with the shadow and the breath, has led many a
people to treat souls as substantial material beings. Thus
it is a usual proceeding to make openings through solid
materials to allow souls to pass. The Iroquois in old times
used to leave an opening in the grave for the lingering soul

[1] Callaway, 'Rel. of Amazulu,' pp. 265, 318, 370.
[2] Homer. Il. xxiii. 100.
[3] Ovid. Fast. v. 457.
[4] Isaiah viii. 19 ; xxix. 4. The Arabs hate whistling (el sifr), it is talking
to devils (Burton, ' First Footsteps in East Africa,' p. 142). "Nicolaus Remi-
gius, whose 'Dæmonolatreia' is one of the ghastliest volumes in the ghastly
literature of witchcraft, cites Hermolaus Barbarus as having heard the voice
sub-sibilantis dæmonis, and, after giving other instances, adduces the authority of Psellus to prove that the devils generally speak very low and con-
fusedly in order not to be caught fibbing" Dr. Sebastian Evans in ' Nature,'
June 22, 1871, p. 140. (Nicolai Remigii Dæmonolatreia, Col. Agripp. 1596,
lb. l. c. 8, "pleræque aliæ vocem illam eam alunt qualem emittunt qui os in
dolium aut restam rimosam insertum habent "—" ut Dæmones e pelvi stridula
voce ac tenui sibilo verba ederent.").

to visit its body, and some of them still bore holes in the
coffin for the same purpose.[1] The Malagasy sorcerer, for
the cure of a sick man who had lost his soul, would make a
hole in the burial-house to let out a spirit, which he would
catch in his cap and so convey to the patient's head.[2] The
Chinese make a hole in the roof to let out the soul at
death.[3] And lastly, the custom of opening a window or
door for the departing soul when it quits the body is to this
day a very familiar superstition in France, Germany, and
England.[4] Again, the souls of the dead are thought susceptible of being beaten, hurt, and driven like any other living
creatures. Thus the Queensland aborigines would beat the
air in an annual mock fight, held to scare away the souls that
death had let loose among the living since last year.[5] Thus
North American Indians, when they had tortured an enemy
to death, ran about crying and beating with sticks to scare
the ghost away; they have been known to set nets round
their cabins to catch and keep out neighbours' departed
souls; fancying the soul of a dying man to go out at the
wigwam roof, they would habitually beat the sides with
sticks to drive it forth; we even hear of the widow going
off from her husband's funeral followed by a person flourishing a handful of twigs about her head like a flyflapper, to
drive off her husband's ghost and leave her free to marry
again.[6] With a kindlier feeling, the Congo negroes ab-
stained for a whole year after a death from sweeping the
house, lest the dust should injure the delicate substance of
the ghost;[7] the Tonquinese avoided house-cleaning during
the festival when the souls of the dead came back to their

[1] Morgan, 'Iroquois,' p. 176.
[2] Flacourt, 'Madagascar,' p. 101.
[3] Bastian, 'Psychologie,' p. 15.
[4] Monnier, 'Traditions Populaires,' p. 142; Wuttke, 'Volksberglaube,'
p. 209; Grimm, 'D. M.' p. 801; Meiners, vol. ii. p. 761.
[5] Lang, 'Queensland,' p. 441; Bonwick, 'Tasmanians,' p. 187.
[6] Charlevoix, 'Nouvelle France,' vol. vi. pp. 76, 122; Le Jeune in 'Rel. de
la Nouvelle France,' 1634, p. 23; 1639, p. 44; Tanner's 'Narr.' p. 292
Peter Jones, 'Hist. of Ojebway Indians,' p. 99.
[7] Bastian, 'Mensch,' vol. ii. p. 323.

houses for the New Year's visit;[1] and it seems likely that the special profession of the Roman "everriatores" who swept the houses out after a funeral, was connected with a similar idea.[2] To this day, it remains a German peasants' saying that it is wrong to slam a door, lest one should pinch a soul in it.[3] The not uncommon practice of strewing ashes to show the footprints of ghosts or demons takes for granted that they are substantial bodies. In the literature of animism, extreme tests of the weight of ghosts are now and then forthcoming. They range from the declaration of a Basuto diviner that the late queen had been bestriding his shoulders, and he never felt such a weight in his life, to Glanvil's story of David Hunter the neat-herd, who lifted up the old woman's ghost, and she felt just like a bag of feathers in his arms, or the pathetic German superstition that the dead mother's coming back in the night to suckle the baby she has left on earth, may be known by the hollow pressed down in the bed where she lay, and at last down to the alleged modern spiritualistic reckoning of the weight of a human soul at from 3 to 4 ounces.[4]

Explicit statements as to the substance of soul are to be found both among low and high races, in an instructive series of definitions. The Tongans imagined the human soul to be the finer or more aeriform part of the body, which leaves it suddenly at the moment of death; something comparable to the perfume and essence of a flower as related to the more solid vegetable fibre.[5] The Greenland seers described the soul as they habitually perceived it in their visions; it is pale and soft, they said, and he who tries to seize it feels nothing, for it has no flesh nor bone

[1] Meiners, vol. L p. 318.
[2] Festus, s. v. 'everriatores;' see Bastian, l. c., and compare Hartknoch, cited below, vol. ii. p. 40.
[3] Wuttke, 'Volksaberglaube,' pp. 132, 216.
[4] Casalis, 'Basutos,' p. 285; Glanvil, 'Saducismus Triumphatus,' part ii. p 161; Wuttke, p. 216; Bastian, 'Psychologie,' p. 192.
[5] Mariner, 'Tonga Is.' vol. ii. p. 135.

nor sinew.[1] The Caribs did not think the soul so immaterial as to be invisible, but said it was subtle and thin like a purified body.[2] Turning to higher races, we may take the Siamese as an example of a people who conceive of souls as consisting of subtle matter escaping sight and touch, or as united to a swiftly moving aerial body.[3] In the classic world, it is recorded as an opinion of Epicurus that "they who say the soul is incorporeal talk folly, for it could neither do nor suffer anything were it such."[4] Among the Fathers, Irenæus describes souls as incorporeal in comparison with mortal bodies,[5] and Tertullian relates a vision or revelation of a certain Montanist prophetess, of the soul seen by her corporeally, thin and lucid, aerial in colour and human in form.[6] For an example of mediæval doctrine, may be cited a 14th century English poem, the " Ayenbite of Inwyt " (i. e. " Remorse of Conscience ") which points out how the soul, by reason of the thinness of its substance, suffers all the more in purgatory:

> " The soul is more tendre and nesche
> Than the bodi that hath bones and fleysche ;
> Thanne the soul that is so tendere of kinde,
> Mote nedis hure penaunce hardere y-finde,
> Than eni bodi that evere on live was."[7]

The doctrine of the ethereal soul passed on into more modern philosophy, and the European peasant holds fast to it still ; as Wuttke says, the ghosts of the dead have to him a misty and evanescent materiality, for they have bodies as we have, though of other kind : they can eat and drink, they can be wounded and killed.[8] Nor was the ancient

[1] Cranz, 'Grönland,' p. 257.
[2] Rochefort, 'Iles Antilles,' p. 429.
[3] Loubere, 'Siam,' vol. I. p. 458 ; Bastian, 'Oestl. Asien,' vol. III. p. 250 ; see 278.
[4] Diog. Laert. x. 67–8 ; see Serv. ad Æn. iv. 654.
[5] Irenæus contra Hæres, v. 7, 1 ; see Origen. De Princip. II. 3, 2.
[6] Tertull. De Anima, 9.
[7] Hampole, 'Ayenbite of Inwyt.'
[8] Wuttke, ' Volksaberglaube,' pp. 214, 226.

doctrine ever more distinctly stated than by a modern spiritualistic writer, who observes that " a spirit is no immaterial substance; on the contrary, the spiritual organization is composed of matter . . . . in a very high state of refinement and attenuation." [1]

Among rude races, the original conception of the human soul seems to have been that of ethereality, or vaporous materiality, which has held so large a place in human thought ever since. In fact, the later metaphysical notion of immateriality could scarcely have conveyed any meaning to a savage. It is moreover to be noticed that, as to the whole nature and action of apparitional souls, the lower philosophy escapes various difficulties which down to modern times have perplexed metaphysicians and theologians of the civilized world. Considering the thin ethereal body of the soul to be itself sufficient and suitable for visibility, movement, and speech, the primitive animists had no need of additional hypotheses to account for these manifestations, theological theories such as we may find detailed by Calmet, as that immaterial souls have their own vaporous bodies, or occasionally have such vaporous bodies provided for them by supernatural means to enable them to appear as spectres, or that they possess the power of condensing the circumambient air into phantom-like bodies to invest themselves in, or of forming from it vocal instruments.[2] It appears to have been within systematic schools of civilized philosophy that the transcendental definitions of the immaterial soul were obtained, by abstraction from the primitive conception of the ethereal-material soul, so as to reduce it from a physical to a metaphysical entity.

Departing from the body at the time of death, the soul or spirit is considered set free to linger near the tomb, to wander on earth or flit in the air, or to travel to the proper region of spirits—the world beyond the grave. The principal conceptions of the lower psychology as to a Future

[1] A. J. Davis, ' Philosophy of Spiritual Intercourse,' New York, 1851, p. 49.
[2] Calmet, vol. I. ch. xli., etc.

Life will be considered in the following chapters, but for
the present purpose of investigating the theory of souls in
general, it will be well to enter here upon one department
of the subject. Men do not stop short at the persuasion
that death releases the soul to a free and active existence,
but they quite logically proceed to assist nature, by slaying
men in order to liberate their souls for ghostly uses. Thus
there arises one of the most wide-spread, distinct, and intelligible rites of animistic religion—that of funeral human
sacrifice for the service of the dead. When a man of rank
dies and his soul departs to its own place, wherever and
whatever that place may be, it is a rational inference of
early philosophy that the souls of attendants, slaves, and
wives, put to death at his funeral, will make the same
journey and continue their service in the next life, and the
argument is frequently stretched further, to include the
souls of new victims sacrificed in order that they may enter
upon the same ghostly servitude. It will appear from the
ethnography of this rite that it is not strongly marked in
the very lowest levels of culture, but that, arising in the
higher savagery, it developes itself in the barbaric stage, and
thenceforth continues or dwindles in survival.

Of the murderous practices to which this opinion leads,
remarkably distinct accounts may be cited from among
tribes of the Indian Archipelago. The following account is
given of the funerals of great men among the savage Kayans
of Borneo:—" Slaves are killed in order that they may
follow the deceased and attend upon him. Before they are
killed the relations who surround them enjoin them to take
great care of their master when they join him, to watch and
shampoo him when he is indisposed, to be always near him,
and to obey all his behests. The female relatives of the
deceased then take a spear and slightly wound the victims,
after which the males spear them to death." Again, the
opinion of the Idaan is " that all whom they kill in this
world shall attend them as slaves after death. This notion
of future interest in the destruction of the human species is

a great impediment to an intercourse with them, as murder goes farther than present advantage or resentment. From the same principle they will purchase a slave, guilty of any capital crime, at fourfold his value, that they may be his executioners." With the same idea is connected the ferocious custom of "head-hunting," so prevalent among the Dayaks before Rajah Brooke's time. They considered that the owner of every human head they could procure would serve them in the next world, where, indeed, a man's rank would be according to his number of heads in this. They would continue the mourning for a dead man till a head was brought in, to provide him with a slave to accompany him to the "habitation of souls;" a father who lost his child would go out and kill the first man he met, as a funeral ceremony; a young man might not marry till he had procured a head, and some tribes would bury with a dead man the first head he had taken, together with spears, cloth, rice, and betel. Waylaying and murdering men for their heads became, in fact, the Dayaks' national sport, and they remarked "the white men read books, we hunt for heads instead."[1] Of such rites in the Pacific islands, the most hideously purposeful accounts reach us from the Fiji group. Till lately, a main part of the ceremony of a great man's funeral was the strangling of wives, friends, and slaves, for the distinct purpose of attending him into the world of spirits. Ordinarily the first victim was the wife of the deceased, and more than one if he had several, and their corpses, oiled as for a feast, clothed with new fringed girdles, with heads dressed and ornamented, and vermilion and turmeric powder spread on their faces and bosoms, were laid by the side of the dead warrior. Associates and inferior attendants were likewise slain, and these bodies

---

[1] 'Journ. Ind. Archip.' vol. II. p. 359; vol. iii. pp. 104, 556; Earl, 'Eastern Seas,' p. 266; St. John, 'Far East,' vol. I. pp. 52, 73, 70, 119; Mundy, 'Narr. from Brooke's Journals,' p. 203. Heads were taken as funeral offerings by the Garos of N. E. India, Eliot in 'As. Res.' vol. iii. p. 28. Dalton, 'Descr. Ethnol. of Bengal,' p. 67; see also p. 46—7 (Kukis).

were spoken of as "grass for bedding the grave." When Ra Mbithi, the pride of Somosomo, was lost at sea, seventeen of his wives were killed; and after the news of the massacre of the Namena people, in 1839, eighty women were strangled to accompany the spirits of their murdered husbands. Such sacrifices took place under the same pressure of public opinion which kept up the widow-burning in modern India. The Fijian widow was worked upon by her relatives with all the pressure of persuasion and of menace; she understood well that life to her henceforth would mean a wretched existence of neglect, disgrace, and destitution; and tyrannous custom, as hard to struggle against in the savage as in the civilized world, drove her to the grave. Thus, far from resisting, she became importunate for death and the new life to come, and till public opinion reached a more enlightened state, the missionaries often used their influence in vain to save from the strangling-cord some wife whom they could have rescued, but who herself refused to live. So repugnant to the native mind was the idea of a chieftain going unattended into the other world, that the missionaries' prohibition of the cherished custom was one reason of their dislike to Christianity. Many of the nominal Christians, when once a chief of theirs was shot from an ambush, esteemed it most fortunate that a stray shot at the same time killed a young man at a distance from him, and thus provided a companion for the spirit of the slain chief.[1]

In America, the funeral human sacrifice makes its characteristic appearance. A good example may be taken from among the Osages, whose habit was sometimes to plant in the cairn raised over a corpse a pole with an enemy's scalp hanging to the top. Their notion was that by taking an enemy and suspending his scalp over the grave of a deceased friend, the spirit of the victim became subjected to the spirit

---

[1] T. Williams, 'Fiji,' vol. L pp. 183—204; Mariner, 'Tonga Is.' vol. II. p. 220. For New Zealand accounts, see R. Taylor, 'New Zealand,' pp. 218, 227; Polack, 'New Zealanders,' vol. L pp. 66, 78, 116.

of the buried warrior in the land of spirits. Hence the
last and best service that could be performed for a deceased
relative was to take an enemy's life, and thus transmit it by
his scalp.[1] The correspondence of this idea with that just
mentioned among the Dyaks is very striking. With a
similar intention, the Caribs would slay on the dead
master's grave any of his slaves they could lay hands on.[2]
Among the native peoples risen to considerably higher
grades of social and political life, these practices were not
suppressed but exaggerated, in the ghastly sacrifices of warriors, slaves, and wives, who departed to continue their
duteous offices at the funeral of the chief or monarch in
Central America[3] and Mexico,[4] in Bogota[5] and Peru.[6] It
is interesting to notice, in somewhat favourable contrast
with these customs of comparatively cultured American
nations, the practice of certain rude tribes of the North-
West. The Quakeolths, for instance, did not actually
sacrifice the widow, but they made her rest her head on her
husband's corpse while it was being burned, until at last
she was dragged more dead than alive from the flames; if
she recovered, she collected her husband's ashes and carried
them about with her for three years, during which any
levity or deficiency of grief would render her an outcast.
This looks like a mitigated survival from an earlier custom
of actual widow-burning.[7]

Of such funeral rites, carried out to the death, graphic

---

[1] J. M'Coy, 'Hist. of Baptist Indian Missions,' p. 360; Waitz, vol. iii.
p. 200. See also Schoolcraft, 'Indian Tribes,' part ii. p. 133 (Comanches).

[2] Rochefort, 'Iles Antilles,' pp. 429, 512; see also J. G. Müller, pp. 174,
222.

[3] Oviedo, 'Relation de Cueba,' p. 140; Charlevoix, 'Nouv. Fr.' vol. vi.
p. 178 (Natchez); Waitz, vol. iii. p. 219. See Brinton, 'Myths of New
World,' p. 259.

[4] Brasseur, 'Mexique,' vol. iii. p. 573.

[5] Piedrahita, 'Nuevo Reyno de Granada,' part. i. lib. i. c. 3.

[6] Cieza de Leon, p. 161; Rivero and Tschudi, 'Peruv. Ant.' p. 200;
Prescott, 'Peru,' vol. i. p. 29. See statements as to effigies, J. G. Müller,
p. 379.

[7] Simpson, 'Journey,' vol. i. p. 190; similar practice among Takulli or
Carrier Ind., Waitz, vol. iii. p. 200.

and horrid descriptions are recorded in the countries across
Africa—East, Central, and West. A headman of the Wa-
doe is buried sitting in a shallow pit, and with the corpse a
male and female slave alive, he with a bill-hook in his hand
to cut fuel for his lord in the death-world, she seated on a
little stool with the dead chief's head in her lap. A chief
of Unyamwezi is entombed in a vaulted pit, sitting on a
low stool with a bow in his right hand, and provided with a
pot of native beer; with him are shut in alive three women
slaves, and the ceremony is concluded with a libation of
beer on the earth heaped up above them all. The same
idea which in Guinea makes it common for the living to
send messages by the dying to the dead, is developed in
Ashanti and Dahome into a monstrous system of massacre.
The King of Dahome must enter Deadland with a ghostly
court of hundreds of wives, eunuchs, singers, drummers,
and soldiers. Nor is this all. Captain Burton thus describes the yearly " Customs :"—" They periodically supply
the departed monarch with fresh attendants in the shadowy
world. For unhappily these murderous scenes are an expression, lamentably mistaken but perfectly sincere, of the
liveliest filial piety." Even this annual slaughter must be
supplemented by almost daily murder :—"Whatever action,
however trivial, is performed by the King, it must dutifully
be reported to his sire in the shadowy realm. A victim,
almost always a war-captive, is chosen; the message is delivered to him, an intoxicating draught of rum follows it,
and he is dispatched to Hades in the best of humours."[1]
In southern districts of Africa, accounts of the same class
begin in Congo and Angola with the recorded slaying of
the dead man's favourite wives, to live with him in the other
world, a practice still in vogue among the Chevas of the
Zambesi district, and formerly known among the Maravis;
while the funeral sacrifice of attendants with a chief is a

[1] Burton, 'Central Afr.' vol. i. p. 124; vol. ii. p. 25; 'Dahome,' vol. II.
p. 18, etc.; 'Tr. Eth. Soc.' vol. iii. p. 403; J. L. Wilson, 'W. Afr.' pp. 203,
219, 394. See also H. Rowley, 'Mission to Central Africa,' p. 229.

thing of the past among the Barotse, as among the Zulus, who yet have not forgotten the days when the chief's servants and attendant warriors were cast into the fire which had consumed his body, that they might go with him, and prepare things beforehand, and get food for him.[1]

If now we turn to the records of Asia and Europe, we shall find the sacrifice of attendants for the dead widely prevalent in both continents in old times, while in the east its course may be traced continuing onward to our own day. The two Mohammedans who travelled in Southern Asia in the ninth century relate that on the accession of certain kings a quantity of rice is prepared, which is eaten by some three or four hundred men, who present themselves voluntarily to share it, thereby undertaking to burn themselves at the monarch's death. With this corresponds Marco Polo's thirteenth century account in Southern India of the king of Maabar's guard of horsemen, who, when he dies and his body is burnt, throw themselves into the fire to do him service in the next world.[2] In the seventeenth century the practice is described as prevailing in Japan, where, on the death of a nobleman, from ten to thirty of his servants put themselves to death by the "hara kari," or ripping-up, having indeed engaged during his lifetime, by the solemn compact of drinking wine together, to give their bodies to their lord at his death. The Japanese form of modern survival of such funeral sacrifices is to substitute for real men and animals images of stone, or clay, or wood, placed by the corpse.[3] Among the Ossetes of the Caucasus, an interesting relic of widow-sacrifice is still kept up: the dead man's widow and his saddle-horse are led thrice round the grave, and no man may marry the widow or mount the

[1] Cavazzi, 'Ist. Descr. de' tre Regni Congo, Matamba, et Angola,' Bologna, 1687, lib. I. 284; Waitz, vol. II. pp. 419—21; Callaway, 'Religion of Amazulu,' p. 212.

[2] Renaudot, 'Acc. by two Mohammedan Travellers,' London 1733, p. 81; and in Pinkerton, vol. vii. p. 215; Marco Polo, book iii. chap. xx.; and in Pinkerton, vol. vii. p. 162.

[3] Caron, 'Japan,' ibid., p. 629; Siebold, 'Nippon,' v. p. 22.

horse thus devoted.[1] In China, legend preserves the memory of the ancient funeral human sacrifice. The brother of
Chin Yang, a disciple of Confucius, died, and his widow and
steward wished to bury some living persons with him, to serve
him in the regions below. Thereupon the sage suggested
that the proper victims would be the widow and steward
themselves, but this not precisely meeting their views, the
matter dropped, and the deceased was interred without attendants. This story at least shows the rite to have been
not only known but understood in China long ago. In
modern China, the suicide of widows to accompany their
husbands is a recognized practice, sometimes even performed in public. Moreover, the ceremonies of providing
sedan-bearers and an umbrella-bearer for the dead, and
sending mounted horsemen to announce beforehand his
arrival to the authorities of Hades, although these bearers
and messengers are only made of paper and burnt, seem to
represent survivals of a more murderous reality.[2]

The Aryan race gives striking examples of the rite of
funeral human sacrifice in its sternest shape, whether in
history or in myth, that records as truly as history the
manners of old days.[3] The episodes of the Trojan cap-
tives laid with the horses and hounds on the funeral pile of
Patroklos, and of Evadne throwing herself into the funeral
pile of her husband, and Pausanias's narrative of the suicide
of the three Messenian widows, are among its Greek representatives.[4] In Scandinavian myth, Baldr is burnt with his

[1] 'Journ. Ind. Archip.' new series, vol. II. p. 374.

[2] Legge, 'Confucius,' p. 119 ; Doolittle, 'Chinese,' vol. I. pp. 108, 174, 192.
The practice of attacking or killing all persons met by a funeral procession is
perhaps generally connected with funeral human sacrifice; any one met on the
road by the funeral of a Mongol prince was slain and ordered to go as escort;
in the Kimbunda country, any one who meets a royal funeral procession is put
to death with the other victims at the grave (Magyar, 'Süd. Afrika,' p. 353) ;
see also Mariner, 'Tonga Is.' vol. I. p. 403 ; Cook, 'First Voy.' vol. i. pp. 146,
216 (Tahiti).

[3] Jacob Grimm, 'Verbrennen der Leichen,' contains an instructive collection
of references and citations.

[4] Homer. Il. xxiii. 175 ; Eurip. Suppl. ; Pausanias, iv. 2.

dwarf foot-page, his horse and saddle; Brynhild lies on the
pile by her beloved Sigurd, and men and maids follow after
them on the hell-way.[1] The Gauls in Cæsar's time burned
at the dead man's sumptuous funeral whatever was dear to
him, animals also, and much-loved slaves and clients.[2] Old
mentions of Slavonic heathendom describe the burning of
the dead with clothing and weapons, horses and hounds,
with faithful servants, and above all, with wives. Thus
St. Boniface says that "the Wends keep matrimonial love
with so great zeal, that the wife may refuse to survive her
husband, and she is held praiseworthy among women who
slays herself with her own hand, that she may be burnt on
one pyre with her lord."[3] This Aryan rite of widow-sacrifice has not only an ethnographic and antiquarian interest,
but even a place in modern politics. In Brahmanic India
the widow of a Hindu of the Brahman or the Kshatriya
caste was burnt on the funeral pile with her husband, as a
sati or "good woman," which word has passed into English
as *suttee*. Mentioned in classic and mediæval times, the
practice was in full vigour at the beginning of the present
century.[4] Often one dead husband took many wives with
him. Some went willingly and gaily to the new life, many
were driven by force of custom, by fear of disgrace, by
family persuasion, by priestly threats and promises, by
sheer violence. When the rite was suppressed under modern British rule, the priesthood resisted to the uttermost,
appealing to the Veda as sanctioning the ordinance, and
demanding that the foreign rulers should respect it. Yet
in fact, as Prof. H. H. Wilson proved, the priests had
actually falsified their sacred Veda in support of a rite en-
joined by long and inveterate prejudice, but not by the

[1] Edda, 'Gylfaginning,' 49; 'Brynhildarqvitha,' etc.
[2] Cæsar. 'Bell. Gall.' vi. 19.
[3] Hanusch, 'Slaw. Myth.' p. 145.
[4] Strabo, xv. 1, 62; Cic. Tusc. Disp. v. 27, 78; Diod. Sic. xvii. 91; xix. 33,
etc.; Grimm, 'Verbrennen,' p. 261; Henandot, 'Two Mohammedans,' p. 4;
and in Pinkerton, vol. vii. p. 191. See Buchanan, Ibid. pp. 675, 682; Ward,
'Hindoos,' vol. ii. pp. 298—312.

traditional standards of Hindu faith. The ancient Brahmanic funeral rites have been minutely detailed from the Sanskrit authorities in an essay by Prof. Max Müller. Their directions are that the widow is to be set on the funeral pile with her husband's corpse, and if he be a warrior his bow is to be placed there too. But then a brother-in-law or adopted child or old servant is to lead the widow down again at the summons, " Rise, woman, come to the world of life ; thou sleepest nigh unto him whose life is gone. Come to us. Thou hast thus fulfilled thy duties of a wife to the husband who once took thy hand, and made thee a mother." The bow, however, is to be broken and thrown back upon the pile, and the dead man's sacrificial instruments are to be laid with him and really consumed. While admitting with Prof. Müller that the more modern ordinance of Suttee-burning is a corrupt departure from the early Brahmanic ritual, we may nevertheless find some reason to consider the practice as not a new invention by the later Hindu priesthood, but as the revival, under congenial influences, of an ancient Aryan rite belonging originally to a period even earlier than the Veda. The ancient authorized ceremony looks as though, in a still more ancient form of the rite, the widow had been actually sent with the dead, for which real sacrifice a more humane law substituted a mere pretence. This view is supported by the existence of an old and express prohibition of the wife being sacrificed, a prohibition seemingly directed against a real custom, " to follow the dead husband is prohibited, so says the law of the Brahmans. With regard to the other castes this law for women may be or may not be."[1] To treat the Hindu widow-burning as a case of survival and revival seems to me most in accordance with a general ethnographic view of the subject. Widow-sacrifice is found in various regions of the world under a low state of civilization, and

[1] Max Müller, 'Todtenbestattung bei den Brahmanen, in Zeitschr. der Deutsch. Morgenl. Ges.' vol. ix. ; 'Chips,' vol. ii. p. 34 ; Pictet, 'Origines Indo-Europ.' part ii. p. 526.

this fits with the hypothesis of its having belonged to the Aryan race while yet in an early and barbarous condition. Thus the prevalence of a rite of suttee like that of modern India among ancient Aryan nations settled in Europe, Greeks, Scandinavians, Germans, Slaves, may be simply accounted for by direct inheritance from the remote common antiquity of them all. If this theory be sound, it will follow that ancient as the Vedic ordinances may be, they represent in this matter a reform and a re-action against a yet more ancient savage rite of widow-sacrifice, which they prohibited in fact, but yet kept up in symbol. The history of religion displays but too plainly the proneness of mankind to relapse, in spite of reformation, into the lower and darker condition of the past. Stronger and more tenacious than even Vedic authority, the hideous custom of the suttee may have outlived an attempt to suppress it in early Brahmanic times, and the English rulers, in abolishing it, may have abolished a relic not merely of degenerate Hinduism, but of the far more remotely ancient savagery out of which the Aryan civilization had grown.

In now passing from the consideration of the souls of men to that of the souls of the lower animals, we have first to inform ourselves as to the savage man's idea, which is very different from the civilized man's, of the nature of these lower animals. A remarkable group of observances customary among rude tribes will bring this distinction sharply into view. Savages talk quite seriously to beasts alive or dead as they would to men alive or dead, offer them homage, ask pardon when it is their painful duty to hunt and kill them. A North American Indian will reason with a horse as if rational. Some will spare the rattlesnake, fearing the vengeance of its spirit if slain; others will salute the creature reverently, bid it welcome as a friend from the land of spirits, sprinkle a pinch of tobacco on its head for an offering, catch it by the tail and dispatch it with extreme dexterity, and carry off its skin as a trophy. If an Indian is attacked and torn by a bear, it is that the

beast fell upon him intentionally in anger, perhaps to revenge the hurt done to another bear. When a bear is
killed, they will beg pardon of him, or even make him con-
done the offence by smoking the peace-pipe with his mur-
derers, who put the pipe in his mouth and blow down it,
begging his spirit not take revenge.[1] So in Africa, the Kafirs
will hunt the elephant, begging him not to tread on them
and kill them, and when he is dead they will assure him
that they did not kill him on purpose, and they will bury
his trunk, for the elephant is a mighty chief, and his trunk
is his hand that he may hurt withal. The Congo people
will even avenge such a murder by a pretended attack on
the hunters who did the deed.[2] Such customs are common
among the lower Asiatic tribes. The Stiens of Kambodia
ask pardon of the beast they have killed;[3] the Ainos of
Yesso kill the bear, offer obeisance and salutation to him,
and cut up his carcase.[4] The Koriaks, if they have slain a
bear or wolf, will flay him, dress one of their people in the
skin, and dance round him, chanting excuses that they did
not do it, and especially laying the blame on a Russian.
But if it is a fox, they take his skin, wrap his dead body in
hay, and sneering tell him to go to his own people and say
what famous hospitality he has had, and how they gave him
a new coat instead of his old one.[5] The Samoyeds excuse
themselves to the slain bear, telling him it was the Russians
who did it, and that a Russian knife will cut him up.[6] The
Goldi will set up the slain bear, call him "my lord" and
do ironical homage to him, or taking him alive will fatten
him in a cage, call him "son" and "brother," and kill
and cut him as a sacrifice at a solemn festival.[7] In Borneo,

[1] Schoolcraft, 'Indian Tribes,' part i. p. 513; part iii. pp. 229, 520;
Waitz, vol. iii. pp. 191—8.
[2] Klemm, 'Cultur-Gesch.' vol. iii. pp. 353, 361; Waitz, vol. ii. p. 178.
[3] Mouhot, 'Indo-China,' vol. i. p. 252.
[4] Wood in 'Tr. Eth. Soc,' vol. iv. p. 36.
[5] Bastian, 'Mensch,' vol. iii. p. 26.
[6] De Brosses, 'Dieux Fetiches,' p. 61.
[7] Ravenstein, 'Amur,' p. 382; T. W. Atkinson, p. 183.

the Dayaks, when they have caught an alligator with a
baited hook and rope, address him with respect and sooth-
ing till they have his legs fast, and then mocking call him
"rajah" and "grandfather."[1] Thus when the savage gets
over his fears, he still keeps up in ironical merriment the
reverence which had its origin in trembling sincerity. Even
now the Norse hunter will say with horror of a bear that
will attack man, that he can be "no Christian bear."

The sense of an absolute psychical distinction between
man and beast, so prevalent in the civilized world, is hardly
to be found among the lower races. Men to whom the
cries of beasts and birds seem like human language, and
their actions guided as it were by human thought, logically
enough allow the existence of souls to beasts, birds, and
reptiles, as to men. The lower psychology cannot but recognize in beasts the very characteristics which it attributes
to the human soul, namely, the phenomena of life and
death, will and judgment, and the phantom seen in vision
or in dream. As for believers, savage or civilized, in the
great doctrine of metempsychosis, these not only consider
that an animal may have a soul, but that this soul may have
inhabited a human being, and thus the creature may be in
fact their own ancestor or once familiar friend. A line of
facts, arranged as waymarks along the course of civilization,
will serve to indicate the history of opinion from savagery
onward, as to the souls of animals during life and after
death. North American Indians held every animal to have
its spirit, and these spirits their future life; the soul of the
Canadian dog went to serve his master in the other world;
among the Sioux, the prerogative of having four souls was
not confined to man, but belonged also to the bear, the
most human of animals.[2] The Greenlanders considered
that a sick human soul might be replaced by the sorcerer
with a fresh healthy soul of a hare, a reindeer, or a young

[1] St. John, 'Far East,' vol. ii. p. 253 (Dayaks).
[2] Charlevoix, 'Nouvelle France,' vol. vi. p. 78; Sagard, 'Hist. du Canada,'
p. 197; Schoolcraft, 'Indian Tribes,' part iii. p. 229.

child.[1] Maori tale-tellers have heard of the road by which
the spirits of dogs descend to Reinga, the Hades of the
departed; the Hovas of Madagascar know that the ghosts
of beasts and men, dwelling in a great mountain in the
south called Ambondrombe, come out occasionally to walk
among the tombs or execution-places of criminals.[2] The
Kamchadals held that every creature, even the smallest fly,
would live again in the under world.[3] The Kukis of Assam
think that the ghost of every animal a Kuki kills in the
chase or for the feast will belong to him in the next life,
even as the enemy he slays in the field will then become his
slave. The Karens apply the doctrine of the spirit or
personal life-phantom, which is apt to wander from the
body and thus suffer injury, equally to men and to animals.[4]
The Zulus say the cattle they kill come to life again, and
become the property of the dwellers in the world beneath.[5]
The Siamese butcher, when in defiance of the very principles of his Buddhism he slaughters an ox, before he kills
the creature has at least the grace to beseech its spirit to
seek a happier abode.[6] In connexion with such transmigration, Pythagorean and Platonic philosophy gives to the
lower animals undying souls, while other classic opinion
may recognize in beasts only an inferior order of soul, only
the "anima" but not the human "animus" besides. Thus
Juvenal:

> " Principio indulsit communis conditor illis
>   Tantùm animas; nobis animum quoque. . . ." [7]

Through the middle ages, controversy as to the psychology
of brutes has lasted on into our own times, ranging between

[1] Cranz, 'Grönland,' p. 257.
[2] Taylor, 'New Zealand,' p. 271; Ellis, 'Madagascar,' vol. I. p. 429.
[3] Steller, 'Kamtschatka,' p. 269.
[4] Stewart, 'Kukis; Dalton, l. c.;' Cross, 'Karens,' l. c.; Mason,
'Karens,' l. c.
[5] Callaway, 'Zulu Tales,' vol. I. p. 317.
[6] Low in 'Journ. Ind. Archip.' vol. I. p. 426. See Meiners, vol. I. p. 220
vol. II. p. 791.
[7] Juvenal. Sat. xv. 148.

two extremes: on the one the theory of Descartes which
reduced animals to mere machines, on the other what Mr.
Alger defines as "the faith that animals have immaterial
and deathless souls." Among modern speculations may be
instanced that of Wesley, who thought that in the next life
animals will be raised even above their bodily and mental
state at the creation, "the horridness of their appearance
will be exchanged for their primæval beauty," and it even
may be that they will be made what men are now, creatures
capable of religion. Adam Clarke's argument for the future
life of animals rests on abstract justice: whereas they did
not sin, but yet are involved in the sufferings of sinful man,
and cannot have in the present state the happiness designed
for them, it is reasonable that they must have it in another.[1]
Although, however, the primitive belief in the souls of
animals still survives to some extent in serious philosophy,
it is obvious that the tendency of educated opinion on the
question whether brutes have soul, as distinguished from
life and mind, has for ages been in a negative and sceptical
direction. The doctrine has fallen from its once high
estate. It belonged originally to real, though rude science.
It has now sunk to become a favourite topic in that mild
speculative talk which still does duty so largely as intellectual conversation, and even then its propounders defend
it with a lurking consciousness of its being after all a piece
of sentimental nonsense.

Animals being thus considered in the primitive psychology
to have souls like human beings, it follows as the simplest
matter of course that tribes who kill wives and slaves, to
dispatch their souls on errands of duty with their departed

<hr>

[1] Alger, 'Future Life,' p. 633, and see 'Bibliography,' appendix II.; Wesley,
'Sermon on Rom. viii. 19—22;' Adam Clarke, 'Commentary,' on same text.
This, by the way, is the converse view to Bellarmine's, who so patiently let
the fleas bite him, saying, "We shall have heaven to reward us for our sufferings, but these poor creatures have nothing but the enjoyment of the present
life."—Bayle, 'Biog. Dic.' The argument in Butler's 'Analogy,' part i. ch. I.
puts the evidence for souls of brutes on much the same footing as that for
souls of men.

lords, may also kill animals in order that their spirits may
do such service as is proper to them. The Pawnee warrior's
horse is slain on his grave to be ready for him to mount
again, and the Comanche's best horses are buried with his
favourite weapons and his pipe, all alike to be used in the
distant happy hunting-grounds.[1] In South America not
only do such rites occur, but they reach a practically
disastrous extreme. Patagonian tribes, says D'Orbigny,
believe in another life, where they are to enjoy perfect
happiness, therefore they bury with the deceased his arms
and ornaments, and even kill on his tomb all the animals
which belonged to him, that he may find them in the abode
of bliss; and this opposes an insurmountable barrier to all
civilization, by preventing them from accumulating property
and fixing their habitations.[2] Not only do Pope's now
hackneyed lines express a real motive with which the
Indian's dog is buried with him, but on the North American
continent the spirit of the dog has another remarkable office
to perform. Certain Esquimaux, as Cranz relates, would
lay a dog's head in a child's grave, that the soul of the dog,
who ever finds his home, may guide the helpless infant to
the land of souls. In accordance with this, Captain
Scoresby in Jameson's Land found a dog's skull in a small
grave, probably a child's. Again, in the distant region of
the Aztecs, one of the principal funeral ceremonies was to
slaughter a techichi, or native dog; it was burnt or buried
with the corpse, with a cotton thread fastened to its neck,
and its office was to convey the deceased across the deep
waters of Chiuhnahuapan, on the way to the Land of the
Dead.[3] The dead Durnet's favourite horse, led saddled to
the grave, killed, and flung in, may serve for a Tatar

---

[1] Schoolcraft, 'Indian Tribes,' part i. pp. 237, 262; part ii. p. 69.
[2] D'Orbigny, 'L'Homme Américain,' vol. i. p. 196; vol. ii. pp. 23, 78;
Falkner, 'Patagonia,' p. 118; Musters, 'Patagonians,' p. 178.
[3] Egede, 'Greenland,' p. 152; Cranz, p. 301; see Nilsson, p. 110. Torquemada, 'Monarquia Indiana,' xili. ch. 47; Clavigero, 'Mexico,' vol. ii.
pp. 64-6.

example.[1] In Tonquin, even wild animals have been customarily drowned at funeral ceremonies of princes, to be at the service of the departed in the next world.[2] Among Semitic tribes, an instance of the custom may be found in the Arab sacrifice of a camel on the grave, for the dead man's spirit to ride upon.[3] Among the nations of the Aryan race in Europe, the prevalence of such rites is deep, wide, and full of purpose. Thus, warriors were provided in death with horses and housings, with hounds and falcons. Customs thus described in chronicle and legend, are vouched for in our own time by the opening of old barbaric burial-places. How clear a relic of savage meaning lies here may be judged from a Livonian account as late as the fourteenth century, which relates how men and women, slaves, sheep, and oxen, with other things, were burnt with the dead, who, it was believed, would reach some region of the living, and find there, with the multitude of cattle and slaves, a country of life and happiness.[4] As usual, these rites may be traced onward in survival. The Mongols, who formerly slaughtered camels and horses at their owner's burial, have been induced to replace the actual sacrifice by a gift of the cattle to the Lamas.[5] The Hindus offer a black cow to the Brahmans, in order to secure their passage across the Vaitarani, the river of death, and will often die grasping the cow's tail as if to swim across in herdsman's fashion, holding on to a cow.[6] It is mentioned as a belief in Northern Europe that he who has given a cow to the poor will find a cow to take

[1] Georgi, 'Reise im Russ. R.' vol. I. p. 312.

[2] Baron, 'Tonquin,' in Pinkerton, vol. ix. p. 704.

[3] W. G. Palgrave, 'Arabia,' vol. I. p. 10; Bastian, 'Mensch,' vol. II. p. 331; Waitz, vol. ii. p. 519 (Gallas).

[4] Grimm, 'Verbrennen der Leichen.' A curious correspondence in the practice of cutting off a fowl's head as a funeral rite is to be noticed among the Yorubas of W. Africa (Burton, 'W. and W.,' p. 220), Chuwashes of Siberia (Castren, 'Finn. Myth.' p. 120), old Russians (Grimm, 'Verbrennen,' p. 251).

[5] Bastian, 'Mensch,' vol. II. p. 335.

[6] Colebrooke, 'Essays,' vol. I. p. 177; Ward, 'Hindoos,' vol. II. pp. 61, 284, 331.

him over the bridge of the dead, and a custom of leading a cow in the funeral procession is said to have been kept up to modern times.[1] All these rites probably belong together as connected with ancient funeral sacrifice, and the survival of the custom of sacrificing the warrior's horse at his tomb is yet more striking. Saint-Foix long ago put the French evidence very forcibly. Mentioning the horse led at the funeral of Charles VI., with the four valets-de-pied in black, and bareheaded, holding the corners of its caparison, he recals the horses and servants killed and buried with præ-Christian kings. And that his readers may not think this an extraordinary idea, he brings forward the records of property and horses being presented at the offertory in Paris, in 1329, of Edward III. presenting horses at King John's funeral in London, and of the funeral service for Bertrand Duguesclin, at St. Denis, in 1389, when horses were offered, the Bishop of Auxerre laid his hand on their heads, and they were afterwards compounded for.[2] Germany retained the actual sacrifice within the memory of living men. A cavalry general named Frederick Kasimir was buried at Treves in 1781 according to the forms of the Teutonic Order; his horse was led in the procession, and the coffin having been lowered into the grave, the horse was killed and thrown in upon it.[3] This was, perhaps, the last occasion when such a sacrifice was consummated in solemn form in Europe. But that pathetic incident of a soldier's funeral, the leading of the saddled and bridled charger in the mournful procession, keeps up to this day a lingering reminiscence of the grim religious rite now passed away.

Plants, partaking with animals the phenomena of life and death, health and sickness, not unnaturally have some kind of soul ascribed to them. In fact, the notion of a vegetable

[1] Mannhardt, 'Götterwelt der Deutschen, etc.' vol. I. p. 319.
[2] Saint-Foix, 'Essais historiques sur Paris,' in 'Œuvres Comp.' Maestricht, 1778, vol. iv. p. 150.
[3] J. M. Kemble, 'Hora Ferales,' p. 68.

soul, common to plants and to the higher organisms possessing an animal soul in addition, was familiar to mediæval
philosophy, and is not yet forgotten by naturalists. But in
the lower ranges of culture, at least within one wide district
of the world, the souls of plants are much more fully
identified with the souls of animals. The Society Islanders
seem to have attributed "varua," i. e., surviving soul or
spirit, not to men only but to animals and plants.[1] The
Dayaks of Borneo not only consider men and animals to
have a spirit or living principle, whose departure from the
body causes sickness and eventually death, but they also
give to the rice its "samangat padi," or "spirit of the
paddy," and they hold feasts to retain this soul securely,
lest the crop should decay.[2] The Karens say that plants as
well as men and animals have their "là" ("kelah"), and
the spirit of sickly rice is here also called back like a human
spirit considered to have left the body. Their formulas for
the purpose have even been written down, and this is part
of one :—" O come, rice kelah, come. Come to the field.
Come to the rice. . . . . Come from the West. Come
from the East. From the throat of the bird, from the maw
of the ape, from the throat of the elephant. . . . .
From all granaries come. O rice kelah, come to the rice."[3]
There is reason to think that the doctrine of the spirits of
plants lay deep in the intellectual history of South-East
Asia, but was in great measure superseded under Buddhist
influence. The Buddhist books show that in the early days
of their religion, it was matter of controversy whether trees
had souls, and therefore whether they might lawfully be
injured. Orthodox Buddhism decided against the tree-
souls, and consequently against the scruple to harm them,
declaring trees to have no mind nor sentient principle,

[1] Mœrenhout. 'Voy. aux Iles du Grand Océan,' vol. i. p. 430.
[2] St. John. 'Far East,' vol. i. p. 187.
[3] Mason, 'Karens,' in 'Journ. As. Soc. Bengal,' 1865, part II. p. 202 ; Cross
in 'Journ. Amer. Oriental Soc.' vol. iv. p. 309. See comparison of Siamese
and Malay ideas ; Low in 'Journ. Ind. Archip.' vol. i. p. 340.

though admitting that certain dewas or spirits do reside in
the body of trees, and speak from within them. Buddhists
also relate that a heterodox sect kept up the early doctrine
of the actual animate life of trees, in connexion with which
may be remembered Marco Polo's somewhat doubtful statement as to certain austere Indians objecting to green herbs
for such a reason, and some other passages from later
writers. Generally speaking, the subject of the spirits of
plants is an obscure one, whether from the lower races not
having definite opinions, or from our not finding it easy to
trace them.[1] The evidence from funeral sacrifices, so
valuable as to most departments of early psychology, fails
us here, from plants not being thought suitable to send for
the service of the dead. Yet, as we shall see more fully
elsewhere, there are two topics which bear closely on the
matter. On the one hand, the doctrine of transmigration
widely and clearly recognises the idea of trees or smaller
plants being animated by human souls; on the other, the
belief in tree-spirits and the practice of tree-worship involve
notions more or less closely coinciding with that of tree-
souls, as when the classic hamadryad dies with her tree, or
when the Talein of South-East Asia, considering every tree
to have a demon or spirit, offers prayers before he cuts one
down.

Thus far the details of the lower animistic philosophy are
not very unfamiliar to modern students. The primitive
view of the souls of men and beasts, as asserted or acted on
in the lower and middle levels of culture, so far belongs to
current civilized thought, that those who hold the doctrine
to be false, and the practices based upon it futile, can
nevertheless understand and sympathise with the lower
nations to whom they are matters of the most sober and
serious conviction. Nor is even the notion of a separable
spirit or soul as the cause of life in plants too incongruous

---

[1] Hardy, 'Manual of Budhism,' pp. 291, 443; Bastian, 'Oestl. Asien,' vol. ii.
p. 184; Marco Polo, book iii. ch. xxli (compare various readings); Meiners,
vol. i. p. 215; vol. ii. p. 799.

with ordinary ideas to be readily appreciable. But the theory of souls in the lower culture stretches beyond this limit, to take in a conception much stranger to modern thought. Certain high savage races distinctly hold, and a large proportion of other savage and barbarian races make a more or less close approach to, a theory of separable and surviving souls or spirits belonging to stocks and stones, weapons, boats, food, clothes, ornaments, and other objects which to us are not merely soulless but lifeless.

Yet, strange as such a notion may seem to us at first sight, if we place ourselves by an effort in the intellectual position of an uncultured tribe, and examine the theory of object-souls from their point of view, we shall hardly pronounce it irrational. In discussing the origin of myth, some account has been already given of the primitive stage of thought in which personality and life are ascribed not to men and beasts only, but to things. It has been shown how what we call inanimate objects—rivers, stones, trees, weapons, and so forth—are treated as living intelligent beings, talked to, propitiated, punished for the harm they do. Hume, whose "Natural History of Religion" is perhaps more than any other work the source of modern opinions as to the development of religion, comments on the influence of this personifying stage of thought. "There is an universal tendency among mankind to conceive all beings like themselves, and to transfer to every object those qualities with which they are familiarly acquainted, and of which they are intimately conscious. . . . . The *unknown causes*, which continally employ their thought, appearing always in the same aspect, are all apprehended to be of the same kind or species. Nor is it long before we ascribe to them thought and reason, and passion, and sometimes even the limbs and figures of men, in order to bring them nearer to a resemblance with ourselves." Auguste Comte has ventured to bring such a state of thought under terms of strict definition in his conception of the primary mental condition of mankind—a state of "pure fetishism, constantly characterized by the free and direct exercise of our primitive tendency to conceive all external bodies soever, natural or artificial, as animated by a life essentially analogous to our own, with mere differences of intensity."[1] Our comprehension of the lower stages of mental culture depends much on the thoroughness with which we can appreciate this primitive, childlike conception, and in this our best guide may be the memory of our own childish days. He who recollects when there was still personality to him in posts and sticks, chairs and toys, may well understand how the infant philosophy of mankind could extend the notion of vitality to what modern science only recognises as lifeless things; thus one main part of the lower animistic doctrine as to souls of objects is accounted for. The doctrine requires for its full conception of a soul not only life, but also a phantom or apparitional spirit; this development, however, follows without difficulty, for the evidence of dreams and visions applies to the spirits of objects in much the same manner as to human ghosts. Everyone who has seen visions while light-headed in fever, everyone who has ever dreamt a dream, has seen the phantoms of objects as well as of persons. How then can we charge the savage with far-fetched absurdity for taking into his philosophy and religion an opinion which rests on the very evidence of his senses? The notion is implicitly recognised in his accounts of ghosts, which do not come naked, but clothed, and even armed; of course there must be spirits of garments and weapons, seeing that the spirits of men come bearing them. It will indeed place savage philosophy in no unfavourable light, if we compare this extreme animistic development of it with the popular opinion still surviving in civilized countries, as to ghosts and the nature of the human soul as connected with them. When the ghost of Hamlet's father appeared armed cap-a-pe,

[1] Hume, 'Nat. Hist. of Rel.' sec. ii.; Comte, 'Philosophie Positive,' vol. v. p. 30.

"Such was the very armour he had on,
When he the ambitious Norway combated."

And thus it is a habitual feature of the ghost-stories of the
civilized, as of the savage world, that the ghost comes
dressed, and even dressed in well-known clothing worn in
life. Hearing as well as sight testifies to the phantoms of
objects: the clanking of ghostly chains and the rustling of
ghostly dresses are described in the literature of apparitions. Now by the savage theory, according to which the
ghost and his clothes are alike real and objective, and by
the modern scientific theory, according to which both ghost
and garment are alike imaginary and subjective, the facts of
apparitions are rationally met. But the modern vulgar who
ignore or repudiate the notion of ghosts of things, while
retaining the notion of ghosts of persons, have fallen into a
hybrid state of opinion which has neither the logic of the
savage nor of the civilized philosopher.

Among the lower races of mankind, three have been observed to hold most explicitly and distinctly the doctrine of
object-souls. These are the Algonquin tribes, extending
over a great district of North America, the islanders
of the Fijian group, and the Karens of Birmah. Among
the Indians of North America, Father Charlevoix wrote,
souls are, as it were, the shadows and animated images of
the body, and it is by a consequence of this principle that
they believe everything to be animate in the universe. This
missionary was especially conversant with the Algonquins,
and it was among one of their tribes, the Ojibwas, that
Keating noticed the opinion that not only men and beasts
have souls, but inorganic things, such as kettles, &c., have
in them a similar essence. In the same district Father Le
Jeune had described, in the seventeenth century, the belief
that the souls, not only of men and animals, but of hatchets
and kettles, had to cross the water to the Great Village, out
where the sun sets.[1] In interesting correspondence with

[1] Charlevoix, vol. vi. p. 74; Keating, 'Long's Exp.' vol. ii. p. 154; Le

this quaint thought is Mariner's description of the Fiji doctrine—"If an animal or a plant die, its soul immediately goes to Bolotoo; if a stone or any other substance is broken, immortality is equally its reward; nay, artificial bodies have equal good luck with men, and hogs, and yams. If an axe or a chisel is worn out or broken up, away flies its soul for the service of the gods. If a house is taken down or any way destroyed, its immortal part will find a situation on the plains of Bolotoo; and, to confirm this doctrine, the Fiji people can show you a sort of natural well, or deep hole in the ground, at one of their islands, across the bottom of which runs a stream of water, in which you may clearly perceive the souls of men and women, beasts and plants, of stocks and stones, canoes and houses, and of all the broken utensils of this frail world, swimming, or rather tumbling along one over the other pell-mell into the regions of immortality." A full generation later, the Rev. Thomas Williams, while remarking that the escape of brutes and lifeless substances to the spirit-land of Mbulu does not receive universal credit among the Fijians, nevertheless confirms the older account of it :—"Those who profess to have seen the souls of canoes, houses, plants, pots, or any artificial bodies, swimming with other relics of this frail world on the stream of the Kauvandra well, which bears them into the regions of immortality, believe this doctrine as a matter of course; and so do those who have seen the foot-marks left about the same well by the ghosts of dogs, pigs, &c."[1] The theory among the Karens is stated by the Rev. E. B. Cross, as follows :—"Every object is supposed to have its 'kelah.' Axes and knives, as well as trees and plants, are supposed to have their separate 'kelahs.'" "The Karen, with his axe and cleaver, may build his house, cut his rice, and conduct his affairs, after death as before."[2]

Jouan, 'Nouvelle France,' p. 59 ; also Waitz, vol. iii. p. 199 ; Gregg, 'Commerce of Prairies,' vol. ii. p. 241 ; see Addison's No. 56 of the 'Spectator.'
[1] Mariner, 'Tonga Is.' vol. ii. p. 129 ; Williams, 'Fiji,' vol. i. p. 212. Similar ideas in Tahiti, Cook's 3rd Voy. vol. ii. p. 169.
[2] Cross, l. c. p. 309, 313 ; Mason, l. c. p. 202. Compare Meiners, vol. i. p. 114 ; Castrén, 'Finn. Myth.' pp. 161-3.

As so many races perform funeral sacrifices of men and animals, in order to dispatch their souls for the service of the soul of the deceased, so tribes who hold this doctrine of object-souls very rationally sacrifice objects, in order to transmit these souls. Among the Algonquin tribes, the sacrifice of objects for the dead was a habitual rite, as when we read of a warrior's corpse being buried with musket and war-club, calumet and war-paint, a public address being made to the body at burial concerning his future path, while in like manner a woman would be buried with her paddle and kettle, and the carrying-strap for the everlasting burden of her heavily-laden life. That the purpose of such offerings is the transmission of the object's spirit or phantom to the possession of the man's is explicitly stated as early as 1623 by Father Lallemant; when the Indians buried kettles, furs, &c., with the dead, they said that the bodies of the things remained, but their souls went to the dead who used them. The whole idea is graphically illustrated in the following Ojibwa tradition or myth. Gitchi Gauzini was a chief who lived on the shores of Lake Superior, and once, after a few days' illness, he seemed to die. He had been a skilful hunter, and had desired that a fine gun which he possessed should be buried with him when he died. But some of his friends not thinking him really dead, his body was not buried; his widow watched him for four days, he came back to life, and told his story. After death, he said, his ghost travelled on the broad road of the dead toward the happy land, passing over great plains of luxuriant herbage, seeing beautiful groves, and hearing the songs of innumerable birds, till at last, from the summit of a hill, he caught sight of the distant city of the dead, far across an intermediate space, partly veiled in mist, and spangled with glittering lakes and streams. He came in view of herds of stately deer, and moose, and other game, which with little fear walked near his path. But he had no gun, and remembering how he had requested his friends to put his gun in his grave, he turned back to go and fetch it. Then he

met face to face the train of men, women, and children who
were travelling toward the city of the dead. They were
heavily laden with guns, pipes, kettles, meats, and other
articles; women were carrying basket-work and painted
paddles, and little boys had their ornamented clubs and
their bows and arrows, the presents of their friends. Refusing a gun which an overburdened traveller offered him,
the ghost of Gitchi Gauzini travelled back in quest of his
own, and at last reached the place where he had died.
There he could see only a great fire before and around him,
and finding the flames barring his passage on every side, he
made a desperate leap through, and awoke from his trance.
Having concluded his story, he gave his auditors this
counsel, that they should no longer deposit so many
burdensome things with the dead, delaying them on their
journey to the place of repose, so that almost everyone he
met complained bitterly. It would be wiser, he said, only
to put such things in the grave as the deceased was particularly attached to, or made a formal request to have
deposited with him.[1]

With purpose no less distinct, when a dead Fijian chief
is laid out oiled and painted and dressed as in life, a heavy
club is placed ready near his right hand, which holds one or
more of the much-prized carved "whale's tooth" ornaments. The club is to serve for defence against the
adversaries who await his soul on the road to Mbulu, seeking to slay and eat him. We hear of a Fijian taking a
club from a companion's grave, and remarking in explanation to a missionary who stood by, "The ghost of the club
has gone with him." The purpose of the whale's tooth is
this; on the road to the land of the dead, near the solitary
hill of Takiveleyawa, there stands a ghostly pandanus-tree,
and the spirit of the dead man is to throw the spirit of the
whale's tooth at this tree, having struck which he is to
ascend the hill and await the coming of the spirits of his

[1] Schoolcraft, 'Indian Tribes,' part ii. p. 68; 'Algic Res.' vol. ii. p. 128;
Lallemant in 'Rel. des Jésuites dans la Nouvelle France,' 1626, p. 3.

strangled wives.[1] The funeral rites of the Karens complete
the present group. They kept up what seems a clear survival from actual human and animal sacrifice, fastening up
near an important person's grave a slave and a pony; these
invariably released themselves, and the slave became henceforth a free man. Moreover, the practice of placing food,
implements and utensils, and valuables of gold and silver,
near the remains of the deceased, was general among them.[2]

Now the sacrifice of property for the dead is one of the
great religious rites of the world; are we then justified in
asserting that all men who abandon or destroy property as
a funeral ceremony believe the articles to have spirits, which
spirits are transmitted to the deceased ? Not so; it is
notorious that there are people who recognize no such theory,
but who nevertheless deposit offerings with the dead. Affec-
tionate fancy or symbolism, a horror of the association of
death leading the survivors to get rid of anything that even
suggests the dreadful thought, a desire to abandon the dead
man's property, an idea that the hovering ghost may take
pleasure in or make use of the gifts left for him, all these
are or may be efficient motives.[3] Yet, having made full

[1] Williams, 'Fiji,' vol. I. pp. 188, 243, 249; Alger, p. 82; Seemann, 'Viti,'
p. 229.
[2] 'Journ. Ind. Archip.' new series, vol. ii. p. 421.
[3] For some cases in which horror or abnegation are assigned as motives for
abandonment of the dead man's property, see Humboldt and Bonpland,
vol. v. p. 626; Dalton in 'Journ. As. Soc. Bengal,' 1866, part ii. p. 191, etc.;
Earl, 'Papuans,' p. 108; Callaway, 'Rel. of Amazulu,' p. 13; Egede, 'Greenland,' p. 151; Cranz, p. 301; Loskiel, 'Ind. N. A.' part i. p. 61, but see
p. 76. The destruction or abandonment of the whole property of the dead
may plausibly, whether justly or not, be explained by horror or abnegation;
but these motives do not generally apply to cases where only part of the property is sacrificed, or now objects are provided expressly, and here the service
of the dead seems the reasonable motive. Thus, at the funeral of a Garo
girl, earthen vessels were broken as they were thrown in above the buried
ashes. "They said, the spirit of the girl would not benefit by them if they
were given unbroken, but for her the fragments would unite again." (Dalton,
'Descriptive Ethnology of Bengal,' p. 67.) The mere fact of breaking or
destruction of objects at funerals does not carry its own explanation, for it
is equally applicable to sentimental abandonment and to practical transmission
of the spirit of the object, as a man is killed to liberate his soul. For good

allowance for all this, we shall yet find reason to judge that many other peoples, though they may never have stated the theory of object-souls in the same explicit way as the Algonquins, Fijians, and Karens, have recognized it with more or less distinctness. It has given me the more confidence in this opinion to find it held, under proper reservation, by Mr. W. R. Alger, an American investigator, who in a treatise entitled "A Critical History of the Doctrine of a Future Life" has discussed the ethnography of his subject with remarkable learning and sagacity. "The barbarian brain," he writes, "seems to have been generally impregnated with the feeling that every thing else has a ghost as well as man. . . . The custom of burning or burying things with the dead probably arose, in some cases at least, from the supposition that every object has its *manes*." [1] It will be desirable briefly to examine further the subject of funeral offerings, as bearing on this interesting question of early psychology.

A wide survey of funeral sacrifices over the world will plainly show one of their most usual motives to be a more

cases of the breaking of vessels and utensils given to the dead, see 'Journ. Ind. Archip.' vol. i. p. 325 (Mintira); Grey, 'Australia,' vol. i. p. 322; G. F. Moore, 'Vocab. W. Australia,' p. 13 (Australians); Markham in 'Tr. Eth. Soc.' vol. iii. p. 188 (Ticunas); St. John, vol. i. p. 68 (Dayaks); Ellis, 'Madagascar,' vol. i. p. 251; Schoolcraft, 'Indian Tribes,' part i. p. 84 (Appalachicola); D. Wilson, 'Prehistoric Man,' vol. ii. p. 196 (N. A. I. and ancient graves in England). Cases of formal sacrifice where objects are offered to the dead and taken away again, are generally doubtful as to motive; see Spix and Martius, vol. i. p. 368; Martius, vol. i. p. 485 (Brazilian Tribes); Moffat, 'S. Africa,' p. 308 (Bechuanas); 'Journ. Ind. Archip.' vol. iii. p. 149 (Kayans).

[1] Alger, 'Future Life,' p. 81. He treats, however (p. 76), as intentionally symbolic the rite of the Winnebagos, who light fires on the grave to provide night after night camp-fires for the soul on its far journey (Schoolcraft, 'Ind. Tr.' vol. iv. p. 55; the idea is introduced in Longfellow's 'Hiawatha,' xix.). I agree with Dr. Brinton ('Myths of New World,' p. 241) that to look for recondite symbolic meaning in these simple childish rites is unreasonable. There was a similar Aztec rite (Clavigero, vol. ii. p. 94). The Mintira light fires on the grave for the spirit to warm itself at ('Journ. Ind. Archip.' vol. i. p. 325*, see p. 271, and compare Martius, vol. i. p. 491). So Australians will light a fire near their camp at night for the ghost of some lately dead relative to sit by (Millett, 'Australian Parsonage,' p. 76).

or less defined notion of benefiting the deceased, whether
out of kindness to him or from fear of his displeasure. How
such an intention may have taken this practical shape we can
perhaps vaguely guess, familiar as we are with a state of mind
out of which funeral sacrifices could naturally have sprung.
The man is dead, but it is still possible to fancy him alive,
to take his cold hand, to speak to him, to place his chair at
the table, to bury suggestive mementos in his coffin, to
throw flowers into his grave, to hang wreaths of everlastings
on his tomb. The Cid may be set on Babieca with his
sword Tizona in his hand, and carried out to do battle as of
old against the unbeliever; the dead king's meal may be
carried in to him in state, although the chamberlain must
announce that the king does not dine to-day. Such childlike ignoring of death, such childlike make-believe that the
dead can still do as heretofore, may well have led the savage
to bury with his kinsman the weapons, clothes, and ornaments that he used in life, to try to feed the corpse, to put
a cigar in the mouth of the skull before its final burial, to
lay playthings in the infant's grave. But one thought beyond would carry this dim blind fancy into the range of
logical reasoning. Granted that the man is dead and his
soul gone out of him, then the way to provide that departed
soul with food or clothes or weapons is to bury or burn them
with the body, for whatever happens to the man may be
taken to happen to the objects that lie beside him and share
his fate, while the precise way in which the transmission
takes place may be left undecided. It is possible that the
funeral sacrifice customary among mankind may have rested
at first, and may to some extent still rest, on vague thoughts
and imaginations like these, as yet fitted into no more
definite and elaborate philosophic theory.

There are, however, two great groups of cases of funeral
sacrifice, which so logically lead up to or involve the notion
of souls or spirits of objects, that the sacrificer himself
could hardly answer otherwise a point-blank question as to
their meaning. The first group is that in which those who

sacrifice men and beasts with the intention of conveying
their souls to the other world, also sacrifice lifeless things
indiscriminately with them. The second group is that in
which the phantoms of the objects sacrificed are traced distinctly into the possession of the human phantom.

The Caribs, holding that after decease man's soul found
its way to the land of the dead, sacrificed slaves on a chief's
grave to serve him in the new life, and for the same purpose
buried dogs with him, and also weapons.[1] The Guinea
negroes, at the funeral of a great man, killed several wives
and slaves to serve him in the other world, and put fine
clothes, gold fetishes, coral, beads, and other valuables, into
the coffin, to be used there too.[2] When the New Zealand
chief had slaves killed at his death for his service, and the
mourning family gave his chief widow a rope to hang herself with in the woods and so rejoin her husband,[3] it is not
easy to discern here a motive different from that which
induced them at the same time to provide the dead man also
with his weapons. Nor can an intellectual line well be
drawn between the intentions with which the Tunguz has
buried with him his horse, his bow and arrows, his smoking
apparatus and kettle. In the typical description which
Herodotus gives of the funeral of the ancient Scythian
chiefs, the miscellaneous contents of the burial-mound,
the strangled wife and household servants, the horses, the
choice articles of property, the golden vessels, fairly represent
the indiscriminate purpose which actuated the barbaric
sacrifice of creatures and things.[4] So in old Europe, the
warrior with his sword and spear, the horse with the saddle,
the hunter's hound and hawk and his bow and arrow, the
wife with her gay clothes and jewels, lie together in the
burial-mound. Their common purpose has become one of
the most undisputed inferences of Archæology.

[1] J. G. Müller, 'Amer. Urrelig.' p. 222, see 420.
[2] Bosman, 'Guinea,' in Pinkerton, vol. xvi. p. 430.
[3] Polack, 'M. of New Zealanders,' vol. ii. pp. 66, 78, 116, 127.
[4] Georgi, 'Russ. R.' vol. i. p. 266; Herodot. iv. 71, see note in Rawlinson's
Tr., etc., etc.

As for what becomes of the objects sacrificed for the dead, there are on record the most distinct statements taken from the sacrificers themselves. Although the objects rot in the grave or are consumed on the pile, they nevertheless come in some way into the possession of the disembodied souls they are intended for. Not the material things themselves, but phantasmal shapes corresponding to them, are carried by the souls of the dead on their far journey beyond the grave, or are used in the world of spirits; while sometimes the phantoms of the dead appear to the living, bearing property which they have received by sacrifice, or demanding something that has been withheld. The Australian will take his weapons with him to his paradise.[1] A Tasmanian, asked the reason of a spear being deposited in a native's grave, replied "To fight with when he is asleep."[2] Many Greenlanders thought that the kayak and arrows and tools laid by a man's grave, the knife and sewing implements laid by a woman's, would be used in the next world.[3] The instruments buried with the Sioux are for him to make a living with hereafter; the paints provided for the dead Iroquois were to enable him to appear decently in the other world.[4] The Aztec's water-bottle was to serve him on the journey to Mictlan, the land of the dead; the bonfire of garments and baskets and spoils of war was intended to send them with him, and somehow to protect him against the bitter wind; the offerings to the warrior's manes on earth would reach him on the heavenly plains.[5] Among the old Peruvians, a dead prince's wives would hang themselves in order to continue in his service, and many of his attendants would be buried in his fields or places of favourite resort, in order that his soul, passing through those places, might

---

[1] Oldfield in 'Tr. Eth. Soc.' vol. iii. pp. 228, 245.
[2] Bonwick, 'Tasmanians,' p. 97.
[3] Cranz, 'Grönland,' pp. 263, 301.
[4] Schoolcraft, 'Indian Tribes,' part iv. pp. 55, 65; J. G. Müller, 'Amer. Urrel.' pp. 88, 287.
[5] Sahagun, book iii. App. in Kingsborough, 'Antiquities of Mexico,' vol. vii.; Clavigero, vol. ii. p. 91; Brasseur, vol. iii. pp. 497, 569.

take their souls along with him for future service. In perfect consistency with these strong animistic notions, the
Peruvians declared that their reason for sacrifice of property
to the dead was that they "have seen, or thought they saw,
those who had long been dead walking, adorned with the
things that were buried with them, and accompanied by
their wives who had been buried alive." [1]

As definite an implication of the spirit or phantom of an
object appears in a recent account from Madagascar, where
things are buried to become in some way useful to the dead.
When King Radama died, it was reported and firmly
believed that his ghost was seen one night in the garden of
his country seat, dressed in one of the uniforms which had
been buried with him, and riding one of the best horses
killed opposite his tomb. [2] Turanian tribes of North Asia
avow that the motive of their funeral offerings of horses and
sledges, clothes and axes and kettles, flint and steel and
tinder, meat and butter, is to provide the dead for his
journey to the land of souls, and for his life there. [3] Among
the Esths of Northern Europe, the dead starts properly
equipped on his ghostly journey with needle and thread,
hairbrush and soap, bread and brandy and coin ; a toy, if it
is a child. And so full a consciousness of practical meaning
survived till lately, that now and then a soul would come back
at night to reproach its relations with not having provided
properly for it, but left it in distress. [4] To turn from these
now Europeanized Tatars to a rude race of the Eastern
Archipelago, among the Orang Binua of Sambawa there
prevails this curious law of inheritance ; not only does each
surviving relative, father, mother, son, brother, and so forth,
take his or her proper share, but the deceased inherits one

[1] Cieza de Leon, p. 161 ; Rivero and Tschudi, 'Peruvian Antiquities,' pp.
186, 200.

[2] Ellis, 'Madagascar,' vol. I. pp. 254, 429 ; see Flacourt, p. 60.

[3] Castrén, 'Finn. Myth.' p. 116 ; J. Billings, 'Exp. to N. Russia,' p. 129 ;
see 'Samoiedia' in Pinkerton, vol. I. p. 532, and Leems, 'Lapland,' ibid.,
p. 484.

[4] Kreeler, 'Ehsten Gebräuche,' p. 69.

share from himself, which is devoted to his use by eating the
animals at the funeral feast, burning everything else that will
burn, and burying the remainder.[1] In Cochin China, the
common people object to celebrating their feast of the dead
on the same day with the upper classes, for this excellent
reason, that the aristocratic souls might make the servant souls carry home their presents for them. These
people employ all the resources of their civilization to perform with the more lavish extravagance the savage funeral
sacrifices. Here are details from an account published in
1849 of the funeral of a late king of Cochin China. "When
the corpse of Thien Tri was deposited in the coffin, there
were also deposited in it many things for the use of the
deceased in the other world, such as his crown, turbans,
clothes of all descriptions, gold, silver, and other precious
articles, rice and other provisions." Meals were set out near
the coffin, and there was a framed piece of damask with
woollen characters, the abode of one of the souls of the
defunct. In the tomb, an enclosed edifice of stone, the
childless wives of the deceased were to be perpetually shut
up to guard the sepulchre, "and prepare daily the food and
other things of which they think the deceased has need in
the other life." At the time of the deposit of the coffin in
a cavern behind the tomb building, there were burnt there
great piles of boats, stages, and everything used in
the funeral, "and moreover of all the objects which had
been in use by the king during his lifetime, of chessmen,
musical instruments, fans, boxes, parasols, mats, fillets,
carriages, &c. &c., and likewise a horse and an elephant of
wood and pasteboard." "Some months after the funeral, at
two different times, there were constructed in a forest near
a pagoda two magnificent palaces of wood with rich furnish-
ings, in all things similar to the palace which the defunct
monarch had inhabited. Each palace was composed of
twenty rooms, and the most scrupulous attention was given
in order that nothing might be wanting necessary for a

palace, and these palaces were burned with great pomp, and
it is thus that immense riches have been given to the flames
from the foolish belief that it would serve the dead in the
other world." [1]

Though the custom is found among the Beduins of array-
ing the dead with turban, girdle, and sword, yet funeral
offerings for the service of the dead are by no means conspicuous among Semitic nations. The mention of the rite
by Ezekiel, while showing a full sense of its meaning,
characterizes it as not Israelite, but Gentile : "The mighty
fallen of the uncircumcised, which are gone down to Hades
with weapons of war, and they have laid their swords under
their heads." [2] Among the Aryan nations, on the contrary,
such funeral offerings are known to have prevailed widely
and of old, while for picturesqueness of rite and definiteness of purpose they can scarcely be surpassed even among
savages. Why the Brahman's sacrificial instruments are to
be burnt with him on the funeral pile, appears from this line
of the Veda recited at the ceremony : "Yadâ gachchátyasuni-
timetâmathâ devânâm vasanirbhaváti,"—"When he cometh
unto that life, faithfully will he do the service of the gods." [3]
Lucian is sarcastic, but scarcely unfair, in his comments on
the Greek funeral rites, speaking of those who slew horses
and slave-girls, and cupbearers, and burned or buried clothes
and ornaments, as for use and service in the world below ; of
the meat and drink offerings on the tombs which serve to
feed the bodiless shades in Hades ; of the splendid garments
and the garlands of the dead, that they might not suffer cold
upon the road, nor be seen naked by Kerberos. For Kerberos was intended the honey-cake deposited with the dead ;
and the obolus placed in the mouth was the toll for Charon,
save at Hermione in Argolis, where men thought there was

---

[1] Bastian, 'Psychologie,' p. 89 ; 'Journ. Ind. Archip.' vol. iii. p. 337. For
other instances, see Bastian, 'Mensch,' vol. ii. p. 332, etc. ; Alger, 'Future
Life,' part ii.

[2] Klemm, 'C. G.' vol. iv. p. 159 ; Ezek. xxxii. 27.

[3] Max Müller, 'Todtenbestattung der Brahmanen,' in D. M. Z. vol. ix.
p. vii.-xiv.

a short descent to Hades, and therefore provided the dead
with no coin for the grim ferryman. How such ideas could
be realized, may be seen in the story of Eukrates, whose
dead wife appeared to him to demand one of her golden
sandals, which had been dropped underneath the chest, and
so not burnt for her with the rest of her wardrobe; or in
the story of Periander, whose dead wife Melissa refused to
give him an oracular response, for she was shivering and
naked, because the garments buried with her had not been
burnt, and so were of no use, wherefore Periander plundered
the Corinthian women of their best clothes, burned them in
a great trench with prayer, and now obtained his answer.[1]
The ancient Gauls were led, by their belief in another life,
to burn and bury with the dead things suited to the living;
nor is the record improbable that they transferred to the
world below the repayment of loans, for even in modern
centuries the Japanese would borrow money in this life, to
be repaid with heavy interest in the next.[2] The souls of the
Norse dead took with them from their earthly home servants
and horses, boats and ferry-money, clothes and weapons.
Thus, in death as in life, they journeyed, following the long
dark " hell-way" (helvegr). The " hell-shoon " (helskó)
were bound upon the dead man's feet for the toilsome
journey; and when King Harald was slain in the battle of
Bravalla, they drove his war-chariot, with the corpse upon it,
into the great burial-mound, and there they killed the horse,
and King Hring gave his own saddle beside, that the fallen
chief might ride or drive to Walhalla, as it pleased him.[3]
Lastly, in the Lithuanian and Old Prussian district, where
Aryan heathendom held its place in Europe so firmly and so
late, accounts of funeral sacrifice of men, and beasts, and
things, date on even beyond the middle ages. Even as they

[1] Lucian. De Lucin. 9, etc.; Philopseudes, 27; Strabo, viii. 6, 12; Herodot.
v. 92; Smith's ' Dic. Gr. and Rom. Ant.' art. ' funus.'
[2] Valet. Max. ll.; Mela, lii. 2. Froins (1565) in Maffei, Histor. Indicarum,
lib. iv.
[3] Grimm, Verbrennen der Leichen,' pp. 232, etc., 247, etc.; ' Deutsche
Myth.' pp. 795-800.

thought that men would live again in the resurrection rich
or poor, noble or peasant, as on earth, so "they believed
that the things burned would rise again with them, and serve
them as before." Among these people lived the Kriwe Kri-
weito, the great priest, whose house was on the high steep
mountain Anafielas. All the souls of their dead must
clamber up this mountain, wherefore they burned with them
claws of bears and lynxes for their help. All the souls
must pass through the Kriwe's house, and he could describe
to the surviving relatives of each the clothes, and horse, and
weapons he had seen him come with, and even show, for
greater certainty, some mark made with lance or other
instrument by the passing soul.[1] Such examples of funeral
rites show a common ceremony, and to a great degree a
common purpose, obtaining from savagery through barbarism, and even into the higher civilization. Now could
we have required from all these races a distinct answer to
the question, whether they believed in spirits of all things,
from men and beasts down to spears and cloaks, sticks and
stones, it is likely that we might have often received the
same acknowledgment of fully developed animism which
stands on record in North America, Polynesia, and Birmah.
Failing such direct testimony, it is at least justifiable to say
that the lower culture, by practically dealing with object-
souls, goes far towards acknowledging their existence.

Before quitting the discussion of funeral offerings for
transmission to the dead, the custom must be traced to its
final decay. It is apt not to die out suddenly, but to leave
surviving remnants, more or less dwindled in form and
changed in meaning. The Kanowits of Borneo talk of
setting a man's property adrift for use in the next world,
and even go so far as to lay out his valuables by the bier,
but in fact they only commit to the frail canoe a few old

---

[1] Duslarg, 'Chronicon Prussiæ,' lii. c. v. ; Hanusch, 'Slaw. Myth.' pp.
308, 414 (Anafielas is the ghost-mountain of Slavonic and German myth, see
Grimm, 'D. M.' p. 786). Compare statement in St. Clair and Brophy,
'Bulgaria,' p. 61 ; as to food transmitted to dead in other world, with more
probable explanation, p. 77.

things not worth plundering.[1] So in North America, the funeral sacrifice of the Winnebagos has come down to burying a pipe and tobacco with the dead, and sometimes a club in a warrior's grave, while the goods brought and hung up at the burial-place are no longer left there, but the survivors gamble for them.[2] The Santals of Bengal put two vessels, one for rice and the other for water, on the dead man's couch, with a few rupees, to enable him to appease the demons on the threshold of the shadowy world, but when the funeral pile is ready these things are removed.[3] The fanciful art of replacing costly offerings by worthless imitations is at this day worked out into the quaintest devices in China. As the men and horses dispatched by fire for the service of the dead are but paper figures, so offerings of clothes and money may be represented likewise. The imitations of Spanish pillar-dollars in pasteboard covered with tinfoil, the sheets of tinfoil-paper which stand for silver money, and if coloured yellow for gold, are consumed in such quantities that the sham becomes a serious reality, for the manufacture of mock-money is the trade of thousands of women and children in a Chinese city. In a similar way trunks full of property are forwarded in the care of the newly deceased, to friends who are gone before. Pretty paper houses, "replete with every luxury," as our auctioneers say, are burnt for the dead Chinaman to live in hereafter, and the paper keys are burnt also, that he may unfasten the paper locks of the paper chests that hold the ingots of gold-paper and silver-paper, which are to be realised as current gold and silver in the other world, an idea which, however, does not prevent the careful survivors from collecting the ashes to re-extract the tin from them in this.[4]

---

[1] St. John, 'Far East,' vol. i. pp. 54, 69. Compare Bosman, 'Guinea,' in Pinkerton, vol. xvi. p. 430.

[2] Schoolcraft, 'Indian Tribes,' part iv. p. 54.

[3] Hunter, 'Rural Bengal,' p. 210.

[4] Davis, 'Chinese,' vol. i. p. 276; Doolittle, vol. i. p. 193; vol. ii. p. 275 Bastian, 'Mensch,' vol. ii. p. 331; see Marco Polo, book ii. ch. lxviii.

Again, when the modern Hindu offers to his dead parent funeral cakes with flowers and betel, he presents a woollen yarn which he lays across the cake, and naming the deceased says, "May this apparel, made of woollen yarn, be acceptable to thee."[1] Such facts as these suggest a symbolic meaning in the practically useless offerings which Sir John Lubbock groups together—the little models of kayaks and spears in Esquimaux graves, the models of objects in Egyptian tombs, and the flimsy unserviceable jewelry buried with the Etruscan dead.[2]

Just as people in Borneo, after they had become Mohammedans, still kept up the rite of burying provisions for the dead man's journey, as a mark of respect,[3] so the rite of interring objects with the dead survived in Christian Europe. As the Greeks gave the dead man the obolus for Charon's toll, and the old Prussians furnished him with spending-money to buy refreshment on his weary journey, so to this day German peasants bury a corpse with money in his mouth or hand, a fourpenny-piece or so, while the placing of the coin in the dead man's hand is a regular ceremony of an Irish wake, and similar little funeral offerings of coin are recorded in the folklore-books elsewhere in Europe.[4] Christian funeral offerings of this kind are mostly trifling in value, and doubtful as to the meaning with which they were kept up. The early Christians retained the heathen custom of placing in the tomb such things as articles of the toilette and children's playthings; modern Greeks would place oars on a shipman's grave, and other such tokens for other crafts; the beautiful classic rite of scattering flowers

[1] Colebrooke, 'Essays,' vol. i. pp. 161, 169.
[2] Lubbock, 'Prehistoric Times,' p. 142; Wilkinson, 'Ancient Eg.' vol. ii. p. 319.
[3] Beeckmann, 'Voy. to Borneo,' in Pinkerton, vol. xl. p. 110.
[4] Hartknoch, 'Alt- und Neues Preussen,' part i. p. 181; Grimm, 'D. M.' pp. 791-5; Wuttke, 'Deutsche Volksaberglaube,' p. 212; Rochholz, 'Deutscher Glaube,' etc. vol. i. p. 187, etc.; Maury, 'Magie,' etc. p. 158 (France); Brand, 'Pop. Ant.' vol. ii. p. 285 (Ireland).

over the dead still holds its place in Europe.[1] Whatever
may have been the thoughts which first prompted these
kindly ceremonies, they were thoughts belonging to far
pre-Christian ages. The change of sacrifice from its early
significance is shown among the Hindus, who have turned
it to account for purposes of priestcraft: he who gives
water or shoes to a Brahman will find water to refresh him,
and shoes to wear, on the journey to the next world, while
the gift of a present house will secure him a future palace.[2]
In interesting correspondence with this, is a transition from
pagan to Christian folklore in our own land. The Lyke-
Wake Dirge, the not yet forgotten funeral chant of the North
Country, tells, like some savage or barbaric legend, of the
passage over the Bridge of Death and the dreadful journey
to the other world. But though the ghostly traveller's feet
are still shod with the old Norseman's hell-shoon, he gains
them no longer by funeral offering, but by his own charity
in life :—

"This a nighte, this a nighte
	Every night and alle;
Fire and fleet and candle-light,
	And Christe receive thy saule.

When thou from hence away are paste
	Every night and alle;
To Whinny-moor thou comes at laste,
	And Christe receive thy saule.

If ever thou gave either hosen or shoon,
	Every night and alle;
Sit thee down and put them on,
	And Christe receive thy saule.

But if hosen nor shoon thou never gave neean,
	Every night and alle;
The Whinnes shall prick thee to the bare beean,
	And Christe receive thy saule.

[1] Maitland, 'Church in the Catacombs,' p. 137 ; Forbes Leslie, vol. II.
502 ; Meiners, vol. II. p. 750 ; Brand, 'Pop. Ant.' vol. II. p. 307.
[2] Ward, 'Hindoos,' vol. II. p. 281.

From Whinny-moore when thou may passe,
   Every night and alle;
To Brig o' Dread thou comes at laste,
   And Christe receive thy saule.

From Brig o' Dread when thou are paste,
   Every night and alle;
To Purgatory Fire thou comes at laste,
   And Christe receive thy saule.

If ever thou gave either milke or drink,
   Every night and alle;
The fire shall never make thee shrinke,
   And Christe receive thy saule.

But if milk nor drink thou never gave neean,
   Every night and alle;
The fire shall burn thee to the bare beean
   And Christe receive thy saule." [1]

What reader, unacquainted with the old doctrine of offerings for the dead, could realize the meaning of its remnants thus lingering in peasants' minds? The survivals from ancient funeral ceremony may here again serve as warnings against attempting to explain relics of intellectual antiquity by viewing them from the changed level of modern opinion.

Having thus surveyed at large the theory of spirits or souls of objects, it remains to point out what, to general students, may seem the most important consideration belonging to it, namely, its close relation to one of the most

[1] From the collated and annotated text in J. C. Atkinson, 'Glossary of Cleveland Dialect,' p. 595 (a = one, neean = none, beean = bone). Other versions in Scott, 'Minstrelsy of the Scottish Border,' vol. ii. p. 367; Kelly, 'Indo-European Folklore,' p. 115; Brand, 'Pop. Ant.' vol. ii. p. 275. Two verses have perhaps been lost between the fifth and sixth. J. C. A. reads 'meate' in vv. 7 and 8; the usual reading 'milke' is retained here. The sense of these two verses may be that the liquor sacrificed in life will quench the fire : an idea parallel to that known to folklore, that he who gave bread in his lifetime will find it after death ready for him to cast into the hellhound's jaws (Mannhardt, 'Götterwelt der Deutschen und Nordischen Völker,' p. 319), a sop to Cerberus.

influential doctrines of civilized philosophy. The savage
thinker, though occupying himself so much with the phenomena of life, sleep, disease, and death, seems to have taken
for granted, as a matter of course, the ordinary operations of
his own mind. It hardly occurred to him to think about the
machinery of thinking. Metaphysics is a study which first
assumes clear shape at a comparatively high level of intellectual culture. The metaphysical philosophy of thought taught
in our modern European lecture-rooms is historically traced
back to the speculative psychology of classic Greece. Now
one doctrine which there comes into view is especially associated with the name of Democritus, the philosopher of
Abdera, in the fifth century B.C. When Democritus propounded the great problem of metaphysics, " How do we
perceive external things?"—thus making, as Lewes says,
an era in the history of philosophy,—he put forth, in
answer to the question, a theory of thought. He explained
the fact of perception by declaring that things are always
throwing off images (εἴδωλα) of themselves, which images,
assimilating to themselves the surrounding air, enter a re-
cipient soul, and are thus perceived. Now, supposing Democritus to have been really the originator of this famed theory
of ideas, how far is he to be considered its inventor?
Writers on the history of philosophy are accustomed to
treat the doctrine as actually made by the philosophical
school which taught it. Yet the evidence here brought forward shows it to be really the savage doctrine of object-
souls, turned to a new purpose as a method of explaining
the phenomena of thought. Nor is the correspondence a
mere coincidence, for at this point of junction between
classic religion and classic philosophy the traces of historical continuity may be still discerned. To say that Democritus was an ancient Greek is to say that from his
childhood he had looked on at the funeral ceremonies of his
country, beholding the funeral sacrifices of garments and
jewels and money and food and drink, rites which his
mother and his nurse could tell him were performed in

order that the phantasmal images of these objects might pass into the possession of forms shadowy like themselves, the souls of dead men. Thus Democritus, seeking a solution of his great problem of the nature of thought, found it by simply decanting into his metaphysics a surviving doctrine of primitive savage animism. This thought of the phantoms or souls of things, if simply modified to form a philosophical theory of perception, would then and there become his doctrine of Ideas. Nor does even this fully represent the closeness of union which connects the savage doctrine of flitting object-souls with the Epicurean philosophy. Lucretius actually makes the theory of film-like images of things (simulacra, membranæ) account both for the apparitions which come to men in dreams, and the images which impress their minds in thinking. So unbroken is the continuity of philosophic speculation from savage to cultured thought. Such are the debts which civilized philosophy owes to primitive animism.

The doctrine of ideas, thus developed in the classic world, has, indeed, by no means held its course thenceforth unchanged through metaphysics, but has undergone transition somewhat like that of the doctrine of the soul itself. Ideas, fined down to the abstract forms or species of material objects, and applied to other than visible qualities, have at last come merely to denote subjects of thought. Yet to this day the old theory has not utterly died out, and the retention of the significant term "idea" (ἰδέα, visible form) is accompanied by a similar retention of original meaning. It is still one of the tasks of the metaphysician to display and refute the old notion of ideas as being real images, and to replace it by more abstract conceptions. It is a striking instance that Dugald Stewart can cite from the works of Sir Isaac Newton the following distinct recognition of "sensible species:" "Is not the sensorium of animals, the place where the sentient substance is present; and to which the sensible species of things are brought, through the nerves and brain, that there they may be perceived by the

mind present in that place?" Again, Dr. Reid states the
original theory of ideas, while declaring that he conceives
it "to have no solid foundation, though it has been adopted
very generally by philosophers. . . . . . This notion of our
perceiving external objects, not immediately, but in certain
images or species of them conveyed by the senses, seems
to be the most ancient philosophical hypothesis we have on
the subject of perception, and to have, with small variations, retained its authority to this day." Granted that
Dr. Reid exaggerated the extent to which metaphysicians
have kept up the notion of ideas as real images of things,
few will deny that it does linger much in modern minds,
and that people who talk of ideas do often, in some hazy
metaphorical way, think of sensible images.' One of the
shrewdest things ever said about either ideas or ghosts was
Bishop Berkeley's retort upon Halley, who bantered him
about his idealism. The bishop claimed the mathematician
as an idealist also, his "ultimate ratios" being ghosts of
departed quantities, appearing when the terms that produced them vanished.

It remains to sum up in few words the doctrine of souls,
in the various phases it has assumed from first to last among
mankind. In the attempt to trace its main course through
the successive grades of man's intellectual history, the evidence seems to accord best with a theory of its development,
somewhat to the following effect. At the lowest levels of
culture of which we have clear knowledge, the notion of a
ghost-soul animating man while in the body, and appearing
in dream and vision out of the body, is found deeply ingrained. There is no reason to think that this belief was
learnt by savage tribes from contact with higher races, nor
that it is a relic of higher culture from which the savage
tribes have degenerated; for what is here treated as the

---

¹ Lewes, 'Biographical History of Philosophy, Democritus' (and see his
remarks on Reid); Lucretius, lib. iv.; 'Early Hist. of Mankind,' p. 6; Stewart,
'Philosophy of Human Mind,' vol. i. chap. i. sec. 2; Reid, 'Essays,' II. chaps.
iv. xiv.; see Thos. Browne, 'Philosophy of the Mind,' lect. 27.

primitive animistic doctrine is thoroughly at home among savages, who appear to hold it on the very evidence of their senses, interpreted on the biological principle which seems to them most reasonable. We may now and then hear the savage doctrines and practices concerning souls claimed as relics of a high religious culture pervading the primæval race of man. They are said to be traces of remote ancestral religion, kept up in scanty and perverted memory by tribes degraded from a nobler state. It is easy to see that such an explanation of some few facts, sundered from their connexion with the general array, may seem plausible to certain minds. But a large view of the subject can hardly leave such argument in possession. The animism of savages stands for and by itself; it explains its own origin. The animism of civilized men, while more appropriate to advanced knowledge, is in great measure only explicable as a developed product of the older and ruder system. It is the doctrines and rites of the lower races which are, according to their philosophy, results of point-blank natural evidence and acts of straightforward practical purpose. It is the doctrines and rites of the higher races which show survival of the old in the midst of the new, modification of the old to bring it into conformity with the new, abandonment of the old because it is no longer compatible with the new. Let us see at a glance in what general relation the doctrine of souls among savage tribes stands to the doctrine of souls among barbaric and cultured nations. Among races within the limits of savagery, the general doctrine of souls is found worked out with remarkable breadth and consistency. The souls of animals are recognized by a natural extension from the theory of human souls; the souls of trees and plants follow in some vague partial way; and the souls of inanimate objects expand the general category to its extremest boundary. Thenceforth, as we explore human thought onward from savage into barbarian and civilized life, we find a state of theory more conformed to positive science, but in itself less complete and consistent. Far on into civilization, men still act as though in some half-meant way they believed in souls or ghosts of objects, while nevertheless their knowledge of physical science is beyond so crude a philosophy. As to the doctrine of souls of plants, fragmentary evidence of the history of its breaking down in Asia has reached us. In our own day and country, the notion of souls of beasts is to be seen dying out. Animism, indeed, seems to be drawing in its outposts, and concentrating itself on its first and main position, the doctrine of the human soul. This doctrine has undergone extreme modification in the course of culture. It has outlived the almost total loss of one great argument attached to it,—the objective reality of apparitional souls or ghosts seen in dreams and visions. The soul has given up its ethereal substance, and become an immaterial entity, "the shadow of a shade." Its theory is becoming separated from the investigations of biology and mental science, which now discuss the phenomena of life and thought, the senses and the intellect, the emotions and the will, on a groundwork of pure experience. There has arisen an intellectual product whose very existence is of the deepest significance, a "psychology" which has no longer anything to do with "soul." The soul's place in modern thought is in the metaphysics of religion, and its especial office there is that of furnishing an intellectual side to the religious doctrine of the future life. Such are the alterations which have differenced the fundamental animistic belief in its course through successive periods of the world's culture. Yet it is evident that, notwithstanding all this profound change, the conception of the human soul is, as to its most essential nature, continuous from the philosophy of the savage thinker to that of the modern professor of theology. Its definition has remained from the first that of an animating, separable, surviving entity, the vehicle of individual personal existence. The theory of the soul is one principal part of a system of religious philosophy, which unites, in an unbroken line of mental connexion, the savage fetish-worshipper and the civilized Christian. The divisions which have separated the great religions of the world into intolerant and hostile sects are for the most part superficial in comparison with the deepest of all religious schisms, that which divides Animism from Materialism.

www.ingramcontent.com/pod-product-compliance
Lightning Source LLC
Chambersburg PA
CBHW020448270326
41926CB00008B/522